Human Stress
and
Cognition

Human Stress
and
Cognition

An Information Processing Approach

Edited by

VERNON HAMILTON

and

DAVID M. WARBURTON

Department of Psychology
University of Reading
England

JOHN WILEY & SONS
Chichester · New York · Brisbane · Toronto

Library of Congress Cataloging in Publication Data:

Main entry under title:

Human stress and cognition.

   1. Stress (Psychology) 2. Human information processing. I. Hamilton, Vernon. II. Warburton, David M.
BF575.S75H85   153.4   78-31691
ISBN 0 471 27572 7

Typeset by Preface Ltd., Salisbury, Wilts
Printed in Great Britain by The Pitman Press, Bath.

*To our wives who supported us
and to our teachers who influenced us*

Contributors

Susan Folkman
Department of Psychology, University of California, Berkeley.

Vernon Hamilton
Department of Psychology, University of Reading.

Robert Hockey
Department of Psychology, Durham University.

Mardi J. Horowitz
Department of Psychiatry, University of California School of Medicine, San Francisco.

James H. Johnson
Department of Psychology, University of Washington, Seattle.

Richard S. Lazarus
Department of Psychology, University of California, Berkeley.

Holger Luczak
Institut für Arbeitswissenschaft, Technische Hochschule Darmstadt.

George Mandler
Department of Psychology, University of California, San Diego.

Roy L. Payne
Department of Psychology, University of Sheffield.

Patrick Rabbitt
Department of Experimental Psychology, Oxford.

Walter Rohmert
Institut für Arbeitswissenschaft, Technische Hochschule Darmstadt.

Irwin G. Sarason
Department of Psychology, University of Washington, Seattle.

Catherine Schaefer
Department of Psychology, University of California, Berkeley.

Hans Selye   *International Institute of Stress, Montreal.*

David M. Warburton   *Department of Psychology, University of Reading.*

Contents

Preface   xi

Acknowledgements   xiii

General Introduction

Human Stress and Cognition: Problems of Definition, Analysis,
and Integration
Vernon Hamilton   3

Basic Mechanisms and Processes

1. The Stress Concept and Some of its Implications
   Hans Selye   11
2. Physiological Aspects of Information Processing and Stress
   David M. Warburton   33
3. 'Personality' and Stress
   Vernon Hamilton   67
4. Current Paradigms and Models in Human Information Processing
   Patrick Rabbitt   115
5. Stress and the Cognitive Components of Skilled Performance
   Robert Hockey   141
6. Thought Processes, Consciousness, and Stress
   George Mandler   179

Coping Processes and Life Event Changes

7. Recent Developments in Research on Life Stress
   James H. Johnson and Irwin G. Sarason   205
8. Psychological Response to Serious Life Events
   Mardi J. Horowitz   237
9. Cognitive Processes as Mediators of Stress and Coping
   Susan Folkman, Catherine Schaefer and Richard S. Lazarus   265

Cognition and Stress in the Working Environment

10. Stress and Cognition in Organizations
 Roy L. Payne   301
11. Stress, Work, and Productivity
 Walter Rohmert and Holger Luczak   339

Stress Vulnerability in Psychopathology

12. Information Processing Aspects of Neurotic Anxiety and the
 Schizophrenias
 Vernon Hamilton   383
13. Physiological Aspects of Anxiety and Schizophrenia
 David M. Warburton   431

Concluding Remarks

Stress and the Processing of Information
David M. Warburton   469

Author Index   477

Subject Index   493

Preface

We have two aims in presenting this book: a scientific and an idealistic.

We have attempted to select well-known contributors who could present the most up-to-date concepts in previously discrete areas of stress and information processing. As a consequence the chapters should be relevant for students, teachers, and research workers in the disciplines of psychology, psychiatry, endocrinology, physiology, sociology, and industrial medicine. Although the aim of achieving a synthesis of all aspects of information processing and stress may be too ambitious, readers will be able to judge whether new levels of understanding have been achieved by the efforts of the contributors.

Since stress is a universal and frequently disabling human phenomenon, we have hoped to show to a wide readership that psychological research can be relevant for behaviour outside the laboratory. Many of the causes are already well understood and new methods of prevention and amelioration are becoming available as a result of the research that is reported here.

We wish to express our gratitude to the contributors to this volume who have so willingly and ably related their own expert knowledge to the new perspectives that we requested them to take.

VERNON HAMILTON
DAVID M. WARBURTON

Acknowledgements

Acknowledgements for permission to reproduce Figures and Tables are made to the following:

American Psychological Association for Figs. 5.2, 5.3, and Tables 7.1, 7.2 and 7.3.

Butterworths, Inc. for Fig. 1.2.

Jossey-Bass, Inc. for Figs. 10.3 and 10.4.

Lippincott, Co. for Fig. 1.1.

Wiley & Sons Ltd., Fig. 10.5.

General Introduction

Human Stress and Cognition: Problems of Definition, Analysis, and Integration

VERNON HAMILTON

How does one justify a book with a title which includes several complex terms, and contributions ranging from the fields of biochemistry to industrial medicine? A broad scientific purpose, of course, is taken for granted, and complexity is unavoidable whenever multivariate and covert processes determine human behaviour. Moreover, the wide range of stress research, yielding a veritable explosion of knowledge and new insights, has led inevitably to highly specialist scientific work. Thus multiple authorship seemed desirable even if agreed generalizations cannot be achieved at this stage.

Whereas the concepts of cognition and information processing are terms with a wide but relatively systematic range of implications for psychologists, neurologists, cyberneticians, and computer scientists, the concept of stress has been part of the vocabulary of everyman for a considerable time. The sense of forcefulness, emphasis, or accentuation has been extended, however, to include analogues of the physical concept of the strength of materials, and the engineering concepts of resilience to load, strain, and 'breaking point'. In this manner, our conception of stress has acquired negative and aversive meaning. It is considered as a state and experience that is unpleasant, that needs to be avoided because its effects on the biochemical and thinking systems of human beings may lead to disease, or to psychosocial incapacities.

If stress has undesirable characteristics and consequences, society may expect those who know something about its antecedents and its mediators to do something about it. After all, society through its industrially productive members ultimately provides the financial support for the acquisition of knowledge through research. It is likely that all the contributors to this book accept at least one aspect of this responsibility, and some of them provide clear evidence in their chapters that they are already attempting to act accordingly.

The application of existing knowledge, however, has another side to it. It brings with it the awareness that one's capacity to help or to alleviate is inadequate. We have no more than a limited understanding of how stressors develop from the complex and sophisticated expectations of our social institutions, its changing conventions, its organizations, and its goals. Can behavioural science really help to increase general well-being, human contentment, and the capacity to generate responsible behaviour on which the institutions depend? Do we really know what we mean by stressful life experience, by the strains of working in automated mass-producing industry? Do we really know what accounts for individual differences in vulnerability to stress? How widely may we define legitimately what we mean by stress without depriving the term of a logically distinct meaning? How do we know that we are under stress, and how and when do we perceive events as stressful? What are the characteristics of the human response systems which generate stress-induced emotionality, stressful knowledge of impending dangers and deprivations, and uncertainties concerning the meaning of events and the utility of one's available responses, at more than one level of consciousness? Under what conditions is there a failure of the human capacity to store, integrate, remember, and selectively attend to a variety of required information, to habits, duties, or important personal goals? And what are the roles of stress-induced aspects of thinking and biochemical reactivity in the development of seriously disabling behaviour disorders?

There appears to be a general feeling that people are now experiencing different types and degrees of stress, some of it reflected in widespread racial and industrial conflicts, for example, or in drug abuse. To a lesser extent there is reference to the increasing information processing demands of the late 20th century. These demands, arise, however, from the increasing changes and elaborations of social structures, institutions, and social role-playing expectations, and the changes and elaborations of rules, ordinances, and laws. The principal cognitive adaptations required of individuals are the rapid acquisition of new knowledge, and the solution of new decision-making conflicts. Although there is already considerable social and experimental evidence of an unfavourable interaction between stress and human cognition, the reasons for this are inadequately understood, parsimonious theories are lacking, and interactions between specialists in different areas of study are infrequent.

The accumulation of studies and models of the nature and components of adaptive cognitive processes seems to have reached the stage at which a first tentative synthesis of their interaction may be usefully attempted. The concepts which are likely to make such an attempt profitable should be derived, in my view, from analyses of human cognitive processes and capacities, and from the recent fast growth of knowledge of the influence of neurotransmitters on speed and organization of attentional and response integrating events. Furthermore, the concepts should be in terms of information processing capacities and strategies.

This volume, therefore, has four general aims:

(1) to present an up-to-date picture of the basic concepts of stress, information processing models, and physiological models of their interrelatedness;

(2) to review the present status of experimental work in psychology on the interaction between stress and the major areas of cognitive functioning;

(3) to consider the major areas of human functioning in which stress is assumed to play a role or to be induced, from the standpoint of human information processing operations and strategies; and

(4) to apply the same conceptual approach to the analysis of two major psychopathological disorders, and their development.

These aims were meant to be the guidelines of all our contributors. This book contains, therefore, discussions of the biochemistry and physiology of the stress response, and a review of current models of the interaction between physiological and electrocortical arousal and the enhancement or attenuation of attention, memory, problem solving, and response selection strategies. The canvas is broadened by a cognitive reinterpretation of personality, and of the adaptive requirements of working in different types of organizational climates, as well as by a fine grain analysis of the physiological stressors of manual and intellectual work. The difficulties of theory building in this complex area of multiple interactions are further illustrated by a close and partially clinical analysis of the cognitive processes of coping with and defending against threats to personal integrity and survival in the face of varying sources of anxiety including those arising from severe illness and bereavement. In addition to a review of methods of assessing the impact of unfavourable life experience, cognitive and physiological models are offered to account for the development of neurotic anxiety and the schizophrenias.

The final chapter will present an evaluation of the theoretical relevance and implications of the ideas of our contributors for research strategies to be favoured in the next two or three years. My own task here, however, is to be prospective, and to indicate briefly how I *expected* various issues to be treated, and what kinds of theoretical developments and reconceptualizations I expected to be initiated here.

A major problem is the definition of the term stress. In the past it appears to have been used to describe the agents of distress as well as its consequences, or the term has been confined to the description of unfavourable and unpleasant outcomes of 'mental' events without considering the effects of effort in muscular or intellectual work. A generalized concept of arousal has been employed to specify a possible unitary agent for distress as well as for performance decrements. The important questions are, however, whether a physiological agent can actually account for individual differences (a) in the experience of distress, (b) for individually and subjectively different *sources* of distress, and (c) for the resulting differences in *types* and *levels* of cognitive processing deficits.

Considerable confusion has been created, in my opinion, by the now fashionable reference to 'environmental stress'. Broadly speaking, we know what this term means. It refers to the aversive effects of an unfavourable physical environment, to the effects of crowding, noise, social and economic deprivations frustrations experienced while commuting to and from work, or to the effects of large-scale housing and industrial developments in a previously quiet rural area. It seems clear that the environmental constraints and changes are fundamentally just stimuli conveying various types and amounts of information in a particular temporal and spatial sequence. The experience of these events as unfavourable, aversive or distressing is, in any event, not universal and a cognitive interpretation of the information is required before the human adaptive systems react with coping or defensive responses. We should talk about environmental stressors, therefore, which lead to responses which are experienced as stressful, and which I would prefer to designate by the term 'strain' or 'load'. Put more simply, I would argue that environmental stress resides in the head and not in the world around us. A 'transaction' does take place, however, and some gains may accrue from a careful taxonomy of environments (Stokols, 1978).

Ecological stressors would seem to be experienced because events present not only opportunities for action, but also because they make demands for adaptation by presenting barriers against subjectively preferred outcomes. The emotions of anxiety, frustration, and anger are important aspects of stressor-strain, and it is now well established that individuals show considerable differences in the ease with which these emotions are generated, as well as in their intensity. Recent studies on people respectively prone and resistant to coronary thrombosis seem to indicate that the former, the so-called 'Type-A', experience higher levels of these emotions than the latter ('Type-B'), with ecological stressors (Rosenman et al., 1975; Glass et al., 1977). This relationship, although previously established less rigorously through psychosomatic medicine, presents us with major explanatory problems. What is the nature of this vulnerability? What are its parameters, and can the differential incidence of heart disease provide us with a new explanatory concept? Can descriptive accounts of public health problems so widely discussed internationally in recent publications (Levi, 1971; 1975; 1978) provide a justification for suggesting an information processing approach to human stress?

The contributors to this volume may give different emphasis to the importance of various subsystems of the responding individual. In my view, a cognitive-informational approach is difficult to avoid, since the perception of an event as a stressor depends fundamentally upon experientially derived predispositions to label events of one type as personally or subjectively acceptable and those of another type as aversive. The greater the number of events previously encoded as aversive, the greater the number of situations which will stimulate long-term memory schemata of this type, and the greater the effort required to avoid their implications and to return to a state of more confortable quiescence. Vulnerability, therefore, seems inevitably linked to a personal cognitive history of experiencing, coping with and defending against stimulation which a given individual codes as aversive or distressing. These, however, are cognitive data representing information of a particular connotation. The larger the data banks for this kind of information, the greater the likelihood that this information will have lower thresholds for selective attention. Since the resources and processing capacities of the cortical information processing system are limited at any given point in time (but with individual differences in resources and capacities), quantitative approaches to the interaction between stress and cognition may not be as fanciful as previously thought. A special difficulty, then, will be the integration of autonomic nervous system and corticosteroid actions and reactions into such a scheme. I am not competent, however, to speculate here, beyond referring to the need to involve conditioning processes, and particularly perhaps, the immediacy, frequency, intensity, and relative permanence of such linkages.

There may be a need, in the service of conceptual integration, to remind ourselves that descriptive or explanatory terms usually associated *either* with 'personality' theory *or* with cognitive processing theory are not restricted to any one of the theories. Conflict, decision-making, and problem solving are three such terms. 'Freudian' or 'schizophrenogenic' conflicts clearly have a different content compared with conflicts due to differences in response bias in a multiple-choice reaction time task, or in serial list learning. In all these cases, however, information has to be received, coded, related to already existing information in memory, and to be selectively attended prior to a response selection process. The difference between types of conflict resolutions has been stated in qualitative terms, but there are those who will continue to argue that qualitative differences are not immune to quantitative restatements. Similar arguments can be advanced for reinterpretations of decision-making and problem solving operations involving 'personality' parameters.

Thus quantitative conceptions are implied in the title of this book, and with it the notion of the data- or information-driven human being. From this is follows that vulnerability to stressors and the deficits from supra-optimal strain may eventually be explained mathematically. I would argue that every stimulus external, internal, physiological, hormonal, involving any sense modality, is in some ways analogous to the position of a pointer on a calibrated dial. The greater the number of dials to be observed simultaneously, the longer the time to process the information they communicate. Also, the greater the number of dials the smaller the possible number of responses, and the greater the probability of making subjectively and objectively inadequate decisions, particularly over extended periods of attention, and when externally paced. The 'strain' or 'load' arising from stressors, likewise, may be seen as information presented on dials, and the number of dials and the pointer positions from which the person has to read it off, is a function of the degree of (conditioned) elaboration and generalization which primary sources of experienced aversiveness have undergone in the preceding years of social reinforcement and adaptation. This is clearly an unsophisticated conceptualization. Its possible merit, however, is my preference for assigning greater weight, than has been customary in cognitive, information processing theory, to internally available and generated *aversive* information. Much of this, however, is fundamentally irrelevant for a particular response.

I cannot be sure that what the contributors to this volume are offering here necessarily constitutes a sufficient number of basic concepts or of established organismic processes to begin a fruitful inductive programme. We did not intend to offer a milestone of achievement. What we have done is to encourage the statement of a number of urgent research problems which could constitute new self-directing tasks. They are those which may be considered to be major prerequisities for the deduction of higher-order principles in the explanation, manipulation, and, eventually, reduction of the adverse effects of stress on social adaptation, intellectual and general performance efficiency, coping capacity, and general lifestyle.

REFERENCES

Glass, D., Singer, J. and Pennebaker, J. (1977). Behavioral and physiological effects of incontrollable environmental events. In D. Stokols (Ed.), *Perspectives on Environment and Behavior*, New York: Plenum Press.

Levi, L. (Ed.) (1975). *Society, Stress and Disease: Vol. 1. The Psychosocial Environment and Psychosomatic Diseases*. London: Oxford University Press.

Levi, L. (Ed.) (1975). *Society, Stress and Disease: Vol. 2. Childhood and Adolescence*. London: Oxford University Press.

Levi, L. (Ed.) (1978). *Society, Stress and Disease: Vol. 3. The Productive and Reproductive Age — Male/Female Roles and Relationships*. Oxford: Oxford University Press.

Rosenman, R., Brand, R. J., Jenkins, C. D., Friedman, M., Strauss, R. and Wurm, M. (1975). Coronary heart disease in the Western Collaborative Group Study: final follow-up experience of 8.5 years. *Journal of the American Medical Association, 233*, 872–877.

Stokols, D. (1978). Environmental psychology. *Annual Review of Psychology, 29*, 253–295.

Basic Mechanisms and Processes

Chapter 1

The Stress Concept
and Some of its Implications

HANS SELYE

1. Introduction
2. Concept of Stress
    (i)   First Mediator
    (ii)   Confusion and Controversy
3. General Adaptation Syndrome
    (i)   Concept
    (ii)   Mechanism
    (iii)   Phenomenon of 'Conditioning'
4. Diseases of Adaptation
5. Neuropsychiatric Implications of Stress
    (i)   Psychosomatic Disorders
    (ii)   Neuroses
    (iii)   Autism and Schizophrenia
    (iv)   Mania and Depression
    (v)   Drug Dependence
    (vi)   Other Psychiatric Conditions
6. Behavioural Implications For Everyday Life
7. References

1. INTRODUCTION

It was more than four decades ago that we performed those first primitive experiments which led to the publication of a 'Letter to the Editor' of *Nature* entitled 'A syndrome produced by diverse nocuous agents' (Selye, 1936). Since that time we have been able to collect more than 120,000 publications (among them several hundred books) which deal with various aspects of what is now known as the stress concept, not only in virtually all fields of medicine, pathology, biochemistry, and medical jurisprudence but also in the behavioural sciences and philosophy. An encyclopaedia quoting 7518 key references from our collection has just been completed under the title *Stress in Health and Disease* (Selye, 1976a), and is meant to act as a detailed guide to the pertinent literature. This voluminous and highly technical treatise appears almost simultaneously with a completely updated edition of *The Stress of Life* (Selye, 1976b), first published about 20 years ago as a simple introduction to this field for general practitioners and medical students, but formulated in a language understandable even by the educated layman.

The panoramic overview of the subject, provided by the re-examination of all aspects of stress research, was necessary for the presentation of the above-mentioned updated synoptic volumes. The compilation of these surveys, as well as the many personal contacts I have had with experts during my lecture tours throughout the world, made it seem opportune at this time to present also the simplest possible synopsis of the main points.

2. CONCEPT OF STRESS

Experiments in 1936 on various species of experimental animals showed (Selye, 1936), that the organism responds in a stereotyped manner to a variety of widely different agents, such as infections, intoxications, trauma, nervous strain, heat, cold, muscular fatigue, and X-irradiation. The specific actions of all these agents are quite different. Their only common feature is that they place the body in a state of stress. Hence, we concluded that the stereotyped response—which is superimposed upon all specific effects — represents a reaction to stress as such.

But what is non-specific stress? The term had long been used in physics to refer to the interaction between a force and the resistance opposed to it. For instance, pressure and tension cause stress in inanimate matter. We thought that the above-mentioned non-specific response represents the biologic equivalent of such physical stress. The term has now been quite generally accepted in medicine not only in English, but — since attempts to translate 'stress' led to much confusion — also in all other languages which have developed a scientific medical literature. We regard as specific actions those which can be elicited only by one or few agents (e.g. the effect of thyrotrophic hormone on the thyroid), while conversely, non-specific actions are those which can be elicited by many agents (e.g. shock, loss of body weight, inflammation, tissue necrosis). Stress is the sum of the non-specific biologic phenomena (including damage and defense), and consequently, a stressor agent is, by definition, non-specific since it produces stress.

You can define stress in various ways, for example, as the wear and tear produced in the body by any type of exposure or, as I have done in all my more recent papers, simply as 'the non-specific response of the body to any demand'.

At an international symposium on 'Society, Stress, and Disease' (Levi, 1971) sponsored by the University of Upsala and the World Health Organization and held in Stockholm in April 1970, Aubrey Kagan presented the following definition: 'Stress is the physiological state that prepares the organism for action'. Having carefully analysed the role of stress in disease and particularly in social maladjustments of various types, he came to the conclusion that, by applying the stress concept to diverse problems of this sort, 'experimental epidemiology, using the disciplines of biochemistry, ethology, mathematics, physiology, psychology, and sociology, may help to replace nature's slow and cruel, and now outmoded, method of "natural selection". It should be more rapid. We will have to make sure that it is also humane and practical.'

In his synopsis of the entire symposium (Levi, 1971), which placed major emphasis upon the normal and morbid psychologic manifestations of responses to stress, Levi suggested that the expression 'Stress (Selye)' be used when the term is employed in my sense, that is, to designate 'the non-specific response of the body to any demand' and that any author wishing to give it another connotation, such as psychogenic stress, burn stress, cold stress, muscular stress, should define the meaning in which he wishes to employ the word.

I would fully concur with this solution but, since most authors use the word in this sense (which corresponds to my definition as previously mentioned), I feel that the addition of my name — though flattering — is not necessary. Besides, I do not think it is objectionable to use such designations as psychogenic, psychosocial, traumatic and other types of stress, as long as it is clearly understood that these qualifying remarks are added merely for the sake of convenience to identify the stressor that called forth the stress reaction in any particular case, since the reaction itself is by definition stereotypical and always identical. The apparent differences are merely due to the specific actions of the stimulus and the specific responsivity of the individual reacting to it and, hence, may be regarded as features superimposed upon stress itself, produced by a particular agent or experienced by a particular individual.

As we shall see later, in man, with his very highly developed central nervous system, psychogenic stress is the most common and by far the most important from a medical point of view. Both an excess and an insufficiency of stimulation may be pathogenic. This is true of somatic activities (unused muscles, or those employed only rarely, undergo atrophy; the same is true of many other organ systems). The fact is particularly evident, however, in the case of the central nervous system. Here, too little input leads to boredom and, under extreme conditions of sensory deprivation, even to hallucinations and severe (though transient) mental disturbances. Such dramatic results have been seen not only under laboratory conditions but even in astronauts and submarine crews on long and uneventful voyages. It is a truism to say that man is a social being. Contact with others to gain support, is indispensable for normal health and its lack may lead to autism, various types of neurotic behaviour, and other disturbances. Such everyday experiences have much in common with the syndrome of 'sensory deprivation'.

(i) First Mediator

In the first paper (Selye, 1936) in which I tried to sketch a blueprint for the possible scientific formulation and analysis of the stress syndrome, I emphasized the fundamental weakness of our inability to identify the mediating factor that conducts the information that a state of stress exists from the primarily affected area to the hypothalamo-pituitary axis. The simplest explanation is that nervous pathways transmit such messages directly to the hypophysiotrophic area of the hypothalamus, but this mechanism is certainly unable to explain the entire role of the first mediator. Even some modern investigators tend to disregard conclusive experiments disproving mediation exclusively through nervous pathways. For example, complete deafferentation of the hypophysiotrophic area by the Halász knife has shown that a variety of stressors can still cause adrenocorticotrophic hormone (ACTH) secretion through humoral pathways (see also section 4, below).

But what could the humoral first mediator be? It must be a substance that can be released into the blood stream from virtually any tissue, since a stressor applied anywhere in the body is able to produce a typical systemic stress reaction. In my first paper (Selye, 1936) I suggested that histamine or some related tissue hormone may represent the first mediator, since it can be liberated from virtually any tissue by virtually any stimulus. Furthermore, intravenous injection of histamine is a potent stimulator of ACTH production.

During the more than four decades since this hypothesis was put forward on purely theoretical grounds, a number of experiments have been published which appear either to confirm or to invalidate it. In addition, more recent observations have brought forth equally convincing and yet debatable arguments that other more or less ubiquitous tissue hormones (e.g. prostaglandins and various protein degradation products) could act in this capacity. All these possibilities deserve careful exploration since the nature of the first mediator is of vital importance in understanding the very basis of stress responses. Yet, it must be admitted that at present this question has not been solved.

Of course, it is by no means essential that the stress reaction is invariably initiated and mediated by the same substance; it might be that the receptors in regulating centres, for example, in the hypothalamus, react stereotypically to a number of chemical messengers brought to them by the blood whenever there is any kind of increased demand anywhere in the body. Indeed, we have no definite proof that the first mediator is a substance or a group of substances rather than a deficiency in some vitally important blood constituent which is 'used up' during any kind of biologic activity. In this respect, stress could be compared with fatigue or energy consumption which likewise are non-specific responses to any demand, pleasant or unpleasant. Moreover, energy utilization for any reason and in any part of the body may result in generalized fatigue, or functional impairments throughout the organism. It is certainly disappointing that after the many years of research since the first description of the 'alarm reaction' during which we have learned so much about the subsequent mediation of the stress response through the hypothalamo-pituitary-adrenal and the sympathetic nervous systems, the nature of the first mediator still remains an enigma.

We do know, however, that the transducers of electric nervous impulses into humoral substances are special cells in the basal hypothalamus which produce polypeptides, such as the corticotrophin-releasing factor (CRF), the structure of which has now been definitely identified. Much less is known about the dynamics of factors produced during stress at lower levels (e.g. hormones) and acting in the opposite direction upon neuropsychiatric processes. Yet, such psychotrophic effects of catecholamines, ACTH, and corticoids have been well established under certain circumstances, in both animal experiments and in man.

(ii) Confusion and Controversy

Some of the most frequently discussed causes of confusion and controversy in stress are related to the role of the nervous system. They have been dealt with recently by J. W. Mason and myself (Mason, 1975a; 1975b; Selye, 1975), but here I would like to call attention only to two points. Firstly, how can the same agent (the stressor) produce diverse manifestations or even different diseases? This is a confusing point but it can be answered by realizing that: (a) Qualitatively different stimuli of equal stressor potency (as judged by their ability to elicit the triad or ACTH and corticoid production) do not necessarily cause the same syndrome in different individuals. (b) Even the same degree of stress induced by the same stimulus may provoke different lesions in different individuals. As a matter of fact, these statements are true not only of nervous maladies but also of every kind of stress disease.

Secondly, why can we not accept emotional arousal as the common cause of stress responses, since it is 'one of the most ubiquitous or relatively "non-specific" reactions common to a great diversity of situations?' This question was foreseen in the first edition of my book *The Stress of Life* (Selye, 1976b). Undoubtedly, in man with his highly developed central nervous system, emotional arousal is the most common cause of stress but this is not so in lower animals or microbes which have no nervous system and yet they also react non-specifically to stress when faced with demands. Furthermore, even in mammals, it has been shown very clearly that the entire hypophysiotrophic area could be surgically isolated from the rest of the brain by a special knife (generally known as the Halász knife) pushed from the cortex down to the base of the skull. Using this instrument, it is possible to accomplish a complete deafferentation of the hypophysiotrophic area, which remains in contact only with the pituitary through the stalk. After this intervention, there is no reduction in basal ACTH secretion; in fact, this is usually above normal, and the anterior lobe can still respond to various physical stressors, such as ether, restraint, tourniquet shock, formalin, etc., by a rise in plasma ACTH, resulting in increased plasma corticoid levels. Even removal of one adrenal still causes hypertrophy of the contralateral gland. These reactions do not occur if the median eminence, in the hypophysiotrophic area, is destroyed. Thus there remains no doubt that neurohumoral stimuli do initiate the stress response, even when emotional arousal or any other cortical stimulus can no longer activate the median eminence of the hypothalamus to secrete CRF for releasing ACTH from the pituitary.

3. GENERAL ADAPTATION SYNDROME

In my early investigations, the most outstanding manifestations of the stress response were: adrenocortical enlargement with histologic signs of hyperactivity, thymicolymphatic involution with certain concomitant changes in the blood count (eosinopenia, lymphopenia, polynucleosis), and gastrointestinal ulcers, often accompanied by other manifestations of damage or shock. We were struck by the fact that, while during this reaction, all the organs of the body show involutional or degenerative changes, the adrenal cortex actually seemed to flourish on stress. We suspected this adrenal response to play a useful part in a non-specific adaptive reaction, which we visualized as a 'call to arms' of the body's defense forces and therefore designated as the 'alarm reaction'.

(i) Concept

It soon became apparent that this alarm reaction was not the entire response. Upon continued exposure to a stressor capable of eliciting the initial reaction, a stage of adaptation or resistance ensued, since no organism can be maintained continuously in a state of alarm. If the stressor is so severe that continued exposure becomes incompatible with life, the animal dies within a few hours or days during the alarm reaction. If it does survive, the initial response is necessarily followed by a stage of resistance during which the symptoms subside. After still more exposure to the stressor, this acquired adaptation is lost again and the animals enter into a third phase, the stage of exhaustion, since the 'adaptation energy' or adaptability of an organism is always finite.

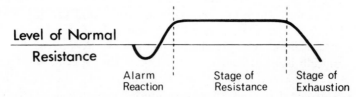

FIGURE 1.1 Resistance during the General Adaptation Syndrome. In the acute phase of the alarm reaction, general resistance to the stressor with which the G.A.S. has been elicited, falls below normal. As adaptation is required, in the stage of resistance, the capacity to resist rises considerably above normal. Eventually, in the stage of exhaustion, resistance drops below normal again. (From *Stress without Distress*, copyright © 1974 by Hans Selye, M. D. Reproduced by permission of J. B. Lippincott Company)

All these observations suggested the need for an all-embracing name for the entire syndrome. We called it the 'General Adaptation Syndrome' (G.A.S.), emphasizing its evolution in three stages (Figure 1.1):

Alarm reaction. This occurs upon sudden exposure to noxious stimuli to which the organism is not adapted. The reaction has two phases:

(a) *Shock phase,* the initial and immediate reaction to the noxious agent. Various signs of injury such as tachycardia, loss of muscle tone, depressed temperature and blood pressure are characteristic symptoms.

(b) *Countershock phase,* a rebound phase marked by the mobilization of defensive forces. This phase merges into the next defensive phase, during which the adrenal cortex is enlarged and secretion of adrenocorticoid hormones is increased.

Stage of resistance. This is marked by full adaptation to the stressor during which symptoms improve or disappear. There is, however, a concurrent decrease in resistance to other stimuli.

Stage of exhaustion. Since adaptability is finite, exhaustion inexorably follows if the stressor is sufficiently severe and applied for a prolonged period of time. Symptoms reappear and if stress continues unabated, death ensues.

Fortunately, most of the physical or mental exertions, infections, and other stressors which act upon us produce only changes corresponding to the first and second stages.

(ii) Mechanism

Subsequent studies showed that alarm signals emanate from stressed tissue and reach coordination centres of the nervous system (Figure 1.2) Then the chief event is the stimulation of the pituitary which initiates the countershock phase. As a result, adrenocorticotrophic hormone (ACTH) is secreted rapidly, in great amounts. In turn, ACTH stimulates the adrenal cortex to discharge the hormones which we named 'corticoids'. Some of these, the pro-inflammatory corticoids, stimulate the proliferative ability and reactivity of the connective tissue; they enhance the 'inflammatory potential'. Thus they help to put up a strong barricade of connective tissue through which the body is protected against further invasion by pathogenic stressor agents. Because of their prominent effect upon salt and water metabolism, these hormones have also been referred to as 'mineralocorticoids' (e.g. desoxycorticosterone, aldosterone, somatotrophic hormone).

However, under ordinary conditions, ACTH stimulates the adrenal much more effectively to secrete anti-inflammatory corticoids. These hormones inhibit the ability of the body to put up granulomatous barricades in the path of the invader; in fact, they tend to cause involution of connective tissue with a pronounced depression of the inflammatory potential. Thus they open the way

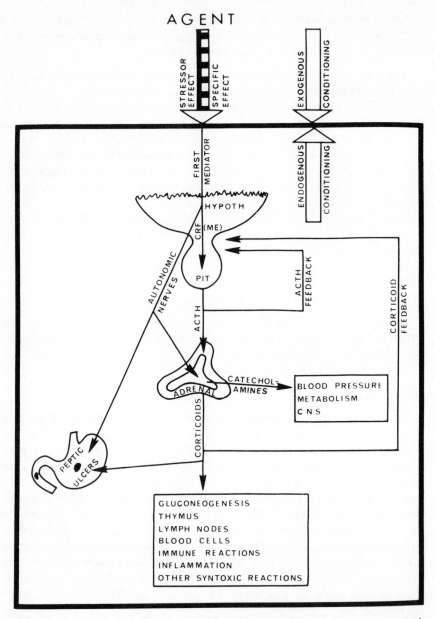

FIGURE 1.2. Principal pathways mediating the response to a stressor agent and the conditioning factors which modify its effect. When an agent acts upon the body (thick outer frame of the diagram), the effect will depend upon three factors (broad vertical arrows pointing to the upper horizontal border of the frame). All agents possess both non-specific stressor effects (solid part of arrow) and specific properties (interrupted part of arrow). The latter are variable and characteristic

to the spreading of infection. Because of their marked effect upon carbohydrate metabolism, I named these hormones 'glucocorticoids' (e.g. ACTH, cortisone, cortisol).

Adrenocorticotrophic hormone usually stimulates the adrenal to produce the various corticoids in more or less fixed proportion and always with a great predominance of anti-inflammatory corticoids. However, STH — the somatotrophic hormone or 'growth hormone' of the pituitary — also increases the inflammatory potential of connective tissue somewhat as the pro-inflammatory corticoids do; hence, it selectively sensitizes the target area to the actions of the latter.

While the basic response to systemic stressors expresses itself in the G.A.S. as outlined above, the fundamental reaction pattern to topical stressors results in a 'local adaptation syndrome' (L.A.S.) in which inflammation and degeneration or necrosis of tissues play important parts. Although these two types of defensive reactions operate through different mechanisms, they resemble each other in that both are non-specific, triphasic, and particularly sensitive to adaptive hormones. The G.A.S. and L.A.S. mutually influence each other, in that local injury activates not only the local, but also the systemic, non-specific defense mechanisms while the resulting G.A.S. can, in turn, regulate the course of topical reactions to stress.

Pretreatment with various systemic and topical stressors can offer non-specific cross-resistance against the production of manifold structurally distinct lesions that are otherwise elicited by diverse pathogens in various organs. In many instances, particularly when the morbid change is essentially an inflammatory lesion, this cross-resistance depends upon an increased anti-inflammatory hormone effect due to activation of the pituitary-adrenocortical axis. Yet, certain types of cross-resistance are demonstrable even in adrenalectomized animals, and in some cases, increased thyroid hormone activity appears to be the cause of the induced tolerance.

The bulk of evidence now available suggests that all forms of cross-resistance cannot be attributed to any single biochemical mechanism. This is true even of those truly non-specific types that are induced by stress itself. We must remember that, although the response to stress is essentially stereotyped and

---

of each individual agent; they will not be discussed here other than to state that they are inseparably attached to the stressor effect and invariably modify it. The other two heavy vertical arrows, pointing toward the upper border of the frame, represent exogenous and endogenous conditioning factors that largely determine the reactivity of the body. It is clear that since all stressors have some specific effects, they cannot elicit exactly the same response in all organs; furthermore, even the same agent will act differently on different individuals, depending upon the internal and external conditioning factors that determine their reactivity. (Reproduced by permission of Butterworths, Reading, Mass., U.S.A. from Selye (1976a))

largely independent of the evocative agent, it represents a mosaic of numerous local and systemic, humoral and nervous reactions, some of which may protect against one pathogen, others against another. Up to now, major emphasis has been placed upon the pathogenic actions of stressors; but it has become abundantly evident that stress also possesses prophylactic and therapeutic value: it can induce non-specific resistance to a great variety of potential pathogens.

There is no doubt that the thyroid gland is also involved in stress reactions and of course it is dependent upon the hypothalamo-pituitary system. Yet despite certain claims, no really convincing evidence is available to show that the thyroid gland plays a significant role in the phenomenon of cross-resistance except in so far as an increase or decrease in metabolism, or more particularly in thyroid hormone secretion itself, does influence virtually every type of biologic reaction.

(iii) Phenomenon of 'Conditioning'

In stress research, the term 'conditioning' is not used in the Pavlovian sense. It is used to express the general concept for which it was originally created, namely, setting the conditions for something to take place (e.g. susceptibility or resistance).

In relation to psychological and psychiatric problems, conditioning factors are undoubtedly of great importance. It had been shown long ago that overdosage with corticoids and similar steroid compounds can cause a state of excitation, followed by deep anaesthesia; mineralocorticoids may produce damage to brain vessels conducive to epileptoid convulsions or serious disturbances of neuromuscular functions, which resemble those seen in familial periodic paralysis. The production of convulsions by 'Metrazol' or electroshock can be greatly influenced by steroid hormones; androgenic and oestrogenic hormones (such as occur not only in the gonads, but also in the adrenals) exert an important effect upon the sexual and fighting behaviour.

The rate of secretion of the adrenal cortex has been measured by circulating lymphocytes. As little as 0.005 micrograms of adrenalin per 100 grams of rat body weight elicits marked lymphopenia, which is one of the signs of an alarm reaction to trauma or sudden stress. Significantly, both rage and injections of ACTH produce lymphopenia. Apparently, emotional excitement initiates activation of the adrenal cortex via the anterior pituitary while this body itself is primarily activated by adrenalin released from the adrenal medulla. Thus research on stress and the G.A.S. has clarified the interaction between the anterior lobe of the pituitary and the adrenal cortex in sustained defense against stress.

4. DISEASES OF ADAPTATION

The pathogenicity of many systemic and local irritants depends largely upon proper functioning of the hypothalamo-pituitary-adrenal axis. The latter may either enhance or inhibit the body's defense reactions against stressors, and disruptions of this adaptive mechanism are the principal factor in the production of certain maladies which, therefore, we consider as essentially diseases of adaptation.

Imperfections of the G.A.S. are not so much the direct results of external agents such as infections or intoxications, but rather consequences of the body's inability to meet these agents by adequate adaptive reactions, that is, by a perfect G.A.S.

Among the disruptions of the G.A.S. which may cause disease, the following are particularly important:

(a) An absolute excess or deficiency in the amount of corticoids and STH produced during stress.

(b) A disproportion in the relative secretion, during stress, of ACTH and glucocorticoids on the one hand, and of STH and mineralocorticoids on the other.

(c) Production of metabolic derangements by stress, which abnormally alter the target organ's response to STH, ACTH, or corticoids (through conditioning).

(d) Finally, we must not forget that although the hypothalamo-pituitary-adrenal mechanism plays a prominent role in the G.A.S., other organs which participate in the latter (e.g. liver, kidney) may also respond abnormally and become the cause of disease during adaptation to stress.

It is common knowledge that maladaptation plays an important part also in nervous and mental diseases. Bodily changes during stress act upon the mind and *vice versa*. Expressions as 'this work gives me a headache' or 'drives me crazy' are not without real significance. Many types of intense headaches or mental breakdowns are actually caused by work to which we are ill adapted. In people with a given hereditary structure, it is often the stress of adjustment to life under difficult circumstances that causes breakdown. In other persons, faulty adaptation may result in cardiovascular, metabolic, digestive, inflammatory or kidney diseases, in sexual disturbances, infections, diabetes, cancer, eclampsia, rheumatic diseases, arthritis, allergies or hypertension, depending upon the site or organ that is most predisposed to be the target of disease. The study of the influence of emotional stress in the aetiology or recurrence of a disease entity began with isolated individual case reports, only to progress more recently to multidisciplinary experimental investigations which attempt to establish correlations between well-defined emotional conflict situations with specific organ responses, and to identify the specific neurophysiologic and neuroendocrine pathways through which the emotional stress exerts its influence.

For a better understanding of the physiological and psychological aspects of stress, it was always deemed most important to explore fully not only the production of steroid hormones during stress, but also their metabolic pathways. Most recent findings at our institute have brought us a great step forward in this direction. Testing hundreds of steroids for their 'catatoxic' (from the Greek *'kata'* meaning 'down or against') activity, we found that certain steroids protect against otherwise fatal poisoning with digitalis, 'Metrazol', and nicotine, the sedative effect of barbiturates and steroid anaesthetics, the calcifying arteriosclerotic lesions elicited by poisoning with vitamin D derivatives and numerous other toxic agents. Certain steroids (glucocorticoids) are 'syntoxic' in that they permit a symbiotic coexistence with the pathogen by merely modifying inappropriate tissue reactions. By contrast, the catatoxic steroids actually destroy the pathogen, usually through the induction of defensive enzymes. The catatoxic effect of such steroids is quite independent of any other steroid hormone activity. It is not yet known to what extent normally excreted stress steroid hormones exert this protective action, but even physiological concentrations are effective in our studies.

5. NEUROPSYCHIATRIC IMPLICATIONS OF STRESS

Innumerable observations have been made on the neuropsychiatric implications of the stress concept, but little would be gained by discussing these at length, especially since an extensive chapter was devoted to this subject in my recent encyclopedia on stress (Selye, 1976a).

Because of the many overlaps, it is very difficult to classify mental diseases into sharply delimited categories but, in order to bring some degree of orderliness into our discussion, we shall try to clarify the most important ones as far as this appears to be possible. In their monograph devoted to *Anxiety and Stress*, Basowitz *et al.* (1954) gave us an excellent description of stress and the G.A.S. with main emphasis upon the correlation between somatic and mental manifestations. A comprehensive review on 'the most important results of stress research (up to 1957) and their significance in psychiatry' was published by D. Langer (1958), quoting several hundred references directly concerned with this interrelation and analysing the data from the psychiatrist's viewpoint. In their famous monograph, *The Vital Balance — The Life Process in Mental Health and Illness*, Karl Menninger and his coworkers (1963) made a careful analysis of the relationship between mental disease and the G.A.S., particularly with regard to the triphasic development of psychologic defenses which—like the somatic ones that we have dealt with — go consecutively through the stages of alarm, resistance, and exhaustion. In the same volume, they also placed special emphasis upon the 'first-order ego-tension disturbance' as the mental equivalent of the alarm reaction. More recently, Donald Oken summarized the whole concept of the stress of daily life and its potential pathogenic effects, from the psychosocial point of view in a language easily understandable to the layman (Miller, 1974).

(i) Psychosomatic Disorders

Undoubtedly, many psychosomatic derangements are due to stress and particularly to disruptions of the G.A.S. Many of these depend not so much upon the apparent pathogen but upon the way we react to it. This was clearly expressed by the much-quoted sentence formulated by Parry in the eighteenth century when he wrote: 'It is much more important to know what sort of a patient has a disease, than what sort of a disease a patient has.' The point is well documented by more modern studies showing that 'clusters of illness' often occur during periods that are significantly stressful for people striving to adapt to conflicting and often threatening demands. As Bastiaans (1973) put it: 'For many years the author, following the concept of Selye's adaptation syndrome, has described psychiatric and psychosomatic syndromes in the framework of Selye's sequence: shock, alarm, adaptation and exhaustion. In this way one may distinguish shock syndromes, alarm syndrome, adaptation syndrome and exhaustion syndrome.'

Many of the psychosomatic derangements can be predicted by questionnaires, such as the 'Schedule of Recent Experiences' of Holmes and Rahe (1967). Among the most common somatic diseases frequently traced to a psychogenic stress situation are: allergies, asthma, skin disorders, gastrointestinal maladies, and derangements of the cardiovascular system, particularly hypertension and coronary heart disease. Even immune reactions can be influenced by psychogenic stress and, in latent diabetics, keto-acidosis is occasionally precipitated by emotional stimuli (Selye, 1976a).

(ii) Neuroses

The most common stress-induced minor nervous derangements are migraine headaches, chronic fatigue, and bruxism as well as various types of neurotic behaviour, which are viewed by numerous authors as manifestations of maladjustments to the stress of life (Dunbar, 1947; Alexander, 1950; Wolff et al., 1950; Hinkle and Wolff, 1957; Wolf, 1963). However, inconvertible objective proof of deranged ACTH or corticoid secretion has not been consistently obtained in psychoneurotic subjects.

Among the neurotic manifestations just mentioned, migraine headaches have received particularly careful attention. Extensive studies have shown that, especially in hereditarily predisposed people, the most frequent precipitating factors are 'emotional reactions to changes in life situation; various psychosocial stressors, periods of overactivity and "letdown" periods. In addition to the operation of the above-mentioned psychological factors, which constitute a psychosomatic sequence of events, there are also mood changes which may accompany an attack of migraine associated with alterations in energy, concentration, and ability to work' (Rees, 1974). It has also been found that 'factors that deplete noradrenalin stores from nerve endings (reserpine, tyramine, phenylethylamine, and stress) may elicit migrainous attacks in sensitive subjects, and in severe headache crisis, catecholamine depletion may be a secondary component of stress' (Parantainen, 1975).

On the other hand, it should be stated that there is an abundance of reliable data concerning the production by stress of *experimental neuroses, including drug consumption in animals* (Liddell, 1952; Casey, 1960; Powell *et al.*, 1966; Cicero *et al.*, 1968; Parker and Radow, 1974). Among these animal models of neuroses, sound-precipitated seizures or convulsions have perhaps been studied most carefully, and a review of 145 papers from the entire world literature was written on the subject as early as 1955 (Bevan, 1955). These conditions show how — in genetically predisposed species of rats, mice, and other animals (as well as occasionally in man) — stress (particularly that of sound) can elicit seizures reminiscent of epilepsy. It is of interest to note that Eränkö and Muittari (1957) found that stress-induced neurosis in rats is associated with hypertrophy of the adrenal cortex — the characteristic indicator of the G.A.S.

(iii) Autism and Schizophrenia

Evidence is particularly strong with regard to the important role played by stress in the pathogenesis of autism. In fact, Tinbergen (1974) devoted his Nobel lecture to 'Ethology and stress diseases', emphasizing that the parents of autistic children are often under stress and that 'at least a large proportion of autists are victims of some kind of environmental stress, whose basic trouble is of an emotional nature'.

According to some authors, autism should really be considered as one type of infantile schizophrenia which requires a special discussion. There seems to be general agreement that stressful life situations can precipitate schizophrenia in genetically predisposed individuals. The first studies pointing to a possible relationship between schizophrenia and the G.A.S. led to the conclusion that schizophrenics — unlike normal subjects — fail to react to various stressors with the usual indications of increased corticoid secretion, sometimes even exhibiting an inverse response. In addition they do not show the normal circadian variations in corticoid production, and some schizophrenics appear to be resistant even to the adrenotrophic effects of exogenous ACTH. Since these patients are regarded as having been 'broken as a result of the stresses of daily life', this basic failure of a fundamental stress-response mechanism is especially interesting (Hoagland, 1947; Pechstein, 1952; Williams, 1953; Binswanger and Meier, 1953; Delay *et al.*, 1953; Fischer and Agnew, 1955; Popoff, 1966; Jacobs, 1972; Serban, 1975) [see also Warburton, Chapter 13 in this book].

According to Lingjaerde (1953), 'acute schizophrenia is an active stage and expression of a deranged homeostasis, an alarm reaction with efforts to adaptation, while the "chronic inactive defect-schizophrenia" is an adaptation disease in Selye's sense'. Particular attention has been given to the often deranged ACTH and corticoid secretion in schizophrenics under stress (Hoagland et al., 1946; Friedlander et al., 1950; Lehmann, 1952; Sachar et al., 1966; Carroll, 1975). However, there is considerable evidence that the metabolism of catecholamines, the other very important group of stress hormones, is likewise abnormal in many schizophrenics (Sachar et al., 1963; Lovegrove et al., 1965).

(iv) Mania and Depression

One of the most frequently emphasized observations, suggesting a relationship between the G.A.S. and manic-depressive diseases, is that the first episode is often precipitated by environmental stressors (Bunney et al., 1972). Furthermore, the corticoid and catecholamine levels of plasma and urine are reportedly high in manic-depressive patients, particularly during acute exacerbations of the disease. In fact, comparative studies on patients with Cushing's syndrome and these mental diseases 'support the possibility of a primary brain state alteration which results in both a depressive affect associated with loss of ego-defense strength and in stimulation of the hypothalamic-pituitary-adrenal axis' (Rubin and Mandell, 1966). Among other pertinent observations, we should mention that the circadian rhythm of corticoid production is allegedly altered in depressed patients (Bunney et al., 1965; Bridges and Jones, 1966; Hullin et al., 1967; Rubin, 1967; Sachar, 1967; Carroll et al., 1968; Carroll and Davies, 1970). Whereas dexamethasone diminishes the plasma cortisol level in manic depressives, lithium carbonate usually raises it, perhaps because it elicits a 'general stress reaction' (Platman and Fieve, 1968).

In a particularly extensive study, depressives showed elevations of plasma and urinary corticoids, with disturbances in the circadian rhythm and resistance to dexamethasone suppression of corticoid production (Butler and Besser, 1968). On the other hand, in some clinical investigations (Carroll et al., 1968), the midnight dexamethasone suppression test was ineffective in depressives and 'resistance to dexamethasone suppression correlated with the clinical rating of the severity of depression while recovery from depression was associated with the return of normal responsiveness to dexamethasone'. Special attention has been given to the fact that many patients suffering from Cushing's disease and from depression share the following disturbances: (a) an abnormal circadian cortisol rhythm, (b) impaired cortisol suppression by dexamethasone, (c) impaired cortisol response to hypoglycaemia, and (d) elevated cortisol secretion rates (Carroll, 1973). According to these investigations, successful lithium treatment of the depression also reverses the hypothalamus-pituitary-adrenal disturbances. The high unbound plasma cortisol levels are likewise uninfluenced by dexamethasone in both Cushing's disease and depression (Carroll, 1975). It appears that men with unipolar depression have a significantly lower cortisol-binding capacity than normals (King, 1973). Finally, biochemical changes allegedly related to depression include derangements in serotonin, adrenalin, noradrenalin, dopamine, free fatty acids, and other components which show characteristic alterations during stress (Funkenstein *et al.*, 1952; Bunney *et al.*, 1965; Bridges and Jones, 1966; Hullin *et al.*, 1967; Rubin, 1967; Sachar, 1967; Carroll *et al.*, 1968; Perez-Reyes, 1969; Carroll and Davies, 1970; Carroll, 1973; 1975; Flach, 1974; Messiha *et al.*, 1974; Schildkraut, 1974; Shopsin *et al.*, 1974).

In his instructive volume, *The Secret Strength of Depression*, Frederic Flach (1974) tells us that 'depression is not limited to specific times and places, however, because it is essentially a reaction to stress . . . and being depressed in the face of stress is still considered by a large number of people as a mark of weakness and hence a source of embarrassment'. Actually, according to him, 'the only healthy reaction to many life situations is depression'. It automatically prevents people from persisting in activities which exceed their powers of resistance.

(v) Drug Dependence

Drug dependence, including alcoholism, have also been ascribed to stress, particularly the distress of being unable to cope with the problems of daily life and the consequent tendency to replace reality with the pleasant sensations offered by drugs. Yet, corticoids have been of little use in the treatment of these conditions. It has been suggested that alcoholics go 'through the stages of alarm reaction, resistance, and eventually exhaustion' (Tintera, 1966). This is very likely, but there is little tangible evidence to support such a view. Although stress is probably involved in drug dependence not much proof has been obtained to show severe and consistent hormonal disturbances in addicts to various drugs (Glickman and Blumenfield, 1967; Margraf *et al.*, 1967; Cushman *et al.*, 1970; Merry and Marks, 1972; Allman, 1973; Takki and Tammisto, 1974).

(vi) Other Psychiatric Conditions

In *senile psychotics* the plasma corticoid and eosinophil responses to the stressor effect of blindfolding are excessive, but their reactions to ACTH remain normal (Kral *et al.*, 1964; 1967). It was supposed that senile psychosis 'might have its cause in a dysfunction of either the pituitary or the hypothalamus or both' (Kral *et al.*, 1967). Yet, there is no clean-cut evidence of a disturbance of neurohormonal reactions to stress in senile psychotics other than the theory suggesting that aging in general is largely the consequence of the cumulative effects of the stressors of daily life.

It is hardly relevant to discuss in detail the rather scanty observations connecting *other neuropsychiatric maladies* with stress, particularly Parkinson's disease, retrograde amnesia, insomnia, multiple sclerosis, Huntington's disease,

Mongoloid idiocy, and the illness common in various parts of Latin America known as 'susto', although our documentation service contains numerous articles attempting to show that stress can be the decisive factor in the pathogenesis of these and many other derangements of the nervous system.

Ever since the introduction of the various *shock therapies* (electroshock, insulin shock, 'Metrazol' shock, cold baths, hot baths, physiotherapy, etc.), some relationships between mobilization of the stress mechanisms and the therapy of neuropsychiatric ailments have been suspected. More recently, an entire monograph was devoted to the review of ancient and modern procedures for relieving distress through modifications of psychological activity (Lande, 1976). These comprise transcendental meditation, yoga, transactional analysis, existential analysis, primal therapy, scientology, biofeedback, Zen, Tibetan Buddhism, all the way to witchcraft and Reverend Moon's Unification Church. Many of these techniques have definitely shown, at least on the basis of empirical evidence, that they do help people to surmount the stresses and strains of daily life. Others, however, are obviously mere superstitions and, often, fraudulent attempts to gain recognition and wealth. It is perhaps rather fortunate that the vast majority of these innumerable 'mindstyles and lifestyles' have been thus brought together for review, between an introduction on modern concepts of stress by myself and a concluding chapter on the philosophy of it all by R. Buckminster Fuller (Lande, 1976).

6. BEHAVIOURAL IMPLICATIONS FOR EVERYDAY LIFE

From what the laboratory and the clinical study of somatic diseases has taught us concerning stress, I have tried to arrive at a code of ethics based not on traditions of our society, inspiration, or blind faith in the infallibility of a particular prophet, religious leader, or political doctrine, but on the scientifically verifiable laws that govern the body's reactions in maintaining homeostasis and living in satisfying equilibrium with its surroundings.

In a recent book *Stress without Distress* (Selye, 1974), which deals with the behavioural implications of the stress concept, and in my autobiography (Selye, 1977), I have attempted to show in more detail how we can adjust our personal reactions to enjoy fully the pleasurable stress of success and accomplishment without suffering the distress commonly generated by frustrated friction and purposeless aggressive behaviour against our surroundings.

Stress is our central concept; however, we must clearly distinguish between an excess of demands which causes *hyperstress* (or overstress) and a deficiency which leads to *hypostress* (or understress). Similarly, a distinction must be made between pleasure, enjoyment, satisfaction, ecstasy, or the sense of fulfilment which we experience during certain stress reactions, referred to as *eustress*, and the frequent and more pathogenic occurrence of unpleasant, unhealthy, or damaging events, that are referred to as *distress*.

Perhaps a word should be said here about the problem of decision-making, which for certain individuals is an extremely difficult task and would fall into the category of hyperstress. On the other hand, it is also a most characteristic symptom in people under stress that they find it very difficult to arrive at decisions and make them only at the price of considerable mental anguish if they feel forced into it. This may well be a consequence of the equally typical disturbance in the ability to concentrate on a certain subject under stress.

When used without any qualifying prefix, the term stress is usually identified with distress in the public mind. I would not object to this since what we usually speak about and want to eliminate during stressful life events is distress. It is quite acceptable to adhere to this usage even in scientific publications as long as the sense of these words is once clearly explained and the terms are more precisely specified whenever necessary.

It is a biologic law that man — like the lower animals — must fight and work for some goal that he considers worthwhile. We must use our innate capacities to enjoy the eustress of fulfilment. Only through effort, often aggressive egoistic effort, can we maintain our fitness and assure our homeostatic equilibrium with the surrounding society and the inanimate world. To achieve this state, our activities must earn lasting results; the fruits of work must be cumulative and must provide a capital gain to meet future needs. To succeed, we have to accept the scientifically established fact that man has an inescapable natural urge to work egoistically for things that can be stored to strengthen his resistance to imbalance in the unpredictable situations with which life may confront him. These are not instincts we should combat or be ashamed of. We can do nothing about having been built to work, and it is primarily for our own good. Organs that are not used (muscles, bones, even the brain) undergo inactivity atrophy, and every living being looks out first of all for itself. There is no example in Nature of a creature guided exclusively by altruism and the desire to protect others. In fact, a code of universal altruism would be highly immoral, since it would expect others to look out for us more than for themselves.

'Love thy neighbour as thyself' is a command filled with wisdom, but as originally expressed it is incompatible with biologic laws; we need not develop an inferiority complex if we cannot love all our fellowmen on command. Neither should we feel guilty because we work for treasures that can be stored to ensure our future homeostatic capacity. Hoarding is a vitally important biological instinct that we share with animals such as ants, bees, squirrels, and beavers.

How can we develop a code of ethics that accepts egoism and working to hoard personal capital as morally correct? That is what I attempted to do in *Stress without Distress* (Selye, 1974) and here I shall summarize the main conclusions in the form of three basic guidelines:

(a) *Find your own natural predilections and stress level.* People differ with regard to the amount and kind of work they consider worth doing to meet the exigencies of daily life and to assure their future security and happiness. In this respect, all of us are influenced by hereditary predispositions and the expectations of our society. Only through planned self-analysis can we establish what we really want; too many people suffer all their lives because they are too conservative to risk a radical change and break with traditions.

(b) _Altruistic egoism._ The selfish hoarding of the goodwill, respect, esteem, support, and love of our neighbour is the most efficient way to give vent to our pent-up energy and create enjoyable, beautiful or useful things.

(c) _Earn thy neighbour's love._ This motto, unlike love on command, is compatible with man's structure, and although it is based on altruistic egoism, it could hardly be attacked as unethical. Who would blame him who wants to assure his own homeostatic capacity and happiness by accumulating the treasure of other people's benevolence towards him? Yet this makes him virtually unassailable, for nobody wants to attack and destroy those upon whom he depends.

These are the main principles derived from observations on the basic mechanisms that maintain homeostasis in cells, people, and entire societies, and which help them face the stressors encountered in their constant fight for survivial, security, and well-being. Once understood and clearly formulated we can use them best by conscious control.

We are still far from accomplishing our final aim, the greatest obligation of science to humanity. Still, it is hoped by many of us that a purely scientific code of ethics would have sufficient appeal, in eastern as well as in western civilizations, to bring about our common ideal of stable peace on earth.

7. REFERENCES

Alexander, F. (1950). _Psychosomatic Medicine. Its Principles and Applications._ New York: Norton.

Allman, L. R. (1973). Group drinking during stress: effects on alcohol intake and group process. _International Journal of the Addictions,_ **8**, 475-488.

Basowitz, H., Persky, H., Korchin, S. J. and Grinker, R. R. (1954). _Anxiety and Stress: An Interdisciplinary Study of a Life Situation._ New York: McGraw-Hill.

Bastiaans, J. (1973). Fixation points in the regulation of aggression and their meaning for syndrome formation. In R. de la Fuenta and M. N. Weisman (Eds.), _Psychiatry_ (Proc. 5th Wld. Congr. Psychiatry, Mexico DF, 1971), Amsterdam: Excerpta Medica, Part 1.

Bevan, W. (1955). Sound-precipitated convulsions: 1947 to 1954. _Psychological Bulletin,_ **52**, 473-504.

Binswanger, H. and Meier, L. (1953). Psychiatrisch-klinische Untersuchungen zur Selyeschen Adaptationslehre. 2. Mitteilung. _Schweizer Medizinische Wochenschrift,_ **83**, 25-30.

Bridges, P. K. and Jones, M. T. (1966). The diurnal rhythm of plasma cortisol concentration in depression. _British Journal of Psychiatry,_ **112**, 1257-1261.

Bunney, W. E. Jr., Hartmann, E. L. and Mason, J. W. (1965). Study of a patient with 48-hour manic-depressive cycles. II. Strong positive correlation between endocrine factors and manic defense patterns. _Archives of General Psychiatry,_ **12**, 619-625.

Bunney, W. E. Jr., Murphy, D. L., Goodwin, F. K. and Borge, G. F. (1972). The 'switch process' in manic-depressive illness. I. A systematic study of sequential behavioural changes. *Archives of General Psychiatry*, **27**, 295–302.

Butler, P. W. P. and Besser, G. M. (1968). Pituitary-adrenal function in severe depressive illness. *Lancet*, June **8**, 1234–1236.

Carroll, B. J. (1973). Hypothalamic-pituitary-adrenal (HPA) function and depression. *International Society of Psychoendocrinology Annual Meeting*, Berkeley, Calif., p. 4.

Carroll, B. J. (1975). Limbic system-adrenal cortex regulation in depression and schizophrenia. *Psychosomatic Medicine*, **38**, 106–121.

Carroll, B. J. and Davies, B. (1970). Clinical associations of 11-hydroxycorticosteroid suppression and non-suppression in severe depressive illnesses. *British Medical Journal*, March 28, 789–791.

Carroll, B. J., Martin, F. I. R. and Davies, B. (1968). Resistance to suppression by dexamethasone of plasma 11-O.H.C.S. levels in severe depressive illness. *British Medical Journal*, August 3, 285–287.

Casey, A. (1960). The effect of stress on the consumption of alcohol and reserpine. *Quarterly Journal of Studies of Alcohol*, **21**, 208–216.

Cicero, T. J., Myers, R. D. and Black, W. C. (1968). Increase in volitional ethanol consumption following interference with a learned avoidance response. *Physiology and Behaviour*, **3**, 657–660.

Cushman, P., Jr., Bordier, B. and Hilton, J. G. (1970). Hypothalamic-pituitary-adrenal axis in methadone-treated heroin addicts. *Journal of Clinical Endocrinology and Metabolism*, **30**, 24–29.

Delay, J., Lainé, B., Azima, H. and Puech, J. (1953). Contribution à l'étude de l'homéostasie dans la schizophrénie et les autres psychoses. *Encéphale*, **42**, 385–406.

Dunbar, F. (1947). *Emotions and Bodily Changes* (3rd edn.). New York: Columbia University Press.

Eränkö, O. and Muittari, A. (1957). Effects of experimental neurosis on the thyroid and adrenal glands of the rat. *Acta Endocrinologia (Kbh.)*, **26**, 109–116.

Fischer, R. and Agnew, N. (1955). A hierarchy of stressors. *Journal of Mental Science*, **101**, 383–386.

Flach, F. F. (1974). *The Secret Strength of Depression*. Philadelphia–New York: Lippincott.

Friedlander, J. H., Perrault, R., Turner, W. J. and Gottfried, S. P. (1950). Adrenocortical response to physiologic stress in schizophrenia. *Psychosomatic Medicine*, **12**, 86–88.

Funkenstein, D. H., Greenblatt, M. and Solomon, H. C. (1952). Nor-epinephrine-like substances in psychotic and psychoneurotic patients. *American Journal of Psychiatry*, **108**, 652–662.

Glickman, L. and Blumenfield, M. (1967). Psychological determinants of 'LSD reactions'. *Journal of Nervous and Mental Diseases*, **145**, 79–83.

Hinkle, L. E. Jr. and Wolff, H. G. (1957). The nature of man's adaptation to his total environment and the relation of this to illness. *Archives of Internal Medicine*, **99**, 442–460.

Hoagland, H. (1947). Scientific capital and the dividends of applied science. *Diseases of the Nervous System*, **8**, 3–8.

Hoagland, H., Elmadjian, F. and Pincus, G. (1946). Stressful psychomotor performance and adrenal cortical function as indicated by the lymphocyte response. *Journal of Clinical Endocrinology*, **6**, 301–311.

Holmes, T. H. and Rahe, R. H. (1967). The social readjustment rating scale. *Journal of Psychosomatic Research*, **11**, 213–218.

Hullin, R. P., Bailey, A. D., McDonald, R., Dransfield, G. A. and Milne, H. B. (1967).

Variations in 11-hydroxycorticosteroids in depression and manic-depressive psychosis. *British Journal of Psychiatry*, **113**, 593–600.

Jacobs, S. (1972). Stress and the schizophrenias. *British Medical Journal*, June 17, 712.

King, D. J. (1973). Plasma cortisol-binding capacity in mental illness. *Psychological Medicine*, **3**, 53–65.

Kral, V. A., Grad, B., Cramer-Azima, F. and Russell, L. (1964). Biologic, psychologic and sociologic studies in normal aged persons and patients with senile psychosis. *Journal of the American Geriatric Society*, **12**, 21–37.

Kral, V. A., Grad, B., Payne, R. C. and Berenson, J. (1967). The effect of ACTH on the plasma and urinary corticoids in normal elderly persons and in patients with senile psychosis. *American Journal of Psychiatry*, **123**, 1260–1269.

Lande, N. (1976). *Mindstyles/Lifestyles*. Los Angeles, Calif.: Price, Stern, Sloan.

Langer, D. (1958). Die wichtigsten Ergebnisse der Stress-Forschung (bis 1957) und deren Bedeutung für die Psychiatrie. *Fortschrift für Neurologie und Psychiatrie*, **26**, 321–354.

Lehmann, H. E. (1952). Stress dynamics in psychiatric perspective. *Psychiatry*, **15**, 387–393.

Levi, L. (Ed.) (1971). *Society, Stress and Disease. 1. The Psychosocial Environment and Psychosomatic Diseases*. London–New York–Toronto: Oxford University Press.

Liddell, H. S. (1952). Effect of corticosteroids in experimental psychoneurosis. In *The Biology of Mental Health and Disease*. New York: Hoeber.

Lingjaerde, P. S. (1964). Plasma hydrocortisone in mental diseases. *British Journal of Psychiatry*, **110**, 423–432.

Lovegrove, T. D., Metcalfe, E. V., Hobbs, G. E. and Stevenson, J. A. F. (1965). The urinary excretion of adrenaline, noradrenaline, and 17-hydroxycorticosteroids in mental illness. *Canadian Psychiatric Association Journal*, **10**, 170–179.

Margraf, H. W., Moyer, C. A., Ashford, L. E. and Lavalle, L. W. (1967). Adrenocortical function in alcoholics. *Journal of Psychiatric Research*, **7**, 55–62.

Mason, J. W. (1975a). A historical view of the stress field. Part I. *Journal of Human Stress*, **1**, 6–12.

Mason, J. W. (1975b). A historical view of the stress field. Part II. *Journal of Human Stress*, **1**, 22–36.

Menninger, K., Mayman, M. and Pruyser, P. (1963). *The Vital Balance — The Life Process in Mental Health and Illness*. New York: Viking.

Merry, J. and Marks, V. (1972). The effect of alcohol, barbiturate, and diazepam on hypothalamic/pituitary/adrenal function in chronic alcoholics. *Lancet*, November 11, 990–991.

Messiha, F. S., Savage, C., Turek, I. and Hanlon, T. E. (1974). A psychopharmacological study of catecholamines in affective disorders. *Journal of Nervous and Mental Diseases*, **158**, 338-347.

Miller, E. (Ed.) (1974). *A Report from Ontario Blue Cross: Stress*. Chicago: Blue Print for Health. Vol. 25, No. 1.

Parantainen, J. (1975). Prolactin, levodopa, and migraine. *Lancet*, February 22, 467.

Parker, L. F. and Radow, B. L. (1974). Isolation stress and volitional ethanol consumption in the rat. *Physiology and Behavior*, **12**, 1–3.

Pechstein, H. (1952). Reaction to stress in schizophrenia. *Psychiatric Quarterly*, **26**, 425–432.

Perez-Reyes, M. (1969). Differences in the capacity of the sympathetic and endocrine systems of depressed patients to react to a physiological stress. *Pharmakopsychiatrie*, **2**, 245–251.

Platman, S. R. and Fieve, R. R. (1968). Lithium carbonate and plasma cortisol response in the affective disorders. *Archives of General Psychiatry*, **18**, 591–594.

Popoff, F. E. (1966). A numerical index for outpatient schizophrenics: its relation to stress concepts. *Hawaii Medical Journal*, **25**, 323–327.

Powell, B. J., Kamano, D. K. and Martin, L. K. (1966). Multiple factors affecting volitional consumption of alcohol in the Abrams Wistar rat. *Quarterly Journal of Studies of Alcohol*, **27**, 7–15.

Rees, W. L. (1974). Personality and psychodynamic mechanisms in migraine. *Psychotherapy and Psychosomatics*, **23**, 111–122.

Rubin, R. T. (1967). Adrenal cortical activity changes in manic-depressive illness. Influence on intermediary metabolism of tryptophan. *Archives of General Psychiatry*, **17**, 671–679.

Rubin, R. T. and Mandell, A. J. (1966). Adrenal cortical activity in pathological emotional states: a review. *American Journal of Psychiatry*, **123**, 387–400.

Sachar, E. J. (1967). Corticosteroids in depressive illness. 1. A reevaluation of control issues and the literature. *Archives of General Psychiatry*, **17**, 544–553.

Sachar, E. J., Harmatz, J., Bergen, H. and Cohler, J. (1966). Corticosteroid responses to milieu therapy of chronic schizophrenics. *Archives of General Psychiatry*, **15**, 310–319.

Sachar, E. J., Mason, J. W., Kolmer, H. S. Jr. and Artiss, K. L. (1963). Psychoendocrine aspects of acute schizophrenic reactions. *Psychosomatic Medicine*, **25**, 510–537.

Schildkraut, J. J. (1974). Biogenic amines and affective disorders. *Annual Review of Medicine*, **25**, 333–348.

Selye, H. (1936). A syndrome produced by diverse nocuous agents. *Nature* (London), **138**, 32.

Selye, H. (1974). *Stress without Distress*. Philadelphia: Lippincott.

Selye, H. (1975). Confusion and controversy in the stress field. *Journal of Human Stress*, **1**, 37–44.

Selye, H. (1976a). *Stress in Health and Disease*. Reading, Mass.: Butterworths.

Selye, H. (1976b). *The Stress of Life* (2nd edn.). New York: McGraw-Hill.

Selye, H. (1977). *The Stress of MY Life*. Toronto: McClelland and Stewart.

Serban, G. (1975). Parental stress in the development of schizophrenic offspring. *Comprehensive Psychiatry*, **16**, 23–36.

Shopsin, B., Wilk, S., Sathananthan, G., Gershon, S. and Davis, K. (1974). Catecholamines and affective disorders revised: a critical assessment. *Journal of Nervous and Mental Diseases*, **158**, 369–383.

Takki, S. and Tammisto, T. (1974). The effect of operative stress on plasma catecholamine levels in chronic alcoholics. *Acta Anesthesiologia Scandinavica*, **18**, 127–132.

Tinbergen, N. (1974). Ethology and stress diseases. *Science*, **185**, 20–27.

Tintera, J. W. (1966). Stabilizing homeostasis in the recovered alcoholic through endocrine therapy: evaluation of the hypoglycemia factor. *Journal of the American Geriatric Society*, **14**, 126–150.

Williams, M. (1953). Psychophysiological responsiveness to psychologic stress in early chronic schizophrenic reactions. *Psychosomatic Medicine*, **15**, 456–462.

Wolf, S. (1963). Life stress and patterns of disease. In H. I. Lief and V. F. Lief (Eds.), *The Psychological Basis of Medical Practice*. New York: Hoeber.

Wolff, H. G., Wolff, S. G. Jr. and Hare, C. C. (Eds.) (1950). *Life Stress and Bodily Disease*. Baltimore: Williams and Wilkins.

Chapter 2

Physiological Aspects of Information Processing and Stress

D. M. WARBURTON

1. Introduction
2. Information Models
3. Information Processing and Stress
4. Physiological Aspects of Attention
5. Electrocortical Activity and Information Processing
6. Drugs, Electrocortical Activity and Cognition
    (i)   Vigilance
    (ii)   Selective Attention
    (iii)   Thinking
    (iv)   An Attentional Mechanism
7. Physiological Stress Response
    (i)   Neural Control of Corticosteroid Release
    (ii)   Corticosteroid Release in Behavioural Situations
    (iii)   Neural Control of Adrenal Medullary Hormones
    (iv)   Catecholamine Release in Behavioural Situations
8. Stress Response, Performance and Fatigue
9. Summary
10. References

1. INTRODUCTION

In everyday conversation how often have we heard expressions like 'a hard day at the office'; 'trying to do two things at once is a strain'; 'it is very wearing adding these figures and trying to ignore the other people's conversation'; 'I got worn out just waiting for you'; 'it is the uncertainty that upsets me'. All of these phrases express the feeling that it is not only physical effort that is tiring, but that mental work and uncertainty can produce feelings of fatigue that are just as strong as those produced by physical work. It is easy to understand that muscular activity produces exhaustion because muscular contraction consumes energy, but it is less clear how mental effort can be just as tiring as physical effort. In this chapter, I will consider how the brain copes with the demands of information processing, and how an inevitable consequence of the attention devoted to the task is the stress response. If the stress response is prolonged, fatigue will result. In the next two sections the concepts of information processing in the nervous system and stress will be considered. In the fourth section the physiological aspects of attention will be outlined. The fifth and sixth section will deal with electrocortical activity, drugs, and cognition. The seventh section will discuss the physiological stress response, and in the eighth section there are speculations about the fatigue that results from mental work.

2. INFORMATION MODELS

The information theory model of human behaviour considered the human organism as a communication channel (Shannon and Weaver, 1949). The model consists of a source, a transmitter, a channel, and a destination. At the transmitter information is encoded and sent along the channel to the destination where it is then decoded. Information is an unpredictable change in sensory input to the destination. To put it another way, there are probabilities associated with a message to the destination, and the amount of information that is conveyed by a message is inversely proportional to its probability of occurrence, i.e. how expected it is or how uncertain it is.

In psychology, the *source* consists of changes of physical energy in the external or internal environment. Such changes impinge upon sense organs, transmitters, which encode the changes in neural energy for transmission — the 'language' of nerves (Segundo, 1970). The encoded information passes along the *channel* of this afferent nervous system, to the central nervous system, and is then transmitted again via the efferent system to some motor unit(s), muscles or glands which constitute the final *destination*. At each destination there is a 'read out' of the information, to use Segundo's (1970) expression, and evaluation.

One of the most important concepts of information theory is the idea of information being transmitted as a 'signal-in-noise'. An information channel has 'noise' which is a statistically regular random process, i.e. predictable change in energy, while the 'signal' is an unpredictable change in energy. In the nervous system there are regular predictable patterns of neural activity and signals are seen as departures from this orderly activity. For the neurophysiologist it is a simple matter to arrange a computer to record the neural activity in a sensory system each time an external source emits a stimulus. The computer will average out the predictable random noise and emphasize the signal wave and curve as the number of stimuli increases. In contrast, the person is only receiving a single stimulus and a decision must be made about whether a stimulus was presented on the basis of a single input. In other words, a statistical decision is being made in the brain about whether a pattern of afferent stimulation differs from expectation. It follows from this idea that external stimuli will not inevitably trigger a stereotyped response, but the occurrence of a response will depend on the probability of a signal in the afferent channel not being a random variation.

Although the information theory model had considerable heuristic value, the complexity of human abilities has demanded more sophisticated cognitive models — information processing models. The information theory approach emphasizes the continuity between input and output, but the information processing model has gone further and has argued that this continuous process can be subdivided into a series of stages for the purpose of experimental analysis even though information may pass continuously through each stage. A typical sequence of stages in an information processing analysis is shown in Figure 2.1.

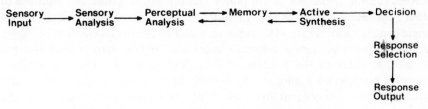

FIGURE 2.1. An Information Processing model

It must be emphasized that there is a continuity between perception and memory, between memory processing and response selection, between response selection and attention, between memory processing and attention, perception and attention and so on. In addition the information processing model has argued that, as different stages can only process limited amounts of information, there must be mechanisms for allocating resources for processing.

3. INFORMATION PROCESSING AND STRESS

In the information processing model that was presented at the end of the last section, it was implied that information is processed by passing through a series of perceptual analyses that extract information for response decisions, and the only restrictions on the decision-making processes are the sensory input (data-limited) and the information processing capacity.

Bainbridge (1974) has defined processing capacity as the information processing operations and strategies which a subject has available. The amount of work done, and performance achieved, by an individual will be a function of the processing capacity and the task demands. Very little seems to be known about many aspects of processing capacity as a function of task demands, although experience seems to play an important part in improving capacity (Bainbridge, 1974; 1978). In this sort of data-driven model [see Rabbitt, Chapter 4] the processing is essentially a passive process. However, it has become clear that these data-driven models are inadequate to explain all aspects of information processing and must be supplemented by active processing models where the analyses are driven by the conceptual organization, so called 'top-down' models.

Some 'top-down' models of information (Kahneman, 1973; Norman and Bobrow, 1975) argue that the resources which an individual can allocate to processing are limited. Thus the organism must allocate resources to one process or another on the basis of some sort of allocation policy. If several processes compete for limited resources then the performance–resource function of each process is crucial in determining which process will be used and ultimately what sort of behaviour will occur (Norman and Bobrow, 1975). A process can fail if the allocation policy distributes the available resources to other processes or if there are not sufficient resources for the demands of a single process. Kahneman (1973) has termed this use of resources in response to task demands as 'mental effort' or 'attention'. In this chapter attention will be used to refer to the process of allocating resources. Thus in selective attention resources are allocated to exclude irrelevant information and select input which is relevant to the task, while divided attention refers to the allocation of resources to processing more than one input and perhaps the exclusion of irrelevant information as well. Effort would be reserved for the proportion of total resources that were devoted to a particular process.

The relationship of mental effort to neural processes has been suggested by Kahneman (1973). He proposed that the limited resources are related to physiological arousal, so that resources and arousal vary together in the low range of arousal levels. They increase and decrease to meet the task demands, and the allocation of resources is based on the level of arousal. Kahneman is not very specific about the nature of the physiological arousal that is related to attentional performance, although he is careful to note that there are sub-types of arousal and that arousal is more than sympathetic dominance. I will be arguing in succeeding sections that the relevant subtype of arousal for attention is electrocortical arousal, and that electrocortical arousal can be related to mental effort. Thus the level of performance will be related to electrocortical arousal.

It seems that people work below maximum effort most of the time, but that they can increase their effort for short periods in an emergency (Bainbridge,1974). However, continuous work at maximum levels of effort results in more rapid onset of fatigue. The conditions which lead to maximum effort can be the result of an interaction between task demands, the person, and the environmental conditions. Work psychologists have tried to conceptualize the nature of this interaction by means of an analogy from physics. In studies of elasticity a load is placed on a body to impose stress, and the effects of this load can be measured as strain (e.g. Russell, 1953). This use contrasts with the use of the term by Selye [Chapter 1, this volume]. He has consistently referred to the organism's physiological response as stress and the agent used to produce the changes as a stressor. This chapter will follow the physics analogy and stress will refer to the imposed load on the information processing system. The consequences of the imposed load will be termed the stress response. In this way the physiological data will be related to that of the work of psychologists, like Luczak (1971) and Bainbridge (1974).

Luczak (1971) proposed that stress was a consequence of mental load, the distribution of task demands over time. Strain would be a consequence of the individual processing capacity and the stress. Note that these terms, stress and strain, are not being used to imply that extreme demands are being made on the system, i.e. overload. Here they are being used in a quantitatively neutral sense. This model can be elaborated, see Figure 2.2, so that performance is a consequence of the attention or mental effort expended to match the strain of the task for the individual. One consequence of the strain and mental effort is the stress response, the physiological correlates of processing. One of the puzzling consequences of prolonged or intense mental effort is fatigue. Evidence for its relation to the stress response will be presented in the last section of this chapter.

The problem with the model is quantification of the variables. Luczak (1971) proposed that mental capacity could be assessed from performance, but Bainbridge (1974) has pointed out that this notion is too simplistic. Performance does not necessarily reflect the amount of processing performed. It will depend on the relation between mental capacity and the task demands. This relation is almost certainly not linear and may be discontinuous if new strategies are adopted. The measurement of strain is less controversial and Luczak (1971) suggested that it could be assessed physiologically. This view

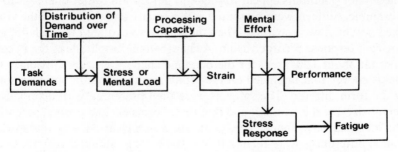

FIGURE 2.2. A model relating task demands, stress, and fatigue

will be adopted here in the sense that the stress response will reflect the mental effort which will be directly related to strain as mental capacity interacts with the task demands. In the model shown in Figure 2.2, it would be argued that if performance was at a high level then the stress response would be directly related to effort which would itself be proportional to strain. However, if mental effort did not match the strain, then the stress response would be poorly correlated with strain.

In the next sections I will discuss the physiological mechanisms that are involved in attention, some of the physiological manifestations of stress, and how the stress response results in fatigue.

4. PHYSIOLOGICAL ASPECTS OF ATTENTION

In the earlier section it was pointed out that there was active processing of information. At the present stage of our knowledge we know some of the simpler forms of analysis that occur in the central nervous system, e.g. feature detection and location detection. The complex aspects of processing are thought to be reflected in the sensory evoked potentials at the cortex.

The sensory evoked response is a cortical potential which represents a change in the continuous random electrocortical activity produced by the input along the sensory pathways. It is partially masked by the random firing of the cortical cells and the form of the potential can only be revealed by computer averaging techniques. If the same stimulus is presented repeatedly the common features of the potential emerge during the averaging while the random noise disappears because it is less related to the stimulus. The evoked potential that is revealed is a plot of amplitude of the wave over time and it shows both negative and positive shifts in electrical potential, the components. The latency of these positive and negative components differs between modalities but there are certain common patterns. The early wave components (P_0, N_1, P_1, N_2) are smaller and relatively invariable while the larger secondary components $(P_2, N_3, P_3,$ and $N_4)$ can be modified by experimental manipulations.

These later potentials appear to relate to perception rather than sensation. For example, subjects were presented with a square and the form of the visual evoked potential was recorded. Then the square was rotated through 45° and the evoked response recorded again. A change in the amplitude of the P_3 component (at about 100 msec) for the diamond shape was seen. Obviously the stimulus energy that impinged on the retina was the same in both cases and only the form differed. The subjects were then presented with diamonds of different sizes, and it would found that these forms elicited evoked potentials of the identical wave shape. These data show in a clear-cut way that evoked potential differences were related to the shape of the stimulus and not to the size of the retinal area stimulated, i.e. to perception rather than sensation (see John, 1967).

This conclusion is brought out more clearly in some later studies. John, Heatherington and Sutton (1967) had already demonstrated that the findings with abstract stimuli could be extended to words. Thus different responses were elicited by different words printed with letters equated for retinal area. There was evidence that the name of the form elicited the same pattern of evoked potential as the geometric form. Even more remarkable but crucial for this chapter was the observation from those experiments (John, 1967) that wave shapes that resembled those of the geometric form could be obtained if the subject viewed a blank screen but imagined the form. These results demonstrate that part of the wave form of the evoked potential reflects the perceptual content of the stimulus rather than its psychophysical aspects. In addition, there is a neural equivalence between external stimuli, a square on a screen, and internal stimuli, and imagined square, i.e. perceptions and thoughts are neurally indistinguishable.

This work has been paralleled by studies that were designed to discover the components of the evoked potential wave that vary with shifts in attention. Many of the early studies were designed to demonstrate the existence of peripheral filtering as a mechanism of selective attention. In his seminal book, *Perception and Communication*, Broadbent (1958) suggested that there was a filtering mechanism in the peripheral parts of the sensory pathways and inputs were selected on the basis of their physical characteristics. However, more recent experiments (see Norman, 1976) have shown that selection cannot be on the basis of physical cues alone and that it cannot be in the peripheral parts of the sensory pathways. Selection seems to be an attenuation of further processing of the inputs on some (therefore non-attended) channels on the basis of expectations about the inputs and only the information in the attended channel is actively processed. Selection must be occurring at a high level in the nervous system where attention could be switched if some channel carried information of high, i.e. important, information content. In addition we often select between incoming information and information that arises within the person, including memories. Obviously, a peripheral filter could not gate out these stimuli, and so there must be some central selection process going on. The most likely site for the selection processes is at the cortex although the mechanism might be controlled from another part of the brain.

Haider, Spong and Lindsley (1964) presented a series of bright (non-signal) and dim (signal) stimuli to subjects in a vigilance experiment. From the responses to the non-signal stimuli the researchers measured any variation in the evoked potential as performance varied during the vigilance task. From the evoked responses to detected and non-detected stimuli it was possible to obtain data which correlated with specific changes in attention and inattention to the signals as defined by the detection performance. During the 80 min. session the amplitude of the evoked potential including the major negative component (N_2) to the non-signal stimuli decreased in parallel with a vigilance performance decrement. Lapses of attention which resulted in detection failures were correlated with smaller amplitude evoked potentials in comparison with the evoked response to detected stimuli.

In a complementary study of attention with distraction, click and flash stimuli were presented alternately to subjects while evoked potentials were recorded from the visual and auditory cortices (Spong, Haider and Lindsley, 1965). In the vigilance condition subjects pressed a key when they detected infrequent weak stimuli in the other modality. During the key-pressing condition subjects pressed for all stimuli in one modality and ignored all stimuli in other modalities. In both conditions, the amplitude of the averaged evoked potential to stimuli in the non-attended modality was attenuated. The most spectacular differences in amplitude found with attention were found in the potentials in the first 30 msec. In another study of intermodality selection, Saterfield (1965) alternately gave subjects clicks and painless shocks to the wrist while they had to detect any decrease in the intensity of the stimuli in one modality and ignore the other input. Averaged cortical evoked potentials were recorded from the auditory and somaesthetic cortex for both the attended and non-attended stimuli. There was typically an increase in the amplitude of the sensory evoked potential when the subject attended to the stimulus, and this was seen for the major negative component (N_1) and a subsequent positive component (P_2) in particular.

These studies have been criticized by Näätänen (1967; 1975). He has pointed out that they gave no evidence for peripheral filtering because the subject could predict the occurrence of the signals on the basis of alternation. Thus the larger evoked potentials were a consequence of differentially enhanced arousal as an anticipatory response to the relevant stimulus. Näätänen (1970) found an 11% change in electrocortical arousal prior to a relevant stimulus when relevant and irrelevant stimuli were alternated. This mechanism corresponds neatly to the idea of Norman (1976) that selection is an attenuation of further processing on the basis of expectations about the stimulus input.

One study in which evoked potential changes may reflect the outcome of a decision between a relevant and irrelevant stimulus is that of Hillyard, Hink, Schwent and Picton (1973). It would be expected that the discrimination between relevant and irrelevant input must occur very early in processing, e.g. 60 – 70 msec from stimulus onset, i.e. by the N_1 component. In a dichotic listening study Hillyard et al. presented 'relevant' tones in one ear and 'irrelevant' tones in the other ear concurrently at such a rate that the subject could only listen to one input at a time if he was to discriminate pitch differences. In these circumstances only the major negative component N_1 of the cortical evoked response of the attended ear was substantially enhanced compared with that evoked by tones in the non-attended ear, while the second positive component P_2 was unchanged. The early latency of the N_1 component (at 60 – 70 msec) suggests that the 'attentional process was a tonically maintained set favouring one ear over the other rather than an active discrimination and recognition of each individual stimulus' (Hillyard *et al.*, 1973, p.179). This attentional process was identified with the stimulus set of Broadbent (1970) which acts to facilitate the recognition of specific task-relevant stimuli. Thus changes in attention were reflected in a change in the major negative component and in some cases in the subsequent positive component. These results do not indicate the locus of the selection mechanism but there is also some physiological evidence which suggests a central locus. (Picton, Hillyard, Galambos and Schiff, 1971). Evoked potential of the cochlear nerve to clock stimuli have been recorded at the same time as the cortical responses to the same stimuli. When the subject was attending to the clocks there was an enhancement of the early components of the cortical evoked potential, but no change was observed in the same components of the cochlear nerve potential, i.e. there was no evidence for peripheral filtering. Therefore, the difference could not be due to peripheral factors like middle ear muscle differences or inhibition at the cochlear nucleus, and must be a central phenomenon.

These data are consistent with the view that there is a two-stage process in which decisions are made about stimuli (Näätänan, 1975). First there is selection on the basis of whether the stimulus is task-relevant or task-irrelevant, and second there is selection about whether the relevant stimulus is a signal or not. If the subject has expectations then there will be increased electrocortical arousal and the first stage will be bypassed. Evidence for the importance of electrocortical arousal in information processing is considered in the next section.

5. ELECTROCORTICAL ACTIVITY AND INFORMATION PROCESSING

It has been suggested already that some evoked potential changes may be a result of expectation which changes electrocortical activity. Electrocortical activity has been divided into four types — alpha, beta, gamma, and theta waves. Beta activity consists of small amplitude (i.e. low voltage) fast waves (13 – 30 cycles per second) and is the most desynchronized activity. Alpha activity has a larger amplitude and is much slower at 8 – 12 cycles per second. The slowest activity in the awake subject is the theta at 4 – 7 cycles per second, and a still large amplitude. When the subject has just fallen asleep there is delta activity which results in large amplitude synchronized waves ranging from $\frac{1}{2}$ – 3 per second.

As we have seen, during prolonged vigilance, subjects become less and less aware of infrequent stimuli with the passage of time, and there is a decrease in the probability of detecting a given stimulus over time. The performance decrement becomes steeper as the task becomes simpler and the frequency of signals decreases. There are individual differences in the rate of decrement and this has been related to the tendency to daydream; the greatest number of errors was found in subjects who reported thoughts while they were performing (Antrobus, Coleman and Singer, 1976). Daydreaming was associated with theta activity at the cortex, and an increased abundance of theta activity was a reliable correlate of the vigilance decrement (Beaty, Greenberg, Deibler and O'Hanlon, 1974). These authors rewarded either the presence or the absence of theta waves and thereby increased the amount of theta activity at the visual cortex. They observed that the monitoring efficiency for visual signals was inversely related to the incidence of theta frequency at the visual cortex.

These data from experimental situations fit in well with correlations between electrocortical arousal and behaviour that had been obtained from introspective reports. Lindsley (1960) proposed a behavioural continuum, including the range from alert attentiveness, relaxed wakefulness, drowsiness, light sleep, and sleep, which would be matched to a continuum of electrocortical arousal. Alert attentiveness which was characterized by selective attention, concentration, anticipation, and set was correlated with fast, low emplitude, mainly desynchronized, beta waves. The state of relaxed wakefulness in which attention wandered and which favoured free association was associated with more synchronized larger amplitude akpha activity. As the person slipped into sleep through states of partial awareness and reverie there was first theta activity and then the appearance of slow large amplitude delta waves.

Brown (1974) has confirmed this continuum by asking subjects to describe their thoughts and feelings when different coloured lights appeared. The electrocortical activity was recorded at the scalp and then filtered for the beta, alpha, and theta frequencies, and these frequences operated three different coloured lights. The subjects did not know which colour represented which sort of brain activity. The subjects agreed to a considerable extent in describing their feelings during beta activity (over 13 cycles per second). Many of them gave introspective reports of alertness, attention, tension, and anxiety at these fast electrocortical frequencies. In contrast, alpha activity was correlated with a feeling of restfulness, relaxation, and lack of concentration on external stimuli. As the activity slowed even more to the theta range (4 – 7 cycles per second) awareness of the external world decreased and subjects reported daydreaming, planning, problem solving, and a general sense of unreality. Thus as the subject engages in problem solving, phantasy and daydreaming he withdraws part of his attention from the external environment, although problem solving seems to be the most common of these activities. Problem solving is an important function for the cognitive life of the individual because it enables him to organize and reorganize information creatively for possible action later on, but the danger of this activity for the individual is that it leads to neglect of external stimuli.

The finding that creative thinking is most effective at lower levels of cortical arousal has been examined from another point of view (Martindale, 1974). Subjects were tested on several tasks that called for imagination, e.g. 'how many alternative uses for a brick can you think of', and simultaneously their electrocortical arousal was measured from the right hemisphere (the side of the brain involved in phantasy according to Sperry, 1969). Subjects who scored highly on these tasks had the lowest levels of arousal, and the most alpha acitivity, while the uncreative subjects produced increased arousal. Creativity seems to be incompatible with concentration and perhaps that is why ideas seem to come to us when we stop thinking about a problem.

All normal people pass through alpha and theta activity as they relax and fall asleep. The transitional phase from wakefulness to sleep is called the hypnagogic state. One study of these states correlated the subjective experiences with electrocortical arousal (Vogel, Foulkes and Trosman, 1966). The early state, when alpha waves occur, was characterized by logical thought processes and the subjects could distinguish easily between internal images and external information. In the intermediate state, when there was slow alpha activity, the subjects had lost contact completely with the external world and reported rather bizarre images and thoughts. During the late hypnagogic state, when theta activity was observed, the images became more plausible and realistic, but there was no contact with external reality. The subjects could not distinguish internal images from reality.

The hypnagogic states seem to be related to hallucinations. A hallucinatory experience is a conscious awareness in which information is represented by means of imagery (Horowitz, 1975). The images are unusually intense from the inner realm of information (increased internal input), and are appraised as if they originated in the outside world (impaired information processing). Hallucinations occur without the sense of conscious intent, or awareness that the image has its origins internally rather than externally (impaired control). Dreams clearly have the first two properties (being of internal derivation but appraised as of external origin at the time), but only occasionally do they possess the second two properties when the subject considers the experience retrospectively. Hypnagogic states have more clearly the four properties that are characteristic of hallucinations.

6. DRUGS, ELECTROCORTICAL ACTIVITY AND COGNITION

In the last section changes in information processing have been correlated with variations in electrocortical activity. Additional evidence for the hypothesis that electrocortical activity is involved with attention comes from studies in which cortical activity has been manipulated by cholinergic drugs, like cholinolytics and cholinomimetics. A discussion of the effects of anticholinesterases is available in Warburton (1975; 1979) and will not be included here. Cholinolytics like atropine and scopolamine, impair cholinergic function by preventing acetylcholine reaching the postsynaptic receptors, while cholinomimetics, like nicotine, imitate acetylcholine at the receptor sites in the synapse. Thus the two drugs produce opposite effects on behaviour and brain activity. In this section we will consider the nature of these changes.

Cholinolytic drugs shifted the spontaneous cortical activity towards slower waves (Grob, Harvey, Langworthy and Lilienthal, 1947; White, Rinaldi and Himwich, 1956; Ostfeld, Machne and Unna, 1960). At first there was a transient augmentation of electrocortical arousal, but then it was reduced (White et al., 1956; Ostfeld et al., 1960). A marked decrease in the duration of electrocortical arousal was seen after single and repetitive visual stimuli. Alpha rhythm (10 – 12 cycles per second) was observed less often after the drug and this continued longer than the reduced duration of arousal (Ostfeld et al., 1960).

Nicotine taken in the form of cigarettes has opposite effects; smoking a single cigarette produced a decrease in the amplitude and an increase in the frequency of the electrocortical activity (Wechsler, 1958; Hauser, Schwartz, Ross and Bickford, 1958). When heavy smokers (over 20 a day) were deprived of cigarettes for 24 hours, there was an increase in the slow frequencies, that is to say, a shift to a less alert pattern of more synchronized activity. These changes were reversed immediately by cigarette smoking.

From the last section it might be expected that the response to stimuli would be diminished by smoking deprivation and enhanced by smoking. Philips (1971) made quantitative spectral analyses of electrocortical responses to visual stimuli and found an enhancement after smoking. The evoked potential to a visual stimulus after smoking deprivation showed a decrease in amplitude, especially in the 100 – 125 msec peaks (i.e. N_2 and P_3 for visual stimuli), which is what would be predicted. There was a return of the amplitude to baseline magnitude when smoking was resumed (Hall, Rappoport, Hopkins and Griffin, 1973). These authors conclude that nicotine alters the manner in which smokers process sensory stimuli and this result fits in very well with the results of studies described in the last section in which electrocortical arousal was allowed to vary naturally.

Most subjects report loss of awareness or alertness, difficulty in concentrating and shortened attention span after cholinolytics (White et al., 1956; Ostfeld et al., 1960; Michelson, 1961; Crowell and Ketchum, 1967; Ketchum et al., 1973). It was difficult to attract the subject's attention and the subject appeared to be in a 'world of his own' or 'daydreaming' (Ketchum et al., 1973). Some subjects described the condition as a sense of detachment from reality (Calloway and Band, 1958). Calloway (Calloway and Dembo, 1958; Calloway and Band, 1958) has argued that these changes represent 'broadened attention'. Broadened attention was defined as an increase in the influence of peripheral factors such as relatively current environmental events which are removed from the central focus of attention by space, time, or by differences of meaning (Calloway and Dembo, 1958).

In contrast, nicotine seems to have opposite effects and smoking is often defended by smokers in terms of its usefulness for preventing lapses in concentration, for example in long-distance driving (Heimstra, Bancroft and De Kock, 1967). Questionnaire investigations of smoking motives have revealed that 70 – 80% of smokers claim that smoking helps them think and concentrate (Russell, Peto and Patel, 1974; Warburton and Wesnes, 1978). In Calloway's terminology nicotine produces 'narrowed attention' in which there is a decreased influence of events that are peripheral in space, time and meaning. Experimental studies of vigilance, selective attention, attention and thinking have confirmed the opposing effects of cholinolytics and nicotine.

(i) Vigilance

In a vigilance task a subject is required to monitor a stimulus source for a brief signal which has an unpredictable and usually low probability of occurrence. As the duration of the task is increased, the probability of correct detection of the experimental signal decreased. The effects of scopolamine on this vigilance decrement have been investigated using the 'continuous clock task' (Wesnes and Warburton, 1978). For this task subjects were isolated and instructed to observe the minute hand of a clock. They were required to detect and respond to brief pauses in the otherwise continuous movement of the clock hand. In comparison with placebo performance, subjects who received a dose of scopolamine prior to the session detected fewer pauses in the minute hand. In other words, scopolamine accentuated the vigilance decrement.

In a study of the effect of smoking, smokers and non-smokers were tested in a vigilance situation that combined central visual guiding with peripheral search (Tarrière and Hartemann, 1964). Measures were made of correct detections, false alarms, and guidance errors, and it was found that smokers who were allowed to smoke showed significantly fewer guidance errors than smokers who were not allowed to smoke and non-smokers. The smoking subjects did not show the normal vigilance decrement over the 150 minute session. In a related study, Heimstra et al. (1967) studied the effects of nicotine on performance on simulated driving. The subjects were allowed to smoke as much as they wanted during the six hour session. Deprived smokers were worse on several aspects of performance. They had more tracking errors (time off the road), they made more meter errors (deflections of a needle), and more brakelight errors than smokers smoking and non-smokers. These meter monitoring and brakelight detection tasks were in effect vigilance tasks and so the results support those of Tarrière and Hartemann (1964), in showing that smoking prevented lapses of vigilance.

In these studies the smokers were allowed to control their own intake of nicotine in terms of the number of cigarettes smoked and by varying the amount of inhalation. Frankenhaeuser (Frankenhaeuser, Myrsten, Post and Johansson, 1971) studied the effects of cigarettes smoked every 20 minutes during simple and complex reaction time tasks. The subjects were all smokers and each was used for both the smoking and no-smoking conditions. Performance in the simple reaction time task was significantly better when the subjects were smoking (Frankenhaeuser *et al.*, 1971; Myrsten *et al.*, 1972). There were no significant effects of smoking on performance in choice reaction time (Myrsten *et al.*, 1972). These findings support the trend observed in the simulated driving study of Heimstra *et al.* (1967).

The effects of smoking on vigilance performance were examined by means of the Mackworth clock (Wesnes and Warburton, 1978), which had previously been used in the scopolamine studies. The first study examined the performance of ten smokers allowed to smoke at 20 min, 40 min, and 60 min while ten non-smokers were given a rod to suck as some sort of control for oral activity. The control subjects showed a vigilance decrement, but the smokers' performance did not deteriorate and even showed slight improvement over initial levels after the second cigarette. In another study with the same task we found that the performance of smokers allowed to smoke showed no deterioration in detection, while smokers who smoked nonnicotine, herbal cigarettes, and non-smokers, deteriorated. In an auditory vigilance task where subjects had to detect faint tones occasionally embedded in noise trials, nicotine again prevented the vigilance decrement. These results confirmed and extended the earlier study of Tarrière and Hartemann (1964). In order to extend these results nicotine tablets containing 1 and 2 mg of drug were used with a group of smokers. It was found that both nicotine doses enhanced detections relative to undrugged vigilance performance.

(ii)   Selective Attention

Some studies have also examined performance in tasks where subjects must filter out irrelevant stimuli. For example, there were more errors on the Stroop test (Calloway and Band, 1958; Ostfeld and Aruguete, 1962) in which the more broadly attending subject will show impaired performance when he must select irrelevant information, e.g. the colour name while identifying the printing colour (e.g. the word 'red' printed in blue). In the Gottschaldt test the subject's task is to find a figure which is embedded within a larger design. It would be predicted that broadly attending subjects would find it more difficult to filter out irrelevant parts of the design. Subjects that have been injected with atropine do experience this sort of difficulty in filtering out the irrelevant stimuli (Calloway and Band, 1958).

Experiments on nicotine (Wesnes and Warburton, 1978) have also used the Stroop test. It was found that nicotine improved performance, i.e.

decreased the effect of the distracting stimuli. This task differs from the vigilance task in being relatively short (less than 15 min) and more interesting. It is of great theoretical importance that nicotine improves performance on the Stroop task and scopolamine disrupts it (Calloway and Band, 1958; Ostfeld and Aruguete, 1962) because they have opposite effects on electro-cortical activity. The effects of nicotine have also been studied in a situation in which subjects process and select information presented at extremely rapid rates. The subjects were instructed to detect and respond to series of three consecutive odd or even numbers presented on a TV screen at a rate of eight signals per minute. Smokers who smoked nicotine-containing cigarettes per-formed at a superior level in comparison with smokers who were given nicotine-free cigarettes or no drug at all (Wesnes and Warburton, 1978). Tests of scopolamine have shown that performance is impaired and so once again drugs which have opposite effects on electrocortical activity have oppo-site effects on performance.

(iii) Thinking

Most subjects who take atropine or scopolamine report decreased clarity of thought with doses of 1.25 mg of atropine (about 15 microgram/kg) and 24 microgram/kg of scopolamine (Crowell and Ketchum, 1967). Tests of arithmetic ability showed a decrement in performance with scopolamine (Crowell and Ketchum, 1967; Ketchum et al., 1973), atropine (Ketchum et al., 1973), and parpanite (Michelson, 1961). Subjects complained of difficulty in following a train of thought. This deficit was manifested in an inability to explain proverbs and to identify word similarities and word differences (Ketchum et al., 1973).

It would be predicted that broadened attention would improve problem solving where a solution depends on attending to peripheral factors such as the Luchins test. This test consists of a series of problems about how a given volume of water can be obtained with three different measures. It was found that subjects receiving atropine discovered the new short method of solving the problems faster than the control group. Calloway and Band (1958) claimed that atropine improved performance by broadening attention, so that the subject attended to aspects of the task which were not essential for the original test, but helped in discovering the simpler method. Atropine also improved performance in a disjunctive reaction time experiment in which the subject had to press one of two keys on seeing a light or hearing a buzzer (Miles, 1955). If one must use a broader focus of attention to respond to two modalities then these results can be understood in terms of this drug broadening attention.

At high doses of cholinolytics most subjects reported hallucinations (Crowell and Ketchum, 1967; Ketchum et al., 1973). These hallucinations were usually visual, but auditory, tactile, olfactory, and gustatory hallucinations did occur

(Abood and Biel, 1962). The visual hallucinations were integrated and extremely realistic with familiar objects and faces (Ketchum *et al.*, 1973). Some subjects smoked imaginary cigarettes (Crowell and Ketchum, 1967) and drank from non-existent drinking glasses (Abood and Biel, 1962; Ketchum *et al.*, 1973). They made appropriate drinking movements and commented on its taste and smell. Subjects heard recognizable voices and music played by single instruments and whole orchestras (Abood and Biel, 1962).

One interpretation of the hallucinations is that they are internal stimuli which are normally filtered out, but are able to reach awareness and influence behaviour as attention becomes broader.

(iv) An Attentional Mechanism

In summary, these studies of natural and drug-induced variations in electrocortical arousal show that variations in attention are correlated with changes in cortical desynchronization and changes in the sensory evoked response. There is an increase in components of the averaged cortical response evoked by sensory stimuli, so that the amplitudes of these initial sensory potentials are proportional to the degree of attention, and the latter components of the evoked responses are increased in duration. Desynchronization is thought to be an enhancement in the random spontaneous activity of some cells in the sensory cortex which is produced by the release of acetylcholine (Krnjević and Phillis, 1963). The increased excitability of the cells would result in a greater number being activated when there is sensory input and consequently the size of the evoked potential will be increased.

The probability of a response will be proportional to the size of the evoked potential at the cortex. When there are many evoked potentials of similar magnitude behaviour will be variable and it will be very stable when there is one dominant potential. Selective activation of one of the sensory cortices, i.e. concentration on one modality, will tend to produce dominant potential. Brown (1974) has shown that people differ with respect to the form, location, and appearance of electrocortical activity. These differences may give some explanation of differences in perception and thought among individuals.

When the cortex becomes more synchronized during lapses in concentration there will be a reduction in the evoked potential size, and less dominant stimuli from external and internal sources of information will intrude producing distraction. The consequences of distraction will be impaired concentration, vigilance, and selective attention. Similarly when the external sensory input is decreased below a critical point then previously stored information may be released into awareness to produce phantasies and images. This critical point will be the size of the externally evoked potentials relative to the internally activated ones. Creative thought consists of establishing connections between previously unconnected information. It involves a person allowing himself to relax the usual organization of the information and allow free rein to his phantasies and images. This process will be facilitated by a synchronized cortical activity of relaxed wakefulness.

The neurochemical substrate for the changes in electrocortical arousal and attention can be inferred from studies with animals. The psychopharmacological research reported in the last section implies that the crucial pathways have cholinergic synapses. There is a considerable body of literature (see Warburton, 1977) that suggests that cholinergic drugs modify stimulus selection mechanisms in animals. Within the constraints imposed by species differences these changes are consistent with the findings in humans; cholinolytics impair stimulus selection while cholinomimetics improve selection. Similarly, cholinolytics produce greater cortical synchronization than placebo and cholinomimetrics produce desynchronization. Direct injections of cholinergic drugs into a number of sites in the rat brain produce changes in stimulus selection and cortical activity, which include the ventral tegmental nuclei (Endroczi, Hartemann and Lissak, 1963a), medial septal nucleus, and hippocampus (Warburton, 1972). These regions are nuclei along the cholinergic pathways identified in the rat brain (Shute and Lewis, 1967).

There are two pathways that ascend to the cortex that stain for acetylcholinesterase and they both have their origins in the ventral tegmental area in the anterior mesencephalon. These neurons are joined by ascending fibres from the nucleus reticularis tegmenti pontis and the combined fibres enter the zona incerta, supramamillary region and the lateral hypothalamic area and run forward to the nuclei in the basal forebrain. All cortical areas of the forebrain are innervated by acetylcholinesterase staining neurons which radiate from nuclei in the basal forebrain (see Figure 2.3). Part of the neocortex is innervated by axons whose cell bodies are located in the globus pallidus and terminate in the lateral cortex above the rhinal or limbic fissure. The lateral cortical areas include regions such as the temporal and occipital cortices that are involved in sensory functions. The pathways most likely to be involved in attention would be the pathway ascending to the lateral areas which include the major sensory areas. Changes in attention would result from shifts in the amount of desynchronization in these areas that are produced by variations in the activity in the pathways ascending from the tegmental area of the reticular formation. The input to this system comes from the external sensory pathways via the hypothalamus from the internal sensory systems, chemoreceptors and visceral sensory system.

In addition to the pathway to the cortex the system has a branch to the hippocampus and from the hippocampus there is a non-cholinergic pathway which returns to the tegmental region. As a result of its clearly defined structure, the electrical activity of the hippocampus has been studied extensively by means of both macro- and microelectrodes. The spontaneous electrical activity of the hippocampus has been studied in acute experiments with the

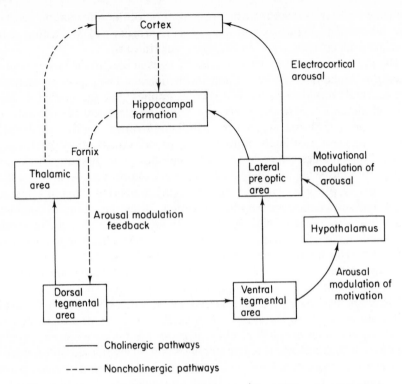

FIGURE 2.3. A schematic diagram of the ascending cholinergic pathway to the cortex that is involved in attention. (After Shute and Lewis, 1967)

anaesthetized cat (Green and Arduini, 1954), and in chronic experiments with animals carrying permanent intracerebral electrodes (MacLean, 1957). The spontaneous hippocampal activity of the unanaesthetized animal is characterized by large amplitude waves irregularly distributed as fast (15 – 30 cps) and slow (4 – 8 cps). This irregular activity is unstable and is interrupted at times by brief periods of synchronization composed of regular sinusoidal waves of 3 – 7 cps, the theta activity. This activity is uniform throughout the hippocampus and has been found in every mammalian species studied.

In the course of spontaneous variations of vigilance, important electrical changes are observed (see Green and Arduini, 1954). Drowsiness is correlated with hippocampal desynchronization in contrast to the cortical synchronization. The cortical and hippocampal responses are not always simultaneous, and often hippocampal desynchronization precedes cortical synchronization (Stumpf, 1965). In deep sleep the differences between cortical and hippocampal activity are smaller. Some polymorphic slow waves occur in both structures and occasionally slow waves spread simultaneously in the cortex and hippocampus. On waking, the differences between cortical and hippocampal activity reappear; cortical desynchronization, consisting of rapid rhythm of multiple frequency and slow voltage, is associated with hippocampal synchronization. The latter is usually transitory and is only distinct when the animal appears alert.

Theta activity is particularly pronounced when it is elicited by novel sensory stimuli, or by reticular, or amygdala stimulation (Green and Arduini, 1954). Novel sensory stimuli in all modalities always induce hippocampal synchronization of brief duration in the resting animal. This effect varies between species; auditory stimuli seem to be most effective for the cat, olfactory for the rat.

The anatomical arrangement of the hippocampus is suitable for a feedback loop to control electrocortical arousal, and stimulation of the hippocampus has been shown to produce changes in electrocortical arousal (see Warburton, 1972). A negative feedback loop is an important part of many physical systems because it prevents unnecessary activation of those systems. For example, a thermostat prevents the unnecessary expenditure of fuel when the temperature is constant. It is possible a similar sort of control over electrocortical arousal is maintained by the hippocampus; it prevents unnecessary electrocortical arousal when the stimuli are repetitive.

The amount of electrocortical arousal is related to the uncertainty of the stimulus input. The organism establishes simple and complex expectancies about the world around him, but novel information represents an increase in uncertainty and produces an increase in electrocortical arousal. The amount of the arousal will be a function of size of the mismatch between expectancy and input (see Pribram, 1967). In information theory terms electrocortical arousal is elicited from high information inputs, that is to say those with a low probability of occurrence for that individual. A repetitive stimulus will have a high probability of occurrence and so low information, and it is proposed that the hippocampus is responsible for identifying simple, low information stimuli and preventing electrocortical arousal via the feedback pathway to the tegmental region (see Figure 2.3). In this way the hippocampus maintains stability by diminishing the response to simple repeated events in the environment (Pribram, 1969). Complex events will be analysed and interpreted at the cortex first and any mismatch between input and expectancy identified and then the cortex will excite the hippocampus. Thus simple expectancies only involve the hippocampus but complex expectancies depend on cortical analysis. As a consequence electrocortical arousal and, according to my hypothesis, attention, will vary in proportion to the information in the inputs. This is particularly important because electrocortical arousal is related to the stress response.

7. PHYSIOLOGICAL STRESS RESPONSE

As Selye has emphasized many times [see Seyle, Chapter 1], the organism responds in the same stereotyped manner to a wide variety of agents such as cold, heat, irradiation, trauma, infections as well as psychological stress. This response is a set of physiological changes that prepares the organism for action. The hormonal aspects of the stress response are well defined; they consist of the release of catecholamines, adrenalin, and noradrenalin, and corticosteroids including cortisone and corticosterone from the adrenal gland. The catecholamines are released from the adrenal medulla and the corticosteroids are released by the adrenal cortex. As shown in Figure 2.4, catecholamine secretion is controlled from the brain by pathways from the sympathetic nervous system. The control of corticosteroid secretion is more complex. Hypothalamic cells close to the median eminence translate the neural stress information into chemical information in the form of corticotrophin-releasing factor (CRF) secreted into a specialized blood vessel system by cells in the hypothalamus. The blood flow carries the corti-

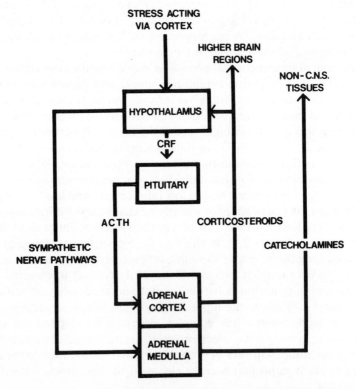

FIGURE 2.4. A schematic diagram of the adrenal systems that are involved in the hormonal stress response

cotrophin-releasing factor to the adrenohypophysis portion of the pituitary where it triggers the release of adrenocorticotrophic hormone (ACTH) into the general blood circulation, and it is carried to the adrenal cortex. The corticosteroids are released into the blood stream and act on many tissues throughout the body, including the brain, to prepare them for action. In contrast, the catecholamines pass through the blood–brain barrier very poorly and their major action is on tissues outside the brain.

(i) Neural Control of Corticosteroid Release

Some of the first studies of stress steroid control gave evidence for catecholamine inhibition of release. Brodie examined the effect of reserpine on the stress steroid response and found that reserpine induced a pattern of change similar to stress, including a release of plasma corticosteroids (Maickel, Westermann and Brodie, 1961) Reserpine depletes dopamine, noradrenalin, and serotonin in the brain which suggests that one of these amines might mediate stress steroid inhibition. In a follow-up study Brodie measured reserpine effects on noradrenalin, serotonin, and plasma corticosteroids and found similar dose-response and time-response effects for noradrenalin depletion and increased corticosteroid release (Westermann, Maickel and Brodie, 1962). Enhanced release of ACTH could also be produced by chlorpromazine which blocks dopamine and noradrenalin and serotonin synapses (De Wied, 1967; Marks, Hall and Bhattachaya, 1970). A later study ruled out the involvement of serotonin. Alpha-methyl-*para*-tyrosine, an inhibitor of noradrenalin and dopamine synthesis, produced an increase in plasma corticosterone in most animals, but in those animals in which alpha-methyl-*para*-tyrosine did not deplete hypothalamic catecholamines, corticosterone was not increased (Scapagnini, Van Loon, Moberg and Ganong, 1970). In order to distinguish between the two catecholamines intraventricular injections of l-dopa, dopamine, l-noradrenalin, and l-isoproterenol, an adrenomimetic, were investigated for their inhibitory properties (Van Loon, Scapagnini, Cohen and Ganong, 1971). All compounds produced inhibition and since the first two are precursors of noradrenalin, but the last two do not form dopamine, it looks as if noradrenalin is the inhibitory transmitter for ACTH release. This hypothesis was supported by a study that used FLA-63 which prevents the synthesis of noradrenalin from dopamine, and so reduced hypothalamic noradrenalin and increased plasma corticosterone (Van Loon *et al.*, 1971).

This conclusion was strengthened by further studies in which dopamine levels were varied independently of noradrenalin concentrations, by combining alpha-methyl-*para*-tyrosine and dihydroxyphenylserine, which is converted directly into noradrenalin but not dopamine. Alpha-methyl-*para*-tyrosine depleted both noradrenalin and dopamine but the dihydroxyphenylserine replenished noradrenalin, whereas the dopamine concentration was reduced. The results showed that dihydroxphenylserine partially prevented the increase in ACTH secretion produced by alpha-methyl-*para*-tyrosine (Scapagnini and Preziosi, 1973). Ganong (1971) plotted a graph of brain noradrenalin levels against plasma steroid levels, showing that there was a threshold level which had to be reached before corticosterone level was reduced to normal.

In studies of direct injections into the brain the effects of various transmitters and their precursors on the stress response have been examined. It was found that l-dopa, dopamine, and l-noradrenalin injected into the third ventricle close to the medial hypothalamus inhibited the rise in plasma corticosteroids that was induced by surgical stress. The biologically inactive d-noradrenalin was ineffectual. Similar results were obtained by intraventricular injections of dopamine and noradrenalin in animals that were stressed by handling (Schiaffini, Motta, Piva and Martini, 1971). Clearly noradrenalin and its precursors block stress-induced increases in plasma stress steroids and the inescapable conclusion is that noradrenalin mediates the inhibitory control of stress steroids.

Direct injections of other compounds into the hypothalamus have suggested that there is a cholinergic system which controls the release of corticotrophin into the blood stream to the pituitary and leads to increased plasma corticosteroids. Krieger and Krieger (1970), found that carbachol, a cholinomimetic, implanted in the median eminence region and mid-mamillary body area induced an abrupt rise in corticosteroid levels but little response was obtained from hippocampal and septal implants. The effects of carbachol were blocked by means of atropine, a cholinergic blocking agent. In a previous experiment, Hedge and Smelik (1968) had implanted annulae in the septum, anterior hypothalamus, and posterior hypothalamus and found that the stress of implantation produced a prolonged release of ACTH, and increased plasma corticosterone levels. Crystalline atropine placed in the anterior hypothalamic cannula reduced plasma corticosterone levels but atropine stimulation at the other two loci was without effect, which showed the specificity of the effect to the median eminence region found to be sensitive to carbachol by Krieger and Krieger. These results were supported by Hedge and De Wied (1971).

In conclusion there is good evidence in favour of a noradrenergic tonic inhibition of stress steroid secretion in balance with tonic cholinergic stimulation. The interaction between the two systems appears to be in the median eminence region which has been implicated in the release of corticotrophin to stimulate the pituitary.

The involvement of a cholinergic pathway in the control of stress steroid release raises the intriguing possibility that it may be related to the cholinergic pathways that control electrocortical arousal. It is clear that there are neurons in the cat which terminate in the median eminence region and have their origins in the ventral tegmental region (Shute and Lewis, 1967). As I mentioned earlier, Endroczi et al. (1963a) showed that injections of carbachol into the ventral tegmental region in the cat produced electrocortical arousal. Injections of carbachol into this same region induced a marked increase in plasma corticosterones (Endroczi, Schreiberg and Lissak, 1963b). This finding indicates that electrocortical arousal and corticosteroid release are related.

Indirect evidence in support of this contention comes from studies of plasma steroids in humans. Over a 24 hour period there is a typical pattern of cortisol secretion. In subjects who sleep from 11.00 p.m. to 7.00 a.m. there is minimal secretion during the late evening and early morning, but about 2.00 a.m. a series of major secretory episodes begin and mean hourly cortisol increases to reach a maximum at 7.00 a.m. Each episode consists of a sharp rise and a decay which is thought to be due to the phasic release of corticotrophin from the hypothalamus to release pulses of ACTH (Weitzman, 1975), and, certainly, there is a similar phasic release of ACTH (Rubin, 1975). It is significant that these episodes are correlated with the periods of cortical desynchronization that occur during dreaming sleep (Rubin, 1975; Weitzman, 1975). These changes occur independently of the content of the dream; a dream of relaxing on the beach can be correlated with massive cortisol secretion. Clearly these results suggest that input information, which produces cortical desynchronization will elicit a corticosteroid response.

(ii) Corticosteroid Release in Behavioural Situations

In section 3, it was argued that cortical desynchronization was a response to high information inputs from the environment, i.e. high uncertainty. It would be predicted from the preceding subsection that stress steroid release will increase in situations of high uncertainty. Some animal studies have indicated that this is the case. In one study (Coover, Goldman and Levine, 1971), uncertainty was introduced by changing the rat's schedule of reinforcement after training; rats were trained to lever press on a continuous reinforcement schedule, and then reinforcement was withheld. Measures of the stress steroids demonstrated a rise in plasma corticosterone during the extinction phase. Levine has argued that during acquisition the situation becomes more predictable for the animal and the corticosterone levels fall, but during extinction 'when the predictability and control that the rats had acquired no longer exist, an increase in pituitary-adrenal function occurs' (Levine, Goldman and Coover, 1972, p. 287).

In a second study Levine et al. (1972) were able to show that the rise was not due to removal of the reinforcement that could have produced some frustration effects. The animals were trained on either a variable-interval schedule or a fixed-interval schedule with the same density of reinforcement, and then switched to the other schedule. Animals switched from unpredictable variable-interval schedule to the predictable fixed-interval schedule showed no change in steroid levels, but rats switched from the predictable fixed-interval to the more uncertain variable interval showed an elevation of plasma corticosterone concentration. Levine *et al*. conclude that the animals develop a set of expectancies with respect to the amount of reinforcement in fixed-interval schedules. When this expectancy is contradicted by the changed schedule, there is an activation of an arousal system which increases pituitary-adrenal activity. It seems likely that this arousal system is the ascending cholinergic pathways which mediate electrocortical arousal. Thus a change in expectancies or the absence of any previously established expectancy results in an increased secretion of ACTH from the pituitary and increased corticosteroid release.

There is very good evidence that a similar pattern of corticosteroid release is found in humans. Healthy young volunteers were admitted to hospital so that their corticosteroid responses could be assessed under standard conditions (Mason, Sachar, Fishman, Hamburg and Handlon, 1965). A total of 60 adults were tested by collecting their urine over a period of 14 days. There was a large secretion of corticosteroids for the first 24 hours and then it dropped markedly although the decline continued over the two weeks. There were some small individual differences in total amount secreted but all subjects showed a decline. The results can be interpreted as an adrenocortical response to a novel and ambiguous environment and all subjects reported some feelings of apprehension that began on the day before admission. The highest levels of corticosteroids were obtained from subjects in the mixed sex groups (Fishman, Mason, Sachar, Hamburg and Handlon, 1962), and it is not too fanciful to suggest that this group experienced more uncertainty than the single sex group — they were certainly processing higher information inputs.

This phenomenon can also be illustrated by considering the pattern of primary corticosteroid excretion which was measured for a group of soldiers in a front-line camp in Vietnam (Bourne, 1969). These soldiers were under constant threat of attack, but they were preparing for an attack on a specific day. (Incidentally, it did not take place.) Urine specimens were collected on the expected day of the attack and for three days before and after that date. On the basis of intuition we might have expected all the soldiers to show dramatic increases in corticosteroid production under the threat of combat. Most of the subjects showed a mean 40 per cent decrease in urinary corticosteroids on the day of the anticipated attack, although the officer and radio operator showed 25 per cent increases. These remarkable differences can be related to the uncertainty to which the two sets of soldiers were operating. On the day of the attack the ordinary soldiers were required to perform tasks in which they were highly trained and which were of a routine nature, e.g.

building defences and maintaining equipment. These tasks were highly trained for and involved little uncertainty because they were so well practised. In contrast, the officer was in a highly unpredictable situation; he was required to stay alert for new instructions which might call for novel decisions and patterns of behaviour. The role of the radio operator was similar in the sense that he was transmitting and receiving new messages and so he, too, was in an unpredictable situation and dealing with high information inputs.

These results show that adrenocortical hormones are released by psychological influences and that psychological stimuli are just as potent as physical stimuli for triggering release of stress steroids (Mason, 1968a). Uncertainty seems to be a common factor of many situations in which there is stress steroid release and this idea would relate to the previous notions of corticosteroid release as an anticipation of activity or coping. The common physiological effect of stimuli which release corticosteroids is an increase in electrocortical arousal and it seems likely that the ascending cholinergic pathways which mediate electrocortical arousal also coordinate stress steroid release. As we pointed out earlier, attentional mechanisms are controlled by these pathways and it would make sense for a common pathway to control anticipation of stimulus input, i.e. attention and anticipation of action. As we will see in the next section corticosteroid release is not the only biochemical secretion during attention situations, there is also release of catecholamines from the adrenal medulla.

(iii) Neural Control of Adrenal Medullary Hormones

The release of hormones from the adrenal medulla is under the control of the splanchnic neurons from the hypothalamus. Thus stimulation of the medial anterior portion of the hypothalamus causes increased secretion by the adrenal medulla. There are two catecholamines, adrenalin and noradrenalin, in the adrenal medulla. There seems to be partially independent release of these compounds so that stimulation of different areas of the anterior hypothalamus releases different proportions of noradrenalin to adrenalin. Clearly there must be partially separate innervation of the different secretory cells for the two hormones so that there is a neural basis for different patterns of secretion that could be controlled from the hypothalamus. The hypothalamic areas seem to be under cortical control and both excitatory and inhibitory cortical areas have been distinguished (Euler and Folkow, 1958). In addition, some cortical areas exert control over adrenal medullary secretion because hypothalamic ablation does not abolish the effects of cortical stimulation. Obviously the presence of these corticofugal pathways are a neural substrate by which cognitive events could influence the secretions of the adrenal medulla. Some of these events will be considered next.

(iv) Catecholamine Release in Behavioural Situations

Performance in any task which involves sustained attention is described as stressful by subjects. One task of this sort which we have described is vigilance in which increased release of adrenal medullary steroids is found. For example, O'Hanlon (1965) required subjects to respond to infrequent increments in illumination during a 90 min session or to watch a relaxing film. An intravenous catheter enabled the experimenters to take serial blood samples without the subjects knowing when the sample was taken. During the vigilance the performance of a proprtion of the subjects decreased markedly. The occurrence of this vigilance decrement was significantly correlated with a decrease in adrenalin secretion. There was no consistent correlation of performance with changes in noradrenalin release. O'Hanlon interpreted these data as evidence for the hypothesis that adrenalin release served an adaptive purpose by increasing arousal which enabled the subject to sustain his concentration. This hypothesis was also proposed by Frankenhaeuser on the basis of her studies of performance and catecholamine secretion.

In another task that involved sustained concentration, Frankenhaeuser and Patkai (1964) measured the catecholamine excretion of a group of university students who were carrying out coding and proof-reading tasks under distracting conditions. They found that these tasks increased the excretion of adrenalin and noradrenalin. Although the secretion of adrenalin was greater and more consistent, small but highly significant correlations between performance in the later stages of the task and noradrenalin excretion was found. Accordingly, Frankenhaeuser has argued that the excretion of catecholamines serves to counteract to some extent the performance decrement found in boring and stressful tasks by increasing arousal. If this interpretation is correct, the effects cannot be due to a direct effect on these arousal pathways, because in amounts excreted by the adrenal medulla, the two catecholamines do not pass from the blood to brain although high physiological quantities may overcome the blood-brain barrier (Vogt, 1975).

In a more naturalistic task Levi (1972) tested a group of invoicing clerks under two conditions of remuneration — salary and piecework. Measures were obtained of the number of invoices that were processed, the number of errors made, the catecholamine excretion, and the subjective reactions of discomfort. During piecework the number of processed invoices doubled without a concomitant rise in errors but performance declined during the late afternoon. There was a dramatic increase in both adrenalin and noradrenalin levels under piecework, but there was no differences between morning and afternoon in excretion rates. Subjective ratings showed that 'fatigue' was significantly increased during piecework compared with salaried work. Thus there was divergence between catecholamine excretion and performance level as well as subjective experience of fatigue which contradicts

Frankenhaeuser's hypothesis. Physiological studies have also shown that insulin produces large increases in catecholamine excretion but no changes in arousal. Thus it seems that arousal leads to the catecholamine secretion rather than the other way round.

The behavioural situations in which catecholamine excretion occur are similar to those in which corticosteroid excretion occurs (Mason, 1968b). However, I am not aware of any evidence that links up the hypothalamic origins of the splanchnic nerve with the ascending cholinergic pathways although it is tempting to speculate on such a relationship. It is known that nicotine does elevate plasma catecholamines (Frankenhaeuser *et al.*, 1971), but the locus of drug action is not known. Another possibility for site of action would be at the cortex since there are direct corticoadrenal pathways.

Although the precise anatomical relations remain to be established it is a fact that the release of corticosteroids and catecholamines, especially adrenalin, are highly correlated. The precise *psychological* determinants of selective adrenalin and noradrenalin release remain to be determined, but there is certainly marked release of corticosteroids and catecholamines in situations that are unpredictable and may require action. Release in these circumstances makes sense in terms of their metabolic actions which mobilize the energy resources that would be required for action. This is an example of the remakable overlap of hormonal effects (Mason, 1968c). The precise reasons for the overlap are unknown but perhaps the adrenal medullary system can provide a rapid short duration response because it is neurally activated and rapidly metabolized, while the corticosteroids provide a slower but more sustained response. The consequences of the joint and synergistic action of the two hormones on performance will be outlined in the last section.

8. STRESS RESPONSE, PERFORMANCE, AND FATIGUE

The corticosteroids produced by the adrenal glands have a marked effect on glucose metabolism, hence their designation as glucocorticoids. Animals without adrenal glands have low levels of blood sugar, but these can be restored and elevated above normal by treatment with appropriate doses of corticosteroids. The experiments are too complicated to describe here, but it seems that the increments in glucose or glycogen are a consequence of increased protein degradation and an inhibition of carbohydrate metabolism (Steele,1975). Consequently in conditions of stress, corticosteroids increase the sugars available in the blood stream. In addition they inhibit the transport of glucose into fat cells and thus increase the release of free fatty acids (Fain and Czech, 1975). Similar changes are observed with the catecholamines, with the most striking metabolic effects on blood sugar and blood fats. They also mobilize glycogen and lipid stores and so raise the blood levels of carbohydrates and free fatty acids (Williamson, 1975). Thus the metabolic consequence of the release of both corticosteroids and catecholamines is to make available to the organism an increased supply of energy for physical and mental effort.

In classical studies of carbohydrate and fat use in work of different intensities, Christensen and Hansen (1939) found that during exhausting work there was a major participation of carbohydrates, and subjective symptons of fatigue disappeared within 15 min of ingesting glucose which raised the blood-sugar levels. The central system has low reserves of sugar and depends on blood sugar for its supply of energy. In man about 60% of the liver sugar output serves brain metabolism, and so exhaustion seems to be mainly a central nervous phenomenon rather than a lack of sugar for muscles (Åstrand and Rodahl, 1970). In support of this argument studies have shown that feelings of fatigue and decreased muscular work have a central nervous component (Åstrand and Rodahl, 1970). Muscular work also uses free fatty acids from the adipose tissues as fuel, but a reduced supply of fats is compensated for by an increased metabolism of glycogen, so that work is not impaired by loss of this fuel, unless the sugars are depleted as well. Thus the stress response of corticosteroids and catecholamine release are important in mobilizing blood sugar and fat for combating fatigue. The superior performance of subjects with higher levels of catecholamines in the study of Frankenhaeuser and Patkai (1964) is probably a direct result of the hormones mobilizing energy to combat fatigue rather than on arousal. Of course, sustained stress will result in a depletion of the fuel reserves and the onset of fatigue, even though the stress hormones are still being secreted at the same level, as in the studies of Levi (1972).

9. SUMMARY

Modern cognitive theories of information analysis have emphasized the active nature of the process. As the task per unit time demands increase, the amount of stress will increase but the amount of strain will depend on the processing capacity of the individual, including the processing strategies that he can adopt. In order to perform adaptively a person must allocate attentional resources to combat the imposed strain. The performance output will reflect the attentional effort. The neurochemical mechanisms that control attention are cholinergic and the pathways are the ascending reticular fibres to the cortex. These pathways control the level of electrocortical arousal at the sensory cortices which interacts with the incoming evoked potentials. This interaction enhances the earlier components of the sensory evoked potential and constitutes stimulus selection. A hippocampal feedback pathway to the tegmental area of the reticular formation prevents low information stimuli producing electrocortical arousal. This process is important because of the intimate link between electrocortical arousal and stress hormone release. Corticosteroid release occurs in the same uncertain (i.e. high information) situations as electrocortical arousal and the two processes seem to be interlinked. Adrenal catecholamines are also released in the same situations. Both corticosteroids and catecholamines mobilize blood sugars and fats, the fuel for action, both mental and physical. In the short term the increased mobilization enables extra effort and high performance levels. However, in the long term the sustained release of sugars and fats leads to depletion and fatigue. Anticipation of action can be just as tiring as the action itself, because uncertainty releases stress hormones. Mental work can be as exhausting as physical work because of the electrocortical arousal and the consequent stress response.

10. REFERENCES

Abood, L. G. and Biel, J. H. (1962). Anticholinergic psychotomimetic agents. *International Review of Neurobiology*, **6**, 218–273.

Antrobus, J. S., Coleman, R. and Singer, J. L. (1967). Signal detection performance by subjects differing in predisposition to daydreaming. *Journal of Consulting Psychology*, **31**, 487–491.

Åstrand, P. O. and Rodahl, K. (1970). *Textbook of Work Physiology*. New York: McGraw-Hill.

Bainbridge, L. (1974). Problems in the assessment of mental load. *Le Travail Humain*, **37**, 279–302.

Bainbridge, L. (1978). Forgotten alternatives in skill and work-load. *Ergonomics*, **21**, 169–185.

Beaty, J., Greenberg, A., Deibler, W. P. and O'Hanlon, J. F. (1974). Operant control of occipital theta rhythm effects performance in a radar monitoring task. *Science*, **183**, 871–873.

Bourne, P. G. (1969). Urinary 17-OHCS levels in two combat situations. In P. G. Bourne (Ed.), *Psychology and Physiology of Stress*. New York: Academic Press.

Broadbent, D. E. (1958). *Perception and Communication*. London: Pergamon.

Broadbent, D. E. (1970). Stimulus set and response set: two kinds of selective attention. In D. G. Mostovsky (Ed.), *Attention: Contemporary Theory and Analysis*. New York: Appleton–Century–Crofts.

Brown, B. B. (1974). *'New Mind — New Body'*. Chicago: Aldine-Atherton.

Calloway, E. and Band, R. I. (1958). Some psychopharmacological effects of atropine. *Archives of Neurology and Psychiatry*, **79**, 91–102.

Calloway, E. and Dembo, D. (1958). Narrowed attention: a psychological phenomenon that accompanies a certain physiological change. *Journal of Neurology and Psychiatry*, **79**, 74–90.

Christensen, E. H. and Hansen, O. (1939). Arbeitsfähigheit und Ehrnähung, *Skandinavische Archiv für Physiologie*, **81**, 160–178.

Coover, G. D., Goldman, L. and Levine, S. (1971). Plasma corticosterone increases produced by extinction of operant behaviour in rats. *Physiology and Behavior*, **7**, 261–263.

Crowell, E. B. and Ketchum, J. S. (1967). The treatment of scopolamine-induced delirium with physostigmine. *Clinical Pharmacology and Therapeutics*, **8**, 409–414.

De Wied, D. (1967). Chlorpromazine and endocrine function. *Pharmacological Review*, **19**, 251–288.

Endroczi, E., Hartemann, G. and Lissak, K. (1963a). Effect of intracerebrally administered cholinergic and adrenergic drugs on neocortical and archicortical electrical activity. *Acta Physiologica Hungarica*, **24**, 207–209.

Endroczi, E., Schreiberg, G. and Lissak, K. (1963b). The role of central nervous activating and inhibitory structures in the control of pituitary-adrenocortical function. Effects of intracerebral and adrenergic stimulation. *Acta Physiologica Hungarica*, **24**, 211–221.

Euler, U. S. von and Folkow, B. (1958). The effect of stimulation of autonomic areas in the cerebral cortex upon the adrenaline and nonadrenaline secretion from the adrenal gland in the cat. *Acta Physiologica Scandinavica*, **42**, 313–320.

Fain, J. N. and Czech, M. P. (1975). Glucocorticoid effects on lipid mobilization and adipose tissue metabolism. In J. Blaschko, G. Sayers and A. D. Smith (Eds.). *Handbook of Physiology: Endocrinology, Vol. 6. Adrenal Gland*. Washington, D. C.: American Physiological Society.

Fishman, J. R., Mason, J. W., Sachar, E. J., Hamburg, D. A. and Handlon, J. H. (1962). Emotional and adrenal cortical responses to new experience. *Archives of General Psychiatry*, **6**, 271–278.

Frankenhaeuser, M., Myrsten, A. L., Johansson, G. and Post, B. (1971). Behavioral and physiological effects of cigarette smoking in a monotonous situation. *Psychopharmacologia* (Berl), **22**, 1–7.

Frankenhaeuser, M. and Patkai, P. (1964). Catecholamine excretion and performance under stress. *Perceptual and Motor Skills*, **19**, 13–14.

Ganong, W. R. (1971). Evidence for a central noradrenergic system that inhibits ACTH secretion. In. W. F. Ganong (Ed.), *Brain–Endocrine Interaction Medicine Eminence: Structure and Function*. Basel: Karger.

Green, J. W. and Arduini, H. (1954). Hippocampal electrical activity in arousal. *Journal of Neurophysiology*, **17**, 533–557.

Grob, D., Harvey, A. M., Langworthy, O. R. and Lilienthal, J. L. (1947). Administration of di-isopropylfluorosphosphate to man: the effect on the central nervous system with special reference to the electrical activity of the brain. *Bulletin of the John Hopkins Hospital*, **81**, 257–266.

Haider, M., Spong, P. and Lindsley, D. B. (1964). Attention, vigilance and cortical-evoked potentials in humans. *Science*, **145**, 180–182.

Hall, R. A., Rappoport, M., Hopkins, H. K. and Griffin, R. (1973). Tobacco and evoked potentials. *Science*, **180**, 212–214.

Hauser, H., Schwartz, B. E., Ross, G. and Bickford, R. G. (1958). Electroencephalographic changes related to smoking. *Electroencephalography and Clinical Neurology*, **10**, 576.

Hedge, G. A. and de Wied, D. (1971). Corticotropin and vasopressin secretion after hypothalamic implantation of atropine. *Endocrinology*, **88**, 1257–1259.

Hedge, G. A. and Smelik, P. G. (1968). Corticotropin release: inhibition by intrahypothalamic implantation of atropine. *Science*, **159**, 891–892.

Heimstra, N. W., Bancroft, N. R. and De Kock, A. R. (1967). Effects of smoking upon sustained performance in a simulated driving task. *Annuals of the New York Academy of Sciences*, **142**, 295–300.

Hillyard, S. A., Hink, R. F., Schwent, V. L. and Picton, T. (1973). Electrical signs of selective attention in the human brain. *Science*, **182**, 177–180.

Horowitz, M. (1975). Hallucinations: an information-processing approach. In R. K. Siegel and L. J. West (Eds.), *Hallucinations*. New York: Wiley.

John, E. R. (1967). *Mechanisms of Memory*. New York: Academic Press.

John, E. R., Heatherington, R. N. and Sutton, S. (1967). Effects of visual form on the evoked response. *Science,* **155**, 1439–1442.

Kahneman, D. (1973). *Attention and Effort*. Englewood Cliffs, N.J.: Prentice-Hall.

Ketchum, J. S., Sidell, F. R., Crowell, E. B., Aghajanian, G. K. and Hayes, A. H. (1973). Atropine, scopolamine and ditran: comparative pharmacology and antagonists in man. *Psychopharmacologia,* **28**, 121–133.

Krieger, H. P. and Krieger, D. T. (1970). Chemical stimulation of the brain: effect on adrenal corticoid release. *American Journal of Physiology,* **218**, 1632–1641.

Krnjević, K. and Phillis, J. W. (1963). Acetylcholine sensitive cells in the cerebral cortex. *Journal of Physiology,* **166**, 296–327.

Levi, L. (1972). Stress and distress in response to psychosocial stimuli. *Acta Medica Scandinavica,* **Suppl. 528.**

Levine, S., Goldman, L. and Coover, G. D. (1972). Expectancy and the pituitary-adrenal system. In R. Porter and J. Knight (Eds.), *Physiology, Emotion and Psychosomatic Illness*. Amsterdam: Elsevier.

Lindsley, D. B. (1960). Attention, consciousness, sleep and wakefulness. In J. Field (Ed.). *Handbook of Physiology: Neurophysiology*, Vol. 3. Washington, D.C.: American Physiological Society.

Luczak, H. (1971). The use of simulators for testing individual working capacity. *Ergonomics,* **14**, 651–660.

MacLean, P. W. (1957). Chemical and electrical stimulation of hippocampus in unrestrained animals I and II. *Archives of Neurology and Psychiatry,* **78**, 113–142.

Maickel, R. P., Westermann, E. O. and Brodie, B. B. (1961). Effects of reserpine and cold exposure on pituitary-adrenocortical function in rats. *Journal of Pharmacology and Experimental Therapeutics,* **134**, 167–175.

Marks, B. H., Hall, M. M. and Bhattachaya, A. N. (1970). Psychopharmacological effects and pituitary-adrenal activity. *Progress in Brain Research*, **32**, 57–69.

Martindale, C. (1974). The relationship of creativity to cortical activation and its operant control. *Journal of Genetic Psychology,* **124**, 311–320.

Mason, J. W. (1968a). A review of psychoendocrine research on the pituitary-adrenal cortical system. *Psychosomatic Medicine,* **30**, 576–607.

Mason, J. W. (1968b). A review of psychoendocrine research on the sympathetic-adrenal medullary system. *Psychosomatic Medicine,* **30**, 631–653.

Mason, J. W. (1968c). 'Over-all' hormonal balance as a key to endocrine organization. *Psychosomatic Medicine,* **30**, 791–808.

Mason, J. W., Sachar, E. J., Fishman, L. A., Hamburg, P. A. and Handlon, J. H. (1965). Corticosteroid responses to hospital admission. *Archives of General Psychiatry,* **13**, 1–8.

Michelson, M. J. (1961). Pharmacologicial evidence of the role of acetylcholine in the higher nervous activity of man and animals. *Activas Nervosa Superior* (Prague), **3**, 140–147.

Miles, S. (1955). Some effects of injection of atropine sulphate in healthy young men. U.K. Ministry of Defence Unpublished Report.

Myrsten, A. L., Post, B., Frankenhaeuser, M. and Johansson, G. (1972) Enhanced behavioral efficiency induced by cigarette smoking. *Psychopharmacologia*, **8**, 64–74.

Näätänen, R. (1967). Selective attention and evoked potentials. *Annales Academiae Scientiarum Fennicae,* **B151**, 1–156.

Näätänen, R. (1970). Evoked potential, E.E.G. and slow potential correlates of selective attention. *Acta Psychologica,* **33**, 178–192.

Näätänen, R. (1975). Selective attention and evoked potentials in humans — a critical review. *Biological Psychology, 2,* 237–307.

Norman, D. A. (1976). *Memory and Attention* (2nd edn.). New York: Wiley.

Norman, D. A. and Bobrow, D. G. (1975). On data-limited and resource-limited processes. *Cognitive Psychology, 7,* 44–64.

O'Hanlon, J. F. (1965). Adrenaline and noradrenaline: relation to performance in a visual vigilance task. *Science,* **150,** 507–509.

Ostfeld, A. M. and Aruguete, A. (1962). Central nervous system effects of hyocine in man. *Journal of Pharmacology,* **137,** 133–139.

Ostfeld, A. M., Machne, X. and Unna, K. R. (1960). The effects of atropine on the electroencephalogram and behavior in man. *Journal of Pharmacology, 128,* 265–272.

Philips, C. (1971). The E.E.G. changes associated with smoking. *Psychophysiology,* **8,** 64–74.

Picton, J. W., Hillyard, S. A., Galambos, R. and Schiff, M. (1971). Human auditory attention: a central or peripheral process? *Science,* **173,** 351–353.

Pribram, K. H. (1967). The new neurology and biology of emotion: a structural approach. *American Psychologist,* **22,** 830–838.

Pribram, K. H. (1969). The neurobehavioral analysis of the limbic forebrain mechanisms: revision and progress report. In D. Lehrman (Ed.), *Advances in the Study of Behavior,* Vol. 2, New York: Academic Press.

Rubin, R. T. (1975). Sleep-endocrinology studies in man. *Progress in Brain Research,* **42,** 73–80.

Russell, M. A. H., Peto, J. and Patel, U. A. (1974). The classification of smoking by factorial structure of motives. *Journal of the Royal Statistical Society Series A,* **137,** 313–346.

Russell, R. W. (1953). Behaviour under stress. *International Journal of Psychoanalysis,* **34,** 1–12.

Saterfield, J. H. (1965). Evoked cortical response enhancement and attention in man. A study of responses to auditory and shock stimuli. *Electroencephalography and Clinical Neurology,* **19,** 470–475.

Scapagnini, U. and Preziosi, P. (1973). Role of brain noradrenaline in the regulation of hypothalamic-hypophyseal adrenal axis. *Progress in Brain Research,* **39,** 171–184.

Scapagnini, U., Van Loon, G. R., Moberg, G. P. and Ganong, W. F. (1970). Effect of a methyl-p-tyrosine on the circadian variation of plasma corticosterone in rats. *European Journal of Pharmacology,* **11,** 266–268.

Schiaffini, O., Motta, M., Piva, F. and Martini, L. (1971). Role of brain transmitters in the control of the pituitary-adrenal axis. In V.H.T. James and L. Martini (Eds.), *Hormonal Steroids.* Amsterdam: Exerpta Medica.

Segundo, J. P. (1970). Communication and coding by nerve cells. In F. O. Schmitt (Ed.), *The Neurosciences.* New York: Rockefeller University Press.

Shannon, B. E. and Weaver, W. (1949). *A Mathematical Theory of Communication.* Urbana, Ill.: University of Illinois Press.

Shute, C. C. D. and Lewis, P. R. (1967). The ascending cholinergic reticular system: neocortical olfactory and subcortical projections. *Brain,* **90,** 497–519.

Sperry, R. W. A. (1969). A modified concept of consciousness. *Psychological Review,* **26,** 532–536.

Spong, P., Haider, M. and Lindsley, D. B. (1965). Selective attentiveness and cortical evoked potentials to visual and auditory stimuli. *Science,* **148,** 395–397.

Steele, R. (1975). Influences of corticosteroids on protein and carbohydrate metabolism. In H. Blaschko, G. Sayers and A. D. Smith (Eds.). *Handbook of Physiology:*

Endocrinology, Vol. 6. Adrenal Gland. Washington, D.C.: American Physiological Society.

Stumpf, C. (1965). Drug action on the electrical activity of the hippocampus. *International Journal of Neurobiology*, **8**, 77–139.

Tarrière, C. and Hartemann, F. (1964). Investigation into the effect of tobacco smoke on a visual vigilance task. *Ergonomics*, Proceedings of the Second International Ergonomics Association Congress, 525–530, Dortmund.

Van Loon, G. L., Scapagnini, U., Cohen, R. and Ganong, W. F. (1971). Effect of intraventricular administration of adrenergic drugs on the adrenal venous M-hydroxycorticosteroid response to surgical stress in the dog. *Neuroendocrinology*, **8**, 257–272.

Vogel, G., Foulkes, D. and Trosman, H. (1966). Ego functions and dreaming during sleep onset. *Archives of General Psychiatry*, **14**, 238–248.

Vogt, M. (1975). Influence of circulating catecholamines on the central nervous system. In H. Blaschko, G. Sayers and A. D. Smith (Eds.). *Handbook of Physiology: Endocrinology, Vol. 6. Adrenal Gland.* Washington, D.C.: American Physiological Society.

Warburton, D. M. (1972). The cholinergic control of internal inhibition. In R. Boakes and M. S. Halliday (Eds.), *Inhibition and Learning.* London: Academic Press.

Warburton, D. M. (1975). *Brain, Drugs and Behaviour.* London: Wiley.

Warburton, D. M. (1977). Stimulus selection and behavioural inhibition. In L. L. Iversen, S. D. Iversen and S. Snyder (Eds.). *Handbook of Psychopharmacology*, Vol. 6. New York: Plenum.

Warburton, D. M. (1979). Neurochemical bases of consciousness. In K. Brown and S. Cooper (Eds.), *Chemical Influences on Behaviour.* London: Academic Press.

Warburton, D. M. and Wesnes, K. (1978). Individual differences in smoking and attentional performance. In R. E. Thornton (Ed.). *Smoking Behaviour: physiological and Psychological Influences.* London: Churchill–Livingston.

Wechsler, R. L. (1958): Effects of cigarette smoking and intravenous nicotine on the human brain. *Federation Proceedings*, **17**, 169.

Weitzman, E. D. (1975). Neuroendocrine pattern of secretion during the sleep–wake cycle of man. *Progress in Brain Research*, **42**, 93–102.

Wesnes, K. and Warburton, D. M. (1978). The effect of cigarette smoking and nicotine tablets upon human attention. In R. E. Thornton (Ed.), *Smoking Behaviour: Physiological and Psychological Influences.* London: Churchill–Livingston.

Westerman, E. O., Maickel, R. P. and Brodie, B. B. (1962). On the mechanism of pituitary adrenal stimulation by reserpine. *Journal of Pharmacology and Experimental Therapeutics*, **138**, 208–217.

White, R. P., Rinaldi, F. and Himwich, H. E. (1956). Central and peripheral nervous effects of atropine sulfate and mepiperphenidal bromide ('Darstine') on human subjects. *Journal of Applied Physiology*, **8**, 635–642.

Williamson, J. R. (1975). The effects of epinephrine on glycogenolysis and myocardial contractility. In H. Blaschko, G. Sayers and A. D. Smith (Eds.), *Handbook of Physiology: Endocrinology, Vol. 6. Adrenal Gland.* Washington, D.C.: American Physiological Society.

Chapter 3

'Personality' and Stress

VERNON HAMILTON

1. Introduction
   (i)   Conceptualizing Personality
   (ii)   Conceptualizing Stress
2. Individual Differences in 'Stress' Tolerance
   (i)   Response to Personal Catastrophies
   (ii)   Predispostions
           (a)   Genetic approaches
           (b)   Learning theory approaches
           (c)   Psychodynamic approaches
3. Personality, Situations and 'Stress'
   (i)   The Interaction Problem
   (ii)   Sources in the Person
   (iii)   Situational Sources
   (iv)   Some Experimental Evidence of Person × Situation Interaction
           (a)   Physical danger
           (b)   Social isolation
           (c)   Work and performance
4. Towards an Information Processing Model of Interaction
5. References

1. INTRODUCTION

The aims of this chapter are tentatively idealistic: to search for a set of explanatory principles of personality and stress which will reflect recent advances in the experimental methodology applied to cognition and the new hypothetical constructs or paradigms which have emerged from them. What seems to be required is a redescription and reconceptualization of what we mean by the time-honoured concept of personality and what actually constitutes *psychological* stress. A restatement, particularly of their unobservable components, must at the same time satisfy the structural, functional, and logical requirements of processes and behaviours which are known to interact.

Oil and water do not mix because of differences in their molecular structure. A reduction of the substances, however, into carbon, hydrogen, and oxygen provides unlimited opportunities for the development of new compounds. This is possible because the simpler structure of atoms 'speaks a language' which all of them can identify and respond to. This analogy, however naive, may be applied to dominant human response dispositions, their goals, and the intensity and persistence with which they are sought. It may also be applied, at several levels of the person, to the frustration, anger, incompetence, conflict, and anxiety which may be experienced during goal-directed behaviour, or as a consequence of a behaviour-controlling environment. The molecules of personality, it may be suggested, are traits, habits, and motives; the molecules of stress are emotional upheaval, disorganization and primitivation of responses, lack of concentration, and distress, to mention just some of the symptoms. The atomic constituents which determine individual behaviour characteristics, as well as the experience of aversiveness and distress, are *cognitive* structures. Cognitive processes, however, combine, separate, and recombine the coded data which the structures contain, because at this reductionist level, the 'language' of personality and stress is neuronal: electrochemical codes carrying information.

In successive sections of this chapter, I will attempt to cite and interpret data which appear to be consistent with a cognitive, information processing analysis of personality characteristics and of stress. It is more than likely that this goal is premature and, therefore, over-ambitious, because it is tied to constructs and paradigms which may be superseded shortly. Since I am aware of my goal, and of my anxiety at exposing myself to academic criticism and even ridicule, and since the task is daunting, I am aware of the stressors and the strain. Awareness, however, requires knowledge of information which can only be communicated by cognitive data and the processes which manipulate them.

(i)   Conceptualizing Personality

There appears to be consensus on two issues: that personality is a multivariate response system and that the system is hierarchically structured. Apart from this limited agreement, theorists and researches have varied widely in their views on the components, on the proportional contribution of physiological or 'mental' processes, on the number of variables sufficient to describe between-subject variance, and in the lexicons they have used to label habits, traits, and types. The issues of genetic and environmental contributions, of the predictability and stability of personality have not been resolved by twin studies, nor by substituting coherence for stability or consistency in the analysis of person × environment interaction. These problems may well remain with us because of the difficulty in defining personality meaningfully and comprehensively in operational terms.

It is easy to underrate the important contribution of the factor-analytic techniques. Their pay-off has been a clearer understanding of the hierarchical structure of the components of characteristic and generalizeable behaviour, even though the experimental tests and probes have been conventional and even dated, and even though the investigators' decisions concerning the crucial components have been inevitably subjective (e.g. Royce, 1973).

Controversies which are now only of historical interest may have prevented us from following up interesting, early conceptions of personality. Wundt's classification of individual differences in temperament and emotionality, derived from the classical Greek personality types, is one of these. A demonstration of three pairs of bipolar orthogonal factors: quick/slow—strong/weak; broad/narrow—deep/shallow; excited/calm — pleasant/unpleasant, might still provide a more meaningful description of individual and group characteristics than does factorial evidence of more grossly defined typologies, in which error variance is substantial, the statistical significance of factors problematical, and orthogonality somewhat spurious and achieved at the expense of untested parameters.

Allport's (1937) attempted omnibus definition of personality is another case which may well repay reassessment. It has always been fundamentally multifactorial in terms of *psychophysical . . . systems . . .* (in) *. . . dynamic organization . . .* (determining) *. . . adjustment . . .* (to the) *. . . environment.* The resulting constellations of personality traits are conceptually quite similar to Guilford's (1967) approach to the analysis of intelligence, and logically guarantee uniqueness as well as meaningfulness.

For our present purposes this approach has added advantages. It prepares the ground for the more complex conceptions of person × environment interactions in which situational variations attenuate the high level of consistency implied by theories of personality traits (e.g. Endler and Magnusson, 1976). More significantly, perhaps, a dynamically conceived organization serving psychophysical adjustment, provides a suitable holistic approach by which to account for the effects of stress and stressors on task- and goal-directed behaviour. It seems doubtful that the first steps towards a cognitive conception of personality (Mischel, 1973; 1974), towards a cognitive interpretation of achievement motivation (Weiner, 1972; 1974), or an information processing analysis of anxiety (Hamilton, 1975; 1976a; 1976b) could have been taken without the conceptual tool of unifying organizational principles in behaviour. In the discussion of individual differences in responding to stress I shall generally disregard, therefore, any remaining disagreements over whether traits or uniqueness of personality are important considerations, or whether predictive consistencies or environmentally determined modulations afford the best approach for explaining characteristic regularities in adaptive goal seeking (Block, 1977; Mischel, 1977).

Instead the primary task will be to aim for a set of conceptual principles, interacting processes and mechanisms which can account parsimoniously for the demonstrated changes in behaviour related to stress and stressors. At this level of analysis, the contributions of autonomic arousal and activation, or of the possibly selective distribution of inhibitory or excitatory corticosteroids, are acknowledged. What may be questioned, directly or by implication, is the logical order of events: whether cognitive events follow upon or of necessity precede activities of the biologically more primitive response systems. In this respect, there seems to be too much contrary evidence to follow the heirs of James and Lange (e.g. Tomkins, 1963; Izard, 1977), though without discarding the possible role of a dual-signal, identification-signal reappraisal feedback system (Mandler, 1975).

Consistent with the orientation of this volume, therefore, personality characteristics are seen as *cognitive* processes and structures which are consistent, modifiable, vulnerable, and susceptible to situational demands. Like less complex habits, these structures provide previously reinforced, goal-reaching expectations and potentials for action, and goal-directed behaviour occurs as the result of decision-making processes at a central response-integrating system. This approach can be seen as a development of the related ideas presented by Weiner (1972), Mischel (1973), and Bolles (1974), but its development was facilitated by attempts to find some *fundamental* causes, for the impairment and limitation of information processing capacity in *anxious* normal children and adults (Hamilton, 1971; 1974; 1975).

(ii) Conceptualizing Stress

All who have followed the progress of Hans Selye's analytic work on the general adaptation syndrome will give ungrudging credit to the man and his concepts [see Chapter 1]. His level of analysis does not immediately help, however, when considering traditional conceptions of emotional tension or strain, their relationship to social vulnerability or to successfully completed, adaptive behaviour, *and the cognitive structures* which must mediate between them. Undoubtedly, steroidal and endocrinological hyper- or hypofunctions play a causal role in the development of the organic features of psychosomatic diorders, where in all probability they capitalize on stress-sensitive physiological structures. But we are left searching for the cognitive trigger of the alarm reaction.

From a cognitive standpoint, the influence of a psychodynamic orientation has been more immediately useful. From early Freud onwards, motivational conflict on more than one level of primary and secondary need systems has been linked with restlessness, displeasure, aversiveness, pain, or anxiety. To the extent that various types of approach-avoidance conflict can be manipulated, the cognitive sources of behavioural tension and indecisiveness are apparent, even in experimental studies of animals. For example, the early experiments of Neal Miller and his students and assistants (Miller, 1944; Brown, 1948) are consistent with a cognitive interpretation of drive conflict. This view is strengthened by the paradigmatic studies of Freudian defence mechanisms such as displacement

(Miller, 1948) and regression (Mowrer, 1940). Unresolved conflicts and their associated anxieties are causally considered in all non-behaviouristic theories of neurosis, and experimental evidence is available that high levels of conflict and anxiety predispose the person towards avoidance of even affectively *neutral* sources of experimental perceptual conflict and ambiguity (Hamilton, 1957; 1960).

It has been easier to define stressful events or stressors than stress itself. Lazarus (1966) suggested that it is difficult to avoid circular definitions, that stress is best defined by the response of people to stressors, i.e. by the sources of stress, which reside in an external or internal aversive event, *as well as* in the disposition or sensitivity of the individual to perceive or conceive aversiveness. The unavailability of concrete demonstrations of a causal agent or force does not present a new or insuperable problem to psychology. In a cogent paper on psychoanalysis and science Frenkel-Brunswik (1954) argued logically and persuasively for the power of constructs to sustain hypotheses about what is not observable, by validating internally consistent predictions which are derived from the constructs. Thus from many points of view, stress and say, repression, do not belong to logical categories essentially different from the construct of gravity. Moreover, they do not appear to be logically different from the mechanical law of the relationship between a force(S) applied, and the modulus of elasticity (λ), of different substances and their products. Unfortunately, for the behavioural scientist, S and λ in human organisms are themselves very complex. It seems prudent to state at this point, therefore, that we *do not* actually carry out experiments on stress. Instead we *do* investigate complexly mediated response states which are substantially influenced by existing levels and ranges of vulnerability (Appley and Trumbull, 1967; Zubin and Spring, 1977), and our dependent variables from which stress is inferred are levels and types of *strain* (Eysenck, 1973; Fröhlich, 1977). This *strain* is the effect of *stressors* on various response systems of the person, it is the type and degree of responding (*deformation*) of adaptive systems which have interpreted given types of stimulation and responding as a *load*. Although the term stress has long been regarded as imprecise and as having too many connotations (Holzman and Bitterman, 1952), it has survived, and cannot be displaced by a more definitive terminology all at once. I have decided to use the compound *stressor-strain* at various points when referring to high demands on the resources of the person which engender discomfort, avoidance strategies, or anxiety. Here *stressors* are the agents and *strain* the effects. *Stressors* and *strain* feedback together define the *load* on the whole system. I have indicated the imprecision of the more usual terms by quotation marks in the following pages.

The terms load and strain may have advantages for conceptualization which are absent from the more descriptive term 'stress'. They may be particularly useful for the development of a generalized quantifiable concept which is relevant to the prediction of stressor-strain from ostensibly quite different sources, impinging on differential capacities for 'stress' tolerance. Ultimately, it should be unnecessary to hold on to definitions of 'stress' as either a class of emotional behaviour elicited by a variety of undesired antecedent stimulation (Janis and Leventhal, 1968), or as states of the organism following the perception of threats to personal integrity and of danger (Cofer and Appley, 1964), because these definitions are too broad and imprecise.

While it is probably correct to assume that high emotionality, and particularly anxiety, are experienced as 'stressful', restricting discussion to these sources of strain diverts attention from the aversive effects of stimulus deprivation (Bexton, Heron, and Scott, 1954; Jones, 1966), from the effects of boredom (Berlyne and McDonnell, 1965; Frankenhaeuser, 1971), from the more clearly cognitive sources of coping strain induced by distracting stimulation (Broadbent, 1971), from protracted high-level skill performance (Davis, 1948; Wilkinson, 1964; Mackie, 1977), and from the effects of carrying out simultaneous tasks under conditions of threat [see Hamilton, Chapter 12].

For a number of years it has been fashionable to account for the effects of aversively experienced stimulation by reference to high arousal and/or high activation of subcortical mechanisms [see Hockey, Chapter 5]. Some recent evidence has shown, however, that the role of physiological arousal in performance decrements may be less important than the role of cognitive structures encoding anxiety which reflect anticipated pain or social censure [see Chapter 12]. These findings support a cognitive explanation of the effects of stressor-strain on performance. They also support an experience-oriented approach to the interpretation of what constitutes a high load on the adaptive system, and to the development of individual differences in strain tolerance. Just as there are developmental individual differences in the perception, and anticipation of levels of pain, so the perception and anticipation of levels of strain is a function of learning superimposed on, and yoked with, biological thresholds. Just as pain experience can be defined by its sources and its language (Melzack, 1973), so we may consider the usefulness of a 'lexicon' of stressor-strain experience. Following Melzack's paradigms, this might be extended from a semantic network describing sensory experience, to a *matrix of events and situations on gradients of intensity* which people describe as aversive, and as being in excess of a comfortable, or manageable, coping level. Each matrix term will reflect one aspect of the learned capacity to identify and to cope with the response requirements. To the extent that acquired strategies of stimulus identification and response selection constitute habits, and to the extent that organized systems of habits contain substantial elements of individual coherence, consistency and predictability, to that extent the stressor-strain processing system defines substantial portions of what is termed personality predisposition. Figure 3.1 represents an over-simplified model of interactions between information processing systems which for the purpose of this chapter are considered most relevant. It amounts to the proposition that strain is a function of stressor-load and coping capacity.

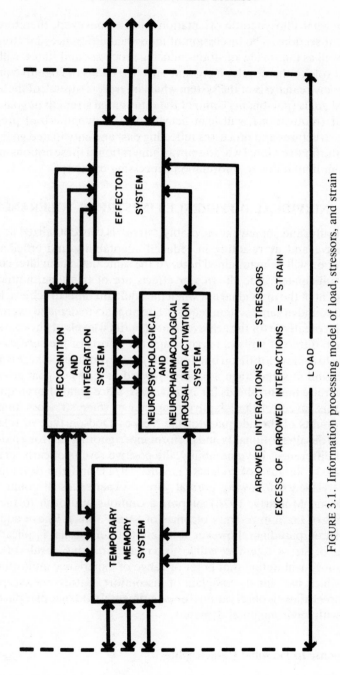

FIGURE 3.1. Information processing model of load, stressors, and strain

A somewhat idiosyncratic orientation will be conveyed, therefore, in the subsequent sections. The discussion of individual differences in 'stress' tolerance, as well as the review of strain-inducing processes and states, will assign a dominant role to the development and selective biases of cognitive processes. Similarly, my reanalysis of the system which interprets 'stress', of the system of individual goals (personality), and of the differential strength of goal-directed behaviour (motivation), will lean heavily on the hypothesized presence of cognitive structures and processes reflecting past and anticipated goal achievement. In the final section, I will attempt an integration of these notions in terms of strain from limitations in information processing capacity.

2. INDIVIDUAL DIFFERENCES IN 'STRESS' TOLERANCE

Historically, and somewhat inevitably, 'stress' is conceptualized as unpleasant, aversive and as resulting in reduced adaptability and efficiency. This interpretation will be maintained here. At the same time some later comments must be anticipated: not all stressor effects are of this type, neither in the development of the individual nor when the adult attempts to achieve his goals. Clearly, a sound organic system requires and appears to demand exercise often to the point of fatigue for the achievement of optimal levels of physical strength. Additional, different stressors accompany the efforts of the success-oriented individual to achieve a difficult but desirable goal. In both cases there is a positive incentive, and at some stage a positive reward in terms of goal achievement which will raise the thresholds for aversiveness. Since great effort requires high arousal, this caveat of the adaptive character of some stressors immediately conveys doubts of the adequacy of the Yerkes–Dodson type of relationship between arousal/emotionality and performance. Ignoring just for a moment the effects of differences in vulnerability, the positive results of early stressors on later 'stress' tolerance of rodents (Levine, 1971), and the development of adaptive resilience following normal 'stress' experiences of young children (Murphy and Moriarty, 1976) support a cautious approach to the general assessment of the nature and outcomes of 'stress'. Since I have adopted the stressor-strain paradigm, however, with all its interactional implications, the discussion of 'stress' tolerance will focus on the *'distressing'* results of stressors, and tolerance will define that point or range of experience and/or behaviour beyond which individuals complain of discomfort, distress, or incapacity, or beyond which there is observational or experimental evidence of reduced ability to cope with environmental demands.

(i) Response to Personal Catastrophies

Many individual differences have been recorded in the maintenance of manageable levels of emotionality, of occupational and problem solving skills, and the habitual organization of capacities to resist changes and aversive events, in response to particularly unpleasant experiences. These may be termed catastrophic, because their speed, their intensity, and the range of behaviour that is stimulated, are well beyond the usual environmental changes to which adaptation is required. Into this category fall the experiences of concentration and labour camp victims, prisoners of war, the victims of natural catastrophies like earthquakes or floods, or knowledge of a terminal illness. Bettelheim's (1960) germinal and moving account of responses to a Nazi concentration camp regimen not only records quite uniquely intense stressors, but distinctive differences in adapting to these. Helpless submission, abdication of *all* freedoms of action and thought, and an almost stuporous acceptance of a non-person status described the lowest point of 'stress' tolerance. In comparison, suicides were evidence of the retention of at least one, albeit unadaptive, area of control, whereas identifying with the agressors, and the direction of attention to situation-avoiding, intellectual issues were evidence of productive coping capacity despite their difference in means–ends evaluations. Although Bettelheim's accounts indicate that strong philosophical beliefs, and a semblance of congruence between grounds for committal and treatment diminished the effects of stressors, we are unable for obvious reasons, to relate differences in personality structure to strain resistance. Anecdotely, it may be noted that many survivors achieved considerable occupational and social success subsequently.

Motivationally considered, there would seem to be adequate grounds for involving the concept of locus of control (Rotter, 1966) to account for a variety of findings in which helplessness, or resistance to it, was the major reported response to stressors. The helplessness of air crews on night sorties (Grinker and Spiegel, 1945), of populations confronted with natural disasters (Janis, 1962), of soldiers in oppressive captivity situations (Biderman, 1967), would seem to be a consequence of a realistic assessment of the inability to control the source of aversive stimulation. Where this inability is experienced as catastrophic, adaptive solutions within the range of the possible are infrequent. Conversely, where self-generated or self-attributed powers of anticipating or minimizing distress are present and used, survival may be achieved (*viz.* the case of Don O'Daniel, Janis, 1971). There are some inconsistencies in studies of the antecedents of internal control beliefs, but generally, and at least for males, it seems that individuals with a warm, supportive but firmly controlled socialization history, with encouragement of independence and achievement, tend towards self-perceptions of being strong and of being capable of controlling the impact of their environment (Weiner *et al.,* 1972; Strickland, 1977).

Individuals faced with a clinical verdict of a potentially terminal illness must accept exposure to the ultimate existential crisis. The initial response is intense anxiety, anger, and depression. Later responses to the knowledge and to the required treatment seem to depend on the intensity of the emotional response, on frank but supportive discussions with hospital personnel and family (Janis and Leventhal, 1968; Janis, 1971), and on the presence and mobilization of what is loosely termed ego strength. All these energize motives and actions conducive to returning to a normal life, and an optimistic view of the final outcome (Surawicz *et al.*, 1976). In Janis' studies, patients with a *moderate* degree of anxiety before their operation, and those who had been informed of their condition and the surgical implications, achieved better post-operative adjustments. This included a greater tolerance of pain and fewer demands for alleviation by narcotics. In addition to the role played by the provision of information in preparing for, containing, and rationalizing the impact of emotionality, these studies suggest that 'stress' is affected by an *accumulation* of 'stressful' events. This relationship has been considered generally as supported by a large variety of studies on the incidence of physical illness after a succession of aversive life-events (e.g. Rabkin and Struening, 1976), or so-called psychosomatic conditions (e.g. Rees, 1977).

Later chapters in this volume will present a more detailed account of the parameters involved in life 'stress'. At this stage it must be sufficient to note that the capacity to withstand the strain from powerful and/or unavoidable stressors depends on at least three major factors: knowledge of the nature of stressors and the resultant strains to be anticipated; the degree of integrated organization of alternative, internally consistent habits for the attainment of the individual's principal goals; and cognitive processes capable of evaluating and integrating the anticipated stressors in relation to the existing goal structures. Unless all these factors can be quantified predictions of 'stress' tolerance must be inaccurate. It is quite likely, for example, that the failure of the O.S.S. studies (1948), to predict response to strain, was due *inter alia,* to the inability to predict the number and types of stressors to which personnel became exposed, and to lack of knowledge at that time of the importance of cognitive processes in coping with stressor-strain experiences.

(ii) Predispositions

Although we must focus here on the individual's characteristics which support resistance to strain, a life-span analysis makes it clear that these characteristics must undergo developmental change, and that sources and types of stressors are themselves developmentally determined. Early experiences of dissatisfaction arising from inadequacies in mother–infant interaction in relation to nutritional and attachment needs (Bowlby, 1951; Escalona, 1968), are followed by stressors arising from increases in mobility, in competence, and in the range of social interaction. These stressors include prevention of excessive independence, experience of illness, awareness of inadequate skills, and competence for a variety of tasks at different ages. Other stressors are implicit in the growth of social role playing in dealing with demands for co-operation, in learning to renounce unattainable goals, and in the postponement of gratifications. *Func-*

tionally similar or identical control and coping demands may well be present, but past theories of personality do not appear to rest on high correlations supporting long-term stability models (Mischel, 1968). It may be argued that high stability of stressor-strain responses would be predicted only on the basis of rather primitive behaviour models, and in the absence of a cognitive approach to stressors and their perception as such, in situations enormously different in complexity. On this basis, the available *evidence of stability* of personality over many years (e.g. Block, 1971; 1977) should be considered remarkable, rather than inadequate. A full discussion of the role of personality predispositions in 'stress' tolerance would require a monograph. In the present context a summary must suffice of the various approaches and models.

(a) *Genetic approaches*

These approaches to 'stress' tolerance usually reflect two related assumptions; that this factor is heritable, and that it determines to a large degree the phenotypical response to stressors. The utility of this approach has been shown in breeding 'emotional' and 'non-emotional' varieties of rats (Broadhurst, 1959), but it has led to controversial results from studies of human behaviour genetics. Eysenck and Prell's (1951) studies produced very high correlations between monozygotic twins in test situations which were assumed to be good measures of neuroticism. Retrospectively considered, however, it is possible that parameters more relevant to disposition to neurotic breakdown might have been chosen. If that had been done, it is likely that lower resemblances might have been found, as for example by Shields (1962) for neuroticism as well as introversion–extraversion. Loehlin and Nichols (1976), working with more than 800 pairs of mono- and dizygotic twins, obtained few correlations higher than 0.50 for personality characteristics, self-concepts, ideals, goals, or interests as assessed by reputable techniques from more than 500 monozygotic twin pairs. As in many other studies, the largest zygosity differences were confined to intellectual capacity variables.

To balance these kinds of results, the relevance of some recent studies by Izard (Izard, 1977) cannot be ignored. Despite the homogeneous influence of an institution, Russian infants 6 months to 2 years old showed wide individual differences in emotion thresholds and emotion-related activities. In so far as carefully controlled clinical observations are reliable and valid indicators of 'stress' tolerance, the studies by Thomas and his colleagures (e.g. Thomas, Chess, and Birch, 1968) must also be considered. The *temperamental* characteristics studies by them are by definition constitutional and heritable. To the extent that infants with early disorders of response intensity, withdrawal from novel stimuli, adaptability and mood, later on required active clinical intervention, a genetic basis for 'stressful' early developmental experience appears to have been demonstrated. In the absence of a co-twin control methodology and a larger and more random subject sample, however, a great deal more confirmation would seem to be required. The critical assumption of most of the genetically oriented studies is that emotionality and particularly its high intensity provide a sufficient definition of strains and that variations in intensity of emotional reactions are a sufficient definition of tolerance of stressors. Neither the main assumption nor its corollaries can be accepted, however, without a considerably up-dated cognitive definition of emotion.

(b) *Learning theory approaches*

These approaches to 'stress' tolerance have taken broadly two directions: conditionability of emotional hyperactivity as a consequence of high avoidance drive, and the acquisition by reinforcement of habits of behavioural and cognitive control and coping strategies. The first direction represents Pavlovian/Hullian conceptions of conditioning, the second assigns greater importance to instrumental responses, although mutually exclusive distinctions between them are now difficult to maintain (Mackintosh, 1974; Bolles, 1975).

Classical association learning depends on the ease with which unconditioned responses can be elicited, which in a stressor context are mainly avoidance responses, and of which eye-blink studies are a good example (e.g. Spence and Farber, 1954; Spence, 1956). The higher the drive and the excitatory potential, the faster the conditioning and the more resistent to extinction is the conditioned response. No clear-cut relationship between Spence's drive concept of conditionability and 'stress' and 'stress' tolerance has ever been developed. Since the model demonstrated an inverse U-shaped relationship between anxiety interpreted as a drive and performance (Spence and Spence, 1966), it is possible to infer that performance decrements with high anxiety reflect the presence of strain in the response system.

H. J. Eysenck's theoretical views are essentially similar in their conception of an interaction of an energizing emotionality component, and level and type of stimulation. The Spence criterion measure of emotionality is the Manifest Anxiety Scale (Taylor, 1953). According to Eysenck this basically measures neuroticism, whereas his criterion variables are introversion–extraversion as well as neuroticism, where sensitivity to stimulation, conditionability, and performance decrements with high scores on introversion are related to biological differences in arousal (ARAS) and activation (ANS) thresholds and processes (Eysenck, 1967; 1970; 1973). The difference between the two classical conditioning approaches is less substantial than it sometimes appears, firstly because Eysenck's model includes high emotionality or neuroticism as a necessary factor in large performance decrements, as well as in the development of neurotic disorders, and secondly, because the criterion I–E questionnaire items still seem to include questions of equal relevance to general anxiety of neuroticism despite the evidence of factorial uniqueness. Eysenck's concepts specify more clearly than Spence's, however, the relationship between sensitivity to level and type of stimulation and 'stress' tolerance: so-called negative hedonic tones appear at lower levels of arousal and activation in introverts than in extraverts. Gray's (1973; 1976) elaboration of Eysenck's conditionability principle is based on postulated separate *physiological* reward and punishment centres. The deduction that introverts are more sensitive to, and learn better with, punishment, and extraverts are more modifiable with reward, does not necessarily follow since 'knowledge of results' must mediate. Thus, the major source of individual differences in strain and 'stress' tolerance may reside in cognitive rather than biological response systems.

Instrumental or effect learning must occur on the basis of knowledge of response consequences; on the ability to make predicitons at some level of stimulus processing of the probability that the same or a related response will have desirable or required outcomes. Therefore, any response that has been experienced as reducing aversive aspects of strain has a high probability of featuring permanently in a response repertoire. Since anticipation precedes knowledge of effect, cognitive structures are required for operant learning. For this reason, *anticipation of, and resistance and adaptation to,* experiences of conflict, frustration, aggression, or anxiety are correctly identified as coping processes in thinking and, in action (Lazarus, 1966; Appley and Trumbull, 1967). These processes and strategies would not have been acquired but for experiencing their effects as strain reducing for a response system which needs to consider at each decision stage the complex interactions of the multiple goals of the individual. It is probably due to these complexities that psychodynamic views of personality continue to be important.

(c) *Psychodynamic approaches*

These approaches to individual differences in 'stress' tolerance make three fundamental assumptions: susceptibility or vulnerability to strain has many of its sources in early experience and coping strategies; the sources and nature of stressors are often not amenable to self-report; protective thought processes often disguise or deny the fact that strain operates. In other words, historical determination, unconscious cognitive processes, and defence mechanisms provide the basis as well as methods of adapting to 'stressful' experience. Again, it must be remembered that not all forms of strain are aversive, so that heightened emotionality from giving pleasure to others, of exultation upon goal achievement, or of sexual love constitute threats and stressor-strain experience only in a minority and mainly pathological cases.

Psychodynamic theorists agree that the greatest single manifestation or source of stressor-strain is anxiety. Freud was probably imprecise in his statements concerning free-floating, objectless anxiety. Since the term anxiety refers to aversive, variously painful, threatening or injurious events which the individual may experience in given circumstances, the anticipation or expectation of these events must guarantee sources. If the sources cannot be reported this does not imply that they are absent, or that the source which is identified is the critical one. 'Unconscious' anxiety, similarly, must logically and necessarily be conceptualized as cognitive data and processes.

Whatever the sources of the person's reporting strategies, their presence guarantees that the necessary associations and choices have been learned. There is, therefore, no necessary antithesis between learning and psychodynamic theories. Equally, any contradiction between the psychodynamic and physical science models of 'stress' tolerance is more apparent than real. The basic component of physiological vulnerability or sensitivity to load is accepted, where load equals *inter alia* approach–approach or approach–avoidance conflicts; frustration or prevention of access to a high-priority goal; anxiety; or the anticipation of threats to self-esteem, pain tolerance, or personal integrity. The greater the load from these sources, the greater the number and the severity of the stressors and the farther the movement towards a limit of 'stress' tolerance. The greater the vulnerability factors, the smaller the number of new stressors of low intensity required to produce maladaptation. Neurosis and psychosis define paradoxical or adaptively primitive attempts to reduce otherwise unmanageable strain, defences which cannot or are too late to defend.

Individuals with a resilient nervous system need not employ ultimate, autonomous avoidance strategies to remain within the limits of 'stress' tolerance. *Conscious detachment* has been described as a usually successful strategy for medical students when first exposed to an autopsy, a situation in which crude humour, which is common in laboratory dissection, would be considered insensitive (Lazarus, 1974). The separation between the cognitive events and aversive or repulsive feelings is facilitated by the teaching situation. In its rational approach and aims this situation is functionally similar to the demonstrated threat-reducing role of preparatory instructions to be objective and rational when observing and reporting upon films depicting physical injuries (Lazarus, 1966; Koriat *et al.*, 1972). Deliberate intentions of *direct self-control* of anxiety about examinations are the most common strategies of dealing with fear of failure in pupils and students (Mechanic, 1962). In all three instances the separation betwen thought and affect is strain reducing, though questions of the actual and fundamental sources of anxiety frequently need to be asked and answered. It is worth noting, perhaps, that while these threat-avoidance strategies reflect commonly successful attempts to separate thought and affect, the individual remains aware of what he has done. Psychoanalytical concepts of the dynamics of obsessive-compulsive neurosis also propose a process of 'splitting' an idea from its affect in the development of a reaction formation defence. An important difference, however, is that the strategy and its outcome are not reportable, and that conscious control cannot be employed to cope adaptively with residual strain.

In more than one way this example could describe the difference between the operations and implications of a coping process as defined by Lazarus (1966; 1971; 1975), and the unconscious defensive distortion and denial processes of psychodynamic models for dealing with unacceptable types and levels of anxiety. Neo-Freudians like Haan (1977) regard coping as the most reality-based cognitive process of regulating 'personality-as-a-process-over-time'. The least effective coping process is fragmentation which occurs presumably when 'stress' tolerance and its defensive supports have been substantially exceeded. An interesting but not quite fully worked out development of this theoretical approach is her suggestion that anxiety and 'stress' control may follow cognitive developmental stages akin to those of Piaget and his school. Thus she argues that '. . . (children's) stress adduce schemata that are disproportionately affective and figurative, rather than cognitive. The more affective and the less cognitive the schemata, the more ready are children to assimilate present to past stress by over-generalizing, and thus they more often defend rather than cope when they are stressed' (Haan, 1977, p.183). It is likely that this approach could become more incisive once it is more generally accepted that these schemata are basically cognitive, and that young children's capacity to reduce strain depends on minimizing the interpretation of experience as stressors. This, in turn, has been shown to be a function of a warm, firmly supportive but controlling parental socialization strategy, accompanied by informative, non-intrusive 'teaching', and by encouragement to achieve age-appropriate goals (e.g. Baumrind, 1967; Hamilton, 1972a; 1972b; 1976a).

A comprehensive account of psychodynamically influenced research orientations and findings relevant to a discussion of difference in 'stress' tolerance is quite beyond the scope of this chapter. It would have to range from a consideration of *perceptual defence,* to *cognitive styles and controls* and to *cognitive dissonance resolution* and *dogmatism.* While these instances of types of conflict resolution and anxiety reduction have not been considered systematically from the point of view of strain avoidance, recent reviews indicate that the avoidance of threating or incongruent cognitive data reflects sometimes consistent and often coherent individual differences in affect control (e.g. Mischel, 1968; Vernon, 1973; Erdelyi, 1974; Hamilton, 1976a). Avoidance, however, is not the only or necessarily the most adaptive strategy for the maintenance of a manageable level of strain: being prepared for exposure to threat assists the coping process. For that reason the sensitization pole of a repression–sensitization dimension (Byrne, 1964) probably characterizes coping individuals rather than defensive individuals, and high levels of attention and anticipation probably indicate that a suitable range of coping mechanisms is available. That these forms of control need not be volitional is strongly suggested by studies in which threatening information was presented in only one half of a stereoscopically viewed field (Dixon and Haider, 1961; Dixon, 1971).

This brief review of approaches to the study of 'stress' tolerance indicates that the normally functioning individual can or does avail himself of a considerable variety of self-protective, controlling or coping processes. What each person does, depends on his constitutional sensitivity, on his history of experienced positive and negative rewards, and on integrated habitual cognitive goal structures which can absorb at all organizational levels rapid changes in the selection of stimuli and responses which maintain him in a perceived state of effectiveness [see Folkman, Schaefer and Lazarus, Chapter 9].

3. PERSONALITY, SITUATIONS AND STRESS

(i) The Interaction Problem

Since differences in 'stress' tolerance are multivariately determined, a more analytic review of some major variables is desirable. In this section, therefore, the components of the interaction equation will be considered separately. When it is stated that 'stress' = f(personality $\times$ situation), the difference between the usefulness of this statement and Hooke's Law is immediately apparent. Not only are there problems concerning scales and units of measurement arising from the complexity of each of the interacting factors, there is the difficulty of reliably and validly isolating their components. A more complex factor impedes the development of adequate explanatory frameworks: that which is termed personality is historically influenced by situational factors, and the range of situations to which individuals are required to adapt is normally a reflection of preceding interactions between personality and situational experience. Therefore, on a priori grounds, exposure to one type of environment is more probable than exposure to others. It follows that personality and situations require additional definition in terms of learned adaptive, coping and/or defensive processes, applicable to all individual goals, and the intensity and consistency with which they are sought. Two additional factors need to be considered which contribute to the difficulties of analysis. On the basis of Hooke's Law it has been assumed that the relationship between load and strain for human behaviour is monotonic (e.g. Eysenck, 1973). This is an over-simplifying extension of a conceptual analogue, because resistance to strain may be apparent only at substantial levels of load, when considering individuals differing in tolerance of stressors. This situation is shown in Figure 3.2(a). Furthermore, individuals with high tolerance of stressors may actually show more strain, defined by decrements on cognitive tasks, than those with low tolerance at low to intermediate levels of load. High tolerance of stressors may be truly indicated only at high levels of load (see Figure 3.2b). Both examples illustrate the influence of adaptive, coping or defensive processes which basically define levels of tolerance of stressors. Situation b is in some respects an analogue of the well-known cross-over effect in the relationship between high and low anxiety and, for example, verbal learning, when the facilitating effect of high anxiety appears only when irrelevant competing responses have been eliminated (e.g. Spielberger and Smith, 1966). Focal

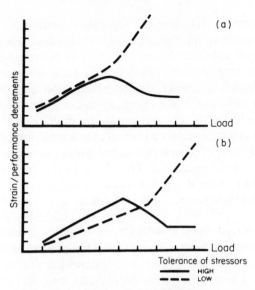

FIGURE 3.2. Non-linear relationships between load and strain

studies in support of these suggestions do not appear to have been carried out.
They would require a reliable and valid indexing of load, a systematic manipulation of the duration over which it is applied, as well as of antecedent stressors, and
of diurnal variations.

   Major potential sources of strain reside in each person's system of needs and
goals because competing responses in attempting to adapt to stressors are
derived from individual histories of adapting to the demands of people, objects,
and situations. In some respects it is valid, therefore, to consider person- or
self-induced sources of strain in isolation from the situational sources, without
thereby rejecting an interactional position. Similarly, there are no *a priori*
reasons why situational sources of strain should not be considered in isolation
from persons, if for no other reason than that a considerable amount of
high-intensity stimulation is commonly experienced by all people as stressing
and strain inducing. We need to cite only fear of falling from great heights, tissue
injuries, sustained demands for vigilance, or demands for responding to multiple, simultaneous stimulation.

   At least two recent symposia have tried to suggest that 'interactional psychology' is a novel field of study, and that it is virtually impossible to disentangle any
identifiable, separate effects attributable to, respectively, personality or situations (Endler and Magnusson, 1976; Magnusson and Endler, 1977). While it is
clearly valuable to be reminded of the importance of interaction processes, this is
neither a novel nor an insoluble problem. Unless, of course, the question asked is
how much each component contributes to each identified response (see Figure

3.5). Years of controversy over the separate contribution of heredity and environment to *measured* intelligence have led to the conclusion that this type of question is less profitable than the analysis of what is actually being measured by the available tools (e.g. Vernon, 1976). Since we are no longer ignorant of the *effects of continuous experience* on the elaboration and differentiation of response dispositions, nor of the *effects of measurement itself* on behaviour, interactional psychologists are overstating the novelty of their endeavours. Many investigators have attempted to clarify the interaction either by statistical design (Endler, 1966), by the use of criterion groups in respect of anxiety (e.g. Sarason, 1972; Spielberger, 1975; Hamilton, 1975), by basic variations or induced variations in arousal (e.g. Wilkinson, 1964), with or without consideration of individual differences in diurnal rhythms (e.g. Colquhoun and Corcoran 1964). These manipulations of independent variables arising primarily within the person have been matched by systematic variations in situational variables that are too numerous to cite here. Our greatest problem so far is the multivariateness of the human response system: the degree of simplicity or complexity with which this system experiences and defines environmental stimulation, and the intensity of cognitive and biological responsiveness which this definition engenders.

(ii) Sources in the Person

When Lazarus (1966) wrote that the degree of threat is limited by the strength of the motive or motives whose gratification is endangered, he adopted the person-centered approach to the development and experience of stressor-strain. A similar approach was adopted by Arnold (1967) by describing 'stress' as a condition of disturbed normal functioning in which extraordinary reactions are required to overcome negative emotions, obstacles to goals, a sense of pressure and demands. We may link these two statements, and propose that obstacles to the gratification of a motive stimulate avoidance of the threat presented by negative emotions and the appraisal of danger. The avoidance of threat and danger requires two supporting processes: arousal and activation which signal negative emotions and energize coping behaviour, and cognitive strategies and skills with which to plan and execute subjectively most favourable responses and outcomes. Biologically oriented theories of personality relate the development of motivation and differences in experimenting and handling stressors to arousal and activation characteristics (e.g. Eysenck, 1967), even to the extent that socially defined introvert or extravert habits and traits are said to be determined by subcortical events and processes. It is probably safer to be less dogmatic, and to assign no more than a *necessary* role to autonomic and subcortical processes in the experience and handling of stressors and their strain effects. Two reasons for this conclusion must suffice here: (1) habituation and higher-order learning are able to reduce what were originally stressors to the level of unremarkable or ordinary stimuli, and (2) biological 'stress' reactions which energize avoidance behaviour are secondary to the cognitive identification of threats of dangers of specific relevance to one particular person and initially precede the biological response.

An additional justification for considering the person-induced aspects of strain separately is that situations can be and often are avoided because we are able to evaluate their stressor capacities in advance, once the required cognitive skills are present. It is rather more difficult for the individual to avoid in the same manner his motivational dangers, conflicts and frustrations which, if they are present, are cognitively coded in a permanent memory system. Let us now briefly consider some of these sources of strain.

The affiliation motive has its origins in the need for maternal comforts, supports, and attachment. Its adult expressions and elaborations are directed towards social companionship, co-operation, the development of friendship ties in occupational and recreational settings, and towards the confirmation of social skills and appreciation by others. A number of studies cited by Wilson (1977) show that affiliation and extraversion are meaningfully related, while the well-known studies by Schachter (1964) confirmed the predicition that affiliative behaviour appears in response to social anxiety. A study by Zimbardo and Formica (1963) showed that with the induction of anxiety, subjects low in self-esteem exhibited a greater affiliation tendency than those with high self-esteem. Additional evidence (Shapiro and Alexander, 1969) suggests that the mediation of affiliation by anxiety is stronger for extraverts than introverts. From this brief account a number of situations can be predicted in which susceptibility to strain is relatable to affiliation needs. For example, criticism, failure, threats of pain by virtue of their anxiety-arousing capacity would increase affiliation needs, particularly for extraverts. The possibility that introverts will have a similar tendency cannot be excluded entirely since the experimental studies were group-behaviour oriented, and the introvert may seek the support of just one trusted person. In the present context the most important stressor seems to be anxiety with its major antecedents in fears of injury, rejection, and inadequacy.

Considerable strain may be experienced in satisfying achievement motivation. It is usual to distinguish here between two types of orientation in the person: to seek or approach success, and to avoid failure. Stressors may be assumed to be potentially present in both orientations. Where, however, there is fear of failure, anxiety tends to be high, and the number of goals and/or the level of goal achievement are reduced, whereas success seeking has been characterized by low levels of anxiety, determination to overcome obstacles, and an optimistic attitude towards outcome (e.g. Atkinson and Feather, 1966; Atkinson, 1977). Recent developments in achievement motivation theory have concerned themselves with achieving distant rather than immediate goals (Raynor, 1974), and the probability of future successes in respect of tasks of increasing difficulty over time. The force-field conception of the theory (Lewin, 1951) seems to be particularly suitable for comparison with models of 'stress', in that load may be analogous to the resultant 'force' (positive or negative) in the direction of the goal. This is a function of goal properties, motivation and distance from goal, and strain may be analogous to the conflict between 'force' and 'barriers' in terms of 'valence' or physical presence. Since 'force' is 'resultant', however, it must involve strain from compromise.

Success seeking has been developmentally related to independence training (Winterbottom, 1953), to high self-esteem (Coopersmith, 1967), and to self-reliance, self-control, and liveliness in children whose parents were predominantly firm, loving, understanding, and demanding (Baumrind, 1967). Fear of failure has been found associated with anxiety in respect of authority and criticism (Cox, 1968; Hill, 1972), and failure in achievement has been demonstrated when social status was 'publicly' tested (Atkinson, 1974a). Individual differences in achievement motivation and anticipation of success and failure in optimally or suboptimally reared children, provide, therefore, a very large number of strain foci, apart from the evidence from the epidemiology of psychosomatic disorders of the effects of stressors in achievement- and status-oriented societies. Strain avoidance then is a function of balancing success and failure orientation by restructuring the hierarchy and values of goals so that non-achievement is not experienced as failure or as damaging to self-concepts.

Conflict, anxiety and frustration have been recurring concepts and responses in this brief analysis of sources of strain in the person. Low thresholds for experiencing them implies that there is a concomitant readiness, and greater anticipation for these negative or aversive experiences. Whether these response predispositions are acquired by 'single-trial, traumatic learning', or by unresolved developmental events at a particular 'psychosexual stage', they clearly have been acquired by some kind of reward contingency, and are brought to environmental situations where they are stimulated by external demands. Whether anxiety is an inevitable or the major experience in relation to conflict or frustration, or whether anger and aggression are primary, is probably an unhelpful question. Observationally, there seems to be a bipolar distribution of responses. It is possible, however, that such evidence is a function of the level of analysis that is adopted. Varieties of approach and avoidance of conflicts and of goal blocking may indeed initially stimulate high-energy responses with physical and physiological signs of anger and aggression. These may be either coping or defensive responses, however, and be representative of a more fundamental fear that goal frustration, inability to decide between goals, or incapacity to overcome the negative or threatening aspects of a desired goal will have damaging consequences for the status, personal acceptibility, or organic integrity of the individual.

In my own view, anxiety — widely and ultimately cognitively defined — is the major and most fundamental source of strain in the person. Since the role of anxiety in strain will be discussed again in Chapter 12, I will confine myself here briefly to two issues: the relationship between anxiety and strain, and what I mean by anxiety. *In my view*, the processes of the autonomic nervous system and ascending reticular activating system concurrently active in generating and sustaining high emotionality, are stressors. Potentially dangerous or threatening stimuli, when identified, equally are stressors, and since their recognition occurs first, they trigger the physiological stressors. The combination of both sources constitutes a major proportion of the total strain (see Figure 3.5). A definition of anxiety as self-generated aversive information assigns priority to cognitive events and, therefore, assigns a dominant role to cognitive sources of strain. These are determined by excessively elaborated anxiety schemata coded in long-term memory with low retrieval thresholds, and reflect historically the individual's *interpretations* of earlier experiences, and consequently his *expectations* of aversive and unfavourable outcomes in subsequent adaptations to the environment. An informational interpretation of anxiety implies a further source of intrapersonal strain: the difficulty level of problem solving is increased by the intrusion of task-irrelevant aversive cognitive data (Mandler and Sarason, 1952; Hamilton, 1972b; 1975; 1976a; 1976b; Sarason, 1975).

Brief mention must be made of two social psychological processes which will contribute to the development of stressor-strain mediated by anxiety, both primarily cognitive and active at different but more specific levels of response selection and interaction. Attribution theory (e.g. Jones *et al.*, 1972) holds that stressors may be erroneously inferred from social events, and that strain may develop as a consequence of identifying false but plausible causes for the behaviour of others. The process described by these theorists is similar to the psychoanalytic concept of projection in which false inference is one of two core cognitive events. The second process relevant to strain induction through anxiety is the strategy of assigning behaviour *control* into the hands of authorities or situations. Where the locus of control is external (Rotter, 1966), and where affiliation and achievement needs have not been adequately met, adaptive coping processes may be unavailable. Stressor-strain due to anxiety over unsatisfied needs may be superseded eventually by resignation, helplessness, or depression.

(iii) Situational Sources

The identification of environmental stressors presents fewer opportunities for controversy. Despite the evidence of universal stressors, it is common knowledge that many people actively seek dangers, social conflicts, or high rates of work output. Explanations for this phenomenon range from labels of psychopathy, masochism or the death wish, to the absence of a long-term goal structure. The only tested explanation is in physiological terms as already discussed earlier on: that inactivity and boredom can be highly arousing physiologically with uncomfortable subjective effects, and that optimal arousal levels, of e.g. extraverts, are higher than for other types of personalities (viz. Bexton, Heron and Scott; Berlyne; Frankenhaeuser; Eysenck; above).

Situational stressors may be grossly but adequately classified under three headings: 'physical dangers'; 'social isolation'; 'work and performance', most of which are discussed in greater detail in other chapters. The first category presents few opportunities for misunderstanding. 'Social isolation', however, is here more complexly defined than usual by events ranging from incarceration to spatial/geographical disorientation, and from 'maternal deprivation' to peer group rejection. The third category contains some of the most carefully studied cognitive operations from vigilance to problem solving under varying conditions assumed to engender strain.

There ought to be a further category which could be superimposed on the other three which, although it belongs to common knowledge, is studied only infrequently. I am referring to the temporal and geographical distance from the subject of an emotion- or strain-inducing event. The increase in anxiety with the approach of examinations is clinically well documented, and Swedish studies (Lundberg and Ekman, 1960) were able to describe the relationship between objective as well as subjective time before an examination adequately by a simple exponential function. Contrasting findings were obtained by Fenz (1964; 1975) who found that strain in experienced sport parachutists was greatest at an intermediate temporal point prior to a jump, but lower than that of novice parachutists. Averill *et al.* (1977) also found stress reactions diminished when subject were able to use a warning signal of impending shock, and Niemelä (1972) similarly found a reduction in physiological, and self-report evidence of strain as the time for the occurrence of situational stressor—an accident film—came closer. The differences between the results of these studies suggest (1) the presence of coping responses in the three last-mentioned studies, and (2) that preparatory set is an important factor in the person × situation interaction in strain control.

(iv) Some Experimental Evidence of Person × Situation Interaction

I have previously indicated that a substantial case can be made out for assigning a dominant role to individual differences in anxiety proneness in the development of strain, as a consequence of interpreting events as stressors. Our brief review of experimental evidence of the relationship between personality and situational stressors will maintain this conceptual stance without, however, suggesting that the involvement of anxiety signifies the presence of pathological processes. It is worth remembering perhaps that when Murray (1938) spoke of a need for 'harm avoidance', he referred to a biologically important capacity for reducing tension and for increasing pleasure and satisfaction. Above I have classified tension-inducing situational domains primarily on the basis of their characteristic capacity to elicit anxiety and, therefore, discomfort. I propose to discuss the person × situation interaction under the same headings, without suggesting, however, that stressors or strain from these sources are *initially* or *exclusively* due to the identification of aversiveness rather than to the informational complexity of the situation.

(a) *Physical danger*

When one considers the relationship between personality and pain tolerance/endurance or pain thresholds, it is pertinent to recall that at least two mediational processes have been considered important. Studies employing criterion groups of introverts and extraverts appear to have worked in a physiological framework of personality and have ignored the cognitive components of adaptation to pain. Melzack (1973 p.102) cites evidence, however, that cognitive components play a possibly decisive role: '. . . cultural values, anxiety, attention and suggestion all have a profound effect on pain experience . . . (which) . . . may affect the sensory-discriminative dimension or the motivational-affective dimension'. Petrie's approach to individual differences in pain tolerance (Petrie, Collins, and Solomon, 1960; Petrie, 1967) employs an 'augmenting–reducing' dimension to describe results obtained from leucotomized or surgical cases, and subjects undergoing experimental sensory isolation or experimental heat pain. With one exception there was higher pain tolerance for the more extravert individuals, albeit with an unconvincing level of statistical significance. The mediating explanatory process employed by Petrie is 'neural satiation', a process first investigates by Köhler and Wallach (1944). Unfortunately, the criterion measure of this process — figural after-effect — is not reliably related to introversion-extraversion (Hamilton, 1959), despite some earlier claims to the contrary (Eysenck, 1957). More recent work on pain tolerance in relation to augmenting or reducing processes has been reviewed by Buchsbaum (1976) in the general context of self-regulation of high-intensity stimulation. His own studies show more significant differences between pain-tolerant and intolerant subjects on average evoked E.E.G. responses (AER). Since AER's are considered to be possibly the most reliable index of arousal, this approach has potential for future work on dual personality-arousal criterion groups.

Apparently reliable differences between levels of pain endurance/tolerance or thresholds for introverts and extraverts have been reviewed by Schalling, who concludes (1976, p. 62), that extraversion-impulsivity is a more important variable for pain tolerance in the laboratory than is anxiety proneness. Her own studies, employing a different personality questionnaire (Schalling, 1971), indicate, however, that experimental methodology may play an important role in this conclusion. Whereas a *continuous* increase in painful stimulation was primarily related to extraversion, increases in stimulation by anticipated discrete increments produced additional significant differences between subjects high and low in neuroticism. Schalling's measure, just as other measures of neuroticism, correlated significantly with measures of anxiety, and a negative relationship between socially defined extraversion and measures of anxiety has never been excluded with full confidence. For these reasons it still seems plausible to believe, bearing in mind Melzack's views, that anxiety — suitably defined — plays a determining role in pain tolerance, even if neurophysiological variables seem crucial for the level of pain *thresholds*. The studies by Janis and others reported in section 2 provide additional support for this conclusion.

It is relevant to refer briefly to Milgram's investigations on obedience to authority (1963) in order to conclude that general and superficial measures of personality may be quite inadequate for the demonstration and prediction of personality differences in response to pain. It should be safe to assume (1) that Milgram's subjects — either 'teachers' or 'learners' — were not chosen on the basis of high extraversion scores; (2) that the conforming 'teachers' similarly were not primarily extraverts; (3) that reluctance to administer painful shock can be due only to identification with the 'learners', that is to say *knowing* about the aversiveness of shock. There are in fact good grounds for arguing the possibility that conforming to sadistic authority demands may require high levels of affiliation needs, which in turn is plausibly relatable to anxiety over social isolation as defined at more than one level.

A good example of a protective response to physical danger is the eye-blink reflex. Studies by Spence and Farber (1954) and Franks (1957) among others, aroused many controversies about the nature of the critical independent variables on which criterion groups of subjects were selected, and about the adequacy of experimental methods. Eysenck (1957) argued persuasively that slow build-up of reactive inhibition and resistance to extinction was characteristic of introverts, and that Franks' data, showing superior conditionability of eye blink to tone by introverts compared with extraverts, supported this proposition. Hamilton (1959), criticized the research methodology for the dubious validity of the personality questionnaires and the unvarying intensity of the UCS. A more recent and more analytic reinvestigation of this issue (Eysenck and Levey, 1971) seems to have confirmed the value of the earlier criticisms. Introverts conditioned better only with a weak UCS and with partial reinforcement, whereas only the sociability and not the impulsiveness component of an extraversion scale diminishes the acquisition of the protective CS. Impulsive extraverts with a strong UCS and 100 per cent reinforcement conditioned as well as, or better than, introverts under optimal conditions. Because partial negative reinforcement was the most successful method of CS establishment in introverts, and because partial reinforcement involves the *unpredictable* occurence and the *anticipation* of an unpleasant stimulus, cognitive processes in identifying the stressor and coping with it cannot be excluded. It seems valid to conclude, therefore, that sensitivity to harm or punishment is a crucial variable in conditioning (Gray, 1972), but that cognitive anxiety is the crucial mediator.

Only brief reference will be made to other danger-stressors, since most of them are discussed more competently elsewhere. More research has focused on individual strategies of *coping* with the stressors of the dangerous sport of parachuting than on the personality traits most frequently found in individuals with this particular hobby, and those conducted by Fenz and his associates have remained the most interesting (see Fenz, 1975, for a recent summary). The most important findings are the differences between unsuccessful trainees, novice jumpers ultimately successful in their training, and experienced successful jumpers, in the control of cognitive and physiological response at various points of a jump sequence. It is possible to conclude that repressor mechanisms are available to the experienced jumper at appropriate preparatory stages, without loss of being repeatedly sensitized, however, to the dangers of this activity.

The careful personnel selection procedures employed for the execution of the United States space exploration programme have been graphically described by Korchin and Ruff (1964). Here the aim was not only the exclusion of anxiety-prone astronauts, but the selection of highly intelligent, unflappable, and high self-esteem men, who characteristically came from the kind of optimal socialization background described by Baumrind (see above), with a particularly strong identification with a co-operative, supportive, and competent father. There is no doubt that the selectors were unusually successful in their predictions of the responses of the men under enormous physical and work performance strain. The *knowledge* that the stressors can be tolerated, is likely to be one factor in reducing the overall level of strain on future generations of space travellers.

(b) *Social isolation*

As suggested earlier on, the ultimate sources of isolation strain may be childhood experiences of rejection or deprivation engendering anxiety, which have remained foci of discomfort. Although other explanations have been offered, they do not appear to me to be sufficiently comprehensive in terms of the range of phenomena that they can explain. The present attempt to search for an information processing explanation of the personality–strain relationship requires, moreover, an historical approach to the development and availability in long-term memory of aversive experiences with unfavourable consequences for the individual. This approach has at least two implications: (1) individuals with this personality structure give high processing priority to the avoidance of non-rewarding, aversive experience, and (2) their responses to achieve this goal have low thresholds so that they are easily triggered off even by situations which are *objectively* unrelated to isolation, rejection, or deprivation. These assumptions appear to be consistent with Gray's theory of the role of frustrative non-reward in personality development (1972; 1973), and with the confirmation of the predicted 'peak-shift phenomenon' in children (Nicholson and Gray, 1971; 1972). Since, however, the behaviour under discussion here is socially, and, therefore, cognitively complex, it seems more logical to look for the causes and dominant effects of anxiety to cognitive interpreting and controlling processes, rather than seeking explanations of these in the limited signal identification capacity of the hippocampus.

Dual sources of anxiety are present in Spielberger's distinction between state and trait anxiety (e.g. Spielberger *et al.*, 1970; Spielberger, 1977) where the trait represents the reservoir of *potential* anxiety responses, and their generalization and intensity. They are determined by physiological activity as well as by anticipating aversive events for which there are developmental justifications. Trait anxiety is a dynamic system of behavioural readiness which is capable of accommodating new experiences which either confirm or falsify the pattern of expectancies. State anxiety, on the other hand, is but a reflection of the predisposing trait, it is situation-specific and is fuelled by transitory arousal and activation processes, some of which are integrated at the level of the hippocampus (Buck, 1976). In the examples of research findings which I propose to cite, trait anxiety is assumed to be the critical variable: independent — when employed for the construction of criterion groups, dependent — when manipulated by threat of pain or by self-esteem-involving instructions.

I have contended in section 3(ii) that the affiliation motive reflects anxiety concerning rejection and isolation. If it is correct that extraverts are less anxious than introverts (see previous subsection), then the seeking of social contact, defined either by proximity or by maintenance of gaze should be more difficult for introverts. Wilson (1977) has summarized some experiments consistent with this conclusion. A similar relationship between eye contact and affiliation under conditions of high and low social completition is reported by Argyle (1977), and long-term schizophrenics are known to avoid eye contact (Rutter, 1977). A neat piece of evidence for the interaction between affiliation, anxiety, and stress is produced in a study by Geen (1976). Figure 3.3 shows that high test-anxious subjects perform substantially worse in terms of anagram solution times when affiliation needs are most threatened, i.e. when evaluated, and when observed as well as evaluated by another person.

It is safe to assume that conflict and, therefore, strain is generated when two important motives are stimulated simultaneously. The conflict may be weak as in the study by French (1956) in which subjects were classified as respectively high and low on affiliation as well as on achievement motivation.

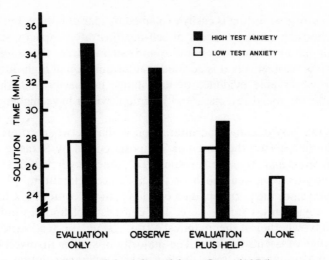

FIGURE 3.3. Adapted from Geen (1976)

She found that those high in affiliation and low in achievement motivation preferred a *non-achieving friend,* whereas subjects high on achievement needs but low on affiliation preferred an *achieving stranger.* These findings have been replicated by Atkinson (1974a). More direct evidence of the presence of strain in motivational conflict comes from an early study by Lazarus (1966). Depending on whether achievement- or affiliation-relevant motives were threatened, those subjects assessed as high on the one that was threatened showed the strongest physiological reaction.

The relationship between achievement orientation and anxiety in status-oriented societies is well established, and does not require much amplification. An infrequently cited research result is the presence of an inverted U-shaped relationship between strength of motivation and performance efficiency, *even when* subjects' ability and a coefficient of efficiency are employed to control for biases (Atkinson, 1974b). As illustrations of stressor-strain in the interaction between anxiety and ahievement motivation, studies by Atkinson and Litwin (1960) and Himmelweit (1947) may be cited, as well as a discussion of the relationship by Hill (1972). Atkinson and Litwin demonstrated that non-anxious, success-oriented subjects more frequently chose tasks of an intermediate level of difficulty. This tendency was much less marked for anxious subjects who more frequently than the non-anxious group chose either low-difficulty or very high-difficulty tasks. Both extreme types of goal settings were shown by Himmelweit to be related to anxiety neurosis, and were described by Hill as indicative of fear of failure, which Heckhausen (1975) has described as a self-reinforcing, self-perpetuating motive system.

Low-difficulty goal setting is easily explained by fear of failure, but perserver-ance in choosing goals in excess of self-demonstrated capacity seems func-tionally similar to the neurotic paradox and can only serve the exacerbation of strain, unless, subjectively it is decided that termination of high-difficulty goal seeking is observable evidence of low status, incapacity and, therefore, a justification for social rejection and isolation, which have higher avoidance priority.

By far the best documented interaction is that between criterion anxiety and performance (see the series of Symposia edited by Sarason and Spiel-berger on *Stress and Anxiety;* Sarason, 1972; Spielberger, 1966; 1972). Since I have recently reviewed much of the evidence (Hamilton, 1975; 1976a; 1976b), and since the pertinent data overlap with the content of Chapter 12, a summary review must suffice here. The consensus of findings indicates that high anxiety, whether of the 'manifest', 'trait', 'state', or 'test' variety, impairs a wide range of cognitive skills. The majority of studies involved the assess-ment of performance on tests of digit span, anagram solution, conceptual problem solving, verbal learning and memory, with or without the simultane-ous manipulation of intelligence, the induction of threats of pain or threats to self-esteem, and, as indicated above, differences in achievement motivation (for additional information see Mueller, 1976; Patty and Safford, 1976; M. W. Eysenck, 1977; Schaie and Goulet, 1977).The majority of explanations offered can be ordered into three groups: supra-optimal arousal; interference from 'worry' and negative self-preoccupation; and the effect of these on coding, attentional and retrieval abilities. I have argued elsewhere [see Chap-ter 12] that the arousal explanation of cognitive impairment is at present more in the nature of a circular description, and that the reduction of cue-utilization proposed by Easterbrook (1959) as the result of increased emo-tionality may be a good explanation for the left-hand side of the inverted U-shaped relationship, but not for the drop in performance with high levels of strain. One reason for this contention is the generally agreed involvement of interference from task-irrelevant self-evaluations which constitute an *increase* in cues presented to an information processing system. The interference proposition itself has also generally remained at a descriptive rather than explanatory level, so that the demonstrations, for example, of the effects of anxiety on memory (Mueller, see above), or of arousal or of introver-sion–extraversion on memory (M. W. Eysenck, see above) are short of rational mediating processes. In relation to the respective roles of strain-inducing physiological arousal and of cognitive anxiety in performance decrement, there are now an increasing number of opinions that the two processes are neither identical nor additive (Wachtel, 1968; Wine, 1971; Bacon, 1974; Basow, 1974). Further evidence in support of a necessary dis-tinction between arousal and anxiety is cited in Chapter 12.

(c) *Work and performance*

Comments here will be confined to a very brief review of the involvement of non-physiological measures of personality, since the greatest number of studies has been concerned with the paradigmatic role of arousal in strain and this area is adequately covered in other chapters [see Hockey, Chapter 5]. Personality–situation interactions appear to have been discussed in relation to three groups of stressors: gross environmental manipulations involving sleep loss, noise, temperature, fatigue, and deprivation of food and oxygen; the length of time and the speed with which responses were required to be made; and the types of experimental situations in which work-strain was assessed such as perceptual vigilance, multiple tasks, and task complexity.

The most frequently used personality criterion measure has been introversion–extraversion. Although there is a fair amount of evidence that strain facilitates performance in extraverts, Broadbent's cautious comments (1971) still apply. Corcoran *et al.* (1977), for example, were unable to confirm a *general* relationship between noise arousal and extraversion and time spent on a vigilance task, and Kennedy (1977) failed to support previous findings regarding smaller decrements in vigilance in the performance of introverts. There appears to be some disconcerting doubt now, as well, concerning the unidimensionality of a vigilance process (Loeb and Alluisi, 1977) so that the relationship with personality and 'stress' may require a more fine-grained approach than can be vouchsafed by single questionnaire scores. In Kennedy's view (see above) differences in the complexity of vigilance tasks have not received sufficient consideration, and a broadband–narrowband attentional dimension reflecting styles of information processing may provide a more profitable approach to performance differences under vigilance strain. This dimension appears to describe individual differences in experiencing and reporting boredom and monotony, subjective ratings of which, as well as ratings on irritation, attentiveness, fatigue, and strain, were found to be significantly related to vigilance in a simulated air traffic control task (Thackray *et al.*, 1977).

The stressor-strain effects of multiple tasks to be carried out simultaneously have been appreciated for a long time. The usual indicators have been increased response times or errors of commission or omission. In studies of cognitive style and control processes, interference processes on the Stroop colour-word test have been construed as evidence of personality constriction mediated by anxiety (Klein, 1954; Hamilton, 1957; 1960). Recent studies by Frankenhaeuser and Johansson (1976) have been able to confirm, by measuring heart rate and catecholamine excretion, that the Stroop task generates stressor effects, which are increased by the introduction of an interfering auditory stimulus. Reports of subjective distress also increased with multiple stimulation.

Multiple tasks require a demanding distribution of attention, and many studies on exposure to central and peripheral stimulation and of incidental learning were cited by Easterbrook to support his proposition of the attention-narrowing effects of emotionality, arousal, or anxiety — terms which were used by him synonymously. There is contrary evidence. Responding by anxious subjects to peripheral cues is *facilitated* by instructions that non-observance will be followed by a noxious event (Wachtel, 1968; Cornsweet, 1969). A study by Launay and Hamilton described in Chapter 12 confirms that test-anxious subjects find dual tasks more difficult in terms of time required, and that arousal is probably not the critical variable. A special problem with multiple-task research is the decision as to which response requirement is central or primary and which of peripheral or secondary importance, as this depends on subjective interpretation of the total task by the subject. Observational evidence suggests that individuals under pressure or conflict may prevaricate and spend an unadaptive amount of effort or time on less essential rather than more important tasks.

Instructions threatening self-esteem have had opposite effects on anxious subjects, depending on the complexity of the task and the measure of anxiety used. Hodges and Spielberger (1969), for example, confirmed the Spence-type prediction that high anxiety facilitates performance once competing responses have extinguished. Sarason (1961) on the other hand, demonstrated the reverse: high anxious subjects under ego-threat, and given a difficult anagram task, performed less well than less anxious subjects. His conclusion that the optimal conditions for generating interfering responses in subjects are a combination of high task difficulty and personal threat, is supported by findings of my own discussed in Chapter 12.

4. TOWARDS AN INFORMATION PROCESSING MODEL OF INTER-ACTION

We have reached the stage in our discussion where the conceptualization behind the title of this volume must be operationalized for the relationship between personality and 'stress'. The recent approaches to the study of attention, perception, and memory owe a great deal of their clarity to advances in computer science and mathematical decision theory. The processing system itself, however, has not changed, only culture-determined factors have altered the data and operations to which information processing is applied. Personality theorists are easy prey to the criticism that they have jumped on the successful band waggon of information processing theory to save themselves from scientific extinction. They might reply with two observations. Firstly, one of the interesting outcomes of cognitive processing experimentation has been the demonstration of irreducible individual differences which used to be discarded as error variances. Secondly, recent studies of the representation of knowledge, of primary orientation towards external data or towards internal conceptualization, of processing limits and the depth of cognitive processing, are all areas of functioning in which individual differences can and do appear (Norman, 1976). These process variables can be held to be at a parallel conceptual level to some variables which are central to personality, and particularly to psychodynamic theories, such as objectivity, subjectivity, distortion, and denial processes, or living according to the pleasure principle.

The major difference between the two orientations towards cognitive processes is not so much the processes themselves, but the informational data and strategies directing attention, perception, and memory. Since cognitive processes cannot work without information, any real antithesis is precluded, provided that our conceptualization of so-called non-cognitive events and data is appropriately revised. First steps in that direction have been taken already (e.g. Weiner, 1972; 1974; Mischel, 1973; Hamilton, 1976a), the results of which can be used as crutches for a first, tentative, informational analysis of stressors, strain, and the personality–'stress' interaction. There is neither the readiness nor the space for formal theory building, although it should be possible to meet some of the requirements of a theory such as offering some explanatory propositions concerning observed relationships and their underlying mechanisms, in the absence of empirical confirmation (Marx, 1976).

The preceding analysis of factors in 'stress' tolerance and the person–situation interaction was intended to convey a conceptualization and reductionist definition of personality, motivation, and stressors, which would supply a cognitive as well as a physiological rationale for interactions which have been observed, or inferred. In the past, these have lacked mediating processes which are consistent with mediators demonstrable in other areas of behaviour. The interactionist truism has seemed to lack facilitating processes. A rationalist position impells the unpopular belief that qualitative characteristics are ultimately expressible quantitatively, that the essence of exultation, happiness, anger, or anxiety are, in the last analysis, electrochemical events. The rejection of this philosophy is substantially due to 'emotional' disquiet, which in itself has its roots in cognitively coded belief systems. But it seems incongruous and unnecessary since the enjoyment of natural beauty, or frustration over an unsuccessful experiment do not in any way preclude a full conceptual analysis of the components: the perpetuation of beauty, or the elucidation of faults and the retention of profitable experimental variables.

To come to the point: if interactions between the domain of personal needs and past habitual responses of characteristic intensities, and external events which disturb them, occur as they do, a *common 'language'* is required to facilitate the interaction. For this reason I have suggested elsewhere (Hamilton, 1976a) that personality and motivation require cognitive-informational redefinition. It was proposed that characteristic strategies and patterns of seeking adaptation or goals, as well as the types and intensities of goal seeking, reflect cognitive schemata encoding the outcomes and evaluations of past responses; the anticipated results of new response requirements; the concepts of self and others as they are relevant to a temporal hierarchy of goals; and the stored cognitive data of previous exposures to pleasure and pain. Consistent with this reformulation is the conceptualization of the personality traits of affiliation, achievement orientation, or anxiety as informational data with specific connotations, differential elaboration, and intensity, defined by retrieval thresholds and the duration, speed, and strength of goal-seeking operations. In view of the evidence of coherence, if not always full consistency, supplied by most people's behaviour, the cognitive organization representing traits and predisposition reflect the presence of rules, and to speak of a *grammar of personality organization* may not be entirely misleading.

Although environmental stimuli contain many elements of objective universality, cross-cultural research supplies powerful evidence that early, society-specific experience, including language, affect the acquisition of goals, of knowledge, and the identification of goal-achieving or avoiding signs (e.g. Cole and Scribner, 1974). Therefore, although there is no controversy about the comparable experience of some pain, injury, danger, or privation stressors, the identification of many other stressors is the result of a much closer relationship between a stimulus, personality-as-defined, and a response, than years of behaviour theory have granted. Since stimuli retrieved from permanent memory have the power of generating responses, it is quite possible that Bolles (1974) is correct in suggesting that a single conceptual matrix may be sufficient to explicate and to predict goal-oriented behaviour. A necessary feature of this system, however, is the reinterpretation of habits as cognitive structures, and the availability of data-codes representing-goals. Goal-selection decisions, and the integration of recognized external stimuli, depend on a common signalling system. The difference between the integrated behaviour domains will then be conveyed by cognitive data differing only in connotation, in size and in density of signal patterns, in their availability, and in their retrieval thresholds.

By the same reasoning, strain will develop in a person–situation interaction if the processing system in responding to multiple input cannot generate responses which satisfy the majority of the different external and internal demands. In Figure 3.4 let S_1 be the stimulus to interact willingly with an experimenter, let S_2 and S_3 be the complexity and information content of a dual experimental task, and let S_4 represent the usually successful stimulation of level of aspiration. The nature and requirements of the four simultaneous stimuli are conveyed by integratable classes of symbols, their frequency, and density or intermittency. Holding and selecting operations followed by a tentative decision process are carried out in 'dashed' area (A), and its results (B_1 and B_2) tested against available matches with memory-bank data (C_1 and C_2).

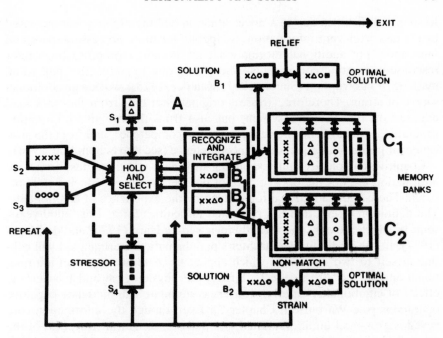

FIGURE 3.4. Stressor-strain and response decrement with multiple stimulus input

Response integration and solution B_2 by its non-match with S_{1-4}, reflects the presence of stressors which engender strain; whereas solution B_1 is experienced as relief. The stressors generating solution 2 may reside in the amount of information or of effort required by S_{1-4}, or in the non-availability of sufficient appropriate data in the memory banks for an adaptive response, as in C_2. Or stimuli as well as experience deficiency (such as past unsuccessful coping responses) may convert response requirements into stressors which in turn engender strain. The strain will be maintained for as long as the stressors are available, which in the present example B_2 means until S_4 or its interpretation is reduced to permit the development of a novel coping response.

This informational redescription of stressors and strain would be incomplete for the example given without drawing attention to the 'stressing' effect of searching long-term memory systems unsuccessfully for habits and strategies appropriate to the situational demands. Within the time limit for producing a response, the individual producing solution 2 needs to carry out a much greater number of matching operations while being required to hold the information from S_2 and S_3 in temporary memory. The longer this period, the greater the probability that memory data reflecting fear of failure, affiliation and status anxiety, and more fundamental anxiety about social isolation, will intrude into information processing operations as additional cognitive data.

Response difficulties due to a novel situation will thereby become increased by (1) task-irrelevant information, competing for finite processing space and time, and (2) by additional information loads on short-term processing and/or response-integrating components. The effects due to retroactive inhibition, masking or interruption (Simon, 1967; Mandler, 1975), provide an additional source of strain. Therefore, stressors originate not only from the work load imposed on the cognitive system, but also from the aversive information generated by the system when experiencing incompetence, and from the anticipated injurious consequences of incompetence (see also Schönpflug, 1976).

Cognitive complexity and responding to it with additional task-irrelevant information are not the only sources of parallel processes inducing stressor-strain. There is the additional role played by the experience of emotionality. The definition of emotion has presented difficulties for at least 2000 years, some of which are ably and recently reviewed by Izard (1977) and de Rivera (1977). In the tradition of Schachter's paradigmatic experiments, I will confine myself to two comments which appear to be required for an informational analysis of 'stress' effects. Firstly, the physiological and biochemical effects of emotionality entering awareness stimulate and modulate cognitive operations [see Warburton, Chapter 2]. Even though the information conveyed is gross and undifferentiated, the persistence and intrusiveness of the physiological effects may constitute an important source of distracting information (Simon Mandler, see above). Distraction, however, will increase the cognitive processing difficulties of tasks and situations which have their own quanta of informational demandingness. A second, much more important, source of distraction and increased information results from the conditioned perceptual processes which identify the type and degree of emotionality. The knowledge conveyed by 'I am angry', 'I am worried', 'I am afraid', 'I am depressed' contains more information than the simple physiological signals of emotionality, and can be assumed to be the second trigger of self-generated, task-irrelevant data which in the above analysis is one of the major sources of strain.

High levels of emotionality have another implication. The level of its arousal and activation components conveys immediacy and urgency to the response-generating system, and *impulsive*, premature closure responses may be made. If this occurs, there is insufficient time to engage in adequate cognitive organizing and matching processes for the selection of the most adaptive response, (i.e. that which has the highest probability of being successful and rewarding), and a possible positive feedback loop between behaviour and emotionality is thereby interrupted. The mechanism for positive feedback appears to be present, since even mild experimental stress has been shown to increase repetitive intrusive thought process (Horowitz, 1975; 1976).

The perseveration of emotion-inducing experiences following exposure to stressors leads fairly naturally to a consideration of the role of some psychoanalytic concepts in cognitive processing analyses of 'stress' proneness and the development of strain. Without engaging in a general and unwarranted apologia for this system of explanation, it needs to be remembered that its present proponents were not usually trained in an experimental science, and that the conceptual language has been traditionally 19th century, idiosyncratic and, therefore, difficult to integrate with advances in experimentally oriented psychology. Resistance to change in theorists and practitioners, however, is not now necessarily greater than in some of their professional opponents. Peterfreund particularly, has shown considerable interest in cognitive processing paradigms (1971; Peterfreund and Franceschini, 1973). For the present purpose three psychoanalytic propositions are sufficient for our discussion of an information processing model of strain induction: unconscious processes, the relevance of historical developmental experience, and mechanisms or processes of defence. I will select for brief examination what I believe to be relevant here for the elaboration of the earlier comments on predispositions to 'stress' tolerance.

All three propositions are fundamentally cognitive. Goal-seeking processes outside awareness and introspection are no less cognitive than those which are involved in sifting a semantic network and discarding unsuitable response words, or those which monitor information coming through a non-attended auditory channel. The processes which reject unwanted response words and those which succeed in achieving recognition of self-relevant stimulation without apparently attending, also defy demonstration, except by inference. When, therefore, our discussion of an informational analysis of strain induction refers to the stimulation of aversive thought processes we must add those that are reported and reportable to the unknown number of cognitive events that cannot be directly or indirectly elicited. Some effects can be demonstrated. For example, sensitivity to conflict and uncertainty in neurotic subjects is greater than in normal individuals when tested by exposure to perceptually ambiguous stimuli (Hamilton, 1957; 1960). One cannot be sure, however, that the total informational load from reportable as well as unreportable events is greater than the load from only those that can be ascertained. The reason for this is that the maximum interference from task-irrelevant processes occurs at the temporary memory and the response-integrating stages, but particularly the former according to my own recent experiments [see Chapter 12].

A substantial part of unconscious, unreportable processes is made up of response predispositions and selection strategies which developmentally and habitually have contributed to subjective states of contentment and strain reduction. It is frequently argued that the more complex habits of adulthood need not reflect the possibly adverse and aversive experiences of earlier phases (Clarke and Clarke, 1976). At the same time, early habits contribute to the structure of adult cognitive schemata, and any review of stress vulnerability shows this to be a frequent sequence in the development of psychopathology. Thus strategies acquired in early or late childhood for meet-ing and/or avoiding frustration, conflict, anxiety, aggression, anger, etc., through being coded in long-term memory, are potentially available for the cognitive elaboration of these emotional experiences and response charac-teristics in later years. Thus as argued before, these events are likely to play some role in the interpretation of stimuli as stressors and in the predisposition to experience strain.

It will have been apparent throughout the discussion of the nature of 'stress' that I have assigned a paradigmatic and major role to anxiety. This has been defined not as primarily emotionality, but as aversive ideation in and outside awareness. The defence mechanisms of psychoanalytic theorists may be redefined with similar plausibility as cognitive processes which attempt to minimize or avoid the participation of aversive experience and expectancy in human behaviour and social interaction [see Horowitz, Chapter 8]. In dis-placement, projection, regression, or isolation, one may perceive the results of schema restructuring, of organizing modes of thinking and action which reduce or obviate the need to experience the anticipation of pain, danger, rejection, or injury to self-concepts. In this respect the effects of coping and defensive strategies are probably identical. Where they may differ, and experimental data are absent and cannot help us, is in the permanence of the learned behaviour and in their generality and stereotypy. Defences are by definition only minimally integrative and are driven by internal cognitive data; coping responses are by definition integrative of internal need *and* external requirements, and maintain the capacity to respond with equal suc-cess to *changes* in situational demands.

Psychoanalytic theorists postulate that the utilization of defence mechan-isms reduces 'stress' tolerance, because emotionality is never absent, only severely controlled. It is possible to rephrase this statement in cognitive, information processing terms. Predisposition to experience disturbing, dis-tracting, and aversive thought processes requires their presence in the form of some coded data. Since these are intended to be diverted from self-knowledge, they must not be permitted to enter a short-term, temporary memory processing stage, that point in a process where knowledge of stimulus denotation is 'read off' after a recognition process involving other long-term memory data. Since repression is a necessary prerequisite of all other defence mechanisms — a requirement not always clearly stated by theorists — this basic avoidance mechanism must be available from among the data-handling strategies. There are three possibilities, at least. It could be either an addi-tional data loop attached to the representation of aversive data which, at a more central data selection stage, denotes 'no further processing' or 'return to data bank'. Or it could be conceived, paraphrasing Broadbent (1971), as a 'low bias' datum attached to a set of past response dispositions so that they would be utilized only rarely, if at all, in generating response decisions.

Thirdly, there appear to be no logical objections to a set of 'pigeon-holes' marked 'undesirable' or 'do not retrieve' by suitable codes. All three possibilities depend on prior learning experience in relation to ease of eliciting and reducing biological dispositions to become unacceptably emotional.

One further point needs to be made. If defence mechanisms in respect of aversive experience are present, and if their data-processing operations are objectively not required to deal with a difficult and prolonged task or with transient danger or social isolation, then the information processing events add irrelevantly to the total load of processing requirements demanded of the individual, with concomitant results for increased stressor-strain.

It must be concluded from the foregoing that coping as well as defensive controls of aversive stimulation require effort, that effort must induce an increase in cognitive processes, and that the additional cognitive processes may not be free of strain potential. This last point is also cogently argued by Averill (1973) when discussing the role of the nature of a critical response and the context in which it is perceived, in a setting where there is personal control over 'stress' exposure. Informational complexity is also being considered now as important for treatment by practising psychoanalysts. For example, the elaborate and goal-avoiding associational memory paths reflected in patients' reports (Palombo, 1973) can be objectified by drawing semi-lattices or semantic networks. Alternatively flow-charts can demonstrate the informational complexity and unadaptive short-circuiting of aversive decision conflicts (Peterfreund and Franceschini, see above).

For all the reasons which I have attempted to discuss, any model of stressor-strain which reflects the effort of person × situation interaction in settings interpreted as unfavourable and demanding by the individual, requires a processing capacity approach to 'stress' tolerance. I would propose, therefore, that the definition of 'stress' should be a cognitive-informational definition, that stressors are stimuli which have information processing effects leading to experiences of discomfort, aversion, and response decrements, and that strain is the representation in total organismic terms of the effects of an unacceptable informational load and its associated stressor experiences. This first tentative model may be misleadingly over-simplified and even false. It has the capacity, however, of accommodating under one superordinate concept a large number of discrete findings; it is potentially quantifiable; it is falsifiable and amenable to a large number of new predictions concerning: cognitive content, decision-making priorities, the relationship between thought and semantic networks, as well as the development of behaviourally abnormal solutions of stressor-strain in neuroses and psychoses.

Figure 3.5 shows in outline and with the customary inaccurate abandon of graphics, how the balance of four areas defining functional personality and situational complexity can determine the level of stressor-strain. Although these parameters have been discussed in some depth in the preceding pages,

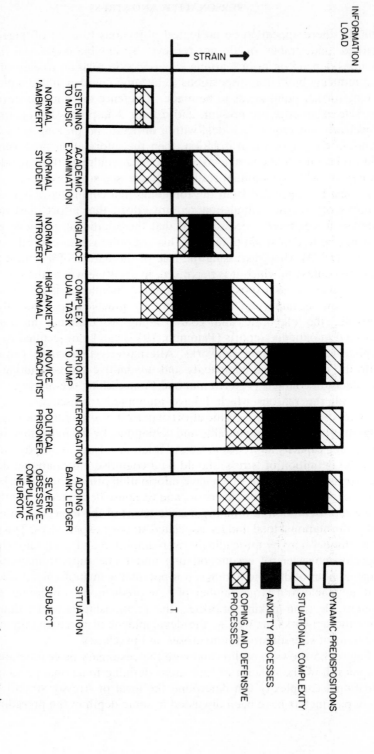

FIGURE 3.5. Hypothetical contribution of types of stressors to information processing load and strain. (T is an assumed average strain threshold.)

their definition, inevitably, is still molar. Let me briefly redefine. *Dynamic predispositions* include emotional arousal and activation levels governed by their thresholds and modifiability, as well as neuropharmacological cortical stimulation, all of which contribute to the effort level of the whole system in assimilating change and accommodating stressors. *Coping and defensive processes* include the whole range of informational analysis, the restructuring and control of associational networks, and the decisional and integrative operations employed in minimizing anxiety. *Anxiety processes* are all those operations which elicit information with aversive denotation arising from historically affected anticipations of physical pain, danger, social rejection, and attacks on self-esteem. *Situational complexity* is defined by the amount, intermittancy, duration, and unusualness of the information from stimulus sources requiring processing, employing whatever index has most rationality: 'number', 'bits', 'steps'.

The situational stressor stimuli in Figure 3.5 have been chosen to reflect some of the sources which have been cited or have been implied by the preceding discussion, but *duration of exposure* has not been considered. The proportional contribution of personal and situational stressors to total information load and thus to strain is highly speculative, of course, and an important and ultimately troublesome dimension — the varieties of interaction and strain-reducing solutions — has been omitted from the illustration. A further omission, of which the attentive reader will have become progressively aware, is a discussion of the possibility that an alternative to ever-increasing sources of information from the data banks and from coping and defensive processes of the person, is the *perseveration of a single group* of cognitive data and processes, which, when other stressor sources increase, will also raise the total level of information load and strain. These, and many other explanatory possibilities await the energy, ingenuity, and 'stress' tolerance of the aspiring investigator.

5. REFERENCES

Allport, G. W. (1937). *Personality*. New York: Holt.

Appley, M. H. and Trumbull, R. (Eds.) (1967). *Psychological Stress — Issues in Research*. New York: Appleton–Century–Crofts.

Argyle, M. (1977). Predictive and generative rules models of P × S. In D. Magnusson and N. S. Endler (Eds.), *Personality at the Crossroads — Current Issues in Interactional Psychology*. Hillsdale: Lawrence Erlbaum.

Arnold, M. B. (1967). Stress and emotion. In M. H. Appley and R. Trumbull (Eds.), *Psychological Stress — Issues in Research*. New York: Appleton–Century–Crofts.

Atkinson, J. W. (1974a). Strength of motivation and efficiency of performance. In J. W. Atkinson and J. O. Raynor (Eds.), *Motivation and Achievement*. Washington, D. C.: Winston.

Atkinson, J. W. (1974b). Motivation determinants of intellectual performance and cumulative achievement. In J. W. Atkinson and J. O. Raynor (Eds.), *Motivation and Achievement*. Washington, D. C.: Winston.

Atkinson, J. W. (1977). Motivation for achievement. In T. Blass (Ed.), *Personality Variables in Social Behaviour*. Hillsdale: Lawrence Erlbaum.

Atkinson, J. W. and Feather, N. T. (Eds.) (1966). *A Theory of Achievement Motivation*. New York: Wiley.

Atkinson, J. W. and Litwin, G. H. (1960). Achievement motive and test anxiety conceived as motive to approach success and to avoid failure. *Journal of Abnormal and Social Psychology*, **60**, 52–63.

Averill, J. R. (1973). Personal control over aversive stimuli and its relationship to stress. *Psychological Bulletin*, **85**, 286–303.

Averill, J. R., O'Brien, L. and DeWitt, G. W. (1977). The influence of response effectiveness on the preference for warning and on psychophysiological stress reactions. *Journal of Personality*, **45**, 395–418.

Bacon, S. J. (1974). Arousal and the range of cue utilization. *Journal of Experimental Psychology*, **102**, 81–87.

Basow, S. A. (1974). Effect of white noise on attention as a function of manifest anxiety. *Perceptual and Motor Skills*, **39**, 655–662.

Baumrind, D. (1967). Child care practices anteceding three patterns of pre-school behavior. *Genetic Psychology Monographs*, **75**, 43–88.

Berlyne, D. E. and McDonnell, P. (1965). Effect of stimulus complexity and incongruity on duration of E.E.G. desynchronization. *Electroencephalography and Clinical Neurophysiology*, **18**, 156–161.

Bettelheim, B. (1960). *The Informed Heart*. New York: Free Press of Glencoe.

Bexton, W. H., Heron, W. and Scott, T. H. (1954). Effect of decreased variation in the sensory environment. *Canadian Journal of Psychology*, **8**, 70–76.

Biderman, A. D. (1967). Life and death in extreme captivity situations. In M. H. Appley and R. Trumbull (Eds.), *Psychological Stress–Issues in Research*. New York: Appleton–Century–Crofts.

Block, J. (1971). *Lives through Time*. California: Bancroft Books.

Block, J. (1977). Advancing the psychology of personality — paradigmatic shift, or improving the quality of research. In D. Magnusson and N. S. Endler (Eds.), *Personality at the Crossroads: Current Issues in Interactional Psychology*. New York: Wiley.

Bolles, R. C. (1974). Cognition and motivation: some historical trends. In B. Weiner (Ed.), *Cognitive Views of Human Motivation*. New York: Academic Press.

Bolles, R. C. (1975). *Theory of Motivation* (2nd edn.). New York: Harper and Row.

Bowlby, J. (1951). *Maternal Care and Mental Health*. Geneva: World Health Organisation.

Bowlby, J. (1973). *Attachment and Loss*. Vol. 1. New York: Basic Books.

Broadbent, D. E. (1971). *Decision and Stress*. London: Academic Press.

Broadhurst, P. L. (1959). The interaction of task difficulty and motivation: the Yerkes–Dodson law reviewed. *Acta Psychologica*, **16**, 321–338.

Brown, J. S. (1948). Gradients of approach and avoidance responses and their relation to level of motivation. *Journal of Comparative and Physiological Psychology*, **41**, 450–465.

Buchsbaum, M. (1976). Self-regulation of stimulus intensity — augmenting, reducing and the average evoked response. In G. E. Schwartz and D. Shapiro (Eds.), *Consciousness and Self-Regulation — Advances in Research*. Vo. 1. London: Wiley.

Buck, R. (1976). *Human Motivation and Emotion*. New York: Wiley.

Byrne, D. (1964). Repression-sensitization as a dimension of personality. In B. A. Maher (Ed.), *Progress in Experimental Personality Research*. Vol. 1. New York: Academic Press.

Clarke, A. M. and Clarke, A. D. B. (1976). *Early Experience — Myth and Evidence.* London: Open Books.

Cofer, C. N. and Appley, M. H. (1964). *Motivation: Theory and Research.* New York: Wiley.

Cole, M. and Scribner, S. (1974). *Culture and Thought.* New York: Wiley.

Colquhoun, W. P. and Corcoran, D. W. J. (1964). The effects of time of day and social isolation on the relationship between temperament and performance. *British Journal of Social and Clinical Psychology,* **3**, 226–231.

Coopersmith, S. (1967). *The Antecedents of Self-Esteem.* San Francisco: Freeman.

Corcoran, D. W. J., Mullin, J., Rainey, M. T. and Frith, G. (1977). The effects of raised signal and noise amplitude during the course of vigilance tasks. In R. R. Mackie (Ed.), *Vigilance — Theory, Operational Performance, and Physiological Correlates.* New York: Plenum.

Cornsweet, D. M. (1969). Use of cues in the visual periphery under conditions of arousal. *Journal of Experimental Psychology,* **80**, 14–18.

Cox, F. N. (1968). Some relationships between test anxiety, presence or absence of male persons, and boys' performance on a repetitive motor task. *Journal of Experimental Child Psychology,* **6**, 1–12.

Davis, R. D. (1948). *Pilot Error.* London: Air Publications, 3139a, H.M.S.O.

de Rivera, J. (1977). *A Structural Theory of the Emotions.* New York: International Universities Press.

Dixon, N. F. (1971). *Subliminal Perception — The Nature of a Controversy.* London: McGraw-Hill.

Dixon, N. F., and Haider, M. (1961). Changes in the visual threshold as a function of subception. *Quarterly Journal of Experimental Psychology,* **13**, 229–235.

Easterbrook, J. A. (1959). The effect of emotion on cue utilization and the organization of behavior. *Psychological Review,* **66**, 183–201.

Endler, N. S. (1966). Estimating variance components from mean squares from random and mixed effects analysis of variance models. *Perceptual and Motor Skills,* **22**, 559–570.

Endler, N. S. and Magnusson, D. (1976). *Interactional Psychology and Personality.* New York: Wiley.

Erdelyi, M. H. (1974). A new look at the New Look: perceptual defence and vigilance. *Psychological Review,* **81**, 1–25.

Escalona, S. K. (1968). *The Roots of Individuality — Normal Patterns of Development in Infancy.* Chicago: Aldine.

Eysenck, H. J. (1957). *The Dynamics of Anxiety and Hysteria.* London: Routledge and Kegan Paul.

Eysenck, H. J. (1967). *The Biological Basis of Personality.* Springfield: C. C. Thomas.

Eysenck, H. J. (1973). Personality, learning and 'anxiety'. In H. J. Eysenck (Ed.), *Handbook of Abnormal Psychology* (2nd edn.). London: Pitman.

Eysenck, H. J. and Levey, A. (1971). Conditioning, introversion–extraversion and the strength of the nervous system. In V. D. Nebylitsyn and J. A. Gray (Eds.), *Biological Bases of Individual Behaviour.* London: Academic Press.

Eysenck, H. J. and Prell, D. B. (1951). The inheritance of neuroticism — an experimental study. *Journal of Mental Science,* **97**, 441–465.

Eysenck, M. W. (1977). *Human Memory — Theory, Research and Individual Differences.* Oxford: Pergamon Press.

Fenz, W. D. (1964). Conflict and stress as related to physiological activation and sensory, perceptual, and cognitive functioning. *Psychological Monographs: General and Applied,* **78**, No. 8, Whole No. 585.

Fenz, W. D. (1975). Stragies for coping with stress. In I. G. Sarason and C. D. Spielberger (Eds.), *Stress and Anxiety.* Vol. 2. New York: Wiley.

Frankenhaeuser, M. (1971). Experimental approaches to the study of human behaviour as related to neuroendocrine functions. In L. Levy (Ed.), *Society, Stress and Disease. Vol. I. The Psychosocial Environment and Psychosomatic Diseases.* Oxford University Press.

Frankenhaeuser, M. and Johansson, G. (1976). Task demands as reflected in catecholamine excretion and heart rate. *Journal of Human Stress,* **2**, 15–23.

Franks, C. M. (1957). Personality factors and the rate of conditioning. *British Journal of Psychology,* **48**, 119–126.

French, E. G. (1956). Motivation as a variable in work partner selection. *Journal of Abnormal and Social Psychology,* **53**, 96–99.

Frenkel-Brunswik, E. (1954). Psycho-analysis and the unity of science. *Proceedings of the American Academy of Arts and Sciences,* **80**, No. 4, 273–347.

Fröhlich, W. D. (1977). Stress, anxiety and the control of attention: a psychophysiological approach. In C. D. Spielberger and I. G. Sarason (Eds.), *Stress and Anxiety.* Vol. 5. Washington, D. C.: Wiley.

Geen, R. G. (1976). The role of the social environment on the induction and reduction of anxiety. In I. G. Sarson and C. D. Spielberger (Eds.), *Stress and Anxiety.* Vol. 3. New York: Wiley.

Gray, J. A. (1972). The psychophysiological nature of introversion–extraversion: a modification of Eysenck's theory. In V. D. Nebylitsyn and J. A. Gray (Eds.), *Biological Bases of Individual Behaviour.* London: Academic Press.

Gray, J. A. (1973). Causal theories of personality and how to test them. In J. R. Royce (Ed). *Multivariate Analysis and Psychological Theory.* London: Academic Press.

Gray, J. A. (1976). The neuropsychology of anxiety. In I. G. Sarason and C. D. Spielberger (Eds.), *Stress and Anxiety.* Vol. 3. New York: Wiley.

Grinker, R. R. and Spiegel, J. (1945). *Men under Stress.* Philadelphia: Blakiston.

Guilford, J. P. (1967). *The Nature of Human Intelligence.* New York: McGraw-Hill.

Haan, N. (1977). *Coping and Defending: Processes of Self-Environment Organization.* New York: Academic Press.

Hamilton, V. (1957). Perceptual and personality dynamics in reactions to ambiguity. *British Journal of Psychology,* **48**, 200–215.

Hamilton, V. (1959). Eysenck's theory of anxiety and hysteria — a methodological critique. *British Journal of Psychology,* **50**, 48–63.

Hamilton, V. (1960). Inperception of Phi: some further determinants. *British Journal of Psychology,* **51**, 257–266.

Hamilton, V. (1971). The effect of maternal attitude on the development of logical operations. *Perceptual and Motor Skills,* **33**, 63–69.

Hamilton, V. (1972a). Continuities and individual differences in conservation. *British Journal of Psychology,* **63**, 429–440.

Hamilton, V. (1972b). Maternal rejection and conservation: an analysis of suboptimal cognition. *Journal of Child Psychology and Psychiatry,* **13**, 147–166.

Hamilton, V. (1974). *The Effect of Maternal Attitude on the Development of Children's Thinking.* S.S.R.C. Report HR 1556/21.

Hamilton, V. (1975). Socialization anxiety and information processing: a capacity model of anxiety-induced performance deficits. In I. G. Sarason and C. D. Spielberger (Eds.), *Stress and Anxiety.* Vol. 2. Washington, D. C.: Wiley.

Hamilton, V. (1976a). Motivation and personality in cognitive development. In V. Hamilton and M. D. Vernon (Eds.), *The Development of Cognitive Processes.* London: Academic Press.

Hamilton, V. (1976b). Cognitive development in the neuroses and the schizophrenias. In V. Hamilton and M. D. Vernon (Eds.), *The Development of Cognitive Processes*. London: Academic Press.

Heckhausen, H. (1975). Fear of failure as a self-reinforcing motive system. In I. G. Sarason and C. D. Spielberger (Eds.), *Stress and Anxiety*, Vol. 2. New York: Wiley.

Hill, K. T. (1972). Anxiety in the evaluative context. In W. W. Hartup (Ed.), *The Young Child — Reviews of Research*, Vol. 2. Washington D.C.: National Association for the Education of Young Children.

Himmelweit, H. T. (1947). A comparative study of the level of aspiration of normal and neurotic persons. *British Journal of Psychology*, **37**, 41–59.

Hodges, W. F. and Spielberger, C. D. (1969). Digit span: an indicant of trait or state anxiety. *Journal of Consulting and Clinical Psychology*, **33**, 430–434.

Holzman, W. H. and Bitterman, M. E. (1952). *Anxiety and Reactions to Stress*. Report No. 6, Project No. 21–37–002. Randolph Field, Texas: School of Aviation Medicine.

Horowitz, M. (1975). Intrusive and repetitive thoughts after experimental stress. *Archives of General Psychiatry*, **32**, 1457–1463.

Horowitz, M. (1976). Stress films, emotion and cognitive response. *Archives of General Psychiatry*, **33**, 1339–1344.

Izard, C. E. (1977). *Human Emotions*. New York: Plenum.

Janis, I. L. (1962). Psychological effects of warnings. In G. W. Barker and D. W. Chapman (Eds.), *Man and Society in Disaster*. New York: Basic Books.

Janis, I. L. (1971). *Stress and Frustration*. New York: Harcourt Brace Jovanovich.

Janis, I. L. and Leventhal, H. (1968). Human reactions to stress. In E. F. Borgatta and W. W. Lambert (Eds.), *Handbook of Personality Theory and Research*. Chicago: Rand McNally.

Jones, A. (1966). Information deprivation in humans. In A. B. Maher (Ed.), *Progress in Experimental Personality Research*, **3**, 241–307.

Jones, E. J., Kanouse, D. E., Kelley, H. H., Valius, S. and Weiner, B. (1972). *Attribution: Perceiving the Causes of Behavior*. New Jersey: General Learning Press.

Kennedy, R. S. (1977). The relationship between vigilance and eye movements induced by vestibular stimulation. In R. R. Mackie (Ed.), *Vigilance — Theory, Operational Performance, and Physiological Correlates*. New York: Plenum.

Klein, G. (1954). Need and regulation. In M. R. Jones (Ed.), *Nebraska Symposium on Motivation*. Lincoln: University of Nebraska Press.

Köhler, W. and Wallach, H. (1944). Figural after-effects. *Proceedings of the American Philosophical Society*, **88**, 269–357.

Korchin, S. J. and Ruff, G. E. (1964). Personality characteristics of the Mercury astronauts. In G. H. Grosser, H. Wechsler and M. Greenblatt (Eds.), *The Threat of Impending Disaster*. Cambridge, Mass.: MIT Press.

Koriat, A., Melkman, R., Averill, J. R. and Lazarus, R. S. (1972). The self-control of emotional reactions to a stressful film. *Journal of Personality*, **40**, 601–619.

Lazarus, R. S. (1966). *Psychological Stress and the Coping Process*. New York: McGraw-Hill.

Lazarus, R. S. (1971). The concept of stress and disease. In L. Levi (Ed.), *Society, Stress and Disease*. Vol. 1. London: Oxford University Press.

Lazarus, R. S. (1974). Cognitive and coping processes in emotion. In B. Weiner (Ed.), *Cognitive Views of Human Motivation*. New York: Academic Press.

Lazarus, R. S. (1975). The healthy personality — a review of conceptualizations and research. In L. Levi (Ed.), *Society, Stress and Disease*. Vol. 2. London: Oxford University Press.

Levine, S. A. (1971). Stress and behavior. *Scientific American*, **224**, 26–31.

Lewin, K. (1951). *Field Theory in Social Science*. New York: Harper and Row.

Loeb, M. and Alluisi, E. A. (1977). An update of findings regarding vigilance and a reconsideration of underlying mechanisms. In R. R. Mackie (Ed.), *Vigilance — Theory, Operational Performance, and Physiological Correlates*. New York: Plenum.

Loehlin, J. C. and Nichols, R. C. (1976). *Heredity, Environment and Personality*. Austin: University of Texas Press.

Lundberg, U. and Ekman, G. (1969). Emotional involvement while anticipating an examination. *Reports from the Psychological Laboratories*, No. 288, University of Stockholm.

Mackie, R. R. (Ed.), (1977). *Vigilance — Theory, Operational Performance, and Physiological Correlates*. NATO Conference Series, Series III: Human Factors. New York: Plenum.

Mackintosh, N. J. (1974). *The Psychology of Animal Learning*. London: Academic Press.

Magnusson, D. and Endler, N. S. (1977). *Personality at the Crossroads — Current Issues in Interactional Psychology*. Hillsdale: Lawrence Erlbaum.

Mandler, G. (1975). *Mind and Emotion*. New York: Wiley.

Mandler, G. and Sarason, S. B. (1952). A study of anxiety and learning. *Journal of Abnormal and Social Psychology*, **47**, 166–173.

Marx, M. H. (1976). Formal theory. In M. H. Marx and F. E. Goodson (Eds.), *Theories in Contemporary Psychology*. New York: Macmillan.

Mechanic, D. (1962). *Students under Stress*. New York: Free Press of Glencoe.

Melzack, R. (1973). *The Puzzle of Pain*. Harmondsworth: Penguin.

Milgram, S. (1963). Behavioral study of obedience. *Journal of Abnormal and Social Psychology*, **67**, 371–378.

Miller, N. E. (1944). Experimental studies of conflict. In J. McV. Hunt (Ed.), *Personality and the Behavior Disorders*. Vol. 1. New York: Ronald Press.

Miller, N. E. (1948). Theory and experiment relating psychoanalytic displacement to stimulus-response generalization. *Journal of Abnormal and Social Psychology*, **43**, 155–178.

Mischel, W. (1968). *Personality and Assessment*. New York: Wiley.

Mischel, W. (1973). Toward a cognitive social learning reconceptualization of personality. *Psychological Review*, **80**, 252–283.

Mischel, W. (1974). Cognitive appraisals and transformations in self control. In B. Weiner (Ed.), *Cognitive Views of Human Motivation*. New York: Academic Press.

Mischel, W. (1977). The interaction of person and situation. In D. Magnusson and N. S. Endler (Eds.), *Personality at the Crossroads: Current Issues in Interactional Psychology*. New Jersey: Lawrence Erlbaum.

Mowrer, O. H. (1940). An experimental analogue of 'regression' with incidental observation on 'reaction formation'. *Journal of Abnormal and Social Psychology*, **35**, 56–87.

Mueller, J. H. (1976). Anxiety and cue utilization in human learning and memory. In M. Zuckerman and C. D. Spielberger (Eds.), *Emotions and Anxiety — New Concepts, Methods and Applications*. New York: Wiley.

Murphy, L. B. and Moriarty, A. E. (1976). *Vulnerability, Coping and Growth — From Infancy to Adolescence*. New Haven: Yale University Press.

Murray, H. A. (1938). *Exploration in Personality*. New York: Oxford University Press.

Nicholson, J. and Gray, J. A. (1971). Behavioural contrast and peak shift in children. *British Journal of Psychology*, **62**, 367–373.

Nicholson, J. and Gray, J. A. (1972). Peak shift, behavioural contrast and stimulus generalization as related to personality and development in children. *British Journal of Psychology*, **63**, 47–62.

Niemelä, P. (1972). Effects of interrupting the process of preparation for film stress. *Reports from the Psychological Laboratories*, No. 361, University of Stockholm.

Norman, D. A. (1976). *Memory and Attention — An Introduction to Human Information Processing*. New York: Wiley.

O.S.S. Assessment Staff (1948). *Assessment of Man*. New York: Rinehart.

Palombo, S. R. (1973). The associative memory tree. In B. B. Rubinstein (Ed.), *Psychoanalysis and Contemporary Science*. Vol. 2. New York: Macmillan.

Patty, R. A. and Safford, S. F. (1976). Motive to avoid success, motive to avoid failure, state-trait anxiety, and performance. In C. D. Spielberger and I. G. Sarason (Eds.), *Stress and Anxiety*. Vol. 4. New York: Wiley.

Peterfreund, E. (1971). Information systems and psychoanalysis: an evolutionary biological approach to psychoanalytic theory. *Psychological Issues*, **7**, Monographs No. 25-26.

Peterfreund, E. and Franceschini, E. (1973). On information, motivation and meaning. In B. B. Rubinstein (Ed.), *Psychoanalysis and Contemporary Science*. Vol. 2. New York: Macmillan.

Petrie, A. (1967). *Individuality in Pain and Suffering*. Chicago: University of Chicago Press.

Petrie, A., Collins, W. and Solomon, P. (1960). The tolerance for pain and for sensory deprivation. *American Journal of Psychology*, **73**, 80–90.

Rabkin, J. G. and Struening, E. L. (1976). Life events, stress and illness. *Science*, **194**, 1013–1020.

Raynor, J. O. (1974). Motivation and career striving. In J. W. Atkinson and J. O. Raynor (Eds.), *Motivation and Achievement*. Washington, D.C.: Winston.

Rees, W. L. (1977). Stress, distress and disease. *British Journal of Psychiatry*, **128**, 3–18.

Rotter, J. B. (1966). Generalized expectancies for internal versus external control of reinforcement. *Psychological Monographs*, **80**, No. 1, Whole No. 609.

Royce, J. R. (1973). The conceptual framework for a multi-factor theory of individuality. In J. R. Royce (Ed.), *Multivariate Analysis and Psychological Theory*. London: Academic Press.

Rutter, D. R. (1977). Visual interaction and speech patterning in remitted and acute schizophrenic patients. *British Journal of Social and Clinical Psychology*, **16**, 359–361.

Sarason, I. G. (1961). The effects of anxiety and threat on the solution of a difficult task. *Journal of Abnormal and Social Psychology*, **62**, 165–168.

Sarason, I. G. (1972). Experimental approaches to test anxiety: attention and the use of information. In C. D. Spielberger (Ed.), *Anxiety — Current Trends in Theory and Research*. Vol. 2. New York: Academic Press.

Sarason, I. G. (1975). Anxiety and self-preoccupation. In I. G. Sarason and C. D. Spielberger (Eds.), *Stress and Anxiety*. Vol. 2. New York: Wiley.

Schachter, S. (1964). The interaction of cognitive and physiological determinants of emotional state. In L. Berkowitz (Ed.), *Advances in Experimental Social Psychology*, **1**, 49–80.

Schaie, K. W. and Goulet, L. R. (1977). Trait theory and verbal learning processes. In

R. B. Cattell and R. M. Dreger (Eds.), *Handbook of Modern Personality Theory*. New York: Wiley.

Shalling, D. (1971). Tolerance for experimentally induced pain as related to personality. *Scandinavian Journal of Psychology*, **12**, 271–281.

Schalling, D. (1976). Anxiety, pain and coping. In I. G. Sarason and C. D. Spielberger (Eds.), *Stress and Anxiety*. Vol. 3. New York: Wiley.

Schönpflug, W. (1976). Cognitive mechanisms — stressed or stressing agents. Unpublished contribution to Symposium on *Information Processing and Stress*. 21st International Congress of Psychology.

Shapiro, K. J. and Alexander, I. E. (1969). Extraversion–introversion, affiliation and anxiety. *Journal of Personality*, **37**, 387–406.

Shields, J. (1962). *Monozygotic Twins Brought Up Apart and Brought Up Together*. London: Oxford University Press.

Simon, H. A. (1967). Motivational and emotional controls of cognition. *Psychological Review*, **74**, 29–39.

Spence, K. W. (1956). *Behavior Theory and Conditioning*. New Haven: Yale University Press.

Spence, K. W. and Farber, I. E. (1954). The relation of anxiety to differential eyelid conditioning. *Journal of Experimental Psychology*, **47**, 127–134.

Spence, J. T. and Spence, K. W. (1966). The motivational components of manifest anxiety: drive and drive stimuli. In C. D. Spielberger (Ed.), *Anxiety and Behavior*. New York: Academic Press.

Spielberger, C. D. (Ed.) (1966). *Anxiety and Behavior*. New York: Academic Press.

Spielberger, C. D. (Ed.) (1972). *Anxiety — Current Trends in Theory and Research*. 2 Vols. New York: Academic Press.

Spielberger, C. D. (1975). Anxiety: state-trait process. In C. D. Spielberger and I. G. Sarason (Eds.), *Stress and Anxiety*. Vol. 1. New York: Wiley.

Spielberger, C. D. (1977). State-trait anxiety and interactional psychology. In D. Magnusson and N. S. Endler (Eds.), *Personality at the Crossroads — Current Issues in International Psychology*. Hillsdale: Lawrence Erlbaum.

Spielberger, C. D., Gorsuch, R. L. and Lushene, R. E. (1970). *Manual for the State-Trait Anxiety Inventory*. Palo Alto: Consulting Psychologist Press.

Spielberger, C. D. and Smith, L. H. (1966). Anxiety (drive) stress and serial position effects in serial-verbal learning. *Journal of Experimental Psychology*, **72**, 589–595.

Strickland, B. R. (1977). Internal–external control of reinforcement. In T. Blass (Ed.), *Personality Variables in Social Behaviour*. Hillsdale: Lawrence Erlbaum.

Surawicz, F. G., Brightwell, D. R., Weitzel, W. D., and Othmer, E. (1976). Cancer, emotions and mental illness: the present state of understanding. *American Journal of Psychiatry*, **133**, 1306–1309.

Taylor, J. A. (1953). A personality scale of manifest anxiety. *Journal of Abnormal and Social Psychology*, **48**, 285–290.

Thackray, R. I., Bayley, J. P., and Touchstone, M. (1977). Physiological, subjective and performance correlates of reported boredom and monotony while performing a simulated radar control task. In R. R. Mackie (Ed.), *Vigilance–Theory, Operational Performance and Physiological Correlates*. New York: Plenum.

Thomas, A., Chess, S. and Birch, H. G. (1968). *Temperament and Behavior Disorders in Children*. New York: New York University Press.

Tomkins, S. S. (1963). *Affect, Imagery, Consciousness: Vol. II. The Negative Affects*. New York: Springer.

Vernon, P. E. (1973). Multivariate approaches to the study of cognitive styles. In J. R.

Royce (Ed.), *Multivariate Analysis and Psychological Theory*. London: Academic Press.

Vernon, P. E. (1976). Development of intelligence. In V. Hamilton and M. D. Vernon (Eds.), *The Development of Cognitive Processes*. London: Academic Press.

Wachtel, P. L. (1968). Anxiety, attention and coping with threat. *Journal of Abnormal Psychology*, **73**, 137–143.

Weiner, B. (1972). *Theories of Motivation: From Mechanisms to Cognition*. Chicago: Markham.

Weiner, B. (1974). *Cognitive Views of Human Motivation*. New York: Academic Press.

Weiner, B., Frieze, I., Kukla, A., Reed, L., Rest, S. and Rosenbaum, R. M. (1972). Perceiving the causes of success and failure. In E. E. Jones, D. Kanouse, H. H. Kelley, R. E. Nisbett, S. Valius, and B. Weiner (Eds.), *Attribution — Perceiving the Causes of Behaviour*. Morristown: General Learning Press.

Wilkinson, R. T. (1964). Effects of up to 60 hours sleep deprivation on different types of work. *Ergonomics*, **7**, 175–186.

Wilson, G. (1977). Introversion–extraversion. In T. Blass (Ed.), Personality Variables in Social Behaviour. Hillsdale: Lawrence Erlbaum.

Wine, J. (1971). Test anxiety and direction of attention. *Psychological Bulletin*, **76**, 92–104.

Winterbottom, M. (1953). The relationship of childhood training in independence to achievement motivation. In J. W. Atkinson (Ed.), *Motives in Fantasy, Action and Society*. Princeton: Van Nostrand.

Zimbardo, P. and Formica, R. (1963). Emotional comparison and self-esteem as determinants of affiliation. *Journal of Personality*, **31**, 141–162.

Zubin, J. and Spring, B. (1977). Vulnerability — a new view of schizophrenia. *Journal of Abnormal Psychology*, **86**, 103–126.

Chapter 4

Current Paradigms and Models
in Human Information Processing

PATRICK RABBITT

1. Introduction
2. 'Data-driven' Models
    (i) Simple Models for Single Indices
    (ii) More Complex Models for Multiple Indices
    (iii) Functional Models for 'Multi-stress' Profiles
    (iv) Linear, Serial, Independent Process Models
3. 'Resource-Driven' Control Process Models
    (i) Transition from 'Data-driven' to 'Resource-driven' Models in Vigilance and Selective Attention
    (ii) Control Processes in Memory
    (iii) Control Processes in Response Output
4. Conclusions
5. References

1. INTRODUCTION

No current models in psychology specify how the functional mechanisms underlying human performance at any simple task may change their characteristics. Yet it is a blatant fact that such changes do occur. When people are practised at simple tasks it is evident that they do not simply learn to perform the same functional operations in the same way. They rather learn to perform in new and more efficient ways (Kristofferson, 1977; Rabbitt, Cumming and Vyas, 1979). Yet after a hundred years of discussion and experimentation we do not even have a model which explains how simple reaction time (RT) improves with practice. Like many other investigators I have data on the effects of practice on simple RT tasks which I have not published because there is currently no useful theoretical framework in which they can be interpreted. Groups of 16 subjects reduced their simple reaction times from an average of 210 msec to an average of 165 msec after 10 days' practice in a task with variable fore-periods. After 30 days of practice they were faster still, and some continued to improve after 40 days. Yet we have no model at all for the way in which such a change comes about. At best we have the simple, unstated assumption that whatever events in the human brain intervene between the onset of a signal and the production of an overt response early in practice also occur in the same order late in practice. The only change is that they occur faster and more efficiently.

This assumption is obviously questionable on logical grounds, and in other simple tasks has been empirically falsified some time ago. Typical young subjects on a two-choice serial self-paced reaction time task average 420 msec with a standard deviation of 98 msec and error rates of 2–5% on their first 500 responses. Ten days and 20,000 responses later they may average 210 msec with a standard deviation of 20 ms and rate 0.4–1.1% of errors. For some individual subjects no single correct reaction time produced early in practice may fall within the entire reaction time distribution for responses later in practice.

All existing models are constrained by the need to account for the effects on reaction time variance of such factors as signal and response information load (Hick, 1952; Hyman, 1953; Audley, 1960; 1973), stimulus and response compatibility (Fitts and Deininger, 1954) or entropy and discriminability (Laming 1968), or the effects of signal and response repetitions and alterations (Rabbitt, 1968; Kornblum 1969a; b; 1973). Yet it has been known for some time that after only moderate practice the effects of the first two factors are greatly reduced or completely abolished (Crossman, 1953; Mowbray and Rhoades, 1959).

The third factor entirely changes the nature of its operation as practice continues (Fletcher and Rabbitt, 1978). After practice subjects cease to identify signals in a two-choice task as unique events and respond merely to constancy or change in the display. In other words the single assumption which actually will *not* serve is that practice simply renders more efficient each one of a set of functional operations, leaving their nature and their sequence of operation intact. When effects of transfer are specifically examined it is clear that subjects improve their performance because they actively discover, and use, increasingly efficient *new* ways in which to process information (Rabbitt, 1967a; b; Kristoffersen, 1977; Fletcher and Rabbitt, 1978; Rabbitt, Cumming and Vyas, 1979).

The lack of models which allow us to describe such changes is a very severe handicap. It is not just that we cannot discuss how performance changes with practice, but that we also cannot discuss other gradual changes in system characteristics such as those which must occur as people grow up or grow old. Indeed any theory of individual differences, which implies that people may be ranked along continua of difference, demands corresponding models of performance which not only describe limiting cases but will also describe inter-mediate transitional states. Useful models for the effects of stressors are also impossible under any other assumptions.

Stressors typically have incremental rather than all-or-none effects on human performance, so that models for their effects should, above all, be models which can describe progressive change. We might therefore hope that by reviewing the stress literature we might find that this problem has been faced, and that we can discover that the kind of model which we require to rehabilitate the rest of human experimental psychology already exists. This expectation is met only to a very limited extent. A brief taxonomy of experi-ments and models in the stress literature may help us to understand how things stand.

When discussing the *kinds* of models of systems used in experimental psychology a very convenient initial distinction is that between models which assume 'data-driven' or 'bottom-up' processing and those which assume 'resource-driven' or 'top-down' control of information flow (Norman and Bobrow, 1975; Bobrow, 1976; Bobrow and Norman, 1976). 'Bottom-up' information processing systems are envisaged as passive, so that system input characteristics are reset by successive inputs. In 'top-down' processing sys-tems some central decision mechanism is assumed to be in control of system input characteristics and can autonomously reset them from time to time. A simple example of a 'bottom-up' system would be an electric typewriter in which output is determined by input alone, however, complex the intermediate linkages may be. A programmable desk calculator, however, can accept the same input on successive occasions (e.g. the number 42) and, under control of its programme, subject it to different transformations (e.g. divide it by log 2 or square it, etc.). Such a system can select what data to process, and can select what operations to perform on such data in ways which are not at all affected by moment to moment changes in data input.

This can very usefully serve as a metaphor to illustrate the historical reci-procity between theoretical models and empirical data in the literature on human performance and stress. Let us consider how 'data-driven' descrip-tions, formulated to answer limited, applied questions fall at one end of a continuum, gradually giving way to 'theory-driven' discussions, almost devoid of empirical prediction, at the other.

2. 'DATA-DRIVEN' MODELS

(i) Simple Models for single Indices

Poulton's (1970) admirably clear and comprehensive handbook on the effects of stressors was written with the needs of engineers and equipment designers in mind. Most of the studies which he describes were carried out to establish critical limits for tolerance of particular stressors in particular situations (e.g. hours of sleep deprivation, critical wet and dry bulb temperatures, atmospheres of compression, etc., etc.). Experimenters who acquire such data are often not at all motivated by theoretical considerations. They must usually respond to a demand for an ideally sensitive diagnostic index of human response to a particular stressor. Obviously the existing performance literature will guide their intuitions as to which experimental paradigms may provide useful indices. However they usually have other applied demands to meet—principally that the indices used should have face-validity as components of some complex skill in real life (e.g. controlling an aeroplane) on which the effects of a stressor are to be investigated. This second demand may even lead them to construct detailed and realistic laboratory simulations of the real-life task (e.g. the 'Cambridge Cockpit' see Davis, 1948).

Experiments of this kind have striking advantages for the development of human experimental psychology. First, they force investigators to consider real-life tasks which tend to challenge naive theoretical assumptions and to draw attention to fresh problems for investigation (Broadbent, 1971). Second, as we see from Poulton's (1970) valuable compendium, these scores of isolated applied studies provide potentially a very rich source of data base against which theoretical assumptions can be tested. Indeed the applied literature is so vast, and as yet so poorly reviewed, that it might be argued that stress research in the 1980s is best carried out in libraries rather than in laboratories.

Unfortunately these data, though rich and varied, are also incoherent and fragmented. It is endlessly frustrating to find that striking speculations and insights are never followed up, and that the observations necessary to test any coherent theory either do not exist, or are tantalizingly incomplete in crucial details, or were made for purposes so oblique to any theoretical question that the experimental methods used cannot sustain any generalization.

(ii) More Complex Models for Multiple Indices

The first step in investigating a stressor is usually a 'one-off experiment'. In the simplest case such an experiment shows that the scores which healthy young subjects attain on a particular laboratory task change significantly when they concurrently experience one, particular, level of a stressor. Out of 97 studies reviewed in Poulton's (1970) handbook some 62 per cent are of this kind. In slightly more developed experiments several levels of a stressor are compared and it may be found that task performance scores covary with levels of stressor experienced.

After such preliminary studies investigators may respond in two general ways, depending on whether they choose to be more, or less, 'data-driven' or 'theory-driven'. I shall suggest that a desirable response is to consider the nature of possible performance models for the particular experimental tasks used, and to consider how particular stressors bring about some, but not other, changes in a variety of different performance indices derived for the same task. The more typical approach has been the 'test battery' or 'psychometric' approach. This line of approach is common to investigators working with particular stressors (e.g. noise, sleep loss, heat, drugs, etc.) but probably originates with investigators who attempt to describe performance of people suffering more or less chronic conditions (after-effects of concussion; old age; stable personality conditions such as introversion or extraversion; or disorders such as schizophrenia). This is an approach encouraged by the applied demand for differential diagnoses: e.g. the applied questions may be 'What sorts of things can a man do, and what sorts of things will he fail to do under heat stress or sleep loss?', 'What sorts of things do old people do relatively well or badly compared to the young?' The typical experimental strategy is to accumulate a number of sensitive tests judged on more or less intuitive grounds to reflect performance in, say, 'memory', 'perceptual processing', or 'psychomotor speed'. These tests are then administered as a 'battery' to groups of subjects under normal and stressed conditions, or to subjects experiencing chronic conditions. Individual sensitive tests will show changes in score between conditions or across groups. These changes may be more marked for some sensitive tests than for others. Changes in test score can be used to present 'profiles' delimiting the effects of a particular stressor or of a particular chronic condition in comparison with different 'profiles' delimiting effects of other stressors or conditions.

As with the application of intelligence test batteries, severe logical difficulties arise if this technique is used for other than very limited practical reasons. If the practical question is whether certain, calibrated levels of performance on particular tasks are, or are not, affected by heat, age, sleep loss, extraversion, or schizophrenia, this can be an eminently sensible approach. Test batteries, when validated against real-life performance, may accurately predict limitations of capacity and tolerable limits of stress. But inferences beyond this are very dubious. For example, suppose that we wish to discover whether memory, reaction time, or perceptual recognition time are *most* affected by heat or old age. We have, somewhat arbitrarily selected sensitive tests for each. We note that age or heat results in changes in reaction time but not in changes in scores for memory or perceptual recognition. Obviously we cannot therefore say that a change of X units on one test score is equivalent to a change of Y units on another. Nor can we even make the simpler statement that *because* some tests show zero effects while other tests show positive or negative effects, *therefore* some aspects of performance are affected while others are not. We have no way of assuring ourselves that our tests are of *equal sensitivity* in any absolute sense. The threshold for stress effects on any test may be higher than that on others. We can therefore only say that tests are not necessarily equally sensitive to changes in the efficiency of the particular *functions* which we hope they tap. We cannot add that the *functions* which these tests allegedly tap are more, or less, sensitive to the stresses which we impose on our subjects. Thus until we have models of the particular functional processes which each involves we cannot say whether any given sensitive test is, or is not, really a *sensitive* index of changes in these, underlying, functional processes.

These logical difficulties cannot be compensated by ingenuity in statistical analysis. For example, a meticulously analysed study of the comparative performance of groups of old and young people on very large and diverse test batteries is reported by Birren, Butler, Greenhouse, Sokoloff and Yarrow (1963). The directions of effects on individual tests are provocative, but the general picture is of global deficit, and the question as to which mechanisms are particularly damaged by age remains obscure. The question as to how these various functions interrelate to each other in normal performance is left completely undiscussed. A similar, very large, study by Heron and Chown (1967) used factor analysis to evaluate strengths of associated changes of scores on a very large number of different tests. Heron and Chown (1967) indeed discovered patterns of association, but these remain uninterpretable because their data provide no way in which we can relate a statistical model for effects, derived from factor analysis, to any functional model of human performance. Further, their tests appear to have been chosen with only the statistical model in mind. They are selected as providing isolated 'sensitive indices' for performance and metabolic efficiency, rather than as representing interrelated indices referring to a particular performance model. I do not argue that it is, in principle, impossible to map correlational relationships derived from test batteries on to schemes of hypothetical causal relationships derived from performance models. I do, however, argue that until our functional models are better than they are at present this is a clumsy and time-wasting procedure.

Fortunately the strategy of deriving a 'test performance profile' for any particular stress, or for any human condition, is not the only option available. It has proved far more useful to invert this approach and to examine changes in performance on particular tasks as subjects experience each of a number of different stressors.

(iii) Functional Models for 'Multi-stress' Profiles

Obviously this approach would be futile if applied to tasks for which we could obtain only a single index of performance. Suppose, for example, we were only able to measure overall average reaction time and not errors. In this case we could only hope to rank order a series of different stresses along a single continuum of reaction time slowing. Such statements as 'Alcohol slows reaction time more than loss of sleep, and loss of sleep slows reaction time more than noise' might be true, but would be of little value except in curiously limited practical situations. Now levels of stressors rather than test scores become incommensurable, and the titration of milligrams of alcohol per blood litre against wet bulb temperature of hours of sleep loss is quite unhelpful.

However, in practice, this approach usefully forces us to design tasks which allow us to measure, simultaneously, not one but several indices of performance in the same experimental situation. Thus if we have multiple performance indices from a given task we can observe variations in these performance indices not merely in relation to task-external factors but also in relation to *each other*. Because we are in a position to observe relations between several performance indices we find ourselves in a position to construct a *functional* model for performance at the task in question and are not merely limited to such statistical models of association as our mathematical ingenuity allows. This fact gives this particular methodology its explanatory power. Let us review the history of one, very simple, task in the stress literature to see how this possibility has worked out in practice.

The '5-choice' serial, self-paced choice response task was used for many years as a standard instrument for evaluating effects of stressors at the Medical Research Council Applied Psychology Research Unit, in Cambridge. It thus provides a rare case where the same paradigm, indeed the same equipment, has been used by a number of different investigators to investigate a number of different stressors. A subject holds a stylus in his preferred hand. When any one of five lamps, arranged at the corner of an equilateral pentagon, is automatically lit, he strikes a brass plate next to it with the stylus point. In the self-paced, unlagged, version of the task, as soon as he hits any plate the light is automatically switched off, and the next light, determined by a pre-programmed random sequence, immediately switches on. He then again strikes the appropriate plate and so continues for half an hour or longer, as fast and as accurately as he can.

In the context of the automatic programming and recording apparatus available in the 1950's there were only three different performance indices which might be extracted from this task. We shall see later how the development of current, better models is due to improvements in this respect. First investigators could measure average reaction time. Since this could only be done by counting the number of responses made within a given time period, this was a gross measure indeed. Second, errors could be counted, (though not independently timed). Finally, some clue could be obtained as to the *distribution of reaction times*, but only by setting an upper fixed time limit such that responses which were faster than this limit and those which were slower than this limit were counted separately.

Using this task Broadbent (1953) found that loud (75 dB) 'white noise' increased the percentage of errors committed. In a later study he confirmed that noise affected error incidence, but found that noise did not affect the average rate of responding, nor did it increase the number of responses slower than a critical limit of 1.5 seconds (Broadbent, 1957). Pepler (1959) found that heat stress also increased errors but did not change average response rate or increase the incidence of unusually slow responses. However the effects of heat stress differed from those of noise in that heat caused an increase in errors early in a session but not towards the end of a session, while noise had the reverse effect.

Wilkinson (1959) found that loss of sleep had quite different effects. Overall average reaction time and error rates were not affected. However, the number of unusually slow responses ('gaps' i.e. reaction times greater than 1.5 sec) sharply increased. Subjects apparently maintained their average reaction times in spite of an increase in the number of gaps because between gaps they briefly speeded up their response rate. Wilkinson et al. (1964) also found that the number of gaps was reduced when subjects had knowledge of results. (This was an early recognition that even in a very simple task subjects can *regulate* their performance within limits by monitoring feedback from the task.)

Subsequently Wilkinson and Colquhoun (1968) have found that ingestion of alcohol, heat, or noise, increase errors but not gaps, and do not affect the average rate of responding.

Thus if only one index of five-choice performance had been available (e.g. average response rate) no effects of any stress would have been found within the limits tested. If only response rate and errors had been measured three stressors would have shown very similar effects and loss of sleep would have shown no effect.

These differences in *patterns* of stress effects are quite uninformative if considered as data from 'psychometric tests'. Note that there is no rationale behind considering 'accuracy', 'slow responses', and 'response rate' as independent 'factors' or as coordinates in a multidimensional space within which stresses may fall into one 'cluster' or another. Such an exercise might be, at best, a prelude to a search for a reasonable *functional* model which intepreted effects of stressors in terms of their *causal* effects on one another through a model for the mechanisms by which signals are identified and responses are selected and made to them. Broadbent (1971) was able to proceed directly from a review of these effects to suggest just such a model.

The logical assumptions underlying this model are particularly interesting, because it is implicitly based upon the powerful technique of 'decomposition of indices' (see Donders, 1868; and a review and extention of Donder's work by Sternberg, 1969; 1975). Stated in its simplest form, Broadbent's assumption was that the human information processing system can be described in terms of the operation of at least three successive independent information processing stages illustrated in Figure 4.1.

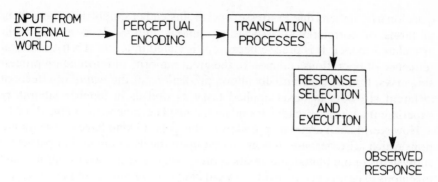

FIGURE 4.1.

Any stressor, or general condition of the system, may potentially affect the operation of any stage but not others. Thus Broadbent noted that errors occurred independently of average reaction time, and independently of the occurrence of unusually long responses: 1.5 sec or longer. He concluded that factors producing errors were independent of factors governing speed of response selection and execution. The system illustrated in Figure 4.1 pointed to the conclusion that those stresses which produced errors did so because they interfered with perceptual analysis. He therefore interpreted the effects of noise, heat stress, and of alcohol as producing momentary diversions of attention which prevented accurate identification of signals. This assumption usefully linked five-choice effects with attentional effects of the same stressors observed in vigilance experiments. Broadbent further pointed out that highly practised subjects who are required to keep up a rapid response rate (and are in conditions of high arousal), may continue responding at this high rate in spite of brief disturbances of sensory input. On this assumption aroused subjects experiencing heat, noise, or alcohol might suffer such disturbances and, as a consequence, make errors because they briefly continued responding without reference to changes in the display. In contrast, subjects suffering from loss of sleep may be assumed to be in a lower state of arousal and so to be less able to maintain a fast response rate. In their case, interruptions of attention to the display of signals would appear as long response times rather than errors.

In terms of the components of Figure 4.1 Broadbent (1971) supposes that all stressors affect perceptual selection and processing, but that only stressors which lower arousal affect response selection. It is in this latter box that the rate at which responses are generated is determined.

This is a concise model, and is satisfying for many reasons. It goes beyond data from a single limited task (the five-choice) to allow prediction of the nature of performance decrements in other tasks in which the response load is small, but the perceptual load may be considerable (e.g. vigilance tasks, cf. Broadbent, 1971). It is also a process model, which considers seriously the question *why* deficits due to stressors occur, instead of simply describing them in terms of correlational associations among indices. It is a very well-articulated model. It is precise because it is stated in terms of a hypothetical sequence of operations common to the great majority of information processing tasks, that is, it potentially allows predictions of the *nature* of effects of different stressors in novel applied tasks as well as in familiar laboratory experiments. It can be readily tested and, if need be, amended or abandoned.

However, I shall argue that models of this general kind have severe limitations which arise because they are based upon the assumption that particular subsystems in the human information processing system may, by appropriate ingenious experiments, be made to yield *independent* indices of performance. If we assume this we may hope that the empirical independence of indices, and arguably therefore, the functional independence of the subsystems whose operation they represent, may be recognized by *post hoc* data analysis. We may hope to do this in two main ways. First, we may decide to apply external variables (e.g. stressors) to a system. We may decide to investigate changes in overall system states (e.g. old age, intoxication, etc.) or we may decide to manipulate task parameters which may bring about changes in one recorded index while not producing changes in others. Second, in some cases our derived performance indices may be treated as components in changes along a single measurable variable. For example Donders (1868) used a subtraction technique to partition overall observed reaction time into time for stimulus analysis and time for response choice. In this case, as Sternberg (1969; 1975) has pointed out, these derived indices must be shown to respond *additively* rather than *interactively* to changes in system state or to task-intrinsic parameters. With these considerations in mind we may consider the formal basis for such models, and the feasibility of the assumptions which they imply.

(iv) Linear, Serial, Independent Process Models

The basic assumptions behind process models of this sort have been so elegantly and precisely stated by Sternberg (1969) that it is convenient to take this model, and the experimental paradigm on which it is based, as a test case for considering the advantages of this methodological ploy. Sternberg (1966; 1967; 1969; 1975) used a simple task in which, on every trial, subjects were rapidly presented with varying numbers of items (usually random digits) which they had to remember briefly. Very shortly after this 'target' set of items subjects were given a test item, or 'probe'. Their task was to respond, as fast as possible, indicating whether the probe was, or was not, a member of the target set. Sternberg's (1968) first findings were that reactions for both positive and negative responses increased linearly, and at the same rate, as the number of items in the target set increased. He explained this by the assumption that subjects always compared input from the probe against representations of all target set items (exhaustive comparison) and that this comparison process was serial, so that each extra target set member required one extra comparison to be made. The slope of the functions relating positive and negative reaction times to target set size was thus a direct index of comparison time. This function had a non-zero intercept. Sternberg (1969) assumed that this intercept represented the time, consumed on each trial, by factors other than successive serial comparisons (e.g. response selection time to move the fingers). Use of degraded probes affected the intercept rather than the slope of the function so that it was reasonable to assume that the time required for perceptual recognition of the probe was additive to, and independent of time for memory comparisons (Sternberg, 1967). Other factors were found to affect the slope, but not the intercept (Sternberg, 1969). This allowed Sternberg to suggest a model of perceptual recognition and response choice which postulated that there were two or more successive, independent, processing stages, and that separate indices of efficiency might be obtained for each of these if changes in overall measured reaction times were 'decomposed' by suitable experiments. Sternberg's paradigm has been enthusiastically taken up by scores of investigators, many of whom have sought to use it to speculate on the implications for individual differences of independent changes in slopes and intercepts of memory scanning functions (see Sternberg, 1975). The reaction time decomposition technique has probably attained its greatest elaboration in studios by Briggs and Swanson, 1970; Briggs and Johnsen, 1973; and Briggs, Johnsen and Shinar, 1974.

It is crucial to recognize that the assumptions which Sternberg states so carefully and tests so well are common to a very large number of performance models in the literature. Such models have typically been used to diagnose the effects of stressors upon underlying functional mechanisms. The idea has been that we may learn something about particular stressors if it turns out that they affect one, but not others, of a series of independent processes occurring sequentially in time. As we shall see, these assumptions have usually hardly been recognized, let alone formally stated and clearly tested as Sternberg's studies show they should be.

In some experiments the logic of 'decomposing' a particular task into an hypothetical sequence of independent 'input', 'transformation', and 'output' stages is compelling, because these three functions can be seen to be separated in time by the structure of the task itself. In this case it is very reasonable to compare the effects of sudden and brief onset of a stressor during one of these component stages with its effects during others. Thus Woodhead (1964) presented brief bursts of noise to her subjects either while they read digits (input) or while they later carried out mental arithmetic on the digits they had read (transformation). Noise during input increased errors significantly, noise during transformation did not. Woodhead's conclusion that noise affects perceptual processing but not transformation is compelling.

Note, however, that the information which we can possibly get from this kind of experimental paradigm is limited in a number of ways. First, we can only say that a given level of noise impairs a particular kind of perceptual input more than it impairs a particular kind of cognitive process (transformation). It is quite feasible that other, higher, levels of noise might have the reverse effect. For example, digit reading might not become less efficient if noise were increased, while cognitive transformations, if impaired at all, might lead to a disastrous increase in errors. As an extension of the same point consider what we could say if noise affected *both* processes, but produced different numbers of errors in each case. It would be difficult to claim that one process was 'more affected' by noise than the other. In a very real sense the two processes are incommensurable. Let us suppose that during an experiment a subject has to input 10 digits for each of 50 runs. Suppose that under noisy conditions he fails to input, at random, one in 20 digits. Since loss of any digit will produce an incorrect answer, and since incorrect answers are all that we can score, the probability of one failure in any random group of 10 will be 0.2, so that we would expect subjects to get about 10 runs wrong because of noise during input. On the most naive model possible we might assign exactly the same proability value, i.e. $p=0.02$, to the likelihood of a noise burst interfering with a particular operation in mental arithmetic, i.e. with one addition of 10 digits. Even if we assume that any interference during mental arithmetic will result in an error, only 1 extra error will result, on average, during a list of 50 different runs. Thus for this reason alone, arithmetical transformation would appear to be 10 times less affected by noise than digit input. Of course, such an argument cannot seriously be sustained because it is based upon *ad hoc* assumptions, but this is precisely the point. Unless we can state our assumptions, and empirically justify them, it is far from clear what such data can possibly mean. For practical purposes, in particular situations, it may be vital to know that noise during digit input produces more wrong answers than noise during transformation. But without reference to particular functional models of input and transformation processes in mental arithmetic this is a statement empty of any theoretical content.

The difficulty that the successive stages in sequential models do different things, and that output from any one stage becomes input for the next is common to all deductions from models of this type. Thus in a model with sequential stages A—B—C—D any external factor which affects B must also affect the nature of information input to the subsequent stages C and D. Thus effects of external factors cannot, without good evidence, be supposed to be specific to the particular stages at which they are introduced. Variables impinging at B are likely also to have an *indirect* effect on C and D so that their effects on measured indices of output from D will be combinatorial rather than additive and separable. If this output is all we can measure, Sternberg's canons of independent and additive contributions to performance indices can never be satisfied in practice.

This difficulty does not arise if we choose not to *intervene* in the system but rather to *monitor* concomitant changes in physiological indices. Thus Kahneman and Wright (1971) report differences in pupillary dilation between presentation, storage, and retrieval stages in a digit-span task. They are thus able to discriminate between arousal states concomitant with various processing stages without any of the difficulties discussed above.

The logical framework in Figure 4.1 is common to a very large number of studies. For example Baddeley (1968) used a model of short-term memory which assumed that 'input', 'storage', and 'retrieval' processes were functionally separable. He tried to discover whether the effects of acoustic confusability of items presented for recall might be referred to one rather than another of these stages. His study is a clever and useful one, but illustrates some interesting conceptual difficulties. These are common to a number of similar designs which have been used in attempts to interpret age changes in memory performance (see a review by Craik 1977; also experiments by Rabbitt, Clancy and Vyas, 1969).

In all such studies no formal test of independence of these hypothetical stages has been made. Moreover, since changes in quality of output from the first and second stages must affect processing in later stages, interpretations of performance indices are likely to remain cryptic. Thus we may be able to say that particular factors do have an effect on one stage or another. But discussions of their *relative* effects on particular stages will hardly be useful. For example, the question asked by Rabbitt, Clancy and Vyas (1969) as to whether old age has differential effects on input, storage, or retrieval functions loses any point.

A further consideration follows from this discussion. Since 'pure' effects are difficult to obtain we are quite unlikely to be able to compare zero effects of interventions on two stages with significant effects of the same interventions on a third stage. Without such separability of indices, as we have seen, the comparison of relative sizes of effects is unhelpful.

Finally, we must be wary what kinds of interventions we choose to make at different stages, and try to secure their *comparability*. Thus Baddeley (1968) uses masking noise at acoustic (letter) input to search for a noise × confusability interaction to compare with, say, a 'delay × confusability' interaction. If these interactions occur they are bound to have different functional aetiologies, irrespective of the question as to whether they affect different processing stages. We are taking three factors, each known on its own to have an effect on probability of recall (confusability, noise, and delay), and we are comparing the size of the *interaction* of the first with either of the other two. (The argument with age as one factor is corrupt in precisely the same way). The derivation of magnitudes of *relative* decrements is, logically, impossible. Similar difficulties occur in other tasks.

A very early, and explicit, use of the reaction time decomposition technique is described by Welford (1960; 1968). Hick (1952) had found that the function relating choice reaction time to the number, N, of signal and response alternatives in a one-to-one signal-to-response mapping task, fitted the simple equation $RT=a+b$ ($\log_2 N + 1$) where a and b are empirically derived constants. Hyman (1953) had found a very similar descriptive relationship. This allowed Welford (1968) to discuss factors affecting choice reaction time in terms of their effects on either a or b (i.e. it raised the possibility that, at least, some factors might have independent effects on the slope and intercept of the choice reaction time function). In these terms Welford (1968) discussed the effects of compatibility, Rabbitt (1963) discussed effects of compatibility and discriminability, and Welford (1958) discussed the effects of age and interactions with practice.

Again, versions of the same difficulties make it dubious whether we can ever discuss *relative* decrement in the various functional processes which are assumed to differentially contribute to these indices. In addition, there is a new and interesting difficulty. One index of performance, the derived zero intercept of the choice reaction time function, is assumed to comprise the time consumed by such factors as physical movements of the fingers. Recent work has shown that all processing necessary to produce reaction time may be completed up to 100 msec before overt finger movements are measurable, and probably even before electromyographical events can be recorded (Megaw, 1972). It follows that considerable variations in processing time, which might also contribute to intercept changes, may be 'masked' because the minimum value for the index to which they contribute is set by another, relatively slow process. This difficulty is familiar as the difficulty encountered when we attempt to analyse performance indices for successive stages in independent sequential process models without adequate justification for the assumption that processes cannot overlap in time (i.e. when we do not know whether processes are parallel or not). An interesting difficulty of interpretation arises when one index has a range from 0 to X units while the other has no actual zero point. We know that the slope of the choice reaction time function may be reduced by practice until no variation of reaction time with number of alternatives is seen (Mowbray and Rhoades, 1959). This index thus has a real lower limit. However the intercept function, by its nature, cannot be reduced to zero. Thus different indices may not merely show different (and incommensurable) sensitivities, but also may show different floor effects. In either case we may be misled into supposing that an external variable, such as a stressor, has independent effects on the operation of two or more subsystems to which we assume our indices refer.

We see from all this that information processing models which postulate linear sequences of successive and independent functional operations have intrinsic methodological limitations. Data generated by experiments designed with such models in mind are very difficult to interpret. Nevertheless, such models have been of enormous service in human experimental psychology.

They have provided standard techniques for the experimental analysis of nearly all tasks we have studied during the last 30 years. Our current state of knowledge would be poor without them. Bearing this in mind, I shall argue that, quite apart from their limitations as methodological tools, they have a crucial limitation as heuristic devices because they do not allow us to discuss the ways in which subjects exercise flexible, continuous control of perceptual processing and of production of responses. The argument is that linear sequential stage models refer to 'bottom-up', or 'data-driven' processing systems, whereas the critical feature of human performance seems to be the way in which subjects use their acquired information about the structure of particular tasks, and about the external world (their 'resources'), in order to actively control their momentary perceptual selectivity and their choice of responses. An exemplary case for the necessity of this transition between 'passive', 'data-driven' linear sequential operation models and 'active', 'resource-driven' heuristics occurs in the literature on vigilance tasks. It is precisely these tasks on which about 80 per cent of the literature on human performance under stress has been based (using a selective count of references in bibliographies of large-scale reviews such as Broadbent, 1958; 1971; and Poulton, 1970).

3. 'RESOURCE-DRIVEN' CONTROL PROCESS MODELS

(i) Transition from 'Data-driven' to 'Resource-driven' Models in Vigilance and Selective Attention

The general pattern of data in vigilance experiments can be very simply described. When people must continuously monitor a particular information source for infrequent signals, they miss signals with increasing frequency as time passes. Broadbent (1971) very elegantly reviews the vigilance literature in terms of the assumption that this decrement can occur at either of two successive processing stages, that is, at perceptual detection or response selection. In his hands this dichotomy has been an extremely productive analytic tool. In fact some circumstantial evidence for its reality is available. Haider (1967) notes that subjects show cortical evoked potential changes during vigilance tasks even to signals to which they *fail* to respond. These evoked potentials are smaller than those which follow signals to which responses are made. Nevertheless their existence may mean that detection of a signal by one system (perceptual system) may occur independently of production of a response by another.

However, as Broadbent (1971) himself points out, an approach to vigilance tasks which questions only whether the main decrements occur in one or the other of these two systems does not help us to interpret all the data now available. Vigilance tasks may either be single-channel tasks in which subjects have to continuously attend to one source, or multi-channel tasks in which they have to distribute their attention across many different sources. The linear 'separate system' model works well for neither situation. As Jerison (1967) has shown, even in single-source tasks subjects cannot be considered to simply passively monitor events showing 'perceptual fading' or 'response blockage' according to the experimenter's presuppositions. They rather actively estimate the overall probabilities of signals, the ratios of signal-to-non-signal events and the contingent probabilities of signals to each other. Their performance can very reasonably be interpreted in terms of a model of strategic sampling behaviour, which postulates that they rationally allocate more or less time to inspection of a display depending on the stochastic models which they develop for task parameters, and their assessment of rewards and penalties for noting or missing signals. Baddeley and Colquhoun (1969) neatly demonstrate that subjects in vigilance tasks learn and use stochastic contingencies. Three groups of subjects began a vigilance task with different 10 min sequences of events during which signal probabilities were high, medium, or low. They then, without interruption, were given identical 50 min sequences with medium signal probability. Subjects who had been introduced to high signal probability maintained a better level of performance than the medium group, while the medium group showed less decrement than the 'low signal probability' group. It is difficult to account for these data except on the assumption that subjects adapt the frequency with which they sample the signal source over time to their estimates of signal probability. Note that a group which has adopted the strategy of sampling the display infrequently will not have their pessimistic hypotheses disconfirmed, since by missing signals they will retain their false impression of signal frequency. If a linear, successive process model is inadequate for single-source tasks it is impossible for tasks in which subjects have to monitor several different information sources at once.

A very early flight simulation study in the 'Cambridge Cockpit' (see Davis, 1948) showed that over prolonged simulated 'missions' pilots in the apparatus regularly checked and reset critical controls such as air-speed indicator and altitude meters, but checked less and less frequently 'minor' instruments such as the fuel gauge. Prolonged vigilance obviously led to increased selectivity among information sources based on reasonable estimates of priorities and of probabilities of change over time. Another early study by Broadbent (1958) showed that subjects who had to monitor banks of several dials at once showed selective decrements in their detections of critical states on peripheral, or low, information sources while they maintained a high level of performance on high information sources. Bahrick et al. (1952), manipulating incentives, found that 'high reward' sources continue to be efficiently monitored while 'low value' sources show marked vigilance decrement. Bursill

(1958) showed that heat stress exaggerated this effect, normally shown by prolonged vigilance. A critical experiment by Webster and Haslerud (1964) showed that a subsidiary auditory task also impaired performance to peripheral rather than to central sources in a multi-display task. Thus by 1964 it was apparent that the important feature of this situation was the subject's ability to flexibly allocate his resources of time, and information processing capacity, over the multiple sources with which he was required to deal.

A brilliant series of analyses by Hockey (1970; 1973) finally made it clear that we can only interpret performance on tasks of this kind if we assume that subjects exercise active, continuous control ('top-down' control) of their moment-to-moment selection between information sources. Hockey showed that external stresses or competing task demands result in attenuation of processing capacity. In this case diminished resources of time and capacity are nevertheless rationally deployed to maximize event detection.

At the same time Hamilton (1969) gave a new turn to the debate as to whether vigilance decrements reflect changes in efficiency of separate and independent perceptual and response systems. He divised a clever technique by which subjects were required to make overt responses in order to inspect signal sources and to determine whether critical events had occurred. Hamilton (1969) and Hamilton, Hockey and Rejman (1977) make the extremely important point that we can distinguish between subjects' *knowledge* of the respective stochastic probabilities of signals from various sources, and their *use* of this knowledge to guide their inspection strategies in vigilance tasks. Using similar techniques Sandford and Maule (1971; 1973) have shown that although old people can state, as accurately as the young, what are the absolute and conditional probabilities of signals from the various sources which they must inspect, the young but not the old actually employ this information to guide their distribution of inspection responses during a vigilance task.

To account for findings of this kind, Hamilton, Hockey, and Rejman (1977) and Hockey [Chapter 5] have put forward a model suggesting that the locus of control of current activity may be passed between levels of operation from the 'top' to the 'bottom' of the human information processing system as task demands require. They thus provide two valuable new ideas and a useful model for interpretation of experimental data. First, human information processing is seen to be under *active* control, so that strategic changes in the selection of information between several sources can usefully be discussed. A second, very original and useful, idea is that the locus of control within a complex system can vary from time to time during a task. The system can be either more or less 'resource-driven' or 'data-driven', depending on task demands and on the systems' idiosyncratic characteristics. The implication for analysis of available data and for design of future experiments is that we can now consider the operation of stressors, or of other system characteristics such as age, as affecting the efficiency with which an interactive processing system can control its own parameters of operation.

We began our discussion of 'top-down' processing systems by discussing how a system may respond to stressors, or to the onset of conditions such as old age, by changing the way in which it allocates its resources. We have, previously, criticized one linear, serial independent stage model for short-term memory on the grounds that it provides a poor tool for analysis of the effects of both task-external and task-internal variables. Let us see whether discussions of the operation of 'top-down' control processes in memory can improve our grasp of the data. This will allow us to extend our discussion of control systems by describing a system quite different from that which Hamilton, Hockey and Rejman (1977) present.

(ii) Control Processes in Memory

Baddeley (1976) and Hitch and Baddeley (1978) introduced the useful concept of 'working memory'. They point out that performance at a wide range of information processing tasks, such as mental arithmetic, forces us to assume that people retain information about recent events in a 'working memory'. They may use this information to guide their responses (memory-driven processing) or omit it when task demands require them to do so.

Caroline Thomas, Frieda Newcombe and I were struck by a monograph by Gronwall and Sampson (1974) which showed that patients recovering from mild concussion had difficulty with a particular paced serial addition task (PASAT). Subjects are given strings of single digit numbers at regular rates (varying from one digit per second to one every three seconds). Subjects have to add each successive pair of numbers together, thus

Numbers received:	8		4	6	3	5	etc.
Correct response:	No response		12	10	9	8	etc.

Thomas (1978) was unable to replicate Gronwall and Sampson's (1976) results but noted that her subjects made a variety of different *kinds* of error on this task. Most errors occur because subjects fail to keep up with the number sequences, and so may neglect to note one or more responses. However, very occasionally, subjects keep up but, sometimes, add the wrong digits, adding a current digit to the last *total* they derived rather than to the last digit given to them.

Digits read:	8	9	4	2	
Response:	None	17	13	15	— rather than 6

Subjects also, sometimes, add a current digit to a digit two or more places back in the sequence, thus:

Responses: None 15 12 11 — rather than 7

Thomas (1978) failed to find differences in the incidence of this kind of error between normal and concussed groups. However Rabbitt and Heptinstall (1979) found that when subjects are stressed by a secondary task (card sorting) while performing the main PASAT task, the number of errors of this kind increases more sharply than the number of omitted responses or errors in other categories.

Errors of this kind cannot be attributed to forgetting, in the conventional sense of loss of information once stored. It seems necessary to suppose that the subject may remember quite well the digits he has recently heard, and the numbers he has emitted as responses. His difficulty is that he has to maintain a 'memory pointer' (analogous to the 'programme location pointer' in a computer) in order to mark *which* of the digits he holds in his short-term memory he must currently deal with. In other words he must keep track of events in memory in order to decide what to do next. Thomas (1978), pursuing this idea, adopted tasks by Yntema and Mueser, (1960) and Yntema and Trask (1963). Thomas (1978) gave her subjects packs of cards to sort, consecutively, into four piles. The cards depicted four different types of symbols, but were sorted in fixed order irrespective of the symbols they bore. At random intervals Thomas stopped the sort and interrogated subjects as to the contents, in order, of one of the four locations into which they had sorted the symbols, or asked them to designate the locations into which a particular class of symbols had been sorted. While other, more conventional, tests of short-term memory efficiency showed no effects of concussion, this task was performed more poorly by recently concussed subjects. In this case subjects do not have to control their ongoing activity by reference to a moving 'memory pointer' which determines what they must do next. Rather subjects must try to simultaneously impose two different kinds of ordering on a series of events which they must remember. They must order classes of symbols according to locations, and tag locations according to the classes of symbols they include. A 'passive', data-driven model of memory function could not account for this process. It seems likely that the decrement shown by concussed subjects must be explained as a loss of capacity for active organization of events in memory rather than simply as accelerated forgetting. There is no evidence from PASAT or from other tasks that forgetting was in any way accelerated for this particular group of mildly concussed subjects.

It is possible to design a third type of task to show that subjects must control their current responses on the basis of either more, or less information held in short-term memory. Rabbitt and Heptinstall (1979) interpreted complaints by subjects that they grow 'absent minded' under stress in this way. They compared the ability of subjects to learn and repeat letter sequences of two types. In one class of sequences each letter occurred only once. This meant that each letter uniquely determined the next response, e.g.

A—B—C—D—E—F—G

In a second type of sequence some letters were repeated, so that at certain points in a sequence a subject could not know what response to make next unless he remembered more than one preceding letter: e.g.

A—B—C—B—D—C—B

Here, when the subject has said 'B', this fact, alone, does not tell him what he has to do next. He has to recall either one, two or three previous letters before his next response is determined. Rabbitt and Heptinstall (1979) found that subjects suffering concurrent distraction from a card-sorting task made more errors in sequences of the second kind. Their errors were associated with repeated letters, and often involved them in iterative 'loops' of three or four letters within a sequence, during which most of the other letters in the sequence were ignored.

In this case, once again, breakdown of performance under distraction appears to result from a breakdown in the way in which subjects can use their memory for some events, to control their selection of responses to others. Such breakdowns in memory-controlled processes are of at least two different kinds. First, the order of events in memory is garbled (the 'memory pointer' is lost) so that responses are not made in the correct sequence. This failure may be characterized as a failure to keep track of the order of events in memory (Thomas, 1973). Second, a distraction task may reduce the size of the sample of recent events which may effectively be held in memory and used to maintain control over response output. In either case we find ourselves forced to employ an active 'top-down' 'memory-driven' process control model rather than a passive 'data-driven' linear sequential system model to explain our data. Like Hamilton, Hockey and Rejman (1977) we may begin to look for the effects of stressors on the structure of active control processes, rather than to attempt to tease out their effects on one or another performance index.

As we saw earlier, the five-choice serial self-paced choice response task is unique in having been employed by various investigators over ten years or longer to compare the effects of different stressors. Broadbent (1971) presents a functional model for five-choice task performance which integrates the different patterns of data obtained from different stressors. Let us see whether a third kind of control process model will allow us to discuss performance in this classic task so as to better understand the effects of the various stressors to which it is sensitive.

(iii)　Control Processes In Response Output

Rabbitt and Vyas (1970) pointed out that subjects who are asked to carry out serial, self-paced, choice reaction time tasks, such as the five-choice task, are faced with a control problem. If they respond too fast they begin to make increasing numbers of errors. This speed–error trade-off function (SETO) relating accuracy to speed marks a stable limit to performance which subjects cannot transgress (Schouten and Bekker, 1967; Pacella and Pew, 1968; Pew, 1969; Rabbitt and Vyas, 1970). The usual experimental instructions given to subjects are 'Go as fast as you can and be as accurate as possible'. Rabbitt and Vyas (1970) pointed out that in novel tasks subjects could not know how fast they might safely respond unless they could increase response rate until errors occurred, detect these errors, and then adjust their rate of responding to avoid risky, fast reaction time bands. If we view the task in this way subjects need to know three things in order to control their performance. First, they need to know when they make errors. A series of papers have shown that indeed they almost invariably do (e.g. Rabbitt, 1966a; b; Rabbitt and Vyas, 1970). Second, they must be able to vary their response speed, and control it so as to 'track' the fastest, safe reaction time band possible to them. Finally, they need to know when they make *slow* responses so that they can reduce the variance of their reaction time distributions.

If we bear these requirements in mind age differences in performance, which are otherwise cryptic or counter-intuitive, can be conveniently explained. Old people have considerably longer mean correct reaction times than the young, but old and young people have almost identical average error reaction times. At first sight we might assume that old people have a less cautious attitude to their speed–error trade-off, and indeed brashly attempt to lower their average reaction times by responding as fast as possible irrespective of increases in error rate. An associated possibility is that old people, unlike the young, cannot detect their errors and so do not know when they are responding too fast. Rabbitt and Vyas (1973) found that this was not the case. Old people detect their errors as efficiently as the young. Also the shape of their reaction time distributions does not indicate that they produce large numbers of fast errors by responding unrealistically quickly. The key seems to be that the *variance* of individual old people's reaction times, is much greater than that of their young controls. It seems that old people cannot control their response speed very accurately. When they attempt to respond faster they overshoot their speed–error trade-off and commit errors. When they try to adjust their response speeds appropriately they respond much too slowly.

Young people can adjust fast response speeds to track their speed–error trade-off, because error detections provide feedback which allows them to avoid fast, risky reaction time bands. However there is no similar source of feedback which can warn subjects when they are going too slowly. Presumably they must control their *upper* reaction time limit by reference to some internal 'clock'. It is evident from the variance of reaction time distributions that such internal clocks are not very accurate instruments. When an external, pacing, time signal is introduced subjects immediately, and dramatically improve their average reaction time without loss of accuracy as reaction time distributions are 'shaped' to fit a narrow reaction time band (Rabbitt, unpublished data).

We therefore have a picture of a system which controls its maximum output rate to observe a speed–error trade-off, and controls its minimum output rate to avoid undesirably slow reaction time bands. To do the latter it must employ some internal or external timing process or 'clock'. On these assumptions we can plausibly explain details of differences in the performance of old and young subjects in terms of increased imprecision in one of these component functions (control of response timing), but not of others (error detection efficiency or maximum response rate).

This model allows us to reinterpret the classic five-choice data. Wilkinson (1959) pointed out that although subjects suffering from sleep loss make occasional very slow responses their average reaction times are not affected because they 'spurt' between slow responses. This picture of increasing drift from an optimal reaction time band, with attempts to adjust performance to maintain constant average reaction time would be characteristic of just such a system as we have described. Noise, heat, and alcohol all increase errors without affecting overall average reaction time or producing occasional slow 'gaps' in responding. The control process model allows us to see that Broadbent's (1971) explanation for this can be checked as one of two separate, equally likely possibilities. On Broadbent's hypothesis, information uptake from signals would become poorer, or become intermittent because of distraction from noise or heat. In this case a speed–error trade-off function measured under noise or heat should be displaced towards a slower reaction time band than when measured under normal conditions. That is to say subjects might make more errors even if they continue to respond at the same rate as they do under normal conditions. That is, they will produce the same distribution of reaction times under normal and stressed conditions, but a shift in speed–error trade-off function will mean that more responses are errors. Alternatively noise, heat or alcohol, like old age, may deprive subjects of fine control over their upper rates of responding. This, again, would increase the number of 'fast' errors, but would produce an identical speed–error trade-off and a changed reaction time distribution. A simple study of reaction time distributions would allow this to be checked for each stressor independently (see Rabbitt and Vyas 1970; 1978). It might very well be that both effects would be found, but in different degrees for different stressors, allowing us to differentiate effects of alcohol, heat, and noise in ways which other models have not allowed us to do.

4. CONCLUSIONS

This paper began with the complaint that our models for human performance have been so limited that they cannot properly account for change of any kind. In particular we noted that no existing linear serial independent process model can even offer a useful description of change with extended practice. Deficiencies of models for simple and choice reaction time were cited to make this point. In fact the control process model described above deals very well with changes in performance with practice in choice reaction time tasks. Hopefully similar models can be extended to other tasks in the future.

As a class of heuristics, control process models are specifically concerned with the description of the ways in which systems discover and control their limits and parameters of operation (McFarland, 1971; Toates, 1976). They are, above, all models of *change*. To the extent that the effects of incremental applications of stressors result in change, control process models may well do exactly what we require. The simple control process models which we have discussed are certainly tentative and crude. Their enthusiastic adoption is unlikely to instantly supersede the patient work of the last thirty years on which our current state of knowledge depends. Nor should it lessen our admiration for the vision and ingenuity with which this work has been carried on. But the old models have limitations which the possible future models can avoid. Best of all, before we are cramped, as we must inevitably be, by the limitations of the new models there are scores of new and useful experiments to be done, and a great deal to be learned.

5. REFERENCES

Audley, R. J. (1960). A stochastic model for individual choice behavior. *Psychological Review*. **67**, 1–15.

Audley, R. J. (1973). Some observations on theories of choice reaction time: a tutorial review. In S. Kornblum (Ed.), *Attention and Performance IV*, New York: Academic Press.

Baddeley, A. D. (1968). How does acoustic similarity influence short-term memory? *Quarterly Journal of Experimental Psychology*, **20**, 249–264.

Baddeley, A. D. (1976). *The Psychology of Memory*. New York, San Francisco, London: Harper and Row.

Baddeley, A. D. and Colquhoun, W. P. (1969). Signal probability and vigilance: a reappraisal of the 'signal rate' effect. *British Journal of Psychology*, **60**, 169–178.

Bahrick, H. P., Fitts, P. M. and Rankin, R. E. (1952). Effect of incentives upon reactions to peripheral stimuli. *Journal of Experimental Psychology*, **44**, 400–406.

Birren, J. E., Butler, R. M., Greenhouse, S. W., Sokoloff, L. and Yarrow, M. R. (Eds.) (1963). *Human Ageing: A Biological and Behavioral Study*. Washington, D.C.: Government Printing Office.

Bobrow, D. (1976). Dimensions of representation. In D. G. Bobrow and A. M. Collins (Eds.), *Representation and Understanding: Studies in Cognitive Science*. New York: Academic Press.

Bobrow, D. G. and Norman, D. A. (1978). Some principles of memory schemata. In D. G. Bobrow and A. M. Collins (Eds.), *Representation and Understanding: Studies in Cognitive Science*. New York: Academic Press.

Briggs, G. E. and Johnsen, A. M. (1973). On the nature of central processing in choice reactions. *Memory and Cognition*, **1**, 91–100.

Briggs, G. E., Johnsen, A. M. and Shinar, D. (1974). Central processing uncertainty as a determinant of reaction time. *Memory and Cognition*, **2**, 417–425.

Briggs, G. E. and Swanson, J. M. (1970). Encoding, decoding and central functions in human information processing. *Journal of Experimental Psychology*, **86**, 296–308.

Broadbent, D. E. (1953). Noise, paced performance and vigilance tasks. *British Journal of Psychology*, **44**, 295–303.

Broadbent, D. E. (1957). Effects of noise on behaviour. In C. M. Harris (Ed.), *Handbook of Noise Control*. New York: McGraw-Hill.

Broadbent, D. E. (1958). *Perception and Communication*. London: Pergamon Press.

Broadbent, D. E. (1971). *Decision and Stress*. London: Academic Press.

Bursill, A. E. (1958). The restriction of peripheral vision during exposure to hot and humid conditions. *Quarterly Journal of Experimental Psychology*, **10**, 113–129.

Craik, F. I. M. (1977). Age differences in human memory. In J. E. Birren and K. W. Schaie (Eds.), *Handbook of the Psychology of Ageing*. New York: Van Nostrand, Reinhold.

Crossman, E. R. F. W. (1953). Entropy and choice time: the effect of frequency unbalance on choice response. *Quarterly Journal of Experimental Psychology*, **5**, 41–51.

Davis, D. R. (1948). *Pilot Error. Air Ministry Publication A.P. 3139A*. London: His Majesty's Stationery Office.

Donders, F. C. (1868). Die Schnelligkeit psychischer Processe. *Archiv der Anatomie und Physiologie*, 657–681.

Fitts, P. and Deininger, R. L. (1954). S-R compatability: correspondence among paired elements within stimulus and response codes. *Journal of Experimental Psychology*, **48**, 483–492.

Fletcher, C. and Rabbitt, P. M. A. (1978). The changing pattern of perceptual analytic strategies and response selection with practice in a two-choice reaction time task. *Quarterly Journal of Experimental Psychology*, **30**, 417–427.

Gronwall, D. M. A. and Sampson, H. (1974). *The Psychological Effects of Concussion*. Oxford: Auckland University Press/O.U.P.

Haider, M. (1967). Vigilance, attention, expectancy and cortical evoked potentials. *Acta Psychologica*, **27**, 246–252.

Hamilton, P. (1969). Selective attention in multi-source monitoring tasks. *Journal of Experimental Psychology*, **82**, 34–37.

Hamilton, P., Hockey, G. R. J. and Rejman, M. (1977). The place of the concept of activation in human information theory: an integrative approach. In S. Dornic (Ed.), *Attention and Performance VI*. New Jersey: Lawrence Erlbaum.

Heron, A. and Chown, S. M. (1967). *Age and Function*. London: Churchill.

Hick, W. E. (1952). On the rate of gain of information. *Quarterly Journal of Experimental Psychology*, **4**, 11–26.

Hitch, G. I. and Baddeley, A. D. (1978). *Working Memory*. Unit 15 in *Open University Cognitive Psychology Course, D.203*. Milton Keynes: The Open University Press.

Hockey, G. R. J. (1970). Effects of loud noise on attentional selectivity. *Quarterly Journal of Experimental Psychology*, **22**, 37–42.

Hockey, G. R. J. (1973). Changes in information selection patterns in multi-source monitoring as a function of induced arousal shifts. *Journal of Experimental Psychology*, **101**, 35–42.

Hyman, R. (1953). Stimulus information as a determinant of reaction time. *Journal of Experimental Psychology*, **45**, 188–196.

Jerison, H. J. (1967). Activation and long term performance. *Acta Psychologica*, **27**, 373–389.

Kahneman, D. and Wright, P. (1971). Changes of pupil size and rehearsal strategies in a short-term memory task. *Quarterly Journal of Experimental Psychology*, **23**, 187196.

Kornblum, S. (1969a). Sequential dependencies as a determinant of choice reaction time: a summary. In W. Koster (Ed.), *Attention and Performance II*. Amsterdam: North Holland.

Kornblum, S. (1969b). Sequential determinants of information processing in serial and discrete choice reaction time. *Psychological Review*, **76**, 113–131.

Kornblum, S. (1973). Sequential effects in reaction time: a tutorial review. In S. Kornblum (Ed.), *Attention and Performance IV*. New York and London: Academic Press.

Kristofferson, M. W. (1977). The effects of practice with one positive set in a memory scanning task can be completely transferred to a different positive set. *Memory and Cognition*, **5**, 177–186.

Laming, D. R. J. (1968). *An Information Theory of Choice Reaction Times*. New York: Academic Press.

McFarland, D. J. (1971). *Feedback Mechanisms in Animal Behaviour*. London: Academic Press.

Megaw, E. D. (1972). Directional errors and their correction in a discrete tracking task. *Ergonomics*, **15**, 633–643.

Mowbray, G. H. and Rhoades, M. V. (1959). On the reduction of choice reaction time with practice. *Quarterly Journal of Experimental Psychology*, **11**, 16–23.

Norman, D. A. and Bobrow, D. G. (1975). On data limited and resource limited processes. *Cognitive Psychology*, **7**, 44–64.

Pacella, R. G. and Pew, R. (1968). Speed-accuracy trade-off in reaction times: effect of discrete criterion times. *Journal of Experimental Psychology*, **76**, 19–24.

Pepler, R. D. (1959). Warmth and lack of sleep: accuracy or activity reduced. *Journal of Comparative and Physiological Psychology*, **52**, 446–450.

Pew, R. (1969). The speed-accuracy operating characteristic. *Acta Psychologica*, **30**, 16–26.

Poulton, E. C. (1970). *Environment and Human Efficiency*. Springfield, Ill.: C. C. Thomas.

Rabbitt, P. M. A. (1963). Stimulus information load and discriminability. *Nature (London)*, **197**, 1029–1030.

Rabbitt, P. M. A. (1966a). Errors and error correction in choice-response tasks. *Journal of Experimental Psychology*. **71**, 264–272.

Rabbitt, P. M. A. (1966b). Error correction time without external error-signals. *Nature, (London)*. **212**, 438.

Rabbitt, P. M. A. (1967a). Learning to ignore irrelevant information. *American Journal of Psychology*, **80**, 1–13.

Rabbitt, P. M. A. (1967b). Time to detect errors as a function of factors affecting choice response time. *Acta Psychologica*, **27**, 131–142.

Rabbitt, P. M. A. (1968). Three kinds of error-signalling responses in a serial choice task. *Quarterly Journal of Experimental Psychology*, **19**, 37–42.

Rabbitt, P. M. A., Clancy, M. and Vyas, S. M. (1969). *Proceedings of the International Congress of Gerontology*, Washington, D.C.

Rabbitt, P. M. A., Cumming, G. C. and Vyas, S. M. (1979). Learning, improvement and retention in visual search tasks. *Quarterly Journal of Experimental Psychology*, in press.

Rabbitt, P. M. A. and Heptinstall, S. (1979). A laboratory simulation of absent-mindedness. Paper in preparation.

Rabbitt, P. M. A. and Vyas, S. M. (1970). An elementary preliminary taxonomy for some errors in laboratory choice RT. tasks. *Acta Psychologica*, **33**, 56–76.

Rabbitt, P. M. A. and Vyas, S. M. (1978). Can slowing in old age be compensated by more sensitive statistical prediction? *Journal of Gerontology*, in press.

Sandford, A. J. and Maule, A. (1971). Age and the distribution of observing responses. *Psychonomic Science*, **23**, 419–420.

Sandford, A. J. and Maule, A. J. (1973). The allocation of attention in multi-source monitoring behaviour: adult age differences, *Perception*, **2**, 91–100.

Schouten, J. F. and Bekker, J. A. M. (1967). Reaction time and accuracy. *Acta Psychologica*, **27**, 143–156.

Sternberg, S. (1966). High speed scanning in human memory. *Science*, **153**, 652–654.

Sternberg, S. (1967). Two operations in character recognition: some evidence from reaction time measurements. *Perception and Psychophysics*, **2**, 45–53.

Sternberg, S. (1969). The discovery of processing stages: extensions of Donders' method. *Acta Psychologica*, **30**, 276–315.

Sternberg, S. (1975). Memory scanning: new findings and current controversies. *Quarterly Journal of Experimental Psychology*, **27**, 1–32.

Thomas, C. M. (1978). Deficits of memory and attention following closed head injury. Unpublished *M.Sc. Thesis*, University of Oxford.

Toates, F. (1976). *Control Theory in Biology and Experimental Psychology*. London: Hutchinson's Education.

Webster, R. G. and Haslerud, G. M. (1964). Influence on extreme peripheral vision of attention to a visual or auditory task. *Journal of Experimental Psychology*, **68**, 269–272.

Welford, A. T. (1958). *Ageing and Human Skill*. London: Oxford University Press.

Welford, A. T. (1960). The measurement of sensory-motor performance: survey and re-appraisal of twelve years' progress. *Ergonomics*, **3**, 189–230.

Welford, A. T. (1968). *Fundamentals of Skill*. London: Methuen.

Wilkinson, R. T. (1959). Rest pauses in a task affected by lack of sleep. *Ergonomics*, **2**, 373–380.

Wilkinson, R. T. and Colquhoun, W. P. (1968). Interaction of alcohol with incentive and with sleep-deprivation. *Journal of Experimental Psychology*, **76**, 623–629.

Wilkinson, R. T., Fox, R. H., Goldsmith, R., Hampton, I. F. G. and Leven, H. E. (1964). Psychological and physiological responses to raised body temperature. *Journal of Applied Physiology*, **19**, 287–291.

Woodhead, M. M. (1964). The effect of bursts of noise on an arithmetic task. *American Journal of Psychology*, **77**, 627–633.

Yntema, D. B. and Mueser, G. E. (1960). Remembering the present state of a number of variables. *Journal of Experimental Psychology*, **63**, 391–395.

Yntema, D. B. and Trask, F. P. (1963). Recall as a search process. *Journal of Verbal Learning and Verbal Behavior*, **2**, 67–74.

Chapter 5

Stress and the Cognitive Components of Skilled Performance

ROBERT HOCKEY

1. Introduction
   (i) Stress and Arousal
   (ii) The Yerkes–Dodson Law
   (iii) Outline of the Chapter
2. Sustained Attention and Continuous Work
   (i) Vigilance
   (ii) Continuous Serial Reaction
3. Memory and Learning
   (i) Survey of Principal Findings
   (ii) Theoretical Problems of Memory and Arousal
4. Alternative Views of Arousal
   (i) Directional Effects of Arousal
   (ii) Autonomic Patterns of Task Orientation
5. Patterns of Performance Under Stress
   (i) Arousal and Selectivity
   (ii) The Mapping of a Stress State
6. Conclusions and Some Speculations
7. References

1. INTRODUCTION

The aims of this chapter are twofold; firstly, to attempt an integrated survey of research findings in the area of stress and performance and, secondly, to propose alternative methodological and theoretical approaches to the experimental study of stress effects in cognition. In reviewing the literature I have concentrated on two main areas of skilled performance, sustained attention and memory. This is primarily because most work has been done in these two fields and the findings are therefore more reliable. In addition, however, and this may be no accident, these two components may be considered as, in some ways, primary in the organization of skilled behaviour. Most of the work which forms the basis for the point of view expressed in the following pages comes from my collaboration with Peter Hamilton. Much of the credit for any value in this contribution should go to him.

(i) Stress and Arousal

One difficulty in writing this chapter concerns the way in which the term 'stress' should be interpreted. Very few studies have examined the effects on performance of the kind of conditions that most people would think of as stressful; chronic anxiety, for example, or prolonged interpersonal tension. This is largely because of the origins of stress research in the performance field, which have emphasized the kinds of relatively mild stress found in normal working conditions; loud noise, fatigue, sleeplessness, and so on. The use of stress in this context tends to refer to the conditions themselves, rather than to the state which it may produce in the person. Although the former class of variables are more correctly called 'stressors', after Selye's (1956) definition of the stress syndrome, I shall follow accepted usage and use these two terms interchangeably. In fact, very little is known about the states produced by stressors, although I have suggested later in the chapter an approach which makes this the central problem in stress research.

Work on sustained attention and on memory has relied on the use of arousal or activation as the major theoretical construct. These two terms are also used synonymously, and refer to the suggested non-specific changes in brain activity which results from stimulation (Hebb, 1955; Duffy, 1957; Malmo, 1959). Arousal theorists have argued that these effects are mediated by changes in the brainstem reticular formation, though the anatomical evidence now suggests that other systems are also involved, notably the diffuse thalamic projection system (e.g. Grossman, 1973). Despite the lack of agreement between physiological psychologists about the functional significance of arousal, the concept has proved a very useful one in accounting for effects on behaviour brought about by general changes in environmental conditions, rather than specific features of the experimental task. In this respect, conditions defined as 'stressful' have usually been thought of in terms of increasing arousal. In some cases, such as sleep deprivation, arousal may be reduced by this form of stress. This is a useful theoretical distinction, which I shall consider in this chapter. It seems, to some extent, to be at odds with the normal meaning of stress, even though sleep deprivation would be regarded as stressful by most people. Lastly, to complicate this picture further, stress has been identified by some theorists specifically with *emotional* arousal, while others have used the term to refer to *any* significant change in the normal environmental input. These are not issues which can be tackled adequately in this context, though they point strongly to the need for a more considered use of arousal as an explanatory concept for stress effects.

An important source of integration here is the research on the measurement of circulating catecholamines, particularly that carried out by Frankenhaeuser's group in Stockholm. I will not have space to deal with this extensive body of work, but one point is worth making here. The response of the adrenal medulla (in the form of increased output of adrenalin and noradrenalin) may be regarded as a measure of the extent to which subjects are coping with stress, and is observed to occur across a very wide range of situations (see, for example, Frankenhaeuser, 1975). The fundamental relationship between stress, arousal, and emotion and effort may be readily appreciated in this area of research, and offers support to Selye's concept of a general bodily reaction to any demands made on it.

In the present chapter an eclectic approach is adopted. I shall consider effects of any conditions which are thought to produce changes in arousal of one form or another. In doing this I will attempt to indicate which of these are best regarded as general effects of arousal, and which are more likely to be specific effects of the particular stressor. While they may well have a high degree of communality in their effects on bodily or behavioural functions it is important to remember that stressors also produce changes which are idiosyncratic.

(ii) The Yerkes–Dodson Law

The use of arousal in stress research is largely based on a complex relationship between arousal, task difficulty, and efficiency, first demonstrated by Yerkes and Dodson (1908) in a study of the effects of electric shock on discrimination learning in mice. This has become the cornerstone of theories of performance under stress. Mice were trained to choose the brighter of two boxes, and given an electric shock for failing to make the discrimination. Increases in the strength of the shock produced faster acquisition for the easiest brightness discriminations, but as the discrimination was made more difficult the optimum level of shock for learning was progressively reduced (see Figure 5.1). This interaction between difficulty of discrimination and level of shock is known as the Yerkes–Dodson law, and may be expressed, in modern terms, as two separate postulates:

(a) For any task there is an optimal level of arousal such that performance is related to arousal in the form of an inverted U.

(b) The optimum level of arousal is a decreasing monotonic function of the difficulty of the task.

There is considerable support for these claims, both from work in animal learning itself, and from research on human learning and performance (see

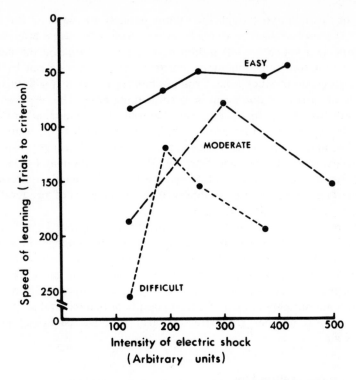

FIGURE 5.1. The relation between drive level and learning.
See text for explanation. (Redrawn from Yerkes and Dodson,
1908)

Hebb, 1955; Broadhurst, 1959). There is also an intuitive appeal about the
proposed form of this relationship, in terms of personal experience. Everyone
'knows' that they are most efficient when neither very sleepy, nor aroused by
strong emotion. We also 'know' that, while we can still change a motor car
wheel when we are tense or anxious, we would not like to have to mend a
watch. These observations are persuasive, and are, I think, the main reason
for the widespread and largely uncritical acceptance of the Yerkes–Dodson
law in human stress research. I do not want to object to its failure to describe
the effects of stress adequately, but it blinds us to the recognition of more
fundamental changes in functioning. The questions that I shall address myself
to in later sections of this chapter are 'What changes underly the observations
embodied in the Yerkes–Dodson law?' 'Why are high levels of arousal bad for
performance?' 'What makes a task difficult?' In general these questions
have been side-stepped in favour of circular reasoning and naive operational
definitions.

(iii) Outline of the chapter

In section 2 I will summarize evidence on the ways in which stressors affect the performance of tasks requiring sustained attention over periods of 30 minutes or more; tasks such as those of vigilance and self-paced serial reaction. These studies, in the tradition of the post-war work on skill, provide us with much of our current knowledge about effects of stress in situations involving attention to the environment and speeded performance. Section 3 looks at research findings from studies of memory and learning. Arousal has always been a central theoretical construct in this work, though very few studies make any explicit claim to be concerned with stress. Logically, however, the relation between the two concepts is similar in the two areas. Section 4 examines alternative views on arousal theory, in conjunction with considerations of methodological problems involved in performance analysis. These ideas are developed more fully in section 5, which attempts to give an account of recent research and theory in stress, and to tie together the separate strands of sections 2 and 3. Some general principles and speculations on the nature of state changes brought about by stresss are presented in section 6.

2. SUSTAINED ATTENTION AND CONTINUOUS WORK

Early work on stress and human work efficiency originated in practical needs arising from industrial and military problems of the 1940's, and was not considered in terms of general theories such as arousal until the early 1960's. The belief underlying much of this work was that stress is an unwanted source of difficulty which can only impair the efficiency of work. The practical aim of many of the early studies was to find out which conditions affected efficiency, and to provide recommendations for guarding against these effects (e.g. Chapanis, Garner, and Morgan, 1949; McCormick, 1957). Thus much of this research is concerned with effects of noise, temperature changes, sleep deprivation, fatigue, and, in more specialized situations, vibration, toxic environments, and gravitational force. For the purposes of this review we shall restrict our discussion to studies carried out in the context of concurrent developments in human performance theory, such as those at the Applied Psychology Unit in Cambridge during the post-war years. This research provides a useful integrated body of empirical data, since it was systematically carried out using a small number of well-developed tasks. It is particularly important from the point of view we have adopted in this chapter, since it illustrates two rather different features of the effects of stressors. One is the fundamental similarity between separate effects, a fact which is clearly consistent with the idea of stress as having general significance for the organism, after Selye's definition of the concept [see Chapter 1]. The other, no less important in developing theories of stress effects, is the presentation of systematic differences between the effects of different stressors. Thus we may say that noise and incentives are similar in their action, as we shall see later, with respect to their arousing effects, yet they differ in the pattern of these effects in important ways (which is one reason why an offer of an increase in the factory noise level would not generally be an acceptable alternative to a bonus scheme). We shall consider briefly the principal findings to emerge from this important body of work and go on to show how the inverted-U concept, and, to a lesser extent, the optimality concept, have proved useful integrating theoretical ideas in this field.

Most of the findings discussed in this section demonstrate some form of impairment in continuous work tasks (extending over 30 minutes or more) when subjects are required to work in what are normally considered to be adverse working conditions. The kinds of tasks in which these effects have been demonstrated are those which demand sustained attention, rather than selective attention for brief periods; tasks such as vigilance and serial choice reaction. It was believed until recently (e.g. Broadbent, 1958) that stress effects would *only* be observed reliably on this kind of task, though it is now clear that selective attention and memory may also show changes with stress.

(i) Vigilance

Sustained attention over long periods is most clearly observed in vigilance tasks, which require subjects to detect and report occasional critical signals. Mackworth (1950) showed that this kind of task is subject to a fairly pronounced decrement in efficiency with time at work, though there is no evidence of sensory or motor fatigue as such. Mackworth himself demonstrated that the extent of this decrement was increased by heat and could be *reduced* by an administration of amphetamine, or by a telephone call half way through the watch, suggesting that decrement may be due to a fall in arousal or motivation. A detailed review of stress effects in vigilance is not attempted here (see Davies and Tune, 1970; Poulton, 1970; Broadbent, 1971). The task has proved sensitive to changes in a wide range of environmental variables, such as loss of sleep (Wilkinson, 1959; Williams, Lubin, and Goodnow, 1959), increases in temperature (Pepler, 1953), and diurnal rhythm (Blake, 1967; Colquhoun, 1971). The effects of noise on vigilance are quite complex, though impairment has been found usually with rather complex tasks (involving more than one signal source, or a high signal rate), while detection is often enhanced in the case of simpler tasks (Hockey, 1970a). The reviews by Hockey (1978) and Broadbent (1971; 1978) give a more detailed discussion of noise effects, and the relationship between task complexity and direction of the effect is dealt with in section 5.

The general picture from this work is that performance is improved by mild stresses that are thought to increase arousal, but to be impaired by sleep loss and fatigue, which are thought to reduce arousal. Noise and heat, both of which have been argued as increasing arousal may have either effect—as one might expect from a simple interpretation of the Yerkes–Dodson law—depending on the level of stress and difficulty of the task. Poulton (1976) argues that all stressors which increase arousal should improve performance, and attempts to dismiss findings to the contrary as artefacts of one kind or another. In the case of noise, impairment is only found, he argues, when the noise prevents subjects from making use of intrinsic auditory cues present in the task (Poulton, 1977). A careful study of the literature from the point of view of the controls used in the studies mentioned by Poulton shows that this clearly is not the case (Broadbent, 1978). Noise consistently impairs detection performance in certain kinds of vigilance task. The important problem is to determine the conditions under which impairment or improvement is found. As I have indicated above, some feature of task complexity is implicated in this.

One reason why vigilance studies have proved difficult to interpret is the use of what may be inappropriate dependent variables in earlier experiments. It is now recognized that performance measurement must take into account not only the proportion of signals detected but also the rate at which subjects make false reports of signals. This approach, based on signal detection theory has thrown new light on many findings. Broadbent and Gregory (1965) showed that noise only reduced detections associated with high false-alarm rates (a risky criterion of report), as is usual, for example, in tasks with high signal rates. Low signal rate tasks, associated with low levels of false alarms (cautious criterion) are less likely to suffer, and may show an improvement in detections. The effect has been interpreted by Broadbent as a change in the decision mechanism rather than in sensitivity to visual signals, though the change appears to be rather complex. What happens in practice is that subjects make less use of intermediate categories of confidence in reporting whether a signal is present or not and, instead, are more confident in both asserting and denying the presence of a signal. This effect is difficult to classify in terms of efficiency. Instead it is illustrative of the more fundamental changes which stress research should perhaps be looking for. This same change in the decision mechanism may, as Broadbent points out, give rise to *either* of the observed effects on detection rates, depending on its suitability for the particular task being carried out. This is a point of view that runs through the whole of this chapter, though I will not dwell on it at this stage. Using the same signal detection approach it should be said that some apparently straightforward effects have also been observed. Wilkinson (1968) showed that stimulus sensitivity (d') was reduced by partial sleep deprivation, when subjects were restricted to two hours sleep or less, while Colquhoun and Goldman (1968) found increases in both detection and false alarms reduction of the criterion measure (β) in subjects working in a high temperature. These effects again tell us more than we could learn from a study of detections alone, and enable us to make statements of greater importance than those concerned with whether performance is worse or not.

Despite the sensitivity to stress effects, vigilance has tended to give rise to performance changes which are rather difficult to interpret. Although the signal detection methodology is now the more widely used approach in the study of vigilance, it has not been used systematically in stress research, so that findings are rather inconsistent. A more clear-cut set of findings is available from studies using serial choice reaction tasks. We will consider this evidence next.

(ii) Continuous Serial Reaction

The five-choice serial reaction task was developed by Leonard (1959) explicitly to provide a sensitive vehicle for examining stress effects. In this task a new stimulus appears as soon as a correct response is made to the present one, and the subject is required to work as quickly as possible over a 30 minute session. Performance under normal conditions shows three types of effect over the duration of the session: (1) no change in the mean work rate, (2) an increase in errors (making the wrong response) and (3) an increase in the number of very long response times, called 'gaps', 'lapses', or 'blocks' (this last term was used by Bills (1931) in an early series of experiments on prolonged serial responding). Loud noise (typically continuous broad-band noise at 100 dBA was shown to produce an increase in errors (Broadbent, 1953), especially towards the end of the session, though rate of work was not affected. Essentially the same finding was obtained in other studies by Broadbent (1957a) and Wilkinson (1963). In one experiment (Corcoran, 1962) the effect of noise was to increase the number of slow responses, again progressively over time, without affecting errors. It has been suggested (Broadbent, 1963) that this may be the result of a trade-off between gaps and errors as the subject becomes more practised, though Corcoran's result is unusual in this respect.

If we compare these findings with those from manipulations of other stresses an interesting pattern emerges. The effect of sleep loss (usually one night without sleep) is also progressive over the task duration, but is more widespread. Rate of work is reduced and the number of long response times is increased, though, when considered as a proportion of the total responses made, no increase in errors is found (Corcoran, 1962; Wilkinson, 1959; 1963). Thus both these stressors impair performance, but do so only after some considerable time at work. Whereas noise tends to induce a higher error rate, sleep loss results in a rather general slowing down of all responses. The pattern of impairment with heat (an increase in ambient temperature) is different from either of these (Pepler, 1959), primarily showing an increase in errors, but throughout the session, rather than only towards the end.

All these results show that performance is impaired by mild stress, though the precise nature of the impairment depends on which stress is employed. Do all these stressors therefore affect the same general function? One way of answering this question is to examine the effects of combined stress conditions. Two variables affecting the same underlying mechanism should give rise to an interaction, whereas two variables affecting different mechanisms would not. This approach to understanding effects of environmental stress has produced some interesting and somewhat surprising results.

As we have seen, both sleep loss and noise adversely affect serial performance. When the two stressors are applied at the same time, however, the effects appear to 'cancel each other out'. Corcoran (1962) found that noise actually reduced the number of gaps in sleep-deprived subjects, while Wilkinson (1963) found the same effect but on errors. The latter result (shown in Figure 5.2a) is a clear example of a crossover interaction, in which the direction of the effect of noise is opposite at the two levels of sleep loss. The same pattern has also been observed in the case of the combination of sleep loss and incentives (or knowledge of results). This latter treatment, while not strictly a stress, has been used to increase motivation and implicit competition between subjects taking the form of a posting of daily performance results: it therefore may be thought of as a stressor in connection with the work we are discussing. Normally all measures of performance are improved by incentives (Wilkinson, 1961). Wilkinson also showed that this variable was capable of almost completely abolishing the pronounced effects of loss of sleep on the task (Figure 5.2b). Interestingly, the effects of incentive were seen to wear off somewhat after subjects had been working on the task two days a week for six weeks. As Wilkinson argues, this cannot be due to a progressive sleep deficit, since subjects lost only one night's sleep each week. Instead, as he suggests, it points to the importance of task novelty, or loss of it in this case, in preserving the goals of the situation. This is a problem, of course, for all laboratory work on stress, where the task is at first novel, and interesting, then becomes familiar and unimportant. This makes it difficult to readily extrapolate findings such as these to everyday situations such as driving or factory work, where task incentives may be assumed to remain fairly constant and relatively high.

These two findings give rise to the conclusion that sleep loss may be effectively counteracted, at least in the short term, by both noise and incentives. Are they therefore equivalent in their effects on performance? After all, noise normally produces worse performance while incentives produce a general improvement. Wilkinson (1963) found that these two stressors did, in fact, interact, and in a rather surprising way. Performance under the noise condition was actually impaired by the addition of an incentive to perform well,

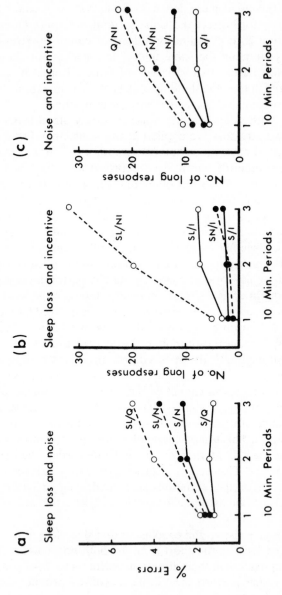

FIGURE 5.2. Evidence for stress interactions on the five-choice task. Abbreviations used in the figure are: S = normal sleep, SL = sleep loss, Q = quiet, N = noise, I = incentive, NI = no incentive. (Redrawn from Wilkinson, 1963 (a, c), and Wilkinson, 1961 (b)) (Copyright 1961 and 1963 by the American Psychological Association. Reprinted by permission)

whereas this variable had its usual facilitatory effect on performance in the control condition (Figure 5.2c).

These results have been interpreted as requiring an explanation based on the inverted-U arousal postulate. Arousal is thought to be related to performance in a curvilinear manner, with arousal level being affected by stress. One difficulty is where to place the stress conditions on the abscissa: all that can be inferred from the stress interactions is that noise and incentives appear to act in the same direction, and opposite to that of sleep loss. Independent evidence suggests that noise produces an increase in activation (Helper, 1957; Berlyne and Lewis, 1963) while sleep loss reduces it (Williams, Lubin, and Goodnow, 1959; Corcoran, 1964). This leads to what seems the most likely arrangement of conditions with incentives being treated as arousing in line with their general motivating effect. This argument is probably current, as far as it goes, although Malmo and Surwillo (1959) found evidence of raised autonomic activity in sleep-deprived subjects. This result is atypical, and almost certainly occurred only because subjects received a painful forehead burn if they did not remain upright and alert. Under normal relaxed conditions, such as those employed by Corcoran, reduced autonomic activity is the rule. The Malmo and Surwillo finding is nevertheless of interest, and fits in well with Wilkinson's (1962) observation that the subjects who best resisted the effects of sleep loss were those who showed the greatest muscle tension. Some mechanism of resistance to stress is implicated here, and we shall return to it in our discussion of the nature of arousal effects later.

To return to the data from the stress interaction studies, we can easily see how the results of the stress interactions may be accommodated within the arousal framework. Sleep loss impairs efficiency by reducing the level of arousal below that which is required by the task; incentive increases arousal level from a point somewhat below the optimal level to the optimum; while noise decreases efficiency by producing too high an arousal level in the subject. Indeed, this analysis seems to be the only way in which these rather complicated findings can be readily accounted for. It is worth mentioning that heat, the other stress examined in these studies, does not interact with any of the three variables included here (Poulton, 1966; Broadbent, 1971), supporting the implication that it is affecting a separate mechanism to the one assumed to underly the above effects.

This is as far as a theoretical analysis of stress effects can go without considering the underlying cognitive processes involved in continuous work. Although it is, in many ways, a valuable chapter in the problem of understanding stress effects, we shall see in later sections the importance of looking more deeply into these underlying processes. Before doing so, however, I shall review briefly research in the area of arousal and memory. Some of these latter issues become more readily discernible in this context.

3. MEMORY AND LEARNING

Whereas the research on environmental stress and sustained attention which we discussed in section 2 is in some ways a model of systematic investigation, making extensive use of convergent operations, the literature which has grown up around work on arousal effects in memory is rather fragmentary. The major reason for this, I think, is the seemingly arbitrary use of the various memory paradigms, as if any test of retention would do. In recent years the approach has become rather more systematic, and some interesting patterns are beginning to emerge. This body of work differs in other ways from the sustained-attention literature. Tests are usually much briefer, levels of stress lower, and the kinds of stress variables used rather different. The clearest link between the two areas concerns effects of noise. This stress has been possibly the one most extensively studied in both fields, and we shall examine this data more closely in order to compare the two sets of findings. The most interesting aspect of work on memory is that effects of stress are observed *at all*, considering that sustained-attention tasks tend to be relatively resistant to these changes until subjects have been working for some time. We shall consider reasons for this later, and offer some suggestions for the relationship between the two areas, using noise as our main link. First, let us examine what has been found in this field.

(i) Survey of Principal Findings

The most generally agreed finding is that higher states of arousal are associated with better long-term recall than low states of arousal. Related to this is a set of data which shows the opposite kind of effect in short-term recall, though this result is by no means as robust, and seems to depend very much on the circumstances of testing. It should perhaps be pointed out that, in the main, the use of 'short-term' in this context refers to presentation-test intervals of up to 20 or 30 minutes, unlike current usage in memory paradigms, where it tends to refer to items still in working memory, that is in current awareness.

The key demonstration of work in this field is that of Kleinsmith and Kaplan (1963) at the University of Michigan. They presented subjects with an eight-item paired associate (P-A) task, with 'emotional' words, of varying degree, such as rape or exam, as the stimuli and digits as the responses. Arousal was inferred from GSR responses to the presentation of each of the words during the task. Each subject's data was sorted into the three items associated with the highest GSR and the three lowest, ignoring the middle two items. Their results, shown in Figure 5.3, indicate the dramatic cross-over interaction between autonomic arousal level and time of testing recall. Responses to low arousal items are best retrieved in immediate tests, then

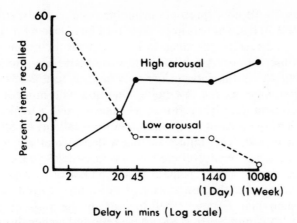

FIGURE 5.3. Interaction between the effects of delay of testing and the arousal value of items. (Redrawn from Kleinsmith and Kaplan, 1963) (Copyright 1963 by the American Psychological Association. Reprinted by permission)

become progressively less accessible. High arousal items, on the other hand, are not only better recalled at longer delays than low arousal items, but actually show a reminiscence effect (i.e. they are recalled better after a delay.

The general pattern of these data has been replicated in a number of studies also carried out in Michigan (e.g. Walker and Tarte, 1963, Kleinsmith and Kaplan, 1963), although the more usual observation is that long-term recall is only *relatively* better for high arousal items. While these findings are not strictly relevant to the question of how memory is affected by stress *per se*, they are clearly related to the more general problem of the role of activation in memory. The distinction between naturally occurring arousal increments produced by particular stimuli and increases in arousal produced by externally applied stressors is pointed out by Craik and Blankstein (1975) in their review of this work. Generally speaking, the same kinds of effects are observed with both types of manipulation, with one or two exceptions. As it is necessary to be somewhat selective in reviewing this evidence I shall concentrate on those studies in which stress has been externally applied in order to produce a shift in arousal level: Craik and Blankstein (1975) provide an excellent summary of research on arousal increments but this literature is strangely bereft of experiments which have examined *downward* shifts in activation. Some recent studies of this kind will be referred to later.

As usual, noise has been the most widely used treatment for increasing arousal in these studies. Berlyne, Borsa, Craw, Gelman and Mandell (1965) found improved delayed recall of responses in a P-A task (24 hours after learning) with 75 dB noise present during the training trials, compared with levels of 35 and 50 dB, whereas immediate recall was worse for the high noise level condition, a result very much in keeping with the original Kleinsmith and Kaplan observations. A similar result was obtained by McClean (1969), although in this case the interaction with time of test was due largely to superior performance in the low noise condition with immediate recall. A further experiment (Berlyne, Borsa, Hamacher and Koenig, 1966) also found a facilitatory effect of noise on long-term recall but no effect on recall in an immediate test. This failure to find a detrimental effect of noise on immediate recall has been observed in several studies (e.g. Farley, 1969; Haveman and Farley, 1969), while a small number of studies also report a failure to demonstrate the superiority of noise for delayed recall (Farley, 1969; Haveman and Farley, 1969 (except in the case of free recall); McClean, 1969). A number of studies have reported higher short-term memory performance at low points in the diurnal rhythm, early in the waking day, for example (Blake, 1967; Baddeley, Hatter, Scott and Shashall, 1970; Hockey, Davies and Gray, 1972), whereas retrieval from long-term memory seems better for material later in the day (Folkard, Monk, Bradbury and Rosenthal, 1977). This pattern of results is clearly consistent with the Kleinsmith and Kaplan findings, if arousal is assumed to be increasing throughout the day (Colquhoun, 1971).

In general it is fair to say that the observed interaction of *relatively* better delayed recall for higher levels of arousal is a reliable finding, and that, independently, delayed recall is normally better for material learned during these states. Immediate memory does, however, appear to depend on a number of other factors. Amongst these are the type of test used (i.e. the type of storage required, whether items of associations between items), and the precise time of the immediate test. Current memory theory makes a quite clear distinction between memory for very recent events (still held in primary memory) and those which were presented some minutes before. The way in which arousal is manipulated in the study is also likely to be of some relevance. Impairment in immediate tests with high arousal has been more commonly observed with naturally occurring changes in phasic arousal such as diurnal rhythm and GSR measures, although the relationship between these various kinds of arousal is still unclear.

(ii) Theoretical Problems of Memory and Arousal

Effects such as these nevertheless point to some fairly consistent effect of arousal upon memory, whether the changes in arousal are the result of natural variations in the effect of stimulus material or whether they occur as a result of some environmental manipulation. Before looking at a number of complications in this body of data, we should perhaps consider the ways in which these findings have been interpreted. The theory that has tended to guide research on arousal and memory is that based on Walker's (1958) action decrement hypothesis. This hypothasis makes considerable use of Hebb's (1949) concept of reverberating circuits, and suggests that memory is laid down gradually as a permanent trace by a process of consolidation. High arousal during learning is regarded as producing a more active consolidation process, and hence, leading to a stronger memory trace, which would account for the normally better retention of high arousal items after long delays. The inhibition of immediate recall in the Michigan studies is explained by reference to the postulated inhibition of retrieval of the trace during consolidation: the more active the trace, the more difficult is immediate recall.

A number of arguments may be levelled against the usefulness of this theory. Firstly, the idea of consolidation as a slow progressive change in neural tissue is questionable in terms of modern work on retrograde amnesia (e.g. Miller and Springer, 1974), though the conclusion that some kind of change takes place over time is, of course, inescapable (Chorover, 1976). In the absence of a strong body of systematic knowledge concerning the physiology of memory, a more serious objection is the fact that a number of behavioural results argue quite strongly against the generality of Walker's theory. It is known from free recall studies that the more an item is rehearsed the more likely it is to be recalled at a later time (Glanzer and Cunitz, 1966; Rundus, 1971). This should imply that rehearsal has the effect of increasing consolidation, and that immediate recall of rehearsed items should be poor. Of course, this is not the case. A number of studies have also found no effect on long-term recall of arousal-inducing treatments applied *after* presentation of the material to be learned (e.g. Berlyne *et al.*, 1969). If, as Walker (1958) argues, the effect of arousal on the consolidation process is non-specific, this increase in stimulation level after presentation should result in the same kind of effect as that found with high arousal during learning.

A further argument against this explanation is provided by the modified P-A study carried out by Hamilton, Hockey and Quinn (1972). In the normal use of this paradigm the order of stimuli is changed from one learning trial to the next, so that intra-pair associations do not become confounded with those between successive pairs of items in the list. Using this arrangement they did find a decrease in initial learning with 85 dBC as opposed to 55 dBC white noise (though not a significant one), but when the order of items was kept constant from study to test trials noise produced much *better* learning. The interaction between noise conditions and list order is illustrated in Figure 5.4, and can be seen to persist for at least the two test trials used in the study. Since the effect of noise depends so critically on whether order information between successive pairs of items is a relevant cue or not, the idea that it impairs short-term recall through its consolidation effect must be rejected. Instead, these data must imply that noise increases the use made of sequential or

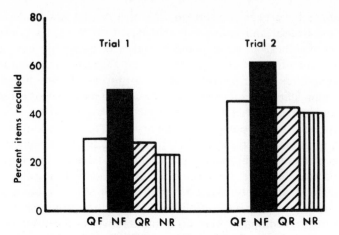

FIGURE 5.4. Paired associate recall as a function of presentation conditions and noise. Abbreviations used in the figure
are: QF = quiet/fixed, NF = noise/fixed, QR = quiet/ran-
dom, NR = noise/random. The data for two test trials are
shown. (From Hamilton, Hockey, and Quinn, 1972)

positional information present in the task. When this is useful, as in the fixed
order case, learning is enhanced; however, if the order of pairs is constantly
changed, such information will actually be likely to interfere with learning by
producing competing responses.

It is not possible, of course, to extrapolate from this result to account for
the Kleinsmith and Kaplan findings, since the effects of arousal produced by a
stimulus word must presumably last for a fairly brief time (otherwise the low
arousal associations in the list would also be affected by increased consolidation), unlike the sustained increase in noise-induced arousal. A fixed versus
random order comparison of this type would certainly be interesting in the
Kleinsmith and Kaplan paradigm, and may throw some light on the distinction between the effects of different kinds of arousal. In conclusion, at least, it
seems clear that the consolidation view cannot be applied generally to results
of arousal–time interactions, though it is still possible that it has some role in
the storage process. Instead, most of the phenomena we have looked at may
be accounted for, I think, by the simple assumption that an arousing stimulus,
or an increase in the tonic level of arousal, is associated with greater attention
at the time of presentation. This would certainly result in stronger registration
and make items more resistant to decay or interference over time. As I have
indicated, effects on immediate recall are ambiguous. If our observations on
order effects are substantiated, it could be argued that increased arousal
results in greater attention not only to items to be remembered but also to
implicit associations within the sequence, such as those provided by the order-

ing of material. This is not entirely *post hoc*; order information is recognized to be an important factor in any learning situation where material is presented in sequence, especially where verbal information is concerned. The P-A task may be seen, in this context, as being atypical in that subjects are required to suppress information about the sequence of inputs, except for the relation between stimulus–response pairs. Poor immediate recall with high arousal may result from this conflict between what is learned and what is required by the test of retention.

The fact that subjects readily make use of this additional information, given the opportunity to do so, is illustrated by the fact that learning can be seen to be much better for both noise and quiet in the fixed order condition of the Hamilton *et al.* study (see Figure 5.4). Some support for this general idea comes from other studies. Dornic (1973) found that immediate serial recall was as good in a number of stress conditions as in the control conditions; the overall impairment in performance with stress was entirely due to a drop in the number of items recalled out of order. Schwartz (1947a; b) has extended these findings to show that effects of high arousal are more serious for the retention of material which does not strongly depend on serial order. Again using noise, he found impairment for the recall of normal sentences (containing much semantic information) but little effect on strings of unconnected words. In a second experiment he found that noise improved the recall of phonemically related lists, but had no effect on words which were semantically related. The implication from these studies is that high arousal (at least in the form of loud noise) biases the system more towards relatively low level processing, based on physical properties of the input, including its sequential pattern, along the lines of Craik and Lockhart's (1972) maintenance rehearsal suggestion. The material is kept more strongly in the form in which it is presented. This would explain why high arousal does not always lead to impairment in immediate recall: only in traditional P-A tasks is this result usually obtained. Where recall of unrelated single words is required as in serial or free recall tasks performance is often improved by high arousal (see Craik and Blankstein, 1975; Eysenck, 1976; for a further discussion of this evidence).

There still remains the problem of long-term recall, which is normally considered to depend more strongly on semantic information: we might, therefore, expect this to be actually worse for items learned under high arousal, rather than better. In fact, most of the tests of long-term memory employed in this field have not relied much on semantic features of the stimulus. Several studies have shown a reduction in semantic clustering with high arousal (Hörmann and Osterkamp, 1966; Daee and Wilding, 1977), implying that tests of semantic retrieval would show such an impairment. A direct test of this in our laboratory, using 85 dBA noise as the arousal agent, and 55 dBA as the control condition shows that this is indeed the case. Subjects were asked to read a factual passage from a science fiction story, then carry out an immediate recall test, followed by a comprehension test after a 10 minute distractor task. Immediate recall (scored in terms of names used in the passage) was better in noise, but comprehension (answering questions about the story) was worse. The overall picture from these studies is that high arousal results in a stronger ordering and verbatim storage of presented material, but one which is less readily accessible in other ways: the learning may be thought of as being in some ways stronger, but less flexible.

A question, which I have not considered, is whether memory, like sustained attention, appears to be explained by the Yerkes–Dodson law. As we shall see later this is not such a straightforward a question as it looks. It is certainly true that some studies, using more than two levels of arousal, have found evidence of optimal levels for the effect of noise intensity (Berlyne *et al.*, 1965; Daee and Wilding, 1977) or, tonic levels of skin conductance (Berry, 1962; Levonian, 1968) on immediate recall, though there appear to be no interaction studies of the type found in the sustained attention literature. In its traditionally stated form the Yerkes–Dodson law is, I believe, a misrepresentation of the way in which stress or arousal affect skilled performance. Part of the difficulty concerns the nature of the assumed arousal process and part is a consequence of the methodology of performance measurement. Let me now turn my attention to some of the more general theoretical problems in this area.

4. ALTERNATIVE VIEWS OF AROUSAL

The traditional view that arousal is a unitary, non-specific process has been assumed by most of the research we have looked at in the previous two sections. In its effects on skilled performance it has tended to be thought of as a kind of 'volume control', simply changing the gain on all operations currently in use. The most obvious alternative to this is that some degree of selectivity is involved, i.e. that changes in activation are associated with a process analogous to 'tuning'. While the first theory postulates a general increase in the 'energy' of all responses, the second may be regarded as a 'constant energy' theory, where the relative likelihood of different responses is changed.

(i) Directional Effects of Arousal

An influential example of the selectivity theory is that put forward by Easterbrook (1959), in a discussion of the effects of emotional arousal on behavioural organization. For many years, theorists have argued whether emotion has an organizing or disorganizing effect on behaviour. Easterbrook illustrates that this conflict is, at least in part, a consequence of the different tasks used in these studies, simpler tasks being more likely to benefit from stress than more complex ones. He put forward the hypothesis that emotional arousal has the effect of progressively restricting the use of cues in the task environment, irrespective of the requirements of the task itself. This has the effect of facilitating performance on simple tasks by the exclusion of irrelevant cues, though the same change may lead to disruption of more complex, multiple-cue operations. While it is true to say that this hypothesis has not been adequately tested in any direct manner, it provides an account of the effects of activation which are *independent* of performance on the task. This feature is missing from most arousal studies, where arousal effects are inferred from changes in the dependent variable—a circular argument. It provides one answer to the question 'What underlies the Yerkes–Dodson law?', by suggesting a directional change in the degree of selectivity of attention as activation is increased (narrow attention) or decreased (broad attention).

I shall consider evidence for this point of view in the next section, though it is intuitively satisfying for at least one important reason. From the stress interaction studies examined in section 2 we have seen how, for example, noise and loss of sleep were assumed to have opposite effects on arousal. Yet, in those studies, it was not possible to observe these opposing influences directly in terms of changes in the dependent variable. Implicit in the reasoning behind this work was a belief that under-arousal and over-arousal effects were, in some way, equivalent. In fact, as we have seen, a close examination of the performance patterns shows that the changes are not symmetrical. Impairment with noise stress tends to take the form of an increase in errors, or a drop in visual detections made with low confidence; loss of sleep, on the other hand, produces slower responding, more gaps, and a marked overall reduction in stimulus sensitivity in vigilance tasks. Why, then, should the one set of effects cancel out the other? Clearly, we can only answer this by knowing the underlying changes which mediate between stress and its observed effects in performance.

This is particularly true of effects of over-arousal, which do not appear to make sense in terms of what is known about CNS activation. While we can readily appreciate the profound effects of a general reduction in the level of brain stimulation (resulting in sleep in the extreme case, and sluggish, uncontrolled responding in states close to sleep), it is by no means clear why very high levels of stimulation should be undesirable. The concept over-arousal, by itself, means nothing of course: implicit in its use is an observation of degradation in performance. As we have seen, the same level of assumed activation may or may not produce such a change in performance. Thus when Easterbrook suggests that the effects of arousal 'depend on the task' he is not avoiding the issue, but pointing us towards an analysis of these effects in terms of this important and largely neglected independent variable. I will deal with this issue in some detail in section 5, since I think we can now say *how* it depends on the task. For the moment I would like to suggest that an analysis of stress effects needs to address itself to a study of this intervening state. What does stress actually do to the mechanism that governs the control of attention and memory?

A somewhat different point of view, but one which also suggests that stress may alter the direction of behaviour, is that of Näätänen (1975). He argues for a monotonic relationship between stress and efficiency, with the drop in performance above the 'optimal' level of activation resulting, indirectly, from a reduction in attention to the task. This may result from distraction brought about by the attention demands of the activation procedure (in the case of dynamometer-induced muscle tension, for example), or from induced anxiety or other cognitive reactions to the stress. The central point of Näätänen's argument is that activation is best considered not as a quantitative variable (as a 'level') but as a patterning of the physiological state. He goes further by suggesting that it is the appropriateness of this patterning with respect to the task in question which is the important determinant of behavioural efficiency. In the case of attempts to increase activation level, the secondary reactions mentioned above are regarded as providing competing patterns of activation to those required for task performance. This point of view is very similar in orientation to our own (Hamilton, Hockey and Rejman, 1977); there are now, I think, sound empirical pointers to a qualitative view of activation effects, and we shall examine these in the next section. It is not necessary to go along with Näätänen in believing that the inverted U is an artifact of activation manipulations however. Some form of directional change in behaviour may well result *directly* from the change in activation state—as a shift in the balance of the operations which are dominant in current information processing, rather than being a product of competing behavioural tendencies.

(ii) Autonomic Patterns of Task Orientation

In the preceding few pages, I have looked at alternatives to the assumption that arousal is a non-specific process. We have seen that there are grounds for believing that its effect on behaviour may be directional, though whether this is a direct effect of activation or a by-product of these more general effects is a point for further discussion. Before considering recent evidence on this let us examine the second assumption of activation theorists, that the process is a unitary one. This has been questioned, in particular, by Lacey (1967), on the basis of two kinds of evidence. Firstly there is often considerable dissociation between indices of behavioural, autonomic, and cortical arousal, although these different forms of activation are often regarded as equivalent dependent variables. Secondly, poor correlations are sometimes observed between different indices of the same kind of activation, notably measures of autonomic activity. If an individual is assumed to be in an aroused state a general pattern of sympathetic dominance should be observed across measures of heart rate, skin conductance, pupil dilation, and so on.

In practice, conditions assumed to increase activation are usually associated with some evidence of autonomic activity, particularly in the case of the three variables mentioned above, although correlations between the autonomic indices are generally modest. Lacey (1959, 1967) demonstrated, however, that different patterns are observed in different situuations. When subjects are required to manipulate information, as in mental arithmetic or reasoning, all these measures tend to show increased levels of activity. If, on the other hand, they are asked to attend to an external source of information a pattern of *directional fractionation* is found, heart rate undergoing deceleration while other measures continue to show autonomic dominance. This effect, which Lacey calls 'situational stereotypy', had previously been observed by Darrow (1929) and by Davis (1957), and has been substantiated by numerous studies since. Lacey suggested that the normal sympathetic dominance pattern occurs in situations where the individual attempts to resist stimulation, either because it is stressful or because it interferes with cognitive processing. The fractionation pattern, on the other hand, is seen as an indication of acceptance of external stimulation, as in most attention situations. He further argues that the heart rate deceleration has a causal role in maintaining attention to the environment, though this has not generally received much support from other work in cardiovascular physiology, and has more usually been regarded as an effect of efforts to meet specific task demands (Kahneman, 1973). This external receptiveness is particularly evident in the foreperiod of a reaction time experiment, where the heart rate deceleration is accompanied by a marked reduction in motor activity and steady gaze (e.g. Obrist, Webb and Sutterer, 1969), inhibition of microsaccades (Findlay, personal communication), and generally increased orienting behaviour. As Kahneman (1973) points out, this kind of pattern is probably very adaptive in such a situation in that irrelevant bodily activity is reduced to a minimum. Some evidence that the motor inhibition pattern and that of cardiac deceleration may themselves be dissociated comes from a study by Elliott (1969) of the Stroop colour-word conflict test. Even though subjects are verbalizing throughout and there is considerable evidence of motor activity the heart rate deceleration is still observed. Elliott argues that it is the *attempt* by the subject to inhibit the conflicting responses in this task which is responsible for the pattern.

Essentially what these findings tell us is that it is possible to distinguish two states of high activation (or, more correctly, alertness). An individual is highly alert both in waiting to receive a signal to be reacted to quickly, and in multiplying together 28 and 37 in his head. Yet, heart rate changes consistently in opposite directions in the two situations. Kahneman suggests that a third pattern of motor inhibition may be differentiated as accompanying active rather than passive attention to the environment, though there is no clear evidence on this. It is not possible to discuss these observations in more detail within the present framework. They show that we must distinguish between different states of activation, rather than simply different levels. Although we are in no position to suggest how or why these patterns are functionally related to the organization of cognitive requirements, it is clear that they are reflecting quite different strategies on the part of the subject to marshall the resources at his disposal. These conclusions dovetail quite neatly with our observations on selectivity changes and the appropriateness of patterning mentioned by Näätänen. There is still a case, I believe, for speaking of levels of activation (in terms of the degree of sympathetic dominance observed, for example, in conductance or pupil measures). This is particularly important in the distinction between states of rest and action. Once the individual is awake and working at a task these more subtle changes are more likely to give us an insight into the ongoing processes. Such changes could be considered to be manifestations of the subject's attempts to direct his cognitive resources effectively, rather than indicators of his basic physiological state. This distinction between the static and dynamic aspects of arousal is usually ignored in favour of more extreme positions. In the present state of evidence both, I think, are important.

5. PATTERNS OF PERFORMANCE UNDER STRESS

Easterbrook's (1959) observations that emotional arousal may be regarded as leading to a decrease in the range of peripheral cues attended to may be generalized to include effects of external stressors such as noise and sleep deprivation and 'life-threat' situations, such as deep-sea diving or parachuting. An early example of this kind of effect is found in the Cambridge Cockpit experiments (Davis, 1948). Prolonged work at the control panel of a simulated flight deck was found to result in selective impairment of responses to spatially peripheral parts of the display, rather than a simple overall degradation in skill. A similar effect was observed by Broadbent (1954) in his 20 dials task. Here, 100 dBA noise did not produce an overall effect in performance, but a selective impairment of detection to centrally located dials. As we saw earlier the effects of fatigue brought about by prolonged work may be rather different to those of situational stressors, though they may have some mechanism in common. More recent evidence of this type of change in performance comes from work using dual-task situations, in which the subject is required to carry out two simultaneous tasks with instructions about what priority to give each component. I will examine the evidence from these studies, then go on to consider results from other experiments, which suggest that these effects are only part of a complex pattern of cognitive changes which occur under stress.

(i) Arousal and Selectivity

Research on this topic is reported in detail elsewhere (Hockey, 1970a; b; c; Hamilton and Copeman, 1970), but a summary of the findings will be useful at this point. The advantage of using a task with a priority structure is that the direction of attention is fixed under all conditions. It is not clear in the Davis (1948) task, for example, whether the observed change with fatigue may be regarded as a narrowing of attention towards important parts of the display or a functional 'shrinkage' of the visual field: in the Broadbent (1954) study, in any case, the impairment with noise is on central locations. Bursill (1958) used a task in which subjects were required to carry out a primary pursuit tracking task and to detect occasional visual signals presented on lamps arranged in a semicircular display around the tracking task. He found that an increase in ambient temperature produced an impairment on the secondary detection task without affecting tracking performance. He argued that this effect was not one of visual restriction but central in origin, since an easier tracking task produced no impairment of secondary task performance. Of course, it could be argued that greater peripheral scanning is possible in the latter case, though there is no data on eye movements, for example, to provide any evidence on this. The task has been used by us in a number of studies (Hockey, 1970a; b; c; Hamilton and Copeman, 1970) and provides general support for the idea that changes in performance with stress are characterized by *selective*, rather than general deterioration.

Noise (100 dBA) is seen to actually improve tracking performance (time on target) over the forty minute task, compared to a control condition of 70 dBA, and to reduce the number of visual signals detected from the four most peripheral lamps only. This effect is dependent on the subject being aware of a clear difference in the probability of signals occurring in central and peripheral locations, supporting the idea that noise is affecting some attentional strategy based on relative priorities or utilities of different actions. It is clearly sensible to pay more attention to sources which are more likely to provide information: this strategy is exaggerated in loud noise. An experiment by Bacon (1974) confirms this interpretation in the case of threat or shock. The activity which suffers most from stress is the one which is given less attentional priority by instructions, and is carried out less efficiently. A further experiment (Hockey, 1970c), using one night's loss of sleep as the stressor, found effects which were essentially opposite to these. While, in this case, impairment was evident over the task as a whole, it was most pronounced on the tracking component, and least on the detection of peripheral signals. This does not mean, of course, that sleep loss makes attention *better* for low priority activities (either in comparison to normal sleep, or with respect to high priority behaviour), but it does suggest that loss of sleep results in a 'levelling' of allocation priorities, such that a sleepy man is unable to give important activities the special attention they require. This kind of allocation policy, to use Kahneman's (1973) term, is inappropriate to the dual-task situation, since it fails to take advantage of the built-in structure of the task, and also makes less use of relevant stored information about goals: in short it makes insufficient use of long-term attentional skills.

These differences can be seen more directly in an observing response situation. Here, the subject presses one of three buttons in order to observe whether the relevant display contains a fault (i.e. flashes briefly). Hamilton (1969) showed that subjects would only sample the display in relation to the probability of finding faults on different sources when they were paced, and when the rate of fault occurrence was high. In other words, checking a source is only important when you are likely to find a fault upon making an observing response. Otherwise, it is simpler to use a fixed sampling order, rather than having to decide which source to look at next. Hockey (1973) showed that noise increased this tendency to sample the high probability source, while loss of sleep produced the opposite effect, resulting in almost unselective observing of the three sources. These data show direct evidence of changes in the pattern of attention with stress, through its effect on responses involved in information selection. The overall picture from both sets of studies is consistent. The selectivity of attention is increased by noise and decreased by sleep loss.

This kind of pattern fits in well, of course, with Easterbrook's observations on emotional arousal, though it suggests a more specific form for the relationship in terms of attentional sampling If noise is regarded as increasing arousal and sleep loss as decreasing it, as was suggested in section 2, then what emerges is a monotonic relation between degree of arousal and level of selectivity. Note that this is *not* an inverted-U function, although it *can* give rise to a relation such as the Yerkes–Dodson law and I shall discuss this possibility in broader terms later. More general support for these interpretations comes from a number of other studies showing attentional changes under stress.Effects similar to those of noise have been observed for induced anxiety (Wachtel, 1968; Bacon, 1974), incentives (Bahrick, Fitts and Rankin, 1952), open sea diving (Weltman and Egstrom, 1966), and other stressors. Baddleley (1972) summarizes much of this literature from the point of view of effects of anxiety induced by perceived danger. Whether all effects of arousing stressors may be considered in this way is not known, though loud noise may certainly be perceived as threatening. This *perception* of stress is probably critical to the effects of an external stressor. Both Wachtel (1968) and Glass and Singer (1972) show that changes in performance are minimized by allowing subjects some degree of 'control' over the situation. In contrast, there have been very few studies of the effects of a *reduction* in stimulation or arousal. In support of the loss of sleep findings, Nakamura and Broen (1965) found that relaxation produced an increase in the proportion of low probability responses made in a two-choice prediction situation, though other apparent forms of low arousal such as fatigue or sensory deprivation do not appear to function in the same way. One problem with low levels of arousal, of course, is that there may be directional differences between states induced by different forms of stress. Loss of sleep may result in a man falling asleep if left alone (this sometimes happens during experiments), while sensory deprivation may make him hyperactive and information seeking (Schultz, 1965): they are not simply both examples of low arousal in any useful sense. Much more work is needed on reduced arousal states, so that the generality of the selectivity/arousal relation may be examined. Unlike high arousal, low arousal is a 'normal' state for approximately a third of each day. It is only stressful if the subject is required to *counteract* this state.

The effects observed in a multiple-source attention task can be shown to operate in other situations such as those involving immediate memory and selective attention. Hockey and Hamilton (1970) presented subjects with a single sequence of eight words on slides and tested immediate recall after a short break. The effect of noise was to marginally improve performance, especially when words were scored correct only if they were in the right position in the sequence. Subjects were then asked to recall in which corner of the slides words appeared (this was a non-salient incidental cue in the presentation). Noise drastically impaired memory for this low priority information. This result has been replicated by Davies and Jones (1975), who also showed that monetary incentives produced the same pattern of change. Andersson and Hockey (1975) have shown that the same effect is found in subjects who have smoked a cigarette. In all cases the arousal-induced selectivity pattern is the same. In another study (Hockey, Dornic and Hamilton, 1975) subjects were asked to read one of two interleaved passages (a version of Neisser's selective reading task suggested by Lindsay and Norman 1972) and were then tested for recognition memory of words from both passages. Although no differences in stimulus sensitivity were found for the unattended passage, noise increased stimulus sensitivity for the passage read. Both these effects may be considered in more specific terms, but they have in common the same increased bias towards dominant aspects of the task. In a rather different context Broadbent and Gregory have found similar effects in tachistoscopic recognition (Broadbent, 1971) in which common words are seen more easily and rare words less easily in noise.

None of the results discussed in this section lead to a conclusion such as 'stress impairs performance'. Instead they point to a qualitative change in the pattern of performance which is more fundamental than the question of efficiency. So far, however, I have suggested that stress affects the selectivity of attention, and that the observed effects on efficiency follow from this. This does not appear to be the whole story. For the rest of this section I will try to sketch the current position with respect to changes in the patterning of performance. What we have tried to do in our research is to build a composite picture of cognition in the noise state, both to serve as a model for looking at other stress states and to provide what we regard as a more useful data base on which to build theories of stress (Hamilton *et al*., 1977).

(ii) The Mapping of a Stress State

One of the most striking patterns to emerge with this approach is a trade-off between two major components of information processing; storage and throughput. In extreme situations involving either immediate recall or speeded classification the subject must attempt to maximize the use of one or the other of these resources. This may be artificial, though, since most real-life tasks involve both components. (I am not suggesting that other processes are not important, but the distinction between these two appears to be a very useful one in our research programme to date.) Effects of this kind have been found for time of day, noise, and sleep loss. As I mentioned in section 3, time of day tends to show an effect on short-term memory rather like the majority of arousal studies: memory is best early in the day (when arousal may be thought to be low) and drops off through the day. On the other hand, tasks such as the five-choice serial reaction test, letter cancellation, and simple additions, all of which require speeded throughput of information, show a steady improvement through the day (Blake, 1967). This dissociation is echoed in other stresses.

We have seen that noise is often associated with poor immediate memory, though the complexity of strategy changes sometimes make these effects difficult to interpret. A clearer demonstration of this is obtained using running memory. In this procedure the subject has to recall only the last few items in a long sequence, and only knows which these are when the list ends. This provides a relatively 'pure' estimate of passive retention, largely uncontaminated by rehearsal strategies. We have found (Hamilton *et al*., 1977) a marked effect of quite a low noise level (80 dB) on this task: the data are illustrated in Figure 5.5. While the last few items are relatively better retrieved in noise, the span is lower. That is, items slightly further back in the sequence (beyond the 4th) are more difficult to remember. While this result may generally be seen as showing a reduction in the use of storage processes in the noise state, the form the data take further illustrates the difficulty of making simple inferences about performance change, even in this relatively 'pure' task. Speeded processing tasks are always performed at least as quickly in noise, and there is some evidence that subjects work faster in noise when the conditions are suitable (Broadbent, 1957b; Hamilton *et al*., 1977), though errors may be increased. Lastly, the trade-off between these two kinds of activities occurs also with sleep deprivation (Hamilton, Wilkinson and Edwards, 1972). Whereas speeded additions are performed more slowly as a

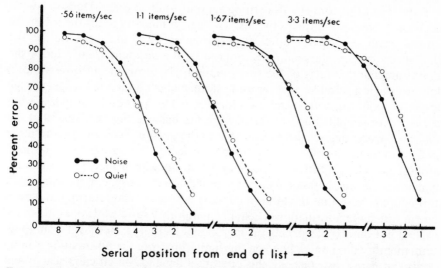

FIGURE 5.5. Running memory as a function of noise level. The abscissa is truncated to allow partial overlapping of data from the four presentation rates used. (From Hamilton, Hockey and Rejman, 1977)

result of a decrease in the number of hours sleep from 7½ to 4 to zero, running memory *improves* steadily with a reduction in sleep. In this case subjects were required to report only the 4th item before the end of the list: loss of sleep enables them to do this more easily.

This last result, in particular, is counter-intuitive, and reinforces the idea that the two kinds of processing are reciprocally related. Fast processing depends on clearing the system quickly of residual input traces, while retention tasks depend on the ability to 'hold' this information, and may be helped in achieving this by a state which is not efficient in 'getting rid' of items quickly: the argument is outlined in more detail by Hamilton *et al.* (1972). The relative contributions of each component to a particular task, on the basis of results such as these, is likely to be critical to the direction in which a stressor affects performance. Two examples, one from a time of day study, and one of our own, may illustrate this. Firstly, Folkard, Knauth, Monk and Rutenfranz (1976) have shown that, whereas a normal visual search task shows a normal peak of performance late in the day, adding a memory requirement to the task progressively shifts the peak towards the early part of the day. Secondly, we have shown that increasing the memory load in a speed transformation task changes the effect of noise from one of clear facilitation to one of clear impairment (Hamilton *et al.*, 1977). In both cases the task is the same, except for an additional requirement to hold a set of items in memory instead of having them available in printed form.

Both results, of course, offer strong support to the Yerkes–Dodson law. In each case, the more difficult the task (with high memory load) the lower the arousal level suitable for efficient performance. Yet, and here we see the limitations of the 'parsimonious' approach, this account clearly hides the more fundamental facts of the two situations. In terms of our observations, low arousal is a suitable state for using storage and a poor one for speed; high arousal is poor for storage and good for speed. The Yerkes–Dodson law is but a gross over-simplification of this shift in the balance of effectiveness of the different processing resources available to the person. Such an interpretation in fact offers a possible way of defining 'difficulty' in relation to the optimal arousal postulate. Difficult tasks may be those with a high memory component, while simple tasks make no demands on memory, emphasizing rapid throughput. Note that the kind of memory resource I am referring to here is one in which the information is held in a temporary store while operations are carried out on it (i.e. working or operational memory). Retrieval from long-term memory does not depend on this limitation since the information is in no danger of being lost. Instead, this operation depends on efficient search and editing, much as visual search or cancellation tasks do. This may explain why high arousal at retrieval may sometimes produce better memory performance in addition to any effects of arousal during the original study period.

Eysenck (1975) has shown that noise facilitates the retrieval of high association items in a probed category recall task and impairs the retrieval of low dominance responses. The result is very similar in character to those found in the studies of attention patterns in monitoring visual displays: in both cases initially dominant activities become even more dominant in noise, while less dominant ones are neglected. A similar effect has also been found in a probability 'guessing' situation, in which subjects must predict which of two lights will come on during each trial (Hamilton et al., 1977). Noise again increases the tendency to select the high probability event, though only when 'irrelevant' outcomes (no light or both lights coming on) are included in the sequence. This is a difficult result to interpret without further evidence, but parallels that found in the observing response task discussed earlier. The potentiation of high probability responses, in both cases, occurs in situations where responses are not always followed by significant events. This may occur because relevant outcomes normally serve to stabilize response probabilities at the level of matching, but the absence of such events leads to greater emphasis being placed on stored information about the statistical properties of the sequence. In this case, as with attention tasks, any existing bias may be exaggerated by noise.

In section 2 I reported the complex pattern of change found in confidence ratings with noise (Broadbent and Gregory, 1965). This showed, in simple terms, an increase in the use of confident responses at the expense of more cautious decisions about the presence of a signal. A similar effect is found in the observing response task in terms of the checking pattern adopted by subjects. Whereas in the control condition a detection of a signal present in the system sometimes follows a second (check) observation on the relevant source, this behaviour is markedly reduced in noise. Subjects either report signals on the first occasion or seem quite sure that no signal was present. Once again, this pattern is reversed in sleep-deprived subjects, who make very few detections without a check.

What, then, are the main features to be represented on our map of noise-induced stress? As a first approximation the following set of characteristics must be considered:

(a) an increase in rate of work, with an increase in errors;
(b) a reduction in primary memory capacity;
(c) an increase in the selectivity of attention;
(d) an increase in the selectivity of response; and
(e) a reduction in the use of intermediate categories of confidence.

These observations are by no means final, and they, themselves, are likely to be altered by further work of a more analytic nature. They do, however, offer a useful baseline for building an adequate theory of stress effects. Although I have focused on noise in these pages, the approach I have suggested may be valuable for the study of any stress state. We have found, in ongoing work, suggestions of a similar dissociation between the effects on separate components of skilled performance of experimental manipulations as different as alcohol hangovers, sleep deprivation, nicotine, menstruation, and fatigue.

The above effects may be quite separate consequences of working in noise, but it seems more likely that they are different manifestations of some fundamental change in the system parameters responsible for the control of behaviour. Broadbent (1978) has concluded that a number of these effects may be seen to have a degree of functional consistency. Thus:

'(through greater selectivity) . . . a more aroused person will select information from a smaller area of the environment. He will therefore pick up less fragmentary and doubtful information outside that area. Consequently he will rarely give qualified and doubtful judgments about, say, visual signals seen in peripheral attention; but will give predominantly confident assertions and denials. This will be good for performance so long as the centre of attention is on the task; early in the work session that will be true most of the time. Any shift away from the task later on, will however give rise to missed signals, or inefficiencies in continuous performance.'

(Broadbent, 1978, p. 1063)

I would add that a person is more likely to work quickly (and so make more errors), since he is ignoring some aspects of the task. The role of the reduced memory capacity, which I have inferred may be primary or secondary in facilitating this speeded, selective operation, is consistent with such a pattern of behaviour, as I have already argued. While such a synthesis is unwarranted on the basis of present evidence it is important, I think, to show that the data are potentially meaningful as a *set*, rather than as separate, unrelated observations. They represent a picture of cognition in the noise state which, we have argued, may be a useful model for stress research as a whole (Hamilton *et al.*, 1977).

6. CONCLUSIONS AND SOME SPECULATIONS

In this sketch of what I see to be the most central findings of work in this area I have proposed an alternative methodology for experimental programmes. The usual research tactic has been to examine the effects of a number of stressors on a single task. This approach has, in many ways, been a productive one, allowing us to make generalizations that are applicable to a range of conditions (assumed to influence arousal in a similar way), rather than to just one. This is as true of the selectivity findings as of earlier work on the five-choice task. The method is, I believe, a sound one, and remains a necessary technique in the systematic study of stress effects. What I wish to propose is that we also adopt an approach of examining the detailed effects of a single stress across a range of tasks. Not only is a broad-band approach such as this valuable both in its own right, and as part of a converging operations methodology, but it produces results which are liable to go unnoticed otherwise. The single-task method will become more useful generally, when it is explicitly realized that performance in different laboratory tasks depends on the use of different processing resources by the subject. This is one reason why the data on sustained-attention tasks and those on memory and learning do not give comparable results, not even on a superficial level of analysis.

What is needed if we are to make progress in this objective, is a realistic functional model of cognitive behaviour, suggesting a closer link with mainstream theory than has been the case in recent years. I am not forgetting, here, that much of the work on sustained attention was quite intimately linked with Broadbent's (1958) theory of information processing. Despite the changes in theoretical views over the past twenty years, much of this work is still valuable for that reason. The memory literature fails in this respect, however, using as its major theoretical basis a view of the relation between short- and long-term memory that was seen to be at best inadequate, and at worst, wrong, even at the time of Kleinsmith and Kaplan's original demonstration. The notable advances in memory theory since that time have had very little influence in this research.

Models of cognition do, of course, exist in plentiful supply, and I believe the information flow type of model still to be the best we have for analysing the different processes involved in human perception and action. What they do not tell us, however, is (a) what the *functionally* significant components of the system are, and (b) how these components are manipulated in the production of a particular behaviour pattern. They have tended to assume a passive, static view of the flow of information through the system, and of the effects of activation which are independent of the processing resources. I do not have an answer to this problem, but there are approaches within the information processing framework which seem promising as a basis for examining the functions of different components, and the ways in which they are affected by changes in bodily state. A clear example of this, is the attempt by Kahneman (1973) to integrate activational and capacity ideas. He shows how arousal may be involved, directly and indirectly, in the deployment of capacity to different activities, in response to the perceived demands of the task. Another approach which comes close to providing this necessary dynamic feature of behaviour is that of Baddeley and Hitch (1974) on the functions of working memory. They ask not only what working memory is like, but what it does as a mental resource. As a last example, Hunt (e.g. Hunt, Luneborg and Lewis, 1975) goes a step further. By identifying the primary processing resources used in mental activity (through a factor analysis of performance in a large range of tasks) he is then able to ask questions about the different use made of these by individuals. This work is important in offering a long-needed information processing analysis for the study of individual differences. One aspect of our current work is based on an approach similar to Hunt's, and indicates clear parallels in the way in which trade-offs in the efficiency of component processes occur between different stress states and different individuals. In both cases some are good with storage and some are not, and the same is true for speeded processing.

This brings me back, full circle, to the distinction between these two processing resources which seems to be important in stress, at least as far as noise is representative of such states. As I said earlier, the distinction is an empirical rather than a theoretical one, and other processes are almost certain to prove at least as important. (An obvious candidate is any process involved in response organization: I have, so far, given little attention to these aspects of skilled behaviour.) Nevertheless, it seems necessary to build into any theory of information processing the kinds of trade-off that appear to occur between functions such as these. This means including stress as an ever-present, central feature of the model, instead of a peripheral, and relatively orthogonal factor. Its importance is that the whole balance of normal functioning may be altered in different states, rather than the level of efficiency simply being uniformly reduced (or augmented). Kahneman (1973) has attempted to do this by placing arousal processes centrally in the control function of the organism, and we have tried to show how state changes (whether brought about by external stress, or by internal operations such as voluntary modulation of alertness) may be implicated in both the enduring and the moment-to-moment control of behaviour (Hamilton et al., 1977). Both these approaches are inadequate, but they are, I believe, a necessary step in the direction of integrating the activational concept into cognitive theory.

One of the most interesting problems in developing such a theory is, I think, the relation between state changes and effort. Kahneman (1973) argues that effort is reflected in the manifestation of arousal that results from the individual's adoption of a particular task set, as a response to the demands of the task on capacity. Without going into the broader implications of Kahneman's viewpoint, we can examine some of the implications of these ideas for the problems raised in this chapter. I have suggested that stress has the effect of shifting the balance of effectiveness of different resources, storage operations being used less optimally, for example, in noise and at later times of the waking day. Quite separately, in my discussion of the theoretical difficulties of arousal, I have indicated the importance of situational stereotypy in the autonomic response to external and internal processing demands.

How, if at all, are these two ideas related? At this stage of our understanding, my guess would be that the tonic changes in state induced by stress result in a *predisposition* towards certain kinds of mental activity. While passive reflective behaviour is difficult when one is emotionally aroused, the experience of increased mental activity is almost universal: thoughts are said to '. . . run through one's head'. Reflective activity, on the other hand, seems all one can manage in states of relaxed tiredness. The change in state may be regarded, then, as setting a limit (though probably a slight one in most cases) on what the individual can do with his mental apparatus. Having said this, however, it is clear that he can be alert to both external and internal events in *either* of these two states. The dramatic effects of incentives on the performance of sleep-deprived subjects (Wilkinson, 1961) is good evidence of the flexibility of the system. The effort involved in meeting these task demands is reflected in the pattern of autonomic activity seen in the situation, which may override any tonic effects of state on autonomic parameters. Under these conditions, the sleepy man may therefore look *more*, rather than less, aroused.

While the two concepts do, therefore, refer to different aspects of the way in which the individual is able to meet the demands of the environment, a possible consequence of this point of view is that we should find asymmetric patterns of situational stereotypy in different stress states. We would expect to observe heart rate acceleration and sympathetic dominance in internal processing tasks more readily in noise, for example, than in a state of sleep deprivation. The system may require less effort to meet these demands in noise, since they are congruent with the basal mode of operation. The fractionation pattern, conversely, may be more difficult to achieve in such 'fast processing' states. The mapping of the two distinctions is not as direct as this, of course, but some such prediction does seem to follow from the views I have expressed. This seems a promising line of research for future work, especially since it emphasizes the analysis of moment-to-moment changes in performance and physiological state. The effects of stress may then be seen in their true perspective as an integral part of the information processing system.

I have tried in the preceding pages to present a personal view of the current state of stress research, as it applies to the area of skilled performance. I hope that this view is not unduly biased towards my own dominant interests, even though the act of writing is often a somewhat stressful one in my experience, and may, therefore, be subject to the same kinds of distortion that are found in the performance of laboratory tasks. In this case, of course, such effects ought to be compensated for by an awareness of their existence and the application of well-learned rules for presenting a 'balanced' point of view. This does, however, raise interesting questions about the kinds of changes I have suggested to occur as a result of exposure to stress. How far can subjects compensate for these effects if they are made aware of them, in driving under the influence of alcohol, for example, or taking part in important political discussions where a lot is at stake? Questions such as these present logical extensions of work on attention and memory into the real-life situation. Our ideas are now sufficiently developed to allow us at least to begin a study of such problems. Unless we do, the net result of all the work I have discussed will be a very pretty theory that doesn't actually help anyone to cope with stress. Above all other considerations this is perhaps the problem that our research should ultimately be focused upon.

7. REFERENCES

Andersson, K. and Hockey, G. R. J. (1975). Effects of cigarette smoking on incidental memory. *University of Stockholm, Department of Psychology Reports*, **455**.

Bacon, S. J. (1974). Arousal and the range of cue utilization. *Journal of Experimental Psychology*, **102**, 81–87.

Baddeley, A. D. (1972). Selective attention and performance in dangerous environments. *British Journal of Psychology*, **63**, 537–546.

Baddeley, A. D. and Hitch, G. J. (1974). Working memory. In G. H. Bower (Ed.), *The Psychology of Learning and Motivation*. Vol. 8, New York: Academic Press.

Bahrick, H. P., Fitts, P. M. and Rankin, R. F. (1952). Effects of incentives upon reactions to peripheral stimuli. *Journal of Experimental Psychology*, **44**, 400–406.

Berlyne, D. E., Borsa, D. M., Craw, M. A. Gelman, R. S. and Mandell, E. E. (1965). Effects of stimulus complexity and induced arousal on paired-associate learning. *Journal of Verbal Learning and Verbal Behavior*, **4**, 291–299.

Berlyne, D. E., Borsa, D. M., Hamacher, J. H. and Koenig, I. D. V. (1966). Paired-associate learning and the timing of arousal. *Journal of Experimental Psychology*, **72**, 1–6.

Berlyne, D. E. and Lewis, J. L. (1963). Effects of heightened arousal on human exploratory behavior. *Canadian Journal of Psychology*, **17**, 398–410.

Berry, R. N. (1962). Skin conductance levels and verbal recall. *Journal of Experimental Psychology*, **63**, 275–277.

Bills, A. G. (1931). Blocking: a new principle of mental fatigue. *American Journal of Psychology*, **43**, 230–245.

Blake, M. J. (1967). Time of day-effects on performance in a range of tasks. *Psychonomic Science*, **9**, 349–350.

Broadbent, D. E. (1953). Noise, paced performance and vigilance tasks. *British Journal of Psychology*, **44**, 295–303.

Broadbent, D. E. (1954). Some effects of noise on visual performance. *Quarterly Journal of Experimental Psychology*, **6**, 1–5.

Broadbent, D. E. (1957a). Effects of noises of high and low frequency on behaviour. *Ergonomics*, **1**, 21–29.

Broadbent, D. E. (1957b). Effects of noise on behaviour. In C. M. Harris (Ed.), *Handbook of Noise Control*. New York: McGraw-Hill.

Broadbent, D. E. (1958). *Perception and Communication*. London: Pergamon Press.

Broadbent, D. E. (1963). Differences and interactions between stresses. *Quarterly Journal of Experimental Psychology*, **15**, 205–211.

Broadbent, D. E. (1971). *Decision and Stress*. New York: Academic Press.

Broadbent, D. E. (1978). The current state of noise research: a reply to Poulton. *Psychological Bulletin*, **85**, 1052–1067.

Broadbent, D. E. and Gregory, M. (1965). The effect of noise and signal rate upon vigilance analysed by means of decision theory. *Human Factors*, **7**, 155–162.

Broadhurst, P. L. (1959). The interaction of task difficulty and motivation: the Yerkes–Dodson law revived. *Acta Psychologica*, **16**, 321–338.

Bursill, A. E. (1958). The restriction of peripheral vision during exposure to hot and humid conditions. *Quarterly Journal of Experimental Psychology*, **10**, 113–129.

Chapanis, A., Garner, W. R. and Morgan, C. T. (1949). *Applied Experimental Psychology*. New York: Wiley.

Chorover, S. (1976). An experimental critique of 'consolidation studies' and an alternative 'models systems' approach to the biophysiology of memory. In M. R. Rosenzweig and E. L. Bennett (Eds.), *Neural Mechanisms of Learning and Memory*. Cambridge, Mass.: MIT Press.

Colquhoun, W. P. (1971). Circadian variations in mental efficiency. In W. P. Colquhoun (Ed.), *Biological Rhythms and Human Behaviour*. London: Academic Press.

Colquhoun, W. P. and Goldman, R. F. (1968). The effects of raised body temperature on vigilance performance. *Ergonomics*, **11**, 408.

Corcoran, D. W. J. (1962). Noise and loss of sleep. *Quarterly Journal of Experimental Psychology*, **14**, 178–182.

Corcoran, D. W. J. (1964). Changes in heart rate and performance as a result of loss of sleep, *British Journal of Psychology*, **55**, 307–314.

Craik, F. I. and Blankstein, K. R. (1975). Psychophysiology and human memory. In P. H. Venables and M. J. Christie (Eds.), *Research in Psychophysiology*. London: Wiley.

Craik, F. I. and Lockhart, R. S. (1972). Levels of processing: a framework for memory research. *Journal of Verbal Learning and Verbal Behavior*, **11**, 671–684.

Daee, S. and Wilding, J. M. (1977). Effects of high intensity white noise in short-term memory for position in a list and sequence. *British Journal of Psychology*, **68**, 735–749.

Darrow, C. W. (1929). Differences in the physiological reactions to sensory and ideational stimuli. *Psychological Bulletin*, **76**, 185–201.

Davis, D. R. (1948). *Pilot Error*. London: His Majesty's Stationery Office.

Davies, D. R. and Jones, D. W. (1975). The effects of noise and incentives upon attention in short-term memory. *British Journal of Psychology*, **66**, 61–68.

Davies, D. R. and Tune, S. (1970). *Human Vigilance Performance*. London: Staples Press.

Davis, R. C. (1957). Response patterns. *Transactions of the New York Academy of Sciences*, Series 2, **19**, 731–737.

Dornic, S. (1973). Order error in attended and non-attended tasks. In S. Kornblum (Ed.), *Attention and Performance*. Vol. IV. New York: Academic Press.

Duffy, E. (1957). The psychological significance of the concept of 'arousal' or 'activation'. *Psychological Review, 64*, 265–275.

Easterbrook, J. A. (1959). The effect of emotion on cue utilization and the organisation of behavior. *Psychological Review, 66*, 187–201.

Elliott, R. (1969). Tonic heart rate: experiments on the effects of collative variables lead to a hypothesis about its motivational significance. *Journal of Personality and Social Psychology, 12*, 211–228.

Eysenck, M. W. (1975). Effects of noise, activation level, and response dominance in retrieval from semantic memory. *Journal of Experimental Psychology: Human Learning and Memory, 104*, 143–148.

Eysenck, M. W. (1976). Arousal, learning and memory. *Psychological Bulletin, 83*, 389–404.

Farley, F. (1969). Memory storage in free learning as a function of arousal and time with homogeneous and heterogeneous lists. *Wisconsin University Center in Cognitive Learning, Technical Reports, 87*.

Folkard, S., Knauth, P., Monk, T. H. and Rutenfranz, J. (1976). The effect of memory load on the circadian variation in performance efficiency under a rapidly rotating shift system. *Ergonomics, 19*, 479–488.

Folkard, S., Monk, T. H., Bradbury, R. and Rosenthal, J. (1977). Time of day effects in schoolchildren's immediate and delayed recall of meaningful material. *British Journal of Psychology, 68*, 45–50.

Frankenhaeuser, M. (1975). Experimental approaches to the study of catecholamines and emotion. In L. Levi (Ed.), *Emotions: Their Parameters and Measurement*. New York: Raven Press.

Glanzer, M. and Cunitz, A. R. (1966). Two storage mechanisms in free recall. *Journal of Verbal Learning and Verbal Behavior, 5*, 351–360.

Glass, D. C. and Singer, J. E. (1972). *Urban Stress*. New York: Academic Press.

Grossman, S. P. (1973). *Essentials of Physiological Psychology*. New York: Wiley.

Hamilton, P. (1969). Selective attention in multi-score monitoring tasks. *Journal of Experimental Psychology, 82*, 34–37.

Hamilton, P. and Copeman, A. (1970). The effect of alcohol and noise on components of a tracking and monitoring task. *British Journal of Psychology, 61*, 144–156.

Hamilton, P., Hockey, G. R. J. and Rejman, M. (1977). The place of the concept of activation in human information processing theory. In S. Dornic (Ed.), *Attention and Performance*. Vol. 6. New York: Academic Press.

Hamilton, P., Hockey, G. R. J. and Quinn, J. G. (1972). Information selection, arousal and memory. *British Journal of Psychology, 63*, 181–190.

Hamilton, P., Wilkinson, R. T. and Edwards, R. (1972). A study of four days partial sleep deprivation. In W. P. Colquhoun (Ed.), *Aspects of Human Efficiency*. London: English Universities Press.

Haveman, J. E. and Farley, F. H. (1969). Arousal and retention in paired associate, serial and free learning. *Wisconsin University Center for Cognitive Learning, Technical Reports, 91*.

Hebb, D. O. (1949). *The Organisation of Behavior*. New York: Wiley.

Hebb, D. O. (1955). Drives and the C.N.S. (conceptual nervous system). *Psychological Review, 62*, 243–254.

Helper, H. M. (1957). The effects of noise on norm output and physiological activation. *AMRL Technical Report, 270*.

Hockey, G. R. J. (1970a). Effect of loud noise on attentional selectivity. *Quarterly Journal of Experimental Psychology, 22*, 28–36.

Hockey, G. R. J. (1970b). Signal probability and spatial location as possible bases for increased selectivity in noise. *Quarterly Journal of Experimental Psychology*, **22**, 37–42.

Hockey, G. R. J. (1970c). Changes in attention allocation in a multi-component task under loss of sleep. *British Journal of Psychology*, **61**, 473–480.

Hockey, G. R. J. (1973). Changes in information selection patterns in multi-source monitoring as a function of induced arousal shifts. *Journal of Experimental Psychology*, **101**, 35–42.

Hockey, G. R. J. (1978). Effects of noise on human work efficiency. In D. N. May (Ed.), *Handbook of Noise Assessment*. New York: Van Nostrand-Reinhold.

Hockey, G. R. J., Davies, S. and Gray, M. M. (1972). Forgetting as a function of sleep at different times of day. *Quarterly Journal of Experimental Psychology*, **24**, 386–393.

Hockey, G. R. J., Dornie, S. and Hamilton, P. (1975). Selective attention during reading: the effect of noise. *University of Stockholm Institute of Applied Psychology, Reports*, **66**.

Hockey, G. R. J. and Hamilton, P. (1970). Arousal and information selection in short-term memory. *Nature* (London), **226**, 866–867.

Hörmann, H. and Osterkamp, U. (1966). Uber den Einfluss von Kontinuierlichem Lärm auf die Organisation von Gedächtnisinhalten. *Zeitschrift für Experimentelle und Angewandte Psychologie*, **13**, 31–38.

Hunt, E., Luneborg, C. and Lewis, J. (1975). What does it mean to be high verbal? *Cognitive Psychology*, **7**, 194–227.

Kahneman, D. (1973). *Attention and Effort*. Englewood Cliffs, N.J.: Prentice-Hall.

Kleinsmith, L. J. and Kaplan, S. (1963). Paired associate learning as a function of arousal and interpolated interval. *Journal of Experimental Psychology*, **65**, 190–193.

Lacey, J. I. (1959). Psychophysiological approaches to the evaluation of psycho-therapeutic process and outcome. In E. A. Rubenstein and M. B. Parloff (Eds.), *Research in Psychotherapy*. Washington, D.C.: APA.

Lacey, J. (1967). Somatic response patterning and stress: Some revisions of activation theory. In M. H. Appley and R. Trumbell (Eds.), *Psychological Stress*. New York: Appleton–Century–Crofts.

Leonard, J. A. (1959). Five-choice serial reaction apparatus. *Medical Research Council, Applied Psychology Unit, Reports*, **326**.

Levonian, F. (1968). Short term retention in relation to arousal. *Psychophysiology*, **4**, 284–293.

Lindsay, P. H. and Norman, D. A. (1972). *Human Information Processing*. New York: Academic Press.

Mackworth, N. H. (1950). *Researches on the Measurement of Human Performance*. London: His Majesty's Stationery Office.

Malmo, R. B. (1959). Activation: a neuropsychological dimension. *Psychological Review*, **66**, 367–386.

Malmo, R. B. and Surwillo, W. W. (1959). Sleep deprivation: changes in performance and physiological indicants of activation. *Psychological Monographs*, **74**, No. 15, Whole No. 502.

McClean, P. D. (1969). Induced arousal and time of recall as determinants of paired-associate recall. *British Journal of Psychology*, **60**, 57–62.

McCormick, E. J. (1957). *Human Engineering*. New York: McGraw-Hill.

Miller, R. R. and Springer, H. D. (1974). Implications of recovery from experimental amnesia. *Psychological Review*, **81**, 470–473.

Näätänen, R. (1975). The inverted-U relationship between activation and performance: a critical review. In P. M. A. Rabbitt and S. Dornic (Eds.), *Attention and Performance*. Vol. 5. New York: Academic Press.

Nakamura, C. Y. and Broen, W. E. (1965). Facilitation of competing responses as a function of 'subnormal' drive conditions. *Journal of Experimental Psychology*, **69**, 180–185.

Obrist, P. A., Webb, D. A. and Sutterer, J. R. (1969). Heart rate and somatic changes during aversive conditioning and a simple reaction-time task. *Psychophysiology*, **5**, 696–723.

Pepler, R. D. (1953). The effect of climatic factors on the performance of skilled tasks by young European men living in the tropics: 4. a task of prolonged visual vigilance. *Medical Research Council, Applied Psychology Unit, Reports*, **156.**

Pepler, R. D. (1959). Warmth and lack of sleep: accuracy or activity reduced? *Journal of Comparative and Physiological Psychology*, **52**, 446–450.

Poulton, E. C. (1966). Engineering psychology. *Annual Review of Psychology*, **17**, 177–200.

Poulton, E. C. (1970). *Environment and Human Efficiency*. Springfield, Ill.: C. C. Thomas.

Poulton, E. C. (1976). Arousing environmental stresses can improve performance, whatever people say. *Aviation, Space and Environmental Medicine*, **47**, 1193–1204.

Poulton, E. C. (1977). Continuous intense noise mask auditory feedback and inner speech. *Psychological Bulletin*, **84**, 977–1001.

Rundus, D. (1971). Analysis of rehearsal processes in free recall. *Journal of Experimental Psychology*, **89**, 63–77.

Schultz, D. P. (1965). *Sensory Restriction: Effects on Behavior*. New York: Academic Press.

Schwartz, S. (1974a). Arousal and recall: effects of noise on two retrieval strategies. *Journal of Experimental Psychology*, **102**, 896–898.

Schwartz, S. (1974b). The effects of arousal on recall, recognition and the organisation of memory. University of Northern Illinois, unpublished manuscripts.

Selye, H. (1956). *The Stress of Life*. New York: McGraw-Hill.

Wachtel, P. L. (1968). Anxiety, attention and coping with threat. *Journal of Abnormal Psychology*, **73**, 137–143.

Walker, E. L. (1958). Action decrement and its relation to learning. *Psychological Review*, **65**, 129–142.

Walker, E. L. and Tarte, R. D. (1963). Memory storage as a function of arousal and time with homogeneous and heterogeneous lists. *Journal of Verbal Learning and Verbal Behavior*, **2**, 113–119.

Weltman, G. and Egstrom, G. H. (1966). Perceptual narrowing in novice divers. *Human Factors*, **8**, 499–506.

Wilkinson, R. T. (1959). Rest pauses in a track affected by lack of sleep. *Ergonomics*, **2**, 373–380.

Wilkinson, R. T. (1961). Interaction of lack of sleep with knowledge of results, individual differences and repeated testing. *Journal of Experimental Psychology*, **62**, 236–271.

Wilkinson, R. T. (1962). Muscle tension during mental work under sleep deprivation. *Journal of Experimental Psychology*, **64**, 565–571.

Wilkinson, R. T. (1963). Interaction of noise with knowledge of results and sleep deprivation. *Journal of Experimental Psychology*, **66**, 332–337.

Wilkinson, R. T. (1968). Sleep deprivation: Performance tests for partial and selective sleep deprivation. In L. A. Abt and B. F. Reiss (Eds.), *Progress in Clinical Psychology*. Vol. 7, New York: Grune and Stratton.

Williams, H. L., Lubin, A. and Goodnow, J. J. (1959). Impaired performance with acute sleep loss. *Psychological Monographs*, **73**, No. 14, Whole No. 484.

Yerkes, R. M. and Dodson, J. D. (1908). The relation of strength of stimulus to rapidity of habit formation. *Journal of Comparative and Neurological Psychology*, **18**, 459–482.

Chapter 6

Thought Processes, Consciousness, and Stress

GEORGE MANDLER

1. Introduction: The Impact of the New Mentalism
   (i)   A Point of View and Some Definitions
   (ii) Consciousness and Problem Solving
   (iii) Consciousness and Memory
   (iv) A Cognitive Definition of Stress
2. Stress and Thought: A Theoretical View
   (i)   The Conditions of Stress
   (ii) The Functions of Autonomic Nervous System Arousal
   (iii) Attentional Effects of Stress and Autonomic Arousal
3. The Yerkes–Dodson Law—Then and Now
4. High Degrees of Stress and Cognitive Efficiency
5. Mastery and Stress
6. Threat and Intellectual Efficiency
7. The Strange and the Unusual—Some Conditions of Stress
8. Memory, Problem Solving, and Stress
9. Acknowledgement
10. References

'Depend upon it, Sir, when a man knows he is to be hanged in a fortnight, it concentrates his mind wonderfully.'

Samuel Johnson (1777)

1. INTRODUCTION: THE IMPACT OF THE NEW MENTALISM

If this chapter had been written 20 or 30 years ago, it would have been both very short and very speculative. Short, particularly if written from a behaviourist point of view; and speculative from a cognitive point of view.

Thought—however defined—referred primarily to mental events as seen from a particular vantage point, namely as the contents of consciousness. For the behaviourist, such events were beyond the pale; for the rest of psychology they were difficult to assess because their accessibility depended on introspective reports.

The ability to write today about the interaction between stress and thought processes—however speculatively—still derives in large part from a reassessment and renascence of cognitive psychology. Mentalism today—the new mentalism—not only does not restrict its domain to the contents of consciousness, much less to the aspects of those contents that can be verbalized but it considers as mental events all those complex processes and mechanisms that need to be ascribed to the organisms in order to make its thoughts and actions comprehensible. In that sense modern cognitive psychology is not just a psychology of knowledge and thought, but rather a psychology rich in complex mechanisms broadly conceived as 'cognitive'. In addition, we have learned to speak both more boldly and more respectfully about consciousness. It is a somewhat saddening commentary that the boldness in part consists in speaking about consciousness at all; yet on the other hand, we speak of it as a theoretical construct—the functions of which still need to be explored, delimited, and described (Mandler, 1975a).

There is one important change in what cognitive psychology is about. Traditionally, and certainly earlier this century, there was a significant tie between cognitive and phenomenological concerns. Cognitive psychologists frequently used as primitive terms of their language those terms of the common language that referred to cognitive processes—and frequently these terms were coextensive with phenomenological usage. Thus intuitively 'obvious' judgmental terms such as 'good' and 'bad', comparative terms such as 'better' and 'similar', and references to processes such as 'conscious' and 'self' formed the basic vocabulary of cognitive theories. The new cognitive psychology, the human information processing approach, instead searches for the processes and mechanisms that generate these terms and usages, and that in fact generate language as such. Such an approach to problems of thought and stress will form one of the themes of the following pages.

(i) A Point of View and Some Definitions

I have outlined my view of the current state of cognitive psychology primarily because it influences critically what I consider to be the problems of thought and stress. First of all we need to specify the kinds of events that are to be included under 'thought processes'. In the first instance we must distinguish between thought considered traditionally—and usually philosophically, and thought in the modern mould.

Traditionally, thought processes have been seen as coextensive with the contents of consciousness. In fact, up until the mid-twentieth century, both thought and mental life were frequently considered to be conscious. All this despite the fact that the notion of unconscious thought has been popular at least since Freud. In the modern sense, and in the sense to be used here, thought processes refer to any and all variety of complex transformations performed on environmental inputs as well as intermediate products of the information processing chain. In that sense the quite 'unconscious' use of proper syntactic rules is just as much a thought process as the 'conscious' process of judging the meaning of a passage of poetry. In considering all such processes as 'thoughts' there is a danger of including all of the organism's inferred activities as relevant to thought processes. To avoid such imperialism, I shall confine myself to those thought processes that are involved in complex activities, particularly problem solving. And consequently, I shall frequently be talking about measures of cognitive efficiency as the observable evidence for the operation of internal (theoretical and postulated) thought processes.

I have stressed that 'thought' processes can be found both in the conscious and the non-conscious mode in order to avoid previous confusions on the topic, but, more importantly, because in the discussion of stress and thought I shall be talking mainly about conscious processes. By such an emphasis I do not mean to restrict 'thoughts' to conscious ones, rather it develops out of the position taken here that the interference between stress (and its consequences) and thought does in fact take place primarily in consciousness states.

My usual reference to 'conscious' states and events will be to the limited capacity system that has variously been identified with consciousness or focal attention. My own preference has been to view that capacity as being limited in the number of organized chunks of information it can simultaneously keep in the conscious state, i.e. that it can apprehend or keep in a working memory. Typically about five such chunks can be accommodated. However, that preference in no sense excludes other interpretations which ascribe that limitation to effort or some other variable. Agreement as to some limitation is now well established and can be assured, regardless of niceties of theoretical interpretations of what it is that is limited or why it is so limited.

The notion that human information processing capacity is limited has been about (in one form or another) for at least a couple of centuries. However, the use of such a view for the explanation of interfering and capacity-limiting events (such as stress) is relatively recent. One influential model relevant to the present discussion is Kahneman's (1973). He assumes that the amount of available capacity varies with arousal (theoretically rather than autonomically defined). Spare capacity is defined as the amount of capacity that remains after most of the capacity available has been supplied to the primary task at hand. I shall argue here that the definition of a 'primary' task is at least difficult and that the amount of capacity available for any task facing the individual is a function of other tasks and other capacity-demanding inputs with which some fixed limit of capacity must be shared.

What is it that becomes conscious? I cannot examine that question in detail here, but a more extended discussion is available elsewhere (Mandler, 1975a; b).

I shall summarize here some of the major characteristics of conscious states, and in particular how and why they function in problem solving and memory tasks. The first set of characteristics deals with consciousness during problem solving in the broad sense and we consider when and why particular structures are in the conscious states, or, to be more precise, when it is that conscious processes are both useful and necessary.

(ii) Consciousness and Problem Solving

In the first instance I assume that the limited capacity characteristic of consciousness serves to reduce further the 'blooming confusion' that the physical world potentially presents to the organism. Just as sensory end organs and central sensory transducers radically reduce and categorize the world of physical stimuli to the functional and manageable world that is in fact registered, so does the conscious process further radically reduce the available information to a small and manageable subset. I assume, somewhat circularly, that the limitation of conscious capacity defines what is in fact cognitively manageable. While we do not know why the reduction is of the magnitude that we observe, it is reasonable to assume that some reduction is necessary. Just consider a need for pairwise comparisons (in a choice situation) among n chunks in consciousness; clearly the number n must be limited if the organism is to make a choice within some reasonable time span.

I shall also emphasize that the human organism is pre-programmed to represent certain events consciously; among these are intense stimuli and, most important for the present discussion, internal physiological events such as autonomic nervous system activity. Whenever such events claim and preoccupy some part of the limited capacity system, other cognitive functions will suffer, i.e. they will be displaced from conscious processing and problem solving activities will be impaired [see also Hamilton, Chapter 12]. Particularly in the case of the interruption or failure of ongoing conscious (and particularly unconscious) intercourse with the world, signals from both the external and the internal world will demand conscious attention.

When are conscious processes most obvious? First of all in the process of construction and integration of mental and action structures. Essentially this refers to the use of consciousness in the learning process. Thoughts and actions are typically conscious before they become well integrated and subsequently automatic. Thus for example, learning to drive a car is a conscious process, while the skilled driver acts usually automatically and unconsciously.

Second, conscious processes are active during the exercise of choices and judgments, particularly with respect to the action requirements of the environment. These choices, often novel ones, require the consideration of possible outcomes and consequences, and frequently involve what the behaviourist literature calls 'covert trial and error'.

Third, conscious processes exercise an important function during 'troubleshooting'. Thus many automatic structures become 'conscious' when they somehow fail in their functions, when a particular habitual way of acting fails or when a thought process cannot be brought to an appropriate conclusion. The experienced driver becomes 'aware' of where he is and what he is doing when something new and different happens; when a near miss, or a police car, or an unexpected traffic light are suddenly registered. The trouble-shooting function of consciousness permits repair on unconscious and automatic structures, and subsequent choice from among other alternatives.

(iii) Consciousness and Memory

Conscious processes also enter into both storage and retrieval mechanisms of memory. While it is commonplace to note that what is not attended to cannot be remembered, it is less clear exactly how consciousness and memorial processes interact. Is consciousness both necessary and sufficient at the time of both storage and retrieval? Despite recent arguments that attention to encoding cues is essential for later retrieval, there is increasing evidence that retrieval is possible through cues that may not have been encoded or attended to at times of storage (cf. Anderson and Pichert, 1977). Fortunately, we need not solve these problems here. All that needs to be noted for present purposes are the conditions where conscious processes obviously interact with memory, so that we can note later how stress interacts with those conditions.

Storage mechanisms that involve consciousness are those where attention is clearly paid to ongoing contexts within which some to-be-remembered events take place. In a sense all conscious current commentary on ongoing environmental events and activities produces some storable structures that may be used for later retrieval and that, conversely, may be interfered with under conditions of stress. We often construct some retrieval structures specifically for the purpose of later use, as, for example, when we note that 'I must remember that John passed his examination and congratulate him the next time I see him'. Both deliberate and incidental mnemonic devices fall into this rubric.

At the retrieval end many memory search processes, particularly those involving complex searches, require conscious processing. Among these are the search processes that involve the generation of possible retrieval candidates ('His name started with an F; what was it?') and specifically search processes that are usually preceded by Wh. . . questions: 'Where did I leave my watch?' 'What is his name?' 'When am I supposed to be in his office?'

I have summarized these major functions of the limited capacity system of consciousness because I shall argue that the most important effect of stresses on thought processes is that they interfere specifically with the smooth operations of these functions. Stress affects consciousness and thereby hampers cogitations and cognitions.

(iv) A Cognitive Definition of Stress

Given that I shall be concerned with thought processes as just defined, I must also restrict my definition of stress within the boundaries of this discourse. I must of course start with a psychological, rather than a physiological definition of stress. External 'stressors' are effective to the extent that they are perceived as dangerous or threatening, that is to the extent that they are cognitively interpreted. One of the difficulties with 'objective' definition of stressors has been the absence of these cognitive mediators. Mason (1975) in a critique of Selye's stress concept notes that 'emotional arousal' is one of the most ubiquitous reactions common to a great many situations that are considered stressful. However, these emotional responses depend on psychological interpretative mechanisms. What determines the emotional quality of an event, such as its noxiousness or attractiveness, is not a question I can deal with in detail here. I shall assume that the major characteristic of such an interpretation or appraisal is the activation of a stress reaction that is psychologically functional, i.e. perceived, such as autonomic nervous system (ANS) activity, and particularly sympathetic activation. Thus a situation is defined as stressful if and when the interpretative cognitive activities of the organism transform the input in such a way that a perceptible internal change results. I shall confine myself here to the interaction between autonomic activity and stress. However, it is also possible to entertain other reactions, such as hormonal release, that would have perceptible effects, as well as conditions under which some physiological activity occurs without direct cognitive interpretation. Thus Selye (1975) in his reply to Mason insists that stress responses (physiologically defined) do and can occur even when no 'emotional' arousal (or appraisal) is observed. If they do, and if they are perceived by the organism, then they properly belong to the rubric of thought and stress.

I shall not consider problems of the 'milder' stresses in this chapter, nor any fine-grained analysis of the limited capacity system. Both tasks were performed admirably by Broadbent (1971). His major concern was not, as he himself notes, to generalize to and from real life stresses, but rather to refine the information model itself, particularly with respect to the decision processes that must be produced within such a system.

2. STRESS AND THOUGHT: A THEORETICAL VIEW

From a theoretical point of view, and following the general position outlined above, the following processes and mechanisms need to be explored. What are the conditions and events that lead to autonomic activity; specifically, how is psychological stress initiated? What is the function of autonomic activity; how does it affect cognitive functioning? How does autonomic arousal affect conscious thought processes?

(i) The Conditions of Stress

The questions about the conditions that produce psychological stress has bedevilled most theories of stress and emotion. The most frequent answer has been in the form of lists of such conditions. These lists consider what might be evaluated as dangerous or noxious, but rarely provide some categorical principle that unites the instances. Psychoanalytic theory has made a stab in that direction when it speaks of the threat or danger (perceived by the individual) of excess stimulation of unmanageable impulses. However, stress theory in general has defined stressors as that class of events that produces stress reactions in the organism. For purposes of this presentation I shall use an approach that I have previously advanced (Mandler, 1964; 1975b), namely interruption theory. That position has cognate but discontinuous predecessors in the so-called conflict theories of emotion dating back at least to Herbart in the early 19th century (cf. Mandler, 1979).

The basic premise of this position is that autonomic activity results whenever some organized action or thought process is interrupted. The term interruption is used in as neutral a sense as possible. That is, any event, external or internal to the individual, that prevents completion of some action, thought sequence, plan, or processing structure is considered to be interrupting. Such interruption might occur because of some active or passive blocking by environmental events; it might occur because some internal thought process prevents or blocks the completion of some other process; or it may occur because one or another plan or processing strategy cannot be brought to completion when it is inconsistent or discrepant with some other currently active processing activity. Interruption can occur in the perceptual, cognitive, behavioural, or problem solving domains—the consequence will always be the same, namely, autonomic activity. It is important to note that interruption should not be imbued with negative characteristics—it simply and neutrally involves lack of structure completion. It is not synonymous with frustration or other related terms. I have noted elsewhere that interruption may be interpreted emotionally in any number of ways ranging from the most joyful to the most noxious.

The degree of autonomic activity depends primarily on two factors: first, the degree of organization of the interrupted process and second, the severity of the interruption. Degree of organization refers to the stereotypy and habitual character of the organization of the act or thought process. An action or thought sequence that is in the process of organization still has much variance associated with it and as a result much irrelevant thought and behaviour occurs within the sequence; thus nothing (and everything) is an interruption. However, when the sequence has become invariant and its parts occur with a high degree of expectancy and even certainty, then the interruptive process will run its course. As far as severity of interruption is concerned, it presumably has its main source in an iterative process. If the environment, for example, not only supports but actually demands the execution of some particular action or cognitive process which is interrupted, then there will be repeated attempts to take up the sequence again, which, when repeatedly interrupted, will potentiate the arousal. In other words, interruption is severe when the process is continuously reinitiated and interrupted. In addition, some cognitive structures are more salient than others to the current plans and goals of the individual, and the more salient the more severe the autonomic reaction to interruption. However, we know relatively little about the psychological structure of 'salience'.

In short, I assume that most (but not necessarily all) psychologically stressful situations are the result of interruption—interruptors are stressors.

(ii) The Functions of Autonomic Nervous System Arousal

If interruption produces autonomic activity, and if that activity produces the major intrapsychic consequences of stress, how does peripheral autonomic activity interact with the information processing apparatus? I shall not discuss here the function of autonomic arousal in potentiating, colouring, distinguishing the experiences usually called 'emotional'. In my book on *Mind and Emotion* (Mandler, 1975b), I have extensively addressed these issues. I noted there that autonomic activity is not merely a homeostatic mechanism related to the internal economy of the organism, but has other important adaptive functions in selecting and coding important events, and in providing a secondary alerting system.

The function of the autonomic nervous system can be viewed as a secondary support system in response to events that require extensive cognitive interpretation. Thus with the individual focused and attending to some set of events, another occurrence in his environment might signal an interruption—an unexpected and unprepared for set of circumstances. This interruption automatically triggers the autonomic nervous system, and the feedback from autonomic events tells the organism that some event is occurring in the environment that requires immediate attention. The system has the paradoxical advantage of being slow, and thus acts as a back-up. During the one to two seconds of its initiation, other cognitive sensory events may take place that 'handle' the situation. If they do not, then the autonomic reaction is available as the second signal (assuming that the first sensory-perceptual one has been ignored). If no appropriate action has been taken to adapt to the new environmental events, then the secondary signal draws the attention of the organism to some, initially cognitively unspecified, emergency. The attention to and cognitive evaluation of that new state of affairs follows the action of the autonomic signal.

The evidence for an attentional effect of autonomic arousal is three-fold. The Laceys (Lacey and Lacey, 1974) have shown that attentional activity is accompanied by cardiac deceleration. Such deceleration would attentuate the internal attention-demanding 'noisy' aspect of cardiac activity (acceleration). Thus the primitive response of the organism is a parasympathetic one which not only conserves energy but also prepares the organism for more adequate coping with the environmental situation. Second, there is an independent response of cardiac deceleration in response to acceleration. Here again, though with a longer latency (1–1.5 sec), a 'noise-reducing response is automatically occurring in response to sympathetic activation. Thus, first, attention reduces internal 'noise', and then internal 'noise' produces its own negative feedback.

The third line of evidence comes primarily from Frankenhaeuser (e.g. 1975; 1976), who has suggested that autonomic activity and the accompanying catecholamine release are not obsolete 'primitive' responses. Rather, she views such activity as facilitating adjustment to cognitive and emotional pressure [see Warburton, Chapter 2]. In brief, there is some evidence that the autonomic nervous system may be involved in environmental scanning and attention to 'important' events.

(iii) Attentional Effects of Stress and Autonomic Arousal

Stress—defined as an emergency-signalling interruption—can have the effect of increasing attention to central or crucial events in the environment. Under these circumstances, the stressful situation produces highly adaptive reactions and improves the coping capability of the organism. On the other hand, I have made reference to autonomic activity as 'noise' in the cognitive system. I am referring here to the organism's conscious perception of autonomic activity, which automatically demands attentional capacity. If the individual attends to these internal events then less focal conscious attention is available for other task-directed and coping activities. To the extent then that autonomic activity is past the point of alerting the individual, continuing autonomic arousal will be registered within consciousness and will interfere with ongoing cognitive efficiency. In that sense then autonomic activity becomes 'noise'.

In a stress situation, there is another aspect that requires attentional or conscious capacity, namely the conditions that themselves produce the stress. These conditions—whether external or internal—are the primary causes of the autonomic 'noise'. As such they may be considered noxious (e.g. interpreted negatively) by the individual and therefore subject to some effort towards their removal. For example, during the performance of some skill or task continuous comments from a coworker, or loud noises may be interpreted as stressful. As a result, some effort, involving conscious capacity, might be made to remove these noxious conditions. Hamilton (1975), following Kahneman's analysis, has drawn attention to these capacity-demanding efforts. In a discussion of anxiety he refers to the attempts at avoiding the stressful conditions as a secondary task that interferes with the primary task engaged by the individual.

In short, the problem of stress is twofold, both the internal autonomic signals and the conditions that generate those signals require part of the conscious capacity, and thereby interfere with the performance of some target task or skill.

I now turn to the specific application of these general theoretical notions to problems of stress and thought. I shall start with a rather ancient but still serviceable notion embodied in the Yerkes–Dodson law which described the relation between efficiency and stress (or stimulation). I will then bring that notion in contact with modern concepts and consider some current evidence on the effect of stress and autonomic activity on attention and consciousness. From that vantage point I shall then consider the more general relation between thought, consciousness, and stress.

3. THE YERKES–DODSON LAW—THEN AND NOW

I have assumed that the effect of physically or environmentally defined stressors depends on their 'analysis' as threats and stresses. There are, of course, stressors which demand a stressful 'interpretation' or which automatically produce stress reactions (particularly autonomic nervous system reactions). When such a demand or effect is obvious we need not speak complexly about cognitive interpretations but can talk directly of stressor effects. Among these are inescapably painful (because extremely intense) stimuli, such as electric shock. The advantage of being able to talk about stressors rather than interpreted stresses and threats is that it enables us to make contact with an older (frequently behaviourist) literature that defined stresses exclusively in terms of environmental, physical variables. Perhaps the oldest and single most important finding in that tradition is enshrined in the Yerkes–Dodson law. Yerkes and Dodson (1908) discovered that while performance on an easy discrimination task improved with increasing shock intensity, performance on a difficult task was worse with weak and strong shocks and optimal with intermediate-level shocks. It is this curvilinear relationship that represents the Yerkes–Dodson law—a surprisingly robust law given the poor track record of psychological generalizations over the years.

In 1940, Freeman confirmed an inverted-U-shaped relationship between arousal and cognitive efficiency. This statement was important because it set the stage for several decades of preoccupation with the rather vague concept of arousal, specifically arousal as a theoretical entity rather than as a measurable and observable set of events that occupy attentional capacity. Indices of arousal have varied widely, from general muscular activity, to sympathetic nervous system activity, to activities of the reticular activating system. In the process it has been pointed out that there is no single unitary and useful concept of arousal (cf. especially Lacey, 1967). I shall avoid the vagueness of the arousal concept by restricting myself to the stress- or threat-induced effects of autonomic nervous system activity; and I shall consequently use the terms autonomic activity and autonomic arousal interchangeably.

The next step in the evolving understanding of the U-shaped function relating to performance, efficiency, and cognitive competence to arousal was Easterbrook's cue-utilization hypothesis. Easterbrook (1959) concluded his review of the literature by suggesting that 'the number of cues utilized in any situation tends to become smaller with increase in emotion'. Since he equated emotion with emotional drive, the jump to a relation to arousal is not only easy, but has frequently been made in the past. Furthermore, Easterbrook related the restricted utilization of cues to change in attention, without however, providing mechanisms for the restriction in attention due to emotion or arousal.

I can now circle back to my initial discussion of the effects of autonomic arousal on the limited capacity system. Given the presence of attention-demanding occurrences, it is to be expected that with increasing autonomic activity the number of events (cues) that can share conscious attention will be limited. Easterbrook had noted that in some cases restrictions in attention (and effective cues) may improve cognitive efficiency. Clearly, when the excluded cues are irrelevant to the thought processes at hand, efficiency will be improved, but when a task requires attention to a wide range of cues, then narrowing of attention will have deleterious effects [see Hockey, Chapter 5].

4. HIGH DEGREES OF STRESS AND COGNITIVE EFFICIENCY

Stress may be experienced in the most innocuous situations. Whether trying to open a door that is stuck, or to complete a complicated bureaucratic form, or to assemble a child's toy, most of us have experienced states of high stress under these, and similar, situations. Repeated attempts to open the door, to follow instructions, or to fit part A between parts B and C may fail, autonomic arousal then increments, irrelevant ideation ('Those idiots, incompetents, and fools!!!'), and panic-like behaviour may ensue. Each failure is an interrupted sequence, and each interruption further potentiates autonomic arousal.

The notion that such sequences have attention-narrowing consequences is not new in the literature. Callaway and Dembo (1958) concluded that 'emotional states, such as anxiety, panic, and orgasm . . . produce a . . . narrowing of attention. . . . (A) correlation between narrowed attention and central sympathomimetic activity is demonstrated'. Similarly, the tendency to engage in task-irrelevant behaviour is well known. Bachrach (1970) has described the psychological problem of panic in deep-sea diving as 'a strong, fearful perception by an individual that he is out of control, that he is not capable of coping with the situation in which he finds himself, leading to behaviors that not only do not solve the problem posed by the danger but actually may work directly against such solution'.

The best analysis and summary of the available evidence on cognitive efficiency in dangerous environments has been presented by Baddeley (1972). His conclusion is well worth citing in full:

> "(It) appears that one way in which danger affects performance is through its influence on the subject's breadth of attention. A dangerous situation will tend to increase level of arousal which in turn will focus the subject's attention more narrowly on those aspects of the situation he considers most important. If the task he is performing is regarded by him as most important, then performance will tend to improve; if on the other hand it is regarded as peripheral to some other activity, such as avoiding danger, then performance will deteriorate. With experience, subjects appear to inhibit anxiety in the danger situation and hence reduce the degree of impairment. We still do not know what mechanisms mediate the effect of arousal on the distribution of attention, or what is involved in the process of adaptation to fear.'

The evidence for Baddeley's conclusion comes from a variety of sources which I shall review briefly, together with other, more recent, evidence. First, Baddeley (1971) and others had found that equal degrees of nitrogen narcosis (when air is breathed at its highest pressures) produced different impairment in efficiency when the test was conducted in the open sea or in a pressure chamber simulation. The greater impairment in the more realistic situation could only be ascribed to the greater degree of danger *perceived* by the subjects. In addition, more anxious subjects were more easily influenced, and impaired, by the increased 'danger' of the more realistic situations.

Given these observations, does the perception of danger behave like 'arousal'; can it be subsumed under the cue-utilization hypothesis of Easterbrook? Hockey (e.g. 1970) showed that an increase in noise improved performance on centrally attended stimuli at the expense of peripheral ones. While Poulton (1976a) has questioned some of Hockey's results on procedural grounds, another study by Bacon (1974) makes the same point more persuasively. Bacon not only found that arousal impaired attention to peripheral cases, but also that it narrows the range of cues processed by systematically 'reducing responsiveness to those aspects of the situation which initially attract a lesser degree of attentional focus'. Bacon notes that this loss is actually due to a diminution in subjects' sensitivity and that arousal affects the capacity limitation directly.

The bridge to the danger situation was provided by Weltman *et al.* (1971) who demonstrated the same diminution of attention to peripheral stimuli in a task simulating danger. Experimental subjects showed both increased autonomic activity and the decrease in attention to peripheral stimuli, but no decrement in performance of a central task.

The conclusion then holds that stress has effects that are very similar to noise in reducing attentional capacity and narrowing it to central tasks. In line with Bacon's results we can assume that what is perceived as psychologically 'central' will be determined by the initial attention assigned to it. What is originally maximally attended to is central, whatever receives less attention is perceived as 'peripheral' and will suffer the greater loss of attention under stress. Whenever the target task is 'central', increased autonomic arousal may well improve performance. That point was made clearly by Baddeley and subsequently adumbrated by Poulton in an attack on the notion that noise necessarily interferes with efficiency (Poulton, 1976b).

Finally, we must deal with the observation that experienced subjects show little or none of the deleterious effects of stress (environmentally defined). First, we note again that stress must be subjectively defined. For the experienced subject the perception of subjectively or objectively defined stress must necessarily be different from that shown by the naive observer. Apart from what is perceived or judged to be stressful, the effect of the stressor differs radically for experienced and inexperienced subjects. Hammerton and Tickner (1967) have shown increased efficiency prior to a parachute jump as a function of previous jumping experience. Similarly, Epstein and Fenz (1965) found that novice jumpers had a high pulse rate before a jump which dropped to a normal level upon landing, while the experienced jumpers showed the reverse effect. The same lack of stress responses has been found for highly trained astronauts and has been explained in the same fashion (Mandler, 1967).

The effect of experience must be related to the proposition that autonomic arousal is to a very large degree related to the interruption of ongoing behaviour, plans, and expectations. Stress, under that explanation, occurs when no available action or thought structures are available to handle the situation which faces the individual. Astronauts, as an example, are trained to have available response sequences, plans, and problem solving strategies for all imaginable emergencies. An emergency then ceases to be one, it is another routine situation—it is by definition not stressful. Similarly, the novice parachutist ruminates on possible outcomes, none of which he is able to handle, emergencies that he either imagines or remembers and for which no action structures are available. At the end of the jump, this interruptive effect, interrupting thoughts about successful completion of the jump, is eliminated—the original plan (to complete the jump successfully) has been achieved. At the more speculative level, one might assume that for the experienced parachutist, who enjoys the jump (both emotionally and cognitively) the completion interrupts that enjoyment, or even elation—more concretely it terminates a complete and competent action structure. Relevant confirming reports are available anecdotally from sky jumpers who cannot wait to go up again for the next jump.

As far as Baddeley's final question about the mechanisms that mediate the effect of arousal on attention is concerned, I have—hopefully—provided such a mechanism in the introductory theoretical passages. Autonomic arousal narrows attention in two ways: first, automatically by the direct action of the autonomic nervous system, and second, indirectly by occupying some of the limited capacity of attention/consciousness and thereby limiting the remaining available attentional capacity to those events or stimuli that have originally been perceived as 'central' (cf. Bacon, 1974).

5. MASTERY AND STRESS

I have noted that stress may result in cognitive processes that draw attention to centrally important aspects of the environment. The common language describes such efforts as relevant to the mastery of stress, to our ability to control a particular situation. Mastery refers to our perception that the events in our personal world may be brought under our control. I have suggested elsewhere that this sense of mastery may be important not so much because of the direct effects it has on our actions, but because a sense of control or mastery colours the cognitive interpretation of our world. It is generally seen as 'good' to be in control of our world, and as the world is appraised as 'good' the emotional tone will be positive. What may frighten us may become amusing when we have a sense of mastery, even though our actual control of the situation has not changed. What has changed is the relevance of the event to our ongoing plans—if they are seen as relevant and as impeding (interrupting) ongoing action they may become frightening. If they are seen as irrelevant, or impeding only in the short term, they may become amusing and tolerable. When a friend and colleague criticizes our work, the remark is often seen as constructive and leading to mastery, while the identical remark from a supervisor may easily appear threatening. The objective absence of control is not necessarily seen as negative; just consider the enjoyment some experience on a rollercoaster, while others are—in the identical situation—just as frightened. It is the subjective sense of control that may be important rather than the objective control of the environment.

There is, however, no doubt that the sense of mastery does in many cases reduce the deleterious effects of stress and does alleviate the subjective sense of emotional disturbance. I assume that this effect may occur under two conditions:

(a) Any action directly related to the threatening, interrupting situation or event may change that event and reduce its threatening, i.e. interrupting effect. In that case an action by the individual has changed the situation from one that is arousing (and interpreted as threatening) to a non-arousing one, and thereby removed its threatening aspects.

(b) Without changing any of its objective aspects, a situation may be reinterpreted in such a way that the events are not perceived as interrupting any more. The overall structure or plan under which the situation and events are perceived is changed significantly to remove its interrupting aspect or to view the interruptive events as beneficial. In the latter case, the autonomic arousal will persist but will be positively interpreted. The rollercoaster seen as a joyful situation that will terminate when planned (at the end of its run) will thus become non-frightening. The other kind of event, the cognitive removal of interruptive aspects, occurs less frequently. Consider the case of the student who has received his graded examination papers with a grade of 66 per cent. He had hoped (planned) for at least a 75 per cent grade in order to pass the course. These plans have been disrupted; he is in a state of autonomic arousal—negatively interrupted. Then he notices a slip of paper appended to the examination which says that the examination was unusually difficult and that 66 per cent was the highest mark which will be recorded as a good passing grade. The same event has now been reinterpreted, its interruptive, as well as negative aspect, has been removed.

This discussion leads us into the general topic of coping, appraisal and reappraisal. The most important contribution to this problem has been made by Lazarus and his colleagues, in whose papers extensive discussions and elaborations of this area can be found (e.g. Lazarus, 1975 [see also Folkman, Schaefer, and Lazarus, Chapter 9]). In a recent paper, Gal and Lazarus (1975) have addressed the issue of mastery and stress. They examined the question why activity as such apparently has the capacity to lower stress reactions. Gal and Lazarus distinguish between threat-related and non-threat-related activities. The former lower stress reactions because they provide a feeling of control or mastery. In the case of non-threat-related activities, however, their effect derives from the fact that they distract or divert attention from threat. It is this latter explanation that should be added to the account I have given here. It is certainly likely that in some cases of threat some restriction of attention may reduce the perception of both the threatening event as well as the internal autonomic activity. However, activity as such is not stress reducing in all cases. In panic situations, for example, continuing interrupted activity not only fails to reduce the experience of stress, but usually actually increments it. In general, the question of mastery and control, as well as of the effects of activity as such, requires detailed analyses of the task, the perceived situation, and the general structures that guide thought and action at each point in time.

6. THREAT AND INTELLECTUAL EFFICIENCY

An area in which questions of mastery of threat and the effect of interpreted threat on efficiency have been of continuing interest is in the realm of performance on complex intellectual tasks. This area of research has permitted us to come relatively close to observing the outcomes of complex thought processes, while at the same time addressing a topic of some practical importance. Specifically, we are concerned with the effect of perceived threat on performance of test-like tasks.

Whereas a reasonable amount of research has been going on in this area over the years, the general conclusions that still hold today derive from a few studies published some twenty years ago. The major strategy is to select individuals who report (on paper and pencil tests) high and low degrees of anxiety or concern about test situations. These test anxiety scales have been variously interpreted as measuring anxiety drives, traits, or attitudes. My own preference (see Mandler, 1972) has been to assume that 'the high anxious subject tells himself that . . . appropriate (not necessarily useful or adaptive) behaviour in a test situation consists of observing his own behaviour, of examining his failures, of ruminating about . . . his emotional reactions . . .' The low anxious individual, on the other hand, 'orients his behaviour and cognitions toward the specific requirements of the task, excluding extraneous ideations . . .'. This line of thought is an elaboration of a distinction between task-relevant and task-irrelevant responses originally proposed by Seymour, Sarason, and me.

In our original study (Mandler and Sarason, 1952) we noted that not only did high anxious individuals perform worse on intelligence test tasks, but also that the absence of any further instructions were most beneficial for the high anxiety people. On the other hand, instructions that tell subjects that they have failed were most helpful for low anxious individuals. In a subsequent study, I. G. Sarason found that high anxious subjects solved anagrams more efficiently than low anxious individuals when the situation was non-threatening, that is when they were instructed that they were not expected to finish all the anagrams because they were very difficult and harder than usual. When the subjects were told that the task was directly related to ones' intelligence level, and that they should finish easily if of average intelligence, the low anxious individual performed significantly better than the high anxious ones (Sarason, 1961).

What these and many other studies in the literature suggest is that many people bring stress into a situation, as the situation brings out their stress potential. Both a potentially threatened individual and a properly interpret-able situation are needed to produce the stress reaction. That reaction in turn is presumably of two forms; first, the individual ruminates—thinks—about the irrelevant aspects of the task, including his own state, performance, and reactions; and second, the threat interpretation produces autonomic activity which is in itself attention demanding. Both of these sets of internal events then vie for limited capacity and thereby reduce attentional, conscious capac-ity available for thought processes required by the task itself [see also Hamil-ton, Chapter 3].

7. THE STRANGE AND THE UNUSUAL—SOME CONDITIONS OF STRESS

In this section I want to explore some further aspects of the events that are usually called stressful, and how they come to be stressful.

It is generally assumed that the strange and the unusual and the unexpected are stressful events. Clearly, this kind of common language label refers exactly to the kind of events that are interruptive in the sense used here. Two major positions in the psychology of stress and emotion have previously emphasized the importance of the strange and the unusual. Bowlby (e.g. 1969) has described, both sensitively and wisely, the general problem of fear and its ontogeny, in the general framework of his attachment theory. Simi-larly, Hebb (e.g. 1946) has talked about the occurrence of fear in response to perceptual discrepancies. It is clear from both expositions that fearfulness of the strange does not occur until familiarity and expectations have been developed first. Stranger anxiety in infants does not occur until schemata for faces have been developed. Chimpanzees are terrorized by detached parts of chimp bodies only after having previously experienced intact bodies. Thus the strange is interruptive because the structures that are evoked in and by a particular situation are violated; the strange is unassimilable. However, apart from specific expectations being violated by the strange and the unusual, there is another characteristic of human cognition that produces fearful (arousing and negatively interpreted) conditions. In the presence of events and perceptions that are new, i.e. for which no current schemata or structures are appropriate, the human individual will search for an appropriate way to interpret the surround— a process which is automatic and which I have previ-ously called 'meaning analysis'. Given the essentially novel characteristic of the situation, no such appropriate structure will be found, but in the process each attempted structure fails of environmental support and is thus inter-rupted. This unavailability of appropriate response or action alternatives, this helplessness in the face of the environment, I consider to be the essential psychological basis of the set of subjective reactions subsumed under 'anxiety'.

Shifting to intrapsychic stressful events, consider first the condition under which ongoing cognitive structures are interrupted by their own consequences. Consider some plan that is not executed but is examined within the conscious system. If a consequence of this plan is discovered to be incompatible with some other, maybe hierarchically higher, plan, or with some expected environmental condition, then we are once again confronted with an interruption, an intrapsychic cognitive one. These thought processes will lead to arousal just as an external event will. For example, planning to attend the theatre, and then remembering a previous engagement at the same time would lead to stress and coping activities.

If we consider the hierarchical structure of plans and cognitive structures (cf. Miller, Galanter and Pribram, 1960), the stress produced by the interruption of a particular plan will vary presumably with the level within the plan hierarchy of the interrupted plan and with the number of other plans (subordinate and superordinate to the interrupted one) that are disrupted at the same time. For example, the interruption of a low-level plan ('I want to have eggs for breakfast but there aren't any in the house') may not be too arousing and stressful because a higher one is not affected ('I want to have breakfast—and might as well eat porridge'). The important point to be noted is that any interruptive event must be analysed in terms of the level of plans and relevant hierarchies involved. Thus when all levels of plans are threatened (cannot be completed) by some event the degree of autonomic arousal will be intense and the stress most severe.

Both action structures and intra-psychic cognitive structures may be interrupted for one of two reasons. One involves the situation where an expected event or sequence fails to occur, the other when something unexpected happens. Both of these involve interruption and both involve automonic arousal and, usually in the kind of situation considered in this chapter, are interpreted as negative and unpleasant. In either case the interruption of a current cognitive structure apparently automatically focuses consciousness on that structure and the interruptive event or thought. I noted earlier that one of the functions of consciousness is that it becomes the arena for trouble-shooting when conscious or unconscious structures fail. This phenomenon has been labelled the law of awareness by Claparède; people become aware of automatic actions when these are disrupted or fail (Claparède, 1934). It is reasonable to assume that one of the adaptive functions of interruption is to bring some problem into consciousness, where repair and coping activities can take place. If such 'snapping into consciousness' takes place we expect the field of focal attention to be narrowed and, under many circumstances, other ongoing activity to be impaired because of the restricted amount of focal capacity that remains available.However, it should be noted that much trouble-shooting will occur without any stressful sequelae. When working on a complex problem, we often expect to find one or more structures to be inadequate for the solution of the problem at hand. In that case, the operative executive plan 'expects' interruptions and the expected does not lead to autonomic arousal. Expected interruptions of this kind will only be innocuous if they are not perceived as destructive of the executive plan. The anxious individual, in contrast, who 'expects' to fail, will perceive these interruptions as fatal or at least deleterious to the goal at hand. I have previously made reference to how well-trained individuals (e.g. the astronauts) have exactly the useful kinds of expectations where trouble-shooting is expected, and interruption may not produce a stress response.

8. MEMORY, PROBLEM SOLVING, AND STRESS

The topic of memory and learning is discussed in a separate chapter [see Hockey, Chapter 5], but I shall indicate briefly, as a concluding note, how stress will affect storage and efficiency of memory and thought.

It is generally agreed that the degree of elaboration of an event will affect how efficiently it is stored and how easily it can be retrieved. The position was introduced under the rubric of 'depth of processing' but has recently been discussed more frequently in terms of elaboration (Craik and Lockhart, 1972; Craik and Tulving, 1975; Mandler, 1978). I have suggested that elaboration describes the complexity of inter-structural links that are developed in the process of coding, and that it is these links that provide better access at the time of retrieval. I have also assumed that these elaborative operations are typically performed in the conscious state of the target structure. Both integrative (intrastructural) and elaborative (interstructural) requirements make demands on conscious capacity and thereby delimit the amount of storage activities possible under various circumstances (see the discussion of isocapacity functions in Mandler, 1978).

Given these assumptions about memory storage and retrieval, the restriction of conscious capacity that occurs as a function of stress should have obvious effects on memory functions. Not only will events be less elaborately coded under conditions of stress (we remember fewer things which occurred under stress and less well), but also—with central focusing during stress—we should remember some few salient events that occurred under stress extremely well. Anecdotal evidence, at least, bears this out. Similarly, one would expect that retrieval under stress should show similar characteristics, with the addendum that the stressful occurrence—the holisitically coded event, cum autonomic arousal—may provide additional retrieval cues.

Unfortunately, there is little experimental evidence available on the effects of stress on complex storage and retrieval processes. What data there are tends to be of rather dated vintage and simply makes the point that stress (frequently defined as failure) impairs memory. Much of that evidence was collected under behaviourist paradigms and therefore tends to emphasize drive–performance interactions and pays little heed to underlying cognitive processes. The only set of extensive data concerns the effect of stress on short-term memory and shows that practically any kind of stress, failure experience, or uncontrollable noise will impair short-term memory retrieval. Since short-term memory, as used in the experimental literature, is—to some extent—coextensive with span of attention or consciousness, such a finding is not surprising and adds little to our understanding of more complex processes. To the extent that short-term memory experiments require the holding in consciousness (or working memory) of the to-be-remembered material, we would naturally expect that any set of events which makes demands on limited processing capacity at the same time will interfere with these short-term 'storage' processes.

If the experimental literature on stress and memory fails to respond to the need to examine underlying cognitive processes, unfortunately experimental work on stress and problem solving fails even more. It has been known, both by laymen and psychologists, that under stress the thought processes involved in problem solving demonstrate the kind of narrowing and stereotyping that we would expect on the basis of the present analysis. If much of problem solving involves the manipulation—in consciousness—of alternatives, choices, probable and possible outcomes and consequences, and alternative goals, then the production of internal 'noise', of stress, and autonomic arousal, should—and does—interfere with such processes. Thought processes become narrowed in the sense that only the available alternatives are considered and no conscious capacity is available to consider new alternatives. In the same sense thought becomes stereotyped and habitual. Conversely, the possibility of bringing in new strategies and considering their possible effect is reduced—thought becomes repetitive and unelaborated. In a sense, the restriction on memorial elaboration refers to the very same elaboration that is restricted during problem solving under stress. We have seen examples of these consequences in the discussion of the available data on the problem of central and peripheral processing under stress.

What is needed are some fine-grained experimental analyses of these processes during problem solving. How, and when, does the introduction of stress (however produced or defined) restrict the available alternatives in the conscious state? Which processes are suppressed or removed from consciousness and in what order? Does the very inability to solve a problem due to stress potentiate further stress reactions because of the interruptive process of the failure to solve a problem? How is hypothesis sampling affected by stress conditions? Under what circumstances can the focusing that occurs under stress become beneficial? How does attention to centrally relevant problems under stress promote more efficient problem solving? The research potential under the aegis of the new mentalism is indeed great, but our preoccupation with the normal unstressed mind has, in recent years, restricted experimental work on these problems.

The present analysis has been presented in part in order to stimulate such explorations. More important, however, is the demonstration—hopefully successful—that modern cognitive and information processing analyses are not confined to purely cognitive problems but can be fruitfully extended to problems that have previously been segregated under discussions of emotions, motivations, and drives.

9. ACKNOWLEDGEMENT

Preparation of this chapter was supported in part by Grant MH-15828 from the National Institute of Mental Health to the Center for Human Information Processing, University of California, San Diego. Some sections have been adapted from *Mind and Emotion*, copyright by the author.

10. REFERENCES

Anderson, R. C. and Pichert, J. W. (1977). Recall of previously unrecallable information following a shift in perspective. *Technical Report*, No. 41, Center for the Study of Reading, University of Illinois, Urbana, Illinois.

Bachrach, A. J. (1970). Diving behavior. In *Human Performance and Scuba Diving*. Chicago: Athletic Institute.

Bacon, S. J. (1974). Arousal and the range of cue utilization. *Journal of Experimental Psychology*, **102**, 81–87.

Baddeley, A. D. (1971). Diver performance. In J. D. Woods and J. N. Lythgoe (Eds.), *Underwater Science*. London: Oxford University Press.

Baddeley, A. D. (1972). Selective attention and performance in dangerous environments. *British Journal of Psychology*, **63**, 537–546.

Bowlby, J. (1969). *Attachment and Loss*. Vol. 1. London: Hogarth Press and Institute of Psychoanalysis.

Broadbent, D. E. (1971). *Decision and Stress*. New York: Academic Press.

Callaway, E. III and Dembo, D. (1958). Narrowed attention: a psychological phenomenon that accompanies a certain physiological change. *AMA Archives of Neurology and Psychiatry*, **79**, 74–90.

Claparède, E. (1934). *La genèse de l'hypothese*. Geneva: Kundig.

Craik, F. I. M. and Lockhart, R. S. (1972). Levels of processing: a framework for memory research. *Journal of Verbal Learning and Verbal Behavior,* **11**, 671–684.

Craik, F. I. M. and Tulving, E. (1975). Depth of processing and the retention of words in episodic memory. *Journal of Experimental Psychology: General*, **104**, 268–294.

Easterbrook, J. A. (1959). The effect of emotion on cue utilization and the organization of behavior. *Psychological Review*, **66**, 183–201.

Epstein, S. and Fenz, W. D. (1965). Steepness of approach and avoidance gradients in humans as a function of experience: theory and experiment. *Journal of Experimental Psychology*, **70**, 1–13.

Frankenhaeuser, M. (1975). Experimental approaches to the study of catecholamines and emotion. In L. Levi (Ed.), *Emotions: Their Parameters and Measurement*. New York: Raven Press.

Frankenhaeuser, M. (1976). The role of peripheral catecholamines in adaptation to understimulation and overstimulation. In G. Serban (Ed.), *Psychopathology of Human Adaptation*. New York: Plenum.

Freeman, G. L. (1940). The relationship between performance level and bodily activity level. *Journal of Experimental Psychology*, **26**, 602–608.

Gal, R. and Lazarus, R. S. (1975). The role of activity in anticipating and confronting stressful situations. *Journal of Human Stress*, **1**, 4–20.

Hamilton, V. (1975). Socialization anxiety and information processing: a capacity model of anxiety-induced performance deficits. In I. G. Sarason and C. D. Spielberger (Eds.), *Stress and Anxiety*, Vol. 2. Washington, D. C.: Hemisphere.

Hammerton, M. and Tickner, A. H. (1967). Tracking under stress. *Medical Research Council Report*, No. APRC 67/CS 10 (A).

Hebb, D. O. (1946). On the nature of fear. *Psychological Review*, **53**, 259–276.

Hockey, G. R. J. (1970). Effect of loud noise on attentional selectivity. *Quarterly Journal of Experimental Psychology*, **22**, 28–36.

Kahneman, D. (1973). *Attention and Effort*. Englewood Cliffs, N. J.: Prentice-Hall.

Lacey, J. I. (1967). Somatic response patterning and stress: Some revisions of activation theory. In M. H. Appley and R. Trumbell (Eds.), *Psychological Stress*. New York: Appleton–Century–Crofts.

Lacey, B. C. and Lacey, J. I. (1974). Studies of heart rate and other bodily processes in sensorimotor behavior. In P. A. Obrist, A. Black, J. Brener and L. DiCara (Eds.), *Cardiovascular Psychophysiology: Current Mechanisms, Biofeedback and Methodology*. Chicago: Aldine-Atherton.

Lazarus, R. S. (1975). The self-regulation of emotion. In L. Levi (Ed.), *Emotions: Their Parameters and Measurement*. NewYork: Raven Press.

Mandler, G. (1964). The interruption of behavior. In D. Levine (Ed.), *Nebraska Symposium on Motivation: 1964*. Lincoln, Nebraska: University of Nebraska Press.

Mandler, G. (1967). Invited commentary. In M. H. Appley and R. Trumbull (Eds.), *Psychological Stress*. New York: Appleton–Century–Crofts.

Mandler, G. (1972). Comments. In C. D. Spielberger (Ed.), *Anxiety: Current Trends in Theory and Research*. New York: Academic Press.

Mandler, G. (1975a). Consciousness: respectable, useful, and probably necessary. In R. Solso (Ed.), *Information Processing and Cognition: The Loyola Symposium*. Hillsdale, N. J.: Lawrence Erlbaum.

Mandler, G. (1975b). *Mind and Emotion*. New York: Wiley.

Mandler, G. (1978). Organization and repetition: an extension of organizational principles with special reference to rote learning. In L. G. Nilsson (Ed.), *Perspectives in Memory Research*. Hillsdale, N. J.: Lawrence Erlbaum.

Mandler, G. (1979). Emotion. In E. Hearst (Ed.), *The First Century of Experimental Psychology*. Hillsdale, N. J.: Lawrence Erlbaum.

Mandler, G. and Sarason, S. B. (1952). A study of anxiety and learning. *Journal of Abnormal and Social Psychology*, **47**, 166–173.

Mason, J. W. (1975). A historical view of the stress field. *Journal of Human Stress*, **1**, 6–12, 22–36.

Miller, G. A., Galanter, E. H. and Pribram, L. (1960). *Plans and the Structure of Behavior*. New York: Holt.

Poulton, E. C. (1976a). Continuous noise interferes with work by masking auditory feedback and inner speech. *Applied Ergonomics*, **7**, 79–84.

Poulton, E. C. (1976b). Arousing environmental stresses can improve performance, whatever people say. *Aviation, Space, and Environmental Medicine*, **47**, 1193–1204.

Sarason, I. G. (1961). The effects of anxiety and threat on the solution of a difficult task. *Journal of Abnormal and Social Psychology,* **62**, 165–168.

Selye, H. (1975). Confusion and controversy in the stress field. *Journal of Human Stress,* **1**, 37–44.

Weltman, G., Smith, J. E. and Egstrom, G. H. (1971). Perceptual narrowing during simulated pressure-chamber exposure. *Human Factors,* **13**, 99–107.

Yerkes, R. M. and Dodson, J. D. (1908). The relation of strength of stimulus to rapidity of habit-formation. *Journal of Comparative and Neurological Psychology,* **18**, 459–482.

Coping Processes and
Life Event Changes

Chapter 7

Recent Developments in
Research on Life Stress

JAMES H. JOHNSON and IRWIN G. SARASON

1. Introduction
2. Life Stress Research: A Selective Overview
3. Conceptual and Methodological Issues
   (i) Assessment of Life Change
   (ii) Interpretation of Results
4. A New Approach to Assessment
   (i) The Life Experiences Survey (LES)
   (ii) Reliability of the LES
   (iii) Life Stress, Anxiety, Academic Performance, and Social Desirability
   (iv) Personal Maladjustment and the LES
   (v) Assessment of Life Change: A Comparison of Approaches
   (vi) Mood States and Reporting of Life Change
   (vii) Efficacy of the LES
5. Moderator Variables in Life Stress Research
6. Causal Relationships in Life Stress Research
7. Summary and Conclusions
8. Acknowledgement
9. References

1. INTRODUCTION

All individuals, in the course of living, experience a variety of events or life changes which may be considered potential stressors. Included here are such diverse events as changes in residence, marriage, separation and divorce, new additions to the family, death or illness of family members, loss of job, changed work responsibilities, among others. These events often require significant social readjustment and adaptation. Although experiencing high levels of life change may be to some degree correlated with variables such as socioeconomic status (Myers, Lindenthal and Pepper, 1974) and minority group membership (Gad and Johnson, 1978), no one is immune from experiencing such changes. Life changes represent ongoing sources of stress to which all individuals are subjected to a greater or lesser degree.

Given the physical and psychological demands involved in coping with high levels of life change, it is not surprising that many clinicians have suggested that the experiencing of major life changes can have a deleterious effect on the functioning of the individual. While speculation concerning the effects of life change has been prominent in the medical and psychiatric literature for many years it is only recently that researchers have begun systematic investigations into the relationships between life stress, health, and psychological adjustment. In this chapter we present an overview of some of the early findings of life stress research, discuss the nature of conceptual and methodological difficulties associated with studies in this area, and describe a series of studies designed to deal with certain of these issues.

2. LIFE STRESS RESEARCH: A SELECTIVE OVERVIEW

The publication by Holmes and Rahe (1967) of an article describing an initial attempt to quantify the impact of life changes on individuals provided a major impetus for research in the area of life stress. This research culminated in the development of an instrument for the assessment of life stress, the Schedule of Recent Experiences (SRE), which has been widely used in subsequent life stress investigations. The popularity of this instrument is no doubt related to the fact that it provided a convenient measure of, not only the extent of life changes experienced by the individual, but also their cumulative impact.

The SRE consists of a list of 42 events. Subjects respond by indicating, for each item, whether they have experienced that event during the recent past and the number of times the event was experienced. To determine scoring weights for specific events Holmes and Rahe had subjects rate each of the 42 events with regard to the amount of social readjustment required to live through the various events. The item 'marriage' was employed as a standard or anchor point in these ratings. This item was given an arbitrary value of 500 and subjects were asked to rate the other items by assigning values of above or below 500 to reflect the degree to which events required more or less readjustment than marriage. Mean adjustment ratings were obtained for each of the items. These values, termed 'Life Change Units', when divided by the constant 10, were taken to represent the average amount of social readjustment considered necessary in response to the SRE events. To illustrate, the event 'death of spouse' is given a value of 100, 'pregnancy' a value of 40, 'change in financial state' a value of 38, and 'minor violations of the law' a value of 11. A total life stress score for the SRE is obtained by determining the events experienced by the respondent and summing the life change units associated with these events.

Since its initial development the SRE and similar measures have been used in numerous studies designed to determine relationships between life stress and indices of health and adjustment. While many of the studies in the published literature are less than elegant methodologically, taken together results of retrospective and prospective studies provide support for a relationship between life stress and a variety of health-related variables. Life stress has, for example, been found to be related to sudden cardiac death (Rahe and Lind, 1971), myocardial infarction (Edwards, 1971; Theorell and Rahe, 1971), pregnancy and birth complications (Gorsuch and Key, 1974), seriousness of chronic illness (Wyler, Masuda and Holmes, 1971), the displaying of symptoms among persons with chronic illness (Bedell, Giordani, Amour, Tavormina and Boll, 1977), as well as to other major health problems such as tuberculosis, multiple sclerosis, and diabetes and a host of other less serious physical conditions (Rabkin and Struening, 1976). While not providing conclusive evidence, these studies provide support for the position taken by Holmes and Masuda (1974) that rather than being related to specific disorders, life stress serves to increase one's overall susceptibility to illness [see Selye, Chapter 1].

In addition to its relationship to physical illness life stress has also been found to be correlated with psychiatric symptomatology (Dekker and Webb, 1974; Paykel, 1974). Several researchers have found life stress scores to correlate with measures of anxiety and depression (e.g. Vinokur and Selzer, 1975) as well as with indices of academic (Harris, 1972) and work performance (Carranza, 1972). These findings suggest that life stress is not only related to physical illness but to mental health and levels of personal effectiveness as well. Reviews of the work in this area have been provided by Dohrenwend and Dohrenwend (1974a) and Rabkin and Struening (1976).

3.   CONCEPTUAL AND METHODOLOGICAL ISSUES

While significant correlations between life stress scores, derived from the SRE, and a variety of dependent variables have been demonstrated there are many unanswered questions and significant unresolved conceptual and methodological issues. A variety of these issues will be considered in the following sections.

(i)   Assessment of Life Change

Although the development of the SRE represented a valuable pioneering attempt at the quantification of the impact of life change, its adequacy as a psychometric measure has been questioned on several counts. First, its construction was based on the general assumption that life changes are stressful regardless of their desirability or undesirability. Both desirable and undesirable events are included in the SRE and are combined in deriving life stress scores. Several investigators, however, have questioned the logic of combining positive and negative events (Brown, 1974; Mechanic, 1975; Sarason, De Monchaux and Hunt, 1975).

It has been argued that (1) undesirable events may have a very different, and more detrimental effect on individuals than the experiencing of positive events and (2) that it may be more reasonable to conceptualize life stress primarily in terms of events that exert negative impacts on individuals. Vinokur and Selzer (1975) have provided information bearing on these two points. They employed a modified version of the SRE which yielded separate values for positive and negative events and were able to determine correlations between life changes and indices of depression, anxiety-tension, aggression, paranoia, and suicidal proclivity. Significant relationships were found only when using the measure of negative change. Positive change was not found to be systematically related to any of these measures. Similar findings have also been reported by Mueller, Edwards and Yarvis (1977). To the extent that positive life changes are uncorrelated with important dependent variables instruments such as the SRE, it would seem necessary to assess desirable and undesirable change separately in the measurement of life stress.

A related issue concerns the quantification of life changes. Individuals vary considerably in how they are affected by life events and whether they perceive a given event as desirable or undesirable (Mueller, Edwards and Yarvis, 1977). As a result, values derived from group ratings (such as those used with the SRE) may not accurately reflect the impact of events on particular individuals. Problems inherent in using group-derived values with individual cases become obvious when it is noted that events listed in the SRE are, in many cases, quite ambiguous. For instance, if a subject responds to the item 'major change in financial status', it is uncertain if the response refers to a major change in a positive or negative direction. It is not clear that the life change unit associated with this event is equally applicable to the person who has recently become bankrupt and the person who has inherited a large sum of money. Indeed, the magnitude of the life change unit itself may have been influenced by the differing perceptions of this event by persons involved in the initial rating of events. As a further example, an event such as pregnancy is likely to be viewed quite differently by a sixteen year old unwed female and a married woman childless during ten years of marriage. While life change units do provide a quantitative index of life change they may not reflect the actual amount of stress resulting from specific events, due to ambiguities inherent in the SRE and to the fact that individuals vary in their perceptions of the desirability or undesirability of events. Given this limitation it would seem that some other method of assessing the impact of life change is needed.

An additional criticism of existing life change measures is that many items which are considered stressful life events may themselves be viewed as symptoms or consequences of illness. Hudgens (1974) has suggested that as many as 29 of the 42 SRE items may fall into this category. Items such as sexual difficulties, change in eating habits, change in sleeping habits, and 'trouble with the boss' are obvious examples. While this possibility of confounding represents a significant methodological issue, there is evidence that when this source of error is controlled (by considering only events judged to be outside the control of the individual), significant relationships between life change and dependent measures are still to be found (Mueller, Edwards and Yarvis; 1977). This would seem to provide support for considering life events as an independent variable in this relationship.

Although acknowledging that the inclusion of events which may be brought about by individuals themselves may create difficulties in interpretation, it may be argued that events such as sexual difficulties, being fired from ones job, etc., regardless of their cause, represent a significant source of stress and that to ignore them is to neglect important assessment information if ones purpose is to determine major sources of life stress experienced by the individual. It would seem reasonable to suggest that life stress measures probably should include events, both within and outside the control of the individual. As suggested by Dohrenwend and Dohrenwend (1974b) this type of measure may have advantages when the major purpose of the investigator is to predict the onset of illness. It would appear, however, that these two types of events should be considered separately when conducting certain types of aetiological research. Further studies investigating correlates of both categories of events are in order.

(ii) Interpretation of Results

In addition to the assessment issues just discussed other factors make it difficult to interpret the findings of life stress research. One important factor is the retrospective nature of many investigations. For example, how does one interpret the finding that a sample of patients who have recently had heart attacks report more recent life changes than do a comparable group of non-patients? Although it might be tempting to conclude that the increased life stress in the cardiac sample contributed to the heart attacks it might just as easily be concluded that cardiac patients simply report experiencing more past events, perhaps due to a need to justify their illness. Brown (1972) describes this as 'retrospective contamination'. If for example, a study of the relationship between life stress and depression yields a significant relationship between the two variables what is to be concluded? Again, while it may be tempting to conclude that life stress leads to depression one must also consider alternative explanations. Depressed individuals, because of their mood state, may simply recall more negative life changes than individuals who are not depressed. If required to rate the stressfulness of events themselves, they may give reported events more negative weightings. An additional explanation might be that individuals who are depressed may, because of their condition, actually experience more life changes than non-depressed individuals. Thus depression might cause an increase in life changes rather than *vice versa*. A similar case might be made regarding correlations between life stress and other variables as well.

Some studies have taken a prospective approach, thus eliminating some of the problems associated with retrospective investigations. An early example of this type of research was provided by Rahe (1968; 1969) who obtained life change scores from a total of 88 physicians. These subjects were then contacted 9 months later and their health status was reassessed. Of the 41 subjects with a life change unit score of at least 250, twenty-four, or 49 per cent, reported some health change. Of the 32 with life change unit scores between 150 and 250, eight (25 per cent) reported illness. Eleven subjects had life change unit scores of less than 150. Only 9 per cent of this group reported any health change. Many other prospective studies have been conducted, and like retrospective investigations, have provided support for a relationship between life stress and health-related variables. Results of these studies do not, however, allow one to infer a causal relationship. Even prospective studies are not sufficient to rule out the possible action of some third variable which might result in both high levels of life stress and lowered levels of physical and psychological functioning.

While significant correlates of life stress have been found in many studies it is instructive to examine the magnitude of the correlations obtained. Although exceptions are to be found, correlation coefficients in the 0.20 to 0.30 range are usually reported, suggesting that life stress accounts for less than 10 per cent of the variance in the dependent measures employed. This rather sobering fact suggests that our ability to make accurate predictions based on life stress scores alone is much less than desirable. The reason for this state of affairs is unclear. Low correlations may simply reflect problems in the quantification of life events, failure to separate positive and negative life changes, and the unreliability of life stress scales. An additional contributing factor may be the failure of investigators to incorporate into their research variables which mediate the effects of life stress.

4. A NEW APPROACH TO ASSESSMENT

Based on the preceding discussion it would appear that there are numerous unanswered questions related to the effects of life stress on individuals and to the most appropriate way of assessing life changes and their impact. During the past three years we have been involved in research dealing with some of the major issues raised here. One aspect of this research involved the construction and development of a new assessment measure, the Life Experiences Survey (LES).

(i) The Life Experiences Survey (LES)

Two major features distinguish the measure to be considered here from the Schedule of Recent Experiences (SRE). First, the new scale was constructed so as to allow for the derivation of both positive and negative life change scores by obtaining individualized ratings of the *desirability* of events. Secondly, the LES provides for individualized ratings of the *impact* of events. Such values were considered preferable to group-derived values, as it was felt that these ratings would provide a more accurate indication of the impact of life changes on particular individuals who may differ in their perceptions of events. Evidence in support of this approach has been provided by the results of a recent study by Yamamoto and Kinney (1976) who found life stress scores, based on self-ratings, to be better predictors than scores derived by employing mean adjustment ratings similar to those used with the SRE. Other investigators (Lundberg, Theorell and Lind, 1975) have also provided evidence that supports the value of self-ratings in assessing the impact of life events.

The Life Experiences Survey (LES) is a 57-item self-report measure and allows respondents to indicate events they have experienced during the past year. The scale has two portions: Section I is designed for all respondents and contains a list of 47 specific events plus three blank spaces in which subjects can indicate other events they may have experienced. The events listed in this section refer to life changes common to individuals in a wide variety of situations. The 10 events listed in Section II are designed primarily for use with students, but could be adapted for use with other populations. Section I is appropriate for use with the general population while both sections are relevant to a student population. (In our research, responses to items from Sections I and II were typically combined in deriving life change scores as much of this research was conducted with college students.)

The LES items were chosen to represent life changes frequently experienced by individuals in the general population. Many of the items were based on existing life stress measures, particularly the SRE. Others were included because they were judged to be events which occurred frequently and which potentially might exert a significant impact on the lives of persons experiencing them. Thirty-four of the events listed in the LES are similar in content to those found in the SRE, but certain SRE items were made more specific. For example, the SRE item 'occurrence of pregnancy' was changed so that the event was now applicable to both men and women. Some events not listed in the SRE but included here are: male and female items dealing with abortion and more general items such as serious injury or illness of close friend, engagement, breaking up with boyfriend/girlfriend, etc. Nine of the 10 school-related items are unique to the LES.

The format of the LES calls for subjects to rate separately the desirability and impact of events they have experienced. They are asked to indicate those events experienced during the past year, as well as (1) whether they viewed the event as being positive or negative, and (2) the perceived impact of the particular event on their life. Ratings are on a 7 point scale ranging from -3 to $+3$. A rating of -3 indicates a negative event judged to have had an extreme impact on the respondent. A rating of $+3$ indicates a positive event having an extreme impact. Summing the impact ratings of events designated as positive by the subject provides a *positive change score*. A *negative change score* is derived by summing the impact ratings of those events experienced as negative by the subject. The LES is presented in Table 7.1. An overview of research with this instrument will be presented here. For a more detailed discussion of the development of the LES see Sarason, Johnson and Siegel (1978).

(ii) Reliability of the LES

Two test–retest reliability studies of the LES have been conducted. Both involved a 5 to 6 week interval between test and retest. There were 34 subjects (undergraduate psychology students) in the first study and 58 in the second. The LES was scored to yield both positive and negative life change scores and Pearson product–moment correlations were employed to determine the relationships between scores obtained at the two testings. Test–retest correlations for the positive change score were 0.19 and 0.53 in the first and second studies, respectively. The significant reliability coefficients for the negative change score were 0.56 and 0.88.

While these correlations vary to some extent, perhaps due to the relatively small sample sizes, they suggest that the LES is a moderately reliable instrument especially when the negative change score is considered. It should be noted that the test–retest reliability coefficients found with instruments of this type are likely to underestimate the reliability of the measure. With a time interval of 5 to 6 weeks between test and retest, subjects may actually experience a variety of events, both positive and negative, which may be reported at the time of retesting. As these changes reflect the actual occurrence of life changes, rather than inconsistencies in reporting, it would be inappropriate to consider the total variability in responding as error. Since subjects generally seem to report somewhat higher levels of positive than negative change on the LES, it seems possible that the lower reliability estimates found with the positive change measure may be due, in part, to the greater likelihood of positive changes occurring within the time interval between test and retest for these particular subject groups.

TABLE 7.1. The Life Experiences Survey. [Reprinted, with permission, from Sarason, Johnson and Siegel (1978). Copyright (1978) by the American Psychological Association.]

Instructions

Listed below are a number of events which sometimes bring about change in the lives of those who experience them and which necessitate social readjustment. *Please check those events which you have experienced in the recent past and indicate the time period during which you have experienced each event.* Be sure that all check marks are directly across from the items they correspond to.

Also, for each item checked below, *please indicate the extent to which you viewed the event as having either a positive or negative impact on your life* at the time the event occurred. That is, *indicate the type and extent of impact that the event had.* A rating of −3 would indicate an extremely negative impact. A rating of 0 suggests no impact either positive or negative. A rating of +3 would indicate an extremely positive impact.

Section I

	0 to 6 mo.	7 mo. to 1 yr.	Extremely negative −3	Moderately negative −2	Somewhat negative −1	No impact 0	Slightly positive +1	Moderately positive +2	Extremely positive +3
1. Marriage									
2. Detention in jail or comparable institution									
3. Death of spouse									
4. Major change in sleeping habits (much more or much less sleep)									

TABLE 7.1. *continued*

	0 to 6 mo.	7 mo. to 1 yr.	Extremely negative −3	Moderately negative −2	Somewhat negative −1	No impact 0	Slightly positive +1	Moderately positive +2	Extremely positive +3

5. Death of close family member:
   a. mother
   b. father
   c. brother
   d. sister
   e. grandmother
   f. grandfather
   g. other (specify)
6. Major change in eating habits (much more or much less food intake)
7. Foreclosure on mortgage or loan
8. Death of close friend
9. Outstanding personal achievement
10. Minor law violations (traffic tickets, disturbing the peace, etc.)
11. *Male:* Wife/girlfriend's pregnancy
12. *Female:* Pregnancy
13. Changed work situation (different work responsibility, major change in working conditions, working hours, etc.)
14. New job

15. Serious illness or injury of close family member:
    a. father
    b. mother
    c. sister
    d. brother
    e. grandfather
    f. grandmother
    g. spouse
    h. other (specify)
16. Sexual difficulties
17. Trouble with employer (in danger of losing job, being suspended, demoted, etc.)
18. Trouble with in-laws
19. Major change in financial status (a lot better off or a lot worse off)
20. Major change in closeness of family members (increased or decreased closeness)
21. Gaining a new family member (through birth, adoption, family member moving in, etc.)
22. Change of residence
23. Marital separation from mate (due to conflict)
24. Major change in church activities (increased or decreased attendance)
25. Marital reconciliation with mate
26. Major change in number of arguments with spouse (a lot more or a lot less arguments)
27. *Married male:* Change in wife's work outside the home (beginning work, ceasing work, changing to a new job, etc.)

TABLE 7.1. *continued*

	0 to 6 mo.	7 mo. to 1 yr.	Extremely negative −3	Moderately negative −2	Somewhat negative −1	No impact 0	Slightly positive +1	Moderately positive +2	Extremely positive +3
28. *Married female*: Change in husband's work (loss of job, beginning new job, retirement, etc.)									
29. Major change in usual type and/or amount of recreation									
30. Borrowing more than $10,000 (buying home, business, etc.)									
31. Borrowing less than $10,000 (buying car, TV, getting school loan, etc.)									
32. Being fired from job									
33. *Male*: Wife/girlfriend having abortion									
34. *Female*: Having abortion									
35. Major personal illness or injury									
36. Major change in social activities, e.g. parties, movies, visiting (increased or decreased participation)									
37. Major change in living conditions of family (building new home, remodeling, deterioration of home, neighbourhood, etc.)									
38. Divorce									
39. Serious injury or illness of close friend									
40. Retirement from work									
41. Son or daughter leaving home (due to marriage, college, etc.)									

42. Ending of formal schooling
43. Separation from spouse (due to work, travel, etc.)
44. Engagement
45. Breaking up with boyfriend/girlfriend
46. Leaving home for the first time
47. Reconciliation with boyfriend/ girlfriend

Other recent experiences which have had an impact on your life. List and rate.

48. _____
49. _____
50. _____

Section II   STUDENT ONLY

51. Beginning a new school experience at a higher academic level (college, graduate school, professional school, etc.)
52. Changing to a new school at same academic level (undergraduate, graduate, etc.)
53. Academic probation
54. Being dismissed from dormitory or other residence
55. Failing an important exam
56. Changing a major
57. Failing a course
58. Dropping a course
59. Joining a fraternity/sorority
60. Financial problems concerning school (in danger of not having sufficient money to continue)

(iii)   Life Stress, Anxiety, Academic Performance, and Social Desirability

In an initial study investigating correlates of positive and negative LES scores, 100 undergraduate psychology students were administered the LES, the State-Trait Anxiety Inventory (Spielberger, Gorsuch and Lushene, 1970), and a short form of the Marlowe–Crowne Social Desirability scale (Strahan and Gerbasi, 1972). Academic transcripts (Grade Point Averages) were available for 75 of these students making it possible to derive grade point averages for the quarter during which the testing occurred. Correlations between life change scores, anxiety, and grade point average are presented in Table 7.2. As can be seen, negative change was found to be correlated significantly and in a positive direction with both state and trait anxiety while the positive change score was unrelated to either measure. Significant correlations between negative change and anxiety have also been found in data collected as part of other investigations, one of them with anxiety measured by the Multiple Affect Adjective Check List (Zuckerman and Lubin, 1965).

As can also be seen in Table 7.2, negative change was found to be significantly correlated with GPA, suggesting that higher levels of life change are related to poorer academic performance. These results are consistent with other studies which have found significant relationships between life stress (assessed by other measures) and measures of anxiety (Constantini, Braun, Davis and Iervolino, 1973) and academic achievement (Carranza, 1972).

As it seemed reasonable that the effects of positive change might, in part, ameliorate the stress produced by negative experiences, a balance or subtractive score (negative − positive) was also computed for each subject and correlated with the dependent measures. In no case was this balance score more predictive than the negative change score. These results are similar to those reported by Mueller *et al.* (1977), and Vinokur and Selzer (1975) who have found such a balance score to be less predictive of stress-related variables than measures of negative life change. No relationship between LES scores and the measure of social desirability was found. This suggests that

TABLE 7.2. Correlations between life change scores, anxiety, and academic achievement. [Reproduced, with permission, from Sarason, Johnson and Siegel (1978). Copyright (1978) by the American Psychological Association.]

Life change scores	Trait anxiety ($N = 97$)	State anxiety ($N = 97$)	Grade Point Average ($N = 73$)
LES positive change	0.04	0.03	−0.21
LES negative change	0.29**	0.46***	−0.38***
LES balance score	−0.21*	−0.36***	0.18

$^*p < 0.05$; $^{**}p < 0.01$; $^{***}p < 0.001$.

responses to the LES are unlikely to be significantly influenced by social desirability response bias.

(iv) Personal Maladjustment and the LES

To determine the relationship between life stress and measures of personal maladjustment, the LES and the Psychological Screening Inventory (PSI) were administered to 75 male and female volunteers drawn from introductory psychology courses. The PSI (Lanyon, 1970; 1973) is a 130 item true-false inventory which yields scores on five subscales; Alienation (Al), Social Non-conformity (Sn), Discomfort (Di), Expression (Ex), and Defensiveness (De). The Al scale was designed for 'assessing similarity to psychiatric patients', and the Sn scale for 'assessing similarity to incarcerated prisoners'. The Di scale has been presented as a measure of neuroticism, the Ex scale as a measure of the introversion–extraversion dimension, and the De scale as a measure of test-taking attitude.

Correlations between life change scores and the PSI scales indicated a significant relationship between negative life change and two measures of maladjustment; the Social Nonconformity and Discomfort scales, suggesting a relationship between negative life change and certain types of personal maladjustment. Only the PSI Expression scale was found to correlate significantly with positive change. The results obtained here are generally in line with those obtained by Constantini, Braun, Davis and Iervolino (1973) in their investigation correlating life stress scores, derived from the Holmes and Rahe (1967) scale, with PSI scores.

Scores on the LES, the Beck Depression Scale (Beck, 1967) and the Locus of Control (I–E) Scale (Rotter, 1966), have also been collected for a research sample. A significant relationship between negative change and scores on the Beck Depression Scale was obtained, but positive change was not significantly correlated with depression. These findings are consistent with evidence presented by Vinokur and Selzer (1975). An additional finding of interest is that individuals who report having experienced high levels of negative change appear to be more externally oriented, perceiving themselves as being less capable of exerting control over environmental events. No relationship between postive change and locus of control was found. Finally employing a sample of 122 subjects, a significant relationship has been found between negative change and MMPI Hypochondriasis scores suggesting that negative change is related to increased somatic preoccupation. Positive change was not correlated with this measure.

Life change scores have also been obtained on a group of students seeking treatment at a university counselling centre for psychological problems. It was expected that this group would differ from randomly selected groups of college students in their negative change scores but not in terms of positive change. No significant differences were obtained when positive change scores were considered, but Counseling Centre clients had significantly higher negative change scores. These findings provide additional support for a relationship between negative life change, as assessed by the LES, and problems of psychological adjustment. It should be pointed out, however, that data of this type may be susceptible to the problem of retrospective contamination discussed earlier.

(v) Assessment of Life Change: A Comparison of Approaches

To the extent that the LES represents an improvement over the SRE, it should be possible to demonstrate that measures derived from this scale are more highly correlated with relevant dependent variables than are SRE scores. Further analyses of data already reported, along with analyses of additional data, were undertaken to provide a basis for comparing these two measures. The comparisons were accomplished by scoring only the 34 items of the LES which are common to the SRE. These items were scored to yield four measures. Three of these measures were LES positive, negative, and total life change scores. The total change score was derived by summing the positive and negative scores. A fourth measure was derived by applying the life change units employed with the SRE to each of the 34 items reported. It was thus possible to derive a measure comparable to the SRE based on responses to these events. Although these measures were based on 34 rather than the entire 42 items of the Holmes and Rahe scale, it was felt that they would provide an adequate basis for comparing the two scoring procedures. Based on previous findings regarding the importance of negative change it was predicted that the LES negative change score would be more predictive of dependent measures than would the Holmes and Rahe measure. No predictions were made regarding the LES positive and total change scores.

In one study, 69 female undergraduates were given the LES, the Beck Depression Scale and the State-Trait Anxiety Inventory. The four life change measures were derived as outlined above. One somewhat surprising finding was that of no significant correlation between any of the life change measures and anxiety. Given the rather consistent finding of a relationship between negative change and anxiety reported earlier, these results might best be attributed to the rather select nature of the samply employed. Significant correlations were obtained, however, between the Beck Depression Scale and negative and total LES scores. There was no significant correlation between the life change unit score, similar to that employed with the SRE and depression, but the difference between the correlations obtained with the LES negative change score and with the Holmes and Rahe score was significant.

A second comparative study of the LES and SRE investigated the relationship between these measures and the scores on the Psychological Screening

TABLE 7.3. Correlations between LES change scores, life change unit scores (34 items) and Psychological Screening Inventory scale scores. [Reproduced, with permission, from Sarason, Johnson and Siegel (1978) Copyright (1978) by the American Psychological Association.]

| Life change score | Psychological Screening Inventory score | |
	Social Nonconformity	Discomfort
LES positive change	0.02	−0.04
LES negative change	0.26*	0.25*
LES total change	0.18	0.12
Life change unit score	0.14	0.15

*$p < 0.05$.

Inventory. As in the original analysis (which employed the entire LES), two Psychological Screening Inventory measures of psychopathology correlated with life change when only 34 items were scored; Social Nonconformity and Discomfort (neuroticism). Correlations between change scores and these measures are presented in Table 7.3. As can be seen, although the LES negative change score was significantly correlated with both measures of maladjustment, no significant relationships were found between these measures and the life change unit score. While the differences between these correlations did not reach statistical significance, the pattern of results seems to support the superiority of the LES measure of negative change.

A further comparative study of the LES and SRE approaches to the assessment of life stress has recently been reported by Pancheri and De Martino (1978). They found LES scores to be more highly associated with a variety of physical (gastro-intestinal disorders, allergic disorders, myocardial infarction, etc.) and psychiatric disorders than were life stress scores derived from the SRE. Although negative change scores were most predictive in the majority of cases, these authors raise the possibility that different patterns of positive and negative life change scores may relate to specific disease entities.

(vi) Mood States and Reporting of Life Change

In developing an assessment instrument it is necessary to provide data indicating that measures derived from the scale are significantly related to relevant dependent variables. Data of this type have been provided by the results of a number of studies reported here. It should also be demonstrated that scores derived from the measure are *unrelated* to certain other variables. For example, it is necessary to demonstrate that scores are not significantly influenced by response sets such as the tendency to place oneself in a socially desirable light. Earlier we presented data suggesting that it is unlikely that LES scores are significantly influenced by this factor. It is possible that still other variables might affect responding to the extent that estimates of life stress derived from this measure would be inaccurate. One such variable is the mood state of the respondent.

As LES positive and negative life change scores are based on subjects' self-ratings of events it is possible that mood state, at the time of testing, may significantly affect the number of events reported as well as the desirability and impact ratings associated with these events. It could be argued, for example, that depressed individuals might tend to report more negative events than non-depressed individuals, and that they may also give these negative events more extreme impact ratings resulting in a high negative life change score. This type of bias might result in finding a significant correlation between negative life change and depression such as that reported earlier in this chapter and elsewhere in the literature. If such factors are operative, this relationship would be more reflective of biased responding than the effects of life stress on individuals.

While further studies are needed to assess the influence of subject variables on responding to life stress measures, one preliminary study has been conducted to specifically examine the possibility that mood state may be a biasing factor. In this study (Siegel, Johnson and Sarason, in press) the effect of experimentally induced mood states on responding to the LES was investigated. Subjects who had previously completed the LES were randomly assigned to one of three experimental conditions; neutral, elation, or depression. By employing an affect induction procedure developed by Velten (1968) it was possible to induce transient states of depression and elation in these subjects. The neutral condition was employed as a control. After the mood induction procedure subjects were given the LES a second time. Although a manipulation check indicated that the affect induction procedure did result in elation and depression (as well as increased anxiety and hostility in the depression condition) in the two experimental groups, mood states had no significant effect on the number of life changes reported, or on LES scores. These results suggest that the significant correlations previously obtained between the LES and depression are not likely to be simply the result of a depressed mood state on responding to the LES. Again, while further research is needed in this area, it would appear that responses to the LES are not unduly influenced by the mood state of the respondent.

(vii) Efficacy of the LES

From this initial work with the LES it appears that the scale will prove a useful instrument in stress research. It has a big advantage over the SRE because it provides separate assessments of positive and negative change and takes into account the impact of the change. In particular, negative changes seem to be associated with many dependent measures that have been used in other life stress studies. The weighting of events for impact made little difference to these relations in our studies because groups of the subjects had experienced only moderate to low levels of life change. However it seems reasonable that impact ratings will assume greater importance for quantifying life changes in populations who have experienced high levels of life change.

5. MODERATOR VARIABLES IN LIFE STRESS RESEARCH

As noted earlier, while many studies have found statistically significant relationships between life stress, assessed in various ways, and a host of stress-related variables, these correlations have usually been quite modest This finding suggests that life stress accounts for a relatively small proportion of the variance in the dependent measures employed and that *by themselves* life stress measures are not likely to be of value for purposes of prediction. A major limitation of research studies in this area seems to be a relative lack of attention given to variables which might mediate the effects of life change. While there has been relatively little research related to this issue, several writers have pointed to the possible role of moderator variables, such as sociological, psychological, and physiological factors, in determining the precise relationship between life stress and other variables (Dohrenwend and Dohrenwend, 1974b; Rabkin and Struening, 1976; Rahe, 1978).

One of the earliest life stress studies to consider the role of moderator variables was conducted by Nuckolls, Cassell and Kaplan (1972) who examined the relationship between life stress and pregnancy and birth complications. Here women were administered the SRE and a specially designed Psychosocial Assets Scale during the thirty-second week of pregnancy. The latter measure was designed to assess the degree to which the women possessed social support systems in their environment. Also obtained was information concerning pregnancy and birth complications. Significant relationships between life change and complications were only found when the social supports measure was taken into account. For subjects with high levels of psychosocial assets, no relationship between life stress and complications was found. Life stress was, however, related to complications among those women with low levels of social supports. Given high life stress scores before and during pregnancy, women with low levels of psychosocial assets had three times the number of pregnancy and birth complications of high life stress women with high psychosocial assets scores. These findings seem to provide support for the notion that the level of social supports in ones environment may be an important variable in determining the effects of life stress. Recent discussions of the role of social supports as a moderator of life stress have been presented by Cobb (1976) and by Dean and Lin (1977).

Another moderator variable has been suggested by the results of a recent study conducted by Smith, Johnson and Sarason (1978). In this study subjects were administered the LES, the Sensation Seeking Scale (Zuckerman, Kolin, Price and Zoob, 1964), and the Discomfort scale of the Psychological Screening Inventory (Lanyon, 1973). The Sensation Seeking measure employed is an instrument designed to assess the tendency of individuals to engage in thrill seeking, risk-taking behaviours. High scorers on this measure are thought to display a high optimal level of stimulation while those scoring low on the scale are thought to display a low optimal level of stimulation. Thus low sensation seekers are thought to often try to minimize arousing stimulus input. The Discomfort scale of the Psychological Screening Inventory has been presented as a measure of neuroticism. Smith *et al.* (1978) reasoned that if the Sensation Seeking measure, in fact, reflects an optimal level of stimulation or arousal then low sensation seekers should be more adversely affected by life stress than high sensation seekers who are presumably more tolerant of change. Results in line with this hypothesis were obtained. While no significant relationships between life change and scores on the Discomfort scale were found among high sensation seekers a signficant relationship between negative change and the Discomfort measure was found when responses of low sensation seekers were analysed.

Support for the role of stimulation seeking as a moderator variable has also been provided by the results of an additional study conducted by Johnson, Sarason and Siegel (1978a). This study investigated the relationship between life change and measures of anxiety, depression, and hostility as a function of subjects' status on the arousal seeking dimension. Partial correlations between these variables for both high and low arousal seekers are presented in Table 7.4. Negative change was significantly correlated with measures of both anxiety and hostility, but only for subjects low on the arousal seeking dimension.

The effects of life change may also vary depending on the degree to which the person perceives events as being under his/her personal control. In a recent investigation Johnson and Sarason (in press) have obtained results that support such a relationship. The Locus of Control Scale (Rotter, 1966) assesses the subjects' perceptions of control over their environment. Low scorers (internals) are thought to perceive environmental reinforcers as being under their personal control. High scorers (externals) are believed to view reinforcers as being controlled by fate, luck, or powerful others. There is considerable evidence that this measure reflects subjects' perception of control over environmental events. Johnson and Sarason (in press) found that negative life change was significantly correlated with measures of both trait anxiety and depression for subjects believing themselves to be controlled by their environment.

In an additional study Siegel, Johnson and Sarason (in press) investigated

TABLE 7.4. Partial correlations between measures of life change and measures of anxiety, depression, and hostility in subjects differing on the arousal seeking dimension

Arousal seeking score	Life change measure	Dependent variables		
		anxiety	depression	hostility
High	Positive change	−0.15	−0.23	0.05
High	Negative change	−0.01	−0.04	0.05
Low	Positive change	−0.18	−0.12	0.00
Low	Negative	0.36*	0.23	0.46**

*$p < 0.05$; ** < 0.01.

the relationship between life stress, as assessed by the LES, and menstrual discomfort. Here a significant relationship between negative life change and discomfort was obtained. This relationship was found, however, to hold only for those subjects not taking oral contraceptives. It seems reasonable to conclude that a number of specific variables may mediate the effects of life changes. To the extent that moderator variables influence the effects of life change, the finding of low correlations between measures of life change and dependent measures is to be expected when such variables are not taken into consideration.

6.   CAUSAL RELATIONSHIPS IN LIFE STRESS RESEARCH

While significant correlations between life change and stress-related variables have been repeatedly demonstrated in the literature, it is impossible to draw firm cause and effect conclusions regarding the effects of life stress on individuals. In order to make causal statements it is usually considered necessary to conduct experiments in which a variable of interest is systematically manipulated and where the effect of this manipulation on behaviour can be observed. For both practical and ethical reasons it is impossible to manipulate life stress as one might a laboratory stressor. Because of this problem studies relating life stress to indices of health and adjustment have necessarily been correlational in nature. While the results of such studies are of interest, one cannot say whether life stress results in problems of health and adjustment, for example, or whether persons with such problems are simply more prone to experience life changes. Further, it is impossible to rule out the existence of other variables which may have resulted in both high levels of life change and health and adjustment problems. Thus research reported, to date, does not permit causal inferences regarding the effects of life stress.

Given that it is desirable to reach the point eventually where causal inferences can be made, and that we will continue to be unable to experimentally manipulate life stress, how then does one proceed? It is likely that no one study, no matter how well designed, will be capable of providing data sufficient to justify the conclusion that a causal relationship exists. It is, in fact, impossible to 'prove' the existence of a causal relationship from correlational data. However, by conducting a variety of studies, specifically designed to investigate and control for specific variables, it may be possible to accumulate a body of information which, when taken together, would allow an inference of causality to be made with some justification.

One potentially fruitful approach to investigating the possibility of a causal relationship in the life stress area would involve the use of a cross-lagged correlational methodology. This quasi-experimental approach, originally suggested by Simon (1954), involves obtaining data on two variables of interest at two points in time and comparing the correlations among these variables from one time period to another. An illustration of this cross-lagged methodology, as applied to life stress research, is presented in Figure 7.1. As can be seen, correlations can be obtained between life stress scores and dependent variables at Time 1 and Time 2. These are the correlations which might be obtained in the typical correlational study. Correlations between life

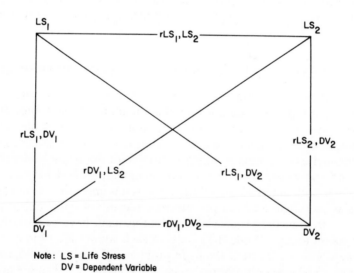

Note: LS = Life Stress
      DV = Dependent Variable

FIGURE 7.1. Cross-lagged panel correlational model. (After Simon, 1954)

stress scores at Time 1 and Time 2 and between dependent measures at Time 1 and Time 2 can also be obtained. These provide information concerning the stability of measures over time. The remaining two correlations are of primary interest in assessing the possibility of a causal relationship. If a causal relationship exists and life stress influences health and adjustment, one would expect life stress, assessed at Time 1, to be significantly correlated with indices of health status and adjustment obtained at Time 2, and that this correlation (rLS_1, DV_2) would be greater than that obtained between health and adjustment, assessed at Time 1, and life stress assessed at Time 2 (rDV_1, LS_2). A significant, and larger, correlation of the latter type would be more suggestive of a causal relationship in which health and adjustment influence subsequent life stress. While this approach would appear to be of value in investigating the possibility of a casual relationship, it does have limitations, one being that it does not entirely eliminate the possibility that some additional variable may cause the two variables of interest (life stress and health status in this case) to covary. For further discussion of this methodology see Kenny (1975).

Data of the type described here have been obtained in a recent study by Johnson, Sarason and Siegel (1978b). Here measures of life stress (previous six months) and several self-report indices of health and adjustment were obtained on a sample of undergraduate psychology students. Seven months later 42 subjects were contacted and these same measures obtained a second

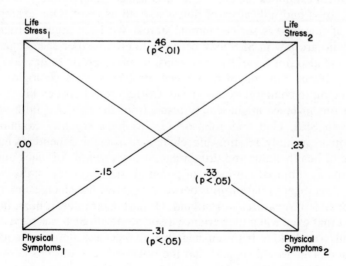

FIGURE 7.2. Cross-lagged correlational analysis of measures of negative life change and the reporting of physical symptoms

time. While the data from this study have not yet been fully analyzed, preliminary analyses seem to be consistent with a causal interpretation, particularly when measures associated with physical health are considered. To illustrate, cross-lagged correlations for three of the dependent measures are presented in Figure 7.2. It may be noted that life stress (negative change) scores at Time 1 are significantly correlated with the reporting of physical symptoms at Time 2. No significant relationship was found between physical symptoms at Time 1 and subsequent life stress scores. Similar findings were obtained with regard to self-ratings of overall physical health, and when a measure of somatic preoccupation (MMPI hypochondriasis scores) was considered.

In general, these correlational data lend tentative support to the view that a causal relationship may exist between negative life change, on one hand, and certain health-related variables on the other. Further, analyses including an examination of the role of events within and outside the control of respondents should shed additional light on the nature of these relationships. A similar study, also employing the cross-lagged correlational approach has recently been conducted by Vossil and Fröhlich (1978). These investigators have examined the relationship between negative life changes, as assessed by the LES, and measures of job tension and task performance effectiveness. The findings of this study were interpreted as being consistent with a causal relationship in the predicted direction (e.g. life stress leads to job tension and decreased performance effectiveness).

In addition to further studies of the type described above, research is also needed which examines the effects of variables considered likely to influence both life stress and indicators of illness and adjustment. One example of a variable of this type is socioeconomic status. We have argued already that persons who are low in SES may be more likely to experience negative life changes and also, for a variety of reasons, be more prone to develop health-related problems. One might also expect problems of psychological adjustment to be more common to this group. Correlations between life stress and illness in this instance might simply result from the fact that both variables covary with SES. Gad and Johnson (1978) have recently examined this interaction in a study relating life change to several dependent measures reflective of health status and drug usage, using a sample of black and white adolescents as subjects. An index of parental socioeconomic status was also obtained. Significant relationships between negative life change and a variety of the dependent measures were found. Of particular interest here, however, is the fact that even when the variance associated with SES was partialled out, significant correlations between negative change and dependent measures were found. This would suggest that the obtained relationships between life change and dependent variables was not due to the common association of these variables with socioeconomic status. Additional studies of this type, investigating other variables, which might exert a common influence on both life stress and health and adjustment, seem to be required.

A neglected area of life stress research has to do with the possible relation-ship between life stress and cognitive variables. To the extent that coping with life stressors may place both physical and psychological demands on individu-als and may be related to increased levels of anxiety and arousal as well as problems of health and adjustment, one might speculate that life stress may have a deleterious effect on cognitive performance. A variety of studies, for example, have suggested that high levels of anxiety and arousal are negatively related to performance on complex tasks (Eysenck, 1976), to ability to utilize semantic cues in recall (Mueller, 1976), and to degree of cue utilization where aroused individuals display a more restricted range of attention (Easterbrook, 1959; Bacon, 1974). Likewise, Broadbent (1971), in considering the effects of specific environmental stressors, has noted that conditions such as noise, high and low temperatures, and sleeplessness also affect performance on vigilance and other tasks. It would not be surprising to find that high life stress subjects display similar problems of attention, memory, and performance, as well as perhaps other difficulties in the processing of information. While little research has been done in this area, the relationship between life stress and such variables would seem to be worth investigation.

7. SUMMARY AND CONCLUSIONS

In this chapter we have focused on one type of stress which is assumed to have negative effects on the physical and psychological well-being of indi-viduals. In considering the effects of life changes it should be pointed out that persons may be exposed to a variety of other types of stress as well. Here one might include a variety of ecological stressors such as high population density (crowding), other facts such as 'noise pollution' and living in extreme envi-ronments. Additionally, it is obvious that there are a variety of other stressors which impinge on the lives of some persons which are not experienced in terms of 'recent life events'. Examples of stressors of this sort might include the knowledge that one has some probability of developing a genetically related disease or that at some earlier time one was industrially exposed to what is now known to be a carcinogen. Other potential stressors such as the realization that one has not reached and probably will not reach goals set earlier in one's career, or that one's level of professional activity is declining may not be fully reflected in terms of specific life changes. Finally, there are undoubtedly a variety of day-to-day situations which do not bring about major life changes and which do not necessitate social readjustment, but which may nevertheless serve as stressors. Thus life changes may best be viewed as one of many sources of stress, albeit an important one. In spite of the fact that changes such as those assessed in life stress research do not tap the totality of stressful situations to which one is exposed, negative life changes do seem to constitute a major type of stress common to the daily lives of individuals. As such, continued research regarding the effects of such life changes on the health, adjustment, and performance of individuals would appear to be important.

Based on previous life stress research and on the results of studies reported here, it would seem possible to begin to draw some tentative conclusions regarding certain important issues in the area and to comment briefly on future directions in which work in this area might proceed.

Taken together, the findings cited here along with those of Mueller, Edwards and Yarvis (1977) and Vinokur and Selzer (1975) suggests that life stress may be most accurately conceptualized in terms of events that exert negative impacts on individuals. This view is supported by the results of a variety of studies which indicate that negative but not positive change is significantly related to stress-related dependent measures. This position, emphasizing the importance of negative change, is at variance with the views of earlier investigators in the area (Holmes and Rahe, 1967) who emphasized the role of change *per se* as the crucial variable.

Considering the distinction to be made between positive and negative life changes, it would appear that the Life Experiences Survey represents a useful step in the assessment of life stress as it allows for the derivation of both positive and negative life change scores. That this measure may be a useful research tool is suggested by the fact that comparisons between the LES and measures similar to the SRE, by ourselves and others, have suggested the superiority of the LES, particularly the negative change score. Although further research with this measure is needed, the results of studies conducted thus far suggest that the LES may have advantages over existing measures.

In spite of the fact that the LES may prove to be useful as a life stress measure, it is the case that life stress does not have a uniform effect on individuals, and that there may be a variety of social, psychological, and perhaps physiological variables which may mediate the effects of life stress (if in fact a causal relationship exists). Further research related to possible moderators of life stress is greatly needed.

While not minimizing the need to consider other major methodological and conceptual issues in the area, it may be argued that it is time to stop simply looking for additional correlates of life stress and begin to determine under what conditions, and with which individuals, observed relationships hold. It is only by identifying and determining the role of moderator variables, and considering such variables within experimental designs, that we can begin to assess the actual implications of life change for the health status, adjustment, and performance of individuals.

Finally, as research is beginning to determine more precisely the nature and effects of life stress and the characteristics of individuals most likely to be affected by life changes, the development of stress management programmes designed to help individuals cope more effectively with such stressors would seem to be a major challenge of the future.

8. ACKNOWLEDGEMENT

Research reported here was funded by the Organizational Effectiveness Research Program, U.S. Office of Naval Research (Code 452), Under Contract N00014-75-C-0905, NR 170-804. The authors wish to acknowledge the contributions of Dr. Judith M. Siegel to much of the research reported here.

9. REFERENCES

Bacon, S. J. (1974). Arousal and the range of cue utilization. *Journal of Experimental Psychology*, **102**, 81–87.

Beck, A. T. (1967). *Depression: Clinical, Experimental, and Theoretical Aspects*. New York: Harper and Row.

Bedell, J. R., Giordani, B., Amour, J. L., Tavormina, J. and Boll, T. (1977). Life stress and the psychological and medical adjustment of chronically ill children. *Journal of Psychosomatic Research*, **21**, 237–242.

Broadbent, D. E. (1971). *Decision and Stress*. London: Academic Press.

Brown, G. W. (1972). Life-events and psychiatric illness: some thoughts on methodology and causality. *Journal of Psychosomatic Research*, **16**, 311–320.

Brown, G. W. (1974). Meaning, measurement, and stress of life events. In B. S. Dohrenwend and B. P. Dohrenwend (Eds.), *Stressful Life Events: Their Nature and Effects*. New York: Wiley.

Carranza, E. (1972). A study of the impact of life changes on high school teacher performance in the Lansing school district as measured by the Holmes and Rahe Schedule of Recent Experiences. Unpublished doctoral dissertation, Michigan State University.

Cobb, S. (1976). Social support as a moderator of life stress. *Psychosomatic Medicine*, **38**, 300–314.

Constantini, A. F., Braun, J. R., Davis, J. and Iervolino, A. (1973). Personality and mood correlates of Schedule of Recent Experience scores. *Psychological Reports*, **32**, 416–418.

Dean, A. and Lin, N. (1977). The stress-buffering role of social support. *Journal of Nervous and Mental Diseases*, **165**, 403–417.

Dekker, D. J. and Webb, J. T. (1974) Relationships of the Social Readjustment Rating Scale to psychiatric patient status, anxiety, and social desirability. *Journal of Psychosomatic Research*, **18**, 125–130.

Dohrenwend, B. S. and Dohrenwend, B. P. (1974a). *Stressful Life Events*. New York: Wiley.

Dohrenwend, B. S. and Dohrenwend, B. P. (1974b). Overview and prospects for research on stressful life events. In B. S. Dohrenwend and B. P. Dohrenwend (Eds.), *Stressful Life Events*. New York: Wiley.

Easterbrook, J. A. (1959). The effect of emotion on cue utilization and the organization of behavior. *Psychological Review*, **66**, 183–201.

Edwards, M. K. (1971). Life crises and myocardial infarction. Unpublished master's thesis, University of Washington.

Eysenck, M. W. (1976). Arousal, learning, and memory. *Psychological Bulletin*, **83**, 389–404.

Gad, M. T. and Johnson, J. H. (1978). Life stress and health status in adolescence as related to race, socioeconomic status, and social support systems. Unpublished manuscript, University of Washington.

Gorsuch, R. L. and Key, M. K. (1974). Abnormalities of pregnancy as a function of anxiety and life stress. *Psychosomatic Medicine*, **36**, 352–361.

Harris, P. W. (1972). The relationship of life change to academic performance among selected college freshmen at varying levels of college readiness. Unpublished doctoral dissertation, East Texas State University.

Holmes, T. H. and Masuda, M. (1974). Life change and illness susceptibility. In B. S. Dohrenwend and B. P. Dohrenwend (Eds.), *Stressful Life Events: Their Nature and Effects*. New York: Wiley.

Holmes, T. H. and Rahe, R. H. (1967). The Social Readjustment Rating Scale. *Journal of Psychosomatic Research*, **11**, 213–218.

Hudgens, R. W. (1974). Personal catastrophe and depression: a consideration of the subject with respect to medically ill adolescents, and a requiem for retrospective life-event studies. In B. S. Dohrenwend and B. P. Dohrenwend (Eds.), *Stressful Life Events: Their Nature and Effect*. New York: Wiley.

Johnson, J. H. and Sarason, I. G. (in press). Life stress, depression and anxiety: internal–external control as a moderator variable. *Journal of Psychosomatic Research*.

Johnson, J. H., Sarason, I. G. and Siegel, J. M. (1978a). Stimulation seeking and the effect of life stress. Unpublished manuscript. University of Washington.

Johnson, J. H., Sarason, I. G., and Siegel, J. M. (1978b). The effects of life stress: a cross-lagged correlational analysis. Unpublished data. University of Washington.

Kenny, D. A. (1975). Cross-lagged panel correlation: a test for spuriousness. *Psychological Bulletin*, **82**, 887–903.

Lanyon, R. I. (1970). Development and validation of a Psychological Screening Inventory. *Journal of Consulting and Clinical Psychology*, **35**, 1–24.

Lanyon, R. I. (1973). *Psychological Screening Inventory Manual*. Goshen, N.Y.: Research Psychologist Press.

Lundberg, V., Theorell, T. and Lind, E. (1975). Life changes and myocardial infarction: individual differences in life change scaling. *Journal of Psychosomatic Research, 19*, 27–32.

Mechanic, D. (1975). Some problems in the measurement of stress and social readjustment. *Journal of Human Stress*, **1**, 43–48.

Mueller, J. H. (1976). Anxiety and cue utilization in human learning and memory. In M. Zuckerman and C. D. Spielberger (Eds.), *Emotions and Anxiety: New Concepts, Methods and Applications*. Hillsdale, N. J.: Lawrence Erlbaum.

Mueller, D. P., Edwards, D. W. and Yarvis, R. M. (1977). Stressful life events and psychiatric symptomatology: change as undesirability. *Journal of Health and Social Behavior*, **18**, 307–317.

Myers, J. K., Lindenthal, J. J. and Pepper, M. P. (1974). Social class, life events, and psychiatric symptoms: a longitudinal study. In B. S. Dohrenwend and B. P. Dohrenwend (Eds.), *Stressful Life Events: Their Nature and Effects*. New York: Wiley.

Nuckolls, K. B., Cassell, J. and Kaplan, B. H. (1972). Psychosocial assets, life crisis and the prognosis of pregnancy. *American Journal of Epidemiology*, **95**, 431–441.

Pancheri, P. and De Martino, V. (1978). Comparison of two life stress events scaling methods as a function of anxiety in psychosomatic and psychiatric patients. Paper presented at Conference on 'Environmental Stress, Life Crises, and Social Adaption', Cambridge, England.

Paykel, E. S. (1974). Life stress and psychiatric disorder: applications of the clinical approach. In B. S. Dohrenwend and B. P. Dohrenwend (Eds.), *Stressful Life Events: Their Nature and Effects*. New York: Wiley.

Rabkin, J. G. and Struening, E. L. (1976). Life events, stress, and illness. *Science*, **194**, 1013–1020.

Rahe, R. H. (1968). Life-change measurement as a predictor of illness. *Proceedings of the Royal Society of Medicine*, **61**, 1124–1126.

Rahe, R. H. (1969). Life crisis and health change. In P. R. A. May and J. R. Wittenborn (Eds.), *Psychotropic Drug Response: Advances in Prediction*. Springfield, Ill.: O. C. Thomas.

Rahe, R. H. (1978). Life change and illness studies: past history and future directions. *Journal of Human Stress*, **4**, 3–14.

Rahe, R. H. and Lind, E. (1971). Psychosocial factors and sudden cardiac death: a pilot study. *Journal of Psychosomatic Research*, **15**, 19–24.

Rotter, J. B. (1966). Generalized expectancies for internal versus external control of reinforcement. *Psychological Monographs*, **80**, No. 1, Whole No. 609.

Sarason, I. G., De Monchaux, C. and Hunt, T. (1975). Methodological issues in the assessment of life stress. In L. Levi (Ed.), *Emotions—Their Parameters and Measurement*. New York: Rover Press.

Sarason, I. G., Johnson, J. H. and Siegel, J. M. (1978). Assessing the impact of life changes: development of the Life Experiences Survey. *Journal of Consulting and Clinical Psychology*, **46**, 932–946.

Siegel, J. M., Johnson, J. H., and Sarason, I. G. (in press). Mood states and the reporting of life changes. *Journal of Psychosomatic Research*.

Simon, H. A. (1954). Spurious correlation: a causal interpretation. *Journal of the American Statistical Association*, **49**, 467–479.

Smith, R. E., Johnson, J. H. and Sarason, I. G. (1978). Life change, the sensation seeking motive, and psychological distress. *Journal of Consulting and Clinical Psychology*, **46**, 348–349.

Spielberger, C. D., Gorsuch, R. L. and Lushene, R. E. (1970). *Manual for the State-Trait Anxiety Inventory*. Palo Alto, California: Consulting Psychologist Press.

Strahan, R. and Gerbasi, K. C. (1972). Short homogeneous versions of the Marlowe–Crowne Social Desirability Scale. *Journal of Clinical Psychology*, **28**, 191–193.

Theorell, T. and Rahe, R. H. (1971). Psychosocial factors and myocardial infarction. I: an inpatient study in Sweden. *Journal of Psychosomatic Research*, **15**, 25–31.

Velten, E. A. (1968). A laboratory task for induction of mood states. *Behaviour Research and Therapy*, **6**, 473–482.

Vinokur, A. and Selzer, M. L. (1975). Desirable versus undesirable life events: their relationship to stress and mental distress. *Journal of Personality and Social Psychology*, **32**, 329–337.

Vossil, G. and Fröhlich, W. D. (1978). Life stress, job tension, and subjective reports of task performance effectiveness: a causal-correlational analysis. Paper presented at Conference on 'Environmental Stress, Life Crises, and Social Adaptation', Cambridge, England.

Wyler, A. R., Masuda, M. and Holmes, T. H. (1971). Magnitude of life events and seriousness of illness. *Psychosomatic Medicine*, **33**, 115–122.

Yamamoto, K. J. and Kinney, O. K. (1976). Pregnant women's ratings of different factors influencing psychological stress during pregnancy. *Psychological Reports*, **39**, 203–214.

Zuckerman, M., Kolin, E. A., Price, L. and Zoob, I. (1964). Development of a sensation seeking scale. *Journal of Consulting Psychology*, **26**, 250–260.

Zuckerman, M. and Lubin, B. (1965). *Manual for the Multiple Affect Adjective Check List*. San Diego: Educational and Industrial Testing Service.

Chapter 8

Psychological Response to Serious Life Events

MARDI J. HOROWITZ

1. Introduction
2. States that follow Serious Life Events
   (i)   Phases
   (ii) Signs and Symptoms During Denial States
   (iii) Signs and Symptoms During Intrusion States
   (iv) Common Intrusive Contents
3. The Effects of Serious Life Events on Cognitive Schemata
4. Cognitive Operations and Controls in Processing the Meanings of Serious Life Events
   (i)   Background
   (ii) Completion Tendency and Active Memory Storage
   (iii) Controls of Information Processing: A More Detailed Examination
   (iv) Controls that Select Information
   (v)   Controls that Select Self-Images and Role Relationship Models
   (vi) 'Format Selection'
5. Concluding Comments
6. Acknowledgements
7. References

1. INTRODUCTION

One of the great paradoxes of the mind is that it must use existing inner models to interpret new events; models based on the past must interpret the present and be revised to meet the future. Evolution and development have favoured the best balance between retention of earlier forms and the acceptance of new stimuli. But the equilibrium between old forms and new information is not easily or quickly balanced when present events are those of loss.

This chapter discusses psychological responses to those serious life events that involve loss, either of a part of the self, or of others; of a world as it once was.

An ideal adjustment to loss, having done what one can to prevent it, is to accept it, to replace that which is lost, and to go on living. But there is an important, painful interval between the first pangs of recognition of loss and adaptation to circumstances as they must be. During that interval, there are states characterized by unusual levels of both intrusion of ideas and feelings and denial of ideas and numbing of emotions. Underlying these shifts in state are changes in inner models of the self, others, and the world; some due to alterations in dominance among models, and others due to formation of new models. Such changes are based on a gradual processing of the new information.

These aspects of psychological response can be systematically studied in any group of persons who experience major life events, and the resulting theory may help in planning the most humane support and treatment for those who experience intense responses to stress.

2. STATES THAT FOLLOW SERIOUS LIFE EVENTS

Considering the general disparities of psychological research, a relatively remarkable concordance is found in the clinical, field and experimental studies of response to the stress of serious events or to vicarious simulations of such events. The frequency of two broadly defined states increases after such occurrences; one epitomized by intrusive experiences, the other by denial and numbing. These seemingly paradoxical, but inextricably interrelated states have been given various names in the extensive literature on stress, (Breuer and Freud, 1895; Freud, 1920; Lazarus, 1966; Janis, 1958; 1969; Parkes 1972; Coehlo, Hamburg and Adams, 1974; Parad, Resnick and Parad 1976). The contents of these state and phase labels are usually specific to each individual. The terms, however, point to the general form of the experience, whatever the particular content (Horowitz, 1976).

(i) Phases

States of intrusion and of denial or avoidance do not occur in any prescribed pattern, but appear to oscillate in ways particular to each person. Nonetheless there is a phasic tendency. An initial period of outcry may occur and be followed by either denial or intrusive states, possibly in oscillation with each other. Then, in a period labelled as working through, the frequency and intensity of each of these states is reduced. When a relative baseline is reached, a period of completion is said to occur. This general sequence and the intensification of these phases is shown in diagrammatic form in Figure 8.1.

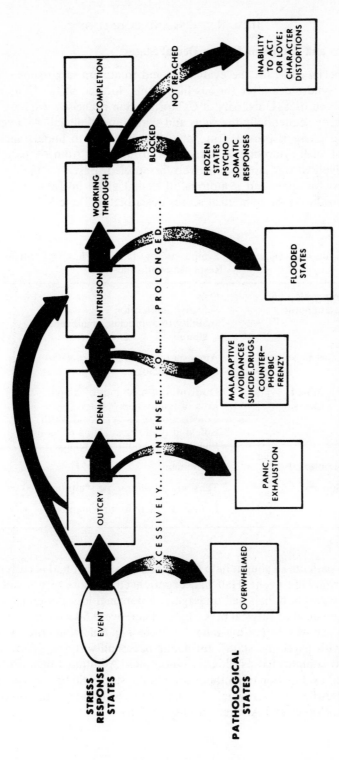

FIGURE 8.1. Phasic organization of denial and intrusion states, where any phase of stress response may be pathologically intense

(ii) Signs and Symptons During Denial States

In a special clinic for the evaluation and treatment of persons with stress response syndromes after serious life events, located at the Center for the Study of Neuroses, University of California, San Francisco, we have attempted to clarify sequentially the signs and symptoms of denial. An overview of the denial phase is provided in Table 8.1. In order to understand the frequency of such symptoms in a relevant group, data from 66 patients seen consecutively at our stress clinic were assembled. Based on the operational definitions for signs and symptoms of denial given in Table 8.2, clinician reports produced the numerical scores described in Table 8.3.

TABLE 8.1 Signs and Symptoms of Denial Phase of Stress Response Syndromes

Perception and attention	Daze Selective inattention Inability to appreciate significance of stimuli
Consciousness	Amnesia (complete or partial) Non-experience
Ideational processing	Disavowal of meanings of stimuli Loss of reality appropriacy Constriction of associational width Inflexibility of organization of thought Phantasies to counteract reality
Emotional	Numbness
Somatic	Tension-inhibition-type symptoms
Actions	Frantic overactivity to withdrawal

The 66 patients all sought help for problem states that had occurred after a recent serious life event. Half had experienced the loss of a loved one by death or separation, half had undergone a personal loss caused by accident, violence, medical or surgical procedures. There were 50 women and 16 men; the mean age was 34 (with a range of 20 to 75). Selection criteria excluded persons with psychotic states, turbulent personality styles, severe ongoing stress, and complicated psychiatric syndromes. Additional data on these 66 people and explanation of methods used in the study will be reported in more detail elsewhere (Horowitz, Wilner and Kaltreider, in preparation; Horowitz, Wilner and Alvarez, in preparation).

TABLE 8.2 Operational Definitions of Some Important Signs and Symptoms of Denial

---

Avoidance of associational connections — inhibiting expectable and fairly obvious personal or general continuations of meaning, implications, contingencies.

Numbness — a present subjective sense of not having feelings, or feeling 'benumbed', include a sense that one is *not* having potential emotions when it *is* a sense, however intuitive, rather than a pure intellectualization.

Reduced level of feeling responses to outer stimuli — include flatness of expectable emotional responses, constriction.

Rigidly role-adherent or stereotyped — carrying on by playing a part, socially automatic response sets.

Loss of reality appropriacy of thought by switching attitudes – going from strong to weak, good to bad, active to passive, liking to disliking, or other changes to the degree that thought about any one meaning or implication is blunted and confused.

Unrealistic narrowing of attention, vagueness, or disavowal of stimuli — include flexibility of attention deployment, lack of centering on a focus, and avoidances of certain otherwise likely perceptual information. Include insensitivity to changes in body.

Inattention, daze — include staring off into space, failure to determine significance of stimuli, clouding of alertness.

Inflexibility or constriction of thought — failure to explore relatively obvious or likely avenues of meaning other than the given theme under contemplation.

Loss of train of thought — temporary or micromomentary lapses in continuation of a communicative experience, or reports of similar inability to concentrate on a line of inner processing of information.

Loss of reality appropriacy of thought by sliding meanings — distorting, minimizing, or exaggerating to the point where real meanings are clouded over.

Memory failure — inability to recall expectable details or sequences of events, amnestic areas, inability to remember in usually expectable manner.

Loss of reality appropriacy of thought by use of disavowal — saying to oneself or others that some meanings, that are or would be fairly obvious, are not so.

Warding off trains of reality-oriented thought by use of phantasy — excessive focus on what might have been, what could be, or imaginative stories as a way of not facing realistic consequences or implications.

TABLE 8.3 Frequency and Means of Signs and Symptoms of Denial Reported by Clinicians for 66 Patients With Stress Response Syndromes After a Recent Life Event

Symptom	Per cent	Group mean*
Numbness	69	1.8
Avoidance of associational connections	69	1.7
Reduced level of feeling responses to outer stimuli	67	1.7
Rigidly role-adherent or stereotyped	62	1.5
Loss of reality appropriacy of thought by switching attitudes	64	1.4
Unrealistic narrowing of attention, vagueness, or disavowal of stimuli	52	1.2
Inattention, daze	48	1.2
Inflexibility or constriction of thought	46	1.0
Loss of train of thought	44	0.9
Loss of reality appropriacy of thought by sliding meanings	41	0.8
Memory failure	34	0.8
Loss of reality appropriacy of thought by use of disavowal	25	0.6
Warding off trains of reality-oriented thought by use of phantasy	15	0.3

*On a scale in which not present = 0, minor = 1, moderate = 3, and major = 5 for intensity of the experience within the past 7 days.

TABLE 8.4 Signs and Symptoms of Intrusiveness Phase of Stress Response Syndromes

Perception and attention	Hypervigilance, startle reactions Sleep and dream disturbance
Consciousness	Intrusive-repetitive thoughts and behaviours (illusions, pseudo-hallucinations, nightmares, ruminations and repetitions)
Ideational processing	Over-generalization Inability to concentrate on other topics, preoccupation Confusion and disorganization
Emotional	Emotional attacks or 'pangs'
Somatic	Symptomatic sequelae of chronic 'fight or flight' readiness (or of exhaustion)
Actions	Search for lost persons and situations, compulsive repetitions

TABLE 8.5 Operational definitions of Some Important Signs and Symptoms of Intrusion

---

Pangs of emotion — a 'spell' or episode or wave of feeling that has a quality of increasing and then decreasing rather than being a prevailing mood or subjective tone.

Rumination or preoccupation — continuous conscious awareness about the event and associations to the event beyond that involved in ordinary thinking through a problem or situation to a point of decision or completion. It has a sense of uncontrolled repetition to it.

Fear of losing bodily control, or hyperactivity in any bodily system — include subjective sensations of urinating, defaecating without will; fears of being unable to control vocalization, arm movements, hiding, running, obvious somatic responses such as excessive sweating, diarrhea, tachycardia.

Intrusive ideas in word form — appearance of sudden and unbidden thoughts.

Difficulty in dispelling ideas — once an idea has come to mind, even if thinking about it were deliberate, the person cannot stop awareness of the idea or topic. Emotions and moods that cannot be stopped are included.

Hypervigilance — the person is excessively alert, overly scanning the surrounding environment, too aroused in the sense of perceptual search, tensely expectant, or more driven towards obtaining stimuli than normal.

Re-enactments – any behaviour that repeats any aspect of the serious life event from minor tic-like movements and gestures to acting out in major movements and sequences. Include enactments of personal responses to the life event, whether or not they were part of the real action surrounding the event.

Bad dreams — any dream with unpleasant subjective experience, not just the classical nightmare with anxious awakenings.

Intrusive thoughts or images while trying to sleep — (see intrusive ideas and intrusive images).

Intrusive images — unbidden sensations in any modality. Any hallucination or pseudo-hallucination would be scored here as well if it came to mind in a non-volitional manner. The emphasis here is on sensory quality, which, however similar to that of ordinary thought images, may be more intense, and occur as a sudden, unwanted entry into awareness.

Startle reactions — flinching after noises, unusual orienting reactions, blanching or otherwise reacting to stimuli that usually do not warrant such responses.

Illusions — a misperception in which a person, object or scene is misappraised as something else; for example a bush is seen for a moment as a person, or a person is misrecognized as someone else.

Hallucinations, pseudo-hallucinations — an imaginary or phantasy-based emotional reaction as if it were real, whether or not the person intellectually thinks it is real. Include 'felt presences' of others in the room. Smell, taste, touch, movement, auditory, and visual sensations, as well as 'out of the body' experiences are included.

(iii)   Signs and Symptoms During Intrusion States

Intrusive experiences commonly alternate with denial or avoidance states and are the essential elements of post-traumatic disorders (Freud, 1920). They can be found after every type of serious life event, and in laboratory analogies to such events, where a variety of emotional responses are evoked (Horowitz, 1975a; Horowitz and Wilner, 1976). In Table 8.4, the overall pattern of such signs and symptoms is organized by the same descriptive sets used in the classification of the denial experiences.

The operational definitions for the assessment of intrusive states used by our clinicians to evaluate persons with stress response syndromes are seen in Table 8.5.

We found that it is very important to query the patient in a particular way after such experiences. Those who are articulate, intelligent, open, and self-confident will, of course, report such experiences spontaneously. But many persons have no experience in communicating the form of their ideas and feelings, and usually describe only the contents. The frequency and means of

TABLE 8.6   Frequency and Means of Signs and Symptoms of Intrusions Reported by Clinicians for 66 Patients with Stress Response Syndromes After a Recent Serious Life Event

Symptom	Per cent	Group mean*
Pangs of emotion	95	3.1
Rumination or preoccupation	90	2.9
Fear of losing bodily control, or hyperactivity in any bodily system	82	2.6
Intrusive ideas (in word form)	77	2.3
Difficulty in dispelling ideas	74	2.1
Hypervigilance	69	1.6
Bad dreams	54	1.6
Intrusive thoughts or images while trying to sleep	51	1.6
Re-enactments	57	1.5
Intrusive images	51	1.4
Startle reactions	34	0.6
Illusions	26	0.6
Hallucinations, pseudo–hallucinations	8	0.2

*On a scale in which not present = 0, minor = 1, moderate = 3, and major = 5 for intensity of the experience within the past 7 days.

clinicians ratings for the signs and symptoms of intrusion in the 66 patients is reported in Table 8.6.

(iv) Common Intrusive Contents

The advantage of the state descriptions given so far lies in their focus on the form of the experiences, a method for facilitating the examination of response tendencies across a variety of stressful events. There are, however, some contents of response that are also generally prevalent across stressful life events. These contents are the themes that may enter consciousness intrusively, or be warded off during periods of denial or avoidance. They have been described in detail elsewhere (Horowitz, 1976), and are briefly listed in Table 8.7, as concepts that frequently take an intrusive form in conscious experience.

Awareness of the frequency and multiplicity of such concerns, is particularly useful to those who help others to master these experiences. No person has only one response to an event, and the idea of working through one constellation may be used as a resistance to further assimilation. Some themes are avoided at the same time that others are intrusively present, adding further complexity to the general ordering of response states over time. Working through each concern to a point of completion requires differentiation of reality from phantasy and continued restructuring of the real world and one's place in it.

To summarize, certain common stress response tendencies can be abstracted from clinical, field and experimental studies among populations reacting to different life events. Simple knowledge of such states helps a person know what to expect and how to assess responses when they occur. Beyond the classification of states of experience, however, understanding why experiences occur may be even more helpful in planning a working-through process. States of mind and transitions from one state to another can be usefully

TABLE 8.7 Common Themes After Loss or Injury

Fear of repetition
Fear of merger with victims
Shame and rage over vulnerability
Rage at the source
Rage at those exempted
Fear of loss of control over aggressive impulses
Guilt or shame over aggressive impulses
Guilt or shame over surviving
Sadness over losses

explained from two points of view: the models or cognitive schemata used to organise information, and the processes of information transformation. These two topics will be taken up in that order.

3. THE EFFECTS OF SERIOUS LIFE EVENTS ON COGNITIVE SCHEMATA

A serious, stress-inducing life event is defined as such because it affects homeostasis. Negative stress stems from experience of loss or injury, psychological or material, real or as phantasied. If action cannot alter the situation, then inner models or schemata must be revised so that they conform to the new reality. No one has just one fully integrated self-image, or just one model of role relationships for his attachments to others. Each person will have several important models that were developed in childhood, and change throughout adult life (Erikson, 1958). Early schemata have been revised, but they are also retained in their earlier forms and can be reactivated during any regression. As a result of a serious life change the hierarchical importance of existing schemata may be altered, and schemata may be revised (Piaget, 1937). The slow revision of models will be discussed later. Here, the rapid changes are conceptualized as a shift induced by initial interpretations of the

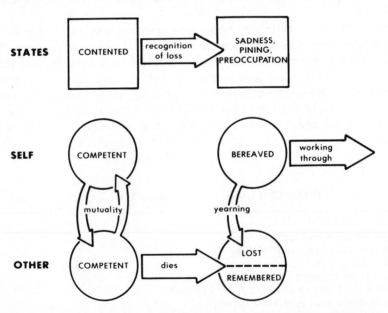

FIGURE 8.2. State shift with bereavement-induced change in self-images and role relationship models

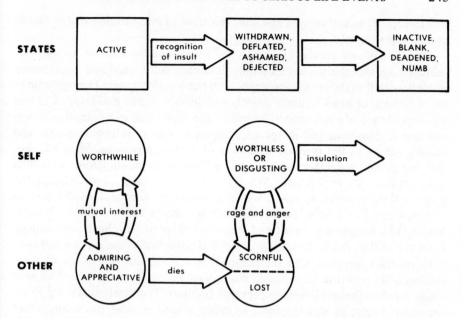

FIGURE 8.3. A state shift in bereavement in a person vulnerable to organizing experience by defective self-images

event and its implications, where models of self and relationships to others function to organize conscious experience and patterns of action.

Bereavement provides one well-studied example. As reviewed elsewhere (Parkes, 1972; Horowitz, 1978a), the loss of the loved one sets in motion a quick shift from previous self-images of mutual attachment and support to self-images as bereft or abandoned. These self-images may originally have been established as a consequence of earlier life experience with real or phantasied separations, however momentary, if not with the actual experience of death. This shift in self-images and role relationship models is one cause of a change in state, as shown diagramatically in Figure 8.2.

Each of the universal themes described earlier in Table 8.7, as well as other individually important themes based on personal history, will contain relevant versions of the person's self-images and role relationships. If a person has an accident with subsequent loss of his arm, or if he is fired from his work, there may be a rapid shift from a competent self-image to an already existent but previously dormant self-image as worthless and defective. Similarly, if a person experiences the death of a loved one who acted to stabilize competent self-images, then among the first effects of the loss may be a shift to usually latent models in which the self is defective and worthless. An example of that type of shift is described in Figure 8.3. The intrusive state is associated with unbidden thoughts of worthlessness and uncontrolled pangs of shame. A defensive shift in self-images can alter the state of mind to one that is blank, numb, and insulated.

The news of any serious life event, and responsive associations to it will be matched against the person's current dominant self-image and relationship models as well as those that are important, but less dominant. The outcome of this matching of news to inner models will depend on the goodness of fit and the importance of each model. Suppose, as a simplified example, that a person has a dominant self-image as competent that is relatively stable and usually serves as the primary organizer of mental processes. Suppose also, that this person has a dormant, inactive self-image as incompetent; a residual from previous life experiences. When that person sustains a loss or insult, the event will be matched against a self-image as competent and a self-image as incompetent. For a time the incompetent self-image may dominate thought, leading to a temporary reaction of increased vulnerability. Such experiences, however, will be brief, partial, or peripheral to central conscious awareness.

In contrast, suppose that the person has a dominant self-image of competence that is brittle or unstable and a usually inactive but important self-image as incompetent based on previous traumas. The newly sustained losses are more likely, in this instance, to cause a shift so that the incompetent self-image dominates. Reactions resulting from this incompetent self-image are likely to be more extended in time, more intense, or more central to experience.

Issues of self-images and role relationship models and the shifts between them have been discussed in detail elsewhere as important components in the theoretical explanation of various states of mind in a particular person (Horowitz, 1978b). Here, the main point is that one component of stress reaction is due to the shift in dominant models of self and others that can occur as part of the internalization of news about serious life events. Working through the news involves relating to it according to several models. Processes interact through shifts in the models evoked by the news, and through changes in the models to meet the new reality. In the short run, ideation and control determine which of a person's models are dominant organizers of experience. In the long run, ideation and control determine if and how models are changed. The remainder of this discussion will deal with ideation and control, based on a central assertion that variations in controls account for much of the variation in stress response states across persons, and in each person as he changes over time.

4.   COGNITIVE OPERATIONS AND CONTROLS IN PROCESSING THE MEANINGS OF SERIOUS LIFE EVENTS

It takes time for a person to assimilate a serious life event. If the event is of sufficient power, there will be signs and symptoms of deflection from normal states to the intrusiveness, denial, or combined intrusion and denial states described. Some persons will enter a stress response state even when a mild but personally significant event occurs. Information processing alters the states; we need to know how this is done. If we know, we can facilitate these natural, healing, adaptive processes when help is requested.

(i) Background

Before Freud's time, psychological traumas such as these were explained by neurologists as altered regulatory capacities induced by a combination of shock resulting from hypnotic states of consciousness, hereditary weakness of the nervous system, and the hope of secondary gains such as compensation after railway accidents (Charcot, 1877). Breuer and Freud (1895) rejected hereditary weakness of the nervous system as an explanation, and replaced it with a theory of psychological conflict. Freud (1920) also attempted to base his theory of neurotic conflict on biological factors, on deflections of drive and energy systems caused by conflict. He explained traumatization as a sudden overload of both information and physical energy. The information processing implications of his theory continue to be developed. The energic and instinctual components of his theory remain speculative.

In Freud's explanation of intrusiveness and denial states after serious life events, excessive stimulation was seen as the inciting cause. Perhaps building on what was then a new concept of physiological homeostasis, he developed a model that included defensive controls, one of the first psychological models to include unconscious information processing and feedback concepts.

Freud theorized along the following lines. When novel perceptions combined with inner meanings to form ideas that evoke strong emotional responses such as fear, controls were activated to regulate levels of tension. A hypothetical 'stimulus barrier' attenuated sensory input; repression and other defence mechanisms attenuated emergent ideas and feelings. Traumatization occurred as controls failed in the face of powerful evocative events. A tension state of high drive characteristics resulted, and the intensification of secondary defences then produced denial states. Episodic defensive failures led to intrusions. Conflict explained these stress states.

Freud then attempted to relate traumatization to libido theory. He puzzled over what drives might be activated by devastating life events. Desires for pleasure seemed out of the question. The horrible combat nightmares that haunted World War I veterans drove some to suicide; they could not be seen as the end product of wish fulfillment. Hypothesizing another level of drives more primitive than the pleasure principle, which he called the repetition compulsion, Freud (1910) speculated on these as a derivative of the death instinct, with aggressive drives seen as another derivative.

It is a well-validated observation that compulsive repetition follows stressful life events, as already noted, but observations are not explanations. The explanatory principle of a drive for repetitiion was re-examined by later theorists. Hartmann (1939), Bibring (1943), and Waelder (1964), each thinking separately, divided the repetition compulsion into two components; one of ego functions, the other of id functions. The ego function of repetition was seen as an automatic, unconscious effort at mastery of an event previously appraised as overwhelming. The id functions were viewed as aggression drives, or as innate tendencies for reproduction of certain types of stimuli. A supergo function of self-punishment by retraumatization was also suggested.

More recently Schur (1966) reviewed this effort to retain Freud's concepts. He questioned the energic and drive components, and suggested efforts to see if the theory of conceptual and emotional mastery could not be expanded to explain the data derived from observations. Rangell (1967, p.80) reviewed the theories for explaining trauma from the various metapsychological points of view and arrived at the following summation of the psychoanalytic theory:

A traumatic occurrence is characterized by the intrusion into the psychic apparatus of a stimulus or series of stimuli (the *traumatic event*), varying in their qualitative manifest contents, in their quantitative characteristics, and in their time relationships, which set off an unconscious train of intrapsychic events (the *traumatic process*) beyond the capacity of the ego to master at that particular time. The dynamics of the traumatic intrapsychic process which ensue lead to the rupture, partial or complete, of the ego's barrier or defensive capacities against stimuli, without a corresponding subsequent ability of the ego to adequately repair the damage in sufficient time to maintain mastery and a state of security. The resulting state (the *traumatic state*) is a feeling of psychic helplessness, in a series of gradations from brief, transitory, and relative to more complete and long-lasting. As a result of insufficient resources on the part of the ego, there is a feeling of lack of control and a vulnerability to further stimuli, without the expectation of adequate containment, mastery, and adaptation.'

The goal of the present attempt is to examine one level of explanation in more detail — that of mental functions that alter the traumatic state to a state of greater stability. This level of explanation falls within the cognitive point of view, and is concerned with the information processing operations that can lead to coping, defence, or defensive failures.

(ii) Completion Tendency and Active Memory Storage

In the section on structure, the mind was described as operating to maintain inner models of self and the world, These inner models are used to interpret new information and are revised to remain true to current reality. Serious life events such as a loss or injury present news that will eventually change the inner models. But change is slow; time is essential for review of the implications of the news and available options for response. The mind continues to process important new information until the situation or the models change, and reality and models of reality reach accord. This important tendency to integrate reality and schemata can be called a *completion tendency*.

Until completion occurs, the new information and reactions to it are stored in active memory. According to this theory, active memory contents will be transformed into representations wherever that process is not actively inhibited (Horowitz and Becker, 1972). This tendency for repeated representations will end only when these are no longer stored in active memory. In the instance of very important contents, termination in active memory will not occur with decay but only when information processing is complete. At that point, the news will be a part of long-term models and revised inner schemata.

As ideas related to the stress event are represented, there will be a very natural comparison of the news with relevant schemata. Because a stress event is, by definition, a significant change, there will be a discrepancy between the implications of the news, and these schemata. This descrepancy evokes emotion. Serious lift events, and the repetition of information related to them, are so different from inner models of attachment that very painful emotional responses occur; emotional states of such power that controls are activated to prevent the threat of unendurable anguish or flooding. This interaction of ideas, emotions, and controls is shown in Figure 8.4.

News and immediate responses to serious life events remain stored in active memory because, on first encounter, the meanings seem to have great personal importance. Because the contents are strongly coded in active memory they tend to be represented intensely and frequently. With each recurrence of the information, comparisons are made again, and emotional activation increases. Emotional responses are also represented, and so become part of the constellation stored in active memory. When other tasks are more immediately relevant, or when emotional responses such as fear, guilt, rage, or sorrow are a threat, controls are initiated. This feedback modulates the flow of information and reduces emotional response.

Excessive controls interrupt the process, change the state of the person to some form of denial and may prevent complete processing of the event. Failures of control lead to excessive levels of emotion, flooding and retraumatization, causing entry into intrusive states. Optimal controls slow down recognition processes and so provide tolerable doses of new information and emotional responses. They lead to working states or less intense oscillations between denial and intrusive states. In this optimal condition some intrusiveness will occur with repeated representation. Some denial will occur when controls operate more pervasively, but the overall result will be adaptive, in that completion will eventually occur. Inner models will eventually conform to the new reality, as in the process of completion of mourning. When this happens, information storage in active memory will terminate, as shown in Figure 8.5.

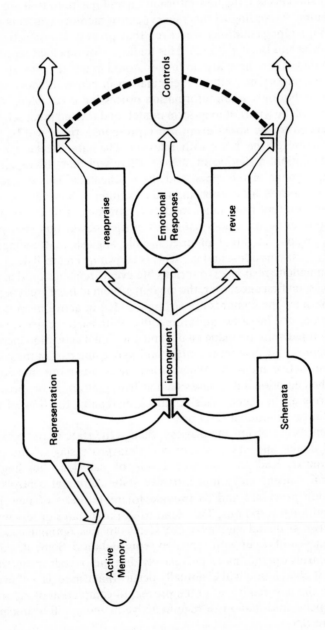

FIGURE 8.4. The interaction of ideas, emotions and controls

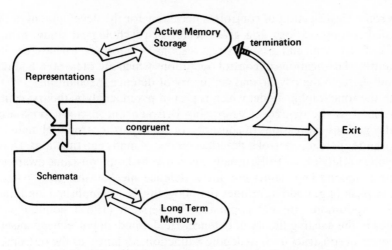

FIGURE 8.5. Termination of active memory

At any given time, different sets of meanings of a stress event will exist in different stages. For example, fear of repetition, or fear of merger with a victim might be a recurrent intrusive experience, while survivor-guilt themes might be completely inhibited and for the moment avoided in experience. Later, in situations of greater safety, this theme might be allowed to enter awareness, and be represented as an intrusive experience.

This model accounts for compulsive repetition, phasic states of intrusion and denial or numbing, variation in the level of experience between different constellations of response, and eventual resolution of stress response syndromes. While general stress response tendencies can be abstracted in this way, persons also respond uniquely. This is due in part to how their developmental history colours personal meanings of an event and to how their current life tasks and environment are effected by the event. Individual variation in response to the same type of life event is also partly due to variations in the habitual style and capacity for control.

(iii) Controls of Information Processing: A More Detailed Examination

An alteration in control functions will lead to change in the ideas and feelings experienced by a person, to a possible change in the dominant schemata for organization of information at a given time, and sometimes to a change in overall state. Persons under stress vary in their use of controls over time, according to specific events and personality differences. Since controls are operations rather than outcomes, they must be inferred from outcomes. That is why there has been no agreement on a general psychological theory of control. Variations account for many differences in the patterning of states, but some classification of controls is necessary for the development of theory related to observations in a given sector of psychological study. From our work of observing and treating stress response syndromes, we have developed tentative classifications of control operations which are presented and related briefly here to the psychoanalytic theory of defence mechanisms.

In the topographic model which is part of psychoanalytic theory, control is described as the degree of censorship between unconscious, preconscious, and conscious expressions of concepts. In the tripartite structural model of id, ego, and superego, control is described as one of many ego functions. Defences are one variety of controls, usually operative without conscious awareness of their function. The names for these defence mechanisms state what they accomplish (e.g. undoing) rather than how this is accomplished, and the cognitive operations are not stipulated. Wallerstein (1967) pointed out this hiatus in the existing theory of defence. He defined 'defence mechanism' as a theoretical construct used to denote a function, 'defence' as the outcome, and 'defensive manoeuvres' as complex configurations.

The term control is used here, instead of defence mechanism, in order to avoid imparting value judgements to the process, as adaptive or maladaptive, developmentally conservative or progressive, consciously or unconsciously operative. Controls can be discussed in terms of psychological or biological systems. Here, discussion is strictly psychological, although inferences to be drawn are consistent with what is known of neurobiological regulatory processes. Since many controls can be postulated at various levels of psychological systems, the focus here is on controls inferred from the observation of change processes in persons passing through a period of response to serious life events.

Controls serve to maintain a state and determine transition from one state to another. The basic controls are inhibition and facilitation, but it is helpful to be more specific about what is inhibited or facilitated. To do so, controls are separated into three levels of abstraction. These levels are (1) the selection of the overall topic and mode of thinking about it, (2) the selection of those self-images and role relationship models that will organize interpretations of information, and (3) the selection of information to form sequences of thought. As controls are discussed within these categories, the common results during stress response syndromes will be described. This will connect the observations of signs and symptoms summarized in earlier tables to the explanatory theory of a completion tendency. Any end result, such as the recurrent and intrusive image of a dead body seen during an automobile accident weeks before, will be a consequence of the operation of many controls. For simple illustration, the tables that follow show each control listed separately along with typical end results of the operation, or failure of operation, of that control.

The most extensive recent review and formulation of the controls that may lead to coping, defence, or failures to successfully cope or defend has been provided by Haan (1977). She calls these failures 'fragmentation'. In the analysis of the development and resolution of stress response syndromes in the clinical context, it has been useful to think of controls as resulting in coping, defence, or relative failure. The particular control processes listed by Haan, however, are not entirely cohesive with our clinical observations.

This is not the appropriate place for a detailed analysis of her system. Since one is always wary of newly developed lists, however, especially lists of defence mechanisms, some salient points ought to be mentioned. Many of her examples of fragmentation occur frequently in psychotic states, and less frequently in the neurotic states that characterize stress response syndromes. For example, tangential concretisms, neologisms, confabulation, delusional ideation, and the like, were seldom noted in the clinical sample we described earlier. But other failures of control have been noted, and lead to the type of signs and symptoms listed in earlier tables.

Haan's list of defensive processes is worded in terms of classical theory (A. Freud, 1936) and we tend to see these more as the outcome of cognitive processes than as the processes themselves. For example, under the cognitive function of 'Delayed Response' Haan lists tolerance of ambiguity as coping, doubt as defence, and immobilization as fragmentation or failure. We, on the other hand, would see tolerance of ambiguity as the result of a variety of cognitive processes and would instead see dosing of information processing by episodic inhibition as the appropriate coping function under 'Delayed Response'. We would see maladaptive extensions of inhibitions as the defensive level of 'Delayed Response'. We would see doubt as the result of cognitive switching between alternative premises on a given topic. Sliding meanings, observed by us as a frequent operation to avoid emotional responses, is hard to find in her classification, as are some other manoeuvres we believe to be important.

Haan divides processes into three other kinds of classifications; those of cognitive functions, attention-focusing functions, and affective-impulse regulations. Here we are in essential, but not complete agreement. It does seem most useful to group several control operations under cognitive functions, and that is where we begin with an overlapping, but somewhat different set. While we agree with her classification of affective-impulse regulations, we find that her formulations do not contain sufficient recognition of contemporary ego psychology (e.g. Kohut, 1971; Blanck and Blanck, 1974; Kernberg 1975), and the importance of mental sets for self-image and role relationship schemata (Horowitz, 1978a). What we believe she means by affective impulse regulations, is subsumed under our heading of controls that select self-images and role relationships, since the cognitive structures include issues of controlling and selecting particulars aims, impulses, and drive derivatives. Attention-focusing functions are also seen by us as 'format selection' controls.

We believe that several different entries are indicated there, not just those listed by Haan, of concentration as coping, denial as defence, and fixation or distraction as fragmentation. Once again, we see concentration as the result of several control operations, that set the topic for sequential organization of thought.

This too brief exposition and comparison of our hypotheses of controls and those of Haan is not meant to indicate sharp disagreement but rather joint construction with some discord. We are still far from a general theory of psychological controls; the field has been as complex as that of personality research, with as many pitfalls. For the time being, it seems that controls, defences and the like have to be defined as patterns relevant to the particular context of observation. What follows is our working model of controls observed in the processing of information about serious life events by persons who have shown some difficulty in mastering their reactions to these experiences.

(iv) Controls that Select Information

The main controls of the flow of simultaneous and sequential arrangements of information are varieties of inhibition and facilitation. These operations lead to such commonly described defences as denial, repression, undoing and reaction formation. It is helpful to define several levels of these basic controls by listing them in an ideal order when there is adaptive, if idealized, working through. This list (Table 8.8) begins with facilitation; the control operation used to choose from recorded impressions those ideas that have the most important and relevant personal implications. Active inhibition of representations is a control that may be used adaptively to dampen ideas and feelings that might distract a person from immediate needs for action. As shown in Table 8.8, these controls can have adaptive, defensive, or maladaptive consequences. These outcomes, however, are only illustrative; any result is the product of multiple processes, not just of a single set of controls.

Switching between sets of information is a higher level of abstraction, a control manoeuvre that requires a subordinate level of inhibition and facilitation. Sliding meanings, including augmentation and reduction of value, is also a complex process, as is shifting the locus of meaning. These controls permit the mind to contemplate and gain perspective on the various implications of a serious life event and responses to it. When switching sets of information is effective, it facilitates emotional balancing and broad appraisals. Sliding meanings along various scales of value enables estimation of the degree of danger and the relative weight of counteractions. Shifting the locus of meaning can differentiate phantasy from reality, a function that is especially important when we consider the universal tendency towards magical thinking about causality.

After the extension and organization of associations selected as most pertinent and realistic, information is then rearranged to arrive at various 'position statements' about the implications of the serious event. Problem solving occurs, and involves choices between alternative implications and possible routes of response. Seeking new information where it is needed, is an effective control that requires attention to gathering knowledge of threat or response tactics. Of a still higher order are those controls based on information processing that revise pre-existent schemata so that new plans can be practised until they become as automatic as those they replace.

(v) Controls that Select Self-Images and Role Relationship Models

The processes of control just described are those that accomplish the more familiar coping and defensive operations. There are also controls that set not only the sequential flow of information, but the organizing schemata that will be used to pattern that information. The assumption here is that multiple self-images and role relationship models are available to every person and that these change in terms of dominance as organizers. A speculative attempt is made in Table 8.9 to specify the controls, at this level of abstraction, that are most prominent during the states that tend to follow serious life events. The three classifications mentioned are setting of controls for schemata of membership, self-images, and role relationships.

As for membership set, any person can view himself as belonging or independent. After a serious life event, he may modulate emotional reactions to a loss of self by increasing the use of schemata in which he is less independent and more unified with a group. This control can lead to coping, as when group coherence reduces combat stress (Borus, 1973). Also, feelings of humanitarian, oceanic or mystical unity may help a person accept his knowledge of impending death. With failures of such controls, the person may experience catastrophic dread with ideas of global annihilation.

Controls also select which of several possible self-images will organize a series of ideas. End results include the various progressions and regressions of identity that commonly occur after serious life events such as the death of a loved one. Failure to select or to stabilize a self-image can lead to chaotic lapses in identity. In a similar manner, one can choose to experience a given self-image as either subject or as object, leading to a variety of common stress responses such as unusually heightened states of self-actualization or depersonalization.

When implications of a serious life event are examined, another way to reduce emotional response levels is to alter the governing model of role relationship between self and others. A common coping response is to see the self as more than usually in need and to seek help and support, or become dependent on others. Common defensive responses are to adopt illusions of

TABLE 8.8 Controls of Information Flow

| Information flow selection process | Common results during stress response states | | |
	coping	defence	control failure
Facilitating	Contemplation*	Rumination*	Inability to think clearly or concentrate*
Inhibiting	Dosing	Denial, repression, suppression, isolation, numbing, dissociations, use of drugs, flight, or suicide as avoidances	Intrusions and emotional flooding
Switching attitudes, premises or schemata	Emotional balancing or counter-weighting	Undoing, reaction formation, doubt, indecisiveness, compulsions	Intrusions and emotional flooding
Sliding meanings and valuations	Humour, wisdom	Rationalizations, distortions, exaggerations or minimization of threats and responses	Intrusions and emotional flooding

Shifting locus of meanings	Useful identifications, acceptance of the nature of life	Externalizations, displacements, inappropriate identifications, self-preoccupations, hypochondriasis	Hallucinosis
Rearranging information	Problem appraisal, problem solving, planning, creative expressions	Comforting illusions and delusions	Confusions
Seeking information	Understanding, learning new skills, hypotheses on future	Intellectualization, searching frenzy	Apathy
Revising inner models of self and expectations	Adaptation, altruism, sublimation, anticipation	Counterphobic self-images, illusional role relationships, inappropriate role reversals	Giving up and hopeless states
Practising new modes	De-automatization and desensitization of outmoded elements and linkages, automatization of new ways	Counterphobic rehearsals	Lack of preparedness

*All results are multiply determined and are simply examples where operation of the particular process makes an important contribution.

TABLE 8.9 Controls of Schemata

Selection	Common result during stress response		
	coping	defense	control failure
Membership set (individual importance vs. group or unity)	Increased ideological conviction, oceanic feelings	Altruistic surrender, self-centered preoccupation and hypochondriasis	Annihilation, dread
Self-schemata set Choice of available self-images	Progressions and regressions in self-concept	Dissociations	Chaotic lapse of identity
Viewing self subjectively or objectively	Heightened sense of identity	Depersonalization	Confusion
Other schemata set choice of available self-actions and other-role schemata	Seeking help from others, pining for attachments, searching behaviour, progressions and regressions in interpersonal patterns	Splitting, introjective experiences	Helplessness, panic

self-sufficiency, to split relationships into those that are all good or all bad, or to heighten introjective experiences in order to maintain an illusion of attachment. When these controls fail, a panic state of helplessness may result.

(vi) 'Format Selection'

Format selection is a broad level of abstraction that refers to choice of topic, mode of thinking about that topic, and in a general way, level of activation. Within this highest level of abstraction, the control operations most relevant to modulating responses to stress are summarized in Table 8.10. Listed first is conceptual area selection, an operation that determines what will be thought about next. In the course of working through the news of a serious event, the event or an aspect of it may be inhibited or facilitated, so that the news is either avoided or confronted. This operation can lead to coping experiences, as when a person doses recognition of a threat by allowing himself time for avoiding unpleasant realities in order to regain composure. An end result, called defensive rather than coping, might be total inhibition with no time spent facing any aspect of the topic. An inability to inhibit and keep from being overwhelmed by the stress event can lead to flooding or dazed states, episodes that could be called defensive or adaptive failures.

Another set of controls involves selection of the mode of organization of information. One such operation involves consideration of the event in relationship to varied temporal contexts, that is, in terms of long or short segments of time. Extremes of such controls are common during response to stressful life events. One frequent end result is concentration on experiencing time in extremely brief intervals, as a person handles a seemingly overwhelming situation by breaking it down into a series of micro-intervals, to be taken one at a time, as he thinks only about what should be done in the next minute or two. A second common response is to scan unusually long sweeps of time in order to place a bitter moment of suffering into the perspective of longer stretches of time so that it either loses significance, or is meaningful in terms of some larger, even cosmic, plan.

Another control for organizing stress-related information is to select sequential set. This determines the kind of flow from one item of information to another. For example, problem solving is a mode in which information is arranged into sets by principles of logic and fidelity to real probabilities. A quite different set is used in phantasy or experiential flows, in which information sets may be associatively linked by sensory similarities and congruencies of wish or fear, rather than by probability or accuracy.

Heightening such controls after a serious life event leads to common responses. After being raped, for instance, a woman might find herself thinking only of what to do next, whom to call, what to say, and would

TABLE 8.10 Controls of 'Format'

Selection	Common result during stress response		
	coping	defence	control failure
Conceptual area (time on and off threats)	Dosing; periods of activity and passivity	Preoccupation and counter-occupation	Dazed state and flooding
Mode of organization Temporal set (viewing over short or long time periods)	Looking at only one step at a time; relating the event to the infinity of time and space	Avoidance of present demands for action	Overwhelmed
Sequential set (problem solving vs experiential or phantasy modes)	Thinking only about what to do next; phantasy about restoration of lost object	Phantasy preoccupation, unrealistic plans	Confusion, freezing or intrusion
Representational set (words, images, enacting)	Problem solving lexically because images evoke too many emotions; intellectualization	Isolation	Intrusive images
Locus set (external or interanal sources of information)	Restorative changes between activity and contemplation	Compulsive action to avoid thought	Flooding, illusions, or hallucinations
Activation level (excitation of various systems)	Healthy cycles of alertness and repose	Hyperalertness, semistuporous, dulling, altered states of consciousness, physiological reactions	Shock

rigorously avoid re-experiencing and remembering the terrifying event or any similar past experience. Another result of such control can occur when the woman phantasizes unlikely revenge stories and avoids thinking about what she has to do next, such as reporting what has happened. Similarly, after a death a person may phantasize restoration of the lost person, and avoid thinking of life functions they must now assume. The results of failures in control may be intrusion of phantasy during problem solving thought, or intrusion of awareness of real problems, with either leading to emotional flooding.

Control of representational set is another way to modulate expression of thought (Horowitz, 1972; 1978c). These controls determine whether the flow of information will proceed in lexical, image, or enactive (motoric) forms. With the use of such controls, some persons remember a serious event such as a car accident only in words, damping out images to avoid emotional arousal from quasi-perceptual thought. Such operations help coping, they also may accomplish defences such as isolation and intellectualization. The episodes of intensive images of bloodied body that might occur weeks after an accident are seen as a combination of the impetus of active memory, other motives, and relative failure of the control operations under discussion.

In a similar manner, other controls search for a relative acceptance of internal or external sources of information. The end results may be a useful search for relevant external information that also wards off the feelings that will emerge when personal implications are contemplated. Levels of activation of various systems can also be controlled. This leads to various altered states of consciousness and also to physiological responses, ranging from hyper- to hypoarousal (Fischer, 1971).

5. CONCLUDING COMMENTS

This chapter has focused on the signs and symptoms commonly found in persons having either unusually intense or ordinary responses to serious life events. It has dealt at some length with how these signs and symptoms are formed as the result of information processing attempts to integrate life events with pre-existent schemata. The past history of the person, and revision of inner models according to the new meanings has been described briefly; a fuller discussion is beyond the cope of this chapter. While past history would account for considerable individual variation, or typological variations, some variance in responsivity is based on differences in habitual controls.

Most persons blend the controls that have been listed in flexible diverse fashions. But in response to stressful life events the prototypical hysterical personality may tend to inhibit, the prototypical obsessional may habitually switch meanings, and the narcissistic personality may tend toward sliding meanings (Horowitz, 1974; 1975b). That is why, since therapeutic intervention often has to do with modifications of controls, a focus on controls as well as meanings is of importance.

Serious life events may lead to stress response syndromes characterized by states of intrusion and of denial. Working through the meanings of the stressful event is part of a general completion tendency aimed at keeping inner models as congruent with reality as possible. Emotional responses to recognition of the discrepancy between inner models and the implications of serious news tends to activate control operations that may, in the long run, either abet or interrupt the completion tendency. Understanding the effect of these controls on the processing of information is an essential precursor to a general theory of traumatization, and an eventual rational strategy for the treatment of such disorders.

6. ACKNOWLEDGEMENTS

Research on which this chapter is based was supported by a Clinical Research Center grant from the National Institute of Mental Health (MH30899), and by research grants from the National Institute of Mental Health (MH24341), the National Institute of Aging (AG00002), and the National Heart, Lung and Blood Institute (HLBI 7580).

Colleagues vital to the stress research effort include Nancy Kaltreider, M.D., John Starkweather, Ph.D., Charles Marmar, M.D., Lydia Temoshok, Ph.D., Robert Wallerstein, M.D., Janice Krupnick, M.S.W., Nancy Wilner, B.A., William Alverez, M.A., Anthony Leong, M.S., and Phyllis Cameron, B.S. Treatments were supervised by Alan Skolnikoff, M.D., Seymour Boorstein, M.D., Dennis Farrell, M.D., Norman Mages, M.D., Richard Lieberman, M.D., and George Kaplan, M.D.

This manuscript was edited by Nancy Wilner and typed by Marsha Jackson. Methodological consultation was provided by William Hargraves, Ph.D. and Clifford Attkisson, Ph.D.

7. REFERENCES

Bibring, E. (1943). The conception of the repetition compulsion. *Psychoanalytic Quarterly,* **12,** 486–519.

Blanck, G. and Blanck, R. (1974). *Ego Psychology.* New York: New York Universities Press.

Borus, J. F. (1973). Adjustment issues facing the Vietnam returnee. *Archives of General Psychiatry,* **28,** 501–506.

Breuer, J. and Freud, S. (1895). *Studies on Hysteria,* **Vol. 2.** Standard Edition, London: Hogarth Press.

Charcot, J. M. (1877). *Lectures on Diseases of the Nervous System.* London: New Sydenham Society.

Coehlo, G. V., Hamburg, D. A. and Adams, J. E. (1974). *Coping and Adaptation* New York: Basic Books.

Erikson, E. (1958). The problem of ego identity. *Journal of the American Psychiatric Association,* **4,** 56–121.

Fischer, R. (1971). A cartography of the ecstatic and meditative states; the experimental and experiential features of a perception-hallucination continuum are considered. *Science,* **174,** 897–904.

Freud, A. (1936). *The Ego and the Mechanisms of Defense.* London: Hogarth Press.

Freud, S. (1920). *Beyond the Pleasure Principle,* **Vol. 18.** Standard Edition. London: Hogarth Press.

Haan, N. (1977). *Coping and Defending.* New York: Academic Press.

Hartmann, H. (1939). *Ego Psychology and the Problem of Adaptation.* New York: International Universities Press.

Horowitz, M. J. (1972). Modes of representation of thought. *Journal of the American Psychoanalytic Association,* **20,** 793–819.

Horowitz, M. J. (1974). Stress response syndromes: character style and brief psychotherapy. *Archives of General Psychiatry,* **31,** 768–781.

Horowitz, M. J. (1975a). Intrusive and repetitive thoughts after experimental stress: a summary. *Archives of General Psychiatry,* **32,** 1457–1463.

Horowitz, J. J. (1975). Sliding meanings: a defense against threat in narcissistic personalities. *International Journal of Psychoanalytic Psychotherapy.* **Vol. 4.** New York: Aronson.

Horowitz, M. J. (1976). *Stress Response Syndromes.* New York: Aronson.

Horowitz, M. J. (1978a). Depressive responses after loss. Presented at Annual Meeting of American Psychiatric Association.

Horowitz, M. J. (1978b). *States of Mind.* New York: Plenum.

Horowitz, M. J. (1978c). *Image Formation and Cognition,* (2nd edn.). New York: Appleton–Century–Crofts.

Horowitz, M. J. and Becker, S. (1972). Cognitive response to stress: experimental studies of a 'compulsion to repeat trauma'. In R. Holt and E. Peterfreund (Eds.), *Psychoanalysis and Contemporary Science.* New York: Macmillan.

Horowitz, M. J., Wilner, N. and Alvarez, W. (In preparation.) Impact of event scale: a measure of presumptive stress.

Horowitz, M. J., Wilner, N. and Kaltreider, N. (In preparation.) Signs and symptoms of post-traumatic stress and adjustment disorders.

Janis, I. (1958). *Psychological Stress.* New York: Wiley.

Janis, I. (1969). *Stress and Frustration.* New York: Harcourt–Brace–Jovanovich.

Kernberg, O. (1975). *The Borderline Conditions and Pathological Narcissism.* New York: Aronson.

Kohut, H. (1971). *Analysis of the Self.* New York: International Universities Press.

Lazarus, R. (1966). *Psychological Stress and the Coping Process.* New York: McGraw–Hill.

Parad, H., Resnick, H. and Parad, L. (1976). *Emergency Mental Health Services and Disaster Management.* New York: Prentice-Hall.

Parkes, C. M. (1972). *Bereavement.* New York: International Universities Press.

Piaget, J. (1937). *The Construction of Reality in the Child.* New York: Basic Books.

Rangell, L. (1967). The metapsychology of psychic trauma. In S. S. Furst (Ed.), *Psychic Trauma.* New York: Basic Books.

Schur, M. (1966). *The Id and the Regulatory Process of the Ego.* New York: International Universities Press.

Waelder, L. (1964). Statements as reported by Gifford S. in Repetition Compulsion. *Journal of the American Psychoanalytic Association,* **12,** 632–649.

Wallerstein, R. S. (1967). Development and metapsychology of the defensive organization of the ego. *Journal of the American Psychoanalytic Association,* **15,** 130.

Chapter 9

Cognitive Processes as Mediators of
Stress and Coping*

SUSAN FOLKMAN, CATHERINE SCHAEFER,
AND RICHARD S. LAZARUS

1. Introduction
2. Emotion and Cognition in Appraisal
   (i) Traditional Views of the Functions of Emotion in Cognition
   (ii) Information processing Approaches to Emotion
3. Ambiguity–Uncertainty and Appraisal
   (i)   Stress-related Research on Ambiguity-Uncertainty
   (ii) Tolerance of Ambiguity (Uncertainty)
   (iii) Ambiguity as a Factor in Coping
4. Evaluation, Secondary Appraisal, and Coping
   (i) Coping Resources
        (a) Health/energy/morale
        (b) Problem solving skills
        (c) Social networks
        (d) Utilitarian resources
        (e) General and specific beliefs
   (ii) Coping Suitability and Goodness of Fit
5. Addendum
6. References

1. INTRODUCTION

There is mounting conviction, and evidence from laboratory, clinical and
field investigations, that the ways people think about a stressful situation
affect how they respond emotionally and how they cope. The rapid growth in

*Writing of this paper was supported in part by research from the National Institute on Aging
(AG 00002) and the National Cancer Institute (CA 19362).

cognitively oriented approaches to the emotional and motivational aspects of adaptation (e.g. Mandler, 1975; Bandura, 1977; Kemper, in press) has even been referred to as the 'cognitive revolution' in psychology (Dember, 1974), although Bolles (1974) holds that psychology has always been cognitive in orientation except for a seventy-year recent period of aberration. If we include in this the cognitive behaviour therapists (e.g. Ellis, 1962; Goldfried and Goldfried, 1975; Mahoney, 1977; Meichenbaum, 1977), the crescendo of interest in cognitive issues in stress, coping, and adaptation cannot be denied.

A wide gap exists, however, between those who look at cognitive processes as a potential guide to understanding individual differences in stress response and those who are concerned normatively with the cognitive processes involved in information processing. This gap is quite similar to the one between the classical perception theorists and the 'New Look' personality-centered cognitivists of the 1940s and 1950s. The question posed by the classicists was always some variant of 'How is it that we perceive accurately what is in the environment, or at least perceive a close enough analogue to be able to act adaptively and survive?' The classical theorists took a normative approach to investigating how people come to perceive their environment similarly. The investigative context was generally 'cool', that is, it was a laboratory situation with an objective stimulus that had little or no meaning for the person's well-being.

In contrast, the New Look psychologists asked some variant of the question 'How is it that different individuals perceive (or learn or remember) the same environmental display differently?' The emphasis of the New Look psychologists was on individual differences, not on people in general, and the sources of variance examined were emotional and motivational. The context of New Look research, therefore, was 'hot', i.e. laden with meaning for the individual. Indeed, a major preoccupation of the New Look theorists came to be their concern with how people defended against emotionally loaded information in the stimulus configuration. Research on perceptual defence, which dominated the New Look period, actually dealt with the avoidance of information, in marked contrast to the concerns of the classical theorists, who were concerned with how people perceive or take in information accurately.

At the time, these divergent perspectives were seen as difficult to combine within the same general theory of perception (cf. Allport, 1955). Yet no theory of perception could be complete without making the integration. Although individual differences are always a major source of variance, humans are, after all, generally able to share perceptions sufficiently to function well in their environment.

Today's interest in theories and research in rational problem solving and information processing parallels the focus of the classical perception theorists. Researchers in this arena are concerned with how people in general correctly process non-emotional information from the environment. On the other hand, investigators in stress and coping are more concerned with individual differences in the cognitive processes that generate differential coping and adaptational outcomes when the person has an important stake in the outcome. This parallels the New Look concern with individual differences in perception due to emotion and motivation.

As in the days of the classical cognitivists and the New Look psychologists, with few exceptions (e.g. Simon, 1967; Kahneman, 1973; Mandler, 1975; Horowitz, 1976; Janis and Mann, 1977) today's information processing and stress and coping researchers seem not to be talking to each other. Indeed, as modern counterparts to the New Look segment, we find little in information processing research that we can use directly to better understand emotional and adaptational issues. Yet both groups must share common concerns with cognitive processes, and perhaps we would both fare better if the connection between the two perspectives could be made more explicit. Our general aims in this chapter are to show in several ways how the two perspectives could interpenetrate or at least complement each other.

Our vantage point is an approach to stress and coping that is essentially cognitive and contains the broad ingredients of what must ultimately be a more elaborate and detailed basis of understanding. In previous writings, for example, Lazarus and his colleagues (e.g. Lazarus, 1966; Lazarus, Averill and Opton, 1970; Lazarus and Launier, in press) have analysed stress in terms of cognitive appraisal and coping, a set of psychological processes that mediate encounters between the person and the environment, and that lead to emotional and adaptational outcomes. These processes determine the person's psychological stress reactions, the various emotions experienced, and the adaptational outcomes. From this standpoint, various forms of stress and emotion are products of the way a person evaluates the present and future significance of such encounters for his or her well-being, encounters that can be actual, imagined, or anticipated. Stress appraisals, which include harm/loss that has already occurred, threat, and challenge, produce negatively toned emotions. In contrast, benign-positive appraisals result in positively toned emotions (Lazarus *et al.* in press). In addition, each emotional intensity level and each specific emotional quality, however complex, has its own particular cognitive appraisal which, in turn, arises from the moment-to-moment interplay of situational and personality factors. Cognitive mediation of this sort is what makes a theory of stress psychological as opposed to sociological or physiological.

In this theory there are three types of appraisal, each of which serves in its own fashion to mediate the relationship: *primary* appraisal, which is the cognitive process of evaluating the significance of an encounter for one's well-being; *secondary* appraisal, which is the process of evaluating an encounter with respect to coping resources and options; and *reappraisal,* which occurs as new information is obtained from internal psychological changes, changes in the environment (often from coping efforts), from further reflection, and from defensive intrapsychic activity which is a form of coping.

The foci of primary and secondary appraisal differ, one being directed at the question'Am I okay or in trouble?', and the other question 'What can I do about it?' Yet the cognitive operations required by these appraisals are similar. Both require attention to and *evaluation* of information in the stimulus configuration, storage, and retrieval of information in memory. Information processing theory and research is concerned with some of these processes. There are, however, three critical aspects of cognitive appraisal that are inadequately considered in traditional information processing models. These relate to emotion, ambiguity or uncertainty, and evaluation of meaning.*

The few information processing models which consider *emotion* (e.g. Simon, 1967; Erdelyi, 1974; Mandler, 1975; Janis and Mann, 1977) generally examine it in terms of its effects on the information processing system. In appraisal and coping processes, however, emotion plays a more central and complex role in its relationship to cognition; we shall discuss this in the first section. *Ambiguity* (or uncertainty) is generally anathema to information processing models, which are concerned primarily with initially meaningless bits of information, and the reduction of ambiguity by cognitive activity. The issue of tolerating ambiguity is totally ignored. Yet most of the information appraised in stressful transactions is characterized by ambiguity, and any formulation that attempts to examine the information processed in stressful encounters must give it serious consideration. Accordingly, our second section deals with ambiguity-uncertainty. Third, appraisal is an *evaluative* process in which information is interpreted in terms of its meaning and significance through the person's experience, values, beliefs, goals, and resources. Traditional information processing models do not extend into this interpretive or evaluative domain. Without an understanding of such evaluative processes, of the meanings specific person–environment transactions have for individuals, the reactions to such transactions, including coping, must remain unclear.

2. EMOTION AND COGNITION IN APPRAISAL

There have been essentially two opposing positions regarding cognition and emotion: the more traditional one that emotion shapes cognition, the other that cognition shapes emotion. The conceptual system presented by Lazarus and his colleagues has emphasized the latter, focusing on the role of cognition as the core influence on the emotional response. Although cognitive proces-

*See Addendum, section 5.

ses do indeed guide emotion – a perspective that has been absent or under-stated in the recent past – it is also true that emotion affects cognition, presumably through its impact on the information processing system. This has been strongly argued and demonstrated in past discussion and research (e.g. Easterbrook, 1959; Young, 1959; Korchin, 1964; Spence and Spence, 1966; Sarason, 1972; Kahneman, 1973; Klinger, 1975; Hamilton, 1976).

Such conceptual one-way streets, that is, that cognition shapes emotion *or* emotion shapes cognition, are in part a product of the laboratory necessity of limiting one's observation and analysis to a specific performance occurring in a brief moment in time rather than looking at the processes as they occur over time, as in the typical stressful encounter or life crisis. A major tenet here is that cognition and emotion, as they unfold over time, are interdependent, one affecting the other in a continuous process. This is a dynamic interpretation which assumes that environmental demands, appraisal processes, coping, and emotional reactions change momentarily as each contributes to, and thereby alters, the ongoing pattern of an adaptational encounter.

(i) Traditional Views of the Functions of Emotion in Cognition

Three functions of emotion in the appraisal process have been previously noted. The first is the *signal* function. In his later writings Freud (1959/1926) treated anxiety as a signal of danger, emphasizing danger from within in the form of instinctual impulses that were proscribed by the environment or by the superego. Unconscious processes and the possibility of dissociation of one mental process from another were central to Freud's formulation. Thus if the source of danger is not assimilated by one portion of the ego system, that is, is not admitted into awareness, then emotion (usually anxiety) serves as an important cue that coping or defensive processes must be set in motion. It is not necessary that the person consciously label the anxiety in order for the signal to be effective. Rather, the concept of signal anxiety implies an automatic process which, once triggered, follows through to its natural conclusion.

There is no attempt in this signal theory of anxiety to account for the phenomenology of experienced emotions and their effect on cognitive processing. Neither is there an easy explanation for how encounters come to be recognized (appraised) as threatening, nor about how information does come to be consciously perceived and subject to deliberation. Cognitive processing is only suggested by Freud, not emphasized or analysed. Further, it is clear why emotion must play this signal function, since any cognitive process or associated fragment could serve (Lazarus, 1966). A case in point is the person with a neurological defect that results in the inability to discriminate pain. In such a case, to survive the person must be trained to cognize and react to the danger of being burned by a match that is held in the hand too long, or of handling sharp objects, and the conditions that engender such danger.

A second major function of emotion that has been described is to *interrupt* ongoing behaviour patterns so that the person can attend to a more salient danger and mobilize to deal with it (Mandler and Watson, 1966; Mandler, 1975). This function is often assumed by arousal or activation theorists such as Lindsley (1951), Duffy (1951), and Malmo (1959) to be the basis for bodily and psychological mobilization for dealing with the threat. Such arousal should not be thought of as necessarily disruptive since it has the function of directing attention and efforts towards goals important for survival or for the person to flourish (Leeper, 1948; Young, 1959). However, it does interrupt ongoing activity. Cognitively oriented theorists, too, have emphasized this function of emotion (e.g. Miller, Galanter and Pribram, 1960; Simon, 1967; Mandler, 1975). Simon (1967, p.29), for example, points out the need for information processing models to have an interrupt system 'having the properties usually ascribed to emotion', one that is capable of temporarily setting aside ongoing programmes when environmental exigencies are encountered. The interrupting and mobilizing function of emotion is also a part of Tomkins' (1963) suggestion that emotions 'amplify' drives when there is a highly salient need or commitment, making the need for an adaptationally relevant action more pressing. Tomkins' idea of 'amplification' has the effect of changing the context from cool to hot, as it were, and it offers one explanation of why emotions are valuable or necessary. Remembering the person without pain sensors described above, such a person is constantly in great danger in the absence of pain to teach him or her what is necessary to avoid. Emotions have traditionally been thought to serve this function, creating a sense of emergency without which adaptive reactions would be too pallid to be serviceable.

Interruption and mobilization (or amplification) seem to us to parallel or encompass one of the functions of anxiety emphasized by Freud (1953/1900) in his earlier writings and by other tension-reduction theorists (e.g. Dollard and Miller, 1950), namely, to serve as a drive tension that motivates behaviour that is tension reducing. Freud (1953/1900) first conceived of anxiety as a painful undischarged drive stimulus, and this pain or tension was the force that mobilized actions against the pain or in the interest of pleasure. Although Freud ultimately dropped this line of reasoning in favour of the more cognitive, signal function of emotion (anxiety), it still receives wide support (e.g. Izard and Tomkins, 1966).

The conceptualization of emotion as having signal and interrupt functions emphasizes an automatic mechanism which, is some species, may be built in phylogenetically. As Arnold (1960) has observed, we become aroused automatically and instantly at a sudden movement or a strong auditory or visual stimulus, and it requires no time for reflection or extensive cognition activity to act defensively and as though endangered.

However, the response of humans to emergencies more often involves an elaborate set of cognitive processes. For example, upon hearing a loud fire alarm in a building, we are likely to feel acute arousal since we recognize instantly through experience that the alarm means danger (primary appraisal of threat). Nevertheless, unless we are panicked, we are likely to further consider how realistic that danger really is; we localize it, assess its potency, and above. all, consider how we might deal with it (secondary appraisal and reappraisal). Secondary appraisal feeds back to the original appraisal of threat, confirming it, enhancing it, or reducing it, depending on our evaluation of coping resources and options. In short, the initial instant of threat experienced at the alarm does not end the cognitive processing but actually initiates a whole chain of cognitive activity, some of it extending over a long period of time and involving complex thoughts, actions, and reactions, all of which make possible finely tuned adaptional responses. The interrupt and signal functions of emotion, therefore, must not be seen merely as automatic equivalents of phyogenetically more primitive adaptive mechanisms observed in mammals, but as setting in motion over time the full gamut of cognitive processes of which an adult human is capable.

In the above illustration we have spoken of survival-related emotions such as fear, and a relatively uncomplicated threat that can be sensed instantly. In our view, however, the most important sources of psychological stress tend to be in the complex meanings that inhere in social relationships, and in the emotions associated with these meanings such as anxiety, anger, guilt, sadness, envy, jealousy, embarrassment and disgust, to mention some of the most commonly recognized ones. The meanings of social stimulus cues are determined by the contents of memory, the belief systems and commitments of the person, by values, immediate goals, and by the resources the person has acquired for handling threat in social contexts – in other words, by multiple *cognitions*. Although the emotions associated with such meanings may facilitate adaptive use of information by further arousing and mobilizing the individual, it would be a mistake to ascribe the initiation of adaptive endeavours solely to emotion in those cases where emotion is a response to complex cognitive activity.

The third function of emotion in appraisal is, perhaps, the most obvious and well researched, namely, its capacity to *interfere* with cognitive processing at various points, say, at the point of paying attention, at registration, in storage, or in retrieval. The extensive discussion and research on test anxiety (e.g. Sarason, 1972), on the restriction of cue utilization (Easterbrook, 1959), and on the facilitating and debilitating effects of anxiety (Allpert and Haber, 1960), are examples. Such research has been reviewed extensively by

Hamilton (1975). Although interference offers one way in which emotion can affect cognitive processes, by itself it is inadequate for explaining the complex two-way relationship between emotion and cognition in the appraisal process.

Thus far we have discussed three ways emotion can affect cognitive activity throughout the appraisal process: it can signal the need for adaptive effort, interrupt less salient activity and produce arousal, and it can interfere with cognitive activity. However, the presence of a strong or distressing emotion can also lead to determined efforts to reduce or regulate it. Not only does coping function instrumentally to solve the problem, i.e. the troubled person–environment relationship that first generated the emotion, but another of its central functions is to regulate the emotional response itself. This is done by a variety of intrapsychic or cognitive coping processes such as avoidance, intellectualized detachment, and denial, to name some of the most common (Lazarus, 1975; Lazarus and Launier, in press). If the person tries not to think about the harm or danger, and succeeds, there need be little or no distress; if the danger is denied, again the distress is short-circuited; and if the personal emotional implications of an encounter are distanced or examined in a detached, intellectualized fashion, here too the potential emotional reaction is diminished by the cognitive regulating process.

Notice, however, what this means for understanding the relationship between emotion and cognition based on information processing modes of analysis. If cognitive activity can be used to regulate emotional states, then the relationship is reversed in a way not suggested in the three major functions of emotion discussed above. In fact, the very cognitive activity used to manage such regulation, for example, avoidance, is apt to be the obverse of attending to, taking in, and storing information about what is happening. The search for and utilization of information is, in effect, aborted or distorted. It is the manipulation of the meaning of the encounter that has come to dominate. The meanings sought by the person are those that make him or her feel better about the encounter. Such a process, and we are certain that it is very frequently found in 'healthy' human coping activity under stress, simply does not fit the information processing form of analysis of cognitive activity. Information processing analysis cannot help us with this aspect of stress and coping. Again, as in the past, we are placed in the position of the New Look perception psychologist who was dealing with individual differences rather than universality, and with a motivated context in which defensive processes and meaning rather than veridical information search become salient, rather than a context in which the stakes to the person are small or absent.

The process of preparing to take the qualifying examination for Ph.D. candidacy serves to illustrate the above theme. In Lazarus's analysis of the cognitive processes likely to be involved in such a transaction (see Lazarus and Launier, in press) there are three basic categories of primary appraisal: irrelevant, in which the person evaluates an event as having no implication for well-being; benign-positive, in which the person regards the event as signifying a positive state of affairs; and stressful, which can take three forms – harm-loss, threat and challenge.

Most students would not appraise the examination as an irrelevant event, because its successful outcome is important to the continuation of their careers. Nor would most students appraise the impending event as benign-positive; examinations are not by nature fun and gala affairs. Most likely, a student will appraise the event as stressful, either as threatening or challenging, although there are clearly exceptions depending on patterns of belief and motivation (Mahl, 1949; Vogel, Raymond and Lazarus, 1959).

Whether a student appraises the examination as a challenge or a threat will depend largely on evaluation of coping resources and options (secondary appraisal). The student might consider whether he or she is generally able to use oral examinations to good account, and may review what must be learned and the amount of time remaining in which to learn it. If the conclusion is drawn that the examination may be failed, or the outcome embarrassing, the oral examination situation cannot be used to good account or the material cannot be learned in time – the appraisal will be threatening and there will be much anxiety. However, the student may also see the possibility for positive gain from the situation. If it is mastered, one has the right to feel pleased and proud of what has been accomplished, and praise can be anticipated. Such a focus involves challenge as well as, perhaps, threat.

The mastering of feelings of anxiety, which could be expected to occur in the context of a threatening or challenging examination, is part of the prospective task, as much as the actual performance and preparation for it. A person's expectations about how intense or controllable the emotion might be also plays a decisive role in anticipated outcome. If the anxiety is intense, coping must also be directed at anxiety reduction, and it will be intrapsychic or cognitive in form. For example, there may be efforts to change the meaning of the examination, that is, cognitive reappraisal that it is less important than originally appraised, or easier to pass, thereby decreasing the sense of threat with its attendant anxiety. Or perhaps the student will engage in cognitive activity aimed at minimizing other threatening aspects of the examination, say, by reappraisal of the examiners in less malevolent terms. If anxiety remains high it may be difficult for the student to engage in the proper planning and preparation. On the other hand, a certain level of threat and anxiety is needed to prompt instrumental coping, such as arranging a rigorous plan of study which, if followed, could help diminish the threat of failure and the anxiety, too. For most students, appraisal will fluctuate with new information about the situation, and the effectiveness of self-reassuring cognitive coping (Mechanic, 1962).

In most cases during the anticipatory period, students will have executed a finely orchestrated series of coping processes designed to meet the requirements of instrumental action and the regulation of the threat-based emotion. In such instances, emotions at times will enhance instrumental coping activity, and at times will pre-empt or interfere with it. Either way, emotions are an important part of the scenario, both affecting cognitive activity and, in turn, being affected by it. Thus when coping activity is turned towards emotion regulation, the direction of the relationship goes from cognition to emotion, since the emotion is raised by threat appraisals in the first place, and lowered by cognitive coping processes.

(ii) Information processing Approaches to Emotion

Efforts to describe the functions of emotion in information processing have usually been in terms of negative feedback loops in which emotions make the system self-correcting and capable of maintaining homeostasis. This negative feedback is analogous to the signal function of emotion described earlier. Similarly, within a psychoanalytic paradigm, Peterfreund (1971) speaks of a system with built-in 'alarms'. In Peterfreund's approach, emotions are conceptualized as resulting from systems that are phylogentically older than thought and 'are able to play especially crucial roles in motivation because of their key positions in over-all organismic programming' (Peterfreund, 1971, p. 181). Exceptions to the tradition of emphasizing negative feedback loops can be found in the work of Tomkins (1963) and Coyne (1976), who talk about the importance of emotions in providing positive feedback.

A different sort of information processing system has been proposed by Erdelyi (1974), who discusses how information is selected for further processing. For Erdelyi, this selection is motivated by emotion. His model emphasizes a multisystem approach to cognitive processing. Within-systems information is multidirectional and can flow backwards as well as forwards. 'Thus examination of the contents of one system by another . . . does not yield storage of the examined information, or consciousness for the materials examined' (Erdelyi, 1974, p. 12). For example, long-term memory may examine and analyse information in a buffer store, which is conceived to have a high capacity but brief duration (cf. Broadbent, 1958; Neisser, 1967), but this examination by itself does not produce storage in long-term memory (or in awareness). Storage is achieved through control commands (e.g. encode the selected information into short-term storage, rehearse and consolidate the information in short-term storage until transfer to long-term memory is achieved, etc.). Further, ongoing storage operation can be interrupted on the basis of analysis of input information held in an earlier buffer; the examining system can terminate further processing through commands to transfer systems (e.g. stop further encoding of the information currently in buffer storage, etc.). Presumably, it is through their operation or influence on such control commands that emotions are thought to influence information processing [see Hamilton, Ch. 12].

These information processing models, while representing advances over models which deal solely with 'cool' processing, serve to point up some of the remaining difficulties in creating an information processing model which can truly incorporate individual differences and the effects of emotion. For example, as we noted in our introduction, the problem with most information processing models is that they have ignored, and possibly do not allow for, information processing in an emotional context, that is, for information that has relevance for well-being. We have referred to this kind of information as 'hot' information. In these cases, emotion and cognition are so tightly intertwined that they can be thought of as fused. Although we can use information processing models such as Erdelyi's (1974) to illustrate how emotion can influence selectivity at various *points* in the processing continuum, even Erdelyi's model does not easily accommodate the *ongoing* effects of fused cognition and emotion, that is, of 'hot' information.

The theory of cognitive appraisal, on the other hand, proceeds from an assumption that people in stressful transactions are dealing with information that is emotional. It must be remembered that cognitive appraisal is but one aspect of a theory of stress and coping. Not only does this model describe how individuals evaluate and cope with a stressful transaction but, more to the point in this discussion, it also considers how people cope with emotional information itself. For example, reappraisal can be employed as a coping strategy to cool or neutralize the information. Consider the individual who is told that he is going to lose his job. The initial appraisal of high threat can be modified through defensive reapraisal in which the person comes to value the job less. Perhaps he decides that the job did not provide much opportunity for advancement, or that the working environment, pay or fringe benefits are less than he 'deserves'. Whatever his method for devaluing the job, the result is that the meaning of the information has been changed so that it is no longer as motivationally salient and hence emotional as it was. We find nothing in traditional information processing analysis that elucidates or even allows us to deal with the above processes, and yet these processes are central to human adaptation.

Another way of looking at the above statement is to say that the nature of emotion as information is unclear. As a result, emotions seem to be conceived of as operating by proxy on cognitions through their influence on programme decision points. Information processing is thereby reduced to a series of binary decisions – will the information be further processed or not? This does not seem faithful to the complex processes that are involved in the creation of meaning which characterizes so many human adaptive activities, and to the possibilities inherent in tacit knowing (Polanyi, 1958). The challenge, then, for stress and coping and information processing theorists, is to construct a comprehensive model which describes the complex cognitive processes that characterize the ways people actually appraise and cope with information that has a vital bearing on the person's well-being.

Furthermore, most information processing systems work in one direction only; that is, emotion is thought to influence cognitive processess. They do not explain how cognitions might produce emotions, although they could attempt to, and they certainly do not allow for the constant interplay of emotions and cognitions across time, as required by our formulation.

3. AMBIGUITY–UNCERTAINTY AND APPRAISAL

Certain information is needed to appraise accurately the significance of any transaction for one's well-being: the imminence of the transaction, the goals or commitments that are at risk, the probable outcome(s) or consequences, and what can be done to control the outcome. Some of these evaluative questions, such as the nature of the outcome, are substantive, while others, such as its imminence, are formal, but all are relevant to primary appraisal – to a judgement of whether the transaction is relevant, benign-positive, or stressful – and to the specific respects in which any of these appraisals apply.

Information is needed to answer the implicit or explicit questions inherent in appraisal, yet in most human affairs, especially those involving threat and challenge, unclear or insufficient information is a common occurrence. When information is unclear or insufficient, it is more difficult to evaluate what the likely outcomes are and how they can best be dealt with. Any information processing model which seeks to address issues of stress, cognitive appraisal, and coping must be able to handle the processing of incomplete and imperfectly explicit information.

We use the term 'ambiguity' to refer to lack of clarity of meaning in the environmental display, and the term 'uncertainty' to refer to a person's mental confusion about its meaning. Remembering that stress refers to transactions between a particular person (with distinctive agendas, beliefs, ways of thinking, and abilities) and a particular environment, an environmental display can be clear as to meaning yet be responded to with uncertainty; such a display can also be ambiguous and yet the person be quite clear about its meaning.

A theoretical model is needed which describes the inferential processes with which people can reduce ambiquity-uncertainty, and which also permits ambiguity-uncertainty to persist. The need to consider the adaptive value of ambiguity is evident in situations where it allows a person to interpret a transaction in a positive light. (This point will be elaborated later in this section.) The absence of a model which allows both reduction and persistence of ambiguity-uncertainty is due, in part, to the assumptions (e.g. veridicality, the computer analogy, universality, etc.) required by information processing language concepts.

There are many ways in which ambiguity and uncertainty can occur. One form that has received much attention concerns the connotative meaning of words (see Osgood, 1952). Another form has to do with not knowing whether an event will occur, when it will occur, or its likely consequences. Among the most stressful instances of ambiguity and uncertainty, however, are those which occur in interpersonal transactions that are significant for our well-being, in other words, are potentially emotional in character. In these transactions inferences are based on complex and ambiguous displays (facial and bodily expressions, complex verbal statements, behaviour patterns in a specific but changing context), and call for judgements about others' intentions, evaluations, and feelings.

Nowhere, incidentally, is the contrast between the veridical, normative, information processing approach and the personalistic, stress-and-coping-centered focus more clear than in the matter of how to interpret emotional expression in faces. The work of Ekman (1956) and Ekman and Friesen (1975) is concerned with evolution-based universals in the meaning of facial muscle patterns that must be decoded by the observer. The assumption is that regardless of culture, each emotional state has its own universal pattern which we can learn to read. If such patterns are not overridden by deceptive presentations of self, or by the person's unique social history, the person who is doing the reading is faced with a highly ambiguous and complex display whose meaning he or she must intuit from a variety of cues.

In our social relationships this state of affairs is the equivalent of a projective technique (such as inkblots) which provides rich opportunities for personal agendas to enter into the inference process to produce great individual differences in appraisals. It is precisely under conditions of environmental ambiguity that there is the greatest latitude for diverse types of appraisal, and in the long range, for coping response. As with many of the New Look writers of the past, our own view is that in stressful transactions, especially in those that are interpersonal, ambiguity and uncertainty are the rule rather than the exception. For this reason, information processing as an approach to stress and coping is, of necessity, dangerously incomplete.

(i) Stress-related Research on Ambiguity–Uncertainty

Considering its importance in stress and coping, and in human affairs in general, research on ambiguity and uncertainty has been surprisingly limited. Until recently investigators have failed to recognize that there are many forms of ambiguity-uncertainty, treating the concept instead in a global and undifferentiated way.

Laboratory investigations have dealt primarily with one type of uncertainty, the probability of an event occurring (cf. Epstein and Roupenian, 1970; Gaines et al., 1977), or what Monat et al. (1972) have called 'event uncertainty'. The latter also contrasted the impact of event uncertainty and 'temporal uncertainty' (the time of an anticipated event) on stress and coping processes. These findings suggested that a high degree of event uncertainty results in increased arousal, although the relationship could well be very complex because of differences in subjective and objective probability (Epstein and Roupenian, 1970). On the other hand, while temporal uncertainty about the occurrence of electric shock (a common stressor in such research) does produce greater stress than when the time of shock is known, as the waiting period grows longer, it results in avoidant forms of intrapsychic coping, with attendant reduction in stress response levels. Thus there is evidence that individual differences in stress responses under conditions of uncertainty could be due, in part, to differences in the form of uncertainty and to mediating cognitive processes.

In addition to uncertainty about whether an event will happen and when it will happen, there can also be uncertainty about what will happen, about the many possible consequences of the event, and about what can be done about it. To our knowledge, these forms of uncertainty have received no attention in the laboratory, yet in real life stress they are likely to be most important. Consider the dilemma of a person facing a breast biopsy for a lump that could be malignant. Event uncertainty and temporal uncertainty are greatly diminished since the patient knows she is to have the surgery the next morning at some given hour. However, even though the immediate event, surgery, is known to a degree, there is uncertainty about whether the surgery is to be restricted merely to a biopsy or extended to a mastectomy. Unless there has been the prior decision to do a two-stage surgical procedure – first a biopsy and then a mastectomy a week or two later – the patient is confronted with not knowing what she will wake up to, and what will transpire afterwards.

Thus the question of what will happen – and remember that this is an emotionally charged question – remains in a high state of uncertainty with at least two broad possibilities: a benign lump will be removed, or some form of mastectomy will be performed. The first outcome is clearly best, although even here there are residual sources of threat concerning the likelihood of future occurrences of biopsy and of later cancer. In the event of mastectomy, there remains the question of the kind of surgery (radical or modified) to be undergone, each with its own attendant threats and uncertainties concerning physical appearance, pain, extended drug therapy, physiotherapy, and physical functioning. Of even greater import to the person is the unresolved issue of the stage of cancer (whether it is localized or has spread), the probability of recurrence and, if so, the temporal aspects of such recurrence, the speed with which the disease progresses, the impact on interpersonal relationships, and the threat of death.

Shalit (1977) has maintained that ambiguity is one of the most important factors in appraisal and coping. He proposes that effectiveness of coping is heavily determined by the ability to resolve ambiguity. Ambiguity, in turn, depends on the structural complexity of a situation as defined by three factors: differentiation, which refers to the number of possibilities of interpretation open to a person; articulation, which is the ease with which the perceived possibilities can be graded or rank ordered; and loading, which is the emotional impact of the situation, whether positive or negative.

After reviewing a large number of studies of adult performance under stress, and examining the demands imposed and the coping outcomes, Shalit selected for further analysis 75 studies representing either good coping, reduced coping, or coping failure. Assessing them on the three dimensions of differentiation, articulation, and emotional loading, and using Multi-dimensional Scalogram Analysis, he concluded that the person's ability to grade or rank order the possibilities (articulation) is most essential to success-ful coping.

While this conclusion may hold up in some situations, especially those in unemotional contexts, there are instances when it might be more adaptive to perpetuate rather than reduce ambiguity. To continue with the previous illustration of a breast biopsy, suppose the surgery reveals extensive metasteses. Would optimum coping be encouraged by explaining to the patient that the odds for recovery are, say, 5 out of 100? If the outcome were less articulated by the physician, to use Shalit's term, that is, less graded, hope and positive morale might remain greater, and with it the motivation to work towards recovery. The maintenance of hope and adaptive efforts may depend to a large extent on outcome uncertainty, and it could be unwise in many instances to conclude that less ambiguity is necessarily related to more effective coping. Other research which might be cited in support of this possibility are Janis's (1958) and Cohen and Lazarus's (1973) studies of patients recovering from minor surgery. Vigilant information search, which might have the function of reducing uncertainty, did not in these instances produce the best postsurgical recoveries. In fact, Janis and Mann (1977) have recently written about 'hypervigilance', which is regarded as counter-productive.

(ii) Tolerance of Ambiguity (Uncertainty)

One of the most interesting directions of past thought and research on uncertainty is the adoption of a personalistic rather than a situation-based perspective. It would seem reasonable to expect that people vary in their ability to remain in a state of uncertainty without undue distress, in which case we would assume that information processing and coping would be differentially disrupted and differentially effective. During the active period of New Look research, Frenkel-Brunswik (1949) labelled this personality characteristic 'tolerance of ambiguity', and its opposite pole 'intolerance', and she regarded it as '. . . one of the basic variables in both the emotional and cognitive orientation of the person toward life . . . .' (p. 113). Those who are intolerant of ambiguity, for example, are likely to arrive at a premature closure often at the neglect of reality. Such premature closure, or closed-mindedness in Rokeach's (1960) term, is highly relevant to coping since it 'requires the shutting out of aspects of reality which represent a possible threat . . . .' (Frenkel-Brunswik, 1949, p. 115). Tolerance of ambiguity, on the other hand, means a willingness to consider multiple aspects of reality and a more flexible adaptation to varying circumstances and degrees of abstraction [see Hamilton Ch. 12].

Loevinger (1976) has also identified tolerance of ambiguity as characteristic of a high level of ego development. She states that:

'A distinctive mark of the Autonomous State is the capacity to acknowledge and to cope with inner conflicts, that is, conflicting needs, conflicting duties, and the conflict between needs and duties . . . the Autonomous person . . . has the courage (and whatever other qualities it takes) to acknowledge and deal with conflict rather than ignoring it or projecting it onto the environment. Where the Conscientious person [a lower form of ego development] tends to construe the world in terms of popular opposites, the Autonomous person partly transcends those polarities, seeing reality as complex and multifaceted . . . there is a high toleration for ambiguity.' (p. 23).

Another theorist with a similar position is Haan (1969; 1977), who has also identified tolerance of ambiguity as a feature of coping, the highest form of ego processing in her tripartite model of coping, defense, and ego failure.

We should note too that in the classical clinical literature a form of uncertainty is expressed in the theme of *ambivalence,* which is both a normal development state and a personality trait especially characteristic of obsessive-compulsion (e.g. Schafer, 1954; Shapiro, 1965). In any case, well-adjusted persons are viewed as being capable of handling ambivalent feelings, such as love and hate, feelings Freud suggested all children direct towards their parents.

There are a host of unresolved empirical issues linked to tolerance of ambiguity-uncertainty. These include the personality traits that dispose to intolerance, and the situational factors that increase intolerance, for example, the imminence of harm, the importance or centrality of the threat, the complexity of the problem, age, intelligence, and so on. The questions we regard as particularly important, however, concern how ambiguity-uncertainty affects cognitive appraisal and coping processes.

(iii) Ambiguity as a Factor in Coping

In certain instances ambiguity-uncertainty will impel a person towards a vigilant search for information on which to predicate cognitive appraisal and coping. Indeed, information search in itself is a basic form of coping (see Hamburg and Adams, 1967; Janis and Mann, 1977; Lazarus and Launier, in press). The person who chooses to engage in information search to reduce ambiguity, however, may well find that the necessary information is unavailable; inferential processes then become critically important. It is through inference that the gaps created by the ambiguous inputs can be narrowed.

Inferences about the meaning of any stressful transaction are based both on partial cues in the transaction and on the person's experience. Schank and Abelson (1977), for example, refer to general and specific knowledge in the person's attempts at comprehension. They write that 'General knowledge enables a person to understand and interpret another person's actions simply because the other person is a human being with certain standard needs who lives in a world which has certain standard methods of getting those needs fulfilled . . . .'. General knowledge permits a person to interpret events even if they have never been observed before. Specific knowledge is used to interpret and participate in events that people have experienced many times. Obviously, then, if a person has a great deal of relevant specific knowledge, the inferential leap will be minimal and uncertainty should be quickly reduced. To the extent that the person's understanding of general rules is accurate and appropriate to the event, inferences made on the basis of general knowledge should be realistic and useful for primary and secondary appraisal (see also Anderson et al., 1977; Stein and Glenn, in press). Individual differences in such knowledge ought to be one of the important bases of cognitive appraisal and of coping.

Inferences about the potential significance and outcome of events are also based on general beliefs about oneself and one's relations with the environment. As noted by Lazarus (1966), '. . . the more ambiguous are the stimulus cues, the more important are general belief systems in determining the appraisal process' (p. 134). For example, whether the environment is viewed as generally unmanageable and hostile, or as supportive and readily subject to control, should affect the appraisal (e.g. threatening or challenging), and the consequent emotional impact. The importance of such beliefs underlies extensive recent research and theorizing on locus of control (Rotter, 1966; Lefcourt, 1976).

On the other hand, ambiguity-uncertainty can encourage the obverse of information search and inferential process, namely, avoidance, denial, or defensive distortion of threatening information. These are forms of coping which, as we have already noted, are actually made easier and more effective by ambiguity. For example, the more ambiguously a physician describes a dangerous or terminal illness, the more the palliative or defensive forms of appraisal are encouraged.

It is important to recognize that such palliative forms of coping need not be viewed as necessarily negative or maladaptive, as is implicit in the previous example dealing with serious illness. Avoidance may be good coping if it adds overall to the quality of life the person experiences and does not obviate adaptive actions. As suggested by Horowitz (1976), avoidance of highly stressful information, if not rigidly used, also allows the person to 'dose' her- or himself strategically with the needed information, thereby avoiding extreme and dysfunctional emotional responses. Moreover, Hamburg and Adams (1967) have observed that a weakened and helpless victim of severe illness (e.g. spinal cord injury, severe burns, polio) may constructively employ denial during the early stages to get past the worst and most debilitating period, but then, when stronger, turn towards more reality-based appraisals and actions aimed at rehabilitation.

In sum, information processing in appraisal must be seen not only in relation to the specific information an individual extracts and uses from the stimulus configuration, but also in relation to the incomplete or ambiguous qualities of that information. Further, a number of personality factors must be given attention. These include the ability to gain additional information and to reason about what is happening, general beliefs and commitments, general and specific knowledge, the emotional consequences of ambiguity as conveyed in concepts such as tolerance for ambiguity, and the available coping possibilities and resources. As the New Look movement has emphasized, ambiguity in the information immediately available to the person in any stressful encounter increases the importance of such personality factors in cognitive appraisal, thus also increasing the variability in the way any event is appraised and in the pattern of coping.

4. EVALUATION, SECONDARY APPRAISAL, AND COPING

We have already discussed the importance of evaluation in primary appraisal where the question is asked, 'Am I okay or in trouble?' and the answer lay in the *meaning* of the information to the individual in terms of values, beliefs, goals, commitments, experience, and resources. In this section we discuss evaluation within the framework of secondary appraisal, in which the answer to the question 'What can I do about the trouble?' centres on evaluation of the availability of *suitable* coping strategies, that is, on the *goodness of fit* among task demands, coping resources, and personal agendas. First, it is important to distinguish between coping resources and coping processes.

Previously, coping has been defined as '. . . efforts, both action-oriented and intrapsychic, to manage (i.e. master, tolerate, reduce, minimize) environmental and internal demands and conflicts among them, which tax or exceed a person's resources' (Lazarus and Launier, in press). Such a definition is process-centred and differs from other approaches that are keyed to generalized personality dispositions or styles such as repression-sensitization (see Lazarus, Averill and Opton, 1970), or that emphasize a built-in hierarchy of coping or defence mechanism (cf. Menninger, 1954; Haan, 1977; Vaillant, 1977). The range of coping processes which can be simultaneously or sequentially employed is broad, encompassing at least four main categories, namely, information search, direct action, inhibition of action, and intrapsychic modes. Moreover, such processes can have at least two main functions, as we noted earlier, namely, to alter the person–environment relationship (instrumental or problem solving) or to regulate the stress and distress reaction (palliative).

A person's coping resources are usually not constant over time, that is, they are likely to expand and contract, some more erratically than others, as a function of experience, degree of stress, time of life, and the requirements of adaptation associated with different styles of life or periods in the life course. Therefore, the presence of a given resource at a given time does not imply that it will be available for the same person to the same extent at another time, although some resources are likely to be more stable than others. For example, general beliefs about one's efficacy may be more resistant to change than morale.

Furthermore, the presence in a person of a general resource such as problem solving skills does not mean that the appropriate resource will be available or used at the time and in the transaction in which coping is required. Every major stressful transaction has its own task requirements: illness makes different coping demands compared with qualifying examinations or a situation requiring that someone in power be influenced. An effective person is likely to be effective across a variety of circumstances, but there will often be occasions when the requisite skills are simply not there, or when some hidden personal agenda or psychological deficit will prevent effective use of coping. Thus it is essential to distinguish between coping resources and the specific coping processes actually used in a given stress situation.

(i) Coping Resources

Coping resources can be drawn from within the person or from the environment, and include at least five categories: *health/energy/morale, problem solving skills, social networks, utilitarian resources* (e.g. money, social agencies), and both *general and specific beliefs.*

Coping resources are relevant to our consideration of information processing and cognitive appraisal in stress and coping for two reasons. First, they provide a key set of data for the person to evaluate when he or she is appraising any transaction for its impact on well-being. Second, they provide the basis of coping action depending, of course, on knowledge about them and how they can be used. As before, we can sense here the two alternative perspectives we have carried throughout this chapter from the beginning, namely, veridical perception versus the personalistic and even idiosyncratic meanings individuals can obtain from their relationships with the environment. We shall examine each major type of resource below.

(a) Health/energy/morale

These are the most obvious coping resources. If a person is frail, sick, tired, or otherwise debilitated, there is less energy to expend on coping than in the case of a healthy, robust person. This should be particularly evident in an enduring problem and in stressful transactions demanding extreme mobilization. The same crisis that a healthy person survives may destroy the weak. In many respects morale operates in a similar way, although it can easily be treated separately. For example, if a person is depressed or otherwise psychologically handicapped, coping effectiveness is reduced. Research on burned patients (Andreasen et al., 1972) demonstrates, for example, that premorbid psychopathology and physical disabilities significantly predict poor adjustment to the immediate trauma of burns, and good premorbid functioning has been shown to correlate better with the prognosis of recovery from reactive schizophrenia than any other measure (Phillips, 1953).

Recent research (Hamburg and Adams, 1967) also suggest that people are capable of managing surprisingly well the most severe life crisis (see also Hamburg et al., 1953; Visotsky et al., 1961; Dimsdale, 1974; Bulman and Wortman, 1977). Often, however, the initial state of mind of the person in crisis or disaster is to be stunned, dependent, and disbelieving. At the outset they are ill-prepared physically and mentally to cope effectively and realistically. However, with time and growing strength, and sometimes following a period of depression when the implications of the disability have become fully assimilated, such persons take increasing responsibility for their own rehabilitation and begin to cope effectively, something they could not do while weak and emotionally drained.

(b) Problem solving skills

These include the ability to search for information, to analyse situations for the purpose of identifying the problem, to generate alternative courses of action, to weigh alternatives with respect to desired or anticipated outcomes, and to select and implement an appropriate plan of action (Janis, 1974; Janis and Mann, 1977). Such generalized, abstract skills ultimately must be actualized through specific acts, in themselves skills, such as changing a flat tyre, managing a boat in a storm, presenting oneself to a prospective employer, preparing for an examination, and so on. Some writers conceptualize skills in somewhat global terms such as dealing with moral dilemmas (Schwartz, 1970), with emergency situations (for reviews see Janis, 1958; Baker and Chapman, 1962; Lazarus, 1966; Appley and Trumbull, 1967; Coelho, Hanburg and Adams, 1974), with role conflict (Katz and Kahn, 1966), with marital conflict (Parsons and Bales, 1955; Levinger, 1966), or with ambiguity (Haan, 1977). Others favour more concrete, day-to-day actions such as one might use in a training manual (cf. Yates, 1976; Meichenbaum, 1977; Rogers, 1977). Both levels of abstraction are important for understanding and for practical intervention.

(c) Social networks

Social networks and support systems have attracted growing interest in stress research, behavioural medicine, and social epidemiology (e.g. Antonovsky, 1972; Nuckolls et al., 1972; Cassell, 1976; Cobb, 1976; Berkman, 1977; Kaplan, Cassel and Gore, 1977). Close positive relationships appear to facilitate good health and morale even under personal crises, and a group of persons which can be characterized as having elaborate social networks at their disposal generally live longer than isolates (Berkman, 1977). Although there are stress situations in which family members exacerbate stress or block coping rather than help, as noted by Mechanic (1962) and Friedman et al., (1963), social support systems can be regarded as an extremely valuable potential coping resource. However, good measures of the quality of social supports as perceived and used by individuals need to be developed, and the details of the impact of social networks and the conditions under which they are used and operate positively need to be fleshed out.

A good example of the use of a social network in daily living is provided by Pearlin's (1975) study of homemakers. Pearlin notes that there are at least three functions performed by social networks. He writes:

'Such networks are, first, a potential source of information pertaining to the recognition and management of problems arising in homemaking. This information provides standards for defining what to ignore, what to get excited about, and how to deal with crises. Social relations, in other words, help place the event and demands of homemaking in a normative framework, thereby clarifying and stabilizing their meaning. Second, social relations may serve as sources of emotional support and encouragement, something to lean on for help when the going is tough. And finally, social contacts and affiliations can provide a haven to which one may flee for a bit of relief from ordinary routines. In this manner social relations function as real safety valves and vehicles of escape for the hassled homemaker' (Pearlin, 1975, pp. 199–200).

(d) Utilitarian resources

Money, tools, instructional manuals, special training programmes, social agencies, etc., are also coping resources, available to some and not others. Such resources greatly increase the coping options available to a person in any stressful transaction, or in just the normal course of living. For example, people with monetary resources have easier and often more effective access to legal, medical, or other professional assistance. It would be unwise to underestimate the value of utilitarian resources in making it possible for a person to cope more effectively in many types of life crisis. This is probably one of the important reasons why socioeconomic status is correlated positively and strongly with nearly every kind of positive adaptational outcome, including health, morale, and social functioning (Syme and Berkman, 1976). People who have an abundance of utilitarian resources, especially if they are aware of their existence and of how to use them, generally fare much better than those without.

(e) General and specific beliefs

Bandura (1977) and others have emphasized the belief in self-efficacy as a general, overarching resource that is critical in coping. Self-efficacy seems to be related conceptually to the locus of control variable as discussed by Rotter (1966) and Lefcourt (1976). Both refer to the conviction that reinforcements are contingent on one's own behaviour rather than being the result of luck, chance or fate, which is unpredictable. To disbelieve in one's own efficacy should generate passivity and disengagement, and at its extreme should be associated with a sense of helplessness and hopelessness, which are in turn linked to depression (e.g. Engel, 1962; Schmale and Iker, 1966; Seligman, 1975; Lefcourt, 1976). Bandura (1977) also makes an important distinction between 'efficacy expectation', which refers to the conviction that one can successfully execute the behaviour required to produce a given outcome, and 'outcome expectation', which refers to a person's estimate that a given behaviour will lead to certain outcomes.

It seems sensible to assume that persons who believe that they can master most demands and threats by doing what is needed or by discovering what to do and how to do it are less likely to be threatened or to feel helpless or hopeless in stressful transactions. The obverse of this is the chronically anxious person who can be thought of as someone who maintains a general belief both that the environment is hostile, and that he or she is incapable of mastery (cf. Lazarus, 1966). Such persons are anxious even in situations in which the ordinary person does not experience threat because the very act of engaging the environment carries with it the implication of danger.

Belief systems of this sort, whether positive or negative, can theoretically vary from the most broad or general, in which virtually every environmental context is a challenge or a threat, to narrower instances in which this or that situation or class of situations is challenging or threatening. For example, a person may be anxious when any ability is being evaluated or only when being evaluated as to mathematical skill or when meeting strangers. Therefore, when we speak of beliefs about self-efficacy, we should recognize that this varies on a dimension from the most general to the specific, and that prediction of threat appraisal ultimately depends on the areas of vulnerability characterizing any given person. One of the more interesting and subtle consequences of living in a large and complex society may be the increase in specialized competence-creating experiences, but the consequent neglect of other such experiences.

At the level of general belief, existential belief systems, such as faith in God, fate, or some higher natural order enable people to create meaning out of life, even out of damaging experiences. Such systems provide answers or explanations for otherwise inexplicable events such as a traumatic accident, death of a loved one, one's own imminent death, and destructive evil such as a Nazi concentration camp. In his study of coping among concentration camp survivors, Dimsdale (1974) gives a graphic example of the importance of meaningful beliefs as a coping resource in a woman of twenty at the time of her imprisonment. Of her experience in the camps, she is quoted as saying:

'I had a belief, a religious belief. I was convinced that all the wrong things had to change and we would be free. My mother put in me the belief that if someone is doing right, he will not always suffer . . . I knew to survive [in Auschwitz] I had to believe, believe that such a bad thing cannot win' (Dimsdale, 1974, p. 793).

In other research, patients who had suffered spinal cord injuries offered the thought that God had a reason for their victimization as the most frequent explanation to the question 'Why me?' (Bulman and Wortman, 1977). One respondent said, for example, 'There must be some reason for it. Could be that He had a reason for it. Maybe somebody else needs my leg more than I do.' Another responded:

'I say, "you were meant to be put in this situation, and so there must be some reason why this situation is." So I try to figure out why, and I say, "Well, I'm put in this situation to learn certain things, 'cause nobody else is in this situation." It's a learning experience. I see God's trying to put me in situations, help me to learn about Him and myself and also how I can help other people' (Bulman and Wortman, 1977, p. 358).

Belief in some higher purpose enabled these persons to look for and see some benefit, some good purpose, in the experiences to which they were subjected (see also Lipowski, 1970). Comparable in effect are beliefs at a more specific level, for example, belief in a helping individual such as a physician, in a particular medicine, in a treatment regimen to cure or prevent illness, in an educational programme, and so on.

As with any coping resource, there is a strong link between beliefs and morale. Morale can be bolstered and hope generated, for example, by the belief that suffering strengthens character. Supportive beliefs as opposed to despair are also probably implicated in positive social functioning as when, for example, patients with advanced cancer continue to struggle to maintain social ties and work commitments (cf. Weisman and Worden, 1975). Whether or not positive general belief systems are functional in the support of somatic health through, say, the generation or maintenance of positive emotions (cf. Cousins, 1976), or life-sustaining actions, still remains uncertain, though a likely hypothesis (Lazarus *et al.*, in press).

In the above discussion we have emphasized belief systems as major factors in appraisal and coping, but we must not make the mistake of assuming that coping effort and coping persistence are explainable solely by such cognitive activity. We must recognize also that potentially emotional transactions are defined by the presence of stakes in the outcomes, that is, commitment or motivational variables (cf. Lazarus, 1966). Clearly, if what is at risk is important to the person, there is a potential for both greater effort and persistence in coping and greater psychological stress (cf. Vogel *et al.*, 1959; Lazarus, 1966), than in transactions appraised as having little motivational relevance.

(ii) Coping Suitability and Goodness of Fit

Secondary appraisal focuses, as we said, on coping resources and options relevant to the choice of coping strategy and tactics. Whether the coping process arises as an impulsive act or a deliberate one that involves information search, feedback and trial and error, and reflection, the various alternatives must be chosen, perhaps intuitively, according to the prospects (e.g. probability) that they can alter the relationship for the better. Bandura (1977) refers to such estimates as 'outcome expectancies', while Averill *et al.*, (1977) use the term 'response effectiveness'. Interesting discussions of the determinants of intuitive predictions about outcomes may be found in Kahneman and Tversky (1973) and Tversky and Kahneman (1971; 1973).

Less often considered is an appraisal-related judgment about the suitability of coping or 'goodness of fit' (1) between the coping strategy and environmental (or task) demands and constraints, and (2) between the coping strategy and other agendas in the person's life. The latter include goals or commitments (both short and long range), personal values, sources of meaning, and well-entrenched styles of thinking and acting. Goodness of fit is at its optimum when the person has coping strategies readily available that will meet the transactional demands without any conflict with the other agendas. When the goodness of fit is less than optimal, coping effectiveness is jeopardized. Far from resulting in stress reduction, it will even increase stress response levels from a variety of sources.

Variants of the concept of goodness of fit are not new since it is an idea based on conflict, which plays a key role in most theories of personality dynamics. When Freud spoke of conflict among id, ego, and superego systems, he was implying a poor fit among internal processes (instinctual drives and internalized societal values) and external or environmental ones (representations of reality). Goodness of fit implies harmony or integration. The concept of person–environment fit has also been emphasized by French et al., (1974) and used in stress research in the work setting, where conflict between the person and institutional roles can be a major source of stress (see also Kahn et al., 1964). We are applying the concept of good fit or misfit to the relationship between coping processes and both internal and environmental demands and constraints (including institutional ones; cf. Mechanic, 1974; Goldschmidt, 1974). The otherwise best coping solution is often proscribed by such demands and constraints.

A recent experiment by Averill et al. (1977) provides provocative support for this line of reasoning by demonstrating that personal agendas create individual differences in coping strategy in spite of common outcome expectancies. Their subjects were given the opportunity to avoid an aversive stimulus, electric shock, by attending to an auditory channel in which a warning would be sounded alerting them to the upcoming shock. Subjects could press a button to avoid the shock with varying rates of known response effectiveness (0%, 33%, 66%, and 100%). Alternatively, subjects could choose to listen to a music channel in which no warning was sounded. Subjects were allowed to switch back and forth between the channels. In effect, a situation had been created in which subjects could choose between two forms of coping, one that had instrumental value but which required constant vigilance, and one that had no instrumental value but which could palliate stress by cognitive avoidance.

Two subject groups are of particular interest here, namely, those 21 subjects (26% of the sample) who chose to listen for the warning in the 0% response effectiveness condition (that is, where there was no way to avoid the shock), and those who chose to listen to the music channel even under conditions of high response effectiveness (5 subjects, 6% of the sample). When asked why they chose to attend to the warning, the former group reported: 'I wanted to prepare for the shock so that it wouldn't hurt so much'; 'I wanted to make a response just in case there was a chance for avoiding shock'; 'I didn't want to be taken by surprise' (p. 413). The authors conceptualize this as a generalized response tendency to exert control over an aversive stimulus even though such control was not possible – in effect, an effort after control. We see in this an example of a poor fit between the choice of coping strategy of seeking control and the lack of possibility for such control in the situation. Consistent with this interpretation, psychological stress was high, as indicated by the fact that subjects in this group described themselves as more tense in the 0% trial than in those trials in which response effectiveness was greater. The problem for these subjects is that they carried an important inner agenda, namely, a strong wish or need to exert control, which dominated their choice of coping strategy despite its poor fit with the external realities.

The latter group, those who chose to listen to the music channel, explained that listening to the tone channel for the purpose of being warned would have made them more anxious. Indeed, as we might anticipate, this group showed higher stress response levels under the condition of 100% response effectiveness than they did under conditions of low response effectiveness – exactly the opposite pattern from the former group. Here too, goodness of fit between the preferred coping strategy of avoidance (the inner agenda) and the coping possibilities inherent in the situation was poor, with consequent heightening of stress response levels. To put it differently, the subjective ranking of coping strategies for the purpose of action (secondary appraisal) was predicated on personal agendas rather than on the actual prospects of mastering the stressor.

Additional support for the importance of personal agendas in understanding differences in stress response is offered by Lundberg and Frankenhaeuser (1978). Stress response under conditions of control and no control over noise intensity was found to be mediated by general expectancies about control. Subjects who characteristically viewed themselves as being in control of significant reinforcers ('internals') had a higher stress level than those who saw themselves as low in such control ('external'). Although the differences between the groups did not reach significance, their findings do emphasize the importance of the goodness of fit between available coping resources and other agendas when explaining the stress response.

We can remind ourselves also that selection of a coping strategy often occurs under conditions of psychological stress and emotion, as we noted at the outset. Such stress can interfere with good decision-making although the rules about when it will interfere, when it will facilitate, and when it will have no effect at all remain unclear (cf. Lazarus and Eriksen, 1952; Lazarus, 1966).

Janis and Mann (1977) have given much attention to the conditions affecting decision-making under stress. Among those identified are the following:

(a) If it is unrealistic to seek a better solution than has been adopted, defensive avoidance will be employed, '. . . the person tries to keep himself from being exposed to communications that might reveal the shortcomings of the course of action he has chosen' (p. 74).

(b) If there is hope of finding a solution but there is no time to search and deliberate, hypervigilance will ensue. The person becomes

'. . . obsessed with nightmarish fantasies about all sorts of horrible things that might happen to him and fails to notice evidence indicating the improbability of their actual occurrence. The person is constantly aware of pressure to take prompt. action to avert catastrophic losses. He superficially scans the most obvious alternatives open to him and may then resort to a crude form of satisficing [sic], hastily choosing the first one that seems to hold the promise of escaping the worst danger' (Janis and Mann, 1977, p. 74).

(c) If there is time to search and deliberate, then the individual can be appropriately vigilant. This includes thorough canvassing of alternatives and objectives, careful evaluation of consequences, thorough search for information with unbiased assessment of it, careful re-evaluation of consequences, and thorough planning for implementation and the contingencies that may befall *en route*. These do not exhaust the conditions on which choice of coping strategy depends. Additional ones, flowing out of our own treatment, might include degree of uncertainty, degree of threat, presence of conflict, and degree of helplessness.

The interplay between appraisal and coping apparent in Janis and Mann's (1977) formulation must be emphasized. Not only does appraisal affect coping, since how a person construes any transaction influences the choice of coping strategy, but coping also affects appraisal, since the strategy with which one copes shapes cognitive processing. Any examination of the cognitive processes mediating between a stressful event and human response must include consideration of the cognitive events that occur in both appraisal and coping, and the interdependence of those events. Moreover, by emphasizing the conditions of choice and the emotionalized processes of avoidance and hypervigilance, Janis and Mann seem to avoid an over-deliberate portrayal of the coping decision, and manage to skirt the machine analogy of binary choice and systematic scanning of alternatives.

It seems to us also, in passing, that it will never be possible adequately to evaluate the quality of coping without having some basis for describing the demands of a stressful transaction, for example, the situational or task requirements. As Hackman (1970) has observed, we have no classificatory system for describing task demands, and hence no way of assessing how well a person is doing with his or her coping strategy, that is, the response effectiveness.

Moreover, multiple values are usually at stake in any stressful encounter, especially when the coping process is considered in the long rather than the short run. For example, a person must balance or harmonize at least three very different values:

(a) controlling the situation instrumentally as effectively as possible so that he or she can move towards important goals or master obstacles or overcome damaging environmental pressures;

(b) maintaining his or her own value integrity and morale; and

(c) keeping the internal environment sufficiently close to homeostatic balance to maintain bodily health despite having to mobilize to cope instrumentally.

Often a person does well with the first, as in vigilance under chronic or repeated danger, but pays a price for this in damage to the second or third value. We need to keep in mind that stressful transactions are a product of two interacting systems, the person and the environment with which that person has continuing commerce.

As we have seen, there is constant interplay between these, mediated by a complex set of ongoing cognitive processes that we have referred to as primary and secondary appraisal. Moreover, these cognitive processes not only affect each other in a continuous flow as events unfold over time and under changing conditions, but they are interpenetrated by stress responses that can further influence information processing and other cognitive activity involved in adaptation. We are convinced that stress and coping cannot be understood until these mediating cognitive processes and their interplay are spelled out in some detail. We seem to have increasing company in this conviction, as is evident in the other chapters of this book. And since so much of cognitive activity occurs in the context of stress or high stakes, it is important for 'cold' information processors to realize that they cannot adequately understand the ways people adapt to their natural settings without finding ways of incorporating what the New Look set out to explore several decades before, namely, the individual difference perspective and the 'hot' context of adaptation. And by the same token, it behoves those working in stress and coping to pay more attention to the cognitive processing and evaluation of adaptational encounters, including what happens in attention, memory, meaning transformations, access, and retrieval. We seem almost as far away from the union of these two outlooks in the 1970s as we were in the 1950s, but if we can break down the barriers to communication, the gain in understanding promises to be great.

5. ADDENDUM

After this paper had been written, we came upon a book by Dreyfus (1972) which adopts a stance like ours, although in a more extensive and explicit treatment. We recommend this book, not well known in psychology, for its sophisticated and carefully reasoned account of the limitations of the computer as a model for human reasoning. Dreyfus' view is exemplified in the quote below:

'The psychological, epistemological, and ontological assumptions [of artificial intelligence and computer simulation] have this in common: They assume that man must be a *device* which calculates according to rules on data which take the form of atomic facts. Such a view is the tidal wave produced by the confluence of two powerful streams: First, the Platonic reduction of all reasoning to explicit rules and the world to atomic facts to which alone such rules could be applied without the risks of interpretation; second, the invention of the digital computer, a general-purpose information-processing device, which calculates according to explicit rules and takes in data in terms of atomic elements logically independent of one another. In some other culture, the digital computer would most likely have seemed an unpromising model for the creation of artificial reason, but in our tradition the computer seems to be the very paradigm of logical intelligence, merely awaiting the proper program to accede to man's essential attribute of rationality.

The impetus gained by the mutual reinforcement of two thousand years of tradition and its product, the most powerful device ever invented by man, is simply too great to be arrested, deflected, or even fully understood. The most that can be hoped is that we become aware that the direction this impetus has taken, while unavoidable, is not the only possible direction; that the assumption underlying the conviction that artificial reason is possible are assumptions, not axioms – in short, that there may be an alternative way of understanding human reason which explains both why the computer paradigm is irresistible and why it must fail' (pp. 143–144).

6. REFERENCES

Allpert, R. and Haber, R. N. 1960, Anxiety in academic achievement situations. *Journal of Abnormal and Social Psychology,* **61**, 207–215.

Allport, F. H. (1955). *Theories of Perception and the Concept of Structure.* New York: Wiley.

Anderson, R. C., Reynolds, R. E., Schallert, D. L. and Goetz, E. T. (1977). Frameworks for comprehending discourse. *American Educational Research Journal,* **14**, 367–381.

Andreasen, N. J. C., Noyes, R., Jr. and Hartford, C. E. (1972). Factors influencing adjustment of burn patients during hospitalization. *Psychosomatic Medicine,* **34**, 517–525.

Antonovsky, A. (1972). Breakdown: a needed fourth step in the conceptual armamentarium of modern medicine. *Social Science and Medicine,* **6**, 537–544.

Appley, M. and Trumbull, I. (Eds.) (1967). *Psychological Stress: Issues in Research.* New York: Appleton–Century–Crofts.

Arnold, M. (1960). *Emotion and Personality.* New York: Columbia University Press.

Averill, J. R., O'Brien, L. and DeWitt, G. W. (1977). The influence of response effectiveness on the preference for warning and on psychophysiological stress reactions. *Journal of Personality,* **45**, 395–418.

Baker, G. W. and Chapman, D. W. (eds.). (1962). *Man and Society in Disaster.* New York: Basic Books.

Bandura, A. (1977). Self-efficacy: toward a unifying theory of behavioral change. *Psychological Review*, **84**, 191–215.

Berkman, L. (1977), Social networks, host resistance, and mortality: a follow-up study of Alameda County residents. Unpublished Doctoral Dissertation, University of California, Berkeley.

Bolles, R. C. (1974). Cognition and motivation: some historical trends. In B. Weiner (Ed.), *Cognitive Views of Human Motivation*. New York: Academic Press.

Broadbent, D. E. (1958). *Perception and Communication*. London: Pergamon.

Bulman, R. J. and Wortman, C. B. (1977). Attributions of blame and coping in the 'Real World': severe accident victims react to their lot. *Journal of Personality and Social Psychology*, **35**, 351–363.

Cassel, J. (1976). The contribution of the social environment to host resistance. *American Journal of Epidemiology*, **104**, 107–123.

Cobb, S. (1976). Social support as a moderator of life stress. *Psychosomatic Medicine*, **38**, 300–314.

Coelho, G. V., Hamburg, D. A. and Adams, J. E. (Eds.) (1974). *Coping and Adaptation*. New York: Basic Books.

Cohen, F. and Lazarus, R. S. (1973). Active coping processes, coping dispositions, and recovery from surgery. *Psychosomatic Medicine*, **35**, 375–389.

Cousins, N. (1976). Anatomy of an illness (as perceived by the patient). *New England Journal of Medicine*, **295**, 1458–1463.

Coyne, J. C. (1976). Toward an interactional description of depression. *Psychiatry*, **39**, 28–40.

Dember, W. N. (1974). Motivation and the cognitive revolution. *American Psychologist*, **29**, 161–168.

Dimsdale, J. E. (1974). The coping behavior of Nazi concentration camp survivors. *American Journal of Psychiatry*, **131**, 792–797.

Dollard, J. and Miller, N. E. (1950). *Personality and Psychotherapy*. New York: McGraw-Hill.

Dreyfus, H. L. (1972). *What Computers Can't Do: A Critique of Artificial Reason*. New York: Harper and Row.

Duffy, E. (1951). The concept of energy mobilization. *Psychological Review*, **58**, 30–40.

Easterbrook, J. A. (1959). The effect of emotion on cue utilization and the organization of behavior. *Psychological Review*, **66**, 183–201.

Ekman, P. (1965). Communication through non-verbal behavior: a source of information about an interpersonal relationship. In S. S. Tomkins and C. E. Izard (Eds.), *Affect, Cognition and Personality*. New York: Springer.

Ekman, P. and Friesen, W. (1975). *Unmasking the Face*. Englewood Cliffs, N.J.: Prentice-Hall.

Ellis, A. (1962). *Reason and Emotion in Psychotherapy*. New York: Lyle Stuart.

Engel, G. L. (1962). *Psychological Development in Health and Disease*. Philadelphia: W. B. Saunders.

Epstein, S. and Roupenian, A. (1970). Heart rate and skin conductance during experimentally induced anxiety: the effect of uncertainty about receiving a noxious stimulus. *Journal of Personality and Social Psychology*, **16**, 20–28.

Erdelyi, M. H. (1974). A new look at the new look: perceptual defence and vigilance. *Psychological Review*, **81**, 1–25

French, J. R. P., Jr., Rodgers, W. and Cobb, S. (1974). Adjustment and person-environment fit. In G. V. Coelho, D. A. Hamburg and J. E. Adams (Eds.), *Coping and Adaptation*. New York: Basic Books.

Frenkel-Brunswik, E. (1949). Intolerance of ambiguity as an emotional and perceptual personality variable. *Journal of Personality*, **18**, 108–143.

Freud, S. (1953). *The Interpretation of Dreams*. Vols. 4 and 5. Standard Edition. London: Hogarth Press. (Originally published, 1900.)

Freud, S. (1959). *Inhibitions, Symptoms, and Anxiety*. Vol. 20. Standard Edition. London: Hogarth Press. (Originally published, 1926.)

Friedman, S. B., Chodoff, P., Mason, J. W. and Hamburg, D. A. (1963). Behavioral observations on parents anticipating the death of a child. *Pediatrics*, **32**, 610–625.

Gaines, L. S., Smith, B. D. and Skolnick, B. E. (1977). Psychological differentiation, event uncertainty, and heart rate. *Journal of Human Stress*, **3**, 11–25.

Goldfried, M. R. and Goldfried, A. P. (1975). Cognitive change methods. In F. H. Kanfer and A. P. Goldstein (Eds.), *Helping People Change*. New York: Pergamon Press.

Goldschmidt, W. (1974). Ethology, ecology, and ethological realities. In G. V. Coelho, D. A. Hamburg and J. E. Adams (Eds.), *Coping and Adaptation*. New York: Basic Books.

Haan, N. (1969). A tripartite model of ego functioning, values and clinical research applications. *Journal of Nervous and Mental Disease*, **148**, 14–30.

Haan, N. (1977). *Coping and Defending*. New York: Academic Press.

Hackman, J. R. (1970). Tasks and task performance in research on stress. In J. E. McGrath (Ed.), *Social and Psychological Factors in Stress*. New York: Holt, Rinehart, and Winston.

Hamburg, D. A. and Adams, J. E. (1967). A perspective on coping: seeking and utilizing information in major transitions. *Archives of General Psychiatry*, **17**, 277–284.

Hamburg, D. A., Hamburg, B. and DeGoza, (1953). Adaptive problems and mechanisms in severely burned patients. *Psychiatry*, **16**, 1–20.

Hamilton, V. (1975). Socialization anxiety and information processing: a capacity model of anxiety-induced performance deficits. In I. G. Sarason and C. D. Spielberger (Eds.), *Stress and Anxiety* Vol. 2. Washington, D.C.: Hemisphere.

Hamilton, V. (1976). Motivation and personality in cognitive development. In V. Hamilton and M. D. Vernon (Eds.), *The Development of Cognitive Processes*. London: Academic Press.

Horowitz, M. (1976). *Stress Response Syndromes*. New York: Aronson.

Izard, C. E. and Tomkins, S. S. (1966). Affect and behavior: anxiety as a negative affect. In C. D. Spielberger (Ed.), *Anxiety and Behavior*. New York: Academic Press.

Janis, I. (1958). *Psychological Stress: Psychoanalytic and Behavioral Studies of Surgical Patients*. New York: Wiley.

Janis, I. (1974). Vigilance and decision making in personal crises. In D. A. Hamburg, C. V. Coelho and J. E. Adams (Eds.), *Coping and Adaptation*. New York: Basic Books.

Janis, I. and Mann, L. (1977). *Decision Making*. New York: The Free Press.

Kahn, R. L., Wolfe, D. M., Quinn, R. P. and Snoek, J. D. (1964). *Organizational Stress: Studies in Role Conflict and Ambiguity*. New York: Wiley.

Kahneman, D. (1973). *Attention and Effort*. Englewood Cliffs, N.J.: Prentice-Hall.

Kahneman, D. and Tversky, A. (1973). On the psychology of prediction. *Psychological Review*, **80**, 237–251.

Kaplan, B., Cassel, J. and Gore, S. (1977). Social support and health. *Medical Care*, **15**, No. 5 Supplement, 47–58.

Katz, D. and Kahn, R. L. (1966). *The Social Psychology of Organizations*. New York: Wiley.

Kemper, T. (In press). Toward a sociology of emotions: some problems and some solutions. *American Sociologist.*

Klinger, E. (1975). Consequences of commitment to and disengagement from incentives. *Psychological Review*, **82**, 1–25.

Korchin, S. J. (1964). Anxiety and cognition. In C. Scheere (Ed.), *Cognition: Theory, Research, Promise.* New York: Harper and Row.

Lazarus, R. S. (1966). *Psychological Stress and the Coping Process.* New York: McGraw-Hill.

Lazarus, R. S. (1975). The self-regulation of emotions. In L. Levi (Ed.), *Emotions — Their Parameters and Measurement.* New York: Raven Press.

Lazarus, R. S., Averill, J. R. and Opton, E. M., Jr. (1970). Toward a cognitive theory of emotion. In M. Arnold (Ed.), *Feelings and Emotions.* New York: Academic Press.

Lazarus, R. S., Cohen, J. B., Folkman, S., Kanner, A. and Schaefer, C. (In press). Psychological stress and adaptation: some unresolved issues. In H. Selye (Ed.), *Guide to Stress Research.* New York: Van Nostrand–Reinhold.

Lazarus, R. S. and Eriksen, C. W. (1952). Effects of failure stress upon skilled performance. *Journal of Experimental Psychology*, **43**, 100–105.

Lazarus, R. S. and Launier, R. (In press). Stress-related transactions between person and environment. In L. A. Pervin and M. Lewis (Eds.), *Perspectives in Interactional Psychology.* New York: Plenum.

Leeper, R. W. (1948). A motivational theory of emotion to replace 'emotion as a disorganized response'. *Psychological Review*, **55**, 5–21.

Lefcourt, H. M. (1976). *Locus of Control, Current Trends in Theory and Research.* Hillsdale, N.J.: Lawrence Erlbaum.

Levinger, G. (1966) Sources of marital dissatisfaction among applicants for divorce. *American Journal of Orthopsychiatry*, **36**, 803–807.

Lindsley, D. B. (1951). Emotion. In S. S. Stevens (Ed.), *Handbook of Experimental Psychology.* New York: Wiley.

Lipowski, Z. J. (1970). Physical illness, the individual and the coping process. *Psychiatry in Medicine*, **1**, 91–102.

Loevinger, J. (1976). *Ego Development.* San Francisco: Jossey-Bass.

Lundberg, U. and Frankenhaeuser, M. (1978). Psychophysiological reactions to noise as modified by personal control over noise intensity. *Biological Psychology*, **6**, 51–59.

Mahl. G. (1949). Anxiety, HCl secretion, and peptic ulcer etiology. *Psychosomatic Medicine*, **11**, 30–44.

Mahoney, N. J. (1977). Cognitive therapy and research: a question of questions. *Cognitive Therapy and Research*, **1**, 5–17.

Malmo, R. B. (1959). Activation: a neuropsychological dimension. *Psychological Review*, **66**, 367–386.

Mandler, G. (1975). *Mind and Emotion.* New York: Wiley.

Mandler, G. and Watson, D. (1966). Anxiety and the interruption of behavior. In C. D. Spielberger (Ed.), *Anxiety and Behavior.* New York: Academic Press.

Mechanic, D. (1962). *Students Under Stress.* Glencoe, Ill.: Free Press.

Mechanic, D. (1974). Discussion of research programs on relations between stressful life events and episodes of physical illness. In B. H. Dohrenwend and B. P. Dohrenwend (Eds.), *Stressful Life Events: Their Nature and Effects.* New York: Wiley.

Meichenbaum, D. (1977). *Cognitive-Behavior Modification.* New York: Plenum.

Menninger, K. (1954). Regulatory devices of the ego under major stress. *International Journal of Psychoanalysis*, **35**, 412–420.

Miller, G. A., Galanter, E. H. and Pribram, K. (1960). *Plans and the Structure of Behavior*. New York: Holt.

Monat, A., Averill, J. R. and Lazarus, R. S. (1972). Anticipatory stress and coping reactions under various conditions of uncertainty. *Journal of Personality and Social Psychology*, **24**, 237–253.

Neisser, U. (1967). *Cognitive Psychology*. New York: Appleton–Century–Crofts.

Nuckolls, K. B., Cassel, J. and Kaplan, B. H. (1972). Psychosocial assets, life crisis, and the prognosis of pregnancy. *American Journal of Epidemiology*, **95**, 431–441.

Osgood, C. E. (1952). The nature and measurement of meaning. *Psychological Bulletin*, **49**, 197–237.

Parsons, T. and Bales, R. F. (1955). *Family, Socialization, and Interaction Processes*. Glencoe, Ill.: Free Press.

Pearlin, L. I. (1975). Sex roles and depression. In N. Datan and L. H. Ginsberg (Eds.), *Life-Span Developmental Psychology: Normative Life Crises*. New York: Academic Press.

Peterfreund, E. (1971). Information systems and psychoanalysis: an evolutionary biological approach to psychoanalytic theory. *Psychological Issues*, **7**, Monograph No. 25/26.

Phillips, L. (1953). Case history data and prognosis in schizophrenia. *Journal of Nervous and Mental Disorders*, **117**, 515–525.

Polanyi, M. (1958). *Personal Knowledge*. Chicago: University of Chicago Press.

Rogers, J. (1977). *You Can Stop: A Smokender Approach to Quitting Smoking and Sticking to it*. New York: Simon and Schuster.

Rokeach, M. (Ed.) (1960). *The Open and the Closed Mind*. New York: Basic Books.

Rotter, J. B. (1966). Generalized expectancies for internal versus external control of reinforcement. *Psychological Monographs*, **80**, Whole No. 609.

Sarason, I. G. (1972). Experimental approaches to test anxiety: attention and the uses of information. In C. D. Spielberger (Ed.), *Anxiety: Current Trends in Theory and Research*. Vol. II. New York: Academic Press.

Schafer, R. (1954). *Psychoanalytic Interpretation in Rorschach Testing*. New York: Grune and Stratton.

Schank, R. and Abelson, R. (1977). *Scripts, Plans, Goals and Understanding*. New York: Wiley.

Schmale, A. and Iker, H. P. (1966). The effect of hopelessness and the development of cancer. *Psychosomatic Medicine*, **28**, 714–721.

Schwartz, S. (1970). Moral decision making and behavior. In J. Macauley and L. Berkowitz (Eds.), *Altruism and Helping Behavior*. New York: Academic Press.

Seligman, M. E. (1975). *Helplessness*. San Francisco: Freeman.

Shalit, B. (1977). Structural ambiguity and limits to coping. *Journal of Human Stress*, **3**, 32–45.

Shapiro, D. (1965). *Neurotic Styles*. New York: Basic Books.

Simon, H. A. (1967). Motivational and emotional controls of cognition. *Psychological Review*, **74**, 29–39.

Spence, J. A. and Spence, K. W. (1966). The motivational components of manifest anxiety: drive and drive stimuli. In C. D. Spielberger (Ed.), *Anxiety and Behavior*. New York: Academic Press.

Stein, N. and Glenn, C. (In press). An analysis of story comprehension in elementary school children. In R. O. Freedle (Ed.), *Discourse Processing: Multidisciplinary Perspectives*. Hillsdale, N.J.: Ablex.

Syme, S. L. and Berkman, L. F. (1976). Social class, susceptibility and sickness. *American Journal of Epidemiology*, **104**, 1–8.

Tomkins, S. S. (1963). Simulation of personality: the interrelationships between affect, memory, thinking, perception and action. In S. S. Tomkins and S. Messick (Eds.), *Computer Simulation of Personality*. New York: Wiley.

Tversky, A. and Kahneman, D. (1971). Belief in the law of small numbers. *Psychological Bulletin*, **76**, 105–110.

Tversky, A. and Kahneman, D. (1973). Availability: a heuristic for judging frequency and probability. *Cognitive Psychology*, **5**, 207–232.

Vaillant, G. (1977). *Adaptation to Life*. Boston: Little, Brown.

Visotsky, H. M., Gross, M. E. and Lebovits, B. Z. (1961). Coping behavior under extreme stress. *Archives of General Psychiatry*, **5**, 423–448.

Vogel, W., Raymond, S. and Lazarus, R. S. (1959). Intrinsic motivation and psychological stress. *Journal of Abnormal and Social Psychology*, **58**, 225–233.

Weisman, A. D. and Worden, J. W. (1975). Psychosocial analysis of cancer deaths. *Omega: Journal of Death and Dying*, **6**, 61–75.

Yates, M. (1976). *Coping: A Survival Manual for Women Alone*. Englewood Cliffs, N.J.: Prentice-Hall.

Young, P. T. (1959). The role of affective processes in learning and motivation. *Psychological Review*, **66**, 104–125.

*Cognition and Stress in
the Working Environment*

Chapter 10

Stress and Cognition in Organizations*

ROY L. PAYNE

1. Introduction
2. A Scheme for Organizing Signs/Symptoms of Psychological Strain
3. Kuhn's Detector, Selector, Effector Model
   (i)   Cross-system Motives
   (ii) Frustration of Cross-system Motives in the DETECTOR
   (iii) Frustration of Cross-system Motives in the SELECTOR
   (iv) Frustration of Cross-system Motives in the EFFECTOR
4. Typology of Organizations
   (i)   Temple structures
   (ii) Web Structures
   (iii) Net of Matrix Structures
   (iv) Cluster Structures
   (v)   Organizational Activities: Maintenance, Breakdown, and Development
   (vi) Rules, Expectations, and Codes
   (vii) Rules, Expectations, Codes, and Organizations
5. Rules, Expectations, Codes, and Kuhn
   (i)   Rules
   (ii) Expectations
   (iii) Codes
6. Summary
7. References

1. INTRODUCTION

Social existence is organized existence: even the family can be viewed as an organization. Most of us then spend most of our time in one form of organiz-

*I would like to thank Bill Starbuck and Dan Gowler for their ideas, interest and encouragement: for me they were, and still are, an example of how organizational life supports and limits stress.

ation or another. This chapter offers some ideas about how we can describe organizations and discusses the relationships between organizational forms and human cognitive processes. Whilst it is fashionable to advertise the amount of stress that occurs in modern organizations, it is also true that one function of organizations is to absorb stress, so that individuals can obtain things together that would be denied them singly. The family and the State nurture and protect in addition to controlling and cajoling us. I shall ride the wave of fashion and concentrate, though not exclusively, on the stresses that arise as we try to make sense of the demands that different organizations make on us.

The organization of the chapter will follow the structure of its title. I shall classify psychological states into two broad classes; those which are stressful (pressure and deprivation) and those which are positively desirable (well-being). I shall then describe a model of human cognitive functioning which posits three interrelated processes given the names of DETECTOR, SELECTOR, and EFFECTOR. The model is taken from Alfred Kuhn's book, *The Logic of Social Systems* (1974). Four organizational forms are then delineated: their structural analogies are the Classical Greek Temple, the Web, the Cluster, and the Net. Each is compared as to the degree to which it is concerned with the three essential organizational activities of Maintenance, Breakdown, and Development. The thoughts on organization are elaborated by enquiring into the social control mechanisms used in organizations to encourage members to perform activities relevant to the achievement of organizational goals. The three control mechanisms described are Rules, Expectations, and Codes, and once again the four organizational forms are compared according to the degree to which they rely on each of these control processes. Finally, the three major concepts of stress, cognitive processes, and organizational settings are brought together by considering the positive and negative consequences (stress) of Rules, Expectations, and Codes for the DETECTOR, SELECTOR, and EFFECTOR functions respectively.

2. A SCHEME FOR ORGANIZING SIGNS/SYMPTOMS OF PSYCHOLOGICAL STRAIN

The definition of psychological stress is a difficult task. One problem is that the word stress is used to describe the cause *and* the outcome. I have chosen the word strain to refer to the psychological state which is caused by some form of 'pressure'. The proposed scheme does not really tackle the definitional problem but it does reveal a range of 'stressful' states.

The problem of understanding psychological strain seems to have three facets:

(a) SOURCE of stimulation (pressure, stress) which is either INTRINSIC to the person or EXTRINSIC.

Source of Stimulation	INTRINSIC						EXTRINSIC					
Level of Stimulation	UNDER			OPTIMUM			OVER			UNDER		
	UNDER			OPTIMUM			OVER					

Duration of Stimulation and following rows:

Duration of Stimulation	L	M	S	S	M	L	S	M	L	L	M	S	S	M	L	S	M	L
Weighting of deviation from optimum	4	3	2	1	0	1	2	3	4	4	3	2	1	0	1	2	3	4
Code letter	A	B	C	D	E	F	G	H	I	J	K	L	M	N	O	P	Q	R

Descriptors by code letter:
- A — Depression (endemic)
- B — Loss of will, self-esteem
- C — Apathy or paralysis
- D — Trying something new and risky
- E — Self directed growth
- F — Self directed and sustained growth
- G — Testing one's limits
- H — Conflicts of values, guilt, "Type A" Behaviour
- I — Obsession, compulsion
- J — Institutionalization, Dependence
- K — Alienation
- L — Apathy, boredom
- M — Inspiration, Challenge
- N — Challenge, encouragement, involving
- O — Commitment
- P — Threat, confusion
- Q — Overload, loss of esteem
- R — Failure, occupational exhaustion

FIGURE 10.1 A Pseudo-facet Analysis of Psychological Strain. S = short, M = medium, L = long

(b) LEVEL of stimulation or arousal (under-, optimum, or over-stimulated).

(c) DURATION of stimulation (short, medium, or long term).

It is possible to distinguish between how long a condition has lasted and how long it is likely to last, and both are important, but for the sake of simplicity they are not distinguished here.

Figure 10.1 presents these three facets in combination to produce 18 broad outcome states. At any moment a person will be experiencing stimulation from intrinsic and extrinsic sources, so in theory every pair of intrinsic and extrinsic states can coexist to produce a different state than either considered alone. This produces 81 possible states.

Let us try and simplify this by assuming that an optimum state of intrinsic and extrinsic stimulation occurs when the duration of stimulation is medium term and of an optimum level. I suggest this rather than long-term optimum, partly because it allows greater symmetry in the 'model', but also because there is some physiological evidence (Kagan and Levi, 1974) that even pleasant states cause wear and tear on the body so that long-term conditions of optimum stimulation might begin to be 'stressful'. Accepting this optimum state we can now ask how far other states depart from it.

Following the facet analysis principle of contiguity (Foa, 1965), long-term/over-stimulation and long-term/under-stimulation are farthest from the optimum; short-term/optimum and long-term/optimum are closest to it. For illustrative purposes these can be given numerical weightings with the optimum given zero and the categories ranked from 1 to 4 as they move away from the optimum (Figure 10). Each *pair* of intrinsic and extrinsic states can now be given a weighting. For example, intrinsic/optimum/medium-term (outcome state E) and extrinsic/optimum/medium-term (outcome state N) have a weighting of zero, so the sum for the pair is zero.

It is also necessary to take into account whether the pairs of intrinsic and extrinsic states are compatible in terms of level of stimulation (e.g. over–over, under–under, under–over, etc.). The principle used here is in terms of how the combination of levels of stimulation affects the overall level of pressure. Thus over–over is seen as increasing pressure and was crudely weighted 3, as was under–under although under–under is seen as decreasing pressure, but increasing deprivation (Figure 10.1). Optimum–optimum is seen as staying at optimum and weighted 1, whilst all other 6 possible combinations were weighted as 2, whether they increased pressure or deprivation. The sum of the weights for each pair of intrinsic/extrinsic states was multiplied by the weights from the compatibility rankings. Thus the pair E and N have a sum of zero multiplied by 1 because they are both optimum levels of duration. The Pair I and R has a sum of $(4 + 4) \times 3$ because it is in the over–over category. These weightings can be calculated for the 81 possible pairs and they may then be simplified into 7 broad clusters as shown in Figure 10.2. The clusters indicate the nature and degree of strain with the intrinsic state always quoted first.

The descriptions of the outcome states in Figure 10.1 are incomplete and are not meant to suggest these are the only outcome states that could occur in any one category. They are merely illustrative and intended to convey the very great differences in types of states which fall under the general heading

DEPRIVATION ◄——————————————— ————————————————► PRESSURE

OPTIMUM–OPTIMUM (Well-being, positive mental health)

(boredom)	OPTIMUM–UNDER*	*OPTIMUM–OVER (harrassed)
(fear of failure)	UNDER–OPTIMUM	OVER–OPTIMUM (anxiety, guilt)

(alienation)   UNDER–OVER   OVER–UNDER ("A-type" behaviour, frustration)

(depression,   UNDER–UNDER   OVER–OVER (combat or occupational institutionalization)   exhaustion)

under the weighting system these two broad clusters get the same average score, though they would obviously indicate very different conditions.

FIGURE 10.2 An ordering of pairs of intrinsic and extrinsic stimulation into clusters

of stress. The deprivation states seem an important part of the problem of stress in work organizations. Caplan *et al.* (1975) compared a variety of indicators across 23 different occupations where the most routine, least demanding jobs showed the worst rates of psychological and somatic complaints. They were the same cases, with low support from home and low participation in decisions that affected their work. The latter might indicate low support from supervisors, too, and this appears to play an important role in alleviating stress (McMichael, 1978). Whilst we might wish to retain 'stress' as an umbrella term for a field of interest, it would seem beneficial to talk of at least three general states rather than just stress: they would be, 'pressure', 'well-being', and 'deprivation' as in Figure 10.2. The same notions could be applied to different domains of the life space (work, family, friends, hobbies or pursuits, etc.) so that an overall indication of well-being, deprivation, or pressure could be obtained. If pressure in all domains proved to be due to intrinsic sources rather than extrinsic sources, then different strategies of intervention would be suggested. Imbalance in the work domain might be compensated for in the family domain and so on. For the remainder of this chapter I shall refer to the three broad outcome states of pressure, well-being, and deprivation.

3. KUHN'S DETECTOR, SELECTOR, EFFECTOR MODEL

Kuhn (1974) has attempted to unify the sub-disciplines of the social sciences with a model of man which is essentially an information processing model. He views man as a *system* in an *environment* to which the system reacts with *adaptive behaviour*. Kuhn proposes that there are three parts to this adaptive process and that they can be named the DETECTOR which receives information about the environment, the SELECTOR which reflects the system's inner tendency to respond in one way rather than another, and the EFFECTOR which executes the behaviour selected. Lack of action can also be a response. The SELECTOR function, 'may be said to contain or reflect the system's tendency, inner logic, goal or goal structure, values or value structure, wants, desires, valences, affective tendencies, needs, strivings and so forth' (Kuhn, 1974, p. 43). Whilst these cover a wide range of concepts in psychology, Kuhn argues that their overall logic is the same – they are about choices – to approach, to avoid, to do nothing. FEEDBACK is built into the system so that after the EFFECTOR has carried out a decision made by the SELECTOR, the DETECTOR may identify changes in the environment arising from the action, and these will be fed into the SELECTOR and ultimately on to the EFFECTOR. It is in this way that learning occurs.

This is called the *main system* and it appears diagramatically in Figure 10.3. The system is elaborated by including DSE *subsystems*. The DETECTOR, SELECTOR, and EFFECTOR functions in the main systems are described as having their own subdetector, subselector, and subeffector systems. The focus of attention for the subsystems is the state of the component function of the main system. The subdetector of the DETECTOR function acquires information about the state of information in the main DETECTOR system. The main DETECTOR will have direct perceptions or images of the real world and the subdetector extracts these. The subselector of the DETEC-TOR identifies the needs or goals for information present in the main DETECTOR system. The subeffector then, obtains, processes, sorts and discards information in the light of the positive and negative values determined by the subselector. This process would account for perceptual distortion, perceptual defence, etc.

The SELECTOR function of the main system is described by the same three components. The subdetector has the task of discriminating the main motives and goals of the SELECTOR system. The subselector registers and chooses the pathways which would most effectively satisfy those motives (e.g. ones which avoid conflict with basic values), and the subeffector then activates and executes plans which allow the pathways to be pursued (e.g. by repressing information which suggests a conflict will occur).

The subdetector of the EFFECTOR in the main system identifies the main EFFECTOR'S skills and capabilities. The subselector refers to its image of the goals and aspirations which the EFFECTOR has for itself in terms of developing new skills and capacities (e.g. of motivating subordinates), and the subeffector then acts to achieve those skill and competence goals (e.g. by

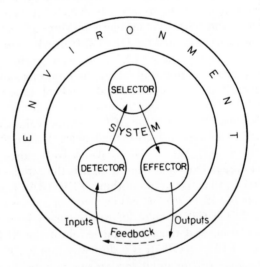

FIGURE 10.3 Behavioural system in an environment (main system only). (Reprinted with permission of Jossey-Bass, San Francisco from Kuhn (1974))

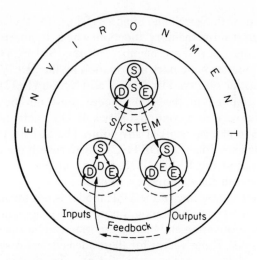

FIGURE 10.4. Behavioural system in an environment (including DSE Subsystems). (Reprinted with permission of Jossey-Bass, San Francisco from Kuhn (1974))

planning to apply for a training course). Figure 10.4 portrays both main and subsystems. Note that the subsystems also have feedback loops and are capable of change or adaptation. It would be misleading to suggest that the three functions are purposive systems. They are not, of course, but it is a convenient way of trying to model what goes on when a human being is engaged in adaptive behaviour.

Kuhn (p. 68) makes the point that all behaviour is an attempt to satisfy inner states, and that behaviour is only determined by the environment in the sense that the environment may affect and alter those inner states. These inner states are represented by concepts and images, and through past experience a stimulus in the environment is more likely to initiate one conceptual pattern rather than another. As Kuhn suggests, in most social behaviour the meaning and consequences of a present stimulus are more a function of past experiences with similar stimuli than they are a function of the stimulus itself.

Newell and Simon (1972) describe the human information processor as having the following characteristics: serial processing (information is processed one bit at a time), short-term memory, infinite long-term memory with fast retrieval but slow storage. This description seems to match well with Kuhn's system. He makes the distinction between sensation and perception and defines the former as involving cognitively-uncoded information and the latter as using coded information. The subdetector of the DETECTOR may register sensation but the subselector quickly acts to interpret that sensation and code it to turn it into a perception. The subsystems themselves act serially which is consistent with Newell and Simon's claims, and their operation fits in well with the short-term memory function which is interpreted by coded information in the short-term memory at the SELECTOR stage. The retrieval of this long-term memory information by the SELECTOR system is of course very fast as observed by Newell and Simon (1972).

The seriality implied in the DSE model must not be taken too far. Behaviour can be seen as a continual series of DSE activities but the cycle around the DSE model can start at any point. The SELECTOR may have a goal or urge which sensitizes the DETECTOR to search the environment for particular things, and the EFFECTOR is then involved in the locomotion necessary to carry out the exploratory activities.

Up to this point the outline of the DSE model is not inconsistent with the influential ideas of Newell and Simon. I now wish to supplement this description to show how motivation and human emotion can be encompassed within the DSE framework. Kuhn's term for these ideas is 'cross-system motives'.

(i) Cross-system Motives

Kuhn has identified four properties which 'cut across' and apply to each of the DSE subsystems. Again he uses purposive imagery by referring to them as motives, but again I emphasize how he is using a human metaphor to illustrate his model. The DSE system does not literally have motives, but the concept is one way of describing their apparent functions: Kuhn does believe that the nature of the DSE system is determined by the neurological system. The four motives are priorities, exercise, efficiency, and frustration.

Priorities: the DSE model assumes an adaptive system and implies that some things are more important to survival than others. Since pain is often associated with events that may threaten survival, unpleasant sensations and perceptions take priority over pleasant ones. At the DETECTOR function we attend to movement which is potentially a sign of threat, and we attend to loud noises because they too are likely to come from large, dangerous objects. There are then inborn priority mechanisms in the DETECTOR, but through learning the DETECTOR may acquire different priorities, such as being alerted by an unnatural silence. Kuhn introduces emotion into his description of the priority setting process and shows how emotions act as priority controls.

He assumes that the SELECTOR acts on the basis that avoidance will take priority over approach since flight from danger is more likely to lead to survival.The role of emotion is to amplify the valence whether negative or positive. Thus fear can mobilize the energy to flee, or if it is too late to flee, then fear produces paralysis and this at least reduces the possibility of being noticed by the predator. This is because movement is dominant for the DETECTOR system and survival for the SELECTOR system. Another way of surviving is counter-attack, but this is more likely to succeed if the probable pain it involves is ignored. The most appropriate emotion here then is anger. Anger can produce a blind rage which prevents people from being aware of serious physical damage they have suffered.

The well-used trilogy of coping responses – flight, fight, and approach – is completed, emotionally speaking, by adding the emotion of love to the list which is the ultimate experience of an approach response. Emotional experiences such as pleasure, joy, worry, annoyance are varieties of these basic emotional responses.

Kuhn says that the EFFECTOR system has no real priorities that cannot be accounted for by another cross-system motive – efficiency.

Efficiency is regarded as having system survival benefits and natural selection works to preserve more efficient modes of functioning. Given the limited short-term memory of the human, tackling things in series is an efficient way of solving problems, particularly when the solutions can be easily and quickly retrieved once they are in the long-term store. This same hierarchical pattern is in evidence at the EFFECTOR function where complex skills are acquired by the eventual integration of overlearned subpatterns: typewriting and piano playing are examples. Concepts about concepts are examples of the same efficiency in intellectual skills.

Examples of efficiency at the DETECTOR stage are similar to the priority motive in that moving objects are likely to contain much information so the DETECTOR scans for these and other large or unexpected patterns. The efficiency of the SELECTOR is found in its tendency to choose goals which it is likely to be able to achieve, and which at the same time bring some positive valence. The literature on Need for Achievement stresses the selection of moderately difficult goals, and such choices can be regarded as having above average survival potential (McClelland *et al.*, 1953).

Exercise, the third cross-system motive, simply means regular use. Exercise is necessary if loss of information (forgetting) is not to occur leading to deterioration in the efficiency and effectiveness of the function: practice not only makes perfect, it makes possible. Exercise not only develops and sustains existing patterns of thinking or behaviour, but by taking the person into new spaces facilitates the formation of new patterns. We know from experiments on sensory deprivation that exploration, and thus exercise, will soon occur if a person is exposed to an unchanging environment for any length of time. The exploration exercises the DETECTOR system.

At the SELECTOR stage the learning of new motives, emotions, and goals has positive valence. Human functions are dynamically homeostatic in that any level of experience can become unstable due to adaptation, therefore, the exercise of selecting new goals and challenges keeps the SELECTOR system alert and this has survival value. The positive valence we achieve from the satisfaction of motives in the past also means that it is pleasant to exercise such motives for their own sake. Too little exercise of the choosing faculty can engender boredom (deprivation), too much of which can result in frustration and strain (pressure).

The EFFECTOR is mainly a skill system, and personal experience is adequate testimony to the enjoyment experienced from exercising established skills and from developing new ones. Both are intrinsically satisfying. Kuhn goes so far as to suggest that self-actualization, curiosity, and self-expression as motives can all be derived from the underlying motive to exercise the DSE system.

Frustration is Kuhn's fourth cross-system motive, and at first sight hardly seems a motive in the same sense that efficiency and exercise are. What Kuhn means is that the system is searching to understand the environment so as to ensure its survival, and it does that by comparing the pattern in the environment with patterns held in the DSE system. Often there is a mismatch between the external pattern and the DSE pattern. Kuhn calls the mismatch *dissonance*. In order to explain this as a motive it might be better to say the system has a motive for *consonance*, but when dissonance occurs the system is motivated to reduce it, in order to achieve consonance.

Dissonance occurs in the DETECTOR when there is a mismatch between the incoming pattern and the pattern (concepts) in the mind. Cognitive dissonance (Festinger, 1957) is reduced by ignoring the discrepancy between the two patterns and fitting the incoming pattern into an already existing one. If the dissonance is not reduced then frustration occurs. If the dissonance is great then the concepts in the main system may have to be changed or new ones developed. Given the efficiency criterion, however, the system has a tendency not to add new concepts or to make radical changes to the old ones. Schroder *et al*. (1967) have suggested that successful problem solving leads to the elaboration of concepts, but there comes a point when the analytical system is too complex and the model becomes too difficult to use given the serial processing and poor short-term memory capacities. Parsimony seems an adaptive as well as a scientific requirement. Failure is held to lead to the simplification of concepts or models and Kuhn points out that when the present conceptual patterns prove inadequate to deal with incoming information, the resulting frustration more quickly leads to vigorous random behaviour, which is adaptively useful in that it might generate a new pattern.

The cross-system motive of frustration (though I prefer to call it the consonance motive) thus helps to explain frustration itself, and frustration is often equated with human stress when stress is defined as a condition where desires remain unfulfilled. It explains coping with stress by dissonance reduction through denying mismatches, and it also explains the 'irrational', 'thrashing about' behaviour that sometimes accompanies frustration. The consonance motive also illustrates the coping failure due to having too complex a pattern – one can't see the wood for the trees.

Kuhn uses the notion of mismatch to explain conflict in the SELECTOR. If the SELECTOR must choose between two positively valued things, or two negatively valued things, then choosing one leads to dissonance since the other must either be lost when it is wanted, or received when it is not wanted. The dissonance creates frustration.

Mismatch at the EFFECTOR occurs when the action pattern selected is blocked by a physical object or skill limitation. It is the mismatch between what was supposed to happen and what actually happened. The common expressions, 'I'll do this if it kills me', and 'I'll finish this before I go' are expressions which illustrate the dissonance resulting from uncompleted patterns in the EFFECTOR.

The final concept that the motive of consonance can throw light upon is the concept of *overload*. Overload is regarded by Kuhn as mismatch between the processing capacity of the person and the amount of information coming to him; or between the amount of work the person is expected to do and the amount he can actually do. This seems another way of saying anxiety can result from the fact that humans are a limited capacity system (Hamilton 1975) and overload of the system produces feelings of threat.

The utility of Kuhn's concepts for exposing the nature of psychological strain in organizations is illustrated in Table 10.1. It summarizes the focus of each cross-system motive for the DSE system and identifies the main sorts of strain to which DETECTOR, SELECTOR, and EFFECTOR are susceptible.

It may help readers unfamiliar with the literature on stress and organizations to have an overview of what organizational stresses are so as to be able to evaluate those encompassed by the cross-system motives. This is most effectively achieved by reference to Figure 10.5 which is taken from Cooper and Marshall (1978). This shows that stresses occur from outside the boundary of the organization (from the family, etc.) as well as from within it. Of those that occur within it, some might be considered more basic than others. The structure of the organization and the climate of values and norms that top management try to create are also determinants of the relationships that occur between bosses and subordinates and among colleagues (Payne and Pugh, 1976), and the intrinsic nature of the work people do (Bonjean and Grimes, 1970). The degree to which roles are specified and defined are largely determined by aspects of the structural arrangements in an organization (Pugh et al., 1968) and this and the climate of trust (Steele, 1975) determines the quantity and quality of role conflict in organizations. Similarly, career decisions are usually taken by managers or specialist advisors so that the stresses arising from career development are also largely produced by those people responsible for the design of the organization. The choices such managers make, however, are constrained by such factors as organizational size, technology, and the scope of the organization's task (Dewar and Hage, 1978). It would be unfair to lay the blame for

TABLE 10.1
Cross-System Motives and their Potential Strains

	Priorities		Exercise		Efficiency		Consonance	
	potential strains	focus	potential strains	focus	potential strains	focus	potential strains	focus
DETECTOR	Unusual/dangerous stimuli	Too much or too little information: overload/underload	Exercise of existing skills and talent; Development of new skills and talents	Boredom through overuse; Boredom through underuse; Exhaustion through over use	Recognizing salient information quickly and accurately	Overload of information; Insufficient information; Conflicting information; No good 'models' to copy	To achieve consonance between incoming information and stored patterns	Ambiguity. Internal patterns under-elaborated: anxiety: Over-elaborated: confusion
SELECTOR	Avoid danger; Approach pleasant situations	Conflicts of preferences; Uncertainty (standards/appreciations not developed)	Satisfaction of familiar goals; Satisfaction of developing goals	Restriction of choice can lead to (a) deprivation and deterioration (b) retreat to exercise in phantasy	Setting goals that are (a) valued and valuable (b) realistically achievable	Goals set are: too easy, too difficult; Lack of feedback to judge efficiency	Solving cost/benefits; problems of approach–approach, avoidance–avoidance conflicts to maximize benefits	Anxiety and frustration about choices made; Lack of feedback about choices *not* taken
EFFECTOR	To act efficiently; The law of 'least effort'	Frustration of not acting efficiently; Self-depreciation; Bodily tension	Practice of familiar skills; Development of new skills	Too little (Deprivation); Too much (Pressure)	Integration of skills and conceptual patterns; Law of 'least effort'	Overload; Underload; Bad organization; Inadequate resources	To act in accordance with standards set by oneself	Tension and emotional blocks (ref. bioenergetics); Inadequate resources/ opportunities leading to frustration

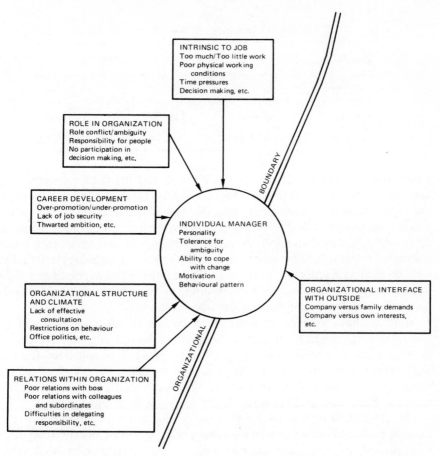

FIGURE 10.5. Sources of managerial stress. (Reprinted from Cooper and Marshall (1978))

organizational stress totally at the feet of managers since they are constrained by the intrinsic nature of social organizations themselves.

It must also be recognized that the stresses that organizations create do not cause damage to most of the people that work in them. This is conveyed in Figure 10.5 by the list of individual factors in the circle. A solid argument can be made that stress is largely in the eye of the beholder (McMichael, 1978), but the more orthodox position is to see it as a consequence of the goodness of fit between the organizational environment and the person's needs, skills, and abilities (Van Harrison, 1978).

(ii) Frustration of Cross-system Motives in the DETECTOR

Reference to Table 10.1 indicates that the DETECTOR gives priority to certain types of information: information loaded with meaning. Meaning

TABLE 10.2
Psychological Outcomes of Six Information States

Familiarity of information	Amount of information		
	too little	enough	too much
Novel	Interest	Pleasure	Overload
Familiar	Frustration	Satisfaction	Annoyance

arises from (a) the novelty of the information and (b) the inpactfulness or amount. Table 10.2 assumes that there can be too little, or too much or about the right amount of information, and that the stimulus can be novel or familiar. The cells are filled with examples of psychological outcomes. Three of these might be called stressful, though the category of annoyance (too much information about familiar things) is unlikely to lead to pathology unless that state of affairs endures for many years. The conditions of overload and frustration can lead to immediate stress resulting eventually in emotional pathology, with long-term influences on organic functioning.

Whilst we have limited our attention to *amount* of information, the more general concept might be amount of *impact* as achieved in good advertising. In organizations information has a greater impact if it emenates from a high-status person. As Captain Queeg says in the film of *The Caine Mutiny*, 'There are four ways of doing things in the Navy: the right way, the wrong way, the Navy way, and my way. On my ship you do things my way!'

The DETECTOR'S need for exercise is frustrated in conditions where existing patterns become so well used that even the routine of exercising them loses positive valence. Frustration also occurs when opportunities to develop new patterns are limited or non-existent. Sensory and perceptual deprivation, whether induced in the laboratory, by imprisonment or poverty, has been shown to be psychologically damaging and in that sense stressful (Bexton *et al.*, 1954).

Whilst such extreme conditions are not produced in work environments, some assembly line jobs have similar characteristics. The high noise and restrictions on movements that some assembly lines involve also prevent people from obtaining novel sensations and experiences through conversation and exploration.

The conditions which frustrate the DETECTOR'S motive for efficiency may also be present in mass production jobs but for different reasons. As Table 10.1 shows, frustration occurs when the DETECTOR cannot function efficiently due to lack of adequate stimuli. This can arise because the stimuli rarely vary so that efficiency becomes irrelevant, or where they vary but are poorly communicated. In mass production organizations the ratio of workers to supervisors increases (Woodward, 1965) and face-to-face communication decreases. The organizations are often large and rely on information posted on notice boards or circulated in house journals; these often go unread. Even though the worker *could* detect relevant changes in his situation, poor communication means that he has to make efforts to seek it for himself, and the efficiency motive, or law of least effort, may inhibit him from bothering. The increasing use of techniques such as job rotation, job enrichment, and worker participation which are designed to improve interest and communications, illustrates the concern over the widespread existence of these impoverished environments.

The consonance motive is frustrated by mismatches between the patterns held by the DETECTOR system and the patterns presented to it. Mismatch can arise because there is insufficient information to confirm or deny the expectations of the DETECTOR. Kahn *et al.* (1964) referred to this condition as role ambiguity. The group of people with whom the focal person interacts are failing to send him clear messages about what they want him to do. Several subsequent studies have shown that experience of ambiguity is associated with reported psychological strain (Caplan *et al.*, 1975). On the other hand the persons, work colleagues or bosses may be sending clear messages, which, however, are in conflict with each other and/or conflict with the pattern in the DETECTOR system. Again, the various types of role conflict have been shown to be associated with increasing strain (e.g. Lyons, 1971). Organizations contribute to the development of such mismatches by poor personnel selection, poor job definition, poor communication, poor training, poor induction, and by blocking peoples' promotion. The latter arises because the person's expectations have changed over time; he may now expect higher status, and the rewards attached to it, as rewards for his loyalty and increased experience.

(iii) Frustration of Cross-system Motives in the SELECTOR

As Table 10.1 shows the SELECTOR gives priority to events which have negative valence, or put the other way round it seeks to maintain positive states (the pleasure principle). The events or conditions which create positive feelings vary enormously for different people, but we have already seen how organizations can create a wide range of frustrating states. Some organizations also create situations where fear or anger occur. Correctional institutions use fear and this often leads to anger. Any hierarchical system can create mild fear for some people: some children are certainly afraid of the headmaster. The fear that adults experience in work organizations in the face of authority is probably generated by the memory of fears developed in childhood rather than by the reality of the situations that face them as adults. This is not to say that the emotion is not powerful. Mistrust is a mild version of fear and several writers on organizations make the development of trusting interpersonal relations central to their theory of how to manage organizations effectively (Argyris, 1962; Steele, 1975).

The exercise of the SELECTOR system occurs when choices have to be made about how to satisfy old, familiar goals as well as new, unfamiliar goals. Where organizations create ultrastable environments the satisfaction of unfamiliar goals is easily frustrated. Much of mass production industry, and much routine clerical work consists of tasks that have these properties. The same is true of many service industries such as nursing the old or mentally ill, issuing social security payments, working in shops and banks. Many of these jobs, however, have the saving grace of involving contact with people and the people themselves create diversity of experience which can lead to the development of new needs and goals. Stable environments lead to the regular use of established skills and this can provide a source of satisfaction in itself: Baldamus (1951) called it 'psychological traction'. On the whole, however, recent years have seen a growing emphasis on the lack of variety and responsibility that much of modern work entails (Hackman and Oldham, 1976; and the provocatively entitled 'Not for Bread Alone', King Taylor, 1972).

In terms of the model of stressful outcomes described in Figure 10.1, many jobs lead to deprivation states. Similar comments apply to the cross-system motive of efficiency. The 'focus' column in Table 10.1 indicates there is a tendency for the SELECTOR to value goals of moderate difficulty so that the person has a reasonable change of achieving them. Achievement of goals produces learning so that after several successes the task will be easier: level of aspiration will rise and only the achievement of slightly more difficult tasks will be satisfying. Since many jobs now set standard performance targets, or limit promotion because of lack of professional qualifications regardless of actual efficiency, there are many jobs in large orgainzations that frustrate the efficiency motive (March and Simon, 1958 describe in detail the dysfunctions of bureaucratic structures). Part of the explanation for some of the industrial 'games people play' (Berne, 1964, e.g. restriction of output – 'cops and robbers'; work to rule – 'Now I've got you you son of a bitch'; industrial sabotage – 'Let's you and him fight'), may lie in the frustration of the efficiency and the effector motives of the SELECTOR. Elliott Jaques (1976) has described a theory of bureaucracy which recognizes the psychological importance of satisfying these motives. He assumes that there are five broad levels of cognitive functioning and that organizations need to be designed so that the needs of people are satisfied with respect to each of these broad ranges of ability. His concept of the 'time-span of discretion' (Jaques, 1962) states that jobs have different lengths of time before performance in them can be evaluated, and that control systems and job rewards should be linked to the time-span. This is another way of recognizing individual differences in capacity. Organizational roles, particularly the number of levels in the hierarchy, and hence the structure of the organization, need to take these differences into account. Much organizational unrest, according to Jaques, is due to the mismatch of psychological needs/capacities and organizational designs which deny people the opportunity to satisfy them.

Frustration of the cross-system motive for consonance occurs for the SELECTOR when a choice has to be made between two situations both of which have positive valences. In more traditional terms it is an 'approach–approach' conflict (Schaffer and Shoben, 1954). 'Avoidance–avoidance' conflict produces dissonance because whatever course is selected a painful experience follows. All organizations produce situations of both types: 'Which of these two promotions would you like?' or 'Put in more effort or you are out of a job!' Whilst all organizations produce dissonance of both types it is very likely that organizations differ in the degree to which different types of dissonance occur.

(iv) Frustration of Cross-system Motives in the EFFECTOR

As Kuhn (1974) says himself, for social system analysis the EFFECTOR system is of less interest than the DETECTOR and the SELECTOR. Consequently it can be dealt with more briefly. The EFFECTOR is frustrated frequently for the same reasons as the SELECTOR since one of its prime goals is to satisfy the choices made by the SELECTOR. Generally, the EFFECTOR'S goal is to function as efficiently and effectively as possible. It is guided by the principle of the 'law of least effort' so that inefficient organizations frustrate its priorities and its motive for efficiency. Jobs which are undemanding in the sense that they do not tax the EFFECTOR also frustrate its need to be exercised. Dissonance arises when tasks are uncompleted and when the body is not exercised. This is why some people go out of their way to make work. This is on the face of it in contradiction of the efficiency motive and its law of least effort, but the contradiction is resolved by recognizing that at some point the needs of the exercise motive take priority over the needs of the efficiency motive. Fragmented tasks, arbitrary control from people higher in the hierarchy, professional boundary disputes, etc. are all aspects of modern organizations which can frustrate the EFFECTOR system of people at all levels of the organization.

I have oultined a general model of cognitive and action processes and examined some ways in which organizations can frustrate the DSE system. It is apparent that there are conceptual similarities between the facet analysis of psychological states and the frustration of the cross-system motives. The notion of consonance in Kuhn has a parallel with those situations which produce psychological well-being (optimum–optimum states in Figure 10.2).

The cross-system motive of priorities in particular is a source of internal stimulation. This is true of exercise and efficiency too, but frustration of these motives is more directly allied to the deprivation states described in the facet analysis. The DSE model describes some of the *mechanisms* which can lead to the outcome states of deprivation, well-being, and pressure. The comments on organizations have treated organizations as if they were homogenous entities, but it is evident that they vary enormously in all sorts of ways: size, purpose, structure, resources. To do justice to their complexity it is now necessary to describe the typology of organizational forms.

4. TYPOLOGY OF ORGANIZATIONS

There are a number of conceptual typologies of organizations (Etzioni, 1961; Blau and Scott, 1962; Kuhn, 1974), but they are all very general and would include all business organizations as single types; though not all would object to having mixtures of their own types, or to grafting other typologies on to their own. The most comprehensive empirically based typology is that of Pugh *et al.* (Pugh and Hickson, 1976; Pugh and Hinings, 1977). This has the advantage of sophisticated measurement, the inclusion of production and service organizations, applicability to a wide range of types of organizations, such as churches and trade unions as well as production and commercial concerns. Most of the measures are only applicable to organizations of around 200 or more people, however, and the typology excludes reference to the philosophy which lies behind the structure of the organization created. In order to include such philosophies and to include organizations from the very smallest to the very largest, I shall rely on a typology which is an amalgamation of ideas from Roger Harrison (1972) and Charles Handy (1976).

Harrison describes four dominating ideologies found in organizations, and Handy describes how they produce, in their ideal forms, four different structural types. The ideologies and the corresponding strucutral forms are:

Ideology	*Structure-stated as an analogy*
Role	Classical Greek Temple (bureaucracy)
Power	Web, with power at centre
Task	Net or matrix structure
Person	Cluster or group (small)

(i) Temple Structures

The role ideology is the counterpart of the ideal bureaucracy (Weber, 1947). The philosophy is that each person be selected to office on the basis of having the appropriate qualifications and experience to do the job as defined. The office holder will be given the necessary authority to carry out his responsibilities and will be clear about the limitations of both his responsibility and authority. Each person should then be an expert in his own role and if everyone is expert then the total system should be effective. This ideaology leads to detailed role specifications and a hierarchical structure which suggests a temple structure in that the columns of the temple are held together by the strength of the roof which brings them together. Large organizations are really a nested series of temples and the work of Pugh *et al.* (Pugh and Hickson, 1976) shows that this structure is strongly associated with organizational size and sophistication of the production system (multiple correlation 0.78). The temple structure is the most conspicuous, if not the most ubiquitous, organizational form to-day. As we describe the remaining types we shall see why large size tends very strongly to produce the temple structure.

(ii) Web Structures

The power ideology usually occurs when the organization is owned or ruled by a charismatic leader whose ideas and wishes dominate events in the system. He is at the center of the web and his minions spend their time doing what he says, and keeping in tune with what the 'governor' is likely to want. The web is a very powerful structure, but it depends very much on the strength of its centre and the willingness of the people who make up its strands to continue to give their support. As organizations grow it becomes more and more difficult for the person at the center to achieve the charismatic influence that this requires. There have been large systems based on the power ideology (Hitler), but the system was supported by a large bureaucracy. Since bureaucracy is also an authority-based system the two ideologies are not too much in conflict and can work well together.

(iii) Net or Matrix Structures

The matrix fits quite well into the bureaucratic or temple structure too. Indeed, one element of the matrix is the functional division of labour found in the horizontal specialization into different departments (production, accounting, marketing, etc.) common to bureaucracies. The other arm of the matrix consists of the specialist skills which are relevant to the particular task in hand. The matrix is based on a task ideology in the sense that a team is built around a task. In large organizations this is often a special project such as the commissioning of a new plant. A project team will be assembled of all the specialist personnel needed and a project manager will be appointed to direct the team. Where the total organization is run on matrix principles any particular person may be working on several projects simultaneously, and as well as having a project boss he will have a functional boss. All engineers will be part of the engineering function and the head of engineering has the job of training and developing his engineers, and of deploying them in the most effective way on the various project teams that are required. The aim is to optimize identification with one's specialist profession and commitment to the particular tasks (projects) to which one is allocated. This system of organization was developed to meet the complex tasks performed under the pressure of severe deadlines which the U.S. National Aeronautics and Space Administration was faced with in the 1960s and 1970s (Sayles and Chandler, 1971). It is an effective and exciting work situation, but one which requires flexibility on the part of everyone, and particularly on the part of the project manager.

(iv) Cluster Structures

The cluster structure can also occur in large organizations but its person-oriented ideology does not fit well with the authority system of the temple, web, and net. It can occur in groups at the top of the organization, and in specialist groups such as research and development groups. It is more common however in much smaller organizations such as professional groups who work together because each respects the need of the other person. The individual takes priority over the needs of the organization: the organization only exists to achieve the satisfaction and personal development of the individuals in it.

It is obvious that I am talking about abstract types and that most organizations have all four types within them, though smaller organizations are much more homogeneous and likely to approximate to the pure types. This is true except for the bureaucracy which only emerges in its ideal form with increasing numbers of personnel. Conceptualizing extremes, however, has the advantage of revealing their more potent consequences. I shall examine these by looking at the major activities carried out by organizations and seeing how the activities vary by organizational type.

(v) Organizational Activities: Maintenance, Breakdown, and Development

Morris and Burgoyne (1973) have posited that all organizations need to carry out three sets of activities which he calls maintenance, breakdown, and development. They are a simplification of Bakke's (1950) more comprehensive descriptions of organizational functioning, but they are adequate to increase the complexity of the organizational typology without making it too complex to use. Maintenance activities are those concerned with maintaining the organization in the steady state for which it is designed: producing goods in manufacturing, administering justice in legal organizations, selling goods in sales organizations. They are the routine activities of the organization which can be programmed because they are predictable. Maintenance activities take up much of any organization's time, including organizations which are working on research and development.

Even organizations which exist in very steady state conditions need to do development work, although it may only be the evolution of new and better routines for controlling the maintenance activities. Development activities are most obvious when concentrated in a specialist department such as a research and development department, but development activities take place in personnel, policy-making departments, organization and methods, and in well-managed organizations at any point in the hierarchy where an individual manager is allowed to use his initiative.

Initiative is the key function of the management of breakdown activities. All organizations have breakdowns at some time or other. They may be due to machinery, to industrial action, to the loss of a key executive, a change in the market place, or in legislation which affects the market or produce, or merely to failure in established routine procedures. Whilst any part of the organization may need to cope with breakdowns, the ultimate responsibility rests with senior management and particularly with departments such as marketing and production. If the image of the organization is involved then the public relations department plays an important role.

Whilst all organizations carry out all three activities, some kind of organizations spend relatively more of their energies on one activity rather than another. For example, by adopting planned maintenance a production department is trying to make a routine what has traditionally been a breakdown activity so that breakdown activities are kept to a minimum. On the other hand, organizations which specialize in research and innovation will often build norms about being unconventional into their culture. They do this to assist the production of ideas of *any* kind in the hope that this generates ideas specific to the actual tasks of the organization. Change for the sake of change might be an appropriate organizational motto. Figure 10.6 grafts the three activities onto the four types of organization structures/ideologies to suggest an elaboration of the types. The solid-lined profiles represent the patterns of activities for each of the four types of organizations in their steady state condition. A more accurate picture could be obtained by presenting profiles for each type under conditions of growth and decay. I have suggested a profile for a cluster structure in a growth period, and for a temple structure in decline. These two profiles appear as dotted lines.

As can be seen from Figure 10.6, the temple and the web have very similar profiles of activities under stable conditions. The reasons behind the profiles are different. Temple structures are built because they handle large-scale routine production and administrative problems. They are high on maintenance, low on development, and moderately low on breakdown. The web derives from a power ideology and much effort is put into maintenance

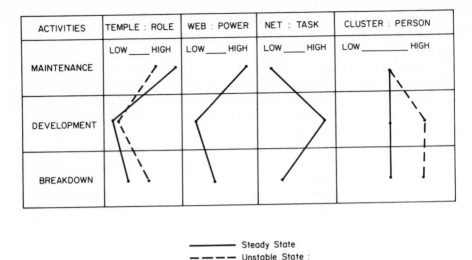

ACTIVITIES	TEMPLE : ROLE	WEB : POWER	NET : TASK	CLUSTER : PERSON
	LOW ___ HIGH	LOW ___ HIGH	LOW ___ HIGH	LOW ___ HIGH
MAINTENANCE				
DEVELOPMENT				
BREAKDOWN				

―――――― Steady State
― ― ― ― Unstable State :
Temple - Decline
Cluster - Growth

FIGURE 10.6. Patterns of activity in four types of organization

activities because the power structure must be preserved, and keeping people in line is a good way of preserving it. Power is also shown, however, by the ability to change things, so development activities are higher than in the temple structure because the charismatic leader is inclined to wish to satisfy his whims for personal excitement as well as to illustrate his power.

Matrix, or net, structures developed in the aerospace industry to meet the demands imposed by complex problems and tight deadlines. Such tasks cannot be made routine, so maintenance activities are at a low level. Problem solving, innovation, and implementation are paramount, so development activities are high, but these bring breakdowns in technical, human, and administrative systems, so breakdown activities are higher than in the temple or web structures.

Breakdown activities are also common in the clusters or small groups of the person-centered organization because the focus on the needs of the individual brings their needs into conflict with the group's needs; this means the breakdowns occur relatively more in the interpersonal system, Breakdowns also occur in the task/technical system since personal development is more important than task performance, and if tasks are not directly relevant to personal growth they may be performed less well than is desirable. But since personal development is important much development occurs as the job and organization is changed to meet the developing needs of the individuals. Maintenance activities are at a moderate level since the organization has to survive, and sensible routines free people for more interesting activities. As the dotted line in Figure 10.6 indicates, there is much more concern with development, and the breakdowns it brings with it, when the group is growing and taking shape as a cluster structure.

Breakdown activities tend to rise in temple structures when they are in decline, but there is rarely an increase in development activities although it would appear that this is really what is required to combat the decline itself. Even in decline, concern with the routines of maintenance activities remains high.

My purpose in describing a typology of organizations is to ask, how do these different types affect man, and particularly, how do they affect him from an information processing point of view? I can also ask, how are men persuaded to engage in these maintenance, breakdown, and development activities? What mechanisms are involved, and what are their implications for an information processing model of man at work? The mechanisms I suggest are rules, expectations, and codes.

(vi) Rules, Expectations, and Codes

Gowler (1977) has suggested three concepts which appear to identify mechanisms which both facilitate and control human interaction. The concepts are rules, expectations, and codes. Rules cover a wide range of phenomena since they range from legally defined rules, to quasi-legal rules such as exist in games. John Morris (1972) suggests three aspects of persons, two of which are very similar to Gowler's concepts. The three aspects of being a person are routines, rituals, and dramas. As Morris neatly puts it '. . . man lives by drama, remembers by ritual and survives by routine,' (p. 90). The similarity of the concepts of routine and rules is obvious and routine is perhaps the more general and useful word. Routines take on the function of rules in that they lead to patterns of behaviour which are frequently repeated and repeated within narrowly defined limits. Rules explicitly serve this purpose whilst routines have the same character without the external sanctions that are inherent in rules. Both rules and routines guide behaviour and save the person thinking afresh about what is appropriate in given situations: in this sense they aid survival. They are particularly useful in facilitating social interaction, and one of the first things we learn as children is how to conduct ourselves with adults: when to say please, thank you, to shake hands, to use titles, etc. In modern organizations there has been a trend to turn routines into rules. Bureaucracy is based on what Weber (1947) called rational-legal authority, and it is this philosophy, combined with technological systems which depend on division of labour, that has led to this high concern with rules and routines.

Routines permeate all aspects of our lives. Sometimes people become almost obsessional about carrying out routines in particular ways. When this happens we sometimes say that it has become a ritual. This indicates the fuzziness about these concepts; it is difficult to say exactly when a routine becomes a ritual, or what the difference is between rules and expectations. Expectations differ from rules in that they are less legalistic. They are tacit agreements amongst people. Expectations almost become rules, but the authority that lies behind them is the authority of people who have informally agreed that this is the way things should be. In work there is often a gap between what the rules say you should do and the expectations that the people have developed for themselves. The rules might say you should work till five o'clock, but actually people expect you to work only until 10 minutes to five; and they will soon let you know if you break their expectations. If you do continue to break their expectations the only sanctions they have are informal pressures to alter your behaviour. If it was a rule that you were breaking, there would be specific formal sanctions that could be used to try and alter your conduct. We have seen that through useage expectations can become rules, but Morris points out that rituals also have the function of making routines meaningful and tolerable. The Harvest Festival is an example, but, as Morris points out, 20th century society has established very few rituals to make its numerous routines meaningful. Office parties might be one ritual (which sometimes become dramas!). Frequently, rituals at work develop in tea and coffee breaks rather than around work itself. Cliques of card players, horse racing syndicates and so on, often develop ritual behaviours to enliven their otherwise meaningless days. To borrow from some distinctions made by Vickers (1973), rules tell us what we can and cannot do and expectations tell us what we should or should not do.

Vickers has a third distinction which involves what we must or must not do. This has some similarity to what Gowler means by codes. The ultimate beliefs or philosophy of a culture are very difficult to identify even for people who have grown up in the culture. They are communicated in symbolic form and in terms of symbols. The actual meaning of the objects which bear the symbolic messages also change over time which makes understanding even more problematic. One literally has to crack the code to come to a real understanding. Codes relate to what we must or must not do in the sense that they are often about moral problems such as sexual relationships, how to treat parents or children, how to deal with death, how to be a good member of the culture. To use another term from Vickers (1968) they arise from the 'appreciations' we make about what is good or bad, what is to be valued, to be sought or avoided. They are codes because we are often not aware of what is guiding our appreciations; we have internalized beliefs which have been transmitted to us over a long period of time and often in symbols and ceremonies of which we are hardly aware. Art and literature are major methods of communicating the values and the dilemmas codes are created to resolve. Once again, these are above all concerned with symbols and meanings. Almost certainly this is because it is not possible to produce answers which could be stated in the form of rules, for the questions at issue are choices about how to make sense of experiences for which there are no obviously attractive answers: sex, death, one's status in society, poverty, and so on.

The deep structures that are the characteristics of codes are well illustrated by the works of the anthropologist Levi-Strauss. An appreciation of their relevance to the analysis of organizational life is contained in an article by Stephen Turner (1977) strikingly titled, 'Complex Organizations as Savage Tribes'. As an example Turner argues that industrial subordination causes asymmetry in relationships and psychological disharmony. Symmetry is re-established for the workers through the 'myth' of brotherhood in the trade union sense.

Gowler (1977) suggests that expectations mediate between rules and codes. Expectations can become routines and through accepting expectations aimed at us by priests, parents, teachers, and other influential persons, we eventually internalize the codes that justify those expectations. At a social level the major function of codes is to create stability. The fact that they are transmitted by symbols makes them slippery to grasp, but it also makes them slippery to capture and destroy. Major changes in individuals do, however, often occur by changing their codes. St Paul's conversion is a convenient example, but on a more prosaic level such changes occur to ordinary people faced by tragedies such as death, divorce, and war. More gradual change occurs through changing expectations, and they may eventually be incorporated into codes, to add to or modify those codes that exist already.

I have emphasized the roles of codes and expectations in the processes of maintaining and changing social systems because recent ideas on organizational development have revealed their power in sustaining what Schon (1971) calls 'dynamic conservatism'. He means the tendency that organizations have to fight to stay as they are. Ten–fifteen years ago, organization development (Bennis, 1966) started with promises to revolutionize relationships in organizations. Presently, that promise remains unfulfilled and various theorists are proposing that it will remain so unless we can find ways of changing the values (codes) that ultimately control what people want from work. Watzlawick et al. (1974) show how trying to make the present rules work better will only serve to maintain the system as it is. In a most exciting book they write vividly about how we have to learn to step outside what is currently happening and try quite different sorts of solutions: in their own language we have to find solutions of a different logical type. A familiar problem will help to illustrate their point: people who can't get to sleep should be encouraged to force themselves to stay awake. Paradoxically this brings sleep.

Argyris and Schon (1978) propose a similar distinction in their book on organizational learning. They distinguish between single-loop learning and double-loop learning. In single-loop learning the organization learns how to detect deviations from a standard (rules or expectations) and to correct things so as to bring the situation back to 'normal'. In double-loop learning the organization has to question the very meaning of what 'normal' is (i.e. what are its values and what codes control them). Having questioned those values it needs to act to change its behaviour and the established patterns of values which mitigate either against the recognition of the need to change, or against the adoption of the new behaviour. In terms of Kuhn's model the DETECTOR does not see the need for change, or if it does, the change is vetoed by the SELECTOR because the values that the behaviour implies are inconsistent with current goals.

Having talked about the new role of codes in organizations in a general way, I now wish to consider the roles of rules, expectations, and codes in each of the four organizational types.

(vii) Rules, Expectations, Codes and Organizations

It will have been apparent that the concept of rules fits well with an organization which has a high concern for maintenance activities. There are parallels between the organizational activities and the mechanisms of co-ordination and control. It is suggested in Figure 10.7 that the four different types of organizations place different degrees of emphasis on rules, expectations and codes. Parallels with John Morris' concepts of routines, rituals, and dramas are included. The temple structure based on the role ideology functions largely by rules and routines, but we know that you cannot work effectively 'to rule' so that it also depends a good deal on expectations. Bureaucracies put little emphasis on codes, or at least on codes which are unique to them. Amongst managers and administrators there may be codes about the professional management role, and the organization as a whole may attempt to inculcate a code about the work ethic. McClelland's work on need for achievement in different cultures (McClelland et al., 1953) would suggest the organization is fighting a losing battle unless there is a set of codes about the work ethic in the society at large. Earlier this century some large employers attempted to create social integration by building a distinctive, all-embracing culture, and they spent much more time in communicating at the level of codes. Organizations such as Cadburys and Lever Brothers actually built villages for their workers and took a very paternal responsibility for their employees. This is still the norm in Japanese factories (Abegglan, 1958). But there is still little activity at the level of codes in large-scale organizations today, and where there is, it is largely aimed at administrative and managerial grades. Social relationships in large-scale organizations are more and more influenced by rules and agreements defined in joint consultation procedures.

The growth of managerial and technical trade unions can be interpreted as

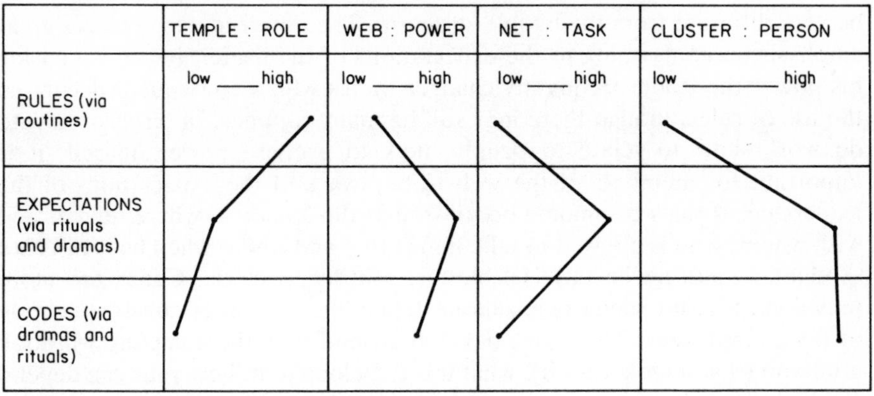

	TEMPLE : ROLE	WEB : POWER	NET : TASK	CLUSTER : PERSON
RULES (via routines)	low ____ high	low ____ high	low ____ high	low _____ high
EXPECTATIONS (via rituals and dramas)				
CODES (via dramas and rituals)				

FIGURE 10.7. Patterns of rules, expectations, and codes in different types of organizations

a sign that codes amongst the managerial staff may be on the wane. Middle management have become conscious of their own 'in the middle' status, just as workers have been conscious of their working-class status. Activities at the level of codes for workers and middle-management grades are now much more in the hands of trade unions. It is they who provide a sense of common problems and qualities. It is they who organize dramas and ceremonies at which the symbols of their culture can be displayed and affirmed. In large or medium-sized organizations where the temple structure dominates, there is little activity at the level of codes. What activity there is is carried out by and for the subcultures that make up the organization. Indeed, it is possible to suggest that, because the high differentiation of roles and statuses in temple structures is supported by differentiation at the level of codes, it will be very difficult to obtain integration between them. Many of the difficulties of communication which appear to arise from failures to communicate routines or expectation, may really be due to conflicts arising from deeper differences rooted in the codes of subgroups in the organization.

As organizations get larger there is a strong pressure on them to assume many elements of the temple structure, so in considering 'pure' examples of the web, matrix, or cluster one is generally concerned with smaller organizations. There are large organizations which have organized as matrix structures, but the pure matrix is likely to be most appropriate to relatively small organizations, or parts of organizations. It is a structure often found within research and development departments of larger organizations. The cluster is almost certainly only to be found in small organizations such as professional partnerships or communes.

The web structure is to be found in small to medium-sized organizations but as Figure 10.7 shows its use of rules, expectations, and codes is considered to be very different from the temple structure. The power ideology places great emphasis on conforming to the expectations of the leader, but in exercising his power the leader frequently changes things with a consequent decline in the use of rules; though there may still be many routines. In terms of how to do work, how to relate to people, how to exercise power oneself, it is important for members of the web to be aware of the expectations of the leadership. Rituals commonly occur around the leader – where he eats and with whom; who is allowed to take him coffee and when; when he is or is not available; ensuring he has His blotter, ashtray, pen. . . . Codes are more prevalent, too, for such organizations depend greatly on establishing a body of loyal employees. The codes develop around how the company will look after you (if you look after it), what it is to belong to it, how your can depend on the leader. At annual dinners these codes are often transmitted as stories about how 'The governor, FJK, Mr. Reginald . . .' pulled off a great deal, got rid of someone who was trying to usurp his power, dealt with a difficult employee. With time, the facts become unimportant and like all effective codes they depend a lot on myths, and the insightful power-oriented leader works hard at developing such myths and the symbols that sustain them. During World War II Churchill's Victory salute became a powerful symbol of the collective consciousness of the British people. Landing a big order or solving one difficult problem can serve the organizational leader in just the same way.

Codes are hardly used at all in the net or matrix structure. If they are then the codes would be assumed to arise from an identity with one's profession or calling. The matrix consists usually of a network of different specialists. Social integration depends largely on the group establishing expectations of each other, and these surround the performance of the task as a whole and the performance of the skills which have justified one's inclusion in the net. Since this structure is usually used to deal with one-off projects, it tends to produce few routines and hardly any rules. It may be subject to rules from the wider structure within which it may be nested, but of itself it generates hardly any. The project leader's job in a matrix structure is to ensure that people are clear about what is expected of them, to encourage necessary co-ordination between the members and to communicate the needs of the members of the matrix to the people for whom it is performing the task. Again, it is a matter of clarifying and communicating their mutual expectations.

Expectations are important in the cluster structure too. The orientation to the needs of the individual means that each member of the group has to communicate clearly his expectations of the others, and his expectations of himself. Only if he does both will the others understand why he wants them to behave in particular ways. Since development involves change, the expectations often change, so that there is great use of expectations in the cluster structure. Rules and routines, and particularly rules, are infrequently used. If they are established, they are much debated and not really backed by

TABLE 10.3
The Implications of Rules, Expectations, and Codes for the DSE System

	Rules		Expectations		Codes	
	advantages	disadvantages	advantages	disadvantages	advantages	disadvantages
DETECTOR	Readily available. Not reliant on short-term memory. If well conceived can reduce ambiguity	Limit choice for Detector. Can cause overload. Rarely well enough conceived to resolve all situations	Allow person room to negotiate for himself so Detector system can generate (b) variety (b) satisfy it's own needs more easily	Signals from several sources lead (a) to ambiguity (b) to conflict between sources (c) to conflict with rules, i.e. detection is more difficult	They can be seen everywhere or nowhere depending on how the Detector chooses	Symbolic expression makes them difficult to detect unless you are immersed in them
SELECTOR	Reduces choice where preferences not already powerful	Often conflict with needs for self-actualization etc. Tend to punish for transgression rather than reward for conformity, so lead to negative valence in the long run	Person can either distort expectations to match his own or negotiate them so they fit his own preferences better	Ambiguity can make choices difficult: anxiety. Conflict can create many situations where negative valence is traded off against more positive valence: frustration	They are the ultimate guides to what is good or bad and can act as the final 'court of appeal' for the undecided. If well articulated and well internalized they simplify many choices	Their generality makes them difficult to apply in particular circumstances. They deal with what is bad and often involve painful choices, conscious and unconscious
EFFECTOR	Direct and ensure some activity e.g. 'working to rule'	Standards set become maximum rather than optimum: can lead to deterioration by reducing exercise of total DSE system	Increased control leads to variety and greater choice of what, how, and when to do it. Less definition of standards of performance.	More dependent on self-direction and control—be difficult for over-dependent, lazy. Feedback about effectiveness of behaviour can be less clearcut	They legitimize all sorts of dedicated behaviour e.g. obsessional work habits, being a monk, personal sacrifice. They can give meaning to tedious actions	Acting in contravention of codes, wittingly or unwittingly, can lead to painful sanctions and retributions. Their symbolic nature sometimes does not lead to clear guides on which to act

the sort of legal sanctions implied by rules since that would be inconsistent with an emphasis on personal choice. Much activity takes place at the level of codes. People in cluster structures will often have regular dinners and outings which provide opportunities to celebrate and establish the group's common identity. Potential recruits to the groups will be carefully vetted, may have to pay a price for their entry, and will almost certainly be subjected to some sort of initiation rites even if they are as innocuous as being taken to a special pub or restaurant. But symbols of belonging, and ritual eating and drinking, are also commonplace in the everyday life of the group, so the codes are transmitted much more frequently than they are in any other form of organization. The cluster structure is more common in non-work organizations such as clubs and societies. It is possibly the most attractive structure to live in.

5. RULES, EXPECTATIONS, CODES AND KUHN

I have tried to show how the DSE model works as an information processing conception of man, and how organizations in general frustrate the working of it. I then described four main types of organizational ideologies and the structures that go with them, and then linked these to different patterns of activities such as maintenance, breakdown, and development. My description of organizational types was then elaborated to show how the different types relied on different balances of communication mechanisms (rules, expectations, and codes) to create the social cohesion necessary for the functioning of the organization. Since these can be seen as communication mechanisms, although they are also mechanisms for co-ordination and control, we can now ask how they relate to the information processing model of the DSE system.

Table 10.3 summarizes the advantages and disadvantages of communicating by rules, expectations, and codes for the DETECTOR, SELECTOR, and EFFECTOR systems separately.

(i) Rules

The advantage of rules for the DETECTOR is that they are available in written form, can be detailed, and therefore limit reliance on memory. For the SELECTOR they limit areas of choice and can thus make selection easier. If past experience has not given the SELECTOR a stock of preferred valences then the provision of rules and set routines considerably reduces anxiety about choosing what to do, how to behave, what standards of performance to aim for. At the level of the EFFECTOR, rules and routines ensure that some level of effort is generated leading to satisfaction of the cross-system motive for exercise. If they are good rules they might also make that exercise efficient and lead to further satisfaction.

Rules also have disadvantages. We know from the destructive effectiveness of 'working to rule' that it is seldom possible to design rules that cover all circumstances, or ones which, if followed, actually lead to efficiency and effectiveness. So most systems of rules still leave uncertainty about some problems which causes difficulties for the DETECTOR system. If the rules are very complex and do cover a wide range of contingencies, then their volume can lead to overload for the DETECTOR even if the rules are written down. Rules also restrict choice for the DETECTOR system and cause frustration for the SELECTOR subsystem of the DETECTOR. The problems for the main system SELECTOR are that rules and routines are often in conflict with the person's need for variety and self-development (Maslow, 1963). Furthermore, rules often lead to an emphasis on punishment for transgression of the rules rather than on reward for having abided by them. Skinner (1969) has expounded the efficacy of using positive rather than negative reinforcement. The punishment involved could be used to explain why rules about work performance tend to turn the *minimum* standards specified into actual standards obtained (March and Simon, 1958). Not only does this lead to poor productivity, but it can lead to underuse of abilities which have long-term deleterious consequences for the individual. Setting standards which are too low can frustrate the exercise motive not only of the EFFECTOR system, but of the DETECTOR and SELECTOR systems too.

Comparing Table 10.3 and Figure 10.7 we can see that organizations which approach the pure type of temple structure and rely heavily on rules and routines will secure the advantages of limited clarity, moderate commitment, and minimally acceptable standards of output. They will suffer from lack of initiative, unwillingness to go beyond the rules, and the inevitable creation of situations where the rules will be inadequate. In the long term, employees may become totally integrated into their roles (Gowler and Legge, 1975) with consequent resistance to change, and immobility of labour. Are not these the symptoms of 'organizational dry rot' that John Gardner (1963) has so eloquently described? The sceptic might ask in return, 'Why don't they collapse then?' One reason is that there is an extensive informal organization based on expectations rather than rules which helps the organization to function effectively enough to survive, and often to prosper. This has always been true, but current moves to enrich jobs and to increase employee involvement in decision-making are both ways of decreasing reliance on rules as control mechanisms, and increasing the use of expectations.

(ii) Expectations

Greater reliance on expectations as communication and control devices has the advantages for the DETECTOR of increasing its ability to search for novelty and variety and generally of being able to satisfy its own valences (as defined by its subselector). This is because expectations are more negotiable. As a member of a work team the person can bargain with the other members of the team as to what he should do, what the group should do, how they should go about doing it, and so on. Since sanctions are less easily applied, and also negotiable, then in the short term at least the DETECTOR can choose to ignore particular expectations without too much danger. This looser structure also brings disadvantages. Since the expectations are defined by different individuals with different needs and goals they are often in conflict with each other (Kahn *et al.*, 1964). If they are not in conflict the expectations are sometimes not clearly transmitted – 'But we expected you to know that' is the kind of comment which describes this situation. Since reliance on rules is ineffective, and the informal system operates on expectations, there is also a situation where the expectations and the rules are in conflict. The disadvantages for the DETECTOR are that the signals are harder to detect. This frustrates the priority motive as well as the efficiency motive, and ambiguity causes mismatches with rules and other expectations thus frustrating the consonance motive. For most people, however, the advantages of expectations as mechanisms of control probably outweigh the disadvantages.

It can be seen from Table 10.3 that conflicts and ambiguities of expectations can also cause difficulties for the SELECTOR. Ambiguity makes it difficult to be certain that particular acts will lead to the positive valences sought: this might be described as anxiety. The conflicts often resolve themselves only by accepting some negative consequences which are traded off against the prospects of more desirable positive outcomes: this might be described as frustration. But again the lack of definition and control in expectations allows the SELECTOR scope to negotiate with others so that the person can improve things to get a better fit with their preferences. Or the person can change their interpretation of the expectations to match the SELECTOR's requirements without immediate and obvious comebacks such as might be involved with distorting what one thought about rules.

The reduction in clarity of what, when and how to do things that is inherent in a system based on expectations, allows the EFFECTOR greater satisfaction of its motives for priority, efficiency, and exercise. However, the lower formality can lead to decreased feedback about performance which can lead to uncertainty about the effectiveness of actions. This means that the person has to develop the ability to evaluate his own progress. He also has to develop the ability to define his own expectations of himself and to apply sanctions to himself when he has transgressed them. In *The Fear of Freedom*, Erich Fromm (1950) describes how threatening this freedom can be. Anyone who has worked at a University will know how easy it is to let one's time for research slip away, and this provides a good example of relatively loose expectations bringing the benefit of autonomy but the problems of self-control. The consequences are negative more often for those who lack self-direction. This characteristic is applicable to young children and perhaps gives a clue as to why rules work better for children than attempts to operate at the level of expectations, though clearly parents have a duty to expose children to both.

(iii) Codes

Symbol is defined in one dictionary (Merriam-Webster, 1972) as, 'a perceptible thing that stands for something unseen or intangible'. The problem for the DETECTOR is to connect the meaning between what is perceptible and the code it represents. In other words, whilst the symbol itself may be perceptible it is not actually seen because it is not connected with a code, or if it is seen it is not recognized for what it is and therefore ignored or misunderstood. Moving within a strange culture immediately causes problems for the DETECTOR because it cannot match incoming information with its own patterns for interpreting information. Middle-class graduates supervising blue-collar workers, men supervising women, the old teaching the young, can feel uncomfortable because they do not recognize the real meanings of actions. They know they are being laughed at but they don't know why.

When the person is immersed in a culture, codes have positive benefits. Since they depend on symbols and interpretation of them, the DETECTOR can see symbols representing the codes wheresoever it chooses. The devout can see good, or evil, wherever he or she wishes, and the same behaviour can be seen as either good or evil depending on the motives of the perceiver. This property potentially allows the DETECTOR to satisfy all four of the cross-system motives at its own whim, provided it has some grasp of the codes themselves. It is disturbing indeed if the DETECTOR does not understand the codes and cannot fit the information into its own patterns. Even more painful is the experience of having one's codes (culture) destroyed so that the myths which guide one's understanding of the world are exposed and nothing that makes sense, to oneself anyway, is put in their place. The alienation and anomie of the Australian Aboriginee and of the North American Indians are the outstanding examples. In our own country the industrial revolution destroyed rural culture in much the same way. The problems of integration (Lawrence and Lorsch, 1967) which face large, fragmented organizations, and society too, can also be seen as failures to establish a common set of codes or beliefs which can give unity and common identity to subcultural diversity.

The desirability of having an ultimate set of beliefs against which one can test one's actions is illustrated by the advantages which such beliefs provide for the SELECTOR. If the SELECTOR finds choices difficult, and moral choices often are, then codes provide the ultimate court of appeal. And the fact that they may have no 'rational' basis in the scientific sense takes nothing away from the ultimate security they provide. As Pepper (1942) says all knowledge is ultimately tested against common sense, and in this sense, codes are common sense. If the codes are well articulated and the person has internalized them then they simplify many choices. The devout Christian, Jew, Organization Man (Whyte, 1956) is much surer than the non-believer about what is the proper thing to do.

The uncertainty of non-believers also reveals another disadvantage of codes; for non-believers and many others, the generality of codes and myths makes them difficult to apply in particular situations. The SELECTOR is left uncertain. This is exacerbated by the nature of the problems with which codes are most intimately concerned – moral and ideological questions. They deal a lot with what is painful or contentious so the SELECTOR may still find it hard to obtain the positive valence it seeks. Self-sacrifice for the sake of one's beliefs indicates the power that such codes have: for the SELECTOR the negative valence of failing one's faith is greater than the negative valence of pain and death.

As Table 10.3 indicates, the advantages for the EFFECTOR system are that tedious activities can be allocated important public symbolic meaning: checking the accounts, opening up the shop are rituals which symbolize the values of commerce or trade, and give dignity and meaning to what are otherwise uninteresting activities. Codes, like the 'protestant ethic', also have the advantage of legitimizing a great variety of statistically unusual behaviours some of which may make it difficult to prevent the person from doing damage to himself or hurting others.

As we have found with all these three modes of communication and control, their strengths are also their weaknesses. The pervasiveness and symbolic expression of codes can lead to lack of clear direction in terms of what one should or should not do. They are easily broken quite unwittingly, and even when sanctions are applied one may not be aware of what part of the code one has transgressed. What might have seemed a good day's work might be seen as sucking up to the management by colleagues. When the codes are well known they provide great comfort, protection and satisfaction, but when they are not known they present perilous pitfalls for the unwary. And falling into pits is an effective way of limiting actions. It is perhaps no accident that we use the term 'drop out' to describe a person who is no longer prepared to act within the codes society has specified.

6. SUMMARY

Having defined a range of psychological states, some of which involve different kinds of stress, I presented a model of how man can be seen to process information from his environment which includes a description of the main ways in which the system could be frustrated. I then developed a typology of organizations based on ideologies and structures and showed how these 'ideal' types of organizations used different proportions of their time on breakdown, maintenance and development activities. These differences were then related to the ways in which managers communicate to and control people in order to manage these activities: the concepts used were rules, expectations, and codes and this comparison also revealed that the different organizational types used differing amounts of these three mechanisms. Finally, we examined the advantages and disadvantages of the different mechanisms from the point of view of satisfying the needs of the three elements in the DETECTOR, SELECTOR, EFFECTOR model. What this analysis revealed was that the effect on the DSE model depends very much on the *degree* to which a particular mechanism was used. If taken too far, rules have negative consequences, but they also have advantages.

Putting the DSE model, the organizational types, and the mechanisms together, it is possible to answer *in general terms* questions about the stresses (deprivation or pressure) that particular types of organizations generate, and some of the ways in which the DSE system copes with them. The concepts could be used to examine *particular* organizations, and the nearer the organizations approach the ideal type the more they might be expected to generate the problems outlined. But ideal types are abstractions and particular organizations will produce idiosyncratic structures, patterns of activities, patterns of social mechanisms, patterns of stresses, and supports for coping with those stresses.

7. REFERENCES

Abegglan, J. C. (1958). *The Japanese Factory*. Bombay: Asia Publishing House.

Argyris, C. (1962). *Interpersonal Competence and Organizational Effectiveness*. London: Tavistock.

Argyris, C. and Schon, D. A. (1978). *Organizational Learning: A Theory of Action Perspective*. Reading, Mass.: Addison-Wesley.

Bakke, E. W. (1950). *Bonds of Organization*. New York: Wiley.

Baldamus, W. (1951). Type of work and motivation. *British Journal of Sociology*, 2, 44–58.

Bennis, W. (1966). *Changing Organizations*. New York: McGraw-Hill.

Berne, E. (1964). *Games People Play*. Harmondsworth: Penguin.

Bexton, W. H., Heron, W. and Scott, T. H. (1954). Effects of decreased variation in the sensory environment, *Canadian Journal of Psychology*, 8, 70–76.

Blau, P. M. and Scott, W. R. (1962). *Formal Organizations*. San Francisco: Chandler.

Bonjean, C. M. and Grimes, M. D. (1970). Bureaucracy and alienation: a dimensional approach. *Social Forces*, 48, 365–373.

Caplan, R. D., Cobb, S., French, J. R. P. Jr., Van Harrison, R. and Pinneau, S. R. Jr. (1975). *Job Demands and Worker Health*. Washington, DC.: National Institute of Occupational Safety and Health, U.S. Government Printing Office.

Cooper, C. L. and Marshall, J. (1978). Sources of managerial and white collar stress. In C. L. Cooper and R. Payne (Eds.), *Stress at Work*. London: Wiley.

Dewar R. and Hage, J. (1978). Size, technology, complexity and structural differentiation: toward a theoretical synthesis. *Administration Science Quarterly*, 23, 111–136.

Etzioni, A. (1961). *A Comparative Analysis of Complex Organizations*. Glencoe, Ill.: Free Press.

Festinger, L. (1957). *A Theory of Cognitive Dissonance*. Stanford: Stanford University Press.

Foa, U. G. (1965). New developments in facet design and analysis, *Psychological Review*, 72, 262–274.

Fromm, E. (1950). *The Fear of Freedom*. London: Routledge and Kegan Paul.

Gardner, J. W. (1963). *Self-renewal*. London: Harper and Row.

Gowler, D. (1977). Private communication.

Gowler, D. and Legge, K. (1975). Occupational role integration and the retention of labour. In B. O. Pittman (Ed.), *Labour Turnover and Retention*. London: Gower Press.

Hackman, J. R. and Oldham, G. (1976). Motivation through the design of work: test of a theory. *Organizational Behavior and Human Performance*, 15, 250–279.

Hamilton, V. (1975). Socialization anxiety and information processing: a capacity model of anxiety-induced performance deficits. In I. G. Sarason and C. D. Spielberger (Eds.), *Stress and Anxiety*. Vol 2. Washington DC.: Wiley.

Handy, C. (1976). *Understanding Organizations*. Harmondsworth: Penguin.

Harrison, R. (1972). How to describe your organization. *Harvard Business Review*, Sept–Oct.

Jaques, E. (1962). *The Measurement of Responsibility*. London: Tavistock.

Jaques, E. (1976). *A General Theory of Bureaucracy*. London: Halstead-Heinemann.

Kagan, A. and Levi, L. (1974). Health and environment – psychosocial stimuli: a review. *Social Science and Medicine*, 8, 225–241.

Kahn, R. L., Wolfe, D. M., Quinn, R. P., Snoek, J. D. and Rosenthal, R. A. (1964). *Organizational Stress: Studies in Role Conflict and Ambiguity*. New York: Wiley.

King Taylor, L. (1972). *Not for Bread Alone*. London: Business Books.

Kuhn, A. (1974). *The Logic of Social Systems*. San Francisco: Jossey-Bass.

Lawrence, P. R. and Lorsch, J. W. (1967). *Organization and Environment*. Boston: Harvard Business School.

Lyons, T. F. (1971). Role clarity, need for clarity, satisfaction, tension and withdrawal. *Organizational Behavior and Human Performance*, 6, 99–110.

McClelland. D. C., Atkinson, J. W., Clark, R. A. and Lowell, E. L. (1953). *The Achievement Motive*. New York: Appleton–Century–Crofts.

McMichael, A. J. (1978). Personality, behavioural and situational modifiers of work stressors. In C. L. Cooper and R. Payne, (Eds.), *Stress at Work*. London: Wiley.

March, J. G. and Simon, H. A. (1958). *Organizations*. New York: Wiley.

Maslow, A. H. (1963). *Towards a Psychology of Being*. New York: Van Nostrand.

Merriam-Webster (1972). *Pocket Dictionary of Synonyms*. New York: Pocket Books.

Morris, J. (1972). Three aspects of the person in social life. In R. Ruddock (Ed.), *Six Approaches to the Person*. London: Routledge and Kegan Paul.

Morris, J. and Burgoyne, J. G. (1973). *Developing Resourceful Managers*. London: Institute of Personnel Management.

Newell, A. and Simon, H. A. (1972) *Human Problem Solving*. Englewood Cliffs N.J.: Prentice-Hall.

Payne, R. L. and Pugh, D. S. (1976). Organizational structure and climate. In M. D. Dunnette (Ed.), *Handbook of Industrial and Organizational Psychology*, Chicago, Rand McNally.

Pepper, S. (1942). *World Hypotheses*. Berkeley: University of California Press.

Pugh, D. S. and Hickson, D. J. (1976). *Organizational Structure in its Context: The Aston Programme 1*. Farnborough: Saxon House.

Pugh, D. S., Hickson, D. J., Hinnings, C. P. and Turner, C. (1968). The dimensions of organization structure. *Administrative Science Quarterly*, 13, 65–105.

Pugh, D. S. and Hinings, C. R. (1977). *Organizational Structure: Extensions and Replications*. Farnborough: Saxon House.

Sayles, L. R. and Chandler, M. K. (1971). *Managing Large Systems: Organizations for the Future*. New York: Harper and Row.

Schon, D. A. (1971). *Beyond the Stable State*. Harmondsworth: Penguin.

Schroder, H. M., Driver, M. J. and Streufert, S. (1967). *Human Information Processing*. New York: Holt, Rinehart, and Winston.

Schaffer, L. F. and Shoben, E. J., Jr. (1954). *The Psychology of Adjustment*. Boston: Houghton Mifflin.

Skinner, B. F. (1969). *Contingencies of Reinforcement*. New York: Appleton–Century–Crofts.

Steele, F. (1975). *The Open Organization*. Reading, Mass.: Addison-Wesley.

Turner, S. P. (1977). Complex organizations as savage tribes. *Journal of Theory of Social Behaviour*, 7, 99–125.

Van Harrison, R. (1978). Person–environment fit and job stress. In C. L. Cooper and R. Payne (Eds.), *Stress at Work*. London: Wiley.

Vickers, G. (1968). *Value Systems and Social Process*. Harmondsworth: Penguin.

Vickers, G. (1973). Motivation theory – a cybernetic contribution. *Behavioral Science*, 18, 242–249.

Watzlawick, P., Weakland, J. H. and Fisch, R. (1974). *Change: Principles of Problem Formation and Problem Resolution*. New York: Norton.

Weber, M. (1947). *The Theory of Social and Economic Organization*. Glencoe, Ill.: Free Press.

Whyte, W. (1956). *The Organization Man*. New York: Simon and Schuster.

Woodward, J. (1965) *Industrial Organization: Theory and Practice*. New York: Oxford University Press.

Chapter 11

Stress, Work, and Productivity

WALTER ROHMERT AND HOLGER LUCZAK

1. Introduction
2. Analysis of Work and Productivity: Ergonomic Aspects
   (i)   Job Analysis
   (ii) Job Demands
3. Analysis and Evaluation of Workload
4. Description of Stressors – Job Description
5. Models and Measurements of Workload (Stressors), Performance/
   Productivity, and Human Effort (Strain)
   (i)   Mainly Physical Work
   (ii) Mainly Non-physical Work
6. Fitting the Subject to his Work by Training
7. Summary
8. References

1. INTRODUCTION

Work is a dominant element of human life in all industrial societies. Work has central importance for the status and development of the national economy (production of goods and services), of the individual worker (status, life events, self-fulfilment) and the persons depending on him directly (family) or indirectly (elderly, sick, and unemployed people). Thus the stress aspects of work are manifold. A comparison of different countries shows that societies with high prosperity can be distinguished from others by their outstanding productivity. This is due partly to the fact that the individuals in these societies experience a strong pressure to aim for more qualified and more profitable work, i.e. more productivity, which causes rapidly changing situations and their consequent stress symptoms. An approach to work and productivity from the point of view of stress can be based on:

(a) the process by which jobs and working places come into existence, change, and disappear, i.e. the economic and sociopolitical aspect;

(b) the process by which humans become workers, i.e. the pedagogical aspect;

(c) the process by which workers and jobs compete in a market for contracts, i.e. the legal and economic aspect;

(d) the process of interaction of different workers in groups, i.e. the sociopsychological and sociological aspect; and

(e) the process of interaction of the individual and his work, i.e. the ergonomic aspect.

Our subsequent presentation and discussion will concentrate on some selected ergonomic problems of man-at-work systems.

Ergonomics attempts to define man in relation to the workplace, working process, and the means of work. It studies the structure and functions of the human body, in order to fit working conditions to human requirements and in order to adapt man to the conditions of work intensity, working environment, and working process. The dynamic behaviour of any man-at-work-system depends on the subsystems 'man' and 'work'. 'Man' can be described by his special qualifications and his workload, the subsystem 'work' by the degree of rationalization, of mechanization of work, or automation. The main tasks of man-at-work-systems are the production of goods or services, in general influencing the flow of energy, material, or information. Work intensity will affect certain parts of man and work. Besides this, work intensity must always be considered as a function of the capabilities of man in relation to certain activities. Furthermore it is necessary to define or to give some advice about suitable or impossible workload intensity which is valid for individuals as well as for groups of different types of workers.

Some remarks are necessary about suitable work intensity. Suitable work intensity involves a prognosis based on data deduced from studies of actual working activities. But there is also the possibility of development of an individual's abilities. Therefore it is sometimes much more correct to evaluate inherent capabilities as is done, for example, in evaluating muscular strength with regard to the possibility of an improvement of muscular strength by means of muscular training.

The notion of suitable work intensity is also related to human society and our knowledge of psychobiology. Acceptability of working conditions as a social–human–technological problem underlies development, which means variability in each sector. There is a development in our social conception of work intensity, for example, in duration of work, length of working life, and work intensities under certain dirty or inconvenient environmental conditions. There is also biological progress that has resulted in higher life expectancy. At the least, our conception of suitable work intensity is influenced by technical developments, with mechanization of heavy muscular work or new activities like air-traffic control tasks. Without taking these changes into account it is impossible to determine values for suitable work intensities numerically. In this paper however only ergonomic aspects of the whole problem are dealt with, although other human, social, or technological aspects must be taken into account in addition to this specific aspect.

2. ANALYSIS OF WORK AND PRODUCTIVITY: ERGONOMIC ASPECTS

Ergonomics is concerned with the study of men at their work from many aspects: the individual, engineering and technology, economics, and society. The main interest is in the relationship between output of work and human input. Ergonomic questions involve also the conditions of human labour and its evaluation, which are regarded as just as important as the output of work. This defines ergonomics as distinct from the mainly technologically or economically oriented disciplines on the one hand, and the mainly man-orientated human or social sciences on the other hand. In ergonomics, techniques and methods from different disciplines have to be combined and new ones must be developed. Work problems cannot be solved by using techniques concerned only with the analysis of what a man is doing at work, work-system interrelations must also be considered. While accepting this, it may be worthwhile summarizing some of the techniques which are available for appraising what man is doing at work.

(i) Job Analysis

Job description or analysis may be made from two different points of view. The more inductively-oriented procedure involves a consideration of occupations (e.g. International Standard Classification of Occupations, 1969) or jobs (e.g. Work Performed Manual, U.S. Department of Labour, 1959), sometimes using algorithmic descriptions (e.g. Krivohlavy, 1966). More deductively-oriented procedures on the other hand, start not with job analysis but with the development of models from which categories can be deduced, for example, in a very simple concept of human work with a hierarchical functional structure: 'job', 'task', 'operation', and 'element' (Beishon, 1967; REFA, 1971). There are other taxonomies, mainly from psychology and human engineering, starting with basic human functions for the perception-, identification-, decision-, and effector-mechanisms (Welford, 1965; Miller, 1967; Christensen and Mills, 1967; Keenan, 1967; Kendrick, 1969; Baker, 1970). Specific models mainly based on the concept of control can be used as an element of job description (Birmingham and Taylor, 1961; Beishon, 1967). It is probably useful to utilize elements from both inductive as well as deductive procedures for job analysis.

Man's task must be clearly defined in the context of the particular work

Work System with	partial fuctions operated by man		
'manual' performance	effecting	controlling	monitoring
mechanized performance	effecting	controlling	monitoring
automatic performance	effecting	controlling	monitoring
	partial functions realized by technical equipment		

FIGURE 11.1. Work system with human and technical functions

system. Two different points of view may be possible: either looking at the role which man plays in the whole system, that is, his part in task completion, or looking at the demands of the job and the effects on man. In any work system the most important areas or partial functions are effecting, controlling, and monitoring. The actual changes in the work objectives will be made by the effecting function and the process will be controlled (or guided) by information processing. Monitoring serves to maintain the functional capacity of the system, that is, the internal checking and clearing of difficulties. The functions of effecting, controlling, and monitoring may be realized by either man or technical equipment. Figure 11.1 demonstrates the steps of technical design logically derived from different possible kinds of work system. The term 'manual' performance means all direct human actions and also non-manual actions such as speaking. The interaction of the human operator with technical equipment is characterized by identifying the steps of technical design which result in distinguishable types of human performance.

(ii) Job Demands

Job demands are influenced not only by the technical sophistication of the work system. Four different design areas are important (Figure 11.2). Objective demands on man result from the aim of the work system and its design in a four-step process. Technological design selects the type of technique and fixes the basis for production capacity and general working conditions. Technical design is related to the utilization of technical equipment based on applied technology. The result of this design is the functional work partition between man and machine (see Figure 11.1). Separating man from the work process, makes him dependent upon the influences of technological and technical design. Ergonomic design covers all aspects of adapting work to man, in

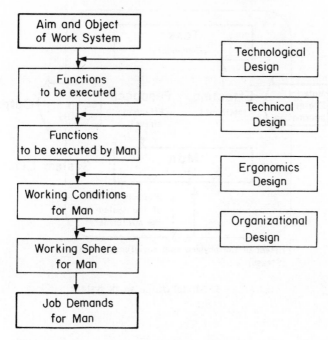

FIGURE 11.2. Job demands for man in a work system, by
different design areas

particular to his abilities and capacities. The main objectives of ergonomic
design are increased output by the man, and improved working conditions.
Organizational design means the division of labour, and problems of specialization and job enlargement have to be solved. In addition, consideration
must be given to problems of the dependence of the different tasks on each
other, on problems of working time and rest pauses, the daily position of work
and rest, and problems of shift work.

Job demands can be described in a very general man-at-work system. This
is defined as a model of the relations between *man* and his *task* (see Figure
11.3). The model will be illustrated for a very complex human task, namely
the task of air-traffic controlling. This task may be considered as a special type
of service man-at-work system. The *task* of the controller is to give external
instructions to a pilot in an aircraft and to make internal coordination with
other controllers. Besides *input* measures like presented information about
the aircraft to be guided and energy to handle miscellaneous material and
technical equipment, the controller needs *methods* for solving his task gained
by training and experience. With these methods he is *effecting* in the work
system. By solving his task, *demands* are put on the controller which present
certain resistances (workload or difficulties) which must be overcome by him

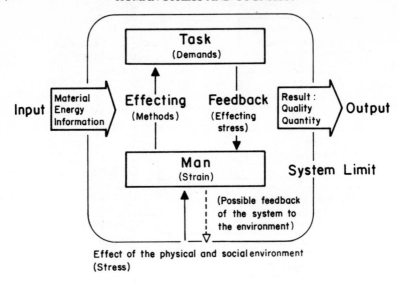

FIGURE 11.3. Model of the work system

and which give *feedback*. The sources of this feedback, which influences man while doing the task, may be called *stressors*. Stressors do not only depend on the workload and the difficulties of the task and its duration, but also on the work *environment* with its physical components (i.e. climate, noise, illumination, etc.) and its social components (i.e. leadership, management relations, communication problems with other controllers or staff, etc.) which are effective as stress components both within and outside the working system limits. Within the person, stress leads to a distinguishable *strain*, dependent not only on stressors but also on different individual controller's capacities, abilities, or skills. The result for the controller's task is shown in both components of *quality* and *quantity* of the control performance. By the *system limits* (i.e. the controller's workplace or his functional area), the relations between man and work are separated from the environment.

Such a general and rough description of the working system 'controller's performance' provides a possible basis for detailed task analysis. With regard to the controller and his control function there are three starting points from which to evaluate the controller's input and his share in the air-traffic control system productivity (see Figure 11.3):

(a) the *demands* of the task (and all concrete elements of the working system), which means a special kind of job evaluation;

(b) the *qualifications* of the air-traffic control officers, which determine differences between the *methods* of working by experienced controllers and trainees respectively; and

(c) the *capacity* of the air-traffic control officers (as a man-related part of the working system, with regard to the quality and quantity of the system's *output*).

To each of these three starting points for evaluating human performance, there is attached the disadvantage that the feedback, which influences man while doing his work, is neglected. All these starting points neglect the evaluation of strain. If, however, an air-traffic control system contains human input and if future developments are going to need the controller's input too, it seems to be really necessary to consider the strain put on man and its contribution to the system's reliability. This is one reason for analysing strain in more detail.

3. ANALYSIS AND EVALUATION OF WORKLOAD

From the study of jobs in actual professional work settings one may deduce specific work contents or types of tasks out of the infinity of possible human tasks. Figure 11.4 shows an order of tasks which are distinctly different in their strain on human organs using specialized human abilities. Strain is explained as the sum of all different effects of stress in man interacting with different individual characteristics. The degree of strain depends on the weight of stressors as well as on the individual characteristics:

$$\text{Strain} = f_1 \text{ (stressors, individual capacities)}$$

Stressors or workload are defined as the sum of all factors influencing man at work, which are perceived or sensed mainly through the receptor system or which put demands on the effector system. In analysing real-life tasks one has to consider that all measures appear as time-dependent values corresponding to alternating work contents. Therefore one has to distinguish between a work-content-related dimension of stressors and a time-related dimension (Rohmert, 1962):

$$\text{Stressors} = f_2 \text{ (intensity of work, duration of work)}$$

In Figure 11.4 work content is defined as generally as possible, but as specifically as necessary. The discrete differences between the specific work contents relatable to strain, have led to specific ergonomic terms. The summary in Figure 11.4 allows a ranking of most tasks found in practical working situations. For mixed tasks the job demands must be generalized to deduce the specific work content. However, one has to consider that different amounts of physical or non-physical work are related to the content of work as well as to its variability. In most industrial situations work content varies during the shift and also the type of strain and the stressors often change in time. This variation of work must be considered in addition to physical and

type of work	specific work content	mainly strain on organs and capabilities	Ergonomics term	examples
mainly physical	producing forces	muscles (in case heart and circulation)	muscular work	handling loads
	coordination of motor and sensory functions	muscles + sense—organs	senso-motor work	assembling, crane operating
mainly non-physical	converting information into reaction	sense—organs + muscles	mainly non-muscular work	controlling
	transformation from input- to output-information	sense—organs + mental abilities		programming, air traffic controlling, book-keeping, translating
	producing information	mental abilities	mental work (in the narrow sense of term)	dictation, designing, problem solving

FIGURE 11.4. Basic types of working tasks

social environment stressors, if a definable task is to be classified in Figure 11.4.

Figure 11.5 shows the close links between the economic and humane aspects in evaluating any man-at-work system design. It is clearly quite illogical to pursue economic aims without considering humane aims, and it is important to remember that, in a wider sociological context, economic aims must always be of service to humanity, otherwise in the long term they become self-destructive and pointless. In order to assess the results of designing human work in the context of an overall men-at-work-system design, apart from the primary aims of humanity and productivity, there are four cardinal criteria which must be fulfilled in order to achieve the primary aims. Therefore the evaluation of any concrete work design has to consider and to satisfy a four-level hierarchy:

(a) level of ability;
(b) level of tolerability;
(c) level of acceptability; and
(d) level of satisfaction.

The ability of man to do the job is a basic prerequisite for productivity. Human capabilities and characteristics must enable man to do the work before the work can be carried out at all. This limit of man's ability means that there is a level of practicability in the use of human input. If the work design does not guarantee the consideration of these maximal, momentary abilities

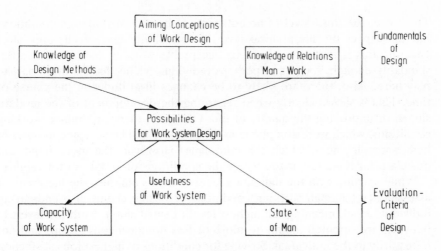

FIGURE 11.5. Aspects and evaluation criteria of work design

of men at their work which are only feasible for a limited time, the designer is obliged to give up all claims to utilize human manpower; he has to design a completely automatic work system. Therefore, the level of practicability of human work makes it imperative to consider human functions (e.g. body dimensions, muscular strength, speed and accuracy of movements, sensory organ functions, etc.).

In most cases, we are not only interested in the execution of the job just once (like in sports) or in one moment, but in a daily repetition in the work of a normal shift's duration over the total period of working life. Under these conditions the demands put on man have to be lower. The highest level of demands which can be endured until the end of the normal working life without any work-related damage to health or normal human functional abilities is called the level of tolerability. The quality and quantitative output of the work a man has to do then affect productivity. Then there is effectiveness in the sense of general efficiency. Not all working conditions are equally conducive to quality and quantitative output or to incurring minimum costs; this in turn, affects productivity. The cardinal criteria for assessing the humanity of work and working conditions are health, well-being, and job satisfaction. However, it is important to see that well-being and satisfaction always include long-term tolerability of work in health terms. Therefore it is imperative to consider the second level of tolerability in assessed work.

The third level of evaluation criteria means that working conditions should be accepted by those who are partners at the shop floor or at the labour agreement level. Unfortunately, conditions can be accepted by agreement as well as even by labour laws which are not tolerable over the total life period.

Therefore, the third level of acceptability of human work-design conditions has to respect the hierarchical level of tolerability first of all; only after ensuring this is it reasonable to fix acceptable working conditions. Understandably enough, social and perhaps individual values have a large part to play here. Also, there are likely to be changes in attitudes in the course of time. This is shown clearly when regarding the development of the modern slogan of improving the quality of life. Of course there are human working conditions, which were acceptable in the past and will be accepted in times of high unemployment, which are inhumane. However, the more important postulate for humanity is to respect the conditions of long-term tolerability.

While starting with the individual level of man's abilities, the hierarchy of assessment of human working conditions or design claims also ends at an individual level, meaning the highest level of satisfaction. Both the levels in between are oriented mainly to more or less homogeneous groups and not necessarily to the individual. Striving for conditions of highest job satisfaction does not guarantee tolerable conditions. For example, if a worker is very content with his working conditions, his workload might still be intolerably high due to the fact that the duration of a stress factor, not necessarily its intensity, is too high. This can occur if a man 'forgets' going home from work at night or forgets any rest pauses, recovery periods, and holidays when he is under the impression of doing a very satisfactory job. Also, the long jumper in the Olympic Games at Mexico City will rest highly content with his performance although he will never succeed in doing this maximal performance at another time in his life.

The two examples given show the importance of the basic levels in the hierarchy as well as the necessity of setting and controlling design aims mainly at the basic levels. Man does not know what is right and useful for him with regard to the defined tolerable conditions of health and well-being, e.g. self-regulation of working time schedules and rest periods. So there is a real need for disciplines, methods, techniques, and knowledge to adapt work to man and *vice versa* man to work for ensuring tolerable working conditions. Here is a real challenge for human sciences, where disciplines like ergonomics may fix standards of work design (cf. the Fachnormenausschuß Ergonomie im Verein Deutscher Ingenieure) primarily upon the basic levels of design assessment.

Figure 11.6 summarizes the general principles of the four-level hierarchy of evaluating either the state of work design or the effects of work asked of man. For each of these four levels there are individual as well as collective standards which allow a ranking in any specific case. Allied to each level we will find methods and techniques from different disciplines which have to be involved in the problems of designing and assessment. By this method one will find important subdisciplines of human sciences. This is not intended to make a claim for a hierarchy of scientific disciplines. Nevertheless, there are a number of disciplines which use the methods and techniques of the natural

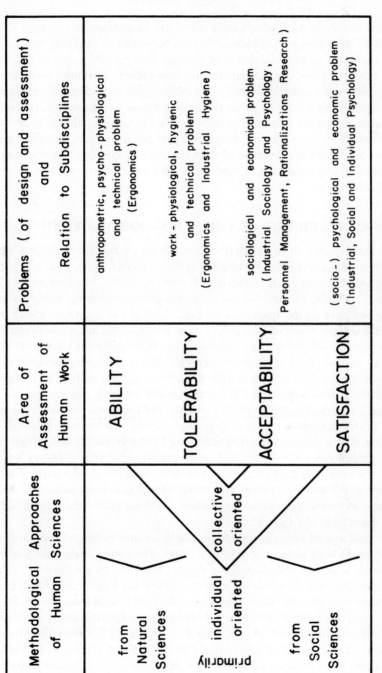

FIGURE 11.6 A four-level hierarchy for assessment of work design

sciences, the results of which have two very important advantages in the context of man-at-work problems: firstly, the results of applying methods of natural sciences to work-design problems are reproducible; one can fix standards concerned with measurement and calculation. Secondly, these results (standards) withstand the test of acceptability and reproducibility, in accordance with human laws as in mathematics. These two facts are, of course, extremely important in the application of knowledge in the field of work design, where policies based on sociopolitical interests exist. In this context, ergonomics, which will be classed with the natural sciences, plays an important role in fixing standards of work design on the evaluation levels of ability and of tolerability.

4. DESCRIPTION OF STRESSORS – JOB DESCRIPTION

For the purpose of an analytical description of the stress factors which possibly occur in various types of work systems, tools for job, position, or task description have been developed (Fleishman, 1975; McCormick, 1976); Hackman, 1970), mostly following information processing concepts of a human operator in the respective system. Taking into account further technological and physiological aspects of man-at-work systems, a comprehensive ergonomic job-description questionnaire has been designed (Rohmert et al., 1975a), named AET (Arbeitswissenschaftliches Erhebungsverfahren zur Tätigkeitsanalyse). It describes with the help of approximately 400 items on alternative or five-step ordinal scales the objects of work, the equipment, the working environment, i.e. system elements and relations, the different tasks to be performed, and the demands imposed on the human operator, see Fig. 11.7. The items are classified according to observation and interview by a highly skilled rater who is trained to an inter-individually constant level of rating, thus reaching high inter-rater and item-reliability coefficients. The raw data are processed by appropriate computer programmes according to the objective in terms of research, evaluation, or design followed (Luczak et al., 1976; Landau et al., 1976).

The structure of stress components can be evaluated by grouping together related items with respect to types of stress. The rating scale values of item groups are added up and plotted in columns. Item groups are derived straightforwardly from the demand-oriented sections of the Ergonomic Job Description Questionnaire. However, they can be derived as well from the results of a factor analysis of the Ergonomic Job Description Questionnaire data and a factor scoring procedure. As an example, Figure 11.8 shows the stressors profile of an air-traffic control officer in the pick-up position of Frankfurt airport approach control. Characteristic demands are combinatory stressors, education, and vigilance. Besides that, stressors caused by work schedule and responsibility are important. The profile shows high workload especially for

A: ANALYSIS OF THE WORKING SYSTEM

1. OBJECTS OF WORK
KIND
CHARACTERISTICS
MAN AS OBJECT OF WORK

2. EQUIPMENT
MEANS OF PRODUCTION
  CHANGE IN THE STATE OF THE OBJECTS
  CHANGE IN THE LOCATION OF THE OBJECTS
  OTHER MEANS OF PRODUCTION
OTHER EQUIPMENT
  FOR CONTROLLING THE STATE
  FOR SUPPORTING HUMAN SENSES
  CHAIR, WORK-BENCH, WORKING ROOM

3. WORKING ENVIRONMENT
PHYSICAL AND CHEMICAL WORKING ENV.
ORGANIZATIONAL AND SOCIAL WORK. ENV.
  TEMPORAL ORGANIZATION OF WORK
  POSITION OF THE WORK WITHIN THE
    OPERATION PROCESS
  POSITION OF THE WORK WITHIN THE
    ORGANIZATIONAL STRUCTURE
  POSITION OF THE WORK WITHIN THE
    COMMUNICATION SYSTEM
PRINCIPLES AND METHODS OF
  REMUNERATION

B: TASK ANALYSIS

TASKS TO BE PERFORMED DURING THE RECEPTION AND PROCESSING OF INFORMATION
JUDGING THE TEMPORAL STATE, JUDGING QUALITY, CONTROLLING,
PLANNING/ORGANIZING, CODING/DECODING, TRANSMITTING INFORMATION,
COUNTING, MATHEMATICAL INVESTIGATION, DISCUSSING, CONSULTING,
NEGOTIATING, CONVINCING, ETC.

TASKS DURING THE PERFORMANCE OF WORK
SETTING/REGULATING, CHANGING MATERIALS/PRODUCTS BY DIRECT MANUAL OPERATION,
ASSEMBLING/DISASSEMBLING, SETTING UP/ARRANGING, LOADING/UNLOADING, ETC.

C: ANALYSIS OF DEMANDS

RANGE OF DEMANDS:
RECEPTION OF INFORMATION

  SENSE ORGANS FOR THE RECEPTION OF
    INFORMATION
  DIMENSIONS OF IDENTIFICATION
  FORMS OF IDENTIFICATION
  ACCURACY NECESSARY FOR THE
    RECEPTION OF INFORMATION
  VIGILANCE

RANGE OF DEMANDS: DECISION
  COMPLEXITY OF DECISION
  TEMPORAL SCOPE OF DECISION
  NECESSARY KNOWLEDGE

RANGE OF DEMANDS: PERFORMANCE
  ORGANS OF PERFORMANCE
  ACCURACY OF PERFORMANCE
  STRESSORS
    CAUSED BY PHYSICAL POSTURE
    CAUSED BY PHYSICAL SUPPORT
    CAUSED BY HEAVY DYNAMIC
      MUSCULAR EXERTION
    CAUSED BY UNILATERAL DYNAMIC
      MUSCULAR EXERTION

FIGURE 11.7. Arrangement and item groups of an ergonomic job description

sensory systems, caused by poorly designed and adapted job aids (i.e. display and information output). Stress factors of information input are caused by the frequency and clearness of signals and information sources. Whereas frequency of signals cannot be changed significantly, clearness of signals – the design of control systems in general – might be improved. Characteristic physical stress factors are static components of muscular work, caused by

STRESSOR PROFILE

Static body positions	
Static muscular work	SSSSSSSSSSS
Extreme body turns	HHHHHHHHHHH
Stressing body movements	
Heavy dynamic muscular work	
Active light muscular work	
Manual activities	WWWWWWWWWWWWWWWWWW
Summary of physical work	SSSSSSSSSSSS
Sensory work	WWWWWWWWWWWWWWWWWWWWWWWWWWWWWWWWWWWWWW
Frequency of signals	HHHHHHHHHHHHHHHHHHHHHHHHHHHHHHHHHHHH
Inadequate signal clearness	HHHHHHHHHHHHHHHHHHHHHHHHHHHHSSSSSSSSSSSS
Discriminatory work	WWWWWWWWWWWWWW
Information sources	HHHHHHHHHHHHHHHHHHHHHHHHHHHHHHHHHHHHH
Vigilance	WWWWWWWWWWWWWWWWWWWWWWWWWWWWWWWWWWWWWWWWWWWWWWWW
Combinatory work	HHHSSSSSSSSSSSWWWWWWWWWWWWWWWWWWWWWWWWWWWWWWWWWWWWWWWWWWWWWWWWWWWWWWWWW
Education	SSSSSSSSSSSSSSSSSSSSSSSSSSSSSSSSSSSSSSSSSSSSSSSSSSSSSSWWWWWWWWWW
Communicative work	HHHHHHHHHHHHHHHHHHHWWWWWWWWWWWWWWWWWWW
Cognitive processes	WWWWW
Work objects	
Tools and equipment	WWWWWWWWWWWWW
Control devices	HHHWWWWWWWWWWWWWWWWWWW
Technical aids	
Physical hazards	SSSSSSSS
Illumination	HHHSSSSSSSSSSSSSSSSSSSSSSSS
Noise	HHHHHHHHHHHHHHHSSSSSSSSSSS
Vibrations	
Climate	
Other negat.environm.cond.	
Risk of accid./occup.diseases	
Work schedule	AAAAAAAAAASSSSSSSSSSSSSSSSSSSSSSSSSSSSSSSSSSSSSSSSS
Paced work	
Repetitive work	
Responsibility	SSSSSSSSSSSSSSSSSSSSSSSSSSSSSSSSSSSSSSSSSSSSSSSSSSSSSSS
Supervision competence	WWWWWWWWWWWWWWWWWWWWWWWWWWWW
Management function	SSSSSSS
Personal contacts	HHHSSSSSSWWWWWWWW
Conflicts	WWWWWWWWWWWWWWWWWWWWW

S = difficulty	W = importance
H = frequency	A = "yes-no" decision

FIGURE 11.8. Stressor profile of an air-traffic control officer in the pick-up position at Frankfurt airport

forced body positions and continuous attention, and extreme body turns for the purpose of work coordination with other operators. Furthermore, there are stressful manual activities using tools.

The importance of this detailed Ergonomic Job Description Analysis method as well as similar approaches lies in four aspects. Firstly, the main stress factors are indicated; with regard to stress one may derive proposals for design activities in various kinds of tasks; priorities for technical development in work-system functions may be deduced. Secondly, advice will be given for finding out relevant methods and techniques for measuring strain caused by the distinguished stressors. Thirdly, advice will be given for finding out suitable methods for personnel selection and training of subjects with regard to the specific demands of their job. Fourthly, comparisons can be made between the demands of specific tasks and the demands of other professional tasks.

The deficiencies of this sort of technique lie in the fact that the specified different stress factors are presented in an isolated form one beside the other. The possibility of summarizing the items is given only by statistical techniques, this does not consider sufficiently their integrative effect on the human organism as strain. Methods of workload analysis which take into account more efficiently the interaction of different stressors, are based on physical or physiological, informational or neuronal models.

5. MODELS AND MEASUREMENTS OF WORKLOAD (STRESSORS), PERFORMANCE/PRODUCTIVITY, AND HUMAN EFFORT (STRAIN)

(i) Mainly Physical Work

Models which are able to connect different stress factors in a theoretical context, are known from biomechanics for physical workload, and from information theory, feedback control theory, theory of graphs, networks, algorithms, and other informational concepts for information workload of a human operator. As examples of this approach to stressor analysis, the biomechanics of work movements of arms and the application of feedback control theory to steering tasks will be considered.

Mechanical workload factors in human motions can be classified (Jenik, 1972) into kinematic and dynamic factors as well as into qualitative and quantitative factors (see Figure 11.9). By combining the qualitative mechanical load factors in various ways, it is possible to define the kind of movements together with the kind of mechanical load of a movement form. Individual quantitative data about the size of movement and the size of load determine an individual movement type. It should be emphasized that the individual's somatotype could be inserted into the model (of Figure 11.9) as a load factor with a corresponding effect on the strain variables. By using the model, many useful results have been obtained, and the computer can be used for a biomechanical analysis of individual types of arm movement. For all these individual types of movement described in the literature or studied in our own research, the nature of mechanical strain variables during a movement cycle can be calculated: angular velocity and acceleration, static and driving movements in the shoulder and elbow joint, mechanical power, and static and dynamic work.

It is interesting to note that during the dynamic motion process a static component of strain is also produced simultaneously as a product of the force and movement time, in contrast to the dynamic component of strain as a product of force and distance. With some difficulty the results of both the mechanical as well as the physiological functioning cycles can be compared on the output side, that is to say, the mechanical power and physiological energy production (or consumption) can be compared. The problems of correlating

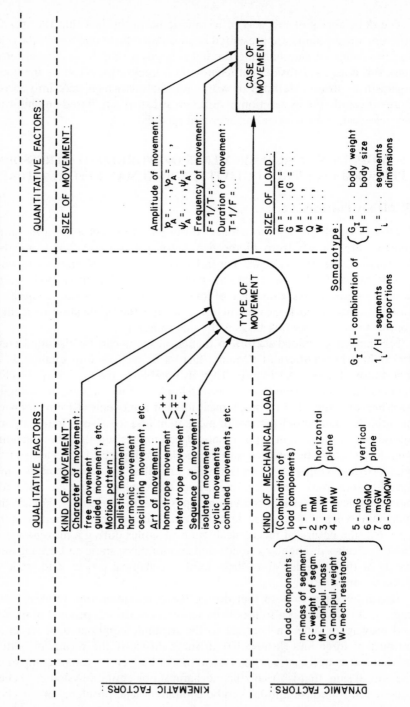

FIGURE 11.9. Factors of mechanical load of work movements of arms

the static work produced during the dynamic action of a motion with the corresponding component of energy expenditure could not be solved in the past. The addition of static and dynamic work in the mechanical work had to be excluded.

The biomechanical computer calculations allow the formulation of a quantitative relation between energy consumption and movement frequency. Simple expressions which include factors that explain the causality of the mechanical processes allow a satisfactorily reliable prediction of the energy expenditure for any individual type of movement. The biomechanical analysis enables the formulation of a logically and causally based *a priori* hypothesis before beginning any laboratory experiment, as well as selecting load factors to reduce the size of expensive and extensive laboratory experiments. Experi-

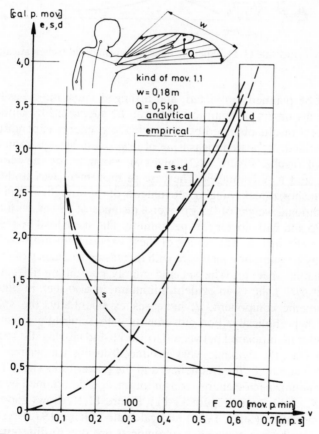

FIGURE 11.10. Correlation between empirical and analytical specific energy consumptions (see text for meaning of symbols)

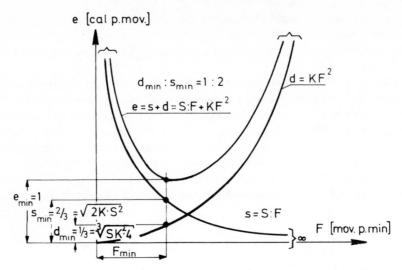

FIGURE 11.11. Specific energy consumption (schematically)

ments can be planned, projected, and arranged much more easily and reliably. Any discussion of empirical data can be supported by objective facts, and incorrect results obtained by measuring, e.g. energy expenditure, can be easily identified. Repeated measuring of fewer variables guarantees a higher accuracy of results. Figure 11.10 gives an example for the biomechanical procedure and its advantages. The case of movement was studied by Stier (1959): free horizontal swinging movements of the straight arm in manipulating an additional weight of 0.5 kp over a distance of 18 cm, with frequencies between 25 and 250 movements per minute. The static load by the additional weight was eliminated. The results of these experiments are well known: the total energy consumption increases with increasing frequency of movement in an exponential manner. The specific energy consumption (related to one movement cycle) shows an evident minimum, as also seen in Figure 11.11.

The dynamic component, d, increases exponentially; the static one, s, decreases hyperbolically. For movements with sinusoidal moving patterns (with weights manipulated between 0 to 1.5 kp and moving distances between 10 and 50 cm), the dynamic work produced during a movement is proportional to the square of the frequency, and the power to its cube. The position of the minimum specific energy consumption, e, is determined by the proportion $d_{min}:S_{min} = 1:2$ (see Figure 11.11). Figure 11.10 shows good agreement between measured (Stier, 1959) and calculated (Jenik 1972) results. (Small deviations for higher movement frequencies are due to different consideration of the movement distance, which were measured in the experiments as a straight line but in the calculations as a ballistic arc, see Figure 11.10).

Corresponding to this approach using biomechanical models, workload, performance, and output of man at work can be evaluated for the special type of muscular work by the measure of energy expenditure. The French chemist Lavoisier discovered (1789) that energy expenditure is increased while man is working. He proposed comparing, by oxygen consumption measurement, the physical and material amount of the activity of any philosopher, author, or composer with any heavy muscular worker. Historically, therefore, this was the first proposal for a scientific job evaluation. We must admire the practical view of this man in applying his discovery for an evaluation of the intensity of different human activities. But 100 years later when work physiology began, it started by stating that any measure of intensity of mental work was 'worthless', if evaluated on the basis of oxygen consumption. There was also no practical evidence because neither the limits of mental capacity nor mental fatigue could be determined, and research workers agreed all over the world to apply Lavoisier's principle only to muscular work. Energy expenditure of more than 100 different activities and more than 100 professions was measured. Today we have tables of results in different languages (Katsuki, 1960; Spitzer and Hettinger, 1964; Passmore and Durnin, 1967). Within these excellent reviews more than 200 references are given about individual experimental work of the different research groups or schools of work physiology all over the world.

Although the number of determined activities and professions is high, there is no complete overview. Therefore we use estimating tables (see Table 11.1)

TABLE 11.1
Estimating Energy Expenditure Per Minute

A Body position or movement	kcal/min (net)	B Type of work		kcal/min (net)
Sitting	0.3	Hand work	light	0.3–0.6
			medium	0.6–0.9
Kneeling	0.5		heavy	0.9–1.2
Crouching	0.5	One-arm work	light	0.7–1.2
			medium	1.2–1.7
Standing	0.6		heavy	1.7–2.2
Stooping	0.8	Both-arms work	light	1.5–2.0
			medium	2.0–2.5
Walking	1.7–3.5		heavy	1.5–3.0
Climbing (without load, inclination 10°)	0.75 per metre height	Whole-body work	light	2.5–4.0
			medium	4.0–6.0
			heavy	6.0–8.5
			very heavy	8.5–11.5

Estimated energy expenditure = $A + B$

which are valid for an average man (1.75 m body height, 70 kp body weight, and 30 years of age). In most cases estimates of A (body position or body movement) will be very easy. In walking, the first kcal/min value in the table relates to a speed of 2 km/h, the last value to 4.5 km/h. When starting with estimate B (type of work) the average value is recommended. Later on with improved skill, estimate can be done in finer steps.

Work physiology started with the classification of intensity of work. By undertaking experiments three questions should be solved:

(a) How much of the consumption of food of a worker is due to his work? In several experiments the measurement of energy expenditure by means of an oxygen meter has proven a simple and reliable method for determining the need of food for identified activities in professions, sports, or in the military area. In some non-voluntary, large-scale experiments it can be shown to what extent lack of nutrition is responsible for low productivity of an entire nation or a group of population, e.g. mining, iron and steel industry (Kraut and Keller, 1961). In very heavy work, with for example 4000 kcal/day, a reduction in food naturally produces the greatest decrease of production; if food intake is only 3400 (3000) kcal/day, production decreases to about 70 (55)%. Even in light work there is an influence because the energy requirement due to basic conditions, rest or leisure time, can only be reduced a little.

By transfering these considerations to a whole nation you may calculate for everyone, heavy muscular workers, children, and elderly people, an average amount of food intake of 3000 kcal per head and per day, while an amount of 1800 kcal excludes any physical work worth mentioning. Efficiency of food, i.e. the ratio between the economically profitable and the total calories, reaches a maximum with 3000 kcal/day. With higher values efficiency drops because of the fact that the additional food intake will not be transformed into work but into body weight increment. Also too low nutrition of a nation will be inefficient because of the decreasing ratio between production and food intake.

(b) For what type of work or type of tool is energy requirement a minimum, and degree of efficiency at a maximum? Research work in this area has brought a good deal of knowledge about basic activities like walking, climbing, carrying a load, weight lifting, cranking, bicycling, etc. A number of practical rules can be learned from this, such as: Work with optimal speed! Lift as little body weight as possible! Use body weight or inertia as contra-force! Never drop on the floor, work pieces such as bricks which have to be piled up again but deliver them at a height of 0.5 m, at least. And further, pack the material in units of at least 15 kp! It should be understood also that the average horizontal distance of transport should be as short as possible. Results of experiments on transport of loads by muscle power show that it is possible for the daily productivity of a man to be doubled by halving the energy consumption for the same pile. From these general rules we obtain many suggestions for mechanization in industry. Knowledge of energy requirement and efficiency is furthermore an important basis for all climatic-physiological calculations.

(c) What is the tolerable amount of daily energy expenditure? Although it was worthwhile transferring engineering thinking about calculations of energy requirements or degrees of efficiency to the problems of man at work, some serious errors were made nevertheless. One got the opinion that suitable energy expenditure would have a certain maximal value for a similar group of people; therefore it would be worthwhile to find out by how much, work in industry or forestry or agriculture exceeds this value. It was an error to think that each increment of the degree of efficiency would facilitate work production. The almost unlimited endurance of machine capacity was transferred also to man and his work. By evaluating all results and experiences with the highest energy requirements a value of 2000 kcal per 8 hours of work was deduced (Lehmann, 1962).

Engineers became very interested in this figure thinking that the necessity for interruptions in work for energy reasons arises from the fact that the human body, considered over fairly long periods of time, has only about 2000 kcal at its disposal to expend on heavy muscular work when using large groups of muscles. An increased output could be covered only with difficulty by the absorption of food and is scarcely found to be exceeded even in practical industrial investigations. On the basis of this daily limit of tolerable energy transformation, the work-free time can be calculated for those operations whose energy transformation exceeds this limit (REFA, 1958). This is to be allotted in the work time in order that 2000 kcal/shift shall not be exceeded. From more recent investigation we know (Rohmert, 1962; Gupta and Rohmert, 1964), however, that keeping to this limit of the daily transformation of energy does not in fact ensure that each prolonged work period is free from fatigue. Accordingly, the allowances calculated for limiting the daily energy transformation should not be described as relaxation allowances.

The decisive factor for the tolerability of muscular work is adequate coverage of the oxygen consumption of the muscles throughout the work time. It is not surprising therefore that at no time did static muscular work fit into the concept of a maximal tolerable limit of energy expenditure. Everywhere in each professional activity, static muscular contractions are involved, which cause muscular fatigue even with very low energy expenditure. To manage this difficulty, work physiology in the past dealt with static muscular load in the same way as with mental load: static muscular work was excluded from practical considerations. It took, furthermore, 50 years to complete this (Monod, 1956; Rohmert, 1960; Scherrer and Monod, 1960).

With regard to tolerable work intensity work physiology was introduced to the definition of Endurance Limit (E.L.) by Müller and his colleagues (Karrasch and Müller, 1951; Müller, 1961). E.L. is a physiological definition which characterizes the ability of the human body to bring different inner balances during muscular work into the highest possible 'steady state' of muscular work. E.L. can be expressed in terms of endurance time, energy expenditure, pulse rate, or other physiological terms. After numerous investigations, the behaviour of the pulse rate in the course of the working and resting periods of the day has proved to be the safest measure for fulfilling the requirement of E.L. From investigations of pulse rate we know that fatigue and tolerable work intensity are not linked unconditionally to the limit of energy expenditure of 2000 kcal/day. Efficiency is almost the same in bicycling (back, legs, and feet) and pedalling (shoulders, arms, and hands), but the mass of the working muscles is three times higher in bicycling, therefore we find three times higher work in terms of physics or in terms of energy expenditure. Similar muscle masses are used in pedalling and shovelling. Although efficiency is different, tolerable energy expenditure is the same when shovelling with a light shovel with small load and high speed of arm movements, while in using a heavy shovel with a greater load and fewer throws a high static load of muscles is involved. Decrease of blood flow through these muscles diminishes work in terms of physics or in terms of energy expenditure.

The examples show three main influences on tolerable work intensity for man: amount of working muscle mass, type of work (static or dynamic muscular work), and speed of movements. In a practical working situation one cannot analyse how heavy muscles have to work statically or dynamically. Knowledge of this is necessary, however, in order to evaluate whether blood flow is sufficient or not. However, neither muscle mass nor blood flow can be measured directly or determined in practical work situations. Therefore the idea of Lavoisier is not suitable for the evaluation of work intensity. Only by analysing the physiological conditions of muscular fatigue and recovery can we deduce tolerable work intensities.

Among all the physiological criteria taken into account as a measure of fatigue the behaviour of pulse rates takes an outstanding place. Christensen (1931), Asmussen *et al.* (1939), Karrasch and Müller (1951), Brouha (1960), Scherrer and Monod (1960), Rohmert (1960; 1962) and others, have studied the correlations between muscular fatigue and pulse rate. Figure 11.12 shows the main energy expenditure differences which are important in physiological evaluation. It shows the non-linear relation between energy expenditure and pulse frequency caused by the type of work, speed of movements, and amount of working muscle mass. There is a further non-linear influence of the duration of work which is not shown in the diagram. By also regarding working time, each curve of Figure 11.12 would have several parameters, which show a steeper increase in pulse rate the longer the work is carried out.

It is still difficult to split up the total stress on a worker, as shown by an increase of pulse rate, into the individual workload components which cause

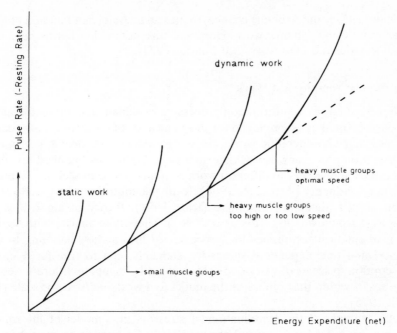

FIGURE 11.12. Pulse rate and energy expenditure in muscular work

the increase (see Rutenfranz *et al.*, 1971). Since the type of workload (activity, environmental or social conditions, etc.), the type of work (heavy dynamic, unilateral dynamic, etc.), and the share of these in the entire work (non-physical components) all have a part to play, it is difficult to obtain any information about the strain on a single muscle from the pulse rate. However, monitoring the electrical discharges (action potentials) which accompany muscular contraction provides a direct measure of the relative strain on a single muscle. A recording of these action potentials in muscles is called an electromyogram and the technique is known as electromyography. The registered electromyogram is transformed into numerical values of the electrical activity by integration, to obtain a criterion for the assessment of muscular strain. For static muscular work it has been shown (see, for instance, Laurig, 1970) that there are reproducible relationships between electrical activity and muscular strength as measured isometrically. It can also be shown that, like pulse rate, where the workload level is constant, electrical activity increases as a function of time when the level of the workload exceeds the endurance threshold, and the gradient of this increase rises with the level of workload (see, for example, Rau and Vredenbregt, 1970).

Thus the derived parameter of strain, 'electrical activity', can be used to assess the strain on different groups of muscles in different bodily postures

(Okada, 1972), and to detect changes in muscular strain, as a function of time, during static and dynamic work. However, this method has hardly been used at all in industrial field work (see Laurig, 1974).

(ii) Mainly Non-physical Work

For the analysis of information processing workload, general mathematical or physical models as employed for mechanical or biomechanical approaches to muscular and energetic work, are not available. The diversity of human information processing in working situations emphasizes the need for different model approaches to different work contents. These models are known as information theory (Attneave, 1968), feedback control theory (McRuer and Weir, 1969), theory of automata (Klix, 1971), theory of algorithms and graphs (Ljapunow, 1962; Klix, et al., 1963). They try to analyse with the help of mathematical techniques the processes of information handling in their logical and time-dependent successive elements, and to transfer from this description to scales of workload. This is done by mapping different descriptive scales within the context of the model to a workload/stressor scale (Luczak, 1975).

An example of the combination of stressors in a model of information processing is feedback control theory. It can be applied to model human behaviour as far as various scales of stressors can be deduced, and the reaction of a human operator to these stressors can be described quantitatively. Continuous signal flow is presupposed in the application of this concept, whereas, for instance, information theory can handle paced and unpaced discrete signal flows. Thus the models of feedback control theory can be applied to types of work such as control and steering tasks. These include information handling of an operator within a man–machine system with defined command signals (trajectory of a flight mission, description of path and speed in a driving task, etc.); disturbance variables (wind, vibrations, etc.); machine characteristics (flight dynamics of an aircraft, manoeuvring characteristics of a ship, longitudinal and lateral dynamics of a car, etc.); and the display configuration and lay-out of the control element. From these elements a man–machine model in terms of differential equations can be derived which combines the different aforementioned elements that determine workload, to predict a certain performance behaviour of the human operator (see overview in *Human Factors* **19**, 4–5 (1977) (Applications of Control Theory in Human Factors, 1977)).

The difficulty of a control task can be quantified firstly, by the bandwidth (i.e. difference between highest and lowest frequencies) of the command signals in a pursuit tracking situation and of the disturbance variables in a compensatory tracking situation (Durand and Jex, 1962; Etschberger, 1975). Secondly, the dynamics of the controlled systems can be quantified in their stress effect on a human operator, by determining the stability reserve from

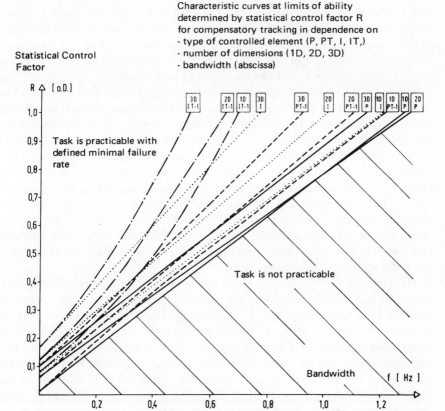

FIGURE 11.13. Limits of ability of human operators as contoller in a feedback control task (after Luczak 1977)

the transfer functions of the respective systems (Taylor and Day, 1961; Smith, 1963; Jex *et al.*, 1966; Leslie and Thompson, 1968). Thirdly, the number of loops under control and their inhomogeneity in bandwidth and system dynamics is important in display and control design. When these elements of external workload are varied in a factorial experiment involving a simulated feedback control task, e.g. with a tracking simulator, a specific dependence of performance on stressors can be found.

On the ordinate of Figure 11.13 the 'statistical control factor', a control theory measure of performance, is drawn (see Etschberger, 1975). The abscissa shows the bandwidth of the disturbance variable; the parameters are the number of loops (1D/2D/3D = 1-/2-/3-dimensional) and the type of the controlled element in control theory terminology. The field of characteristic curves divides the plane of performance within this diagram into a part in which the combination of stressors cannot be handled by a human operator (level of ability), and a part where the task can be fulfilled with minimal failure for a short time. By calculating the amount of variance accounted for in the measurement of performance by the stressors, we find that the bandwidth is the most important factor, the type of controlled element is the second main influence, and the number of loops is not very important if the different loops are homogeneous in bandwidth and controlled element. The values measured for this diagram are based on experiments which lasted only 3 minutes. Taking into account time-series aspects of the performance measurements, we find that the 'statistical control factor' does not remain constant in the short term under defined stressor conditions, but increases as a function of time, at first slightly, later on dramatically up to a value where the human operator as controller only adds noise to the signal flow of the control circuit. The time when the operator passes the limit between the region of stabilizing the circuit and the region of making it more unstable by his effector input, can be taken as maximal endurance. Under this assumption maximal endurance in this information handling task can be quantified as a function of the main stressors (see Figure 11.14).

The abscissa of Figure 11.14 gives the bandwidth of the disturbance variable with maximal endurance on the ordinate, and the type of the controlled element in a single-loop task as parameter. The measured values for the duration of acceptable performance/productivity were approximated by hyperbolic exponential functions. In this field of characteristic curves two important areas can be distinguished: Firstly, for a bandwidth of more than 6 rad/s $\approx$ 1 Hz maximal endurance is nearly independent of the type of the controlled element and is very small, i.e. 3–5 minutes. This is a supplementary result to other experimental findings in the literature, which indicate that the level of ability of a human operator is 'exceeded' beyond 1 Hz. Secondly, for a bandwidth below 1 rad/s maximal endurance increases considerably independently of the controlled element. It seems that even a rather difficult but stable controlled element can be handled for a long period below this limit. The mean asymptotic line to the different curves is approximately 0.5 rad/s, i.e. the level of permanently tolerable workload seems to be reached.

Maximal endurance can be prolonged if sufficient rest allowances are given. Experimentally varying the duration of rest pauses in the aforementioned control task, the difference between values of maximal endurance with and without pauses increases steadily (see Figure 11.15). Contrary to findings on the allocation of rest pauses in muscular workload, the distribution of pauses within the work shift is not very important for the recovery effect, if the pause is given in the period between 50–80% of maximal endurance time under the defined stressor conditions. Similar results were found by Schmidtke (1963), with a dominant effect of the duration in comparison with the distribution of the rest period. Additionally, it could be stated that a relatively short rest period is sufficient for recovery. It seems that the neutral processes of fatigue

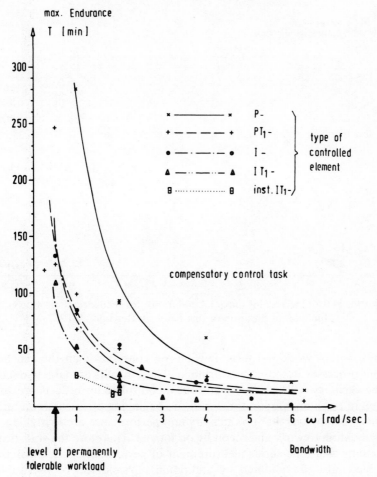

FIGURE 11.14. Maximal endurance as a function of stressor conditions in a single-loop feedback control task (after Luczak 1977). The type of the controlled element is given in control theory terminology. A system to be handled by a human operator can be described by its transfer function, i.e. mostly a differential equation, which caracterizes the behaviour of a technical system (vehicle, ship, aircraft a.s.o.) and thus an aspect of the difficulty of a task. The equations for the input signal x_{in} to output signal x_{out} relationship for the different controlled elements are as follows:

$$P : x_{out}(t) = K x_{in}(t)$$

$$I : x_{out}(t) = K_1 \ x_{in}(t) dt$$

$$PT_1 : T_1 \frac{dx_{out}(t)}{dt} + x_{out}(t) = K x_{in}(t)$$

$$IT_1 : T_1 \frac{dx_{out}(t)}{dt} + x_{out}(t) = K_1 \ x_{in}(t) dt$$

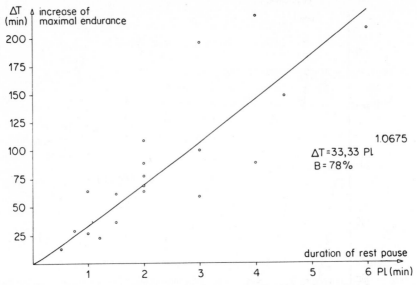

FIGURE 11.15. Increase of maximal endurance for feedback control tasks as a function of duration of rest pauses (after Luczak 1977)

in information workload have fewer time constants than the biochemical fatigue processes in muscular workload. These results are largely dependent on the accuracy with which the statistical control factor reflects processes of fatigue in the human operator. From the beginning of research on fatigue it has become obvious that productivity and performance are firstly dependent on motivation to work and secondly on fatigue. Therefore the statistical control factor as a time series measurement of performance, i.e. a behavioural variable, must be validated by additional physiological or psychophysical measurements to ensure that maximal endurance is not due to a lack of motivation but is an organic fatigue process.

Work motivation has obvious consequences in performance and productivity for self-paced and self-induced tasks. If the stressors of a task are imposed on the working subject without any possibility of the individual varying his work content, a motivational effect can be found in failure rates, quality of production, and maximal endurance. Normally limits of tolerability are not hurt in those cases by high motivation. In tasks which offer degrees of freedom in their operational structure, possible interdependencies of stress effects and motivation are more critical. Limits of tolerability are voluntarily exceeded by the subjects because of motivational incentives given by high work satisfaction. Stressors are not perceived psychophysically to be embarrassing and dangerous, individual health status can be influenced negatively without the normal warning signals.

In both cases of information workload, i.e. either imposed stressor conditions and the risk of overestimating strain, or free choice of stressor conditions and the risk of underestimating strain on behavioural variables, additional variables from psychophysics and physiology should be taken into account. Physiological variables have the advantage that they cannot easily be influenced voluntarily by subjects, whereas psychophysical scales of strain are superimposed by individual decision components, i.e. cost–risk evaluation of the respective subjects (Stevens, 1961; Coombs *et al.*, 1970). Physiological indicators of strain and effort can be measured partly simultaneously to work, partly successively, because of total blocking of sensory or motor functions by the measurement technique. The successive measurement techniques have the disadvantage that an analysis of strain as a time series phenomenon is impossible, and that only the integrative strain over a long period of workload can be evaluated without identifying the risk of instantaneous crossings of limits of intolerable workload or effort.

Physiological indicators should be selective with respect to different types of workload and to time. The more selective a physiological indicator is, the more information it contains for an ergonomic evaluation of different types of strain. Time selectivity means that a variable reacts without great time constants to a variation of workload. Workload selectivity means that a noise ratio caused by simultaneous artefacts and other irrelevant types of stressors is not superimposed on the required signal ratio for the stressor considered. An additional important criterion of a physiological indicator of strain is intra-individual and inter-individual reproductivity/reliability, i.e. the reaction should be homogeneous in kind and type of reaction. If these presuppositions are respected in an evaluation of different strain indicators, only a few measurement techniques remain, because ergonomic measurement techniques must be proven in industrial field situations and not in the isolated conditions of physiological and psychological laboratories.

For the successive measurement of effects of work strain, sensor-oriented methods, for instance flicker fusion frequency (Schmidtke, 1965), motor-oriented methods, for instance tremor (Sälzer, Schreiber and Rohmert, 1973), and biochemical methods are used. This is based on the theory that physiological systems react proportionally or integrally to stress (difficulty and duration of a task), and those reactions are not compensated for after exposure for a short period. Thus a difference between a before and after workload measurement can contain some information on the subject's condition in the reaction to the stressors. One biochemical method, used in ergonomics for the evaluation of mental and emotional strain, is catecholamine secretion (Klimmer *et al.*, 1972). During the neuronal activity concomitant with information processing procedures of a human operator, adrenalin and noradrenalin are secreted from the adrenal medulla. These catecholamines are transported by blood flow to the kidneys and into the urine, where their concentration can be measured. Several tasks, which from the result of work description were different in mental and emotional stress, could be separated after catecholamine measurements (Klimmer *et al.*, 1972).

Methods, which can be applied in ergonomics simultaneous with the working activities of a human operator, are mainly electrophysiological measurements (Venables and Martin, 1967). Their utility rests on their organic selectivity, their time selectivity, and the availability of sophisticated instrumentation suitable for computer processes. From electroencephalographical measurements (Rohracher, 1935) patterns of spontaneous rhythms and evoked potentials have been derived, to obtain information on the sleep–awakeness continuum in supervisory (vigilance) tasks (Haider, 1969), on the separation of different defined stressor conditions (Bartenwerfer, 1960), and on the prediction of blocking, i.e. missed signals in information processing (Böttge, 1972; Holoch, 1972). The complicated application of this method and the considerable noise ratio cause them to be restricted to mainly laboratory oriented investigations. Field research with corresponding and validating results is missing.

Electromyography is used mainly in the analysis of muscular effort (strain), especially static work of isolated muscles (Bigland and Lippold, 1954; Laurig, 1970), and active light dynamic work (Laurig, 1974). By measurement on muscles which do not have a direct function in the production of strength, electromyographic signals contain some information on the activity of motor neurons which correlate with the level of activation of the nervous system (Groll-Knapp, 1969), and with mental and emotional strain in a task. From electro-oculography (Shackel, 1967) visual fixation activity and the frequency of eyelid blinks can be derived. The integrated electro-oculographical signal gives some information on the activity of an operator in a supervisory task, for instance in air-traffic control tasks (Rohmert, 1973), but the filtered blinking frequency seems to be correlated with the level of arousal and activation in control and steering tasks (Haider and Rohmert, 1976).

Electrocardiographical recordings have a diagnostic value for the solution of ergonomic problems, for example R–R intervals, from which heart rate and arrhythmia/heart rate variability can be calculated (see the symposium on heart rate variability published in *Ergonomics*, 16, 1 (1973)). Because heart rate is sensitive primarily to muscular strain, only in situations with high mental and emotional stressors dominating the energetic and effectory stressors is an evaluation of information workload possible (Rohmert, 1973; Rohmert *et al.*, 1973). As soon as heart rate itself does not show a reaction, heart rate variability can give some additional hints on strain, because the decrease in rate correlates with mental load in a variety of information handling tasks.

Single successive as well as single simultaneous measurement techniques suffer from weak correlations with information workload. Coefficients of validity and reliability, stressor and time selectivity, are rather small for all known single-measurement techniques. Therefore a polygraphic measurement concept with a time series registration of different physiological variables seems to be more appropriate to reach a sufficient level of confidence in the evaluation of different stressor conditions relatable to strain and fatigue. When a polygraphic measurement concept is applied, the problem of connecting the different variables in an evaluation procedure arises. A method of evaluation, proposed by Rohmert and Luczak (1973), takes into account time series characteristics of all measured variables. The summary evaluation procedure is based on the theory of destabilization of physical and psychic functions as a function of workload and shift time, as soon as these functional systems are strained above endurance limits. Using results of the aforementioned behavioural (performance) and physiological measurements, fatigue can be identified as time-dependent behaviour, providing functional bottlenecks of the organism are taken into account by a measured variable. Symptoms of fatigue are detected in the measurements by a trend test to verify the destabilization. The detected symptoms in the different measurements cannot be regarded as equally straining for the organism. Following the classification of Schmidtke (1965) for phases of fatigue which follow one another as a function of time under workload above endurance limits, conclusions for degrees of fatigue can be drawn as shown in Figure 11.16.

Firstly disturbances/destabilizations can be identified in the peripheral organic systems which are directly involved in performing the informational task, i.e. normally eye fixation, measured by electrooculograms, and the effector function of the extremities, measured by the appropriate electromyograms. The respective classification is 'degree of fatigue 1'. *Secondly*, as soon as the disturbances/destabilizations reach a level such that they are perceived by the individual, another grade of fatigue is reached. In this phase the mean value of performance is not yet affected, but performance variability may increase. Subjects with sufficient motivation usually try to compensate for the peripheral functional deficits by increased motivational effort. A reaction in central indicators of arousal and activation can be expected, mainly electroencephalographical indicators, electromyographical registrations from muscles not directly involved in the production of strength within the context of the task, heart rate and heart rate variability. The respective classification is 'degree of fatigue 2'. *Thirdly*, performance decreases. Because of disturbances in central processes of integration and activation of motivation this 'degree of fatigue 3' can be called fatigue induced by lack of motivation to utilize capacity. In this phase organic functions not directly affected by the task are simultaneously impaired. The higher degree of fatigue may include the lower level fatigue symptoms.

In support of investigations with this procedure under laboratory conditions on simulators (Haider, 1977), and using idealized feedback control as

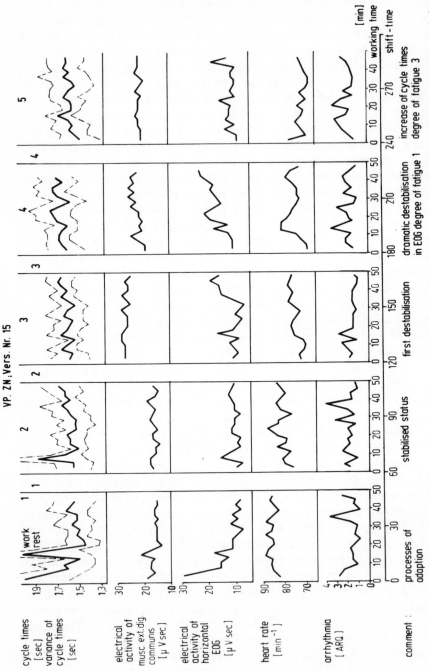

FIGURE 11.16. Successive destablization of different performance and physiological measurements in an unpaced discrete information handling task (field research on letter dotting)

well as paced and unpaced information theory tasks (Luczak, 1977), the
method could be validated in field research on video letter coding (Rohmert
and Luczak, 1978), on inspection of bottles (Rohmert and Luczak, 1974),
and on several industrial mainly sensory-motor tasks (Rohmert, Rutenfranz
and Luczak, 1975b).

6. FITTING THE SUBJECT TO HIS WORK BY TRAINING

Through training the subject is able to increase performance and productivity and simultaneously to decrease strain by adapting his abilities. This is true
predominantly for sensory-motor tasks, which frequently occur in industry.
Most studies on training in sensory-motor performance only use output
criteria to evaluate productivity. By sequential repetitions of the working
cycle (active training), observation of activity of other subjects (observational
training), or mental practice through repeated imagination of the elements of
the working cycle (mental training), a better motor coordination can be
reached which leads to increased performance (Rohmert, Rutenfranz and
Ulich, 1971). Rohmert and Schlaich (1966) found that there was no performance limit in repeating a very simple assembling task (assembling a washer
on a plug) even after four months of repetitions of ca. 1 hour per day (= 1296
assemblings) in 4 subjects (see Figure 11.17). A longer weekend is clearly

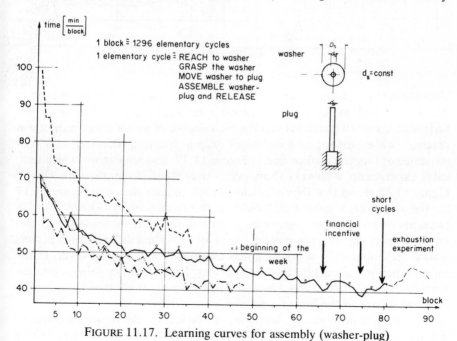

FIGURE 11.17. Learning curves for assembly (washer-plug)

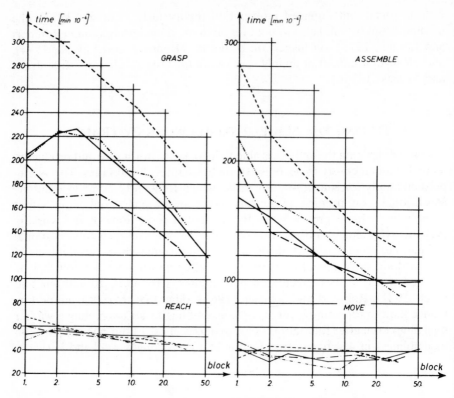

FIGURE 11.18. Learning curves of single motion elements

distinguished (circles in Figure 11.17) by a lower mean performance even in the state of high motor skill. Increasing a financial incentive improves performance about 10 per cent even if a high degree of motor coordination was reached, while performance decreases despite financial incentive as a consequence of fatigue (broken line in Figure 11.17, and long arrow which indicates experiments with very short cycles over small distances of reaching). Figure 11.18 shows that improvement in performance shown in Figure 11.17 for the 4 subjects is gained exclusively in the more sensory-oriented motion elements of grasping and assembling and not all in the motor-oriented elements of reaching and transporting. Also, all individual differences in performance are found only in grasping and assembling and not, however, in the motor functions of reaching and transporting. Thus the major gains in productivity in sensory-motor tasks are achieved by an automation of the informational processes of the human operator.

Evaluation of productivity, however, should include the subjective strain of the operator, i.e. human effort to reach the respective productivity. Taking

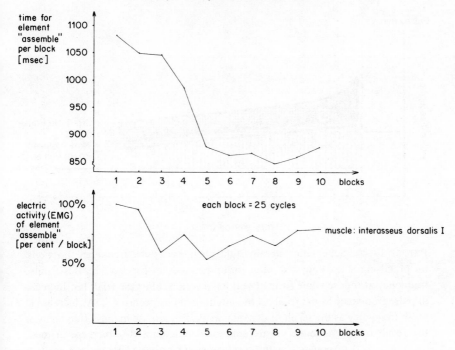

FIGURE 11.19. Simultaneous decrease of cycle times and peripheral physiological strain

into account *peripheral* neuronal processes, quantified by the EMG of the muscle which mainly is involved in the task, a simultaneous decrease of cycle times for the working element 'assemble' and of the electric activity of the muscle can be found (see Figure 11.19).

Even central processes are involved in training procedures. In different tracking experiments, Rutenfranz, Rohmert and Iskander (1971) studied changes in heart rate in relation to the conditions of massed or distributed practice. Figure 11.20 shows heart rate under these conditions while subjects were performing a 60 minute Rotary Pursuit Apparatus Tracking Task. Heart rate is divided into physical and non-physical portions. There is an increasing heart rate due to static load (SA), while the fraction of heart rate due to dynamic work (DA) remains small and constant. A non-physical fraction as the result of psychogenic mainly emotional reactions (P), disappears during the experiments. Also another non-physical fraction is explained as the result of an intentional basic tension (IG) that decreases but does not disappear completely. With respect to the input/output relation in work productivity, i.e. performance per human effort, an additional gain can be demonstrated. Conditions with massed versus interrupted practice (with pauses) proved to

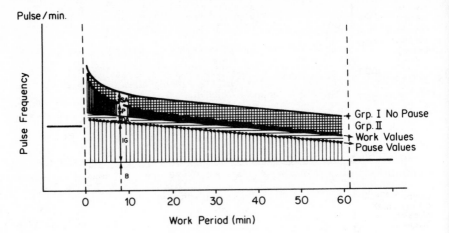

FIGURE 11.20. Schematic diagram of the changes of pulse frequency 'fractions' on practising a tracking task after different kinds of practice. B: Basic pulse frequency at repose while sitting (working position) after the trial. IG: Increase in pulse frequency as the result of the intentional basic tension. DA: Increase in pulse frequency as the result of dynamic work. P: Increase in pulse frequency as the result of psychogenic, mostly emotional reactions. SA: Increase in pulse frequency as the result of static muscle work

be less efficient, as far as gain in performance and physiological processes of strain are concerned.

7. SUMMARY

The process of interaction of the individual worker and his work, i.e. the ergonomic aspect of the problem 'work and productivity', is dealt with in the paper with special reference to suitable work intensity and duration. For this purpose some techniques are first of all considered which are available for appraising what man is doing at work, i.e. tools of job description and analysis. Types of human performance and job demands are derived from models of the division of work between man and machine, their relation to stress and strain is outlined and some criteria for the evaluation of stress and strain are discussed, referring especially to a hierarchical concept for the assessment of human working conditions.

For a comprehensive documentation of single stressors an ergonomic job-description questionnaire is described which contains nearly 400 items on different stressor scales. Suggestions are made for handling the relationship between different types of stressors by appropriate physical or physiological, informational, or neuronal models.

For mainly physical work the biomechanical analysis of work movements is introduced, their relationship to energy consumption is outlined, and suitable values of energy expenditure for different stressor configurations are discussed. This discussion leads to pulse frequency registrations as the basis for limits of tolerable work intensity and duration for heavy dynamic and static work, as well as for the physiological conditions of muscular fatigue and recovery. Considering isolated muscular reactions, the technique of electromyographical recording is introduced for static and light dynamic work.

For mainly non-physical work, diverse models of information processing are mentioned. For example, feedback control theory is chosen to demonstrate the modelling of human behaviour with respect to a special information processing working situation. Stressors, described in control theory terms, are related to predictions of human performance (level of ability), and duration of the respective task (level of tolerability). Physiological indicators of strain, and their simultaneous or successive reaction to stressor conditions are discussed in the context of working situations, especially catecholamine excretion, tremor, flicker fusion frequency, electroencephalography, electromyography, heart rate and its variability. A method for the detection of symptoms of fatigue in polygraphic time series measurements of these variables is presented, and a classification of degrees of fatigue is discussed.

Training procedures and their effect on increase of performance with simultaneous decrease of physiological peripheral and central indicators of strain for types of sensory-motor tasks are also considered.

8. REFERENCES

Applications of Control Theory in Human Factors (1977). Special Issues, *Human Factors*, **19**, No. 4/5.

Asmussen, E., Christensen, E. H. and Nielsen, M. (1939). Pulsfrequenz und Körperstellung. *Skandinavian Archives of Physiology*, **81**, 190.

Attneave, F. (1968). *Informationtheorie in der Psychologie*. Bern/Stuttgart/Wien: Huber.

Baker, J. D. (1970). Quantitative modelling of human performance. *Ergonomics*, **13**, 645–664.

Bartenwerfer, H. (1960). *Beiträge zum Problem der psychischen Beanspruchung*. Köln-Opladen: Westdeutscher Verlag.

Beishon, R. J. (1967). Problems of task description in process control. In W. T. Singleton and P. Spurgeon (Eds.), *The Human Operator in Complex Systems*. London: Taylor and Francis.

Bigland, B. and Lippold, O. C. (1954). Motor unit activity in the voluntary contraction of human muscle. *Journal of Physiology*, **125**, 322–335.

Birmingham, H. P. and Taylor, F. V. (1961). A design philosophy for man-machine control systems. In H. W. Sinaiko (Ed.), *Selected Papers on Human Factors in the Design and Use of Control Systems*. New York: Dover Publications.

Böttge, H. (1972). *Beitrag zur Theorie und Praxis der Analyse des spontanen Elektroencephalogramms*. München: Dissertation.

Brouha, L. (1960). *Physiology in Industry*. Oxford: Pergamon.

Christensen, E. H. (1931). Beiträge zur Physiologie schwerer körperlicher Arbeit. *Arbeitsphysiologie*, **4**, 453–469.

Christensen, J. M. and Mills, R. G. (1967). What does the operator do in complex systems? *Human Factors*, **9**, 329–340.

Coombs, C. H., Dawes, R. M. and Tversky, A. (1970). *Mathematical Psychology*. Englewood Cliffs: Prentice-Hall.

Durand, T. S. and Jex, H. R. (1962). Handling qualities in single loop tracking tasks: Theory and simulator experiments. *ASD-TDR-62-507, Nov*.

Etschberger, K. (1975). Leistungsfähigkeit und Regelungsverhalten des Menschen bei der Nachführung stochastischer Signale. *Biological Cybernetics*, **17**, 81–98.

Fleishman, E. A. (1975). Taxonomic problems in human performance research. In W. T. Singleton and P. Spurgeon (Eds.), *Measurement of Human Resources*. London: Taylor and Francis.

Groll-Knapp, E. (1969). Die Messung physiologischer Aktivierungsindikatoren. In W. Schönpflug (Ed.), *Methoden der Aktivierungsforschung*. Bern/Stuttgart/Wien: Huber.

Gupta, M. N. and Rohmert, W. (1964). Muscular fatigue during transport of load in the horizontal plane. New Delhi: Ministry of Labour and Employment, Industrial Physiology Division, Report No. 5.

Hackman, J. R. (1970). Tasks and tasks performance in research on stress. In J. E. McGrath, (Ed.), *Social and Psychological Factors in Stress*. New York: Holt, Rinehart and Winston.

Haider, E. (1977). Beurteilung von Belastung und zeitvarianter Beanspruchung des Menschen bei kompensatorischen Regeltätigkeiten. *Fortschritt-Berichte der VDI-Zeitschriften*. Dusseldorf: VDI-Verlag.

Haider, E. and Rohmert, W. (1976). Untersuchungen zur Lidschlußfrequenz bei vierstündiger simulierter Kraftfahrzeugfahrt. *European Journal of Applied Physiology*, **35**, 137–147.

Haider, M. (1969). Elektrophysiologische Indikatoren der Aktiviertheit. In W. Schönpflug, (Ed.), *Methoden der Aktivierungsforschung*. Bern/Stuggart/Wien: Huber.

Holoch, J. (1972). *Wachsamkeitsprognose mittels Computeranalyse des spontanen Elektroenzephalogramms*. München: Dissertation.

International Standard Classification of Occupations (1969). Geneva: International Labor Office.

Jenik, P. (1972). *Biomechanische Analyse ausgewählter Arbeitsbewegungen des Armes*. Berlin/Köln/Frankfurt: Beuth Vertrieb.

Jex, H. R., McDonnell, J. D. and Phatak, A. V. (1966). A critical tracking task for manual control research. *IEEE Transactions on Human Factors in Electronics*, Dec.

Karrasch, K. and Müller, E. A. (1951). Das Verhalten der Pulsfrequenz in der Erholungsperiode nach körperlicher Arbeit. *Arbeitsphysiologie*, **14**, 369–382.

Katsuki, S. (1960. Relative metabolic rate of industrial work in Japan. *Metabolic Rate, Food and Nutrition Committee-Japan*.

Keenan, J. J. (1967). Interactionist models of the variety of human performance in complex work systems. *Annals of Reliability and Maintainability*, **6**, 76–85.

Kendrick, P. (1969). Analytical training of operators in the process industry. *International Symposium on Man Machine Systems*. Vol. 1.

Klimmer, F., Aulmann, H. and Rutenfranz, J. (1972). Catecholaminausscheidung im Urin bei emotional und mental belastenden Tätigkeiten im Flugverkehrskontroldienst. *Internationales Archiv für Arbeitsmedizin*, **30**, 65–80.

Klix, F. (1971). *Information und Verhalten*. Bern/Stuttgart/Wien: Huber.

Klix, F., Neumann, J., Seeber, A. and Sydrow H. (1963). Die algorithmische Beschreibung des Lösungsprinzips einer Denkanforderung. *Zeitschrift für Psychologie*, **168**, 1–2.

Kraut, H. and Keller, W. (1961). Arbeit und Ernährung. In *Handbuch der gesamten Arbeitsmedizin, Vol. 1. Arbeitsphysiologie.* Berlin/München/Wien: Urban and Schwarzenberg.

Krivohlavy, J. (1966). Möglichkeiten der Anwendung von algorithmischen Analysen. In F. Klix *et al.* (Ed.), *Ingenieurpsychologie und Volkswirtschaft.* Berlin: VEB Deutscher Verlag der Wissenschaften.

Landau, K., Luczak, H. and Rohmert, W. (1976). Clusteranalytische Untersuchungen zum Arbeitswissenschaftlichen Erhebungsbogen zur Tätigkeitsanalyse – AET. *Z. f. Zeitschrift für Arbeitswissenschaft*, **30**, 31–39.

Laurig, W. (1970). *Elektromyographie als arbeitswissenschaftliche Untersuchungsmethode zur Beurteilung von statischer Muskelarbeit.* Berlin/Köln/Frankfurt: Beuth-Vertrieb.

Laurig, W. (1974). *Beurteilung einseitig dynamischer Muskelarbeit.* Berlin/Köln/Frankfurt: Beuth-Vertrieb.

Lehmann, G. (1962). *Praktische Arbeitsphysiologie.* Stuggart: Thieme.

Leslie, J. M. and Thompson, D. A. (1968). Human frequency response as a function of visual feedback delay. *Human Factors*, **10**, 67–78.

Ljapunow, A. A. (1962). *Probleme der Kybernetik.* Vol. 1 and 3. Berlin: Akademie Verlag.

Luczak, H. (1975). Untersuchungen informatorischer Belastung und Beanspruchung des Menschen. *Fortschritts-Berichte der VDI-Zeitschriften*, Reihe 10. Düsseldorf: VDI-Verlag.

Luczak, H. (1977). *Arbeitswissenschaftliche Untersuchungen von maximaler Arbeitsdauer und Erholungszeiten bei informatorisch-mentaler Arbeit nach dem Kanal- und Regler-Mensch-Modell sowie superponierten Belastungen am Beispiel Hitzearbeit.* Darmstadt: Habilitationsschrift.

Luczak, H., Landau, K. and Rohmert, W. (1976). Faktorenanalytishe Untersuchungen zum Arbeitswissenshaftlichen Erhebungsbogen zur Tätigkeitsanalyse – AET. *Zeitschrift für Arbeitswissenschaft*, **30**, 22–30.

McCormick, E. J. (1976). Job and task analysis. In M. D. Dunette (Ed.), *Handbook of Industrial and Organizational Psychology.* Chicago: Rand McNally.

McRuer, D. T. and Weir, D. H. (1969). Theory of manual vehicular control. *Ergonomics*, **12**, 599–633.

Miller, R. B. (1967). Task taxonomy: science or technology? In W. T. Singleton and P. Spurgeon (Eds.), *The Human Operator in Complex Systems.* London: Taylor and Francis.

Monod, H. (1956). *Contribution á l'étude du travail statique.* Paris: Institut National de Sécurité.

Müller, E. A (1961). Die physische Ermüdung, In *Handbuch der gesamten Arbeitsmedizin, Vol. 1. Arbeitsphysiologie.* Berlin/München/Wien: Urban und Schwarzenberg.

Okada, M. (1972). An electromyographic estimation of the relative muscular load in different human postures. *Journal of Human Ergology*, **1**, 75–93.

Passmore, R. and Durnin, J. V. G. A. (1967). *Energy, Work and Leisure.* London: Heinemann.

Rau, G. and Vredenbregt, J. (1970). The electromyogram and the force during static muscular contractions. Institute for Perception, Onderzock, Eindhoven, Annual Progress Report 5, 174–178.

REFA (1958). *Das REFA-Buch, Part 2, Zeitvorgabe.* München: Hanser.

REFA (1971). *Methodenlehre des Arbeitsstudiums, Part 1, Grundlagen.* München: Hanser.

Rohmert, W. (1960). *Statische Haltearbeit des Menschen.* Berlin/Köln/Frankfurt: Beuth-Vertrieb.

Rohmert, W. (1962). *Untersuchungen über Muskelermüdung und Arbeitsgestaltung.* Berling/Köln/Frankfurt: Beuth-Vertrieb.

Rohmert, W. (1973). *Psychophysische Belastung und Beanspruchung von Fluglotsen.* Berlin/Köln/Frankfurt: Beuth-Vertrieb.

Rohmert, W., Laurig, W., Philipp, U. and Luczak, H. (1973). Heart rate variability and work load measurement. *Ergonomics*, **16**, 33–44.

Rohmert, W. and Luczak, H. (1973). Zur ergonomischen Beurteilung informatorischer Arbeit. *Internationale Zeitschrift für Angewannte Physiologie*, **31**, 209–229.

Rohmert, W. and Luczak, H. (1974). Détermination de la charge de travail sur le terrain: evaluation et aménagement d'une tâche d'inspection. *Le Travail Humain*, **37**, 147–164.

Rohmert, W. and Luczak, H. (1978). Ergonomics in the design and evaluation of postal video-letter-coding. *Applied Ergonomics*, in print.

Rohmert, W., Luczak, H. and Landau, K. (1975a). Arbeitswissenschaftlicher Erhebungsbogen zur Tätigkeitsanalyse – AET. *Zeitschrift für Arbeitswissenschaft*, **29**, 199–207.

Rohmert, W., Rutenfranz, J. and Luczak, H. (1975b). *Arbeitswissenschaftliche Beurteilung der Belastung und Beanspruchung an unterschiedlichen industriellen Arbeitsplätzen.* Bonn: Bundesminster für Arbeit und Sozialordnung.

Rohmert, W., Rutenfranz, J., and Ulich, E. (1971). *Untersuchungen über das Anlernen sensumotorischer Fertigkeiten.* Frankfurt: Europäische Verlagsanstalt.

Rohmert, W. and Schlaich, K. (1966). Learning of complex manual tasks. *International Journal of Production Research*, **5**, 137–145.

Rohracher, A. (1935). Die gehirnelektrischen Erscheinungen bei geistiger Arbeit. *Zeitschrift für Psychologie*, **136**, 308–324.

Rutenfranz, J., Rohmert, W. and Iskander, A. (1971). Über das Verhalten der Pulsfrequenz während des Erlernens sensomotorischer Fertigkeiten unter besonderer Berücksichtigung der Pausenwirkung. *Internationale Zeitschrift für Angewannte Physiologie*, **29**, 101–118.

Sälzer, M., Schreiber, H. J. and Rohmert, W. (1973). Tremor und Arbeitssicherheit — Eine Dokumentation und Systematisierung der Literatur. Dortmund: Forschungsbericht Nr. 103 der Bundesanstalt für Arbeitsschutz und Unfallforschung.

Scherrer, J. and Monod, H. (1960). Le travail musculaire iocale et la fatigue chez l'homme. *Journal de Physiologie*, **52**, 419–501.

Schmidtke, H. (1963). Untersuchungen über den Erholungszeitbedarf bei psychischer beanspruchender Tätigkeit. In REFA (Ed.), *Arbeitsstudien heute und morgen.* Berlin/Köln/Frankfurt: Beuth-Vertrieb.

Schmidtke, H. (1965). *Die Ermüdung.* Bern/Stuttgart: Huber.

Shackel, B. (1967). Eye movement recording by electrooculography. In P. H. Venables and I. Martin (Eds.), *A Manual of Psychophysiological Methods.* Amsterdam: North-Holland.

Smith, R. H. (1963). On the limits of manual control. *IEEE Transactions on Human Factors in Electronics.* Sept., 56–59.

Spitzer, H. and Hettinger, Th. (1964). *Tafeln für den Kalorienumsatz bei körperlicher Arbeit.* Berlin/Köln/Frankfurt: Beuth-Vertrieb.

Stevens, S. S. (1961). The psychophysics of sensory function. In W. A. Rosenblith (Ed.), *Sensory Communication*. Cambridge, Mass.: MIT Press.

Stier, F. (1959). Die Geschwindigkeit von Armbewegungen. *Internationale Zeitschrift für Angewannte Physiologie*, **18**, 82.

Taylor, L. W. and Day, R. E. (1961). Flight controllability limits and related human transfer functions as determined from simulator and flight tests. *NASA-IND-D-746*.

Venables, P. H. and Martin, I. (1967). *A Manual of Psychophysiological Methods*. North-Holland, Amsterdam.

Welford, A. T. (1965). Performance, biological mechanism and age: a theoretical sketch. In A. T. Welford and J. E. Birren (Eds.), *Behavior Ageing and the Nervous System*. Springfield Ill.: C. C. Thomas.

Work Performed Manual (1959). Washington: U.S. Department of Labour.

Stress Vulnerability in Psychopathology

Chapter 12

Information Processing Aspects of Neurotic Anxiety and the Schizophrenias

VERNON HAMILTON

1. Introduction
2. Some Basic Concepts
    (i) Neurotic anxiety
    (ii) The Schizophrenias
3. Towards an Information Processing Model of Neurotic Anxiety
    (i) Introduction
    (ii) Mediating Processes in Cognitive Development
    (iii) Anxiety as Aversive and Competing Information
    (iv) The Utility of the Physiological Arousal Model
    (v) Stimulus and Response Uncertainty, and Anxiety
    (vi) Predictions from Model and Some Experimental Results
4. Towards an Information Processing Model of the Schizophrenias
    (i) Introduction
    (ii) Development of Deviant and Unadaptive Cognitive Structures
    (iii) Retrospective and Predictive Implications of Model
    (iv) Postcript on Subtypes
5. Concluding Comment
6. References

1. INTRODUCTION

A volume on human stress and cognition would be incomplete without reference to the ten or twelve per cent of the unselected population who are unable to lead a life free from severe strain and the incapacities associated with it. In this chapter, therefore, and in the next one, we shall consider neurotic anxiety states and the schizophrenias as extreme examples of the effects of stressors on behaviour. The present chapter, however, will be entirely devoted to a *cognitive* analysis of neurotic anxiety and schizophrenia and will refer only peripherally to the role of physiological and pharmacological stressors. The one exception will be a critical assessment of the role of arousal in behaviour disorders.

Consistent with the formulations which I presented in Chapter 3 on 'Personality and Stress', my analysis of the antecedents of incapacity or breakdown will be in terms of cognitive determinants, of the inadequacies of adaptive cognitive coping and defensive structures, and of the role of developmental experience in cognitive vulnerability.

These antecedents will be interpreted as actual or potential stressors, and the information processing load engendered by them will be interpreted as strain. Strain will be interpreted as the general determinant of abnormal behaviour, behaviour which fails to satisfy the need for freedom from anxiety, psychotherapeutic support, chemotherapy, or custodial care.

The unusual plan of discussing anxiety and schizophrenic disorders under one heading will be defended in subsequent pages by a model derived from experimental work with normally and neurotically anxious children and adults, and from experimental and applied studies of chronic schizophrenic men. After discussing some cognitive processing deficits found in association with neurotic anxiety, I shall present an information processing interpretation of neurotic deficit. This will constitute an elaboration of an information processing model of anxiety which has now gone through several modifying stages (Hamilton, 1972a; 1975; 1976a; 1976b). I shall then discuss some cognitive processing deficits in schizophrenia. Finally, and with reference to developmental antecedents, I shall apply the information processing model of anxiety to schizophrenic behaviour in an experimental and a natural setting. The proposition is that anxiety may be the most important single factor in the development of schizophrenic conditions. This informational anxiety model is an attempt to account for the overall behavioural improvement of chronic schizophrenics participating in an industrial rehabilitation programme (Hamilton and Salmon, 1962; Hamilton, 1963b; Hamilton, 1966), in whose lives nothing changed prior to normal re-employment except the information processing demands of industrial tasks carried out in a benevolent, anxiety-reducing therapeutic workshop setting.

Any attempt, such as the present one, to advance cognitive-developmental hypotheses in the explanation of adult disorders has to overcome the semantic and conceptual problems presented by the procedures and nomenclature of clinical child psychiatry. These are well illustrated in many psychiatric textbooks (e.g. Howells, 1965; Slater and Roth, 1969), and convey the importance of 'diagnosis' on the basis of a methodical application of structured case history taking. The summary assessment of type and causation of abnormality may or may not be supported by 'psychological test' data containing evidence of levels of types of intelligence, of educational achievement, and to a lesser or greater degree interpretations of responses to 'projective' stimuli. These are gross and generally unhelpful data for the assessment of predictive validity, and particularly for the isolation of critical cognitive parameters in the development of behaviour disorders.

The problem of low reliability of predictions from early childhood behaviour are squarely faced by the investigators of the New York 'temperament' studies (e.g. Rutter *et al.*, 1964; Chess, Thomas and Birch, 1968). The categories of child reactivity which were phenomenologically assessed were more analytic than those of the St. Louis longitudinal study (O'Neal and Robins, 1958), but contain only observational validity checks. The long-term effects of negative mood, intensity, irregularity and non-adaptability, and their interaction assessed in infancy and before the onset of overt symptoms, are difficult to assess. It is likely, however, that these characteristics play a substantial role in the child's general capacity to adapt to and cope with environmental demands (Rutter, 1972).

The difficulties encountered in the selection of relevant and valid parameters in the classification of abnormality are not confined to longitudinal studies commencing in infancy. They are present in any study or theory which is exclusively dependent on a very small number of, or even single, gross dimensions of measured behaviour on which a statistically infrequent score defines abnormality. Thus a high score on tests of 'manifest anxiety', 'extraversion', or 'neuroticism', even well within the range of scores of clinically identified diagnostic groups, is a quite insufficient criterion of general behavioural abnormality. Furthermore, neither single-factor scores, nor positions in bi- or tri-factorial space, necessarily provide either relevant or valid criteria. Descriptions of abnormal behaviour and processes depend for their power, their theoretical as well as therapeutic relevance, on the specificity of the critical variables. It is inadequate to designate a given behaviour by referring to, say, subjective attentional preoccupation. This is a normal state of many people on many occasions. A more appropriate designation would be based on *frequency, duration, intensity, periodicity,* and *content,* and particularly on the nature of external, antecedent events which in a systematic investigation can be shown to be related to other indices of abnormality.

2. SOME BASIC CONCEPTS

(i) Neurotic Anxiety

Past shortcomings in the reliability and validity of diagnostic classifying procedures, and the slow development of sophisticated techniques and methods in educational psychology and child psychopathology, may have deprived us so far of really useful concepts of neurosis and of anxiety. Thus we have little knowledge of the attentional strategies of children from pathogenic social backgrounds, their differential patterns of perceptual and conceptual differentiation, or the development of differentially elaborated schemata for types of people, objects, and situations.

My attempt to redefine abnormal behaviour in cognitive processing and processing capacity terms cannot but be influenced by existing theoretical statements of the nature and development of neurotic anxiety. Since there is no shortage of textbooks of Abnormal Psychology, my analysis of the existing concepts will be brief and selective for my own purpose. The two most influential theoretical statements incongruously have been derived from historically opposed systems of explanation: psychodynamic and learning theories. Despite the frequent hostile statements about each other's explanations, there has been little disagreement about the objective signs of pathological anxiety and neurosis. Thus physiological emotional over-arousal in association with cardiovascular and/or gastrointestinal dysfunction; irrational and debilitating fears; intrusions of involuntary rituals and repetitive acts; behaviour inhibition from feelings of helplessness; or inexplicable fainting attacks, amnesia, and sensory or motor incapacities – all, in the absence of organic pathology – have been unanimously regarded as abnormal and neurotic. (The American Psychiatric Association has now recommended in its new *Diagnostic and Statistical Manual – DSM III –* that the term 'neurotic' should be abandoned.) With respect to disorders in which anxiety can be clearly perceived to play a decisive role, apprehension, irritability, tension, indecisiveness through the perception of conflict, and impairment of attention and concentration are the major distinguishing features. The ultimate and agreed criterion is incapacity to lead a normal social and occupational life.

According to the two dominant theoretical positions the sources of neurotic anxiety are found, respectively, in the association between an intense, or intensely experienced, aversive stimulus and a conditioned avoidance response, or in the aversive consequences of motivated behaviour. The latter, by virtue of their verbal, cognitive, symbolic content reflect or restimulate unresolved motivational conflicts and aversive consequences belonging to earlier developmental stages. For learning theorists anxiety is a secondary drive in which a single or several conditioned stimuli operate as signals of danger or aversiveness, whose avoidance is experienced as secondary reinforcement, and whose avoidance habits constitute the neurosis. For psychodynamic theorists anxiety is also a signal, but the *mechanics* of its induction are less important than the reservoir of unresolved conflicts which result in the evaluation of present decision-making as fraught with potential danger. In this respect, the latter approach has been consistently more cognitive than the former, and the psychodynamic interpretation of stressors has been more comprehensive because it could contain the role of physiological as well as cognitive components as integrated as well as additive sources of strain.

While the drive hypothesis of neurotic anxiety has added considerably to knowledge of the physiology of the human energizing system, and while it has yielded a novel therapeutic method for some types of behaviour disorders, it must be considered theoretically inadequate. The major reason for this contention is the failure of the behaviourist model, until quite recently, to regard habits as cognitive structures, and stimuli as events to be interpreted by the analysing system on the basis of existing cognitive structures and schemata.

Existing inadequacies of our concepts of all degress of anxiety could well be due to the historical problems of attempting to distinguish between fear and anxiety, and to theoretical preoccupations with the utility of conditioning paradigms in the explanation of human behaviour. A close reanalysis of these issues is highly desirable and overdue, but must be deferred to another occasion. Statements of the relationship, and the difference and similarity between fear and anxiety are heterogeneous. They range from a somewhat bald acceptance of Hullian postulates in which anxiety is a learned or conditioned form of fear (Yates, 1970), to quasi-definitions that an ability to identify the source of fear requires the label of anxiety for certain types of emotional behaviour, or that one should distinguish between 'tangible and intangible', 'focal and diffuse fears' (Rachman, 1974). In Mowrer's terminology (1947), fear is an emotional response produced by stimuli acting as danger signals in association with incremental reinforcement, and anxiety is the secondary stimulus which leads to the avoidance of the primary danger signals. This outcome is labelled secondary reinforcement because the relief from fear is rewarding. The theory suggests how anxiety responses are acquired and avoided, but it does not address itself to what anxiety is, or why neurotic anxiety should be maintained in the absence of continuing reinforcement. At least one other author suggests that the bulk of human anxiety responses is unconditioned, and that a predisposition to an anxiety response is analogous to a predisposition to experience pain (Costello, 1976). Operant conditioning explanations are appropriately a-theoretical, and inevitably circular: anxiety is a response to a stimulus which preceded another, aversive stimulus, and escape from a punishing stimulus is fear, both defined by observed emotional behaviour (Skinner, 1953).

A fairly recent statement by H. J. Eysenck (1976) attempts to buttress Pavlovian concepts in the explanation of neurotic anxiety and the neurotic paradox. Anxiety fails to extinguish in the absence of an aversive unconditioned stimulus because exposure to conditioned stimuli only enhances conditioned anxiety responses by the processes of incubation and preparedness. This is an interesting model, but for the human neurotic quite untenable without a cognitive conceptualization of its two key processes.

Since neurotic anxiety does not remit even when the person avoids all environmental contact with *conditioned* anxiety stimuli, habituation is prevented, and incrementation must occur as the result of *self-generated stimulation*. If that premise were accepted, Eysenck's model would move very close to psychodynamic views of neurosis, and my own suggestion that anxiety is primarily aversive cognitive structures or schemata.

Motivation theorists in general differentiate between fear and anxiety, partly because of the assumed utility of the Mowrer approach, partly because of their difficulty in distinguishing between anxiety and arousal. Epstein, for example, defines anxiety as unresolved fear, or alternatively as unpleasant and undirected arousal (1972; 1976). The latter statement ignores the fact that arousal associated with anger, frustration, or pain is also unpleasant, and that arousal gains direction only from the cognitive experience that has been previously associated with it. There are two main historical reasons for associating undirected arousal and anxiety: existing emotional definitions of anxiety (all pre-Schachter), and selective interpretations of Freud's discussion of neurotic free-floating anxiety. In his New Introductory Lectures, Freud, however, actually uses the term *expectant* anxiety. This is not object-less anxiety, or physiological arousal usually associated with aversive events, but expectancies that events from a range A – Z previously associated with aversive experience may recur. Free-floating anxiety, therefore, is anticipation of unfavourable events within or outside consciousness for which cognitive structures exist which have acquired certain probabilities of retrieval.

Some probabilistic events with unfavourable outcomes seem to be genetically coded, so that for many species, stimuli of high intensity, sudden onset or change, incongruity, or occurring in response-limiting settings, elicit unlearned avoidance behaviour. It is this evidence which seems to be primarily responsible for the historical distinction between fear and anxiety. There are no good reasons, however, why primary fear cannot be termed primary anxiety, if for no other reason than that even in the so-called primary situations the certainty of aversive outcomes is probabilistic. The customary association between fear and flight does not seem to present an insuperable barrier to this conclusion, since the avoidance behaviour associated with many states of high anxiety has functionally similar goals: to put the safest possible 'distance' between a threat and its source. Therefore, fear and anxiety may be qualitatively different only to the extent that they differ on the quantifiable stimulus dimensions of intensity, suddeness, and temporal-spatial distance, on the response dimensions of amount, intensity, and probability of aversive expectancies, and with respect to the range and complexity of available avoidance strategies. A unitary concept of fear and anxiety is also favoured by McReynolds (1976), but he interprets anxiety as fear. This is more analogous to 'fear of fear', and avoids commenting on the fact that threat and aversiveness are in the first and determining instance the result of cognitive decisions. In this area, the layman may be more correct than the expert when he uses the phrases 'I am afraid of ....' and 'I am afraid *that* .....' to reflect similar feelings and anticipations of outcome.

The distinction between normal and neurotic anxiety becomes difficult if one is searching for philosophical truths rather than pragmatic operationism. In accordance with the latter aim, however, there is general agreement that neurotic anxiety is perceived to be and/or experienced as a handicap which restricts the achievement of realistic personal, occupational, and social goals. This deficiency is accompanied by distress, and in the majority of cases by undesirable and uncontrollable actions and behaviours referred to as symptoms or habits depending on the theoretical orientation of the observer.

(ii) The Schizophrenias

In an area where so much has been written by so many with possibly so little effect, it is necessary to simplify. To consider in detail not only the major theoretical orientations but also the enormous number of individual investigations is impossible for reasons of space. It is not that the variety of evidence is unimportant or irrelevant, but there are very special difficulties – at least at present – in the study of aetiology: no-one has as yet been able to establish that there are valid analogues of any of the schizophrenic subcategories. Moreover, precise details of the precursors and developmental history of this group of disorders are lacking. It is inevitable, therefore, that the majority of studies to date should present findings which are *consequences* of a schizophrenic adaptation to stressors and intolerable strain, rather than valid *determinants*. While this criticism applies equally to the study of severe anxiety, it is less damaging because anxiety is widely experienced, and differences in intensity can be reliably and validly identified. 'Low intensity' schizophrenics leading restricted but otherwise normal lives do not exist. The term schizophrenia should be applied, therefore, only to cases with abnormalities of logical thought; non-thought-disordered schizophrenia is a contradiction of terms.

Although there may be differences of opinion as to the most promising models of the schizophrenias, two groups may be regarded as the most influential: the medical, biochemical, and genetic, and the psychodynamic, sociological, and experimental psychological. The latter may or may not involve information processing theory.

The medical model assumes that any form of schizophrenia is an 'illness' or 'disease' with genetic determination, mediated by biochemical and electrophysiological dysfunctions. A recent authoritative review from the medical point of view by Leonard (1976) correctly points out that improvements in research methodology have diminished logical support for the genetic thesis. This view is shared by Gottesman and Shields (1972) following their review and analysis of a large number of studies, and by Stabenau and Pollin (1967) on the basis of data from 100 monozygotic schizophrenic twins discordant for schizophrenia. Furthermore, the clinical description of schizophrenic deficit by psychiatry lists dominant areas of dysfunction which fall into non-medical psychological areas such as language, memory, perception, thinking, judgment, motivation, personality, social communication (Bleuler, 1968; 1976). This makes the model more psychological than medical. Moreover, deficits in one of these may or may not be related to any one or all of the others, and it is logically fallacious to term widely varying profiles of dysfunction as 'illness' or 'disease', particularly if no single pathogenic agent can be identified, and if quantitative indices can place normal people, neurotics, psychotics, and organics on the same multiple dimensions (Hamilton, 1964; 1966). In other words, the term 'illness' as applied to measles, diabetes, or syphilis should not be extended to hetero-genous functional disorders.

Possible biochemical and electrophysiological dysfunctions in the development and maintenance of schizophrenic psychoses have been recently reviewed (Warburton, 1975; Lader, 1975), and there seems to be little doubt that there are dysfunctions in the biological processes of schizophrenics. This evidence comes from the analysis of corticosteroid metabolism, from 'model psychoses' observed with hallucinogenics, and from evidence of autonomic hyperarousal in acute and chronic schizophrenics. This evidence is fully discussed by my co-editor [see Chapter 13] and I shall select only two points for further comment.

The first of these concerns the possible role of anxiety in the development of a schizophrenic psychosis. I shall argue that anxiety is aversive information in the first instance, that hyperarousal is a secondary consequence of cognitive analysis, and with Mednick (1958), that a positive feedback loop may link these two processes. I shall further argue that irrelevant as well as aversive data stimulated by excess arousal in early childhood will lay the basis for cognitive as well as emotional vulnerability. Where early aversive experience and arousal are severe, optimal, age-appropriate cognitive structures may not develop, and with increasing social demands on the vulnerable person stressors, load and strain will reach a point at which all semblance of rational adaptation disappears and psychotic incongruity takes its place. It is of considerable interest, therefore, to note the degree of similarity of the psychophysiological characteristics of anxiety neurotics and schizophrenics observed by Lader (1975). The two types of patients, he writes, behave similarly to a greater or lesser extent in lack of reactivity, slowness to adapt and habituate, and poor stimulus discrimination (p. 185).

The second comment to be made, which is also supported by Lader, is that psychophysiological responses follow upon cognitive analysis and do not in themselves determine the *content* of basic cognitive data, unless these data were themselves encoded under conditions of high arousal. These two points appear to me to be important to emphasize because they contribute to the conclusion that for the present the group of medical, biological, and genetic models has been unable to state an explanatory basis for perceptual/conceptual incongruity, and bizarre and deteriorated behaviour.

Fundamental explanations are also lacking in sociological approaches. The original findings of the relationship between low socioeconomic group (S.E.G.) membership and the incidence and prevalence of the schizophrenias (Hollingshead and Redlich, 1958; Goldberg and Morrison, 1963), still apply. The effects of low S.E.G. have been extended, however, to all types of behavioural abnormalities (Dohrenwend and Dohrenwend, 1969; Brown *et al.*, 1975), with some provisos recently discussed by Rutter and Madge (1976). The latter authors are unable to explain the meaning of this association (p. 214). In the absence of any degree of reductionism which would hand the responsibility of investigation to others, sociologists and psychiatrists will inevitably experience incompetence from what is a superficial level of enquiry. The 'social drift' answer to the S.E.G. 'cause', also now seems to be invalid in view of Brown *et al.'s* (1975) findings of the greater number of stressors in the lower social groups.

The nature of these stressors has been very ably summarized by Kohn (1976). His deduction from an anlysis of more than 50 studies carried out in different countries and cultures leads him to an interactional model of genetics, stress, and social class. In this, limited conception of social reality, social power, and competence in utilizing resources, supply the sufficiency criterion for the development of schizophrenia. However speculative this deduction, it plausibly relates the experience of stressors to feelings of incompetence, to helplessness, and to fearfulness and distrust of forces to which the person can only respond reluctantly by conformity. What we have here, I would argue, is a first cognitive-sociological explanation of social stressors and strain, and of the relationship between anxiety and relative cognitive incompetence. It supplies a new reason for the established relationship between low S.E.G. and average to below average intelligence, without the additional evidence, however, to justify a general statement concerning the relationship between intelligence and schizophrenic psychopathology.

Psychodynamic formulations of the nature and the development of the schizophrenias have deservedly attracted strong criticisms of their terminology, their processes and their non-rigorous deductions. It is certainly true that these formulations have never achieved the level of internal coherence which characterized statements about anxiety and neurosis. The question here really seems to be a fundamental one for the scientist: dare he ignore badly phrased speculations about unobservable events which contain elements of self-evidence or plausibility? These two positive qualities probably apply to claims that schizophrenics live in a world of phantasy, that they construct for themselves a pseudo-community, that their category boundaries for self, people, objects, and situations are fragile, permeable, or non-existent (Blatt and Wild, 1976), that early parent–child communication plays a substantial role in abnormal cognitive development (Bateson *et al.*, 1956), and that primary motives and social anxieties are probably the most pathological and influential factors in schizophrenics' inadequate structuring and experience of reality (Holt, 1967). Of additional importance in any analysis of the role of stressors and strain in behaviour disorders should be the fact that process schizophrenia has its peak age of onset during and towards the end of adolescence when many new and difficult role-playing demands have to be adaptively met.

At the lowest level of evaluation, psychodynamic hypotheses are developmentally oriented and cognitive (Arieti, 1955), and from Freud onwards have never excluded a necessary role for genetic and psychophysiological vulnerability. Their major idiosyncrasy lies in their statements about the content of schizophrenogenic or schizophrenic cognitive structures. The postulated function of reality-remote associations in the control of anxiety, which paradoxically it does not achieve, is said to account in schizophrenics for the lack of a coherent representation of the external world. This determines their inability for social interaction through communication, their inconsistency, and their lack of emotional control.

Probably the most important contribution of psychodynamic theorizing has been the impetus it has given to psychological studies of the role of socialization in the development of schizophrenic psychosis. Most of these were conceived prior to the new, rigorous, methodological influences associated with cognitive processing analyses of stimuli, their registration, encoding, and retrievability. Psychodynamic predictions are difficult to verify, therefore, because they are phrased in terms of *inferences* about intra-familial communication and role-playing goals whose stimulus properties are only grossly defined. They include assessments of the personality characteristics and concept formation abilities of patients' parents, of the influence of paralogical modes of thought and communication in the family setting ('transmission of irrationality'), and of intra-parental disharmony of 'schism' or 'skew' affecting the distribution of dominant and dependent, sex-appropriate role playing (Wynne and Singer, 1963a; 1963b; Lidz *et al.*, 1965). Wynne has also emphasized the rigidity of role structures in the families of schizophrenics, and evidence of the denial of emotions in intra-familiar communication. The Bateson *et al.* (1956) 'double-bind' hypothesis belongs to this set of social/environmental 'transactional style' variables, anchored largely in assumptions about unconscious processes in patients and their families, which propose a set of complex conflicts acting as stressors, and to which schizophrenic incongruity and withdrawal reflect one particular type of solution (Singer and Wynne, 1965a; 1965b; Alanen, 1976).

There are many difficulties attached to these hypotheses. Projective techniques used in isolation possess dubious validity; family interaction assessments suffer from the presence of the investigator; and thought disorder in parents of schizophrenics not themselves diagnosed, as patients or as requiring treatment, may be due to anxiety over their pathological offspring (Jacob, 1975; Goldstein and Rodnick, 1975; Schopler and Loftin, 1969). Nevertheless, in view of the admitted heterogeneity of the schizophrenic group of disorders, and the practical and methodological difficulties of ascertaining psychotic thinking and diagnosing schizophrenia, it would seem premature to exclude consideration of issues which are difficult to substantiate, but seem to be plausible contributors to a comprehensive theory. Evidence continues to accumulate that disturbed parents and anxiety in their offspring contribute to risk for schizophrenia (Jones *et al.*, 1977), and to lowered cognitive development in 'at-risk' children (Gamer *et al.*, 1976). If anxiety is also still present in the long-term hospitalized schizophrenic (Steingart *et al.*, 1976), it is pertinent to enquire about the role of anxiety in schizophrenia, and about the role of socialization and social interaction experiences in the development of anxiety and of schizophrenic disorders. It seems to be entirely unproductive to engage in arguments which respectively attempt to ignore or down-grade evidence from familial or from genetic/adoption studies in order to sustain *unilateral* hypotheses (Lidz, 1976; Kety *et al.*, 1976; Gottesman and Shields, 1976). None of the protagonists has at his disposal reliable and valid criteria of schizophrenia, and certainly not sufficiently fine-grain measures of cognitive deficit which are specific to this nosological category (see also Chapman and Chapman, 1975).

3.   TOWARDS AN INFORMATION PROCESSING MODEL OF NEUROTIC ANXIETY

(i) Introduction

A great deal more effort and financial support has been expended on the study of psychotic behaviour disorder during recent years than on research into neurosis (Segal *et al.*, 1975). Apart from the much greater number of neurotic anxiety cases in the general population, this uneven division of work is surprising because neurosis is relatively less complicated than any of the schizophrenias, and neurotic patients yield far more reliable data. A recent N.I.M.H. Report states that 'research on neurosis has been fragmentary' (Segal *et al.*, 1975, p. 187). Whether one agrees with this statement, particularly in relation to evidence of the role of learning principles, or not, it seems to be the case that there is no comprehensive agreed statement of why people become neurotic, why they exhibit a variety of neurotic symptoms, or even why anxiety impairs performance on tasks which are not the objective of anxiety.

There are many good reasons for the lack of satisfactory theory here. My suggestions concerning an information processing analysis of strain ('stress') in Chapter 3 lead me to conclude that the demonstrations of multivariateness have not been logically utilized. Situational complexity in association with a subjective anticipation of aversive events, danger or threats (which, of course, partly define environmental complexity), represent a given level of demand on the adaptive processing system of the person. This load may contain contributions from threats of social rejection, injury to self-esteem, of pain, or of more indirect ambiguous threats as suggested, for example, by Zuckerman (1976) in a recent study. All these stimuli may have acquired stressor implications through some learning contingency or other, without thereby clarifying the issues of neurotic collapse. Nothing better could be expected, however, from theoretical efforts which regard responding as a simple linear programme. This notion does not seem to bear any relationship to the picture of distress, despair, and panic which in the acute stage characterize the anxiety neurotic's failure to cope with and control his interaction with people, objects, and situations. It is 'all too much' for him, we are told, and so quite unintentionally we are presented with a possible quantitative approach to the issue.

The legitimate question of what defines excess here can be answered briefly at this stage. I shall argue that neurotic anxiety is *excessive aversive and/or threatening information*. This information resides in cognitive data which encode in schemata an individual's expectancies and anticipations of pain, rejection, isolation, and personal incompetence. It resides in conflicts over classifying stimuli as to their potential threat, in continuous uncertainty over stimulus meaning and response adequacy, and in data-handling strategies which grossly defend but do not adaptively solve a mixture of semi-realistic and spurious problems. The structure of aversive schemata, and their role in analysing stimulus input is analogous to the function of schemata in remembering (Bartlett, 1932; Neisser, 1967), and in perceiving (Vernon, 1955). They provide a relatively coherent and consistent predisposition to apply threat-oriented inferences and search processes in the analysis of the environment. This predisposition has a strong developmental foundation.

(ii) Mediating Processes in Cognitive Development

Any developmental model of cognition must refer to at least three general mediating relationships which take account of the multidimensional stimuli which operate in the child-rearing settings:

(a) that between the socialization strategies and personality characteristics of parents and the development of children's personality and motivational structures;

(b) that between the verbal, object and situational stimulus content of children's early environment, and the subsequent establishment and use of cognitive skills and structures reflecting it; and

(c) that between children's personality and motivation as influenced by caretaker characteristics, and the children's cognitive skill and power.

All these have been reviewed in some detail elsewhere (Hamilton, 1976a).

For example, one of the rather better controlled studies (Baumrind, 1967) on 3–4 year olds show that child control, demands for age-appropriate behaviour, with clarity of parental communication and warm affectionate support, are associated in the children with effectiveness of reinforcing agents, self-assertiveness and affiliation, self-reliance, conformity, high aspirations, and buoyant behaviour. Where the parental characteristics deviate from this optimal level, child characteristics tended towards the dyphasic (anxious, unhappy, angry, obstructive) and poor peer relationships, or towards dependence and immaturity. These differences in habitual and characteristic modes of responding and of seeking goals, have plausibly predictable effects on cognitive development.

The second mediating relationship relates to the cognitive effects of environmental stimulus richness. The effects of unstimulating socialization on cognitive development and capacity have been amply illustrated by the particapants of the Iowa and Fels Research Institute Studies, the Berkeley Growth Studies, as well as by British work on retardation (e.g. Clarke and Clarke, 1974). Although the term deprivation which has tended to be applied here appears to be insufficiently analytic, the relationship is generally regarded as confirmed. A warning to over-confidence is sounded, however, by e.g. Wachs, Uzgiris and Hunt (1971), Tulkin and Kagan (1972), and Cohen, Glass and Singer (1973). Amount of stimulation from radio, TV, street noise, frequent visits to and from neighbours, and intrusive verbalizations not initiated by the child, appears to reduce the quality of consequent cognitive skills.

It would appear that the interaction between children's so-called non-cognitive and their cognitive processes is the most completely documented interaction. Thus we have evidence from infancy on the effects of physical contact and handling on infant attention (e.g. Fantz and Nevis, 1967; White, 1969), and demonstrations of lowered attention in association with the low reward value of maternal non-responsiveness (Lewis and Goldberg, 1969). The effects of children's personality and motivational characteristics, as mediated by those of the maternal caretaker, on response to strangers, and strange and novel environments, are reflected in caution, reluctance or avoidance in exploratory situations (e.g. Rubinstein, 1967; Ainsworth et al., 1971; Bronson, 1971). This evidence must mean that socialization which is experienced as suboptimal by children may lead to delays in using available sensory information, and to interactions between aversive and desirable expectancies in exploration or play which may have long-term effects upon the development of some very basic conceptual structures. Consistent with this interpretation are the findings of a relationship between low maternal emotional and verbal responsiveness and delayed language development in children (Wulbert et al., 1975), and between rejecting and otherwise suboptimal maternal characteristics and suboptimal development of conservation (Hamilton 1972a; 1972b; 1975). The role of child and adult anxiety in suboptimal cognitive performance is well documented (e.g. Taylor and Spence, 1952; Sarason et al., 1964; Hill and Sarason, 1966), but until recently explanations of this unfavourable interaction had been phrased by general reference to arousal, drive, or interference (e.g. Spielberger, 1966; 1972), which appear descriptive rather than explanatory, or even tautological.

(iii) Anxiety as Aversive and Competing Information

Information is here defined as sensory data to which lexical, semantic, or pictorial memory registers have attached codes or connotative labels which facilitate the selection and organization of code-relevant responses from appropriate data banks in long-term memory (LTM). Aversive information is postulated as being of two types: (a) non-specific and low grade in terms of unpleasant autonomically driven somatic feeling tones including the perception of strain due to high arousal as in cardiac and intestinal dysfunctions; (b) highly specific conceptual data. This aversive conceptual information may be retrieved from LTM stores when matching and recognizing operations are applied to short-term memory (STM) inputs. This occurs when people anticipate stimuli which conditionally are associated with 'danger', incompetence, social isolation, or assaults on self-esteem. The model suggests that the aversive LTM structures of anxious people predispose towards: (a) low retrieval thresholds for these data; (b) excessive elaboration of these structures through autonomous self-stimulation; (c) external scanning for subjectively aversive stimuli rather than objective relevance; (d) excessive deployment of matching processes for the identification and recognition of STM input which may be *potentially* aversive.

Given these processes and strategies, high anxiety limits the amount of processing space and time available for objective situational requirements. If, furthermore, information processing capacity at any given point in time is finite (Norman and Bobrow, 1975), it would follow that the capacity to process adaptively relevant cognitive data becomes reduced when effort to cope simultaneously with anxiety absorbs the spare processing capacity of the system (Kahneman, 1973; Hamilton, 1975; 1976b). While this outcome must be a function of the limited physiological and cognitive capacity of the system, it does not require the construct of a *single* processing channel (Broadbent, 1971). It is equally likely that parallel processing *at different levels* (Broadbent, 1977) will exhaust the holding and identifying capacity of the *components* of the processing system.

The suggested model has been formalized by writing an expression for *successful* task performance in problem solution. This reads

$$APC + SPC > I_{e_{(p)}} + I_{i_{(C)}} + I_{i_{(A)}}$$

where *APC* is average processing capacity, *SPC* is spare processing capacity, $I_{e_{(p)}}$ is externally presented primary task information, $I_{i_{(c)}}$ is internally generated, task-relevant, competing information, and where $I_{i_{(A)}}$ indicates the level of internally generated aversive information, i.e. anxiety. Information of the anxiety type in this context is seen as making demands on the processing system at the STM as well as at a central response selection and integrating stage. The allocation of effort and attention to simultaneous identifying processes, according to Kahneman (1973), would put a strain on available capacity, and highly anxious people should exhibit, therefore, greater impairment with all problems of adaptation. While the adverse effects of anxiety on learning, memory, and problem solving have been reliably demonstrated already (e.g. Spielberger, 1966; 1972; Denny, 1966; Dunn, 1968; Hodges and Spielberger, 1969; Sarason, 1972; 1975), the model offered here suggests *why* this unfavourable interaction may occur. It thus elaborates models of information transmission in conditions of overload (Miller, 1960), as well as the insufficiently specified interfering role assigned to worry (Liebert and Morris, 1967), and to anxious self-preoccupation (Mandler and Sarason, 1952; Wine, 1971; Sarason, 1975). My students and I have carried out a series of experiments which appear to be consistent with the informational interpretation of anxiety, and with a processing limitation analysis of neurotic anxiety. Before I review these briefly, however, some comments are required concerning the status of the physiological arousal model of anxiety, and on the role of stimulus and response uncertainty in neurosis.

(iv) The Utility of the Physiological Arousal Model

In Chapter 3 I have argued already that the neurophysiological and neuropharmacological arousal and activation systems make a substantial contribution to stressor-load and -strain. In Figure 3.5 this contribution to instability through excessive information processing demands has been called dynamic predispositions. I argued there that arousal explanations of maladaptations were historically influenced by rather dated non-cognitive definitions of emotionality. For many years, therefore, arousal explanations of behavioural abnormality have accrued considerable plausibility (e.g. Eysenck, 1973; Claridge, 1975; Lader, 1975). In this approach, cognitive events and processes have been largely ignored, and arousal and anxiety were incautiously equated.

Although temporary covariation between measures of anxiety and of physiological arousal can be demonstrated, correlations between them are generally low (see McReynolds, 1976, for a recent summary). It seems plausible to suggest that cognitive identification and evaluation of actual or anticipated aversive stimuli precedes arousal (e.g. Melzack, 1975; Lader, 1975), except to the extent that any stimulus generates arousal in the process and in support of orientation (Sokolov, 1963; Pribram and McGuinness, 1975). When arousal mechanisms are triggered by the identification of an aversive stimulus, they fulfil an energizing role for the emergence of avoidance responses, preceded by further analysis of the meaning of the stimulus (e.g. Mandler, 1975).

A postulated feedback relationship between two discrete processes of anxiety and arousal contrasts markedly with the currently more influential models of the interaction between a monistic process of 'stress' with performance, such as the 'noise' model, and the postulated similarity between behavioural/cognitive effects of white noise and of incentive rewards (Broadbent, 1971), or an anxiety-drive model (e.g. Spence and Spence, 1966). The Yerkes–Dodson model which has been used to underpin these conceptions has always been descriptive rather than explanatory: it cannot specify cognitive as distinct from physiological mediating processes, and, for ethical reasons, has not been derived from systematic, *extreme* variations of either general emotionality, arousal or anxiety applied to human subjects. Therefore, with respect to the right-hand side of the inverted-U curve, it offers only circular reasoning: poor performance is due to high arousal etc., and high arousal etc. leads to poor performance. An apparent exception to this may be the type of study reported by Sjöberg (1977) in which arousal measured by heart rate and blood pressure was raised by physical exertion. It is doubtful, however, that this type of 'stress' provides a valid analogue for arousal-stress functionally related to anticipated injury or insult to self-esteem.

Restrictions in the range of cue utilization in states of high emotionality, arousal, or anxiety were postulated to account for changes in attentional strategy and performance decrements (Easterbrook, 1959). Because of the general acceptance, however, of the proposition that emotive/arousal states of the organism facilitates the emergence of competing responses, this type of explanation is more relevant to *optimal* performance through the *exclusion of task-irrelevant* cues, than to poor performance in which an excessive number of the organism facilitate the emergence of competing responses, this type of drive-arousal model. It is likely, therefore, that high emotionality, arousal, or anxiety increase rather than decrease the range and amount of information presented to an information processing system, where relevant and irrelevant, central as well as peripheral cues, and task- as well as 'affect'-relevant information, are simultaneously present [see Hockey Ch. 5].

(v) Stimulus and Response Uncertainty, and Anxiety

If anxiety is defined as aversive information, then uncertainty over the potential aversiveness of stimuli and response outcomes engenders an extended preoccupation with aversive anticipations, and, therefore, an increase in the cognitive processing load. For the highly anxious person uncertainty itself has always been considered aversive. Kirkegaard (1944) used the term 'possibility' to refer to it, and argued that its acceptance as well as its avoidance were essential in self-realization and communication with others.

Stimulus uncertainty refers to situations – experimental as well as naturalistic – exhibiting lack of definition, lack of structure, multiple classifactory cues or incongruity which may defy unilateral classification or subjective reality. All stimuli which cannot trigger unequivocal responses are subsumed here, with the implication that the task and response setting becomes thereby more complex because of an increase in the number of recognition and response-organizing processes. The availability of equally probable alternative identifications and responses has been considered to induce conflict. Conflict and anxiety, however, have always been causally realted to each other as well as to neurotic disorders. Low tolerance of ambiguity can be predicted to result from exposure to stressors; from the structural complexity of situations; and from an existing high level of conflict and anxiety.

There is evidence for all these propositions which were variously influenced by Frenkel-Brunswik's lucid and cogent theorizing (1948; 1949). Smock (1955) defined intolerance of ambiguity by premature closure – responding before optimal defining information is available – and predicted successfully that exposure to 'stress' would increase this tendency. A recent paper by Shalit (1977) addresses itself methodologically to the relationship between coping capacity and degree of successful performance of men and women in structurally complex and thereby ambiguous physical, social and experimental situations as described in over 300 studies. He demonstrates by multiple scalogram analysis that coping potential decreases (failure in performance) as structural ambiguity increases. For the purpose of an informational analysis of anxiety it is particularly interesting to note Shalit's definition of ambiguity along three dimensions: the number of alternatives perceived; the differentiation and ranking of these alternatives; and the emotional positive or negative loading associated with the situation. In other words, coping is impaired with increases in information, or with appraisal and reappraisal demands.

Hamilton (1957; 1960) predicted successfully that neurotics show significantly greater avoidance of ambiguity than normal people in operationally neutral settings, and that patients whose symptoms defended them most strongly against conflict and anxiety should present the most marked avoidance behaviour. Strategies indicative of imposing structure and certainty in situations in which indecision and non-classification were the most appropriate response defined intolerance of ambiguity. While the original prediction was in terms of conflict and thus anxiety avoidance, it is now possible to argue that this strategy inevitably involves a forced reduction in information processing. Where categorical responses are contraindicated, classification of stimuli on reduced information is a suboptimal response, but it serves to confine processing requirement and strain within manageable limits. This conclusion would be difficult to reach, however, without a cognitive interpretation of anxiety.

These interactions can be redefined in the terms of the informational model of anxiety discussed earlier. If task complexity $I_{e(p)}$ and the cognitive data from internally generated anxiety $I_{i(A)}$ occupy a substantial part of a person's overall processing capacity $(APC + SPC)$, and if these stimuli cannot be excluded from the STM and response-integrating components of the system, but a response is required, then only the task-relevant responses $I_{i(C)}$ can be reduced in order to prevent substantial confusion and disorganization of the system. This reduction of information, however, requires a simplification of stimulus structure, and a reduction, avoidance, or exclusion of ambiguity, response competition, or ranked alternative solutions [see Folkmanetal, Ch. 9].

(vi) Predictions from Model and Some Experimental Results

Whether we utilize the symbolic statement above on the contribution of anxiety to information processing limitations, or the graphical illustrations in Chapter 3 (Figures 3.4 and 3.5) of the relationship between strain and dynamic predispositions, situational complexity, anxiety processes, and coping and defensive operations, the predictions of the effects of high anxiety on performance would be the same. To test the model we need an independent measure of cognitive anxiety, tasks with systematically increasing processing demands, a valid manipulation of threat, danger or aversiveness, and an independent measure of physiological arousal. To gain support for the model it would have to be shown that high anxious subjects perform consistently worse than low anxious subjects on tasks with systematic increases in informational complexity, and when exposed to threat of pain or to ego stressors. It would need to be shown that these relationships are not covariant with arousal or changes in arousal level.

Several experiments have been carried out recently which generally support the model. They were based on paradigmatic studies of the effects of suboptimal maternal socialization strategies on conservation (Hamilton, 1972a; 1975; 1976a). Difficulty of a conservation task was here defined by a validated index derived from the minimal number of equations or steps which had to be processed to obtain an identity or equivalence response (Hamilton and Moss, 1974). The support obtained for a negative relationship between socialization anxiety and information processing capacity in a conversation task led to studies of the relationship between direct measures of test anxiety (S. B. Sarason *et al*., 1960; I. G. Sarason, 1972) and simultaneous task of increasing difficult; mathematico-symbolic problem solving tasks; speed of word recognition; and, most recently, iconic and buffer memory store capacity.

The first study demonstrated that high test-anxious children aged 7–9 performed significantly worse than low anxious children on the tasks of visual RT and simultaneous digit rehearsal and recall (Hamilton, 1976a). This experimental design was subsequently applied to high and low test-anxious

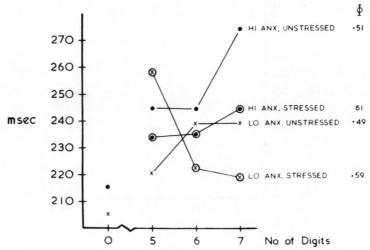

FIGURE 12.1. Visual RT while rehearsing digits, anxiety criterion groups, with and without false feedback of poor performance. *N*'s = 12

student subjects with two modifications: with and without false feedback of goodness of reaction time performance, and with continuous monitoring of skin conductance. The measure of arousal was the range-corrected index for output ϕ (Lykken and Venables, 1971). Figure 12. 1 shows with varying degrees of statistical reliability the relative slowness of high anxious subjects in coping with an increase in the number of digits to be recalled while attending to a reaction time signal. Since the level of arousal for the groups within each condition was virtually identical, the difference in dual-task performance is not primarily due to arousal. On the contrary: high induced arousal improved the performance of the high test-anxious subjects, probably by energizing effort reserves which, however, may not be available for an indefinite period, or when situational demands engender more stressors. (This experiment was conducted by Gilles Launay.)

A subsequent experiment employed a series of mathematical equations, where components of the expression were sequentially transformed and rewritten in alternative forms. Student subjects were asked whether both sides of a final mathematical statement were still equal, or whether the left side was larger or smaller than the right side. The tests were designed as an adult analogue of the conservation skill, and the progressive increase in difficulty of items was defined by the minimum number of identity operations or steps subjects had to carry out before arriving at a solution. This number of operations defined the informational complexity of the item. It was correctly predicted that the solution times for high anxious subjects under ego-involving conditions would be significantly longer than for less anxious

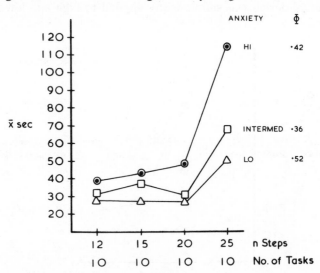

FIGURE 12.2. 'Symbolic conservation' tasks—solution times.

N's = 8

subjects, and that the anxiety × difficulty interaction would be significant. The results of the experiment are shown in Figure 12.2, and indicate at the same time the results are not due to covariation with arousal. (This experiment was conducted by Amanda Prail.)

A third experiment investigated the difference between high and low test-anxious student subjects in speed of recognizing sameness or difference for pairs of anagrams or non-words of increasing letter length. The task was carried out under non-arousal and aroused conditions, where arousal was manipulated by threat of electric shock at a level previously selected by volunteer subjects themselves. Shock, however, was not given at any time. Figure 12.3 not only shows that the arousal manipulations was successful, but also that it cannot plausibly explain the unfavourable interaction between high anxiety and speed of the cognitive recognition processes. Performance errors in these three studies were very low because there was no or only moderate pacing. Short inter-trial intervals would inevitably increase errors. (This experiment was conducted by Annemarie Robinson.)

The data from the studies illustrated in Figures 12.1 and 12.2 strongly implicate the temporary, short-term or buffer memory store stage of the information processing sequence. This would be expected on the proposition that the anticipation of aversive stimulation by the high anxious person would lead to task-irrelevant search and identification processes at the earliest stage of an input system. An analogy would be the finding of Posner *et al.*, (1969) that a visual code can be disrupted by a concurrent memory task.

In a recent completed study, iconic storage and buffer store recall capacity were assessed on 20 high and 20 low test-anxious children aged 10–11 years, while simultaneously monitoring skin conductance and heart rate. Twelve

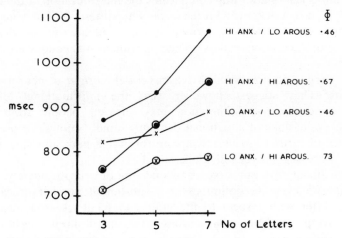

FIGURE 12.3. RT word recognition, varying word length, expecting shock, anxiety *x* arousal subgroups. *N*'s = 5

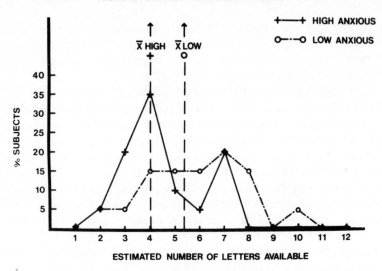

FIGURE 12.4. Iconic/short-term buffer memory capacity of children differing in 'test anxiety'.

stimulus cards were successively exposed at a speed of 300 msec, following a practice session with smaller arrays. Sperling's (1960) partial report technique was adopted. The difference between the two groups for the estimated number of letters available for recall was significant at the 1 per cent level, and is shown in Figure 12.4. The correlation between arousal and performance was 0.05, but the high anxious had significantly lower reading ability, and correlations between reading and test anxiety was also significant. Although this last relationship complicates the interpretation of the results of this study, it does not controvert the anxiety hypothesis. Not only may we ask why poor readers are anxious, more pertinent is the question of why anxious children should be poor readers. (This experiment was conducted by Nicola Hancock.)

These studies do not establish reasons for the *origin* of neurotic anxiety symptoms. They suggest, however, that the informational load from self-generated aversive stimulation may prevent people from making objective evaluations of situational demands rapidly enough to prevent the emergence of further anxiety. Symptom formation may subsequently occur through processes not yet fully understood.

Normal anxiety can but serve as an analogue of neurotic anxiety. The two types may be even discontinuous in a substantial number of cases, and certainly differ with respect to the effects of feedback from pronounced disabling symptoms. For similar reasons scores on questionnaires of manifest, trait or state anxiety or neuroticism are but poor analogues of the informational processes and cognitive strategies of phobic, obsessive-compulsive, reactive depressive or conversion hysteric patients. Given, however, the impairment of cognitive capacity in anxious individuals, it has seemed reasonable to me to consider the possible role of developmentally-early anxiety, not only in the development of neurosis, but in the emergence of schizophrenic psychosis.

4. TOWARDS AN INFORMATION PROCESSING MODEL OF THE SCHIZOPHRENIAS

(i) Introduction

In this section I would like to offer some generalizations derived from the preceding cognitive analysis of anxiety, and the conceptualizations of schizophrenic deficit discussed in section 2. I propose to state the outline of a general model which bypasses biochemical and psychophysiological models of schizophrenic dysfunction which are discussed in Chapter 13, and instead apply the cognitive processing load concepts outlined in Chapter 3 and in section 3 above. At the end of this chapter I shall attempt to discuss the utility of these alternative concepts in the development of two characteristic schizophrenic behaviour patterns or syndromes: the dependent, inadequate, withdrawn type and the impulsive, paranoid/grandiose type. This attempt will leave many obvious conceptual gaps, and in the present state of knowledge, can be sufficiently queried to the point of being considered false.

My justification for formulating these hypotheses lies in the results of research projects carried out by me in the early 1960's. (These were carried out with the help of two assistants, Dr. Phillida Salmon and Dr. Patrick Phillips, on a grant awarded to Dr. Morris Markowe of Springfield Hospital, London.) The projects were concerned with the evaluation of different work therapies on the rehabilitation of long-term schizophrenic men. Our findings supported predictions of the effects of normal industrial work, which were more favourable than those of 'occupational therapy' and non-variation in usual custodial patient activities (Hamilton and Salmon, 1962; Hamilton, 1963b; 1964). Improvements in patients were obtained across a wide spectrum: clinical status, social competence, test intelligence, reaction time, motor speed and response coordination, and congruous deductive thinking. All patients were receiving unchanged doses of phenothiazines. It was concluded that social role-relevant work of only gradually increasing complexity in a 'factory' setting, but with supportive conditions, enabled patients to regain some of their (limited) capacities, and in many instances enabled them to accept and succeed in normal industrial employment. Because of the differences obtained between novel and traditional therapeutic activity techniques, it was concluded that the effects of institutionalization and chemotherapy did not account for the findings.

Instead, I felt encouraged to search for the mediators of improvement in the role of anxiety in cognitive processing deficits, and in the influence of the basic, developmentally early, cognitive skills of perceptual constancy and conservation in schizophrenic perception and thinking (Hamilton, 1963a; 1966; 1972b). Since these basic skills appear to be reliably impaired, and since their normal development occurs at a time when socialization pressures from conforming parents, particularly, are stepped up, a cognitive-developmental approach to schizophrenic dysfunction seemed indicated.

(ii) Development of Deviant and Unadaptive Cognitive Structures

The major components determining progress and directions of cognitive development are probably informational encoding, functional differentiation, and dimensional integration.

The *amount and quality of encoding* depends on the amount and complexity of externally available stimuli, on their pacing, on the degree to which they are experienced as positively or negatively reinforcing, and on the available capacity of the processing system at given points in time. Initially phonemic or graphemic stimuli are gradually coded in semantic, pictorial, or symbolic registers, from whence they are transferred to more permanent data stores. Selective retrieval from these stores achieves age- and experience-based progressive competence in identifying stimulus patterns which pass through the different stages of STM components. The sequences and speed of recognizing and matching skills are clearly interdependent and contribute equally to LTM development and to immediate response-selecting and response-integrating processes.

The ranges of available experience and elicited responses determine the degree of *functional differentiation* of LTM stores. Two hypothetical types of differentiation of cognitive structures in long-term memory are sketched in Figures 12.5(a) and 12.5(b) to illustrate two extreme developmental outcomes. Figure 12.5(a) shows a highly differentiated system with considerable freedom for integration of functional areas, and only two unintegrated or encapsulated experience structures as indicated by the heavy lines. Figure 12.5(b) represents a grossly differentiated and relatively unintegrated experience system. If it is assumed that the content of each functional area consists of hierarchical conceptual subunits down to the level of purely sensory data, we may infer that the integrative capacity for relational operations is under-developed in structural system (b). Also, the differentiated cognitive structures would find complex information difficult to identify because (i) fine-grain or high-level conceptual matches are not readily available, and (ii) input data would decay in iconic and early buffer stores while LTM stores are searched for relevant identifiers. This type of

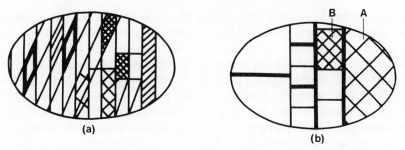

FIGURE 12.5. Hypothetically differentiated cognitive structures

cognitive system has closed and undifferentiated structural boundaries. With the inclusion of the area labelled B—signifying dependence, and the area labelled A— signifying anxiety, it might represent the proportionately over-differentiated dependence and anxiety functions as well as the assumptions of suboptimal cognitive development of the withdrawn, inadequate schizophrenic. Our analysis and representation of functional cognitive structures owes rather less to the Lewinians than to the conceptualizations of the schema by Bartlett (1932), Neisser (1967), or Piaget and Inhelder (1973). At the same time it remains incomplete without a model describing the integrative processes which the development of schemata subsumes as well as facilitates.

Dimensional integration is the process underlying concept formation. It occurs in categorizing and in grouping by combining information from more than one sensory, semantic or attributional source, and requires abstracting and generalizing skills dependent on already differentiated cognitive data in LTM stores. Sensory information yields data only on the surface qualities, and equivalence transformations yielding higher-order commonalities require the utilization of intrinsic and extrinsic functional perspectives (Bruner and Olver, 1963). A *strong* concept is arrived at by integrative information from a large number of different combinations of degrees of dimensional similarities and differences (Schroder, Driver, and Streufert, 1967), whereas a *weak* concept is likely to be unidimensionally determined, and/or by reference to perceptual data alone in conjunction with over-simplified rules for dealing with relational and contextual settings.

Two factors appear to combine in producing impairments of the level and power of LTM structures:

(a) environments presenting either over-complex or over-simplified information, and
(b) response settings eliciting aversive cognitive structures which are irrelevant, interrupting, and interfering in the process of stimulus analysis.

In the context of our model it seems plausible to suggest that inadequate, process schizophrenics, particularly, are characterized by the *weak* conceptual type of LTM structures. This conclusion is consistent with Cameron's (1938) influential views of schizophrenia as a fundamental disorder of concept formation and of pre-logical reasoning. It would appear to derive additional support from repeated findings of suboptimal conserving capacity, and abnormal degrees of over-constancy and under-constancy in the perception of size over distance in non-paranoid schizophrenics (Hamilton, 1963a; 1966; 1972b). Significantly, these basic skills develop during the years of maximum socialization pressure, when a variety of external demands may exceed the capacity of an already suboptimal system. In such a system self-perception of incompetence, censure from the family, and other already developed aversive cognitions, would become additive in exhausting the effort reserves of the processing apparatus. As a consequence, basic cognitive skills such as conservation may have only weak structural support which would diminish further when the processing demands on the system are increased by self-generated, internal information, i.e. subjective aversive preoccupations during and after behavioural collapse. On the basis of the previously elaborated informational model of anxiety, therefore, it could be predicted that process, non-paranoid schizophrenics would perform particularly poorly on conservation problems presenting a large number of necessary steps in order to arrive at a correct solution. This prediction has been confirmed (Hamilton, 1976b).

There is considerable evidence that such deficits are a normal feature of the pre-adolescent development of children (e.g. Osler and Kofsky, 1965; Wickens, 1974) where they reflect incompleteness of (a) structural differentiation, (b) higher-level integrative concepts, and (c) the adaptive redundancy and chunking of information which depends on these changes. In the absence of the resulting processing economies, the identification of stimulus input would have to proceed on the basis of a large number of discrete and frequently unrelated search–scan–match operations (Newell and Simon, 1972).

There are two major lines of evidence suggesting that information processing activity is high in schizophrenic patients who are apparently unable to respond adaptively to external stimulation. The first of these derives from Venables and his associates (e.g. Venables, 1964; 1975) and indicates that skin conductance and other arousal measures show high reactivity for some withdrawn, process schizophrenics which concurrently exhibit input dysfunctions. The second line of evidence derives from the study of children at high risk for schizophrenia who at a premorbid stage show similar high levels of reactivity as well as habituation deficits (e.g. Mednick and Schulsinger, 1972; Mednick, Schulsinger and Garfinkel, 1975). These groups of investigators have veered towards an explanation of damage of hippocampal structures due to birth and pregnancy complications which has not remained unchallenged (Kessler and Neale, 1974), and their interesting hypotheses concerning the effects of supraoptimal arousal on attention deployment appear to be as yet correlational rather than explanatory.

In contrast, the model offered here suggests that the abnormalities of arousal in the morbid state are a concomitant of self-generated data-processing functions which, because of their basic aversiveness for the individual, increases adrenal catecholamine and corticosteroid processes. Thus schizophrenics exhibiting high arousal may do so because they are subjectively preoccupied with cognitive anxiety and with strategies for avoiding its aversiveness. Cognitive as well as various biochemical defences may simultaneously effect a reduction in stimulus input and in the internal selection of chains of thought, which by their conceptual distance from aversiveness are strongly reinforcing. Looked at from the point of view of cognitive development, the findings by Mednick *et al.* of high arousal and poor habituation accompanied by phasic, fast returns to baseline, suggest that encoding of a loud noise stimulus may become excessively elaborated and generalized in a high-risk population, because an adequate memory structure reflecting a *non-noxious identification* of the aversive stimulus cannot be established. In this event a higher than necessary proportion of LTM space and structures becomes devoted to the registration of cognitively aversive data and to weak objective identifiers. A low-threshold high-reactivity arousal system ensures that retrieval thresholds for these cognitive data are permanently low. If these processes occur at an early stage of development, they would set up a response system that is pre-programmed to scan for aversiveness rather than affectively neutral objects, events and their veridical attributes, so that the establishment of basic concepts occurs under suboptimal conditions, and is thereby more difficult.

Postulating an unfavourable interaction between anxiety and conceptual learning, requires evidence that anxiety adversely affects mnemonic storage processes, rather than the capacity to retrieve and utilize securely stored adequate concepts. While some support for this conclusion comes from studies of Goulet and Mazzei (1969), Mueller (1976), and M. W. Eysenck (1977), there are considerable difficulties in the way of generating a satisfactory model of the interaction between personality variables, levels of task difficulty, levels of cognitive processing, and the components of remembering. One of the major reasons for these difficulties seems to be a reluctance to define anxiety in terms of its cognitive components. As a result, effects continue to be conceptualized as due to non-specific drive, arousal or activation, a position which I have critically assessed in section 3(iv) above.

At this point we may summarize the principal features of a cognitive-developmental model of the schizophrenias. In view of the very large gaps in empirical knowledge, we must confine ourselves, however, to

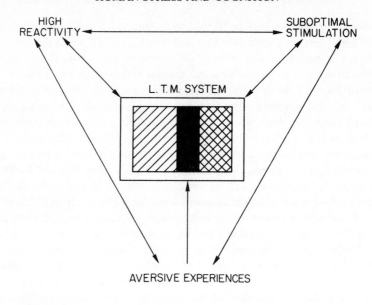

FIGURE 12.6. The development of types of memory structures in
the 'vulnerable' individual

just three major aspects of the development, and of the effects, of abnormal
LTM structures. The first of these is sketched in Figure 12.6. It represents the
necessary interaction in the development of a satisfaction- and
equilibrium-seeking organism of physiological and environmental processes
and data in the development of different types of LTM structures. It shows
the hypothesized outcome for a child with low reactivity thresholds,
suboptimal mothering, and a suboptimal early environment which contains
either too much information and is thus too complex, which contains too little
stimulation and is cognitively impoverished, or which has a low capacity to
elicit the development of integrative, yet differentiated cognitive structures
because of affectively loaded interference. Interactively, these parameters
would produce an unfavourable balance between *strong* structures, concepts
or schemata, and *weak,* and *aversiveness-signifying* long-term conceptual
information.

The second developmental aspect has been fully discussed in Chapter 3 and
section 3 above and refers to the decremental effects of processing
simultaneously anxiety interpreted as aversive information, and objective
task or problem stimuli. The effects are not limited to discrete stimulus
settings, because the suboptimal response will contribute to a progressive

development of conceptually weak and poorly integrated, rather than strong and differentiated structures. Weak LTM structures thus reflect also the consequences of externally paced and/or self-paced demands for excessive parallel processing in early stages of cognitive development.

The third aspect to be considered refers to the cumulative effect of this type of suboptimal LTM development. In the context of the preceding discussion it has been assumed that weak concepts are the results, as well as the determinants, of inadequately differentiated and integrated experience and conceptual systems. In the absence of identifiers or recognizers organized in higher-order schemata, the internal search process must become protracted through successive matching operations with single, concrete, and even sensory schemata. If we now add the information processing goals of an affectively oriented system, it is possible to demonstrate that a suboptimal LTM system needs to work much harder and with more – though inadequate – information than a system that is less vulnerable by virtue of its physiological predisposition and its more economic conceptual structures. There are good reasons for assuming, therefore, that the capacity of the ionic and first durable buffer components of a premorbid STM of some schizophrenics may be lower than in the normal system. Support for this assumption has been obtained recently for under-inclusive schizophrenics (Knight *et al.*, 1977), who, therefore, show deficits which I have reported in section 3(iv) above for anxious normal children. These assumed events and their probable consequences for immediate adaptive response selection are shown diagrammatically in Figure 12.7(A). The lower half (B) presents the hypothesized outcomes for a normally developed system. In the abnormal system they consist primarily of a reduction in the processing of externally available information, and, through stimulus input decay, of decision-making on sparse, possibly unrepresentative and idiosyncratic data. This may satisfy internal rather than external criteria. These criteria are likely to be determined by defensive attempts to control anxiety with at least two possible further strategies: input reduction through withdrawal, mediated by an attentional scanner, or excessive, but superficial scanning (not shown in Figure 12.7) to search out additional potential sources of aversive information. The latter strategy would have the effect of increasing the load on the iconic and more durable STM components with all the built-in implications for increased decay and backward masking.

Our model has assumed that socialization stimuli remain homogeneously suboptimal. It is clear that this is not necessarily the case in all instances. Moreover, since the capacity of the human information processing system for handling connotative input is large, it is implausible that all aspects, sources or goals of cognitive processes become homogeneously impaired. It is likely, however, that increasing age-related demands for adequate social role playing will eventually exceed the processing and effort reserves of a system which

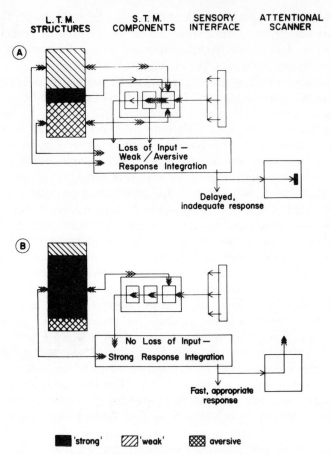

FIGURE 12.7. The role of types of memory structures in the selection and organization of inadequate and appropriate responses

starts off with unfavourable physiological responsiveness. Moreover, a suboptimal set of LTM schemata has been developed for simplifying and integrating inputs which otherwise would constitute an overload for the system, and exceed its appraisal and thus its coping capacities.

The distinction between the cognitive processes and structures of schizophrenia and those of mental subnormality really requires extensive consideration. This is especially so since neurotic anxiety features and bizarre as distinct from impoverished thinking characteristics are not infrequently found in subnormals. In a recent application of information processing paradigms to subnormal cognitive development Odom-Brooks and Arnold (1976) suggest that the processing deficits of subnormals are quantitatively rather than qualitatively defined. They argue in favour of impoverished assimilation and accommodation processes – that is a *fundamental incapacity* for dimensional integration – to which experimentally confirmed STM deficits are likely to make a substantial contribution. In schizophrenia, however, those deficits are not to be considered as endogeneous but due to interference at the encoding stage, and from subsequent self-generated elaboration of aversive expectancies.

(iii) Retrospective and Predictive Implications of Model

In a single chapter it is not possible to relate the aetiological suggestions I have offered to all the dominant research orientations. Moreover, there does not seem to exist any stable set of explanatory coordinates which can simultaneously encompass hypotheses centering on drive/arousal; language deficits; thought disorder; stimulus input or response bias dysfunctions; or ego- and concept boundary deficiencies. Three dominant explanatory preferences appear to have emerged under which schizophrenic deficit has been subsumed: interference, speed of processing, and attention. Subsidiary processes included here are stimulus and response generalization, memory, over- and under-inclusiveness, and deficits in primitive cognitive skills.

The interference hypothesis, despite valiant efforts (Buss and Lang, 1965; Lang and Buss, 1965), does not seem fundamental enough and veers towards the descriptive. It would raise many questions such as *what* it is that interferes, *why* interference leads to impoverished skills and bizarre behaviour, and *how* this interference is mediated. In the light of the preceding discussion, I would argue that interference is caused by threat-, danger-, or aversiveness-related data which preoccupy patients. To cope with these internally generated stimuli patients have recruited avoidance strategies of subjective value but objective incongruence, in which affect-driven mediation between total stimulus input and response output occurs both at a short-term memory and central response-integration stage.

The findings of decrements in speed of motor and cognitive responses in non-paranoid schizophrenics by Yates and his colleagues (Yates, 1966; Court and Garwoli, 1968; Yates and Korboot, 1970) would be interpreted here as a reflection of an uneconomical processing and selection system. In his system response time suffers not only because of a larger number of internal matching and scanning operations, but also because from the start the schizophrenic is already operating on task-irrelevant data and anxiety-avoidance strategies which even for a simple external task may be programmed out only after considerable delay. It is quite likely that these same factors account for the decrements in reaction time with preparatory intervals of increasing length (Shakow, 1962; Zahn, 1975; Zubin, 1975).

The present model appears to be complementary to the arousal explanations of input dysfunctions in so-called responding schizophrenics (e.g. Venables, 1964; Venables and Warwick-Evans, 1968; Gruzelier and Venables, 1972; Gruzelier and Venables, 1973; Gruzelier, 1975). However, whereas Venables *et al.* postulated a primary causal role for arousal, the present model suggests the sequence: cognitive identification of aversive events–arousal–elaboration of aversive cognition–arousal increments–break of positive feedback loop through post-search selection of non-aversive information which satisfies subjective criteria. This formulation is functionally similar to the views of Broen (1968) and Broen and Storms (1966) that a lawful disorganization of schizophrenic behaviour occurs because high drive quickly raises dominant habits to a response ceiling that is lower than in normals, and then generalizes to non-dominant habits and responses. These, presumably must be positively reinforcing, lowering drive or responsiveness in order to break a positive feedback loop. The present model, however, defines the drive component in terms of arousal-supported aversive information, and specifies that non-dominant habits or equivalences are derived from the involvement of cognitively suboptimal, non-integrative LTM structures, rather than conceptually or behaviourally rare alternatives.

Recent studies by Gruzelier (e.g. 1978) report further evidence that non-paranoid schizophrenics may be divided into subgroups of responders and non-responders when exposed to an auditory orienting stimulus testing habituation. The implications for a cognitive processing model of the schizophrenias of bilateral asymmetry with a left hemispheric deficit, as suggested by Gruzelier, are difficult to assess. As with arousal generally, we do not know whether we are dealing with cause or effect. If the former, then this is a legitimate *organic* factor, and the term schizophrenia is logically misapplied, even though it could account parsimoniously for a long-term process. If left-hemisphere dysfunction is an effect, then we would have to account for the loss of hippocampal inhibition. This could be supplied, however, by a chronic high cortical arousal level which is the result of preoccupation with aversive information and behavioural self-evidence of incompetence, particularly in verbal communication (Giora, 1975).

In respect of its conceptual deficit component the present information processing model is closest to Cameron's (1938) early views. Payne's proposition (e.g. 1973) of a dominant abnormal process of over-inclusiveness represents a fine-grain empirical development of this. It would seem, however, that over-inclusiveness, or over-exclusiveness as implicit in Chapman's (1958) dominant-meaning hypotheses, or in Hamilton's notions of deficiencies in cue responsiveness as shown in abnormal size-constancy and conservation skills (1963a, 1972b), reflect the presence of weak concepts in LTM structures. Also, differentiated, integrative structures are lacking which could strengthen those conceptual operations depending on contextual cues. There are suggestions that over-inclusion is not specific to schizophrenia (e.g.

Andreasen and Powers, 1974). But it is not unlikely that an integration deficit is one of the factors leading to redundant and irrelevant responses (McDowell et al., 1975).

The construct of a dysfunction of the attentional selective filter (e.g. Payne, 1973; Hemsley and Zawada, 1976) has been utilized to explain the results of experiments in perception of speech and of distraction of schizophrenics (McGhie and Chapman, 1961; Lawson, McGhie and Chapman, 1964; McGhie, Chapman and Lawson, 1965; McGhie, 1966). Inability to recall verbal material approximating to English, even with help provided by content cues, and distraction by auditory stimulation in multiple-stimulus situations particularly, support the proposition of information processing deficits with a semantic focus. More specifically, the findings by McGhie et al. may be interpreted as demonstrating deficiencies in semantic LTM registers. Susceptibility to selective filter dysfunction and to auditory interference is consistent with the present model's proposition of parallel, ongoing processing of anxiety interpreted as information. This, because it must use semantic codes and pathways to convey its goals, is likely to compete for the very same data-processing pathways as other semantically coded information. For the same reason auditory reaction time may be paradoxically slower than visual reaction time in schizophrenics fitting these criteria (viz. Venables and O'Connor, 1959). Further support for the possible role of anxiety in the schizophrenias comes from renewed evidence of greater perceptual generalization, from correlations between generalization and 'manifest' anxiety, and from significantly higher anxiety in schizophrenics than normal controls (Al-Issa et al., 1975). Clearly relevant is the relationship between social stress and loose associations in reactive schizophrenics with an assumed higher level of cognitive development (DeWolfe and Youkilis, 1974).

Callaway (1970) was one of the first to place the role of memory dysfunction in schizophrenics in the context of response selection. Since then, a large number of studies has been carried out on schizophrenics' memory (e.g. Neale, 1971; Koh et al., 1973; 1976; 1977; Bauman and Kolisnyk, 1976; Traupman et al., 1976; Braff, Callaway and Naylor, 1977; Knight et al., 1977). The experiments differ substantially in the selection and type of patients, methodology, stimulus material, and type of memory investigated. It is difficult, therefore, to draw any general conclusions. The findings include differences between schizophrenics, and non-schizophrenics and normals, and between paranoid and non-paranoid schizophrenics, on speed in STM scanning, and contradictory conclusions on whether encoding is impaired or not. There is also evidence of impaired very short-term memory and interference proneness at the output rather than the input stage of information processing. No other cognitive predispositions or strategies were controlled except by Knight et al. These investigators found that partial recall from an iconic store was normal in over-inclusive subjects, but poor in under-inclusives and poor premorbids who also did not benefit from the full report method, and showed abnormally slow rates of decay. The explanations of Knight *et al.* include difficulty in cue utilization and in transfer to first durable buffer store, as well as broadened rather than excessively narrowed attention.

On balance, the evidence favours abnormal iconic store and decay capacity, and, therefore, the more fundamental explanation seems to be an attentional one. Peripheral attentional deficits, however, as shown by eye movements (Cancro, 1975; Holzman *et al.*, 1976; Shagass *et al.*, 1976), would appear to be at the most *concomitants* of a more central process of input control (Hamilton, 1976b). One reason for the continued acceptability of the proposition that anxiety/arousal narrows attention is the supportive findings obtained with assumed analogues of arousal: noise, sleeplessness, and stimulants [see Hockey's lucid Chapter 5 in this volume]. As I have tried to indicate before, this analogue is conceptually suspect because it ignores attentional broadening from the cognitive determinants of anxiety. While it is possible to account for some of the memory deficits in schizophrenia by reference to narrowed attention, explanations referring to broadened attention cannot be ignored.

Is it possible that this antithesis is apparent only and may be resolved? I believe that this is the case. I would argue that selective attention is anything but unitary, that there are, in fact, four parallel selective attentional processes. These are divided between stimulus-relevant and response relevant processes, and between externally generated and internally generated stimuli. In my view, therefore, reductions in cue utilization and in iconic or more firmly coded memory do not necessarily indicate that there is a *reduction* in selective attention. On the contrary, hyperactivity and over-arousal, particularly if accompanied by withdrawal and performance decrements, in so-called responding schizophrenics, whether non-paranoid, paranoid, acute or chronic (Depue and Fowles, 1973), suggest excessive attentional processes. In this case, however, these processes involve self-generated, task-irrelevant, subjectively important stimuli and response strategies. Furthermore, I would argue that this proposition is fully consistent with evidence and propositions of informational overload and defective filtering of irrelevant stimuli in schizophrenics (e.g. Payne, 1973; Hemsley, 1975, 1976; Heilbrun, 1977).

With an internal as well as an external source of information, selective processes must operate in two directions, and normality and competence are indicated by the selective inhibition of what is irrelevant in a motivated task orientation. Where internal stimuli signalling threat, danger, or aversiveness are inappropriately numerous, and where anxiety-reducing strategies require primary attention to these, processing capacity limitations of space and time reduce the capacity to deal relevantly with externally paced demands. If this were true, then it might be assumed that all schizophrenias without an organic basis represent over-active systems, and that evidence to the contrary is misleading. The behavioural differences, however, between schizophrenic subtypes is real, fundamentally not in *amount* of selective attention, but by virtue of the schematic structures and their elaboration and differentiation which determine the complexity of self-generated stimuli and their intrusiveness.

The developmentally oriented processing capacity model seems to fit the common Verbal-Performance scale IQ differences of patients, and the suggestions that pre-schizophrenic children *may* have lower IQ's than their non-index twins (Lane and Albee, 1970; Jones and Offord, 1975). The model also appears quite consistent with the summary findings on cognitive characteristics of the index children of at-risk studies which commenced more recently than the Danish studies by Mednik *et al.*, to which I have referred earlier. The former have been recently reviewed by Garmezy (1975). The proposed model suggests, furthermore, that the success of token economy (e.g. Ullman and Krasner, 1965) and of graded industrial occupational rehabilitation strategies (see section 4(i)), appears to occur for similar reasons: a reduction in signals which might activate the cognitive components of anxiety, and a clarification and simplification of external task- or behaviour-relevant information. These appear to be the most parsimonious explanations for progressive changes in behaviour without changes in medication, and despite massive doses of de-arousing drugs which often induce lethargy and sleepiness.

If the cognitive-developmental model appears plausible and accrues evidence of validity, a large number of predictions ensue which are not necessarily limited to the antecedents of the schizophrenic disorders. We may take any situation in which response competition occurs in *association* with reported high anxiety, and predict that in the appropriate area of functional differentiation, conceptual structures coded in LTM would show a comparatively lower and thus weaker level of integration and organization of semantic and symbolic codes. In association with genetically programmed ease of eliciting autonomic and cortical arousal, the occurrence in a developmental sequence of aversively experienced stimuli may contribute to our knowledge of LTM structures, and possibly provide us with some predictions of the development of the schizophrenic subtypes, and the development of schizotypy (Meehl, 1962) and of anxiety neurosis. Existing evidence and theory suggest, for example, that the development of neurotic responses occurs during phases of cognitive 'fixation' or traumatic learning. We may say that in these phases aversive information receives subjective, unwarranted elaboration *at the cost of* objectively driven integrative processes and of optimal LTM differentiation in concurrently developing cognitive skills and structures. Since, however, many fundamental integrative cognitive structures are intact in neurotics, deficits determined by information overload must occur at an earlier developmental stage in the schizophrenias.

A specific prediction can be made in conjunction with the findings of the Danish at-risk studies. If physiological lability and poor habituation are fundamental to subsequent schizophrenic development, they should be demonstrable in infancy, and their cognitive effects reduced by systematic management of the informational load and content of the early environment. A general project conceived along these lines has commenced in Mauritius (Bell *et al.,* 1975), but it appears to have excluded a detailed examination and manipulation of information input especially in early infancy. This omission seems unfortunate because of the existing evidence of dysfunction of some important basic cognitive skills such as size constancy and conservation (Hamilton, see above), and of the conceptual use of colour and form by schizophrenics (Kay and Singh, 1975; Kay *et al.,* 1975).

There are obvious points of contact between the parameters of the present model and McReynolds' (1960) propositions of the developmental role of inappropriate assimilation of perceptual stimuli, and the avoidance of novel stimuli which may generate anxiety. Predictions of their effects on response capacity and response hierarchies in young at-risk children may be tested in relation to conceptual learning and long-term serial recall involving an increasing number of categorical dimensions. Lowered levels of performance compared with the performance of appropriate controls would additionally fit Callaway's (1970) general concept of a 'malfunctioning computer'.

Probably more contentious, but possibly of equal relevance, are predictions derived from psychoanalytically oriented propositions concerning 'ego-boundary' disturbances in pre-schizophrenics and in patients. In a recent well-argued book Blatt and Wild (1976) have assembled a considerable amount of support from many sources for this unpopular explanatory concept. From the point of view of the present model, it is important to be reminded of reports of body image and body-boundary disturbances in schizophrenics and of confusions between self, others and objects, because this type of knowledge, consensually, develops in very early stages of cognitive development. Evidence is already available that amount and quality of maternal care have marked effects on the development of object permanence (Bell, 1970) and cognitive-perceptual modalities (White, 1969; Clarke-Stewart, 1973). Two mediating processes appear to be operating: perception and interpretation of maternal feeling through quality of physical contact, and the effect of experienced levels of satisfaction or aversion on explorations of self and the immediate and subsequently wider environment. The present model would predict that early psychomotor and sensorimotor skills would be particularly impaired in suboptimal maternal contacts which present an excessive amount of *unassimilable* experience and thus of excessive information. These effects would be predicted to occur in conjunction with abnormal arousal characteristics due to hyperactivity, and particularly in family settings distinguished by intrapersonal conflict and ambiguities in verbal and non-verbal communication (e.g. Singer and Wynne, 1965a; b). So-called 'ego-boundary' disturbances may be redefined, therefore, as poorly differentiated, unintegrated LTM structures, which while temporarily adaptive and perhaps anxiety reducing, would ultimately reduce conceptual power when aversiveness is experienced. These events would ensue as the increasing information processing requirements of the socializing environment make demands which the suboptimal data banks of the child's response system cannot meet either to his own satisfaction, or to the satisfaction of his principal caretakers.

(iv) Postscript on Subtypes

Statements that process non-paranoids have regressed, or that paranoids are confused and impusively misinterpret events because of a flood of interfering stimuli, could be interpreted as implying, respectively, that the stage which regression has reached or the nature of interfering thoughts reflect an inappropriate use of *otherwise normal* skills or data. Since there is unanimous agreement that genetics play at least a necessary role in the development of the schizophrenias, this implication must be rejected, and to speak of good premorbidity may be logically false.

In addition to the original lability and low habituation rate data from the Copenhagen studies (Mednick and Schulsinger, 1972), there is supportive evidence of behavioural and autonomic developmental lag in at-risk children (Grunebaum *et al.*, 1974; Herman *et al.*, 1977). More recent findings obtained by members of the Copenhagen group confirmed electrodermal hyperactivity in the adopted children of schizophrenics (Van Dyke *et al.*, 1974), and recognizably abnormal E.E.G. in auditory evoked potential investigations (Itil *et al.*, 1974).

If there is evidence of biological vulnerability, it seems quite unsafe to assume that either early or later sensorimotor or conceptual skills necessarily develop in a normal manner. On the contrary, and as I have argued in relation to the model I have offered. Vulnerability must lead to a greater number of stressors which in turn permit of a quantitative assessment of their information load. A system, however, which at an early age must cope with environment stressors *and* biological vulnerability cannot be expected to lay down sound cognitive structures on which to build adult, conceptual units which must be complexly labelled for flexible use in a variety of changing stimulus and response settings.

In section 3(iii) above it was suggested that adequate levels of information processing capacity are a function of externally and internally generated stimuli including aversive stimuli which represent anticipation of danger threat or pain, and of the average and spare processsing capacity of the whole system. It would seem possible to relate this formulation to two schizophrenic subtypes: the withdrawn, inadequate, process non-paranoid, and the hyperactive, partially competent, reactive paranoid, I would propose that the former type has genetically limited processing capacity, and that even the reduced processing demands of a low socioeconomic group family and social setting are too great. Contributing factors are stimulus ambiguity, forced responding, severe criticism, inconsistent reward schedules, and lack of opportunity from an early age onwards to assimilate and accommodate to any single representative stimulus without premature interference from a new set of inputs. All this is experienced as aversive so that stimulus-irrelevant cognitive events will interfere with the veridical coding of stimuli and thus with the development of well-differentiated, flexible schemata. Self-evidence of incompetence in the absence of capable sympathetic parental understanding will reinforce social withdrawal, preoccupation with childish satisfactions and a subjectively acceptable view of reality. A labile, hyper-reactive arousal system ensures that otherwise normal events become stressors because the identification and search processes which it energizes do not in fact lead to a perceived state of success. While arousal levels will remain high, externally focused attention will be reduced, and internally directed selective attention will be biased towards primitive satisfactions.

The hyperactive paranoid type with higher intelligence and often a long period of apparently adequate social competence presents a more difficult conceptual problem. Again, however, physiological vulnerability ensures that there are low thresholds for experiencing aversive stimuli, but because of the higher potential for inductive and deductive logic of this type, there is additionally a lower threshold for avoiding cognitive uncertainty and ambiguity. Cognitive structures are likely to become over- rather than under-elaborated by virtue of making inferences and rationalizations about events which would otherwise be difficult to categorize. Inability to classify, however, would maintain a state of conflicting meaning, which, if meaning and response readiness are felt to be important, are aversive because threats cannot be readily met. The accent is on control here and any event or person who appears to undermine this requirement may become the object of anger or aggression. (I do not wish to comment on the 'homosexual' explanation of paranoid delusions because it is difficult to substantiate in every case, and because it seems to me to be primarily one instance of failure to achieve an anxiety-free classification of a person.)

There are at least two, possibly related, outcomes to this need to control stimulus meaning and response outcome: to project the controlling intention on to another person or 'organization' in order to avoid anxiety from evidence of classificatory incompetence and from processing overload, or to construct a false self-image of powerful control. Colby (1975), and Faught, Colby and

Parkison (1977) suggest that avoidance of humiliation, shame, and self-blame accounts for projection, but I would wish to add that these are avoided because they are a threat to self-esteem and social acceptability. Colby's lengthy computer analogue subroutines indicate, however, that the cognitive processing demands in this type of case are substantial even at the general level of super-ordinate belief systems. I would suggest that the development of persecutory and megalomanic delusions represents a premature and false closure of decision-making processes which have become too complex and aversive for the vulnerable individual. This state has been reached by an accumulation of strain-inducing stressors, and by an involvement of overelaborated, only partially relevant cognitive data in the decision-making processes. These data represent the total information processing load contributed by excessive need-directed external scanning, by overelaborate input identification, by the involvement of irrelevant stimulus identifiers, and by an excess of participating cognitive structures representing failure to inhibit self-induced expectations of threat and danger.

5. CONCLUDING COMMENT

In essence I have argued that neurotic anxiety and schizophrenic disorders are the result of a combination of stressors and that their behavioural characteristics reflect unadaptive solutions to otherwise unmanageable strain. I have posited that anxiety is information with a particular and aversive meaning, that cognitive deficits in conjunction with anxiety are evidence of cognitive processing overload, and that neurotic symptoms reflect attempted solutions to experiences of cognitive overload.

A necessary but not sufficient role was assigned to biological vulnerability represented by peripheral and cortical arousal levels in the development of neurosis and the schizophrenias. Developmentally early experiences of anxiety were regarded as necessary for the development of process as well as reactive schizophrenia. The non-paranoid and the paranoid variants were considered as examples of undifferentiated and of over-differentiated information processing systems for which, respectively, social withdrawal and behavioural incompetence, and delusional rationalizations were subjectively acceptable reductions of unacceptable levels of organismic strain.

It was stated or implied that the differential incidence of the neuroses and the schizophrenias is a complex function of endogenous sensitivity, neurological competence and association forming, and of suboptimal and aversive socialization experience. Since no single factor supplies explanatory sufficiency, and since stressors cannot be experienced without exposure to events which induce them, I am bound to conclude that the development of all types of functional behaviour disorders is potentially preventable by environmental manipulations in early childhood.

6. REFERENCES

Ainsworth, M. D. S., Bell, S. M. V. and Stayton, D. J. (1971). Individual differences in stranger-situation behavior of one-year olds. In H. R. Schaffer (Ed.), *The Origins of Human Social Relations*. London: Academic Press.

Alanen, Y. Ö. (1976). Schizophrenia – the family setting. In S. Krauss (Ed.), *Encyclopaedic Handbook of Medical Psychology*. London: Butterworths.

Al-Issa, I., Bakal, D. and Larkin, N. (1975). Stimulus generalization and anxiety in schizophrenic and normal subjects. *British Journal of Social and Clinical Psychology*, **14**, 371–378.

Andreason, N. J. C. and Powers, P. J. (1974). Overinclusive thinking in mania and schizophrenia. *British Journal of Psychiatry*, **125**, 452–456.

Arieti, S. (1955). *Interpretation of Schizophrenia*. New York: Brunner.

Bartlett, F. C. (1932). *Remembering*. Cambridge: Cambridge University Press.

Bateson, G., Jackson, D., Haley, J. and Weakland, J. (1956). Toward a theory of schizophrenia. *Behavioral Science*, **1**, 251–264.

Bauman, E. and Kolisnyk, E. (1976). Interference effects in schizophrenic short-term memory. *Journal of Abnormal Psychology*, **85**, 303–308.

Baumrind, D. (1967). Child care practices anteceding three patterns of pre-school behavior. *Genetic Psychology Monographs*, **75**, 43–88.

Bell, B., Mednick, S. A., Raman, A. C., Schulsinger, F., Sutton-Smith, S. and Venables, P. H. (1975). A longitudinal psychophysiological study of three-year old Mauritian children: preliminary report. *Developmental Medicine and Child Neurology*, **17** 320–324.

Bell, S. M. (1970). The development of the concept of object as related to infant–mother attachment. *Child Development*, **41**, 292–311.

Blatt, S. J. and Wild, C. M. (1976). *Schizophrenia: A Developmental Analysis*. New York: Academic Press.

Bleuler, M. (1968). A 23-year longitudinal study of 208 schizophrenics and impressions in regard to the nature of schizophrenia. In D. Rosenthal and S. S. Kety (Eds.), *The Transmission of Schizophrenia*. Oxford: Pergamon Press.

Bleuler, M. (1976). Schizophrenia: course and outcome. In S. Krauss (Ed.), *Encyclopaedic Handbook of Medical Psychology*, London: Butterworths.

Braff, D. L., Callaway, E. and Naylor, H. (1977). Very short-term memory dysfunction in schizophrenia. *Archives of General Psychiatry*, **34**, 25–30.

Broadbent, D. E. (1971). *Decision and Stress*. London: Academic Press.

Broadbent, D. E. (1977). Levels, hierarchies and the locus of control. *Quarterly Journal of Experimental Psychology*, **29**, 181–201.

Broen, W. E., Jr. (1968). *Schizophrenia: Research and Theory*. New York: Academic Press.

Broen, W. E., Jr. and Storms, L. H. (1966). Lawful disorganization: the process underlying a schizophrenic syndrome. *Psychological Review*, **73**, 265–279.

Bronson, G. W. (1971). Fear of the unfamiliar. In H. R. Schaffer (Ed.), *The Origins of Human Social Relations*. London: Academic Press.

Brown, G. W., Bhrolchain, M. N. and Harris, T. (1975). Social class and psychiatric disturbances among women in an urban population. *Sociology*, **9**, 225–254.

Bruner, J. S. and Olver, R. R. (1963). Development of equivalence transformations in children. *Monographs of the Society for Research Child Development*, **28**, Serial No. 86.

Buss, A. H. and Lang, P. J. (1965). Psychological deficit in schizophrenia: I. effect, reinforcement and concept attainment. *Journal of Abnormal Psychology*, **70**, 2–24.

Callaway, E. (1970). Schizophrenia and interference: an analogy with a malfunctioning computer. *Archives of General Psychiatry*, **22**, 193–208.

Cameron, N. S. (1938). Reasoning, regression and communication in schizophrenia. *Psychological Monographs*, **50**, 1–33.

Cancro, R. (1975). Visual attention in schizophrenia. *A.P.A. 128th Annual Meeting Scientific Proceedings*, 118–119.

Chapman, J. L. (1958). Intrusion of associative responses into schizophrenic conceptual performance. *Journal of Abnormal and Social Psychology*, **56**, 374–379.

Chapman, L. J. and Chapman, J. P. (1975). How to test hypotheses about schizophrenic thought disorder. *Schizophrenia Bulletin, Issue No. 12*, 42–59.

Chess, S., Thomas, A. and Birch, H. G. (1968). Behavior problems revisited: findings of anterospective study. In S. Chess and A. Thomas (Eds.), *Annual Progress in Child Psychiatry and Child Development*. New York: Bruner/Mazel.

Claridge, G. S. (1975). Psychophysiological indicators of neurosis and early psychosis. In M. L. Kietzman, S. Sutton and J. Zubin (Eds.), *Experimental Approaches to Psychopathology*. New York: Academic press.

Clarke, A. M. and Clarke, A. D. B. (1974). *Mental Deficiency: The Changing Outlook* (3rd edn.). London: Methuen.

Clarke-Stewart. K. A. (1973). Interactions between mothers and their young children: characteristics and consequences. *Monographs of the Society for Research in Child Development*, **38**, Serial No. 153.

Cohen, S., Glass, D. C. and Singer, J. E. (1973). Apartment noise, auditory discrimination and reading ability in children. *Journal of Experimental Social Psychology*, **9**, 407–422.

Colby, K. M. (1975). *Artificial Paranoia*. New York: Pergamon.

Costello, C. G. (1976). *Anxiety and Depression*. Montreal: McGill-Queen's University Press.

Court, J. H. and Garwoli, E. (1968). Schizophrenic performance on a reaction time task with increasing levels of complexity. *British Journal of Social and Clinical Psychology*, **7**, 216–223.

DeWolfe, A. S. and Youkilis, H. D. (1974). Stress and the word associations of process and reactive schizophrenics. *Journal of Clinical Psychology*, **30**, 151–153.

Denny, J. P. (1966). Effects of anxiety and intelligence on concept formation. *Journal of Experimental Psychology*, **72**, 596–602.

Depue, R. A. and Fowles, D. C. (1973). Electrodermal activity as an index for arousal in schizophrenia. *Psychological Bulletin*, **79**, 233–238.

Dohrenwend, B. P. and Dohrenwend, B. S. (1969). *Social Status and Psychological Disorder: A Causal Enquiry*. New York: Wiley.

Dunn, R. F. (1968). Anxiety and verbal concept learning. *Journal of Experimental Psychology*, **76**, 286–290.

Easterbrook, J. A. (1959). The effect of emotion on cue utilization and the organization of behavior. *Psychological Review*, **66**, 183–201.

Epstein, S. (1972). The nature of anxiety with emphasis on its relationship to expectancy. In C. D. Spielberger (Ed.), *Anxiety — Current Trends in Theory and Research*. New York: Academic Press.

Epstein, S. (1976). Anxiety, arousal and the self-concept. In I. G. Sarason and C. D. Spielberger (Eds.), *Stress and Anxiety*, Vol. 3. New York: Wiley.

Eysenck, H. J. (1973). Personality, learning and 'anxiety'. In H. J. Eysenck (Ed.), *Handbook of Abnormal Psychology*. London: Pitman.

Eysenck, H. J. (1976). The learning theory model of neurosis – a new approach. *Behaviour Research and Therapy*, **14**, 251–267.

Eysenck, M. W. (1977). *Human Memory: Theory, Research and Individual Differences*. Oxford: Pergamon.

Fantz, R. L. and Nevis, S. (1967). Pattern preferences and perceptual-cognitive development in early infancy. *Merrill-Palmer Quarterly*, **13**, 77–108.

Faught, W. E., Colby, K. M. and Parkison, R. C. (1977). Inferences, effects and intentions in a model of paranoia. *Cognitive Psychology*, **9**, 153–187.

Frenkel-Brunswik, E. (1948). Dynamic and cognitive categorization of qualitative material: II. interviews of the ethnically prejudiced. *Journal of Psychology*, **25**, 261–277.

Frenkel-Brunswik, E. (1949). Intolerance of ambiguity as an emotional and perceptual personality variable. *Journal of Personality*, **18**, 108–143.

Gamer, M. S., Gallant, D. and Grunebaum, H. (1976). Children of psychotic mothers: an evaluation of one-year olds on a test of object permanence. *Archives of General Psychiatry*, **33**, 311–317.

Garmezy, N. (1975). The experimental study of children vulnerable to psychopathology. In A. Davis (Ed.), *Child Personality and Psychopathology: Current Topics*. New York: Wiley.

Giora, Z. (1975). *Psychopathology: A Cognitive View*. New York: Gardner Press.

Goldberg, E. M. and Morrison, S. L. (1963). Schizophrenia and social class. *British Journal of Psychiatry*, **109**, 785–802.

Goldstein, M. J. and Rodnick, E. H. (1975). The family's contribution to the etiology of schizophrenia: current status. *Schizophrenia Bulletin, Issue No. 15*, 48–63.

Gottesman, I. I. and Shields, J. (1972). *Schizophrenia and Genetics: A Twin Study Vantage Point*. New York: Academic Press.

Gottesman, I. I. and Shields, J. (1976). A critical review of recent adoption, twin and family studies of schizophrenia: behavioral genetics perspectives. *Schizophrenia Bulletin*, **2**, 360–401.

Goulet, L. R. and Mazzei, J. (1969). Verbal learning and confidence thresholds as a function of test anxiety, intelligence and stimulus similarity. *Journal of Experimental Research in Personality*, **3**, 247–252.

Grunebaum, H., Weiss, J. L., Gallant, D. and Cohler, B. J. (1974). Attention in young children of psychotic mothers. *American Journal of Psychiatry*, **131**, 887–891.

Gruzelier, J. H. (1975). The cardiac responses of schizophrenics in orienting, signal and non-signal tones. *Biological Psychology*, **3**, 143–155.

Gruzelier, J. H. (1978). Bimodel states of arousal and lateralised dysfunction in schizophrenia: the effect of chlorpromazine on psychophysiological, information-processing and endocrine measures. In L. Wynne, R. Cromwell and S. Matthysse (Eds.), *Nature of Schizophrenia: New Findings and Future Strategies*. New York: Wiley.

Gruzelier, J. H. and Venables, P. H. (1972). Skin conductance orienting activity in a heterogeneous sample of schizophrenics. *Journal of Nervous and Mental Diseases*, **155**, 277–287.

Gruzelier, J. H. and Venables, P. H. (1973). Skin conductance responses to tones with and without attentional significance in schizophrenic and non-schizophrenic patients. *Neuropsychologia*, **11**, 221–230.

Hamilton, V. (1957). Perceptual and personality dynamics in reactions to ambiguity. *British Journal of Psychology*, **48**, 200–215.

Hamilton, V. (1960). Imperception of Phi: some further determinants. *British Journal of Psychology*, **51**, 257–266.

Hamilton, V. (1963a). Size constancy and cue responsiveness in psychosis. *British Journal of Psychology*, **54**, 25–39.

Hamilton, V. (1963b). I.Q. changes in chronic schizophrenia. *British Journal of Psychiatry,* **109**, 642–648.

Hamilton, V. (1964). Techniques and methods in psychological assessment: a critical reappraisal. *Bulletin of the British Psychological Society,* **17**, 27–36.

Hamilton, V. (1966). Deficits in primitive perceptual and thinking skills in schizophrenia. *Nature* (London), **211**, 389–392.

Hamilton, V. (1972a). Maternal rejection and conservation: an analysis of suboptimal cognition. *Journal of Child Psychology and Psychiatry,* **13**, 147–166.

Hamilton, V. (1972b). The size constancy problem in schizophrenia: a cognitive skill analysis. *British Journal of Psychology,* **63**, 73–84.

Hamilton, V. (1975). Socialization and information-processing: a capacity model of anxiety induced performance deficits. In I. G. Sarason and C. D. Spielberger (Eds.), *Stress and Anxiety.* Vol. 2. New York: Wiley.

Hamilton, V. (1976a). Motivation and personality in cognitive development. In V. Hamilton and M. D. Vernon (Eds.), *The Development of Cognitive Processes.* London: Academic Press.

Hamilton, V. (1976b). Cognitive development in the neuroses and schizophrenias. In V. Hamilton and M. D. Vernon (Eds.), *The Development of Cognitive Processes.* London: Academic Press.

Hamilton, V. and Moss, M. (1974). A method of scaling conservation of quantity problems by information content. *Child Development,* **45**, 737–745.

Hamilton, V. and Salmon, P. (1962). Psychological changes in chronic schizophrenics following differential activity programmes. *Journal of Mental Science,* **108**, 505–519.

Heilbrun, A. B. (1977). An analogue study of disattentional strategies in schizophrenia. *Journal of Abnormal Psychology,* **86**, 135–144.

Hemsley, D. R. (1975). A two-stage model of attention in schizophrenia research. *British Journal of Social and Clinical Psychology,* **14**, 81–89.

Hemsley, D. R. (1976). Attention and information processing in schizophrenia. *British Journal of Social and Clinical Psychology,* **15**, 199–209.

Hemsley, D. R. and Zawada, S. L. (1976). 'Filtering' and the cognitive deficit in schizophrenia. *British Journal of Psychiatry,* **128**, 456–461.

Herman, J., Mirsky, A. F., Ricks, N. L. and Gallant, D. (1977). Behavioral and electrographic measures of attention in children at risk for schizophrenia. *Journal of Abnormal Psychology,* **86**, 27–33.

Hill, K. T. and Sarason, S. B. (1966). The relationship of test anxiety and defensiveness to test and school performance over the elementary school years: a further longitudinal study. *Monographs of the Society for Research in Child Development,* **31**, (104).

Hodges, W. F. and Spielberger, C. D. (1969), Digit span: an indicant of trait or state anxiety? *Journal of Consulting and Clinical Psychology,* **33**, 430–434.

Hollingshead, A. B. and Redlich, F. C. (1958). *Social Class and Mental Illness.* New York: Wiley.

Holt, R. R. (1967). The development of the primary process: a structural view. In R. R. Holt (Ed.), *Motives and Thought: Psychoanalytic Essays in Honor of David Rapaport. Psychological Issues,* **18/19**, 345–383.

Holzman, P. S., Levy, D. L., and Proctor, L. R. (1976). Smooth pursuit eye movements, attention and schizophrenia. *Archives of General Psychiatry,* **33**, 1415–1420.

Howells, J. G. (1955). *Modern Perspectives in Child Psychiatry.* Edinburgh and London: Oliver and Boyd.

Itil, T. M., Hsu, W., Saletu, B. and Mednick, S. A. (1974). Computer EEG and auditory evoked potential investigations in children at high risk for schizophrenia. *American Journal of Psychiatry*, **131**, 892–900.

Jacob, T. (1975). Family interactions in disturbed and normal families: a methodological and substantive review. *Psychological Bulletin*, **82**, 33–65.

Jones, J. E., Rodnick, E. H., Goldstein, M. J., McPherson, S. R. and West, K. L. (1977). Parental transactional style deviance as a possible indicator of risk for schizophrenia. *Archives of General Psychiatry*, **34**, 71–74.

Jones, M. B. and Offord, D. R. (1975). Independent transmission of I.Q. and schizophrenia. *British Journal of Psychiatry*, **126**, 185–190.

Kahneman, D. (1973). *Attention and Effort*. Englewood Cliffs: Prentice-Hall.

Kay, S., Singh, M. M. and Smith, J. M. (1975). Colour Form Representation Test: a of cognitive dysfunction in schizophrenia. *British Journal of Social and Clinical Psychology*, **14**, 387–399.

Kay, S., Singh, M. M. and Smith, J. M. (1975). Colour Form Representation Test: a developmental method for the study of cognition in schizophrenia. *British Journal of Social and Clinical Psychology*, **14**, 401–411.

Kessler, P. and Neale, J. M. (1974). Hippocampal damage and schizophrenia: a critique of Mednick's theory. *Journal of Abnormal Psychology*, **83**, 91–96.

Kety, S. S., Rosenthal, D., Wender, P. H. and Schulsinger, F. (1976). Studies based on a total sample of adopted individuals and their relatives: why they were necessary, what they demonstrated and failed to demonstrate. *Schizophrenia Bulletin*, **2**, 413–428.

Kirkegaard, S. (1944). *The Concept of Dread*. Princeton: Princeton University Press. (First published 1844).

Knight, R., Sherer, M. and Shapiro, J. (1977). Iconic imagery in overinclusive and underinclusive schizophrenics. *Journal of Abnormal Psychology*, **86**, 242–255.

Koh, S. D., Kayton, L. and Berry, R. (1973). Mnemonic organization in young nonpsychotic schizophrenics. *Journal of Abnormal Psychology*, **81**, 299–310.

Koh, S. D., Kayton, L. and Peterson, R. A. (1976). Affective encoding and consequent remembering in schizophrenic young adults. *Journal of Abnormal Psychology*, **85**, 156–166.

Koh, S. D., Szoc, R. and Peterson, R. A. (1977). Short-term memory scanning in schizophrenic young adults. *Journal of Abnormal Psychology*, **86**, 451–460.

Kohn, M. L. (1976). The interaction of social class and other factors in the etiology of schizophrenia. *American Journal of Psychiatry*, **133**, 177–180.

Lader, M. (1975). *The Psychophysiology of Mental Illness*. London: Routledge and Kegan Paul.

Lane, E. A. and Albee, G. W. (1970). Intellectual antecedents of schizophrenia. In M. Roff and D. F. Ricks (Eds.), *Life History Research in Psychopathology*. Minneapolis: University of Minnesota Press.

Lang, P. J. and Buss, A. H. (1965). Psychological deficit in schizophrenia: II. interference and activation. *Journal of Abnormal Psychology*, **70**, 77–106.

Lawson, J. S., McGhie, A. and Chapman, J. (1964). Perception of speech in schizophrenia. *British Journal of Psychiatry*, **110**, 375–380.

Lazarus, R. S. (1966). *Psychological Stress and the Coping Process*. New York: McGraw-Hill.

Leonard, K. (1976). Schizophrenic disorders: survey and classification. In S. Krauss (Ed.), *Encyclopaedic Handbook of Medical Psychology*. London: Butterworths.

Lewis, M. and Goldberg, S. (1969). Perceptual-cognitive development in infancy: a generalized expectancy model as a function of the mother–infant interaction. *Merrill-Palmer Quarterly*, **15**, 81–100.

Lidz, T. (1976). Commentary on 'A critical review of recent adoption, twin and family studies of schizophrenia: behavioral genetic perspectives'. *Schizophrenia Bulletin*, **2**, 402–412.

Lidz, T., Fleck, S. and Cornelison, A. R. (Eds.), (1965). *Schizophrenia and the Family*. New York: International Universities Press.

Liebert, R. M. and Morris, L. W. (1967). Cognitive and emotional components of test anxiety: a distinction and some initial data. *Psychological Reports*, **20**, 975–978.

Lykken, D. T. and Venables, P. H. (1971). Direct measurement of skin conductances: a proposal for standardization. *Psychophysiology*, **8**, 656–672.

McDowell, D., Reynolds, B. and Magaro, P. (1975). The integration defect in paranoid and nonparanoid schizophrenia. *Journal of Abnormal Psychology*, **84**, 629–636.

McGhie, A. (1966). Psychological studies of schizophrenia. *British Journal of Medical Psychology*, **39**, 281–288.

McGhie, A. and Chapman, J. (1961). Disorders of attention and perception in early schizophrenia. *British Journal of Medical Psychology*, **34**, 103–116.

McGhie, A., Chapman, J., and Lawson, J. S. (1965). The effect of distraction on schizophrenic performance: 2. perception and immediate memory. *British Journal of Psychiatry*, **111**, 383–390.

McReynolds, P. (1960). Anxiety, perception and schizophrenia. In D. D. Jackson (Ed.), *The Etiology of Schizophrenia*. New York: Basic Books.

McReynolds, P. (1976). Assimilation and anxiety. In M. Zuckerman and C. D. Spielberger (Eds.), *Emotions and Anxiety: New Concepts, Methods, and Applications*. Hillsdale, N. J.: Lawrence Erlbaum.

Mandler, G. (1975). *Mind and Emotion*. New York: Wiley.

Mandler, G. and Sarason, S. B. (1952). A study of anxiety and learning. *Journal of Abnormal and Social Psychology*, **47**, 166–173.

Mednick, S. A. (1958). A learning theory approach to research in schizophrenia. *Psychological Bulletin*, **55**, 316–327.

Mednick, S. A. and Schulsinger, F. (1972). A learning theory of schizophrenia: thirteen years later. In M. Hammer, K. Salzinger and S. Sutton (Eds.), *Psychopathology*. New York: Wiley.

Mednick, S. A., Schulsinger, F., and Garfinkel, R. (1975). Children at high risk for schizophrenia: predisposing factors and intervention. In M. L. Kietzman, S. Sutton and J. Zubin (Eds.), *Experimental Approaches to Psychopathology*. New York: Academic Press.

Meehl, P. E. (1962). Schizotaxia, schizotypy, schizophrenia. *American Psychologist*, **17**, 827–838.

Melzack, R. (1975). *The Puzzle of Pain*. Harmondsworth: Penguin.

Miller, J. G. (1960). Information input overload and psychopathology. *American Journal of Psychiatry*, **116**, 321–332.

Mowrer, O. H. (1947). On the dual nature of learning – a reinterpretation of 'conditioning' and 'problem solving'. *Harvard Educational Review*, **17**, 102–148.

Mueller, J. H. (1976). Anxiety and cue utilization in human learning and memory. In M. Zuckerman and C. D. Spielberger (Eds.), *Emotions and Anxiety: New Concepts, Methods and Applications*. Hillsdale, N. J.: Lawrence Erlbaum.

Neale, J. M. (1971). Perceptual span in schizophrenia. *Journal of Abnormal Psychology*, **77**, 196–204.

Neisser, U. (1967). *Cognitive Psychology*. New York: Appleton–Century–Crofts.

Newell, A. and Simon, H. A. (1972). *Human Problem Solving*. Englewood Cliffs, N.J.: Prentice-Hall.

Norman, D. A. and Bobrow, D. G. (1975). On data-limited and resource-limited processes. *Cognitive Psychology,* **1**, 44–64.

Odom-Brooks, P. H. and Arnold, D. J. (1976). Cognition development in mental subnormality. In V. Hamilton and M. D. Vernon (Eds.), *The Development of Cognitive Processes.* London: Academic Press.

O'Neal, P. and Robins, L. N. (1958). The relation of childhood behavior problems to adult psychiatric states: a 30-year follow-up of 150 subjects. *American Journal of Psychiatry,* **114**, 961–969.

Osler, S. F. and Kofsky, E. (1965). Stimulus uncertainty as a variable in the development of conceptual ability. *Journal of Experimental Child Psychology,* **2**, 264–279.

Payne, R. W. (1973). Cognitive abnormalities. In H. J. Eysenck (Ed.), *Handbook of Abnormal Psychology* (2nd edn.). London: Pitman.

Piaget, J. and Inhelder, B. (1973). *Memory and Intelligence.* London: Routledge and Kegan Paul.

Posner, M. I., Boies, S. J., Eichelman, W. H. and Taylor, L. (1969). Retention of visual and name codes of single letters. *Journal of Experimental Psychology,* **7**, 1–16.

Pribam, K. H. and McGuinness, D. (1975). Arousal, activation and effort in the control of attention. *Psychological Review,* **82**, 116–149.

Rachman, S. (1974). *The Meanings of Fear.* Harmondsworth: Penguin.

Rubinstein, J. (1967). Maternal attentiveness and subsequent exploratory behavior in the infant. *Child Development,* **38**, 1089–1100.

Rutter, M. (1972). *Maternal Deprivation Reassessed.* Hamondsworth: Penguin.

Rutter, M., Birch, H. G., Thomas, A. and Chess, S. (1964) Temperamental characteristics in infancy and the later development of behaviour disorders. *British Journal of Psychiatry,* **110**, 651–661.

Rutter, M. and Madge, N. (1976). *Cycles of Disadvantage: A Review of Research.* London: Heinemann.

Saltz, E. (1970). Manifest anxiety: have we misread the date? *Psychological Review,* **77**, 568–573.

Sarason, I. G. (1972). Experimental approaches to test anxiety: attention and the uses of information. In C. D. Spielberger (Ed.), *Anxiety — Current Trends in Theory and Research.* New York: Academic Press.

Sarason, I. G. (1975). Anxiety and self-preoccupation. In I. G. Sarason and C. D. Spielberger (Eds.), *Stress and Anxiety,* Vol. 2. New York: Wiley.

Sarason, S. B., Davidson, K. S., Lighthall, F. F., Waite, R. R. and Ruebush, B. K. (1960). *Anxiety in Elementary Schoolchildren: A Report of Research.* New York: Wiley.

Sarason, S. B., Hill, K. T. and Zimbardo, P. G. (1964). A longitudinal study of the relation of test anxiety to performance on intelligence and achievement tests. *Monographs of the Society for Research in Child Development,* **29** (98).

Schopler, E. and Loftin, J. (1969). Thinking disorders in parents of young psychotic children. *Journal of Abnormal Psychology,* **74**, 281–287.

Schroder, H. M., Driver, M. J. and Streufert, S. (1967). *Human Information Processing.* New York: Holt, Rinehart, and Winston.

Segal, J., Boomer, D. S. and Bouthilet, L. (1975). *Research in the Service of Mental Health.* Rockville, Mld.: N.I.M.H.

Shagass, C., Roemer, R. A. and Amadeo, M. (1976). Eye-tracking performance and engagement of attention. *Archives of General Psychiatry,* **33**, 121–125.

Shakow, D. (1962). Segmental set: a theory of the formal psychological deficit in schizophrenia. *Archives of General Psychiatry,* **6**, 1–17.

Shalit, B. (1977). Structural ambiguity and limits of coping. *Journal of Human Stress,* **3,** 32–45.

Singer, M. T. and Wynne, L. C. (1965a). Thought disorder and family relations of schizophrenics: III. methodology using projective techniques. *Archives of General Psychiatry,* **12,** 187–200.

Singer, M. T. and Wynne, L. C. (1965b). Thought disorder and family relations of schizophrenics: IV. results and implications. *Archives of General Psychiatry,* **12,** 201–212.

Sjöberg, H. (1977). Interaction of task difficulty, activation and work load. *Journal of Human Stress,* **3,** 33–38.

Skinner, B. F. (1953). *Science and Human Behavior.* London: Collier-McMillan.

Slater, E. and Roth, M. (Eds.), (1969). *Clinical Psychiatry* (3rd edn.). London: Bailliere, Tindall, and Cassell.

Smock, C. D. (1955). The influence of psychological stress on the 'intolerance of ambiguity'. *Journal of Abnormal and Social Psychology,* **50,** 177–182.

Sokolov, E. W. (1963). *Perception and the Conditioned Reflex.* New York: MacMillan.

Spence, J. T. and Spence, K. W. (1966). The motivational components of manifest anxiety: drive and drive stimuli. In C. D. Spielberger (Ed.), *Anxiety and Behavior.* London: Academic Press.

Sperling, G. (1960). The information available in brief visual presentations. *Psychological Monographs,* **74,** No. 11.

Spielberger, C. D. (Ed.), (1966). *Anxiety and Behavior.* New York: Academic Press.

Spielberger, C. D. (Ed.) (1972). *Anxiety – Current Trends in Theory and Research.* New York: Academic Press.

Stabenau, J. R. and Pollin, W. (1967). Early characteristics of monozygotic twins discordant for schizophrenia. *Archives of General Psychiatry,* **17,** 723–734.

Steingart, I., Grand, S., Margolis, R., Freedman, N. and Buchwald, C. (1976). A study of the representation of anxiety in chronic schizophrenia. *Journal of Abnormal Psychology,* **85,** 535–542.

Taylor, J. and Spence, K. W. (1952). The relationship of anxiety level to performance in serial learning. *Journal of Experimental Psychology,* **44,** 61–64.

Traupman, K. L., Berzofsky, M. and Kesselman, M. (1976). Encoding of taxonomic word categories by schizophrenics. *Journal of Abnormal Psychology,* **85,** 350–355.

Tulkin, S. R. and Kagan, J. (1972). Mother–child interaction in the first year of life. *Child Development,* **43,** 31–41.

Ullman, L. and Krasner, L. (1965). *Case Studies in Behavior Modification.* New York: Holt, Rinehart and Winston.

Van Dyke, J. L., Rosenthal, D. and Rasmussen, P. V. (1974). Electrodermal functioning in adopted-away offspring of schizophrenics. *Journal of Psychiatric Research,* **10,** 199–215.

Venables, P. H. (1964). Input dysfunction in schizophrenia. In B. A. Maher (Ed.), *Progress in Experimental Personality Research,* **1,** 1–47.

Venables, P. H. (1975). Signals, noise, refractoriness and storage: some concepts of value to psychopathology. In M. L. Kietzman, S. Sutton and J. Zubin (Eds.), *Experimental Approaches to Psychopathology.* New York: Academic Press.

Venables, P. H. and O'Connor, N. (1959). Reaction time to auditory and visual stimulation in schizophrenics and normals. *Quarterly Journal of Experimental Psychology,* **11,** 175–179.

Venables. P. H. and Warwick-Evans (1968). The effect of stimulus amplitude on the threshold of fusion of paired light flashes. *Quarterly Journal of Experimental Psychology,* **20,** 30–37.

Vernon, M. D. (1955). The function of schemata in perceiving . *Psychological Review,* **62**, 180–192.

Wachs, T. D., Uzgiris, I. G. and Hunt, J. McV. (1971). Cognitive development in infants of different age levels and from different environmental backgrounds: an explanatory investigation. *Merrill-Palmer Quarterly,* **17**, 283–317.

Warburton, D. M. (1975). *Brain, Behaviour and Drugs.* London: Wiley.

White, B. L. (1969). Child development research: an edifice without a foundation. *Merrill-Palmer Quarterly,* **15**, 49–79.

Wickens, C. D. (1974). Temporal limits of human information processing: a developmental study. *Psychological Bulletin,* **81**, 739–755.

Wine, J. (1971). Test anxiety and direction of attention. *Psychological Bulletin,* **75**, 92–104.

Wulbert, M., Inglis, S., Kriegsmann, E. and Miller, B. (1975). Language delay and associated mother–child interactions. *Developmental Psychology,* **11**, 61–70.

Wynne, L. C. and Singer, M. T. (1963a). Thought disorder and family relations of schizophrenics: I. a research strategy. *Archives of General Psychiatry,* **9**, 191–198.

Wynne, L. C. and Singer, M. T. (1936b). Thought disorder and family relations of schizophrenics: II. a classification of forms of thinking. *Archives of General Psychiatry,* **9**, 199–206.

Yates, A. J. (1966). Psychological deficit. *Annual Review of Psychology,* **17**, 111–144.

Yates, A. J. (1970). *Behavior Therapy.* New York: Wiley.

Yates, A. J. and Korboot, P. (1970). Speed of perceptual functioning in chronic nonparanoid schizophrenics. *Journal of Abnormal Psychology,* **76**, 453–461.

Zahn, T. P. (1975). Psychophysiological concomitants of task performance in schizophrenia. In M. L. Kietzman, S. Sutton and J. Zubin (Eds.), *Experimental Approaches to Psychopathology.* New York: Academic Press.

Zubin, J. (1975). Problem of attention in schizophrenia. In M. L. Kietzman, S. Sutton and J. Zubin (Eds.), *Experimental Approaches to Psychopathology.* New York: Academic Press.

Zuckerman, M. (1976). General and specific traits and states: new approaches to the assessment of anxiety and other constructs. In M. Zuckerman and C. D. Spielberger (Eds.), *Emotions and Anxiety: New Concepts, Methods and Applications.* Hillsdale, N. J.: Lawrence Erlbaum.

Chapter 13

Physiological Aspects of Anxiety and Schizophrenia

DAVID M. WARBURTON

1. Introduction
2. Anxiety
3. Physiological Changes in Anxiety
    (i) Electrocortical Arousal
    (ii) Stress Steriod Release
4. Steroid Action on the Brain and Anxiety
5. Drug Therapy of Anxiety
6. Anxiety Reduction by Coping Strategies
7. Therapy of Anxiety
8. Anxiety and Schizophrenias
9. Physiological Changes in Schizophrenias
    (i) Stress Steroid Release
    (ii) Electrocortical Arousal
10. Anxiolytic Drugs and the Schizophrenias
11. Cholinergic Hypothesis of the Schizophrenias
12. Pharmacotherapy of the Schizophrenias
13. Dopamine Hypothesis
14. Dopamine–Acetylcholine Balance Hypothesis
15. Therapy of the Schizophrenias
16. Conclusions
17. References

1. INTRODUCTION

In the past there was a dichotomy between neurologists who believed that there was a structural defect or toxic chemical that produced mental disorder and psychiatrists who believed in psychological causation, but were unable to explain the success of somatic therapies except in the most trivial terms. The more extreme psychonalytically oriented therapists even regarded drugs as chemical straightjackets that had no therapeutic value and, on the contrary, could actually interfere with the process of psychotherapy (Meerloo, 1955; Szasz, 1957). However, more eclectic therapists conceive of experiences of the mind as the result of an interplay of many levels (Mandell, 1968). Neural activity is the result of dynamic chemical changes in the nervous system. There is complex interaction between the cortical and subcortical structures, and the balance of activity in the neural networks is a consequence of the external environment and past experience which determines the cognitive interpretation at the cortex. This view will be called the mind-brain interaction model.

In accord with this eclectic model, therapy is not based on the structural change model of mental illness but on the view that mental illness is produced as a consequence of environmental events which act on the nervous system. This view does not deny that there may be some genetic influences which may be important in the aetiology. However, the illness is usually precipitated in the adult by the action of psychological factors on the nervous system. In this scheme childhood experience can have two possible influences; first, by acting on the nervous system directly and modifying the pathways before they are fully developed and second, by determining the sorts of adult experience which will be likely to precipitate illness. In addition, the precise symptoms displayed by the patient will have their origins in the development of the individual.

This mind–brain interaction model will be discussed with reference to anxiety and schizophrenia.

2. ANXIETY

One of the earliest theories of emotion was proposed by William James and by Carl Lange at about the same time. The essence of their ideas was that emotion was the feeling of the bodily changes that occur in response to our awareness of an exciting situation. It follows from the James–Lange conception of emotion that every emotion must result from a separate bodily change and that bodily changes produced by drugs or other physiological manipulations will alter the emotional state. This idea has proved to be inadequate to explain the facts. For example, both a gentle kiss and a painful burn will release the stress steroids, cortisol and corticosterone (Selye, 1956) and yet the accompanying emotion is usually different for the experiencing person. An extension of the James–Lange formulation to account for such differences has been described by Stanley Schachter. He suggested that the individual identifies and interprets the bodily changes within the framework of the present situation and his past experience (Schachter, 1964). Thus the emotional state will be a function of a state of physiological arousal and of a cognitive interpretation applied to this state of arousal. Therefore, a person will label the bodily sensations in terms of the knowledge of the immediate situation and, in most circumstances, the cognition will be relevant to the bodily state. However, it need not be, and cases where there is a divergence provide crucial evidence for the extended theory. Let us examine these notions with respect to anxiety.

Anxiety can be characterized as an unpleasant emotional state which is directed towards the future and this anticipatory element distinguishes it from fear which is the result of a response to an actual threat. All normal people are subject to anxiety prior to critical and uncertain events, like examinations, public appearances and so on. The magnitude of the emotional experience will depend on the amount of uncertainty in the environment. In normal life, an organism tries to reduce uncertainty and establish expectancies about the world, but any novel stimulus input represents an increase in uncertainty and produces an increase in electrocortical arousal. The amount of this arousal will depend on the size of the match and mismatch between expectancy and stimulus input (see Pribram, 1967). Mandler (1967) argues that by 'anticipation', or expectancy, we mean that the subject has some available behaviour which can be performed when the appropriate stimuli occur. A situation is 'ambiguous' or unpredictable, when no single set of behaviours is clearly relevant to the situation, and anxiety occurs when no situationally relevant behaviour is available to the organism.

In classical psychoanalytic theory Freud (1963) distinguished three types of anxiety. One form of anxiety is related to an object or situation, i.e. a phobia. A second kind is a general apprehensiveness which the patient attaches to any idea so that 'People who are tormented by this type of anxiety always forsee the most frightful of all possibilities, interpret every chance event as a premonition of evil and exploit every *uncertainty in a bad sense*' (e.g. p. 86, italics mine). The third form is completely divorced from any determinants and is inexplicable to both patient and therapist. Freud seemed to consider these states as variants of the same state, but there is at least an operational distinction between the situation-bound phobias and situationally-independent anticipatory anxiety.

In this chapter anxiety will be used specifically to refer to the situationally-independent anticipatory experience which results from both uncertainty about what will happen and uncertainty about the action to be taken. It will be considered as a person's label for the bodily states, resulting from the feedback of the stress steroids to the brain, experienced in situations perceived as unpredictable. It is beyond dispute that feelings of anxiety are correlated with the release of stress steroids from the adrenal glands but in this paper I will give evidence for a casual relationship.

In Chapter 2 it was pointed out that the secretions of the adrenal glands are controlled from the pituitary by means of hormones released into the blood stream from the hypothalamus. The pituitary releases adrenocorticotrophic hormone (ACTH) into the general blood circulation, and it is carried to the adrenal cortex which secretes corticosteroids, like cortisol and corticosterone. At the moment the evidence favours the hypothesis that there is adrenergic inhibition of ACTH release in parallel with a cholinergic releasing system. Part of the adrenergic inhibition seems to be mediated via the hippocampus and the control of secretion is by means of the cholinergic pathways ascending from the reticular formation, which are involved in electrocortical arousal and attention (Warburton, 1975b). Thus stress steroids are released whenever there is electrocortical arousal. Electrocortical arousal is controlled by the cholinergic pathways ascending from the reticular formation and, in this chapter, the emphasis will be on the contribution of the hippocampal circuit. This forms part of a feedback loop providing recurrent regulation of the internal and external inputs to the ascending cholinergic electrocortical arousal pathways. As a result of this regulation, redundant, i.e. 'expected', stimuli from the external and internal milieu are prevented from arousing the cortex. This implies that there must be some sort of storage of information about stimulus regularities in the internal and external environments at a simple level in the hippocampus and at a more complex level at the cortex. This characterization is based on the idea that the hippocampus via the midbrain maintains internal stability by diminishing the response to most repeated events in the internal and external world (Pribram, 1969). A mechanism of this kind would prevent the stress steroid response [see Chapter 2]. If the hippocampal formation and cortex 'recognize' a state of mismatch between actual input and expected input, specific changes are produced in the hippocampal output to the hypothalamus and the tegmental region. One of the major consequences of the output to the hypothalamus will be the release of stress steroids. It is argued that it is the action of these hormones on the brain chemistry, combined with the cognitive interpretation of the situation, that constitutes the emotion that is experienced as 'anxiety'. The first point of evidence for this argument will be considered in the next sections on neurochemical changes correlated with anxiety.

3. PHYSIOLOGICAL CHANGES IN ANXIETY

(i) Electrocortical Arousal

When normal subjects are put in a test situation, especially when they have electrodes attached to their scalp, they are apprehensive because of the uncertainty about the procedure, the test situation and so on. Typically, the record of electrocortical activity showed a large amount of beta activity, cortical desynchronization, and very few alpha waves (Lindsley, 1944; 1950). As the person became more familiar with the situation, the amplitude of the waves increased as the frequency decreased and alpha waves developed. If the subject was frightened or embarrased by the experimenter, the beta activity increased (Lindsley, 1944). Many other studies have confirmed this finding (see Lindsley, 1951). Thus in a normal population of subjects uncertainty increased beta activity, i.e. electrocortical arousal.

Equivalent results have been obtained in surveys of patients that were suffering from chronic anxiety. Alpha activity was observed less frequently in groups of normal subjects and beta activity was much more typical (Strauss, 1945; Lindsley, 1950). More sophisticated qualititative electrocortical research has confirmed the results of the older studies that patients with anxiety states show more cortical synchronization. When flashes of light are presented to a subject the electrocortical activity can be driven harmonically and in anxiety groups there is better driving at the higher frequencies than in normals, which shows that the endogenous rhythm is faster in the anxious groups.

On the basis of the finding of cortical desynchronization in anxiety a number of predictions about behaviour can be made from the data in Chapter 2. It would be expected that there would be greater attention to central stimuli and less attention for peripheral stimuli as well as better performance in simple perceptual situations and poorer performance in more complex perceptual tasks. Evidence in support of these statements comes from a study of performance in a dangerous situation (Weltman, Smith and Egstrom, 1971). Novice divers simulated a dive in a pressure chamber after all the potential dangers and emergency procedures had been explained to them, they were required to perform a central task and at the same time monitor a faint peripheral light. On the surface the subjects had no difficulties with the central task and the peripheral monitoring but in the simulated dive there was a clear impairment on the peripheral monitoring, but no decrement on performance of the main task. A questionnaire established that the subjects experienced considerable anxiety during the simulated dive. Clearly there has been a narrowing of attention in the dangerous situation and the adaptive value of this change for this situation can be readily seen.

The same changes in attentional performance can be seen in the vigilance performance of a group of dysthymic neurotics, whose main symptom was anxiety (Claridge, 1960). They were required to detect signals, three odd digits, in noise over a 30 min session. Normal subjects showed a vigilance decrement, but the dysthymic group was able to maintain vigilance during the monotonous task. However, when subjects were required to divide their attention by responding to both three odd digits and to the number six, the dysthymics performed worse than normal subjects.

It would be expected that stress would disrupt creative thinking. Divergent thinking is thought by Guilford (1967) to be the most important factor in creativity. An analysis of the effects of stress on thinking, induced by a film of a subincision ritual, supported this hypothesis (Krop, Alegre and Williams, 1969); divergent thinking was disrupted by stress but convergent thinking was not affected.

(ii) Stress Steroid Release

In Chapter 2, the effect of uncertainty on corticosteroid levels was discussed. In this section this material will be extended by considering how these changes in adrenocortical function are associated with anxiety-provoking situations. In normal people apprehension leads to corticosteroid release as one would have predicted from the electrocortical arousal changes we have just discussed. For example, in a comprehensive study of stress steriod response (Bliss, Migeon, Branch and Samuels, 1956) a set of normal subjects was assessed in situations involving experimental and natural stress. In the experimental situation attempts were made to control the amount of stress given to the subjects in order to compare the effects with those induced by naturally occurring, uncontrolled circumstances. Two public speaking tests were used: in one test subjects were merely told to talk about themselves in front of a one way mirror for 15 minutes. In the second test students were asked to discuss their psychology course when they believed that their course grade would be based on their performance. Increases in stress steroids were observed, but a smaller change was found in subjects who showed little or no disturbance by the procedure (e.g. 'I'm an experienced public speaker, this did not bother me much') in comparison with subjects who were upset by the ordeal because they felt that they did not know how to handle the situation.

In contrast to the rather modest elevation of steroids in the experimental situation, more drastic changes were seen in subjects who had faced a real-life emergency. They were medically well individuals who had arrived at a hospital emergency room usually with a sick releative, e.g. a daughter who had accompanied her father when he was brought to hospital with severe compound fractures of the leg after a car crash. Since the samples were taken at different times of the day a correction was made for the diurnal rhythm. The corrected values showed a 90 per cent increase over the normal values for a similar population. Thus the more unstructured the situation was, the greater the objective uncertainty and so the steroids were elevated more. However, an important variable was the subjective uncertainty, the person's own evaluation of his ability to handle the situation (Bliss et al., 1956).

Bliss et al. (1956) also took samples from subjects just before another less emotionally disturbing natural experience, examinations in medical school. The plasma steroid levels were significantly elevated in comparison with other students who were not being examined. In a variation of the study fourteen students were used as their own control. They were tested on a non-examination day as well as on day of the test. Eleven out of the fourteen candidates showed an elevation on the examination morning. The most dramatic reversal pattern was seen in a subject who reported that he was not very anxious about the examination. The other two candidates had nearly equal values for the two samples of plasma.

In a related study, the pituitary-adrenal activity of students who were taking an oral examination was studied. Blood corticotrophin levels and cortisol levels were determined for this group and compared with the levels of similar group of students who were not taking medical examinations. Adrenocorticotrophic hormone (ACTH) could not be detected in the blood of the control subjects (it is estimated as 0.1 nanograms per 100 ml of blood in normal subjects), but subjects taking the examination had levels of 6–9 nanograms per 100 ml of blood. In conjunction with the ACTH increase the blood cortisol of examinees was double the values in the control subjects. This increase was greater than that obtained with physical stress and suggests that emotional stress is a much more powerful activator of pituitary-adrenal activity (Jones, Bridges and Leak, 1970). In a related study Bloch and Brackenridge (1972) measured the plasma cortisol levels of students who were undergoing the same sort of examination. In addition, they assessed their emotionality by means of the Taylor Manifest Anxiety Scale, and found that the subjects with the highest anxiety scores had the higher plasma cortisol levels. In other words there was an interaction between the individual and the situation which determined the pituitary-adrenal response. Other groups (Curtis, Fogel, McEvoy and Zarate, 1970) have found correlations between Manifest Anxiety scores and corticosteroid levels in plasma and urine.

The interaction between the individual and the situation has been revealed even more clearly in patients with pathological anxiety. A number of studies (e.g. Bliss *et al.*, 1956), have found that plasma steroid levels were up to 70 per cent higher than normal in patients with high levels of anxiety. The elevated steroid levels in the anxious patients can be taken as evidence that the hypothalamic-pituitary-adrenal system in anxious patients is 'set' to release corticosteroids at an increased rate in response to any situation-person interaction.

In the study of Persky *et al.* (1956) patients were assessed as being anxious or anxiety prone by covert observation and by the patients' verbal reports at psychiatric interviews. They were subjected to a 30 min stressful interview. The interview was designed to evoke overt anxiety in the patients by discussing problems that were known to be disturbing to them. The fact that three subjects withdrew from the study at this time suggests that the technique was effective. Plasma samples were collected and the plasma hydrocortisone levels were assessed. Although the levels in the patients were considerably higher than normal, their steroid levels were raised even further by the interview and the magnitude of the increase was correlated with the patient's estimate of the stress intensity. The increases were not very large because the stress stimulus could not be too traumatic for ethical reasons.

Thus there is a good correlation between anxiety level and corticosteroid levels. This relation seems to hold up irrespective of the psychiatric diagnosis. Lingjaerde (1964) examined plasma hydrocortisone in a variety of patients with mental illness, including schizophrenia and depression. Elevated plasma hydrocortisone occurred in many types of illness, but the one discriminating factor appeared to be the anxiety that the patients reported experiencing.

4. STEROID ACTION ON THE BRAIN AND ANXIETY

In the last section a correlative relationship between the experience of anxiety and stress steroids was demonstrated. However it is fallacious reasoning to argue that the stress steroids caused anxiety from the evidence that has been presented so far. In this section evidence will be presented for the hypothesis, originally discussed by Warburton (1975a), that the hormones do reach the brain and that high levels of endogenous and exogenous hormones increase proneness to anxiety.

It is known that the levels of corticosterone are kept stable by negative feedback of steroids to receptors in the hypothalamus. Injection of corticosteroids into the hypothalamus (Chowers, Feldman and Davidson, 1963) and other regions like the mesencephalic reticular formation decreased the secretion of ACTH, and produce atrophy of the adrenal cortex. As well as feedback to the hypothalamus it has been found (Pfaff, Silva and Weiss, 1971) that corticosterone produced decreases in hippocampal unit activity, starting 10 to 40 minutes after injection and lasting for at least two hours. This prolonged effect would be characteristic of a substance binding intracellularly in the hippocampal formation and inhibiting activity to the pyramidal cells.

Studies of the effects of stress steroids on brain chemistry have shown that brain levels of noradrenalin decrease after exposure to a variety of stressors (Maynert and Levi, 1964; Levi and Maynert, 1964; Corrodi, Fuxe, Lidbrink and Olson, 1972). This change can be interpreted as feedback of stress steroids to the brain activating adrenergic neurons, which include the inhibitory neurons in the median eminence that reduce the production of corticotrophin releasing factor (as part of the negative feedback mechanism for steroid control). Serotonin neurons also appear to be affected by the feedback of stress steroids. Exposure to stressors (Curzon and Green, 1968; Fuxe, Corrodi, Hokfelt and Jonsson, 1970) depleted brain serotonin when tryptophan hydroxylase, the rate-limiting synthesizing enzyme, was inhibited. These results in themselves are not convincing, but cortisol (Curzon and

Green, 1968) and corticosterone (Scapagnini, Moberg, Van Loon, de Groot and Ganong, 1971) also produce depletion showing that it is the steroid feedback that releases the serotonin. This increased rate of release would be expected to reduce the functional serotonin, if there was not a compensatory increase in synthesis. Some evidence for corticosteroid control of synthesis has come from studies where synthesis inhibitors were not injected and the serotonin levels remained constant after stress (Levi and Maynert, 1964; Maynert and Levi, 1964). This increased synthesis appears to be due to increased tryptophan hydroxylase activity produced by corticosteroids. (Azmiţia and McEwen, 1969; Azmitia, Algheri and Costa, 1970; Fuxe, Corrodi, Hokfelt and Jonsson, 1970). This result is consistent with the hypothesis that it was the low level of corticosterone in the adrenalectomized animals which reduced serotonin synthesis and that doses of corticosteroids increase serotonin synthesis. In other words corticosteroids increase the functional amounts of serotonin by increased synthesis and release.

If the feedback of corticosteroids acting on the neurochemical systems in the brain form part of the sensations experienced as anxiety then we would expect increased proneness to anxiety when corticosteroid levels are increased. Some evidence for this hypothesis comes from studies of patients with Cushing's disease in which the plasma levels of ACTH are not abnormal but the plasma corticosteroid levels are increased enormously. Psychiatric disturbance occurs in over seventy per cent of the cases (Michael and Gibbons, 1963) and this is not merely a reaction to the disfigurement and malaise that constitute a major part of the syndrome. Furger (1961) reported that a universal feature was emotional lability which took the form of gross over-reaction to emotional stimuli. In some cases there are grossly disturbed episodes of tension and acute anxiety (Cleghorn, 1957). Frequently patients are driven to avoid contact with events which are likely to trigger emotional responses. Treatment which reduces hormone levels leads to psychological improvement (Michael and Gibbons, 1963).

After cortisone treatment similar changes have been observed; the patients are in a tense alerted state marked by irritability, emotional lability, and anxiety. Although the patients invariably become more tense, anxiety was not always increased which suggests that the plasma cortisol was producing proneness to anxiety, but that anxiety did not occur unless the cognitive component was present. In experimental investigations the plasma corticosteroid level was raised rapidly by an intravenous injection of hydrocortisone and the subjects' anxiety levels assessed by a battery of tests. It was found that this steroid did not affect the immediate experience of anxiety, but their proneness to anxiety was enhanced (Weiner, Dorman, Persky, Stach, Norton and Levitt, 1963). A later study (Persky, Smith and Basu, 1971) found that intravenous doses of the naturally occurring corticosterone B and corticosterone F produced slight increases in anxiety measured on the same anxiety scales used by Weiner *et al.* (1963). In order to examine the joint role of the corticosteroids and cognitions in producing feelings of anxiety, subjects were given a cortisone injection and an anxiety-provoking suggestion while in a hypnotic trance. These subjects responded to the suggestion with a more prolonged anxiety response than subjects receiving a placebo injection (Levitt, Persky, Brady and Fitzgerald, 1963).

More evidence for the importance of the biochemical component for the experience of anxiety comes from the reports of subjects in stress experiments. Even though they were debriefed at the end of an experiment they still experienced tension and anxiety. The subjects who were most upset in the public speaking test of Bliss *et al.* (1956), continued to experience tension later. For example, one reported that 'Knees shook, felt foolish. For some reason couldn't cope with situation. Felt very upset for at least an hour after test was concluded' or 'Felt self-conscious and silly. Thought I did stupidly. Seldom if ever got more tense than that. Even more tense after task was over'.

Taken together, these studies give strong evidence for steroids acting on the brain and the consequent changes in biochemistry are an important part of the feelings that are labelled as anxiety.

5. DRUG THERAPY OF ANXIETY

If anxiety depends on the feedback of corticosteroids to the brain, then any drugs will reduce anxiety if they either block the corticosteroid release mechanisms in the brain or reverse the effects of the corticosteroids on the brain. The drug could reduce corticosteroid release either by blocking the cholinergic release mechanism, by activating the adrenergic inhibitory system, or by blocking the increase in functional serotonin that is produced by corticosteroids.

More recently a number of anti-anxiety compounds have been developed which have some of these properties. The most frequently used drugs in the treatment of anxiety states are the benzodiazepines, including chlordiazepoxide ('Librium'), diazepam ('Valium'), and oxazepam ('Serax'). The effects of the benzodiazepines on acetylcholine have suggested that the diazepam increased the cortical levels of the transmitter by decreasing release at the terminals of the ascending cholinergic pathways (Ladinsky, Consolo, Peri and Garattini, 1973). Decreased functional acetylcholine would reduce the activity in the cholinergic releasing pathways for ACTH and reduce the secretion of corticosteroids. In addition the benzodiazepines act on noradrenalin and serotonin neurons, i.e. the pathways believed to be affected by the feedback of corticosteroids to the brain. Assays of the effect of the benzodiazepines on the synthesis, storage, release, receptor interaction and inactivation of these transmitters indicate that the major benzodiazepines chlordiazepoxide and diazepam) did not change the levels of noradrenalin in any part of the rat brain (Taylor and Laverty, 1969). However, the static levels of transmitter are not good indicators of functional transmitter in the brain. Electric shock increased noradrenalin turnover in all regions of the rat brain (Bliss, Ailion and Zwanziger, 1968) as one would expect from the action of corticosteroids on noradrenalin, but the benzodiazepines blocked this effect and maintained the noradrenalin levels close to their control values (Taylor and Laverty, 1973). A human anti-anxiety potency order was found in these studies, so that nitrazepam was the most effective and chlordiazepoxide was the least effective in maintaining the noradrenalin turnover.

Benzodiazepines also reduced the rate of depletion of serotonin in the cortex, and other parts of the brain (Lidbrink, Corrodi, Fuxe and Olson, 1973) by blocking serotonin release (Chase, Katz and Kopin, 1970). Both single and repeated doses of oxazepam (Wise, Berger and Stein, 1972) reduced serotonin turnover in the midbrain–hindbrain region, and contrasts with the marked tolerance that developed in the noradrenalin system after repeated doses. This finding suggests that serotonin is the transmitter system that is important in mediating the effects of repeated benzodiazepine doses.

Tests of the hypothesis that it is the reduction of functional serotonin which is responsible for the anti-anxiety properties of the benzodiazepines have been carried out by Stein and his coworkers. They argued that serotonin blockers and serotonin synthesis inhibitors would produce the same effects on behaviour as those produced by the benzodiazepines. They injected methysergide, the antogonist, and released the suppressed responding in a conflict situation (Stein, Wise and Berger, 1973). Similar results were obtained with *para*-chlorophenylalanine, the synthesis blocker, and the suppressed behaviour could be reinstated by repletion of serotonin by injecting the precursor, 5-hydroxytryptophan (Stein *et al*., 1973). The serotonin agonist, alpha-methyltryptamine and serotonin both enhanced the suppression of responding in the conflict situation (Stein *et al.,* 1973), as one would have predicted from the other results. In a final test of the hypothesis, Stein *et al.* (1973) injected oxazepam, releasing the suppressed responding, and then introduced serotonin directly into the brain which restored the suppressed responding. The neurochemical pathways on which the oxazepam was acting are not known, although Stein *et al.* (1973) suggested serotonin fibres arising in the dorso-medial tegmental region of the midbrain. The terminals of these pathways are mainly in the limbic system (Anden, Dahlstrom, Fuxe, Larsson, Olson and Ungerstedt, 1966), the regions involved in the control of corticosteroid release. Electrophysiological studies of the benzodiazepines show that they act on these structures. Tests of chlordiazepoxide disclosed that there was a decreased duration of neural after-discharge of the septal area, and hippocampus, and a decreased amplitude of after-discharge in the amygdala (Schallek and Kuehn, 1960). Chlordiazepoxide also slowed the electrical activity in the septal area, amygdala, and hippocampus, but not the cortex, of the unanaesthetized animals (Schallek, Kuehn and Jew, 1962).

Experiments by Gray (1976a and b) have focused on the action of anxiolytic drugs on hippocampal activity. He found that rats who were subjected to uncertainty (e.g. novel environment or non-reward) showed characteristic hippocampal theta activity in the 7.5 to 8.5 Hz band (Gray and Ball, 1970). The sensitivity of the hippocampus in various frequency bands can be decreased by implanting an electrode in the septal area and stimulating the pathway to the hippocampus. More emotional strains, e.g. Maudsley reactive rats, as well as the more emotional male rats show a lower threshold for activity in this 7.5 to 8.5 Hz band especially at 7.7 Hz (Gray, 1976b). The lower threshold at 7.7 Hz could be abolished by drugs with anti-anxiety properties like alcohol and chlordiazepoxide (Gray, 1972).

Numerous studies have demonstrated the superiority of benzodiazepines to placebos and other anxiolytics like the barbiturates. In a controlled double-blind comparison of chlordiazepoxide with amylobarbital and placebo, Jenner, Kerry and Parkin (1960) found that in a two week trial chlordiazepoxide was more effective in relieving anxiety in neurotic patients than placebo. As a result of the improvement of the symptoms 'many patients were able to live more normal lives to travel on buses or walk in the streets alone without severe discomfort even after prolonged incapacity' (Jenner et al., 1961). The more recent benzodiazepines like diazepam ('Valium') may be better than chlordiazepoxide ('Librium') for the relief of anxiety with minimum side effects. Kerry and Jenner (1962) found diazepam was preferred by 35 of the 75 patients, while 10 selected chlordiazepoxide and 30 felt that the drugs were of equal value from the point of view of relief of symptoms. Only eight patients felt that chlordiazepoxide had few side effects while 31 had no preference. Few studies of the benzodiazepines have been carried out on changes in performance. It is known that untreated anxiety may result in seriously impaired driving ability (Rickels, 1977), but there are no studies which investigated the changes in the anxious person that result from anxiolytic medication. As far as I can trace, only one study investigated the performance after medication of workers who were suffering from anxiety and tension for various reasons (Proctor, 1962). It was carried out on 50 women working in a hosiery mill looping thread in the knitting machines on piecework. Their output had declined because of the anxiety and tension symptoms probably due to the uncertainty of this method of payment. Use of other anxiolytics impaired the loopers' dexterity and coordination so chlordiazepoxide was tried with considerable success; all but eight were relieved of their anxiety symptoms and their average production returned to normal in 32 of the women. No undesirable side effects of lowered mood, ataxia, and drowsiness were reported and obviously coordination was not affected, since their production returned to normal. Of course a more certain, humane form of payment would have eliminated the anxiety and obviated the need for anxiolytics in most of the workers. In the next section psychological methods of reducing anxiety will be discussed.

6. ANXIETY REDUCTION BY COPING STRATEGIES

In the last section the discussion was centered on biochemical methods of reducing the anxiety experienced by an individual. Normally stress steroids are released as a consequence of that individual's interpretation of his situation as uncertian in terms of events and, or, actions, and so individual variations in the analysis of some circumstances should result in differences in the stress response and the experienced emotion. Any types of analysis which reduce the stress response will be adaptive in the sense that they reduce the experienced anxiety in the short term although the strategy could be maladaptive in the long term by producing other sorts of psychological problems [see Horowitz, Chapter 8]. This process is analogous to homeostatic motivation where behaviour is directed towards restoration of some chemical imbalance within the body; drinking impure water may restore the water balance in a thirsty person, but lead to poisoning later. Some examples of these coping strategies and their effectiveness in reducing the stress response will be considered next.

Medically well subjects who are exposed to prolonged threat differ in their response. In an early study parents of fatally ill children were assessed psychologically and biochemically (Wolff, Friedman, Hofer and Mason, 1964); Wolff, Hofer and Mason, 1964). The psychological assessment consisted of two interviews; the first session was devoted to getting the parent to describe his experience of having a fatally ill child and the second dealt with the parent's life history. From the two interviews the effectiveness of his psychological defences were assessed in terms of an affect criterion (amount of overt distress), a function criterion (amount of impairment of function), and a 'defensive reserve' criterion (the ability to cope with other superimposed stressful experiences). Predictions were made from the interview data about the mean level of corticosteroid excretion, with no knowledge of the actual levels. One method of analysis of the data compared the estimated and actual mean values according to predetermined definitions of high, middle, and low; 23 of the 31 predictions were correct. A correlation between the predicted values was significant for both mothers and fathers in spite of the rather crude psychological assessment that was made. There was no evidence that a particular defensive strategy was associated with low steroids, rather it was the effectiveness of whatever defence was available that determined the stress response. One of these defences was denial of the existence of illness in the child and it was effective in maintaining low levels of stress steroid. This strategy was maladaptive, both with respect to parental functioning and also in terms of possible long-range consequences to the person when child did die. Although therapeutic care was given to parents who lived in the hospital with the child there was no evidence that the stress response was reduced in comparison with parents who lived outside the hospital and received no care. Unfortunately, there are no details of the sort of therapeutic aid that was offered to these unfortunate parents.

In the paper of Bourne (1969) discussed in Chapter 2, soldiers in combat also showed marked differences in their stress response which were related to the amount of uncertainty that they experienced. However, one fascinating aspect of these studies was the way in which the servicemen had developed strategies for coping with the stressful situations and the consequent threat of death and mutilation. The less intellectually capable individual developed ritualistic compulsive behaviour so that his tasks were performed in a painstaking systematic manner. In this way he was able to make the situation more predictable and subjectively less uncertain. In other cases the probability of a dangerous incident was minimized either intellectually by computing the probability of being harmed on a specific day or by a religious belief that they were operating under divine protection. As a consequence corticosteroid levels on action days were very little above those on rest days for these servicemen.

Similar strategies were described by Sachar (1970) in his study of a group of women in hospital for breast surgery. They were faced with the possibility of having breast cancer and breast surgery but only a few women showed elevated cortisol levels and these were only 25–35% above normal levels. There was a good correlation between the cortisol levels and psychiatric distress. Most women coped very well by means of ritualistic behaviour, intellectualizing the experience or by religious faith, and so the adrenocortical response was minimized. Only those women who confronted the danger directly had high corticosteroid response and experienced anxiety.

Thus a person can cope with stressful situations by developing strategies of various kinds to minimize uncertainty. As Masserman (1972) has expressed it '. . . no one is ever quite sure of his continued health; or of the reliability of his friends or, for that matter, the verity of his beliefs – and the intensities of his anxieties are in direct proportion to unpredictabilities in any or all of these spheres' (p. 187). The implications for human socialization are that we should be trained to cope with these major vicissitudes of life with strategies that are adaptive in both the short term and the long term. In the case of pathological anxiety the aim of the therapist should be to help the patient develop more effective strategies for intractable situations and better still encourage the person to change his lifestyle to avoid these situations in the future.

7. THERAPY OF ANXIETY

The treatment of any illness has both long- and short-term aims; the short-term aim is the reversal of the presenting symptoms and the long-term aim is the prevention of future breakdown. Obviously, the best treatment would completely reverse the symptoms, and there would be no residual effect and no reoccurrence of the disorder after treatment had been discontinued. This form of cure is only achieved in medicine in the case of some infectious diseases. In most of modern medicine, physicians aim for symptomatic treatment rather than cure, and it is strange that treatment in psychiatry is criticized for not providing 'cures'. At the present stage there is probably no form of psychiatric treatment that leaves no residue of the disorder or can prevent reoccurrence of the disorder completely.

The results of drug therapy and the implications of psychotherapy suggest that the most beneficial effects on anxious patients could be achieved by combining pharmacotherapy with psychotherapy. (In this chapter psychotherapy is used in the broad sense and not confined to psychoanalysis.) The simplest consequence of the combination would be an additive effect where the effect of the combined therapy would be equal to the sum of the effects of the two forms of therapy alone. The more complex effect would be an interactive one where the therapeutic benefit of the combined therapy was different from the combined simple effects.

The interactive treatment effect could be better or worse than the single effect. Thus the drug might modify the neurochemical state of patients so that they could function more effectively in the therapeutic situation and be able to make use of the therapeutic insights outside the clinic. For example, the drug could enable them to communicate and learn more constructively. It might reduce distractability, improve attention and stimulate more efficient problem solving ability, and enable them to think more rationally in all situations. On the basis of studies cited earlier on the effects of anxiety on information processing, these changes could be predicted. On the other hand, a negative interaction might occur; the drug might lull the patient into a false sense of security, an illusion of being cured so that they neglect therapy and may even abandon it (Szasz, 1957). Many psychoanalysts believe that emotional arousal enhances the effectiveness of psychotherapy and must be maintained (Frank, 1974). In addition, the patient may become psychologically dependent on the drug to control anxiety and ignore the environmental and personal factors that resulted in the disorder.

Studies of combined therapy have proved very difficult to set up and carry out (Group for the Advancement of Psychiatry, 1975). Special problems of treatment interaction are likely and the practical problems of controlling two forms of therapy are immense. Patient compliance must be elicited to ensure that both forms of therapy are obtained according to schedule. There are problems of defining adequate drug therapy (e.g. fixed or flexible doses) and psychotherapy (e.g. type of therapist and amount of treatment). There are problems of patient matching especially if there is a high attrition rate as patients dissatisfied with one form of treatment may drop out and there is some evidence that dissimilar patients have different treatments.

It is not surprising, therefore, that very few studies of any kind of combined therapy come close to satisfying rigorous scientific criteria. One of these studies is a double-blind investigation of combining psychotherapy with chlordiazepoxide ('Librium') (Lorr, McNair and Weinstein, 1965). Psychoneurotic men who attended an outpatient clinic were assigned randomly to one of six groups: (a) no treatment; (b) psychotherapy for one hour each week; (c) placebo with psychotherapy; (d) placebo without psychotherapy; (e) 'Librium' and psychotherapy; (f) chlordiazepoxide alone. In the first week patients in chlordiazepoxide groups reported more improvement than subjects who had no chlordiazepoxide and the latter groups felt better than the subjects who had no prescription. In other words, there was a positive placebo effect, but the anxiolytic had a greater positive effect on anxiety. Over a four week period, the therapists felt that the pharmacotherapy had facilitated psychotherapy for a third of the patients and had not interfered with the progress of psychotherapy in the remainder. This interactive effect was supported by the reports of patients which showed that chlordiazepoxide was superior to placebo and no drug in the psychotherapy groups. There was no evidence that the drug suppressed anxiety, so that the patient was less motivated to continue psychotherapy and less able to benefit from it. The suggestion from the studies is that the drug improved the information processing abilities of the patient so that they obtained more benefit from psychotherapy. The problem of this study was the high attrition rate which could have attenuated the differences and obscured the interaction. The attrition was 25 per cent for the psychotherapy groups compared with 17 per cent for groups not receiving psychotherapy. As attrition biases results in favour of the group with the highest rate, because they are the ones who feel that they have not been helped, it is likely that psychotherapy was less effective (May, 1971).

Unfortunately, there have been no studies of information processing in anxiety neurotics before, during, and after drug therapy, which would lend support to this notion. Studies of the effects of anxiolytics on the performance of normal subjects are not relevant because there is abundant evidence that effects differ qualitatively as well as quantitatively from those obtained from abnormal populations. For example, chlorpromazine impairs information processing in normal subjects, but improves schizophrenic performance.

These studies suggest that the anxiolytics provide relief from anxiety and that they also facilitate psychotherapy and so it is to the advantage for the therapist to use this form of medication to help the patient acquire coping strategies for his life. However, the drugs should not be used as a substitute for a change in strategies and lifestyle. The success of the drug in reversing the symptoms should not blind us to the fact that only change will minimize the reoccurrence of the disorder.

8.   ANXIETY AND THE SCHIZOPHRENIAS

Many hypotheses about the genesis of the schizophrenias are based on the notion that there is a continuum from anxiety to the psychosis. Many psychodynamic therapists have interpreted the symptomatology and communications of schizophrenics in terms of expression of unbearable anxiety, as an attempt to reduce this anxiety and prevent it from reaching awareness (Sullivan, 1948; Arieti, 1955). Like Freud (1963). They believed that anxiety had its origins in childhood socialization, but it remains effective throughout people's lives in response to disapproval and rejection, with individual variations in threshold. Full-blown anxiety was considered to be a disturbing and disconcerting experience and, as a consequence, schizophrenics show disturbed and disconcerted behaviour. Altogether the symptoms of schizophrenia represent a break with reality that was precipitated by overwhelming anxiety which leads to regression. Arieti (1955) elaborated this regression hypothesis on the basis of his experience of treating schizophrenic patients by psychoanalysis. He argued that anxiety interfered with higher neural centres and produced a functional paralysis of higher mental processes like logical thought. Lower neural centres are released from the inhibiton of the higher centres and more primitive thinking occurs. At this lower level of cognitive functioning there is less anxiety so that this regression is adaptive.

One of the learning theories of anxiety and schizophrenia which has stimulated considerable amount of research was proposed by Mednick (1958). Mednick postulated that the pre-psychotic person is prone to anxiety and recovers very slowly from a stressful experience. The anxiety acts as a drive and high drive levels lead to stimulus generalization. As a consequence the increased generalization during high anxiety will lead to more events being associated with anxiety. This is a positive feedback situation: as more anxiety-evoking stimuli are added, the anxiety levels rise further leading to greater generalization.

'As the spiral of anxiety and generalization mounts, his drive level may increase to an almost insupportable degree. As this is taking place, his ability to discriminate is almost totally eclipsed by his generalization tendencies. Any unit of a thought sequence might call up still another remote associate . . . His speech may resemble a "word salad". He will be an acute schizophrenic with a full-blown thinking disorder' (Mednick, 1958, p. 322).

According to Mednick the high anxiety acting as a drive is pushing remote and irrelevant thought patterns above the awareness threshold. However, this process leads to a change to a lower anxiety state. The occurrence of remote associations will divert the individuals attention from the anxiety-provoking stimuli and so anxiety will be reduced. Since anxiety reduction, i.e. drive reduction, is reinforcing in classical learning theory, Mednick argues that disorganized thinking will be reinforced. Consequently chronic schizophrenics will show thought disorders, but a low anxiety level because of the acquisition of these avoidance responses (Higgins and Mednick, 1963).

These hypotheses have been cited to show how information processing changes in schizophrenia have been interpreted as a response to extreme anxiety. Certainly in schizophrenia there is often sudden overwhelming anxiety and feelings of unreality. Renee described in the *Autobiography of a Schizophrenic Girl* (Sechehaye, 1951) the mental distress that occurred during these anxiety episodes.

'It was New Year's when I first experienced what I called *Fear*. It literally fell on me, how I know not . . . Suddenly Fear, agonizing, boundless Fear, overcame me, not the usual uneasiness of unreality, but real fear, such as one knows at the approach of danger, of calamity . . . I remained unaware of the basis for the fear which from then on came over me at any moment of the day . . .' (pp. 13–14). 'During the earliest attacks of Fear and intense unreality, I sometimes uttered these . . . words: "I should prefer to escape into madness to avoid this consuming fear". Alas, I did not know what I was saying. In my ignorance I believed that madness was a state of insensibility . . . (and) no responsibility. Never . . . had I even imagined what "to lose one's reason" actually meant . . .' (p. 23). 'In the endless silence and the strained immobility, I had the impression that some dreadful thing about to occur would break the quiet, something horrible, overwhelming. I waited, holding my breath, suffused with inquietude; but nothing happened. The immobility became more immobile, the silence more silent, things and people, their gestures and their noises, more artificially, detached one from the other, unreal, without life. And my fear increased, became inexpressible, shattering, intolerable' (p. 25).

On the basis of the earlier description of anxiety it would be predicted that if anxiety was the immediate cause of the disorder, schizophrenics would display (a) high levels of electrocortical arousal, (b) high levels of corticosteroids, and (c) that the disorder would be best treated by anti-anxiety drugs and psychotherapy. We will examine each of these predictions in the next three sections.

9. PHYSIOLOGICAL CHANGES IN SCHIZOPHRENIAS

(i) Stress Steroid Release

The anxiety hypothesis would predict that corticosteroid levels would be higher than normal. As part of the mammoth study of Bliss *et al.* (1956)

mentioned earlier, 64 measurements of corticosteroids were made on 26 schizophrenics who had been ill for five years or more. Their average steroid values were very slightly but not significantly above normal. In contrast, a group of emotionally disturbed patients, mostly schizophrenic, who were tested on admission showed higher than normal levels. In general the corticosteroid levels were correlated with level of disturbance (assessed on a five-point scale from calm to disintegrative panic). Assessment of the chronic patients showed that their manifest anxieties and psychological turmoil were low. Bliss *et al.*, suggest that anxieties and tensions and corticosteroid levels were low in chronic schizophrenics because of their withdrawal from reality and this idea is consonant with the hypothesis of Arieti (1955) and Mednick (1958) that schizophrenics adopt a lower level of cognitive functioning in order to lower anxiety.

Evidence on this point also comes from the work of Sachar on the changes over time in steroid levels in disturbed patients. Sachar's longitudinal studies of schizophrenic patients revealed that there was a marked change in steroid levels as the psychosis changed (Sachar, 1970). At the onset of the schizophrenic breakdown the patients were confused and felt that they had lost identity, i.e. total uncertainty, and this was correlated with massive corticosteroid excretion. Over time there was a change in the levels of anxiety and corticosteroid release. In some patients their 'mental reintegration' and premorbid coping mechanisms returned and corticosteroid levels fell. In other patients a psychotic solution developed in which a fixed delusional system was formed and also corticosteroid levels fell. Frequently this pathological coping mechanism involved strategies for reducing uncertainty, e.g. catatonia or compulsive behaviour. Once again we see that psychological coping mechanisms reduced the stress response. This work is clearly in accord with theories of schizophrenia that suggest that acute schizophrenia is on a continuum from severe anxiety, but that in chronic schizophrenia there has been an adaptation which lowers the anxiety level.

(ii) Electrocortical Arousal

Evidence which can be fitted to this idea comes from studies of electrocortical activity in schizophrenic populations. Unfortunately, many studies have merely studied schizophrenics without further classification (see Mirsky, 1969). It seems clear that much of the confusion in the literature is a consequence of this failure to classify the population in any way. In this discussion only studies which have subclassified the group in some way will be cited. For example, Kortchinskaia (1965) compared a set of patients who were subdivided into groups which fit the process-reactive distinction. The 'process' group had poor premorbid adjustment, in the sense that the disorder was enduring, while the 'reactive' group tended to have episodic psychoses, often with paranoia. The process patients were characterized by diffuse, slow, electrocortical activity and poor alpha blocking (i.e. beta activity) response to light stimulation. In contrast the reactive group had alpha activity at rest and showed alpha blocking to a light flash. Automatic frequency analysis have extended these findings. Young schizophrenics, i.e. those likely to be 'process', showed more delta (0 – 3.5 cps) and theta activity (3.6 – 7.5 cps) and less high beta activity (20 – 26.6 cps) than other groups (Fink, Itil and Clyde, 1965).

The inescapable conclusion of these studies and others like them (Mirsky, 1969) is that there are two schizophrenic populations, at least. The process-non-paranoid who have grossly slow, electrocortical activity and the reactive-paranoid who show normal to fast electrocortical activity. There has been considerable discussion about the validity of this dichotomy and it seems that the two forms may represent the end points of a continuum rather than a true dichotomy. Herron (1962) suggested that the 'most process' patient represents the extreme form of personality disintegration, while the 'most reactive' patient represents the extreme form of schizophrenic integration. I would argue the opposite point of view: that the 'most process' form represents schizophrenic integration and the 'most reactive' form represents personality disintegration. Let us examine this idea further.

The major characteristic of the reactive form of schizophrenic is the sudden change from an apparently well-adjusted personality to disintegration as the result of a stressful experience. In contrast the 'process' patient has an integrated pathological personality which would suggest that chronic stress has acted insidiously and unrelentingly on the person and there is adaptation on the part of the patient. In order to cope with and rationalize the disorder the patient develops coping patterns of activity. For example, McGhie and Chapman (1961) quote a patient who said 'If you move fast without thinking, coordination becomes difficult and everything becomes mechanical. I prefer to think out movements first before I do anything, then I get up slowly and do it' (p. 108). This patient, and others in the same article, expressed the feeling that they were in danger of losing control over their own mind and body. It is no wonder that many rationalized this frightening experience by developing delusions of control from outside themselves. As the disorder continues the delusion system becomes an elaborate, completely integrated set of beliefs. It follows from this view that if a reactive patient was not separated from the stressful situation, he could become adapted to the disorder and develop an integrated schizophrenic personality, as Arieti (1955) and Mednick (1958) have suggested.

10. ANXIOLYTIC DRUGS AND THE SCHIZOPHRENIAS

The most obvious prediction of the anxiety hypotheses is that schizophrenic symptoms should be alleviated by drugs that have proved effective in the treatment of pathological anxiety, especially in acute, reactive patients. In two studies of a total of 58 newly admitted schizophrenics diazepam was tested with little success (Hollister, Bennett, Kimbell, Savage and Overall, 1963). In the first study the drug produced improvement in a minority (9 out of 25) of patients whose predominant symptoms were anxiety, depression and somatic complaints, i.e. those who could be classified as 'pseudo-neurotic'. In a second study of 33 patients who had fewer of these symptoms, even less success was obtained and the only significant change was an exacerbation of the symptoms of unusual thought content and hallucinations which many people would consider as some of the core symptoms of schizophrenia. For comparison purposes a similar set of patients were tested on acetophenazine and perphenazine, two phenothiazines. The improvement of the phenothiazine group was far superior to the diazepam group even with the 'pseudo-neurotic' patients included. They concluded – 'Neither study provided encouragement for using diazepam in schizophrenics though it was obvious that the drug had some therapeutic effects in a minority of patients' (p. 748).

Similar conclusions were drawn from studies of chronic patients. For example, in a well-designed study (Holden, Itil, Keskiner and Fink, 1968), 22 chronic schizophrenics were tested double-blind, with chlordiazepoxide, thioridazine, and a combination of thioridazine (a phenothiazine) and chlordiazepoxide (an anxiolytic). The actively psychotic patients were assigned to the rows of a cross-over design in which the eight week treatment periods were separated by eight week placebo periods. Patients were assessed on global clinical improvement and for individual psychopathological symptoms like affect, association, delusions, communication, and so on. Deterioration occurred with five patients principally those on chlordiazepoxide. Both thioridazine and the combination of thioridazine and chlordiazepoxide alleviated the primary and florid secondary symptoms of schizophrenia while chlordiazepoxide had a mild anti-anxiety effect without changes in basic psychopathology. In conclusion, chlordiazepoxide was ineffective in altering the basic schizophrenic process while thioridazine improved affect, association, thought content, will, and mood.

Many other negative studies could have been cited with different anxiolytics. The unanimous conclusion of the standard texts in psycho-pharmacology is that anxiolytics are ineffective in the treatment of the core symptoms of schizophrenias – the cognitive disorder. Thus although anxiety is a common symptom of schizophrenias, anxiety is not the *immediate* cause of the disorder.

11. CHOLINERGIC HYPOTHESIS OF THE SCHIZOPHRENIAS

If acute schizophrenic episodes are characterized by an attentional disorder (see McGhie and Chapman, 1961), high electrocortical arousal, high corticosteroid and anxiety levels, an alternative solution is to suggest that the disorder is a consequence of changes in the ascending cholinergic pathways which result in disturbed attention and concomitant corticosteroid release. A secondary consequence of the corticosteroid release would be that the steroid will feed back to the brain and, combined with the awareness of the attentional disturbance, anxiety will be experienced.

Feldberg and Sherwood (1954; 1955) studied the intracerebral effects of acetylcholine and cholinergic drugs in cats and man and found that anticholinesterases induced changes in awareness. This effect could also be obtained by putting lesions in the diencephalon-containing fibres connecting the dorsal and ventral tegmental nuclei (Sherwood, 1958). This region is the origin of the ascending cholinergic pathways to the cortex (Shute and Lewis, 1967) that are thought to control attention (see Chapter 2). Feldberg and Sherwood suggested that changes in the cholinergic activity in the lower parts of the brain produced a modification of general awareness, and that this might be the basis of the disorder in some schizophrenics.

One piece of evidence in favour of this hypothesis is that anticholinesterases should exacerbate the symptoms of schizophrenia. Tests showed that in 30 per cent of schizophrenic patients the psychosis was activated; there were auditory hallucinations, ideas of reference, thought disorder, and bizarre behaviour, and these changes persisted for some months after the injection. This was not a form of toxic delirium because there was no disorientation, the brain electrical activity was not characteristic of delirium and the florid symptoms were characteristic of the patients' earlier symptomatology (Rowntree, Nevin and Wilson, 1950).

A second finding is that agents which reduced functional brain acetylcholine ameliorated the symptoms of some schizophrenics. Sherwood (1952) injected cholinesterase and the cholinergic blockers pentamethonium iodide intraventricularly into chronic catatonic patients. Forty per cent of chronic patients returned to normal at one time or another, and in one case this lasted for four years and two years in another without further injections. A second set of studies which support the prediction that a reduction in brain cholinergic activity will be therapeutic for some schizophrenics comes from clinical studies of atropine therapy (reviewed by Forrer, 1956; and Forrer and Miller, 1958). Treatment of chronic schizophrenics with high doses of atropine resulted in a marked improvement, in terms of a marked increase in accessibility, better contact with the surroundings and less affective dulling (Forrer and Miller, 1958). Schizophrenics showing high anxiety levels seem to be the most improved (Forrer, 1956; Grisell and Bynum, 1956).

A third finding is that the electrocortical activity of some schizophrenics is similar to that of normal subjects dosed with an anticholinesterase. It has been found that some schizophrenics have slow voltage arrhythmic activity with greater amounts of alpha activity (8–12 Hz) and that sensory stimulation does not block this activity. Improvement of the patient's behaviour was obtained after injection of some cholinesterase, and this was correlated with changes in the alpha activity with the frequency becoming more uniform, i.e. 'more normal', and alpha disappearing with sensory stimulation (Farrell and Sherwood, 1956).

Although these pieces of evidence support the notion, major evidence against the simple cholinergic hypothesis of schizophrenia comes from the drug therapy of the disorder.

12 PHARMACOTHERAPY OF THE SCHIZOPHRENIAS

The first drugs to be effective for the treatment of schizophrenia were the phenothiazines. Chlorpromazine was first introduced in the mid 1950s and the phenothiazines led to a rapid reduction in the number of patients in hospital. In the early 1960s the butyrophenones, like haloperidol, were introduced. A common criticism in the early days of anti-psychotic drug therapy was that these compounds were merely acting as chemical straightjackets that lower function and mask symptoms, i.e. a 'tranquillizer' (Szasz, 1957). Clinical research has not supported this assertion and on the contrary, there is compelling evidence that anti-psychotic drugs alleviate the cardinal symptoms of schizophrenia.

The definitive study of the action of phenothiazines was organized by the National Institute of Mental Health – Psychopharmacology Service Center (NIMH-PSC Collaborative Study Group, 1964). The nine hospitals ranged from a large state institution to a small intensive-care unit. There were wide variations in the type of patient, doctor attitude, staff–patient ratio, and hospital milieu. Although as one might expect the results confirmed major institutional differences, the most dramatic effects were due to the drugs. Three different phenothiazines and a placebo were tested double-blind on 463 patients with over 110 in each group. Thirty per cent of the placebo subjects dropped out due to clinical worsening, while only two per cent of the phenothiazine patients lapsed for this reason. Ninety-five per cent of the patients showed some degree of improvement within six weeks with over 50 per cent of them considered very much improved or much improved, while only 30 per cent of the placebo patients were very much improved or much improved. The withdrawn, under-active hallucinating patient showed just the same improvement as the over-active disturbed patient. The drugs were acting as more than a tranquillizer because the core symptoms of apathy, withdrawal, retardation were most improved in comparison with placebo. Most changes occurred in the first week and the majority of improvement occurs within six weeks (Goldberg, Klerman and Cole, 1965).

Although all the phenothiazines produced the same general improvement, the question arises whether differential drug action might be demonstrated if the schizophrenic patients could be subdivided into reliable, meaningful subgroups. Differences of action on subgroups would have considerable theoretical importance because different biochemical subtypes might be inferred from the differences in the biochemical mode of action of the drug. The data of the study came from two NIMH-PSC studies, one of which has been discussed already. There were no basic differences in the general effectiveness of chlorpromazine in the two studies which enabled the samples in the two studies were consistent and that the data could be pooled to give a total population of 700 patients. It was established at a statistically significant level from the combined studies that patients improved more if assigned to a drug of choice. Thus the most improved patients on chlorpromazine had auditory hallucinations, and were retarded, apathetic confused, irritable, poor self-care, poor social participation, and feelings of unreality, i.e most of the core symptoms of the disorder. In contrast the most improved patients on thioridazine had fewer of the core symptoms and the drug seemed to improve patients with agitation and feelings of unreality more than the other drugs. However, the predictor patterns for most improved patients could not be interpreted as patient types. Patients assigned to the 'worst' drug improved more on average than placebo-treated patients and the difference between patients assigned to the drug of choice and those randomly assigned to a drug was not as great as the random drug *vs*. placebo difference. In other words, the similarities in the clinical effectiveness of the phenothiazines is far greater than their differences so that less harm will be done to the patient by giving the 'wrong' phenothiazine than by giving no drug at all. Thus the phenothiazines seem to act on the brain in some way to produce an improvement in the symptoms of schizophrenia.

An interesting question is whether there are changes in information processing during recovery. Studies of acute schizophrenic patients are extremely difficult to carry out because of the problem of obtaining any sort of co-operation and patients, who co-operate, may represent a biased sample. Nevertheless, one study (Landau, Buchsbaum, Carpenter, Strauss and Sacks, 1975) examined the changes in averaged visual evoked potential of acute unmedicated schizophrenics at admission in comparison with a group of disturbed but non-schizophrenic patients and with a set of normal subjects. At admission the schizophrenic group had markedly reduced amplitude of response in the P100-N140 component in comparison with normal subjects. This component has been related to attentional shifts [see Chapter 2]. As a whole the group showed an increase in the size of the response towards the normal after being on phenothiazine medication, although medication had been discontinued for at least 14 days at the time of the study. Patients who showed most improvement showed the greatest increase and these patients tended to have relatively good premorbid histories. The authors argue that this reduction may be evidence for a mechanism which is operating to reduce a sensory overload after a breakdown of the attention mechanisms.

Improvements in attentional function have been reported for schizophrenics during recovery (Spohn, Lacoursière, Thompson and Coyne, 1977). They tested a number of aspects of information processing before and during phenothiazine medication (chlorpromazine). All patients were on medication prior to the study but the drugs were replaced with placebo for six weeks prior to the initial test. Patients who showed a severe relapse were removed from the study and given medication which biased the sample and reduced the drug–placebo difference. In spite of this factor, differences were obtained in attentional measures. In a continuous performance test where the patients had to respond to the letter X in a serially presented random series of letters, the drug enhanced detections, i.e. improved vigilance in comparison with placebo. In a size estimation task the drug treatment reduced the overestimation found with the schizophrenics and increased the accuracy of perceptual judgement. This change was interpreted as an increase in the efficiency of selective attention, in particular the reduced fixation time suggested that increased accuracy was a consequence of a reduction in excessive attention to the standard stimulus [cf. Hamilton, Chapter 12]. At brief durations there was an improvement in span of apprehension for letters which the experimenters inferred was an increase in the rate of pre-cognitive information processing (e.g. attention) as a result of drug treatment. The changes in attention were correlated with clinical improvement which is consistent with the hypothesis that attentional dysfunction is the essential characteristic of schizophrenic psychopathology. Phenothiazine treatment restored normal attentional function, and consequently normal information processing, which resulted in a return towards normality. In terms of the treatment criteria which were listed earlier the phenothiazines suppress the major symptoms and facilitate the patient's adjustment. However, the drugs do not seem to 'cure' in the sense of leaving no residual effects. A question of current importance is whether the patients can be withdrawn from the drug after remission of the major symptoms or whether drug treatments have to be maintained as in diabetes. The answer seems to be that drug treatment as a low dose must be continued to maintain the patient close to normality otherwise relapse occurs (May, 1968). As Jarvik (1970) wrote in *The Pharmacological Basis of Therapeutics*

'Chlorpromazine and other phenothiazines are not considered truly curative in psychotic disorders, since most patients usually display some residual psychotic symptomatology even following considerable improvement. Individual patients may require phenothiazine medication for years, perhaps for a lifetime. It must be pointed out, however, that some patients are so benefitted by the drugs that psychopathology is not detectable even by highly skilled observers' (p. 167).

13. DOPAMINE HYPOTHESIS

The dopamine hypothesis of schizophrenia developed from observations on the biochemical mode of action of the major anti-psychotic drugs that were discussed in the last section. Carlsson and Lindqvist (1963) found that chlorpromazine increased the levels of dopamine metabolites while promethazine, a related phenothiazine which has no anti-psychotic properties, did not. The increase in metabolites was due to a blockade of the dopamine synapses that resulted in compensatory increased dopamine release. Haloperidol, a more potent anti-psychotic drug produced a greater increase than chlorpromazine. Carlsson and Lindqvist suggested that the anti-psychotic properties were a consequence of this dopamine blockade. More recent studies have confirmed that there is a remarkable correlation between clinical potency of anti-psychotic drugs and dopamine receptor binding (Creese, Burt and Snyder, 1976; Creese and Snyder, 1978).

It follows from this notion that drugs, which act in the opposite way to the anti-psychotic drugs, might produce psychotic symptoms. Amphetamine releases dopamine at synapses and large doses of amphetamine are taken. A psychotic state is induced that is sometimes misdiagnosed as acute schizophrenia when the drug-taking history is not known, and Kety (1959) suggested that this amphetamine psychosis might be a model for schizophrenia. Evidence that this psychosis may be more than a model comes from studies that administered amphetamine and a related drug, like methylphenidate ('Ritalin'), to schizophrenics whose illness was in remission. Small doses of the drugs exacerbated the symptoms of schizophrenia markedly. The patients reported that they felt that the disorder was like their original illness and was not merely a toxic psychosis superimposed on the other disorder (Janowsky, El-Yousef, Davis and Sekerke, 1973). Anti-psychotic drugs reversed the psychotic symptoms in these patients (see Snyder, Banerjee, Yamamura and Greenberg, 1974).

On the basis of these results it would be predicted that any compound that increased the brain levels of dopamine would also exacerbate schizophrenic symptoms. In a test of this prediction, chronic schizophrenics who were receiving maintenance neuroleptic medication were given placebo doses for 10 days, and their psychotic symptoms increased (Angrist, Sathananthan, and Gershon, 1973). Subsequently they were given l-dopa, a precursor for dopamine, and seven of the patients showed an even more marked deterioration in terms of increased hallucinations and paranoia. Their status improved when the l-dopa was discontinued, although most of them required phenothiazines to restore baseline functioning. Other studies of this type are discussed in Meltzer and Stahl (1976).

The paradox of these data is that the major anti-psychotic drugs appear to be acting on a dopamine system in the brain, whereas the evidence points to an attentional deficit in the schizophrenias. One way of resolving the paradox has been proposed by Matthysse (1974; 1977). He suggested that there might be a dopamine system that functions in a manner analogous to the nigro-striatal pathway. The nigrostriatal dopamine pathway seems to act by dis-inhibition to permit the emergence of motor movements from their sub-threshold state. So Matthysse argued that preconscious thought and images are like subthreshold motor commands and a dopamine system controls the threshold for these thoughts and phantasies. In schizophrenia this 'disinhibit-ory' system is over-active and so a mass of irrelevant thoughts becomes avail-able to awareness to produce distraction. Anti-psychotic drugs block the dopamine synapses and reduce the activity in this 'disinhibitory' system and prevent the emergence of distracting ideas.

The locus of this postulated dopamine disinhibitory system could be in the limbic system or cortex. Matthysse (1977) has suggested that it may be a pathway which interlinks the mesolimbic dopamine pathway of the nucleus accumbens septi, with substantia innominata and parietal lobe. More recent evidence on the dopamine neurons that project to the cortex indicates that three terminal systems can be distinguished in the frontal lobe area. The origin of these fibres of the frontal lobe and peripheral projections appear to be in the A10 region, the ventral tegmental area in the reticular formation, and passes close to or through the nucleus accumbens (Lindvall, Björklund and Dinac, 1978). Thus the mesocortical pathway is closely associated with the mesolimbic pathway and may even comprise a single system of cells. Of course, it could be that the brain region that malfunctions is not a system which is dopaminoceptive or dopaminergic, but is in an area which is modulated by dopamine neurons (Meltzer and Stahl, 1976). Drugs which reduced function in the dopamine pathways would still be anti-psychotic, but it would be possible to find other anti-schizophrenic drugs which act on the malfunctioning neurons directly. One possibility for an alternative system is the cholinergic system that was discussed earlier. This combined hypothesis will be considered in the next section.

14. DOPAMINE–ACETYLCHOLINE BALANCE HYPOTHESIS

At many synapses in the nervous system there are opposing synaptic transmitters and many behavioural functions seem to be controlled by neural systems which have opposing transmitters (Warburton, 1975b). For example, the excitatory transmitter for the control of water intake is acetylcholine and the inhibitory transmitter is noradrenalin, while in motor control there appears to be a dynamic balance between acetylcholine and dopamine in the basal ganglia (see Warburton, 1975b, for a review of this work). Thus there is a precedent for proposing that psychoses may be a result of an imbalance between two transmitters. The two candidates for transmitters involved in schizophrenia are dopamine and acetylcholine on the basis of the evidence that was cited in the earlier section on the simple cholinergic hypothesis and the last section on the simple dopamine hypothesis.

The evidence for cholinergic involvement was that reduction of functional acetylcholine in normal subjects produces attentional deficits [see Chapter 2], and attentional deficits are one of the cardinal symptoms of schizophrenia. Large reductions of the functional acetylcholine produce thought disorders and auditory hallucinations (Warburton, 1979). Drugs like cholinomimetics and anticholinesterases which increase the activity in cholinergic pathways reduce schizophrenic symptoms. As we saw in the last section, increased activity in the dopamine pathways exacerbated the symptoms of schizophrenia. One piece of crucial evidence for a dopamine-cholinergic imbalance in the production of the psychotic symptoms was the finding that although methylphenidate exacerbated the symptoms of schizophrenia, the occurrence of symptoms was prevented by physostigmine, which increases the functional levels of acetylcholine (Janowsky and Davis, 1974).

15. THERAPY OF THE SCHIZOPHRENIAS

One of the most impressive controlled studies of drugs and psychotherapy was coordinated by May (1968). Two hundred and twenty eight schizophrenic patients in the middle third of the prognostic range were divided into four major groups: (a) no treatment; (b) psychotherapy alone; (c) psychotherapy and 'Stelazine', a phenothiazine; (d) 'Stelazine' alone. The evaluation criteria included release rate, a nurse's rating, a therapist's rating of symptoms and thought processes, an independent psychoanalyst's rating of insight and anxiety. Overall these measures showed that there was a very powerful drug effect, but no significant effect for psychotherapy alone. Psychotherapy plus drug therapy was significantly superior to psychotherapy alone. However, the difference between psychotherapy with pharmacotherapy and drug therapy was rather small. There was no evidence of a significant negative interaction between the two forms of therapy, and if anything there was slight positive interaction in the combined therapy.

This interaction seems to be most evident in patients who had good premorbid information processing ability. Certainly phenothiazine medication has different effects on patients with good and poor premorbid adjustments. Premorbid adjustments represent the coping behaviour prior to the onset of the episodes and it seems that the drug therapy restores the patient to his premorbid coping level. It is at this stage, as information processing improves, that psychotherapy becomes important (May, 1968). Drugs lead to an increased awareness of the situation and the insight must be maintained by an alteration in the patient's lifestyle and/or environment. Psychotherapy can provide help with this change.

16. CONCLUSIONS

In Chapter 3 of this volume, I outlined some of the neurochemical mechanisms that were involved in human information processing and showed that the release of stress hormones was an inevitable consequence of these processes. In this chapter it was argued that interpretation of a situation as uncertain resulted in increased activation of the electrocortical pathways, i.e. cortical desynchronization and stress steroid release. The stress steroids feed back to the brain and produce changes in brain chemistry. Anxiety is the label that we give to the bodily feeling produced by the steroids combined with our interpretation of the environment. The therapy of anxiety can be directed at one or preferably both components of the experience. Psychotherapy can change the interpretation of the situation to reduce the cognitive component and drug therapy can reduce the neurochemical effects of the stress steroids. Drug therapy is an important adjunct to psychotherapy and can assist therapeutic processes.

The majority of schizophrenics share many of the same symptoms – anxiety, high stress steroid levels in their plasma, and cortical desynchronization. However anxiolytic drugs only reduced the anxiety symptoms and do not modify the information processing deficits of schizophrenics. Instead it seems that the underlying deficit is in the control of electrocortical arousal, perhaps the balance between cholinergic-dopaminergic neural systems at the cortex. Anti-psychotic drugs restore this balance and normal information processing. Psychotherapy seems to produce little improvement on its own but once information processing has returned to its premorbid levels, psychotherapy may be a useful adjunct to drug therapy in producing a relapse.

As I indicated in the Introduction a hypothesis of a neurochemical change does not contradict hypotheses that emphasize, genetic predisposition, the importance of childhood experiences and adult precipitating factors in the aetiology of mental illness. However treatment must take into account the neurochemical changes and drugs can be used to aid return to normal function.

17. REFERENCES

Anden, N.-E., Dahlstrom, A., Fuxe, K., Larsson, K., Olson, L. and Ungerstedt, U. (1966). Ascending monoamine neurons to the telencephalon and diencephalon. *Acta Physiologica Scandinavica*, **67**, 313–326.

Angrist, B., Sathananthan, G. and Gershon, S. (1973). Behavioral effects of L-DOPA in schizophrenic patients. *Psychopharmacologia*, **31**, 1–12.

Arieti, S., (1955). *Interpretation of Schizophrenia*. New York: Brunner.

Azmitia, F. C., Algheri, S., and Costa, E. (1970). Turnover rate of *in vivo* conversion of tryptophan into serotonin in brain areas of adrenalectomized rats. *Science*, **169**, 201–203.

Azmitia, E. C. and McEwen, B. S. (1969). Corticosterone regulation of tryptophan hydroxylase in midbrain of the rat. *Science*, **166**, 1274–1276.

Bliss, E. J., Ailion, J. and Zwanziger, J. (1968). Metabolism of norepinephrine, serotonin and dopamine in rat brain with stress. *Journal of Pharmacology and Experimental Therapeutics*, **164**, 122–131.

Bliss, E. J., Migeon, C. J., Branch, C. H., and Samuels, L. T. (1956). Reaction of the adrenal cortex to emotional stress. *Psychosomatic Medicine*, **18**, 56–76.

Bloch, S. and Brackenridge, C. J. (1972). Psychological performance and biochemical factors in medical students under examination stress. *Journal of Psychosomatic Research*, **16**, 25–33.

Bourne, P. G. (1969). Urinary 17–OHCS levels in two combat situations. In P. G. Bourne (Ed.), *Psychology and Physiology of Stress*. New York: Academic Press.

Carlsson, A. and Lindqvist, M. (1963). Effect of chlorpromazine and haloperidol on formation of 3-methoxytyramine and normetanephrine in mouse brain. *Acta Pharmacologica et Toxicologica*, **20**, 140–144.

Chase, T. N., Katz, R. I. and Copin, I. J. (1970). Effect of diazepam on fate of intracisternally injected serotonin-C^{14}. *Neuropharmacology*, **9**, 103–108.

Chowers, I., Feldman, S. and Davidson, J. M. (1963). Effects of intrahypothalamic crystalline steroids on acute ACTH secretion. *American Journal of Physiology*, **205**, 671–673.

Claridge, G. S. (1960). The excitation–inhibition balance in neurotics. In H. J. Eysenck (Ed.), *Experiments in Personality*. Vol. 2, London: Routledge and Kegan Paul.

Cleghorn, R. A. (1957). Steroid hormones in relation to neuropsychiatric disorders. In H. Hoagland (Ed.), *Hormones, Brain Function and Behavior*. New York: Academic Press.

Corrodi, H., Fuxe, K., Lidbrink, P. and Olson, L. (1971). Minor tranquillizers, stress and central monoamine neurons. *Brain Research*, **29**, 1–16.

Creese, I., Burt, D. R. and Snyder, S. H. (1976). Dopamine receptor binding predicts clinical and pharmacological potencies of antischizophrenic drug. *Science*, **192**, 481–483.

Creese, I. and Snyder, S. H. (1978). Behavioral and biochemical properties of the dopamine receptor. In M. A. Lipton, A. DiMascio and K. F. Killam (Eds.). *Psychopharmacology: A Generation of Progress*. New York: Raven Press.

Curtis, G., Fogel, M. C., McEvoy, D. and Zarate, C. (1970). Urine and plasma corticosteroids, psychological tests and effectiveness of psychological defenses. *Journal of Psychiatric Research*, **7**, 237–247.

Curzon, G. and Green, A. R. (1968). Effect of hydrocortisone on rat brain 5-hydroxytryptamine. *Life Science*, **7**, 657–663.

Farrell, J. P. and Sherwood, S. L. (1956). An alpha correlate to behaviour changes produced in psychotics by intraventricular injections. *Electroencephalography and Clinical Neurophysiology*, **8**, 713.

Feldberg, W. and Sherwood, S. L. (1954). Injection of drugs into the lateral ventricle of the cat. *Journal of Physiology*, **123**, 148–167.

Feldberg, W. and Sherwood, S. L. (1955). Recent experiments with injections of drugs into the ventricular system of the brain. *Proceedings of the Royal Society of Medicine*, **48**, 853–863.

Fink, M., Itil, T. and Clyde, D. (1965). A contribution to the classification of psychoses by quantitative E.E.G. measures. *Proceedings of the Society for Biological Psychiatry*, **2**, 5–17.

Forrer, G. R. (1956). Symposium on atropine toxicity therapy. *Journal of Nervous and Mental Disease*, **124**, 257–283.

Forrer, G. R. and Miller, J. J. (1958). Atropine coma: a somatic therapy in psychiatry. *American Journal of Psychiatry*, **115**, 455–458.

Frank, J. D. (1974). Therapeutic components of psychotherapy. *Journal of Nervous and Mental Disease*, **159**, 325–342.

Freud, S. (1963). *Introductory Lectures on Psychoanalysis*. London: Hogarth Press.

Furger, R. (1961). Psychiatrische Unterzuchungen beim Cushing-Syndrom. *Schweizer Archiv für Neurologie und Psychiatrie*, **88**, 9–39.

Fuxe, K., Corrodi, H., Hokfelt, T. and Jonsson, G. (1970). Central monoamine neurons and pituitary-adrenal activity. *Progress in Brain Research*, **32**, 42–56.

Goldberg, S. C., Klerman, G. L. and Cole, J. O. (1965). Changes in schizophrenic psychopathology and ward behaviour as a function of phenothiazine treatment. *British Journal of Psychiatry*, **111**, 120–133.

Gray, J. A. (1972). The structure of the emotions and limbic system: a theoretical model. In R. Porter and J. Knight (Eds.), *Physiology, Emotion, and Psychosomatic Illness*. Amsterdam: Ciba Foundation.

Gray, J. A. (1976a). The neuropsychology of anxiety. In I. G. Sarason and C. D. Spielberger (Eds.), *Stress and Anxiety*. Vol. 3. Washington, D.C.: Hemisphere.

Gray, J. A. (1976b). The behavioural inhibition system: a possible substrate for anxiety. In P. Feldman and A. Broadhurst (Eds.), *Theoretical and Experimental Bases of Behaviour Modification*. London: Wiley.

Gray, J. A. and Ball, G. C. (1970). Frequency-specific relations between hippocampal theta rhythm, behavior and amylobarbital action. *Science*, **168**, 1246–1248.

Grisell, J. L. and Bynum, H. J. (1956). A study of the relationship between anxiety level, ego strength and response to atropine toxicity therapy. *Journal of Nervous and Mental Disease*, **124**, 265–268.

Group for the Advancement of Psychiatry (1975). *Pharmacotherapy and Psychotherapy*. New York: Mental Health Materials Center.

Guilford, J. P. (1967). *The Nature of Human Intelligence*. New York: McGraw-Hill.

Herron, W. G. (1962). The process-reactive classification of schizophrenia. *Psychological Bulletin*, **59**, 329–333.

Higgins, J. and Mednick, S. A. (1963). Reminiscence and stage of illness in schizophrenia. *Journal of Abnormal and Social Psychology*, **66**, 314–317.

Holden, J. M., Itil, T. M., Keskiner, N. and Fink, M. (1968). Thioridazine and chlordiazepoxide in the treatment of chronic schizophrenia. *Comprehensive Psychiatry*, **9**, 633–643.

Hollister, L. E., Bennett, J. J., Kimbell, I., Savage, C. and Overall, J. E. (1963). Diazepam in newly admitted schizophrenics. *Diseases of the Nervous System*, **25**, 746–750.

Janowsky, D. S. and Davis, J. M. (1974). Dopamine, psychomotor stimulants, and schizophrenia: effects of methylphenidate and the stereoisomers of amphetamine in schizophrenics. In E. Usdin (Ed.), *Neuropsychopharmacology of Monoamines and their Regulatory Enzymes*. New York: Raven Press.

Jonowsky, D. S., El-Yousef, M. K., Davis, J. M. and Sekerke, H. J. (1973). Provocation of schizophrenic symptoms by intravenous administration of methylphenidate. *Archives of General Psychiatry*, **28**, 185–191.

Jarvik, M. (1970). Drugs used in the treatment of psychiatric disorders. In L. S. Goodman and A. Gilman (Eds.), *The Pharmacological Basis of Therapeutics*. New York: MacMillan.

Jenner, F. A., Kerry, R. J. and Parkin, J. (1961). A controlled comparison of methaminodiazepoxide (chlordiazepoxide, 'Librium') and amylobarbitone in the treatment of anxiety in neurotic patients. *Journal of Mental Science*, **107**, 583–589.

Jones, M. T., Bridges, P. K. and Leak, D. (1970). Correlation between psychic and endocrinological responses to emotional stress. *Progress in Brain Research*, **32**, 325–335.

Kerry, R. J. and Jenner, T. A. (1962). A double-blind crossover comparison of diazepam ('Valium') with chlordiazepoxide ('Librium') in the treatment of neurotic anxiety. *Psychopharmacologia*, **3**, 302–312.

Kety, S. S. (1959). Biochemical theories of schizophrenia. A two-part critical review of current theories and of the evidence used to support them. *Science*, **129**, 1528–1532; 1590–1596.

Kortchinskaia, E. J. (1965). Étude électroencéphalographique comparée de malades atteint de schizophrénie greffée et de malades atteint de schizophrénie non compliquée à évolutions maligne. *Zhurnal Nevropatologii Psikhiatrii*, **65**, 263–267.

Krop, H. D., Alegre, C. E. and Williams, C. D. (1969). Effect of induced stress on convergent and divergent thinking. *Psychological Reports*, **24**, 895–898.

Ladinsky, H., Consolo, S., Peri, G. and Garattini, S. (1973). Increase in mouse and rat brain acetylcholine levels by diazepam. In S. Garattini, E. Mussini, and L. O. Randall (Eds.), *The Benzodiazepines*. New York: Raven Press.

Landau, S. G., Buchsbaum, M. T., Carpenter, W., Strauss, J. and Sacks, M. (1975). Schizophrenia and stimulus intensity control. *Archives of General Psychiatry*, **32**, 1239–1245.

Levi, R. and Maynert, E. W. (1964). The subcellular localization of brain stem norepinephrine and 5-hydroxytryptamine in stressed rats. *Biochemical Pharmacology*, **3**, 615–621.

Levitt, E. E., Persky, H., Brady, J. P. and Fitzgerald, J. A. (1963). The effect of hydrocortisone infusion on hypnotically induced anxiety. *Psychosomatic Medicine*, **25**, 158–161.

Lidbrink, P., Corrodi, H., Fuxe, K. and Olson, L. (1973). The effects of benzodiazepines, meprobamate and barbiturates on central monoamine neurons. In S. Garattini, E. Mussini and L. O. Randall (Eds.), *The Benzodiazepines*. New York: Raven Press.

Lindsley, D. B. (1944). Electroencephalography. In J. McV. Hunt (Ed.), *Personality and the Behavior Disorders*. New York: Ronald Press.

Lindsley, D. B. (1950). Emotions and the electroencephalogram. In M. T. Reymert (Ed.), *Feelings and Emotions*. New York: McGraw-Hill.

Lindsley, D. B. (1951). Emotion. In S. S. Stevens (Ed.), *Handbook of Experimental Psychology*. New York: Wiley.

Lindvall, O., Björklund, A. and Dinac, T. (1978). Organisation of catecholamine neurons projecting to the frontal cortex in the rat. *Brain Research*, **142**, 1–24.

Lingjaerde, P. T. (1964). Plasma hydrocortisone in mental disease. *British Journal of Psychiatry*, **110**, 423–432.

Lorr, M., McNair, D. M. and Weinstein, G. J. (1965). Early effects of chlordiazepoxide ('Librium') used with psychotherapy. *Journal of Psychiatric Research*, **1**, 257–263.

McGhie, A. and Chapman, J. (1961). Disorders of attention and perception in early schizophrenia. *British Journal of Medical Psychology*, **34**, 103–116.

Mandell, A. (1968). Psychoanalysis and psychopharmacology. In J. Marmor (Ed.), *Modern Psychoanalysis*. New York: Basic Books.

Mandler, G. (1967). The conditions for emotional behavior. In D. C. Glass (Ed.), *Neurophysiology and Emotion*. New York: Rockefeller University Press.

Masserman, J. H. (1972). Psychotherapy as the mitigation of uncertainties. *Archives of General Psychiatry*, **26**, 186–188.

Matthysse, S. (1974). Schizophrenia: relationships to dopamine transmission, motor control and feature extraction. In F. O. Schmitt and F. G. Worden (Eds.), *Neurosciences: Third Study Program*. Cambridge, Mass.: MIT Press.

Matthysse, S. (1977). Dopamine and selective attention. *Advances in Biochemical Pharmacology*, **16**, 667–669.

May, P.R.A. (1968). *Treatment of Schizophrenia*. New York: Science House.

May, P.R.A. (1971). Psychotherapy and ataraxic drugs. In A. E. Bergin and S. J. Garfield (Eds.), *Handbook of Psychotherapy and Behavior Change*. New York: Wiley.

Maynert, E. W. and Levi, R. (1964). Stress-induced release of brain norepinephrine and its inhibition by drugs. *Journal of Pharmacology and Experimental Therapeutics*, **143**, 90–95.

Mednick, S. A. (1958). A learning theory approach to research in schizophrenia. *Psychological Bulletin*, **55**, 316–327.

Meerloo, J. A. (1955). Medication into submission: the danger of therapeutic coercion. *Journal of Nervous and Mental Diseases*, **122**, 353.

Meltzer, H. Y. and Stahl, S. M. (1976). The dopamine hypothesis of schizophrenia: a review. *Schizophrenia Bulletin*, **2**, 19–76.

Michael, R. P. and Gibbons, J. L. (1963). Interrelationships between the endocrine system and neuropsychiatry. *International Review of Neurobiology*, **5**, 243–302.

Mirsky, A. F. (1969). Neuropsychological bases of schizophrenia. *Annual Review of Psychology*, **20**, 321–348.

NIMH-PSC Collaborative Study Group (1964). Phenothiazine treatment in chronic schizophrenia. *Archives of General Psychiatry*, **10**, 528–553.

Persky, H., Grinber, R. R., Hamburg, D. A., Sabshin, M., Korchin, S. J., Basowitz, H. and Chevalier, J. A. (1956). *Archives of Neurology and Psychiatry*, **76**, 549–562.

Persky, H., Smith, K. D., and Basu, G. K. (1971). Effect of corticosterone and hydrocortisone on some indicators of anxiety. *Journal of Clinical Endocrinology and Metabolism*, **33**, 467–474.

Pfaff, D. W., Silva, M. T. A. and Weiss, J. M. (1971). Telemetered recording of hormone effects on hippocampal neurons, *Science*, **172**, 394–395.

Pribram, K. H. (1967). The new neurology and biology of emotion: a structural approach, *American Psychologist*, **22**, 830–838.

Pribram, K. H. (1969). The neurobehavioral analysis of the limbic forebrain mechanisms: revision and progress report. In D. Lehrman (Ed.), *Advances in the Study of Behavior*. Vol. 2. New York: Academic Press.

Proctor, R. C. (1962). Clinical use of chlordiazepoxide. In J. H. Nodine and J. H. Mayer (Eds.), *Psychosomatic Medicine*. Philadelphia: Lea and Febiger.

Rickels, K. (1977). Drug treatment of anxiety. In M. E. Jarvik (Ed.) *Psychopharmacology in the Practice of Medicine*. New York: Appleton–Century–Crofts.

Rowntree, D. W., Nevin, S. and Wilson, A. (1950). The effects of di-isopropylfluorophosphonate in schizophrenia and manic depressive psychosis. *Journal of Neurology, Neurosurgery and Psychiatry*, **13**, 47–62.

Sachar, E. J. (1970). Psychological factors relating to activation and inhibition of the adrenocortical stress response in man: a review, *Progress in Brain Research*, **32**, 316–324.

Scapagnini, U., Moberg, G. P., Van Loon, G. R., De Groot, J. and Ganong, W. F. (1971). Relation of brain 5-hydroxytryptamine content to the diurnal variation in plasma corticosterone in the rat. *Neuroendocrinology*, **7**, 90–96.

Schachter, S. (1964). The interaction of cognitive and physiological determinants of emotional state. In L. Berkowitz (Ed.), *Advances in Experimental Social Psychology*. Vol. 1. New York: Academic Press.

Schallek, W. and Kuehn, A. (1960). Effects of psychotropic drugs on limbic system of cat. *Proceedings of the Society for Experimental Biology and Medicine*, **105**, 115–119.

Schallek, W., Kuehn, A. and Jew, N. (1962). Effects of chlordiazepoxide ('Librium') and other psychotropic agents on the brain stem of the brain. *Annals of the New York Academy of Science*. **96**, 303–312.

Sechehaye, M., (1951). *Autobiography of a Schizophrenic Girl*. New York: Grune and Stratton.

Selye, H. (1956). *The Stress of Life*. New York: McGraw-Hill.

Sherwood, S. L. (1952). Intraventricular medication in catatonic stupor. *Brain*, **75**, 68–75.

Sherwood, S. L. (1958). Consciousness, adaptive behaviour and schizophrenia. In D. Richter (Ed.), *Schizophrenia: Somatic Aspects*. London: Pergamon Press.

Shute, C. C. and Lewis, P. R. (1967). The ascending cholinergic reticular system. neocortical, olfactory and subcortical projections. *Brain*, **90**, 497–520.

Snyder, S. H., Banerjee, S. P., Yamamura, H. T. and Greenberg, D. (1974). Drugs, transmitters and schizophrenia. *Science*, **184**, 1243–1253.

Spohn, H. E., Lacoursiere, R. B., Thompson, K. and Coyne, L. (1977). Phenothiazine effects on psychological and psychophysiological dysfunction in chronic schizophrenics. *Archives of General Psychiatry*. **34**, 633–644.

Stein, L., Wise, C. D. and Berger, B. D. (1973). Antianxiety action of benzodiazepines: decrease in activity of serotonin neurons in the punishment system. In S. Garattini, E. Mussini, and L. O. Randall (Eds.), *The Benzodiazepines*. New York: Raven Press.

Strauss, H. (1945). Clinical and encephalographic studies: the encephalogram in psychoneurotics. *Journal of Nervous and Mental Diseases*, **101**, 19–27.

Sullivan, H. S. (1948). The meaning of anxiety in psychiatry and in life. *Psychiatry*, **11**, 1–13.

Szasz, T. S. (1957). Some observations in the use of tranquillizing drugs. *Archives of Neurology and Psychiatry*, **77**, 86–91.

Taylor, K. M. and Laverty, R. (1969). The effect of chlordiazepoxide, diazepam, and nitrazepam on catecholamine metabolism in regions of the rat brain. *European Journal of Pharmacology*, **8**, 296–301.

Taylor, K. M. and Laverty, R. (1973). The interaction of chlordiazepoxide, diazepam and mitrazepam with catecholamines and histamine in regions of the rat brain. In S. Garattini, E. Mussini, and L. O. Randall (Eds.), *The Benzodiazepines*, New York: Raven Press.

Warburton, D. M. (1975a). Modern biochemical concepts of anxiety. *International Pharmacopsychiatry*, **9**, 189–205.

Warburton, D. M. (1975b). *Brain, Drugs and Behaviour*. London: Wiley.

Warburton, D. M. (1979). Neurochemical bases of conciousness. In K. Brown and S. J. Cooper (Eds.), *Chemical Influences on Behaviour*, London: Academic Press.

Weiner, S., Dorman, D., Persky, H., Stach, T. W., Norton, J. and Levitt, E. E. (1963). Effect on anxiety of increasing the plasma hydrocortisone level. *Psychosomatic Medicine*, **25**, 69–77.

Weltman, G., Smith, J. E. and Egstrom, G. H. (1971). Perceptual narrowing during simulated pressure-chamber exposure. *Human Factors*, **13**, 79–107.

Wise, C. D., Berger, B. D. and Stein, L. (1972). Benzodiazepines: anxiety-reducing activity by reduction of serotonin turnover in the brain. *Science*, **177**, 180–183.

Wolff, C. T., Friedman, S. B., Hofer, M. A. and Mason, J. W. (1964). Relationship between psychological defenses and mean urinary 17-hydroxysteroid excretion rates: a predictive study of parents of fatally ill children. *Psychosomatic Medicine*, **26**, 576–591.

Wolff, C. T., Hofer, M. A. and Mason, J. W. (1964). Relationship between psychological defenses and mean urinary 17-hydroxycorticosteroid excretion rates. II. methodologic and theoretical considerations. *Psychosomatic Medicine*, **26**, 592–598.

Concluding Remarks

Stress and the Processing of Information

DAVID M. WARBURTON

Writing a book is a learning process which involves the distillation of the thoughts of others. Editing a book turns out to be even more educational because a group of contributors has done much of the difficult work first, and all that an editor has to do is learn. In these final comments I would like to present what I have learned, although this is obviously a very personal selection that is influenced by my own biases. This version is only one of many ways to summarize these chapters and it would take another book of 3–400 pages to do justice to the many provocative ideas of the contributors.

One apparent stumbling block to integration that any reader will notice is the two distinct uses of the word 'stress' in the papers. Stress is used to refer to certain types of agents which act on people, and to the responses of the people to certain types of agents. More careful reading shows that the divergence is illusory and that there is considerable agreement among the contributors about the agents, which I will refer to as stressors, and the psychological and physiological consequences, the stress response. It soon becomes clear that all the authors are talking about the same thing – the *stress phenemenon*.

The initiating factor in the stress phenomenon is the stressor. A whole range of physical stimuli act as stressors which Rohmert and Luczak [Chapter 11] have discussed in relation to muscular work and the assessment of work load. In addition, restraint, heat, cold, noise, pain, shock, injury, and the infection can all elicit stress responses as well as their specific actions (e.g. burn from heat). The common factor of these physical stressors is that they subject the body to extreme stimulation, and this might justify a simple model in which stress responses are a simple monotonic function of the physical intensity of the stimulus. This model can be easily extended to explain some of the effects of stressors on information processing; stress responses will increase in direct proportion to the amount of information to be processed per unit time with the largest responses being produced by extreme information overload. Unfortunately, this simple intensity model has serious flaws which become evident as the various contributors tell their stories.

One problem is in the definition of stressor in terms of physical intensity and frequency. Some psychological stimuli are stressors because of their distribution in time, not merely their frequency. Stimuli produce a much greater stress response if they are presented at unpredictable intervals than if they occur regularly, even though the density of these stimuli over time is the same (Warburton, Chapter 2). One solution to the problem could be based on the old, 'data-driven' information theory in which information in an input was inversely proportional to its uncertainty. Highly predictable inputs give little information while novel inputs have high information content. Novel inputs would be 'interruptors' in terms of Mandler's hypothesis [see Chapter 6.] In theory, stressors could be quantified in terms of their uncertainty and the stress response would be directly related to the amount of information.

The flaw in this solution is that predictability or uncertainty of input cannot be evaluated independently of the person who perceives it. Thus the magnitude of a stressor will depend on the interaction between the environment in which the person first evaluates the information content of the input, its significance. Folkman, Schaefer, and Lazarus [Chapter 9] point out that after this primary appraisal there is a secondary appraisal which is an evaluation of the possible courses of action that are available. Thus they argue that as well as uncertainty about *whether* an event will happen and *when* it will happen there is also uncertainty about *what* event might occur and *what* action can be taken. As Hamilton [Chapters 3 and 12] discusses, the cognitive interpretation of the situation gives it meaning for the individual; thus ambiguity is a consequence of the many alternative meanings that the input has for the person, coupled with the available response strategies from which a choice must be made. This orientation has shifted the emphasis completely and has shown that uncertainty must be defined subjectively. Consequently, stressors cannot be quantified independently of the individual.

The analysis of real-life stressors by Johnson and Sarason [Chapter 7] make this point even clearer. The early studies tried to quantify life event stress in terms of the number of recent life changes, but individuals will vary considerably in their appraisal of the same event, and even whether they perceive it as desirable or undesirable. Pregnancy is a qualitatively and quantitatively different event for unmarried teenagers, in comparison with a middle-aged childless couple.

In a similar fashion, work stressors must be evaluated with reference to the organization, and how the individual perceives himself with respect to that organization. Payne [Chapter 10] discusses how work stressors arise from the structure of the organization, and the climate of norms and values that the management tries to create. They will depend on the rigidity with which roles are defined, and on the climate of trust. Rigid hierarchical work organizations are perceived as threatening, which gives rise to mistrust. All the evidence points to the fact that stress effects are greatest among the unskilled workers at the bottom of the hierarchy, with least participation in decision-making. Although their work involves low uncertainty in the sense that it is routine, their future (*what* will happen) is highly uncertain because they do not have any say in it. In summary, work stressors will depend both on how the person processes information, and on how he perceives himself and his job with respect to the organization. Clearly stressors cannot be defined independently of the person.

This view of the person as an active processor of information fits neatly with the recent information processing models reviewed by Rabbitt in Chapter 4. He shows that the human organism is not merely a passive, 'data-driven' processor, but instead there is active, 'top-down' control of information flow and that the locus of this control varies with the task demands [see also Hockey in Chapter 5]. Rohmert and Luczak [Chapter 11] describe how there is an interaction between experience and task demands, so that different strategies of operation may be adopted as workload increases. At another level, past experience can modify information processing capacity. Hamilton [Chapters 3 and 12] makes the important point that 'top-down' effects of pathological thought processes that were developed in the past will impair information processing. This problem is exacerbated in the highly anxious people who will use up processing capacity by internally generated information, thoughts about their own state and abilities. The same point is taken up by Mandler [Chapter 6] in his discussions of stress and thought processes.

In summary, psychological stressors must be considered with respect to the individual, and the stress response will be a function of the person's evaluation of the input. This definition of stressors in subjective terms does not differentiate 'psychological' stressors from 'physical' stressors. All physical stressors (work, noise, pain, etc.) have psychological effects, and it is impossible to separate out the respective stress effects on the person. Mason (1971) suggests that the stress should be considered as a behavioural concept, not a physiological concept, because of the involvement of the higher levels of the central nervous system. Certainly the stress responses are the same for 'pure psychological' and 'pure physical' stressors.

As Selye [Chapter 1] has indicated, the stress response is a non-specific response to any demand and it prepares the organism for action. All the evidence suggests that the response is stereotyped and independent of the nature of the stressor. At a physiological level [see Warburton, Chapter 2], there is cortical desynchronization and release of stress hormones from the adrenal medulla and adrenal cortex. The hormones mobilize energy resources as fuel for the demands of mental as well as physical effort. The measurement of these physiological responses enables some estimate to be made of the subjective intensity of a stressor. These measures have proved extremely useful in the ergonomic analysis of workload [see Chapter 11 by Rohmert and

Luczak]. In order to try and bridge the gap between the physical properties of the stimulus and the changes in behaviour, experimental psychologists postulated an intervening variable, arousal, that they thought could be assessed from the physiological measures.

One of the most widely used explanatory devices using arousal for relating performance to stressors, is the Yerkes–Dodson law. This law postulates that for any task there is a level of arousal which is optimal for performance, and which varies inversely with task difficulty. Arousal levels which are less than, or greater than, the optimum level will produce inferior performance, i.e. an inverted-U shaped relation between perfomances and arousal. This 'law' can be related to stressors by means of the U-shaped relationship between stressor magnitude and the stress response that was hypothesized by Levi (1972). In this model the stress response is lowest for intermediate levels of stimulation and increases for both stimulus deprivation and excessive stimulation. Hockey [Chapter 5] has made cogent criticisms of the use of the Yerkes–Dodson law in stress research. [See also Hamilton, Chapter 12.] He shows that it is a gross over-simplification to think of information processing performance as a unitary activity because stressors change the balance of effectiveness of the cognitive resources. Thus increasing the magnitude of a stressor increases the selectivity of attention, but decreases primary memory capacity; selectivity of responses increases, but the use of intermediate categories of response decreases; work rate will increase, but accuracy will decrease. Thus the changes in performance in a particular task will be a function of the involvement of different cognitive capacities in performance and the precise relation of these changes to various physiological measures.

From what has been discovered, it seems that the cognitive changes also represent preparations for action in an emergency. In a dangerous situation it is obviously more adaptive to be highly selective in the stimuli processed than to store information; to act quickly and risk mistakes rather than act slowly and carefully; to focus on one problem than to think divergently and creatively. Altogether the stress response consists of a pattern of physiological and cognitive changes that have evolved for mental and physical action.

The changes in physiological response that have been observed in the laboratory are also seen in real-life situations [see Warburton, Chapter 2]. Similarly, Horowitz [Chapter 8] has listed the psychological responses of patients who had experienced severe life events, like personal injury or bereavement. These signs and symptoms included shifts in attentional selectivity, memory loss, feelings of hyperactivity, and autonomic activation (desire to urinate, excessive sweating, etc.). Sensations of this kind arouse fears of losing bodily control which intrude into conscious experience, and, as Mandler suggests, may impair thought processes because they are attention demanding, although Hamilton [Chapter 12] regards the physiological signals as 'low-grade' information in comparison with cognitive information. A more serious problem is that the sustained release of hormones leads to mental and physical fatigue, due to depletion of energy reserves, and in the long term to the serious, and sometimes fatal physical changes that are discussed by Selye. These deterious consequences make it imperative for the person to reduce the experience of the stressors and the resulting stress responses.

Of course, the shift in the balance of cognitive capacities, mentioned by Hockey, will provide extra resources for problem solving that will prevent the stressor–person interaction that generated the stress response. However, for many types of life stress there is no solution. For example, we cannot escape from the threat of death to us and our loved ones, and from actual bereavement. Folkman *et al.* and Horowitz discuss the cognitive regulating processes that are adopted to minimize the stress response (palliatives). Two of the common strategies are denial and intellectualizing. In denial the person interprets the information as incorrect ('there is no danger'), and so minimizes the stress response, while, alternatively, the person may interpret the implications of the information in an intellectual manner ('the chances of being killed are 10,000 to 1'), which also minimizes the stress response. As Folkman *et al.* show, the regulating cognitive activity aborts or distorts information processing. These coping strategies can be handled very neatly by the 'top-down' models of information processing that are discussed by Rabbitt [Chapter 4].

Denial as a coping mechanism is usually viewed as maladaptive because the confrontation with reality will be all the more intense when it occurs, e.g. denial of terminal illness of a close relative. However, Horowitz has observed that denial may serve two purposes. It may dampen ideas and feelings that would distract the person from action that was needed immediately. Second, it allows the person to adjust gradually to unpleasant information (loss of a limb of disfigurement) – a process called 'dosing'. Clearly denial, as a temporary defence mechanism, is extremely important immediately after some stressful experiences. More research needs to be undertaken in therapeutic situations to understand in what circumstances its use may be cencouraged, and in what way it might retard recovery. In the same way, Horowitz considers that the other defence or control operations may aid or impair adjustment and a rational strategy for the treatment of stress disorders depends on obtaining an understanding of these control operations.

One of the controversial problems of the therapy of stress disorders is the function of drug treatment. At one time it was thought that drug therapy might impair the psychological changes that were required for recovery. However, Warburton reviews the action of anxiolytic drugs and concludes that anxiolytics not only provide relief from anxiety but also facilitate psychotherapeutic processes. Of course, anxiolytic therapy should not be used, as it often is, as a substitute for psychotherapy. Psychotherapy which provides the patient with more effective coping strategies is essential for minimizing the reoccurrence of the disorder. Drug therapy is thus an important adjunct to psychotherapy in the treatment of anxiety.

In contrast, for the schizophrenias, the roles of drug therapy and psychotherapy are reversed; psychotherapy can be considered as an adjunct to drug therapy. The schizophrenias have been considered as a consequence of stressors by a number of theorists, whether these are internally or externally generated. When the anxiety cannot be coped with by the individual there are compensatory changes in information processing that constitute the cardinal symptoms of the schizophrenias [see Chapter 12 by Hamilton]. It is certainly true that schizophrenia is characterized by disturbed information processing and a large stress response, at least in the acute phases [see discussion by Warburton in Chapter 13]. However, anxiolytic drugs which block the stress response are ineffective for the treatment of acute and chronic schizophrenia, which suggests that the anxiety is not the *immediate* cause of the breakdown. The evidence from drug therapy suggests that the basis of the disorder is an impairment in mechanisms of information processing [see Warburton in Chapter 2], and the stress response results from this change, not the other way round. However, since people are not merely 'bottom-up' processors of information, various coping strategies are adopted to minimize the dysphoric experience. The success of these strategies, including the psychotic solutions can be seen in the reduced physiological stress response. As information processing disorders, schizophrenias are also helped by treatments like those suggested by Hamilton [Chapter 12] which simplify the information and reduce information load.

If anxiety is not the immediate precipitating factor in schizophrenic disorders it seems likely from the work of Hamilton [Chapter 12] that childhood anxiety is a crucial factor in the development of the adult psychosis. It seems clear that aversive events in childhood give rise to anxiety and that maladaptive cognitive structures may develop. Both of these factors will increase vulnerability; excessive activation of the immature electrocortical pathways would make them more sensitive to later cognitive load and inadequate information processing structures will increase the strain on the information processing capacities and over-activate the electrocortical arousal systems. As Hamilton points out, the higher incidence of schizophrenia in lower socioeconomic groups can be attributed to a great extent to the excessive stress that must inevitably occur in children of this group. The study of the socialization processes of children, especially the underprivileged groups, must be of high priority in the near future.

From what has been said, it is clear that the stress phenomenon is an integral part of normal everyday life. Only when we are 'in neutral', a state of relaxed wakefulness, is the stress response very low. As soon as we start to concentrate and do something, the brain prepares us for action, psychologically and physiologically. Thus some stress responses are a natural consequence of any human information processing. The major problem for future research is how we can organize our society so that we can have the 'stress without distress' for which Selye argues. From the work cited in this volume it seems that distress occurs when the stressor-person interaction is too intense, too uncertain, and too prolonged. Obviously we cannot control genetic vulnerability to stress, but we can study the socialization processes which lower a person's ability to experience stress and minimize distress. An integral part of socialization should be preparing the child for coping with the vicissitudes of life effectively. After all, everyone's life is marked by stressful life events, like bereavement, but few of us are equipped to minimize distress that results from these sorts of events.

However, life event stressors are only isolated episodes in our lives. A much more pervasive problem is work. Over half our working lives are spent at work and it is as a consequence of work that most distress occurs. One of the causes of work stress is that the person cannot handle the total information input. As we come to understand the way in which we process information and develop integrated cognitive models as Rabbitt suggests, then we can train people to optimize their processing capacities. When we understand the changes that occur with information overload, we will be able to design tasks to allow for the inevitable shift in the balance of cognitive abilities that occurs with high levels of stressors. In the next decades the conditions under which people work will be changing rapidly in the technological age, but too little thought has been devoted to designing task demands to fit the worker. In many jobs the person is working under threat of failure to handle all the information. There is a pernicious tendency to attribute the consequent distress to the person's 'failure-to-cope' rather than to excessive, and so inhuman, task demands. In other words, there is something wrong with the individual not with the psychological work conditions that were imposed on him. It is imperative that industrial planners take heed of the results of psychological stress research, both present and future, to rectify this false reasoning.

REFERENCES

Levi, L. (1972). Stress and distress in response to psychosocial stimuli *Acta Medica Scandinavica*, Supplement 528, 119–142.
Mason, J. W. (1971). A re-evaluation of the conept of 'non-specificity' in stress theory. *Journal of Psychiatric Research*, **8**, 323–328.

Author Index

Abegglan, J. C. 326, 335
Abelson, R. 281, 297
Abood, L. G. 48, 61
Adams, J. E. 236, 262, 281, 282, 284, 285, 294, 295
Agnew, N. 24, 30
Aghajanian, G. K. 63
Ailion, G. 441, 460
Ainsworth, M. D. S. 396, 422
Alanen, Y. Ö. 393, 422
Albee, G. W. 417, 426
Alegre, C. E. 436, 462
Alexander, F. 23, 29
Alexander, I. E. 85, 112
Algheri, S. 439, 459
Al-Issa, I. 415, 422
Allman, L. R. 26, 29
Allpert, R. 271, 293
Allport, F. H. 266, 293
Allport, G. W. 69, 105
Alluisi, E. A. 95, 110
Alvarez, W. 238, 263
Amadeo, M. 416, 428
Amour, J. L. 207, 231
Andén, N. E. 441, 459
Anderson, R. C. 183, 199, 281, 293
Andersson, K. 165, 173
Andreason, N. J. C. 284, 293, 415, 422
Antonovsky, A. 285, 293
Antrobus, G. S. 42, 61
Appley, M. H. 71, 72, 79, 105, 107, 285, 293
Arduini, H. 50, 51, 62
Argyle, M. 92, 105
Argyris, C. 316, 325, 335
Arieti, S. 392, 422, 447, 449, 450, 459
Arnold, D. J. 412, 428
Arnold, M. B. 84, 105, 270, 293
Artiss, K. L. 32
Aruguete, A. 46, 47, 61
Ashford, L. E. 31
Asmussen, E. 360, 375

Åstrand, P. O. 60, 61
Atkinson, J. W. 85, 86, 93, 105, 106, 309, 326, 336
Attneave, F. 362, 375
Audley, R. J. 116, 137
Aulmann, H. 367, 368, 376
Averill, J. R. 88, 103, 106, 109, 267, 278, 283, 288, 289, 293, 296, 297
Azima, H. 30
Azmitia, E. C. 439, 459, 460

Bachrach, A. J. 190, 199
Bacon, S. J. 94, 106, 163, 164, 173, 190, 191, 192, 199, 229, 231
Baddeley, A. D. 127, 130, 132, 137, 138, 154, 164, 171, 173, 190, 192, 199
Bailey, A. D. 30
Bainbridge, L. 35, 36, 37, 61
Bahrick, H. P. 130, 137, 164, 173
Bakal, D. 415, 422
Baker, G. W. 285, 293
Baker. J. D. 341, 375
Bakke, E. W. 320, 335
Baldamus, W. 316, 335
Bales, R. F. 285, 297
Ball, G. C. 442, 461
Band, R. J. 44, 46, 47, 61
Bandura, A. 266, 286, 288, 294
Bancroft, N. R. 45, 62
Banerjee, S. P. 456, 464
Bartenwerfer, H. 368, 375
Bartlett, F. C. 394, 407, 422
Basow, S. A. 94, 106
Basowitz, H. 22, 29, 437, 463
Bastiaans, J. 23, 29
Basu, G. K. 439, 463
Bateson, G. 392, 422
Bauman, E. 415, 422
Baumrind, D. 81, 86, 91, 106, 395, 422
Bayley, J. P. 112
Beaty, G. 42, 61
Beck, A. T. 219, 220, 231

Becker, S. 249, 263
Bedell, J. R. 207, 231
Beishon, R. J. 341, 375
Bekker, J. A. M. 135, 140
Bell, B. 418, 422
Bell, S. M. V. 396, 418, 422
Bennett, J. J. 451, 461
Bennis, W. 325, 335
Berenson, J. 31
Bergen, H. 32
Berger, B. D. 441, 464
Bergin, A. E. 463
Berkman, L. F. 285, 286, 294, 298
Berkowitz, L. 464
Berlyne, D. E. 72, 88, 106, 151, 153, 154, 155, 158, 173
Berne, E. 316, 335
Berry, R. 158, 173, 415, 426
Berzofsky, M. 415, 429
Besser, G. M. 25, 30
Bettelheim, B. 75, 106
Bevan, W. 24, 29
Bexton, W. H. 72, 88, 106, 314, 335
Bhattachaya, S. 53, 63
Bhrolchain, M. N. 392, 422
Bibring, E. 248, 262
Bickford, R. G. 44, 62
Biderman, A. D. 75, 106
Biel, G. H. 48, 61
Bigland, B. 368, 375
Bills, A. G. 148, 173
Binswanger, H. 24, 29
Birch, H. G. 77, 112, 385, 423, 428
Birmingham, H. P. 341, 375
Birren, J. E. 120, 137
Bitterman, M. E. 71, 109
Björklund, A. 457, 462
Blake, M. J. 146, 154, 166, 174
Black, W. C. 30
Blanck, G. 253, 262
Blanck, R. 253, 262
Blankstein, K. R. 153, 157, 174
Blatt, S. J. 392, 418, 422
Blau, P. M. 318, 335
Bleuler, M. 390, 422
Bliss, E. J. 436, 437, 440, 441, 448, 449, 460
Bloch, S. 437, 460
Block, J. 69, 77, 106
Blumenfield, M. 26, 30
Bobrow, D. G. 36, 64, 117, 137, 139, 397, 428

Böttge, H. 368, 375
Boies, S. J. 403, 428
Boll, T. 207, 231
Bolles, R. C. 70, 78, 98, 106, 266, 294
Bonjean, C. M. 311, 335
Boomer, D. S. 393, 394, 428
Bordier, B. 30
Borge, G. F. 30
Borsa, D. M. 153, 154, 173
Borus, J. F. 255, 262
Bourne, P. G. 57, 61, 444, 460
Bouthilet, L. 393, 394, 428
Bowlby, J. 76, 106, 195, 199
Brackenridge, C. J. 437, 460
Bradbury, R. 154, 175
Brady, J. P. 440, 462
Braff, D. L. 415, 422
Branch, C. H. 436, 437, 440, 448, 449, 460
Brand, R. J. 8
Braun, J. R. 218, 219, 231
Breuer, J. 236, 247, 262
Bridges, P. K. 25, 26, 29, 437, 461
Briggs, G. E. 125, 137, 138
Brightwell, D. R. 112
Broadbent, D. E. 39, 41, 61, 72, 95, 102, 106, 118, 121, 122, 123, 129, 130, 134, 136, 138, 146, 147, 148, 151, 162, 163, 165, 166, 168, 169, 170, 174, 184, 199, 229, 231, 274, 294, 397, 398, 422
Broadhurst, P. L. 77, 106, 144, 174, 461
Brodie, B. B. 53, 63, 65
Broen, W. E. 164, 177, 414, 422
Bronson, G. W. 396, 422
Bronha, L. 360, 375
Brown, B. B. 42, 48, 61
Brown, G. W. 208, 209, 231, 391, 422
Brown, J. S. 70, 106
Brown, K. 464
Bruner, J. S. 407, 422
Buchsbaum, M. 89, 106
Buchsbaum, M. T. 454, 462
Buchwald, C. 393, 429
Buck, R. 92, 106
Buckminster Fuller, R. 26
Bulman, R. J. 284, 287, 294
Bunney, W. E. 25, 26, 29, 30
Burgoyne, J. G. 320, 336
Bursill, A. E. 130, 138, 163, 174
Burt, D. R. 456, 460
Buss, A. H. 413, 422

Butler, P. W. P. 25, 30
Butler, R. M. 120, 137
Bynum, H. J. 452, 461
Byrne, D. 81, 106

Calloway, E. 44, 45, 46, 47, 61, 190,
  199, 415, 418, 422, 423
Cameron, N. S. 408, 414, 423
Cancro, R. 416, 423
Caplan, R. D. 305, 315, 335
Carlsson, A. 456, 460
Carpenter, W. 454, 462
Carranza, E. 207, 218, 231
Carroll, B. J. 25, 26, 30
Casey, A. 24, 30
Cassel, J. 223, 232, 285, 294, 295, 297
Chandler, M. K. 320, 337
Chapanis, A. 145, 174
Chapman, D. W. 285, 293
Chapman, J. 415, 427, 450, 451, 462
Chapman, J. P. 393, 415, 423
Chapman, L. J. 393, 415, 423
Charcot, J. M. 247, 262
Chase, T. N. 441, 460
Chess, S. 77, 112, 385, 423, 428
Chevalier, J. A. 437, 463
Chodoff, P. 285, 295
Chorover, S. 155, 174
Chowers, I. 438, 460
Chown, S. M. 120, 138
Christensen, E. H. 60, 61, 341, 360,
  375, 376
Cicero, T. J. 24, 30
Clancy, M. 127, 139
Claparède, E. 196, 199
Claridge, G. J. 398, 423, 435, 460
Clark, R. A. 309, 326, 336
Clarke, A. D. B. 101, 107, 395, 423
Clarke, A. M. 395, 423
Clarke-Stewart, K. A. 418, 423
Cleghorn, R. A. 439, 460
Clyde, D. 450, 460
Cobb, S. 223, 231, 285, 289, 293, 294,
  305, 315, 335
Coelho, G. V. 236, 262, 285, 294
Cofer, C. N. 72, 107
Cohen, J. B. 279, 294, 296
Cohen, R. 53, 65
Cohen, S. 395, 423
Cohler, B. J. 419, 424
Cohler, J. 32
Colby, K. M. 420, 423, 424

Cole, J. O. 453, 461
Cole, M. 98, 107
Coleman, R. 42, 61
Collins, W. 89, 111
Colquhoun, W. P. 84, 107, 122, 130,
  137, 140, 146, 147, 154, 174
Consolo, S. 440, 462
Constantini, A. F. 218, 219, 231
Coombs, C. H. 367, 376
Cooper, C. L. 311, 313, 335
Cooper, S. J. 464
Coopersmith, S. 86, 107
Coover, G. D. 55, 61, 63
Copeman, A. 163, 175
Corcoran, D. W. J. 84, 95, 107, 148,
  149, 151, 174
Cornelison, A. R. 392, 427
Cornsweet, D. M. 96, 107
Corrodi, H. 438, 439, 441, 460, 461,
  462
Costa, E. 439, 459
Costello, C. G. 387, 423
Court, J. H. 413, 423
Cousins, N. 288, 294
Coyne, J. C. 274, 294
Coyne, L. 455, 464
Cox, F. N. 86, 107
Craik, F. I. 127, 138, 153, 157, 173,
  174, 197, 199
Cramer-Azima, E. 31
Creese, J. 456, 460
Crossman, E. R. F. W. 116, 138
Crowell, E. B. 44, 47, 48, 61, 63
Cumming, G. C. 115, 116, 139
Cunitz, A. R. 155, 175
Curtis, G. 437, 460
Curzon, G. 438, 460
Cushman, P. 26, 30
Czech, M. P. 59, 62

Daee, S. 157, 158, 175
Dahlstrom, A. 441, 459
Darrow, C. W. 161, 174
Davidson, J. M. 438, 460
Davidson, K. S. 401, 428
Davies, B. 30
Davies, S. 154, 176
Davis, D. R. 118, 130, 138, 146, 162,
  163, 165, 174
Davis, J. 218, 219, 231
Davis, J. M. 456, 458, 461
Davis, K. 32

Davis, R. C. 161, 174
Davis, R. D. 72, 107
Dawes, R. M. 376
Day, R. E. 363, 379
Dean, A. 223, 231
De Goza, S. 284, 295
de Groot, J. 438, 463
Deibler, W. P. 42, 61
Deininger, R. L. 116, 138
Dekker, D. J. 207, 231
De Kock, A. R. 45, 62
Delay, J. 24, 30
De Martino, V. 221, 232
Dember, W. N. 266, 294
Dembo, D. 44, 45, 61, 191, 199
De Monchaux, C. 208, 233
Denny, J. P. 397, 423
Depue, R. A. 416, 423
De Rivera, J. 100, 107
Dewar, R. 311, 336
De Wied, D. 53, 54, 62
De Witt, G. W. 106, 288, 289, 293
De Wolfe, A. S. 415, 423
Dimsdale, J. E. 284, 287, 294
Dinac, T. 457, 462
Dixon, N. F. 81, 107
Dodson, J. D. 143, 144, 177, 188, 201
Dohrenwend, B. P. 207, 209, 223, 231, 391, 423
Dohrenwend, B. S. 207, 209, 223, 231, 391, 423
Dollard, J. 270, 294
Donders, F. C. 122, 124, 138
Dorman, D. 439, 464
Dornic, S. 157, 165, 175, 176
Dransfield, G. A. 30
Dreyfus, H. L. 292, 293, 294
Driver, M. J. 310, 337, 407, 428
Duffy, E. 142, 175, 270, 294
Dunbar, F. 23, 30
Dunn, R. F. 397, 423
Durand, T. S. 362, 376
Durnin, J. V. G. A. 357, 377

Easterbrook, J. A. 94, 107, 158, 159, 162, 164, 175, 189, 199, 229, 231, 269, 271, 294, 399, 423
Edwards, D. W. 208, 209, 230, 232
Edwards, M. K. 207, 231
Edwards, R. 166, 175
Egstrom, G. H. 164, 177, 201, 435, 464
Eichelman, W. H. 403, 428

Ekman, G. 88, 110
Ekman, P. 277, 294
Elliott, R. 161, 175
Ellis, A. 266, 294
Elmadjian, F. 30
El-Yousef, M. K. 456, 461
Endler, N. S. 69, 83, 84, 107
Endroczi, E. 49, 55, 62
Engel, G. L. 286, 294
Epstein, 191, 199, 278, 294, 388, 423
Eränkö, O. 24, 30
Erdelyi, M. H. 81, 107, 268, 274, 275, 294
Eriksen, C. W. 290, 296
Erikson, E. 244, 263
Escalona, S. K. 76, 107
Etschberger, K. 362, 363, 376
Etzioni, A. 318, 336
Euler, U. S. von 57, 62
Eysenck, M. W. 94, 107, 157, 168, 175, 229, 231, 409, 424
Eysenck, H. J. 71, 77, 78, 82, 84, 88, 90, 107, 387, 388, 398, 423

Fain, J. N. 59, 62
Fantz, R. L. 395, 424
Farber, I. E. 78, 90, 112
Farley, F. H. 154, 175
Farrell, J. P. 453, 460
Faught, W. S. 420, 424
Feather, N. T. 85, 106
Feldberg, W. 452, 460
Feldman, P. 461
Feldman, S. 438, 460
Fenz, W. D. 88, 91, 107, 108, 191, 199
Festinger, L. 310, 336
Fieve, R. R. 25, 31
Fink, M. 450, 451, 460, 461
Fisch, R. 325, 337
Fischer, R. 24, 30, 261, 263
Fishman, J. R. 56, 62, 63
Fitts, P. M. 116, 137, 138, 164, 173
Fitzgerald, J. A. 440, 462
Flach, F. F. 26, 30
Fleck, S. 392, 427
Fleishman, E. A. 350, 376
Fletcher, C. 116, 138
Foa, U. G. 303, 336
Fogel, M. C. 437, 460
Folkard, S. 154, 167, 175
Folkman, S. 296, 470, 473
Folkow, B. 57, 62

Formica, R. 85, 113
Forrer, G. R. 452, 400, 461
Foulkes, D. 43, 65
Fowles, D. C. 416, 423
Fox, R. H. 140
Franceschini, E. 101, 103, 111
Frank, J. D. 445, 461
Frankenhaeuser, M. 46, 58, 59, 60, 62, 63, 12, 88, 95, 108, 143, 175, 187, 199, 200, 290, 296
Franks, C. M. 90, 108
Freedman, N. 393, 429
Freeman, G. L. 189, 200
French, E. G. 92, 108
French, J. R. P. Jr. 289, 294, 305, 315, 335
Frenkel-Brunswik, E. 71, 108, 280, 295, 399, 424
Freud, A. 236, 263
Freud, S. 236, 247, 262, 263, 269, 270, 289, 295, 388, 392, 433, 461
Friedman, M. 8
Freidman, S. B. 285, 295, 443, 465
Friesen, W. 277, 294
Frieze, I. 113
Frith, G. 107
Fröhlich, W. D. 71, 108, 228, 233
Fromm, E. 332, 336
Fuenta, R. de la 29
Funkenstein, D. H. 26, 30
Furger, R. 439, 461
Fuxe, K. 438, 439, 441, 459, 460, 461, 462

Gad, M. T. 206, 228, 231
Gaines, L. S. 278, 295
Gal, R. 193, 200
Galambos, R. 41, 64
Galanter, E. H. 196, 200, 270, 297
Gallant, D. 393, 419, 424, 425
Gamer, M. S. 393, 424
Ganong, W. F. 53, 54, 62, 64, 65, 439, 463
Garattini, S. 440, 462, 464
Gardner, J. W. 331, 336
Garfield, S. J. 463
Garfinkel, R. 408, 427
Garmezy, N. 417, 424
Garner, W. R. 145, 174
Garwoli, E. 413, 423
Geen, R. G. 92, 93, 108
Gelman, R. S. 153, 173

Gerbasi, K. C. 218, 233
Gershon, S. 32
Gibbons, J. L. 439, 463
Giora, Z. 414, 424
Giordani, B. 207, 231
Glanzer, M. 155, 175
Glass, D. C. 6, 8, 164, 175, 395, 423, 462
Glenn, C. 281, 297
Glickman, L. 26, 30
Goetz, E. T. 281, 293
Goldberg, E. M. 391, 424
Goldberg, S. 396, 426
Goldberg, S. C. 453, 461
Goldfried, A. P. 266, 295
Goldfried, M. R. 266, 295
Goldman, L. 55, 61, 63
Goldman, R. F. 147, 174
Goldschmidt, W. 289, 295
Goldsmith, R. 140
Goldstein, M. J. 393, 424, 426
Goodnow, J. J. 146, 151, 177
Goodwin, F. K. 30
Gore, S. 285, 295
Gorsuch, R. L. 112, 207, 218, 232, 233
Gottesman, I. I. 390, 393, 424
Gottfried, S. P. 30
Goulet, L. R. 94, 111, 409, 424
Gowler, D. 323, 325, 331, 336
Grad, B. 31
Grand, S. 393, 429
Gray, J. A. 79, 91, 92, 108, 111, 442, 461
Gray, M. M. 154, 176
Green, A. R. 438, 460
Green, J. W. 50, 51, 62
Greenberg, A. 42, 61
Greenberg, D. 456, 464
Greenblatt, M. 30
Greenhouse, S. W. 120, 137
Gregory, M. 147, 165, 168, 174
Griffin, R. 44, 62
Grimes, M. D. 311, 335
Grinker, R. R. 29, 75, 108, 437, 463
Grisell, J. L. 452, 461
Grob, D. 44, 62
Groll-Knapp, E. 368, 376
Gronwall, D. M. A 132, 138
Gross, M. E. 284, 298
Grossman, S. P. 142, 175
Grunebaum, H. 393, 419, 424
Gruzelier, J. H. 414, 424
Guilford, J. P. 69, 108, 435, 461

Gupta M. N. 359, 376

Haan, N. 81, 108, 253, 254, 263, 280, 283, 285, 295
Haber, R. N. 271, 293
Hackman, J. R. 291, 295, 316, 336
Hage, J. 311, 336
Haider, M. 39, 40, 62, 81, 107, 129, 138, 368, 369, 376
Haley, J. 392, 422
Hall, M. M. 53, 63
Hall, R. A. 44, 62
Hamacher, J. H. 154, 173
Hamburg, B. 284, 295
Hamburg, D. A. 56, 62, 63, 236, 262, 263, 281, 282, 284, 285, 294, 295, 437, 463
Hamilton, P. 131, 132, 134, 138, 142, 155, 156, 157, 160, 163, 164, 165, 166, 167, 168, 170, 171, 175, 176
Hamilton, V. 69, 70, 71, 81, 84, 87, 89, 90, 94, 95, 96, 97, 101, 108, 109, 188, 200, 269, 272, 295, 311, 336, 384, 390, 395, 396, 397, 400, 401, 405, 406, 408, 414, 416, 418, 424, 425, 470, 471, 472, 474
Hammerton, M. 191, 200
Hampton, I. F. G. 140
Hancock, N. 404
Handlon, J. H. 56, 62, 63
Handy, C. 318, 336
Hanlon, T. E. 31
Hansen, O. 60, 61
Hare, C. C. 32
Harmatz, J. 32
Harris, P. W. 207, 232
Harris, T. 392, 422
Harrison, R. 318, 336
Hartemann, F. 45, 46, 65
Hartemann, G. 49, 62
Hartford, C. E. 284, 293
Hartmann, E. L. 29
Hartmann, H. 248, 263
Harvey, A. M. 44, 62
Haslerud, G. M. 131, 140.
Hatter, J. E. 154, 173
Hauser, H. 44, 62
Haveman, J. E. 154, 175
Hayes, A. H. 63
Heatherington, R. N. 39, 63
Hebb, D. O. 142, 144, 155, 175, 195, 200
Heckhausen, H. 93, 109
Hedge, G. A. 54, 62

Heilbrun, A. B. 416, 425
Heimstra, N. W. 45, 46, 62
Helper, M. M. 151, 175
Hemsley, D. R. 415, 416, 425
Heptinstall, S. 133, 134, 140
Herman, J. 419, 425
Heron, A. 120, 138
Heron, W. 72, 88, 106, 314, 335
Herron, W. G. 450, 461
Hettinger, T. 357, 378
Hick, W. E. 116, 127, 138
Hickson, D. J. 311, 318, 319, 337
Higgins, J. 448, 461
Hill, K. T. 86, 93, 109, 396, 425, 428
Hillon, J. G. 30
Hillyard, S. A. 40, 41, 62, 64
Himmelweit, H. 93, 109
Himwich, H. E. 44, 65
Hinings, C. R. 311, 318, 319, 337
Hink, R. F. 40, 62
Hinkle, L. E. 23, 30
Hinnings, C. P 337
Hitch, G. J. 132, 138, 171, 173
Hoagland, H. 24, 25, 30, 460
Hobbs, G. E. 31
Hockey, G. R. J. 131, 132, 134, 138, 146, 154, 155, 156, 160, 163, 164, 165, 167, 173, 175, 176, 190, 200, 471, 472, 473
Hodges, W. F. 96, 109, 397, 425
Hofer, M. A. 443, 465
Hokfelt, T. 438, 439, 461
Holden, J. M. 451, 461
Hollingshead, A. B. 391, 425
Hollister, L. E. 451, 461
Holmes, T. H. 23, 30, 206, 207, 219, 220, 230, 232, 233
Holoch, J. 368, 376
Holt, R. R. 392, 425
Holzman, P. S. 416, 425
Holzman, W. H. 71, 109
Hopkins, H. K. 44, 62
Hörmann, H. 157, 176
Horowitz, M. 43, 62, 100, 109, 236, 238, 242, 243, 245, 246, 249, 253, 261, 262, 263, 267, 282, 295, 443, 472, 473
Howells, J. G. 384, 425
Hsu, W. 419, 425, 426
Hudgens, R. W. 209, 232
Hullin, R. P. 26, 30
Hunt, E. 171, 176
Hunt, J. McV. 395, 430

Hunt, T. 208, 233
Hyman, R. 116, 128, 138

Iervolino, A. 218, 219, 231
Iker, H. P. 286, 297
Inglis, S. 396, 430
Inhelder, B. 407, 428
Iskander, 361, 373, 378
Itil, T. M. 419, 425, 426, 450, 451, 460, 461
Izard, C. E. 70, 77, 100, 109, 270, 295

Jacob, T. 393, 426
Jacobs, S. 24, 31
Jackson, D. 392, 422
James, W. 432
Janis, I. 72, 75, 76, 109, 236, 263, 267, 268, 279, 281, 284, 285, 290, 291, 295
Janowsky, D. S. 456, 458, 461
Jaques, E. 316, 336
Jarvik, M. 455, 461
Jenik, P. 353, 356, 376
Jenkins, C. D. 8
Jenner, F. A. 442, 461, 462
Jerison, H. J. 130, 138
Jew, N. 442, 464
Jex, H. R 362, 363, 376
Johansson, G. 46, 62, 63, 95, 108
John, E. R. 38, 39, 63
Johnsen, A. M. 125, 137, 138
Johnson, J. H. 206, 212, 213, 218, 221, 222, 224, 227, 228, 231, 232, 233, 470
Jones, A. 72, 109
Jones, D. M. 165, 174
Jones, E. J. 87, 109
Jones, J. E. 393, 426
Jones, M. B. 417, 426
Jones, M. T. 25, 26, 29, 437, 461
Jonsson, G. 438, 439, 461

Kagan, A. 13, 303, 336
Kagan, J. 395, 429
Kahn, R. L. 285, 289, 295, 315, 332, 336
Kahneman, D. 36, 63, 127, 139, 161, 164, 171, 172, 176, 181, 200, 267, 269, 288, 295, 298, 397, 426
Kaltreider, N. 238, 263
Kamano, D. K. 32
Kanner, A. 296
Kanouse, D. E. 109
Kaplan, B. H. 223, 232, 285, 295, 297

Kaplan, S. 152, 153, 154, 156, 170, 176
Karrasch, K. 359, 360
Katsuki, S. 357, 376
Katz, D. 285, 295
Katz, R. I. 441, 460
Kay, S. 418, 426
Kayton, L. 415, 426
King Taylor, L. 316, 336
Keenan, J. J. 341, 376
Keller, W. 358, 377
Kelley, H. H. 109
Kemper, T. 266, 296
Kendrick, P. 341, 376
Kennedy, R. S. 95, 109
Kenney, D.A. 226. 232
Kernberg, O. 253, 263
Kerry, R. J. 442, 461, 462
Keskiner, N. 451, 461
Kesselman, M. 415, 429
Kessler, P. 409, 426
Ketchum, J. S. 44, 47, 48, 61, 63
Kety, S. S. 393, 426, 456, 462
Key, M. K. 207, 232
Kimbell, I. 451, 461
King, D. J. 26, 31
Kinney, O. K. 211, 233
Kirkegaard, S. 399, 426
Klein, G. 95, 109
Kleinsmith, L. J. 152, 153, 154, 156, 170, 176
Klerman, G. L. 453, 461
Klimmer, F. 367, 368, 376
Klinger, E. 269, 296
Klix, F. 362, 376, 377
Köhler, W. 89, 109
Koenig, I. D. V. 154, 173
Kofsky, E. 408, 428
Koh, S. D. 415, 426
Kohn, M. L. 391, 426
Kohner, H. S. 32
Kohut, H. 253, 263
Kolin, E. A. 224, 233
Kolisnyk, E. 415, 422
Kopin, I. 441, 460
Korboot, P. 413, 430
Korchin, S. J. 29, 91, 109, 269, 296, 437, 463
Koriat, A. 80, 109
Kornblum, S. 116, 139
Kortchinskaia, E. J. 449, 462
Knauth, P. 167, 175
Knight, R. 411, 415, 416, 426
Kral, V. A. 26, 31

Krasner, L. 417, 429
Kraut, H. 358, 377
Krieger, D. T. 54, 63
Krieger, H. P. 54, 63
Kriegsmann, E. 396, 430
Kristofferson, M. W. 115, 116, 139
Krivohlavy, J., 341, 377
Krnjević, K. 48, 63
Krop, H. D. 436, 462
Kuehn, A. 441, 442, 464
Kuhn, A. 302, 305, 306, 307, 308, 309
310, 311, 317, 318, 326, 336
Kukla, A. 113

Lacey, B. C. 187, 200
Lacey, J. I. 160, 161, 176, 187, 189, 200
Lacoursière, R. B. 455, 464
Lader, M. 390, 391, 398, 426
Ladinsky, H. 440, 462
Lainé, B. 30
Laming, D. R. J. 116, 139
Landau, K. 350, 377
Landau, S. G. 454, 462
Lande, N. 27, 31
Lane, E. A. 417, 426
Lang, P. J. 413, 422
Lange, C. 432
Langer, D. 22, 31
Langworthy, O. R. 44, 62
Lanyon, R. I. 219, 224, 232
Larkin, N. 415, 422
Launay, G. 96, 402
Launier, R. 272, 281, 283, 296
Laurig, W. 361, 362, 368, 377
Lavalle, L. W. 31
Laverty, R. 441, 464
Lavoisier, A. 357
Lawrence, P. R. 333, 336
Lawson, J. S. 415, 427
Lazarus, R. S. 71, 79, 80, 81, 84, 93,
109, 193, 200, 236, 263, 267, 269,
272, 273, 279, 281, 283, 285, 288,
290, 294, 296, 297, 298, 426, 470, 473
Leak, D. 437, 461
Lebovits, B. Z. 284, 298
Leeper, R. W. 270, 296
Lefcourt, H. M. 281, 286, 296
Legge, K. 331, 336
Lehmann, G. 359, 377
Lehmann, H. E. 25, 31
Lehrman, D. 463
Leonard, J. A. 148, 176

Leonard, K. 389, 426
Leslie, J. M. 363, 377
Leven, H. E. 140
Leventhal, H. 72, 76, 109
Levey, A. 90, 107
Levi, L. 6, 8, 12, 13, 31, 58, 60, 63, 303,
336, 472, 475
Levi, R. 438, 439, 462, 463
Levine, S. 55, 56, 61, 63, 74, 110
Levinger, G. 285, 296
Levitt, E. E. 439, 440, 462, 464
Levonian, F. 158, 176
Levy, D. L. 416, 425
Lewin, K. 86, 110
Lewis, J. 151, 171, 176
Lewis, J. L. 173
Lewis, M. 396, 426
Lewis, P. R. 49, 55, 64, 452, 464
Lidbrink, P. 438, 441, 461, 462
Liddell, H. S. 24, 31
Lidz, T. 392, 393, 427
Liebert, R. M 397, 427
Lief, H. I. 32
Lief, V. F. 32
Lighthall, F. F. 401, 428
Lilienthal, J. L. 44, 62
Lin, N. 223, 231
Lind, E. 207, 211, 232, 233
Lindenthal, J. J. 206, 232
Lindqvist, M. 456, 460
Lindsay, P. H. 165, 176
Lindsley, D. B. 39, 40, 42, 62, 63, 270,
296, 434, 435, 462
Lindvall, O. 457, 462
Lingjaerde, P. S. 24, 25, 31
Lingjaerde, P. T. 438, 462
Lipowski, Z. J. 287, 296
Lippold, O. C. 368, 375
Lissak, K. 49, 55, 62
Litwin, G. H. 93, 106
Ljapunow, A. A. 362, 377
Lockhart, R. S. 157, 174, 197, 199
Loeb, M. 95, 110
Loehlin, J. C. 77, 110
Loevinger, J. 280, 296
Loftin, J. 393, 428
Lorr, M. 446, 462
Lorsch, J. W. 333, 336
Lovegrove, T. D. 25, 31
Lowell, E. L. 309, 326, 336
Lubin, A. 146, 151, 177
Lubin, B. 218, 233

Luczak, H. 37, 63, 350, 362, 363, 365, 371, 377, 378, 469, 471, 472
Lundberg, U. 88, 110, 290, 296
Lundberg, V. 211, 232
Luneborg, C. 171, 176
Lushene, R. E. 112, 218, 233
Lykken, D. T. 402, 427
Lyons, T. F 315, 336

Machne, X. 44, 64
MacLean, P. W. 50, 63
Mackie, R. R. 72, 110
Mackintosh, N. J. 78, 110
Mackworth, N. H. 146, 176
Madge, N. 391, 428
Magaro, P. 415, 427
Magnusson, D. 69, 83, 107, 110
Mahl, G. 273, 296
Mahoney, N. J. 266, 296
Malmo, R. B. 142, 151, 176, 270, 296
Mandell, A. J. 25, 32, 432
Mandell, E. E. 153, 173
Mandler, G. 70, 87, 100, 110, 180, 182, 185, 186, 191, 194, 197, 200, 266, 267, 268, 270, 296, 397, 398, 427, 433, 462, 470
Mann, L. 267, 268, 279, 281, 285, 290, 291, 295
March, J. G. 316, 331, 336
Margolis, R. 393, 429
Margraf, H. W. 26, 31
Marks, B. H. 53, 63
Marks, V. 26, 31
Marmor, J. 462
Marshall, J. 311, 313, 335
Martin, F. I. R. 30
Martin, I. 368, 378, 379
Martin, L. K. 32
Martindale, C. 43, 63
Martini, L. 54, 64
Marx, M. H. 97, 110
Maslow, A. H. 331, 336
Mason, J. W. 15, 29, 31, 32, 56, 57, 59, 62, 63, 184, 200, 285, 295, 443, 465, 471, 475
Masserman, J. H. 444, 462
Masuda, M. 207, 232, 233
Matthysse, S. 456, 457, 463
Maule, A. J. 131, 140
May, P. R. A. 446, 455, 458, 463
Mayer, J. H. 463
Mayman, M. 31

Maynert, E. W. 438, 439, 462, 463
Mazzei, J. 409, 424
McClean, P. D. 154, 176
McClelland, D. C. 309, 326, 336
McCormick, E. J. 145, 176, 350, 377
McDonald, R. 30
McDonnell, J. D. 376
McDonnell, P. 72, 106
McDonell, D. 415, 427
McEvoy, D. 437, 460
McEwen, B. 439, 460
McFarland, D. J. 137, 139
McGhie, A. 415, 427, 450, 451, 462
McGuinness, D. 398, 428
McMichael, A. J. 305, 313, 336
McNair, D. M. 446, 462
McPherson, S. R. 393, 426
McReynolds, P. 388, 398, 418, 427
McRuer, D. T. 362, 377
Mechanic, D. 80, 110, 208, 232, 273, 285, 289, 296
Mednick, S. A. 390, 408, 409, 417, 418, 419, 422, 425, 426, 427, 447, 448, 449, 450, 463
Meehl, P. E. 417, 427
Meerloo, J. A. 432, 463
Megaw, E. D. 128, 139
Meichenbaum, D. 266, 285, 296
Meier, L. 24, 29
Melkman, R. 109
Meltzer, H. Y. 456, 457, 463
Melzack, R. 72, 89, 110, 398, 427
Menninger, K. 22, 31, 283, 297
Merriam–Webster 333, 336
Merry, J. 26, 31
Messiha, F. S. 26, 31
Metcalfe, E. V. 31
Michael, R. P. 439, 463
Michelson, M. J. 44, 47, 63
Migeon, C. J. 436, 437, 440, 448, 449, 460
Miles, S. 47, 63
Milgram, S. 90, 110
Miller, B. 396, 430
Miller, E. 22, 31
Miller, G. A. 196, 200, 270, 297,
Miller, J. G. 397, 427
Miller, J. J. 452, 461
Miller, N. E. 70, 71, 110, 270, 294
Miller, R. B. 341, 377
Miller, R. R. 155, 176
Mills, R. G. 341, 376

Milner, H. B. 30
Mirsky, A. F. 419, 425, 449, 463
Mischel, W. 69, 70, 77, 81, 97, 110
Moberg, G. P 53, 64, 436, 463
Monat, A. 278, 297
Monk, T. H. 154, 167, 175
Monod, H. 359, 360, 377, 378
Morgan, C. T. 145, 174
Moriarty, A. E. 74, 110
Morris, J. 320, 323, 324, 326, 336
Morris, L. W. 397, 427
Morrison, S. L. 391, 424
Moss, M. 400, 425
Motta, M. 54, 64
Mowbray, G. H. 116, 128, 139
Mowrer, O. H. 71, 110, 387, 388, 427
Moyer, C. A. 31
Müller, E.A. 359, 360, 376, 377
Mueller, D. P. 208, 209, 218, 232
Mueller, J. H. 94, 110, 229, 232, 409, 427
Mueser, G. E. 133, 140
Muittari, A. 24, 30
Mullin, J. 107
Murphy, D. L. 30
Murphy, L. B. 74, 110
Murray, H. A. 88, 110
Mussini, S. 462, 464
Myers, J. K. 206, 232
Myrsten, A. L. 46, 62, 63

Näätänen, R. 40, 41, 64, 160, 162, 176
Nakamura, C. Y. 164, 177
Naylor, H. 415, 422
Neale, J. M. 409, 415, 426, 427
Neisser, U. 274, 297, 394, 407, 427
Neumann, J. 362, 377
Nevin, S. 452, 463
Nevis, S. 395, 424
Newcombe, F. 132
Newell, A. 307, 308, 336
Nichols, R. C. 77, 110
Nicholson, J. 92, 111
Nielsen, M. 360, 375
Niemelä, P. 88, 111
Nodine, J. H. 463
Norman, D. A. 36, 39, 40, 64, 96, 97, 111, 117, 137, 139, 165, 176, 397, 428
Norton, J. 439, 464
Noyes, R. Jr. 284, 293
Nuckolls, K. B. 223, 232, 285, 297

O'Brien, L. 106, 288, 289, 293
Obrist, P. A. 161, 177
O'Connor, N. 415, 429
Odom–Brooks, P. H. 412, 428
Offord, D. R. 417, 426
O'Hanlon, J. F. 42, 58, 61, 64
Okada, M. 362, 377
Oken, D. 22
Oldham, G. 316, 336
Olson, L. 438, 441, 459, 461, 462
Olver, R. R. 407, 422
O'Neal, P. 385, 428
Opton, E. M. Jr. 267, 283, 296
Osgood, C. E. 277, 297
Osler, S. F. 408, 428
O. S. S. Assessment Staff 76, 111
Osterkamp, U. 157, 176
Ostfeld, A. M. 44, 46, 47, 64
Othmer, E. 112
Overall, J. E. 451, 461

Pacella, R. G. 135, 139
Palombo, S. R. 103, 111
Pancheri, P. 221, 232
Parad, H. 236, 263
Parad, L. 236, 263
Parantainen, J. 24, 31
Parker, L. F. 24, 31
Parkes, C. M. 236, 245, 263
Parkin, J. 442, 461
Parkison, R. C. 421, 424
Parry, C. H. 23
Parsons, T. 285, 297
Passmore, R. 357, 377
Patel, A. A. 45, 64
Patkai, P. 58, 60, 62
Patty, R. A. 94, 111
Paykel, E. S. 207, 232
Payne, R. C. 31
Payne, R. L. 311, 336, 470
Payne, R. W. 414, 415, 416, 428
Pearlin, J. I. 285, 297
Pechstein, H. 24, 31
Pennebaker, J. 8
Pepler, R. D. 122, 139, 146, 149, 177
Pepper, M. P. 206, 232
Pepper, S. 334, 336
Perez–Reyes, M. 26, 31
Peri, G. 440, 462
Perrault, R. 30
Persky, H. 29, 437, 439, 440, 462, 463, 464

Peterfreund, E. 101, 103, 111, 274, 297
Peterson, R. A. 415, 426
Peto, J. 45, 64
Petrie, A. 89, 111
Pew, R. 135, 139
Pfaff, D. W. 438, 463
Phatak, A. V. 376
Philips, C. 44, 64
Phillips, L. 284, 297
Phillips, P. 405
Phillis, J. W. 48, 63
Piaget, J. 244, 263, 407, 428
Pichert, J. W. 183, 199
Picton, I. 40, 41, 62, 64
Pincus, G. 30
Pinneau, S. R. 305, 315, 335
Piva, F. 54, 66
Platman, S. R. 25, 31
Polanyi, M. 275, 297
Pollin, W. 390, 429
Popoff, F. E. 24, 32
Posner, M. I. 403, 428
Post, B. 46, 62, 63
Poulton, E. C. 117, 118, 129, 139, 146, 147, 151, 177, 190, 191, 200
Powell, B. J. 24, 32
Powers, P. J 415, 422
Prail, A. 403
Prell, D. B. 77, 107
Preziosi, P. 54, 64
Pribram, K. 51, 64, 196, 200, 270, 297, 398, 428, 433, 434, 463
Price, L. 224, 233
Proctor, L. R. 416, 425
Proctor, R. C. 442, 463
Pruyser, P. 31
Puech, J. 30
Pugh, D. S. 311, 318, 319, 336, 337

Quinn, J. G. 155, 156, 175
Quinn, R. P. 289, 295, 315, 332, 336

Rabbitt, P. 36, 115, 116, 127, 128, 133, 134, 135, 136, 138, 139, 140, 471, 473, 475
Rabkin, J. G. 76, 111, 207, 223, 233
Rachman, S. 387, 428
Radow, B. L. 24
Rahe, R. H. 23, 30, 206, 207, 210, 219, 220, 223, 230, 232, 233
Rainey, M. T. 107
Raman, A. C. 418, 422

Randall, L. O. 462, 464
Rangell, L. 248, 263
Rankin, R. E. 137, 164, 173
Rappoport, M. 44, 62
Rasmussen, P. V. 419, 429
Rau, G. 361, 377
Raymond, S. 273, 288, 298
Raynor, J. O. 85, 105, 111
Redlich, F. C. 391, 425
Reed, L. 113
Rees, W. L. 24, 32, 76, 111
Rejman, M. 131, 132, 134, 138, 160, 167, 175
Resnick, H. 236, 263
Rest, S. 113
Reymert, M. T. 462
Reynolds, B. 427
Reynolds, R. E. 281, 293
Rhoades, M. V. 116, 128, 139
Rickels, K. 442, 463
Ricks, N. L. 419, 425
Rinaldi, F. 44, 65
Robins, L. N. 385, 428
Robinson, A. 403
Rodahl, K. 60, 61
Rodgers, W. 289, 294
Rodnick, E. H. 393, 424, 426
Roemier, R. A. 416, 428
Rogers, J. 285, 289, 297
Rohmert, W. 350, 359, 360, 361, 367, 368, 369, 371, 373, 376, 377, 378, 469, 471
Rohracher, A. 368, 378
Rokeach, M. 280, 297
Rosenbaum, R. M. 113
Rosenblith, W. A. 377
Rosenman, R. 6, 8
Rosenthal, D. 393, 419, 426, 429
Rosenthal, J. 154, 175
Rosenthal, R. A. 315, 332, 336
Ross, G. 44, 62
Roth, M. 384, 429
Rotter, J. B. 75, 87, 111, 219, 224, 233, 286, 297
Roupenian, A. 278, 294
Rowntree, D. W. 452, 463
Royce, J. R. 69, 111
Rubin, R. T. 25, 26, 32, 55, 64
Rubinstein, J. 395, 428
Ruebush, B. K. 401, 428
Ruff, G. E. 91, 109
Rundus, D. 155, 177

Russell, L. 31
Russell, M. A. H. 45, 64
Russell, R. W. 37, 64
Rutenfranz, J. 167, 175, 361, 367, 368, 371, 373, 376, 378
Rutter, D. R. 92, 111
Rutter, M. 385, 391, 428

Sabshin, M. 437, 463
Sachar, E. J. 26, 32, 56, 62, 64, 444, 449, 463
Sacks, M. 454, 462
Safford, S. F. 94, 111
Saletu, B. 419, 425, 426
Salmon, P. 384, 405, 425
Saltz, E. 428
Sälzer, M. 367, 378
Sampson, H. 132, 138
Samuels, L. T. 436, 437, 440, 448, 449, 460
Sandford, A. J. 131, 140
Sarason, I. G. 84, 87, 94, 96, 111, 194, 201, 208, 212, 213, 218, 221, 222, 224, 227, 232, 233, 269, 271, 297, 397, 401, 428, 470
Sarason, S. B. 87, 110, 194, 200, 396, 397, 401, 425, 427, 428
Saterfield, J. H. 40, 64
Sathananthan, G. 32
Sayles, L. R. 320, 337
Savage, C. 31, 451, 461
Scapagnini, U. 53, 54, 64, 65, 438, 463
Schachter, S. 85, 111, 432, 464
Schaefer, C. 296, 470, 473
Schafer, R. 280, 297
Schaie, K. W. 94, 111
Schallek, W. 441, 442, 464
Schallert, D. L. 281, 293
Schalling, D. 89, 112
Schank, R. 281, 297
Scherrer, J. 359, 360
Schiaffini, O. 54, 64
Schiff, M. 41, 64
Schildkraut, J. J. 26, 32
Schlaich, K. 371, 378
Schmale, A. 286, 297
Schmidtke, H. 364, 367, 369, 378
Schmitt, F. O. 463
Schon, D. A. 325, 335, 337
Schönpflug, W. 100, 112, 376
Schopler, E. 393, 428

Schouten, J. F. 135, 140
Schreiber, A. J. 367, 378
Schreiberg, G. 55, 62
Schroder, H. M. 310, 337, 407, 428
Schulsinger, F. 393, 408, 417, 418, 419, 422, 426, 427
Schultz, D. P. 165, 177
Schur, M. 248, 263
Schwent, V. L. 40, 62
Schwartz, B. E. 44, 62
Schwartz, S. 157, 177, 285, 297
Scott, D. 154, 173
Scott, T. H. 72, 88, 106, 314, 335
Scott, W. R. 318, 335
Scribner, S. 98, 107
Sechehaye, M. 448, 464
Seeber, A. 362, 376, 377
Segal, J. 393, 394, 428
Segundo, J. P. 34, 64
Sekerke, H. J. 456, 461
Seligman, M. E. 286, 297
Selye, H. 11, 12, 13, 14, 15, 16, 19, 22, 23, 25, 26, 28, 32, 52, 142, 177, 184, 201, 432, 464, 471
Selzer, M. L. 207, 208, 218, 219, 230, 233
Serban, G. 24, 32
Shackel, B. 368, 378
Shaffer, L. F 317, 337
Shagass, C. 416, 428
Shakow, D. 413, 428
Shalit, B. 279, 297, 399, 400, 429
Shannon, B. E. 34, 64
Shapiro, D. 280, 297
Shapiro, J. 411, 415, 416, 426
Shapiro, K. J. 85, 112
Shashall, A. 154, 173
Sherer, M. 411, 415, 416, 426
Sherwood, S. L. 452, 453, 460, 464
Shields, J. 77, 112, 390, 393, 424
Shinar, D. 125, 138
Shoben, E. J. Jr. 317, 337
Shopsin, B. 26, 32
Shute, C. C. D. 49, 55, 64, 452, 464
Sidell, F. R. 63
Siegel, J. M. 212, 213, 218, 221, 222, 224, 227, 232
Silva, M. T. A. 438, 463
Simon, H. A. 100, 112, 226, 233, 267, 268, 270, 297, 307, 308, 316, 331, 336, 408, 427
Sinaiko, H. W. 375

Singer, J. E. 8, 164, 175, 395, 423
Singer, J. L. 42, 61
Singer, M. T. 392, 393, 419, 429, 430
Singh, M. M. 418, 426
Singleton, W. T. 375, 376
Sjöberg, H. 398, 429
Skinner, B. F. 331, 337, 387, 429
Skolnick, B. E. 278, 295
Slater, E. 384, 429
Smelik, P. G. 54, 62
Smith, B. D. 278, 295
Smith, J. E. 201, 435, 464
Smith, J. M. 418, 426
Smith, K. D. 439, 463
Smith, L. H. 82, 112
Smith, R. E. 224, 233
Smock, C. D. 399, 429
Snoek, J. D. 289, 295, 315, 332, 336
Snyder, S. H. 456, 460, 464
Solomon, A. C. 30
Solomon, P. 89, 111
Sokoloff, L. 120, 137
Sokolov, E. W. 398, 429
Spence, J. T. 78, 112, 269, 297, 398, 429
Spence, K. W. 78, 90, 112, 269, 297, 396, 398, 429
Sperling, G. 404, 429
Sperry, R. W. A. 43, 64
Spiegel, J. 75, 108
Spielberger, C. D. 82, 84, 92, 94, 96, 109, 112, 218, 233, 396, 397, 425, 429
Spitzer, H. 357, 378
Spohn, H. E. 455, 464
Spong, P. 39, 40, 62
Spring, B. 71, 113
Springer, H. D. 155, 176
Spurgeon, P. 375, 376
Stabenau, J. R. 390, 429
Stach, T. W. 439, 464
Stahl, S. M. 456, 457, 463
Stayton, D. J. 395, 422
Steele, F. 311, 315, 337
Steele, R. 59, 64
Stein, L. 441, 464
Stein, N. 281, 297
Steingart, I. 393, 429
Sternberg, S. 122, 124, 125, 140
Stevens, S. S. 367, 379
Stevenson, J. A. F. 31
Stier, F. 356, 379

Strahan, R. 218, 233
Strauss, H. 435, 464
Strauss, J. 454, 462
Strauss, R. 8
Streufert, S. 310, 337, 407, 428
Strickland, B. R. 75, 112
Struening, E. L. 76, 111, 207, 223, 233
Stokols, D. 6, 8
Storms, L. H. 414, 422
Stumpf, C. 50, 65
Sullivan, H. S. 447, 464
Surawicz, F. G. 76, 112
Surwillo, W. W. 151, 176
Sutterer, J. R. 161, 177
Sutton, S. 39, 63
Sutton–Smith, S. 422
Swanson, J. M. 125, 138
Sydrow, H. 377
Syme, S. L. 286, 298
Szasz, T. S. 432, 445, 453
Szoc, R. 415, 426

Takki, S. 26, 32
Tammisto, T. 26, 32
Tarrière, C. 45, 46, 65
Tarte, R. D. 153, 177
Tavormina, J. 207, 231
Taylor, F. V. 341, 375
Taylor, J. 78, 112, 396, 429
Taylor, K. M. 441, 464
Taylor, L. W. 363, 379, 403, 428
Thackray, R. I. 95, 112
Theorell, T. 207, 211, 232, 233
Thomas, A. 77, 112, 385, 423, 428
Thomas, C. M. 132, 133, 134, 140
Thompson, D. A. 363, 377
Thompson, K. 455, 464
Tickner, A. H. 191, 200
Tinbergen, N. 24, 32
Tintera, J. W. 26, 32
Toates, F. 137, 140
Tomkins, S. S. 70, 112, 270, 274, 295, 298
Touchstone, M. 112
Trask, F. P. 133, 140
Traupman, K. L. 415, 429
Trosman, H. 43, 65
Trumbull, I. 285, 293
Trumbull, R. 71, 79, 105
Tulkin, S. R. 395, 429
Tulving, E. 197, 199
Tune, S. 146, 174

Turck, I. 31
Turner, C. 311, 325, 337
Turner, S. P. 337
Turner, W. J. 30
Tversky, A. 288, 295, 298, 376

Ulich, E. 371, 378
Ullman, L. 417, 429
Ungerstedt, U. 441, 459
Unna, K. R. 44, 64
Usdin, E. 461
Uzgiris, I. G. 395, 430

Vaillant, G. 283, 298
Valius, S. 109
Van Dyke, J. L. 419, 429
Van Harrison, R. 305, 313, 315, 335, 337
Van Loon, G. L. 53, 64, 65, 438, 463
Velten, E. A. 222, 233
Venables, P. H. 368, 378, 379, 402, 408, 414, 415, 422, 424, 427, 429
Vernon, M. D. 394, 430
Vernon, P. E. 81, 84, 112, 113
Vickers, G. 324, 337
Vinokur, A. 207, 208, 218, 219, 230, 233
Visotsky, H. M. 284, 298
Vogel, G. 43, 65
Vogel, W. 273, 288, 298
Vogt, M. 58, 65
Vossil, G. 228, 233
Vredenbregt, J. 361, 377
Vyas, S. M. 115, 116, 127, 134, 135, 136, 139, 140

Wachs, T. D. 395, 430
Wachtel, P. L. 94, 96, 113, 164, 177
Waelder, L. 248, 263
Waite, R. R. 401, 428
Walker, E. L. 153, 155, 177
Wallach, H. 89, 109
Wallerstein, R. S. 252, 263
Warburton, D. M. 24, 33, 43, 45, 46, 47, 49, 51, 65, 390, 430, 434, 438, 457, 458, 464, 470, 471, 472, 473, 474
Warwick–Evans, L. A. 414, 429
Watson, D. 270, 296
Watzlawich, P. 325, 337
Weakland, J. 325, 337, 392, 422
Weaver, W. 34, 64

Webb, D. A. 161, 177
Webb, J. T. 207, 231
Weber, M. 318, 323, 337
Webster, R. G. 131, 140
Wechsler, R. L. 44, 65
Weiner, B. 69, 70, 75, 97, 109, 113
Weiner, S. 439, 464
Weinstein, G. J. 446, 462
Weir, D. H. 362, 377
Weisman, A. D. 288, 298
Weisman, M. N. 29
Weiss, J. L. 419, 424
Weiss, J. M. 438, 463
Weitzel, W. D. 112
Weitzman, E. D. 55, 65
Welford, A. T. 127, 128, 140, 341, 379
Weltman, G. 164, 177, 191, 201, 435, 464
Wender, P. H. 393, 426
Wesnes, K. 45, 46, 47, 65
West, K. L. 393, 426
Westermann, E. O. 53, 63, 65
White, B. L. 395, 418, 430
White, R. P. 44, 65
Whyte, W. 334, 337
Wickens, C. D. 408, 430
Wild, C. M. 392, 418, 422
Wilding, J. M. 157, 158, 174
Wilk, S. 32
Wilkinson, R. T. 72, 84, 113, 122, 136, 140, 146, 147, 148, 149, 150, 151, 166, 172, 175, 177
Williams, C. D. 436, 462
Williams, H. L. 146, 151, 177
Williams, M. 24, 32
Williamson, J. R. 60, 65
Wilner, N. 238, 242, 263
Wilson, A. 452, 463
Wilson, G. 85, 92, 113
Wine, J. 94, 113, 397, 430
Winterbottom, M. 86, 113
Wise, C. D. 441, 464
Wolf, S. 23, 32
Wolfe, D. M. 289, 295, 315, 332, 336
Wolff, C. T. 443, 465
Wolff, H. G. 23, 30, 32
Woodhead, M. M. 125, 140
Woodward, J. 315, 337
Worden, F. G. 463
Worden, J. W. 288, 298
Wortman, C. B. 284, 287, 294
Wright, P. 127, 139

Wulbert, M. 396, 430
Wurm, M. 8
Wyler, A. R. 207, 233
Wynne, L. C. 392, 393, 419, 429, 430

Yamamoto, K. J. 211, 233
Yamamura, H. T. 456, 464
Yarrow, M. R. 120, 137
Yarvis, R. M. 208, 209, 230, 232
Yates, A. J. 387, 413, 430
Yates, M. 285, 298
Yerkes, R. M. 143, 144, 177, 188, 201

Yntema, D. B. 133, 140
Youkilis, H. D. 415, 423
Young, P. T. 269, 270, 298

Zahn, T. P. 413, 430
Zarate, C. 437, 460
Zawada, S. L. 415, 425
Zimbardo, P. G. 85, 113, 396, 428
Zoob, I. 224, 233
Zubin, J. 71, 113, 413, 430
Zuckerman, M. 218, 224, 233, 394, 430
Zwanziger, J. 441, 460

Subject Index

ability 346–347
abnormality 383–385
academic performance 218
acceptability level 347–348
accident 238
acetylcholine, brain 54–55, 440
achievement motivation 85–86, 92–94, 326
action, preparation for 12–13, 192, 472, 474–475
Action Decrement Hypothesis (Walker) 155
activation, *see* Arousal
accuracy 472
adaptation 186–187, 305–318, 450
  diseases of 16, 20–22, 24–25
adrenocorticotrophic hormone (ACTH) 14, 15, 16, 17, 19, 20, 21, 53–56
  and neurosis 23
  and schizophrenia 24–25
affiliation motive 85, 92–93
aggressive behaviour 20, 27
alarm reaction 14, 16, 17, 20, 23, 26
alcohol 123, 136
alcoholism 26
ambiguity 17–27
  and anxiety 394
  and appraisal 276–282
  and inference 24–27, 281–282
  information search 281–282
  intolerance of 279, 280, 399–400
  ambivalence 280
amphetamine 146
amphetamine psychosis 456–457
antipsychotic drugs 446, 451, 458, 459
anxiety 270, 273, 471, 473, 474
  and arousal 400–405
  and cognitive deficit 396–405
  and coping 190, 443–444
  and drugs 440–443, 445, 473, 474
  and electrocortical arousal 434

and processing capacity 194–195, 395–405
  and psychotherapy 445–446
  and schizophrenia 447–448, 450–451
  and stress 22, 86–87, 160, 436–438, 439–444, 449
  and uncertainty 195, 394, 399–400, 433
  defined 72–73, 89–90, 94–96, 164, 188, 194–195, 396, 403–421, 433, 447
  expectant 388
  fear 387–389
  free-floating 79, 388
  manifest 437
  social aspects 92–94, 332, 394–396
  state-trait and life changes 219
  test 194
  unconscious 79–80
appraisal, cognitive, and ambiguity 276–282
  and coping 282–293
  and defence 281–282
  and emotions 267–276
  and information processes 267–268
  and stress 267–268
arousal, autonomic 151, 196, 472
  and expectancy 185, 186, 192, 193, 196
  and performance 152–153, 160–162, 182, 187–188, 189, 190, 191–192, 197
arousal, concept of 36, 141–144, 160–162, 189
  and anxiety 88, 400–405
  and attention 156, 190–191
  and cognitive deficit 398–399
  and cue utilization 94, 96, 398–399
  and performance 95, 123, 126–127, 143–144, 146, 154–157, 158–162, 168, 181, 189
  and stress 151, 184
arousal, electrocortical 36, 40, 60–61, 471, 474

and anxiety 434–435
and behaviour 160–162
and drugs 43–44
and evoked potentials 38
and expectancy 51, 55–57, 434
and information processing 41–50, 55, 160–162, 451–452
and schizophrenia 449–450, 454
and stress response 51, 54–55, 57, 434–435
arousal, emotional 142, 159, 162, 164, 184, 445
arrhythmia 368, 370
assimilation 195
atropine 43–49
and selective attention 46–47, 48
attention 36, 37, 42, 162, 238, 472
and arousal 156, 159, 162, 164, 187, 190–191
and drugs 44–47, 49, 455
and electrocortical arousal 42, 43–47, 48–51, 451–452
and evoked potential 48, 129, 161–162
and performance 35, 39, 145–151, 156, 163, 190
and schizophrenia 452, 455
and stress 123–124, 162, 163, 164, 199, 434
and stress hormones 57, 190–192
broadened 44–45, 46, 47
narrowed 45, 190, 196
physiological aspects of 38–41, 42, 43–47, 48–51, 57, 129, 161–162, 190, 191–192, 451–452
selective 46–47, 165
theories of 39, 40–41, 48–51
autism 24–25
aversive information 394–405, 405–422
avoidance 240, 243
awareness, law of 196

behaviour and environment feedback 306–307
benzodiazepines 440, 441
bereavement 238, 245
biomechanical analysis 351, 353, 354, 355, 357
boredom 13, 72
buffer store memory 403–404
bureaucracy 316, 318, 320, 323, 326

capacity 345
catastrophies 74–76
catatoxic hormones 22
catecholamine release and performance 187
catecholamines, see Adrenaline, Noradrenaline, and Dopamine
catecholamines, adrenal, 58–59
and attention 58–59
and brain 57, 58
and depression 25–26
and energy resources 59–61, 471–472
and performance 58–59, 60, 187
and schizophrenia 25
and stress 15, 25, 59–61, 471–472
and uncertainty 59
release 53–54, 59, 143, 367–368
catecholamines, brain 438–439, 441
and stress 53–54
choice 183
cholinergic pathways 49–50, 452
cholinolytics 43, 44–47, 48, 49, 452, see also Atropine and Scopolamine
closure 280
codes and stress 323–335
cognition in organizations 301–335
cognitive consonance 310
cognitive controls, serious life events 246–262
cognitive deficit, anxiety 396–405
arousal model 398–399
cognitive development, deviant 406–413
long term memory 406–413
mediators 395–396
socialization strategies 395–396
cognitive dissonance 310
cognitive efficiency and stress 189–192
cognitive functioning, Kuhn's model (D.S.E.) 302, 305–318
and organizational codes 326–335
and organizational expectations 326–335
and organizational rules 326–335
cognitive mismatch and stress 310–313
cognitive performance, life stess 229
cognitive resources 472
cognitive salience 186
cognitive schemata 6
inner models 244
in the schizophrenias 406–408, 416–421
personality traits and habits as 97–100, 103

relationship models 244
self image 244
serious life events 244–246
cognitive structures, development 406–413
  deviant 406–413 (see also
    Schizophrenia, Anxiety, Stress,
    Stressors, Strain)
  differentiation 406–408, see also
    Anxiety, Schizophrenia, Stress,
    Stressors, Strain
  dimensional integration 406–408, see
    also Anxiety, Schizophrenia,
    Stress, Stressors, Strain
  mediators of vulnerability 70
cognitive style, cognitive controls 95
cold stress, see Physical stress
communication mechanisms, organizational 301–335
compatibility, stimulus–response 116, 128
competing information, anxiety 396–398, 412–418
completion tendency 248–251
compulsive behaviour 444, 449
concentration, see Attention
concussion 119, 132, 133
conditioning, stress 20, 21
conflict 70–71, 80, 86, 185, 310–313, 317
confusion 240
consciousness 180–184
conservation 396, 401, 402, 406, 408, 418
consolidation 155–158
consonance, cognitive 310
control processes, response 134–136
convulsions 24, 27
coping 57, 193
  and ambiguity 239–279, 281–282
  and information processing 248
  and schizophrenia 449, 450
  and stress 196, 449
  individual differences 265–268
coping processes 265–293
  evaluation 282–293
  goodness of fit 288–293
  individual differences 289–290
  morale 284, 288
  self-efficacy 286–288
coping resources 283–288
  and beliefs 286–288

and health 284
and problem-solving skills 284–285
social 285
utilitarian 286
coping strain, cognitive interpretation 72–74
coping strategies 102–105, 283, 288–293, 443–444, 473, 474
coronary thrombosis 6
corticosteroids, and brain 59, 433–434
  and depression 25–26, 438
  and energy resources 59–61
  and neurosis 23
  and schizophrenia 25, 437, 438
  and uncertainty 55–57, 59
  electrocortical arousal 54–55, 57
  release of 15–17, 19, 21, 53–57
countershock phase 17
cross resistance 19, 20
cue utilization 189–191, 398–399
cure, medical 445, 455
Cushing's disease 25, 439

danger 89–91, 472
data-driven model 117–129, 133–134, 470, 471
data-limited model 35, 471
day dreaming 41–42, 44
decision making and sleep loss 169
  and stress 168–169, 291–293
decomposition indices 122, 124–129
defences, psychological and stress steroids response 247, 443–444
defensive failures 248
defensive processes 251–262
degree of control 164
denial 236–237, 239, 443
depression 87
  and stress hormones 25–26, 438
  life stress 207–208, 219, 220
depth of processing 197–199
destabilization 369
desynchronization, see Electrocortical arousal
detector system 305–318
dexamethasone 25
digit span, simultaneous task 401–402
disavowal 238
dissonance, cognitive 310
distraction 40, 47, 48, 58, 72, 134–136, 160
distress 27–28

directional fractionation 161
diurnal rhythm 166
dopamine pathway 457
dreams 43, 55, 242
drug dependence 26
drug therapy and anxiety 440–443, 445, 450–451
dual tasks and anxiety and arousal 401–402

effector system 305–318
efficiency, cognitive 145, 160, 165, 190, 194–195
ego development 280
ego functions 248
egoism 28, 29
elaboration, see also Depth of processing 197
electrocardiography 368, 370
electroencephalography 368
electromyography 361, 368, 370
electrooculography 368
emotion and perception 277
emotions as interference 271–272
    as interruptions 270–271
    as signals 269–270
    cognitive appraisal 267–268, 268–276
    information processing 273–276
    mobilization 270
    theories of 100–103, 432–433
endurance limit 359–360, 362
energy expenditure 355–358
ergonomics 341–345
eustress 27, 28
evaluation, coping processes 27–42, 282–293
evoked potential, cortical 38–41, 44, 48, 129, 454
exercise 371–374
exhaustion, stage of 16, 17, 23, 26, 27
expectancy 39, 40, 41, 56–57, 186, 195, 196, 197, 323–325, 434
experience and processing 36, 116, 190, 344
experiences, intrusive 236–237, 241
extraversion–introversion 78–79, 84, 85, 88, 89–92, 95, 119
eyeblink reflex 90

fatigue 12, 13, 14, 23, 33, 36–38, 58, 60, 61, 122, 146, 159, 162, 163, 165, 166–167, 357, 364–366, 369
fear 191, 387–389

feedback 306–307
feedback-control theory 362–365
flicker-fusion-frequency 367
free fatty acids (FFA) 26
frustration 86, 313–318, 330

General Adaptation Syndrome (G.A.S.) 16–20, 21, 22, 23, 24, 25
glucocorticoids 21, 22
'grammar' of personality organization 97–98
group membership, controls 255

hallucinations 13, 43, 47–48, 240, 241, 441, 451, 454, 455, 456
headache 23, 24
heart rate 368, 370
heat stress, see Stress, heat, noise
hippocampus 49, 50–51
histamine 14
homeostasis 28, 29
hyperactivity in the schizophrenias 419–421
hyperstress (overstress) 27
hypnagogic state 43
hypostress (understress) 27
hypothalamo-pituitary-adrenal axis 14, 15, 20–21, 25

iconic memory in the schizophrenias 403–404, 411, 415–416
id functions 248
illusions 240
incentives 146, 149, 151, 164
individual differences, coping 265–268, 289, 290
    stress, stressor, strain tolerance 74–82
industrial rehabilitation therapy in schizophrenia 384, 405–406
infection 12, 17, 21, 22
inflammation 12, 17, 19, 21
inflexibility 238
information, aversive 7
information coding, development 406–413, see also Anxiety, Schizophrenia, Stress, Stressors, Strain
    in subnormality 412–413
information flow, control 254–255
information load 116
    in stress, stressors, strain 70–105
information measure 34
information overload, and anxiety 395–405

in organizations 311–318
in the schizophrenias 406–413,
    416–421
information processing, and anxiety 445
    and electrocortical arousal 41–50
    and pupil dilation 127
    and schizophrenia 389–393, 406–421,
        447, 454–455
    and stress 35–38
    cognitive appraisal 267–268
    coping 248, 273–274
    defensive controls 248–262
    emotions 274–276
    in neurotic anxiety 383–421
    Kuhn's model 306–308
    models 115–137
information processing capacity, and
    anxiety 396–397
information processing load 82–83
information processing model, of
    anxiety 384
    of personality and stress 96–105
    of the schizophrenias 405–421
information processor, human 307–308
information search, ambiguity 281–282
    inference 281–282
information structures, organizations
    301–335
information theory models 34–35, 38,
    170–171
integration, mental 182
internal clock in reaction time 136
interruption and autonomic arousal 193,
    196
interruption theory 191–192, 195
    and stress 185–188, 191–192, 195,
        196–197
intolerance of ambiguity 101, 399–400,
    see also Ambiguity
introversion–extraversion 78–79, 84, 85,
    88, 89–92, 95, 119
intrusion states 242–243

job description 341–342, 350–353
job design 342–343
job enrichment 315
job rotation 315
job satisfaction, intrinsic 310–318
judgments 183

'lexicon', personality traits and
    habits 97–100, 103

Librium, see Benzodiazepines
life changes 207–209, 219, 220–221, 225
life crises 284
life events 246–262
life experience survey (LES) 211–230
life stress 205–230
    academic performance 218
    anxiety 218
    cognitive performance 228, 229
    depression 207–208
    job tension 228
    pregnancy and birth complications
        223
    social desirability 218
locus of control 75, 87, 219, 224, 281,
    286–287
loss 235–236

man-at-work-system 340–345
manic-depression 25–26
mastery and stress 192–194
meaning analysis 195
memory 132–134
    and arousal 95, 154–158
    and attention 39, 156
    and autonomic arousal 152–153, 197
    and consciousness 183–184
    and stress 127, 152–158, 166, 168,
        197–199
    cognitive controls 274
    in anxiety 95
    information load 98–99
    in the schizophrenias 411, 415–416
    long-term 307–308, 310
        and anxiety 396, 405–421
        and noise stress 153–154
    primary (short term) 472
    retrieval 126, 127
    scanning 125
    short term 127, 132–133, 152–153,
        198, 307–308, 310
        and concussion 133
        and noise stress 156, 165
    storage 126, 127, 183
        and stress 183, 197
        completion tendency 248–251
    structures, 'strong' vs. 'weak', 406–413,
        see also Anxiety, Schizophrenia,
        Stress, Stressors, Strain
    working 132, 181
mental capacity 37
mental effort 36–38, 471, 474–475
mental load 37

mental work 362–371
mentalism 180
migraine 23–24
mind–brain interaction 432
mineralocorticoids 17, 20, 21
mismatch 310–313
model, cue utilization 189, 190–191,
     398–399
models, data-driven 117–129, 133–134,
     470, 471
  information processing 115–137, 128
  resource-driven 129–136, 473
moderator variables and life stress
     research 223–225
mood and life changes 221–222
motivation, cognitive analysis, 70, 72–74
motives, motivation 306–307, 366
  cross-system 308–313
  efficiency 309, 316–318
  exercise 309
  frustration 310–318
  priority 308–309
'myth' of industrial brotherhood 325

neuroses 23–24
neurotic anxiety 383–421,
  see also Anxiety
neuroticism 78–79, 84, 85
nicotine 44, 45–47
nightmares 240, 241
noise stress, see Stress, noise
noradrenalin 24
novelty 51, 56, 195
numbing 236–237, 238, 239, 240

occupational role integration 331
old age 119–120, 127, 135–136
organizational activities 320–323
organizational climate 311–318
organizational control mechanisms 302,
     330–335
organizational development 325
organizational ideology 318
organizational size 319
organizational structure 302
organizational typologies 318–330
organizations, role conflict 314–316
  stress in 301–335
  work 470–471, 475
outcry 238
overarousal 159

pain 89–90

pangs 240
panic 190, 193
perceptual processing 119, 123, 125,
     126, 129
performance 362, 363, 364
  and anxiety 194
  and arousal 143–144, 168, 189
  and drugs 45–48, 136, 165, 455
  and fatigue 122, 146, 159, 163,
     165, 166–167
  and old age 135–136
  and stress response 58–61
  and stressors 117, 121–122, 136, 146,
     147, 159, 167, 169, 228
  profile 119–120, 162
  theories 158–162
person–environment interaction 69
personality, and cognitive schemata
     97–100, 103
  conceptualizations 68–70, 72–73,
     96–105
  consistency vs. coherence 69, 77
  'lexicon' 97–100, 103
  motivation 70
  multi-factorial definition 69
  organization, 'grammar' 97–98
  temperament 69
personality and stress, information pro-
     cessing model 91–94, 96–105
personality × situations interac-
     tions 82–96
phantasy 42–43, 238–239, 240, 241
phasic tendency 236
phenothiazines, see Antipsychotic drugs
phenylethylamine 24
physical stress 469, 470, 471
physical work 351–357
pituitary (hypophysis) 15, 17, 20
plans 192, 196
post-traumatic disorders 238
problem solving 42–43, 181–183, 196,
     284–285
  and anxiety 194–195, 402–403
  and stress 191, 197–199
processing capacity 35–37, 38, 60, 119,
     130, 181, 182, 188, 189, 194–195,
     310–313, 472, 474, 475
processing strategies 35, 60, 132
productivity and stress 339
prostaglandin 14
psychoanalysis 71, 100–103, 252
psychosomatic disorder 23, 70

psychotherapy 473, 474
pulse rate 360–361
punishment, sensitivity to 59, 79, 91
pupil dilation 127

reaction time (RT), and atropine 47
    and autonomic arousal 161–162
    and simultaneous tasks 401–402
    and smoking 45
    band 135
    choice 116, 121–124, 128, 134–135,
        136, 146
        and heat stress 148–149
        and noise stress 148–151
        and sleep loss 149–151
        and stress 122
    internal clock 136
    simple 115–116, 124–125
    stress 128
recognition and noise stress 165
rehearsal 155
repetition compulsion 248
resistance, stage of 16, 17, 26
resource allocation 36, 163–164
resource-driven models 131
resource limited model 36
response inhibition 161–162
response output, control processes
    134–136
response selection 472
representational set, control 261
repression-sensitization 81
rest pauses 364–366
retrieval 183
    and stress 197
rituals and stress 323
role ambiguity 332
role conflict in organizations 313–315
role relationship models, controls 255
rules and stress 323–335
rules, codes, expectations relationship
    between 325

satisfaction, level of 350, 351
salient cognitive structures 186
scanning 396
schedule of recent experiences
    (S.R.E.) 23, 206, 207, 208
schema(ta), aversive information 394
    and expectancy 195
    in the schizophrenias 407, 411–412
schizophrenia 119

and ACTH 24–25
and amphetamine 456
and anticholinesterases 452
and anti-psychotic drugs 446, 451,
    455, 458, 459
and anxiety 447–448, 450–451
and anxiolytics 450–451
and attention 452, 455
and catecholamines 25
and cholinolytics 452
and coping 449, 450
and cortical evoked potential 454
and corticosteroids 25, 437, 438
and electrocortical arousal 449–450,
    454
and general adaptation syndrome
    24–25
and hallucinations 454, 455, 456
and information processing 447,
    454–455
and stress steroids 448–449
and stress, stressors, strain 383–421
anxiety model 390
at-risk studies 392–393, 408–409,
    418, 419
category boundaries 392, 418
cholinergic hypothesis 451–453
cognitive-developmental
    model 409–413
cognitive impoverishment
    hypothesis 419–420
cognitive over-elaboration
    hypothesis 420–421
computer analogues 420–421
concepts 389–393
deviant cognitive development
    406–413
dopamine-acetylcholine hypothesis
    457–458
double-bind hypothesis 392–393
ego boundaries 392, 418–419
family communication 392–393
hemispheric asymmetry 414
hippocampal damage 408–409, 418
hyperactive, reactive, paranoid 405,
    420–421
iconic memory 411, 415–416
industrial rehabilitation 384, 405–406
information overload 406–413,
    416–421
information processing aspects
    383–421

information processing model
  405–421
input dysfunction hypothesis 414
intelligence 417, 419–420
interference hypothesis 413
medical and genetic model 389–391
memory 411, 415–416
paranoid 449–450
pharmacotherapy 450–451,
  453–455, 458–459
precursors 392–393
process 449–450
processing speed hypothesis 413
psychodynamic model 391–393
psychotherapy 458
reactive 449–450
regression hypothesis 419
schemata 407, 411–412, 420
selective attention hypothesis
  414–417
size constancy 406, 408
socialization effects 392–393, 410,
  418–420
socio-economic status 391
sociological model 391
withdrawn, inadequate, process, non-
  paranoid 405, 420
schizophrenias 474
scopolamine 45–48
selector system 305–318
self-esteem 86
self-image models, controls 255
semantic networks anxiety 72
  in the schizophrenias 417
senile psychosis 26
sensation seeking 224
sensory deprivation 13, 165
separation 238
serotonin and benzodiazepines 441
  and depression 26
  and stress steroids 438–439
sexual behaviour 20, 21
shock phase 17, 23
short-term memory with anxiety and
  arousal 403–404
short term (working) memory information load 98–99
signal detection and sleep loss 147–148
signal detection theory 148
signs of denial 238–243
size constancy in the schizophrenias 406,
  408, 418

skilled performance and stress 141–173
sleep 41, 42, 43, 50
sleep loss 119, 142, 146, 165
  and arousal 151
  and attention 163
  and choice reaction time 149–151
  and decision making 169
  and performance 122, 123, 146, 159,
    163, 166–167
  and signal detection 147–148
  and vigilance 147–148
sliding meanings 254
smoking see nicotine
  and electrocortical arousal 44
  and performance 165
  and reaction time 45
  deprivation 44, 45
social complexity and anxiety 394
socialization 474, 475
  and anxiety 395–396
  effect in the schizophrenias 392–393,
    410, 418–420
  strategies and cognitive develop-
    ment 395–396
somatotrophic hormone (STH) 19, 21
speed-error-trade-off function
  (SETO) 135–136, 148–149,
  166
startle reactions 241
stimulation, barrier 247
stimulation, excessive 247
stimulus deprivation 72
strategies 37
  and vigilance 131–132
Stroop test 47
subnormality, information coding
  412–413
superego functions 148
surgical procedures 238
sympathetic nervous system 15
syntoxic hormones 22
strain 37–38, 345–346
  motivational 311
  psychological 302–305
stress and anxiety 160
  and attention 164
  and autonomic arousal 184
  and brain catecholamines 53–54
  and cognitive efficiency 189–192
  and cognitive mismatch 310–313
  and coping 196, 265–293
  and death 17

and decision making 168–169, 291–293
and depression 25–26
and disease 12–13
and distraction 160
and efficiency 160, 165, 194
and frustration 310–318
and hierarchy of plans 196
and information processing 35–38
and interruption theory 185–188, 196–197
and mastery 192–194
and memory 152–158, 197–199
and memory storage 183
and novelty 195
and organization expectations 323–335
and organizational codes 323–335
and organizational rules 323–335
and performance 167
and problem solving 191, 197–199
and productivity 339
and rituals 323
and skilled performance 141–173
and thinking 185–188, 435
and uncertainty 195, 277–279
and vigilance 146, 148
benefits of 20
cognitive appraisal 267–268
cold 12, 13
concept of 12–13
control of schemata 255
coping strategies 288–293
definition 5, 184, 191, 302–305
environmental 6
extrinsic 302–303
first mediator of 14–15
format of control 26, 259–261
heat 12, 13, 119, 146
    and attention 123–124, 163
    and choice reaction line 148–149
    and performance 122, 146
hormones 471
individual differences 265–268
intrinsic 302–303
life (see Life stress)
life event 470, 472–473, 474–475
managerial 310–313
noise 119, 145–146
    and arousal 151
    and attention 123, 166, 199
    and choice reaction times 148–151

and long term memory 153–154
and memory 127, 157–158, 168
and performance 121–122, 125–126, 136, 146, 147, 159, 169, 191
and recognition 165
and short term memory 156, 165, 166
non-specific 12, 13, 14, 15, 19, 20
occupational differences 304–305
organizational 301–335
psychogenic 13, 15, 21–22, 23, 28, 36–37, 57, 436–437
Stress response 33, 37, 52–53, 123, 238, 443–444
    and electrocortical arousal 52–53
    and performances 59–61
    defined 12–13, 37, 471–473
stress steroids, and anxiety 434–438, 439–440, 443–444, 449
    and brain 438–439
    and brain catecholamines 438–439
    and coping 449
    and electrocortical arousal 434–435
    and schizophrenia 448–449
    and serotonin 438–439
    and uncertainty 436, 443–444, 449
    control release of 434
    feedback 438–439
stress, stressors, strain anxiety 86–87
    catastrophies 74–76
    definitions 70–74
    duration 105
    in neurotic anxiety 383–421
    in the schizophrenias 383–421
    information load 70–105
    information processing definition 72–74
    organizational typologies 318–330
    parallel cognitive processes 96–105
    person sources 84–87
    personality × situations interactions 82–96
    physical danger 89–91
    situational sources 87–88
    temporal aspects 88
    vigilance tasks 95
    vulnerability to 101–105
stress, stressors, strain tolerance 71–72, 74–82, 119
    cognitive interpretation 96–105
    genetic influences 77–78
    learning theory 78–79
    individual differences 74–82

predispositions 76–82
psychodynamic theory 79–82
socialization in 74, 80
stress vulnerability 6
stressors 344, 345, 346, 350–353
and performance 117
defined 469, 470–471
ecological 6
informational analysis 7–8
organizational 311–318
psychological 37
tolerance 118

task demands 36, 37, 38, 143–144,
342–346, 471–472, 475
thinking 41–43, 48
and atropine 47–48
and consciousness 181–183
and cortical evoked potential 39
definition 180, 181
and scopolamine 47–48
and stress 185–188, 435
threat and efficiency 194–195
thyroid hormones 12, 20
tolerability, level of 347
'top-down' model see resource-limited
training 371–374, 475
traumatization 247–248
tremor 368
trouble shooting 183 see problem
solving
tyramine 24

ulcers 16
unadaptive cognitive structures, development 406–413
uncertainty 34, 51, 55–57, 470–471

and adrenal catecholamine 59
and anxiety 195, 399–400, 433
and appraisal 276–282
and corticosteroids 55–57, 59
and corticosteroid release 56–57
and electrocortical arousal 433–434
and stress 195, 277–279
and stress steroids 436, 443–444, 449
and therapy 445
under-arousal 159

vigilance 27, 39, 41, 50, 58, 123,
129–130, 146–148, 368
and arousal 146
and scopolamine 45–46
and sleep loss 147–148
and stress 147, 148
decrement 45–46, 130–131
and adrenal catecholamines 58–59
and electrocortical activity 42
stress, stressor, strain 95
violence 238
vulnerability stress, stressors, strain 71,
80, 101–105

word recognition 403
work assessment 346, 351
intensity 340, 345
load, see task demand
movements 353–355
muscular 361
working through 243–244
X-radiation 12

Yerkes-Dodson law 143–144, 147, 151,
158, 159, 164, 168, 188–189, 398,
472